*Included in *The Norton CD-ROM Masterworks*, vol. 1.

(continued on back flyleaf)

Darla

The Enjoyment of
Music

W · W · NORTON & COMPANY · *New York* · *London*

The Enjoyment of

Music

AN INTRODUCTION
TO PERCEPTIVE LISTENING

Joseph Machlis

Professor of Music Emeritus,
Queens College of The City University of New York

Kristine Forney

Professor of Music, California State University, Long Beach

Eighth Edition / Standard

The text of this book is composed in Minion with display set in Bauer Bodoni.
Composition by U.G.
Manufacturing by R.R. Donnelley
Cover illustration: Helmut A. Preiss, *Mandolin* (1996), collage and acrylic paint;
    collection of the artist.
Editor: Michael Ochs
Developmental editor: Susan Gaustad
Production manager: Roy Tedoff
Editorial assistants: Martha Graedel, Anne White
Design: Antonina Krass
Cover design: Joan Greenfield
Coordinator of photography: Neil Ryder Hoos
Layout: Sue Crooks
Proofreader: Rosanne Fox
Indexer: Marilyn Bliss

Machlis, Joseph, 1906–
      The enjoyment of music: an introduction to perceptive listening/
Joseph Machlis and Kristine Forney.—8th ed., standard.
         p.   cm.
      Includes bibliographical references and index.
      ISBN 0-393-97290-9
      1. Music appreciation.   I. Forney, Kristine.   II. Title.
      MT90.M23 1998a
      780—dc21   98-34248

W. W. Norton & Company, Inc., 500 Fifth Avenue, New York, N.Y. 10110
http://www.wwnorton.com
W.W. Norton & Company Ltd., 10 Coptic Street, London WC1A 1PU
1 2 3 4 5 6 7 8 9 0

FOR EARLE FENTON PALMER

Contents

Part 2

The Nineteenth Century

Contents

Part 3

More Materials of Music

Part 5

Medieval and Renaissance Music

Part 7

The Twentieth Century

Listening Guides

Cultural Perspectives

Preface

What's new in the eighth edition of *The Enjoyment of Music*? The answer is, a lot: more diversity, more technology, more visual and aural stimulation, and more pedagogical resources within the same dependable package of teaching materials. We continue to offer the book in three formats: the Chronological and the Shorter (both of which take a historical approach), and the Standard (which begins with the accessible and familiar sounds of Romantic music). All three versions feature Listening Guides to supplement the prose descriptions of the primary repertory, a reference listing (with dates and original titles) of Principal Works for each major composer, introductory chapters on the arts and intellectual climate of each historical era, and discussions of the transitions between eras (along with helpful outline comparisons of the style traits for consecutive eras).

This new edition offers more breadth of styles than ever before. While the book retains its focus on the classics of Western art music, the international flavor of the seventh edition has been broadened through comparative discussions of world and traditional musics in relation to Western art and popular music. These occur throughout the book, most notably in the form of Cultural Perspectives—text "windows" that open fascinating new topics to students through engaging descriptions and familiar references to popular culture. The twenty-four Cultural Perspectives in this edition delve into the cultures of African Americans, Latin Americans, and Asian Americans, and into the musics of Canada and Mexico as well as those of Africa and the Far East. Among the new topics explored here are music in the ancient world, music for films, and women and music (from a feminist viewpoint). Students can pursue any of these topics further electronically through the *Enjoyment* web site, which offers additional material and links to other informative sites.

One notable area of expansion in this edition is the inclusion of four world music examples as primary repertory, all of which are integrated into comparative discussions of styles rather than isolated in their own chapters. Two works—an eastern African drumming example and a Chinese instrumental piece played on traditional instruments—are each preceded by a Western composition that clearly draws inspiration, stylistic concepts, and musical techniques from the non-Western culture paired with it. This approach is designed to introduce students and faculty to new musical cultures from a familiar vantage point. In addition, two well-known world music ensembles introduce popular contemporary styles—the South African *a cappella* group Ladysmith Black Mambazo, with an antiracism song (in Zulu and English), and The Chieftains, performing a set of traditional Irish dances.

Some new repertory was selected to appeal to the increasingly diverse student populations on many campuses today: these works include, in addition to the non-Western music examples, *Spiral*, a "pan-Asian" chamber piece by the Cambodian-American composer Chinary Ung; the fiery Spanish *Feria* from Ravel's *Rapsodie espagnole* and the electrifying Latin *Mambo* from Bernstein's *West Side Story* (we retain the *Habanera* from Bizet's *Carmen*); Scott Joplin's ever-popular *Maple Leaf Rag* and Lillian Hardin Armstrong's jaunty *Hotter Than That* (as well as Ellington's blues *Ko-Ko*).

Some newly added works serve to better grab the attention of today's students: Smetana's memorable symphonic poem *The Moldau*, the commanding *March to the Scaffold* from Berlioz's *Symphonie fantastique* (along with the closing *Dream of a Witches' Sabbath*), Mendelssohn's songful Violin Concerto, the delightful Rondo alla turca from Mozart's Piano Sonata in A major, K. 331, Liszt's tintinnabulary *La campanella*, the unforgettable *La donna è mobile* and Quartet from Verdi's *Rigoletto*, and the dramatic *Tonight* Ensemble from *West Side Story*. Other new additions provide excellent teaching examples: there are the theme and variations movements from Haydn's Symphony No. 94 (*Surprise*) and from Schubert's *Trout* Quintet (along with the song *The Trout*), a serious Italian madrigal rich with word painting (Monteverdi's *A un giro sol*), more accessible early music examples (a Machaut chanson and the fifteenth-century Burgundian work *Il sera pour vous / L'homme armé*), works featuring early instruments (the monophonic *Royal estampie* No. 4 and Giovanni Gabrieli's polychoral motet *O quam suavis*), solo and choral selections from Haydn's inspiring oratorio *The Creation*, the concisely constructed Third Symphony of Brahms, and Bartók's *Concerto for Orchestra*, one of the great masterworks of the twentieth century.

A new edition allows us to keep pace with contemporary composition. Accordingly, in addition to the Ligeti piano etude (*Désordre*, 1985) carried over from the previous edition, we have included four new works written since 1985: Libby Larsen's tribute to Handel in *Symphony: Water Music* (1985), Chinary Ung's multicultural *Spiral* (1987), Paul Lansky's computer music work *Notjustmoreidlechatter* (1988), and Steve Reich's *City Lights* (1995), for orchestra and samplers.

A record number of seven women composers are represented in the primary repertory: in addition to Hildegard of Bingen, Elisabeth Jacquet de la Guerre, and Clara Schumann, the eighth edition introduces Fanny Mendelssohn (with her last work, the poignant song *Mountain Yearning*), Amy Cheney Beach (with the lilting scherzo from her Violin Sonata), Lillian Hardin Armstrong (with *Hotter Than That,* which she recorded with Louis Armstrong and his Hot Five), and the contemporary composer Libby Larsen (with her symphonic homage to Handel and to nature, mentioned above). Numerous women performers are featured as well, some of whom can be directly associated with the primary repertory. These include the famed Singing Ladies of Ferrara, for whose patron Monteverdi intended his madrigal *A un giro sol;* women pianists of the Classical era, including the student for whom Mozart wrote his Piano Concerto in G major, K. 453; and notable women interpreters of twentieth-century music, opera, and blues. The professional opportunities available to women are discussed in the opening chapter to each historical era, and the Cultural Perspective "Women and Music: A Feminist View" elaborates on issues surrounding the participation of women in the music world in the nineteenth and twentieth centuries.

We have augmented the coverage of chamber music with a Romantic chamber work (Beach's Violin Sonata) and two contemporary pieces (*Spiral,* by Ung, and the powerful *Quartet for the End of Time,* by Messiaen). There is substantially more coverage of American music, with the addition of a chapter dedicated to Amy Beach and the nineteenth-century New England School and the inclusion of a nostalgic song by Charles Ives (*The Things Our Fathers Loved*), as well as the jazz and contemporary selections mentioned earlier. Coverage of Canadian music has been expanded in the Cultural Perspectives, illustrations, and recording package.

Five complete multimovement works help students get the "whole picture" of important absolute forms: included in their entirety are Vivaldi's *La primavera,* Mozart's *Eine kleine Nachtmusik* and Piano Concerto in G major, K. 453, and Beethoven's Fifth Symphony and Piano Sonata, Op. 13 (*Pathétique*). Extra movements have been added for Berlioz's *Symphonie fantastique* (the fourth and fifth are now featured) and for Bach's *Brandenburg Concerto* No. 2 (the first and second movements).

The opening chapters present the basic concepts and building blocks of music with a broad focus on all styles—Western and non-Western, art and traditional. Music examples throughout these elements chapters provide a multicultural perspective, and the discussion of instruments and ensembles goes beyond those of Western art music. New Listening Activities using examples from the accompanying sound package appear in each elements chapter to reinforce the student's comprehension of vocabulary. As in earlier editions, chapters discussing advanced concepts of harmony and form appear later in the book.

A new eye-catching design, with vibrant colors, highlighting, and abundant illustrations, leads the reader easily to the book's various parts. Maps—including a chart of the medieval Crusade routes, an eighteenth-century plan of the main compositional centers of Western Europe, and a full-opening world map—provide useful reference material. The text remains eminently readable, preserving the composer biographies (the "story material") and adding a new feature, marginal quotes ("In His/Her Own Words") from composers' letters or writings that provide a glimpse of their personalities and creative goals; these help bring the musicians alive to students.

As in previous editions, most of the operas and ballets discussed in the text are available on videocassettes, which can enliven and enrich the classroom experience for students. Two recording packages are available with this edition: one with eight CDs or cassettes, including all the primary repertory discussed in the Chronological and Standard editions; and one with four CDs or cassettes, which accompanies the Shorter version and contains forty-seven listening examples. Electronic Listening Guides are provided for all selections on the Shorter recordings, allowing interactive study—either in the classroom or individually; they can also be downloaded from the web, for users of the longer edition and recording package. The in-depth Masterworks CD-ROM of twelve primary examples, featured with the previous edition, remains a fine enhancement for this teaching package.

Any project of this size depends on the expertise and assistance of many to make it a success. We would like first to thank the numerous users of *The Enjoyment of Music* who took the time to send helpful comments relating to the previous edition; their ideas form the basis from which we begin our plan for each new edition. We further extend our appreciation to the members of the focus groups held in Pittsburgh (at the American Musicological Society conference), at the University of California, Santa Barbara, and at California State University, Long Beach; these forums encouraged a free exchange of ideas on teaching methods, appropriate repertory, and the use of various ancillary materials in the classroom.

Several specialists offered their expertise in reviewing this new edition, including Daniel Kazez of Wittenberg University (elements of music); Martin Brenner and Martin Herman, both of California State University, Long Beach (technology and music); Dolores Hsu of the University of California, Santa Barbara (Chinese traditional music); and Richard Crawford of the University of Michigan, Helen Myers of Trinity College, and Gordon Thompson of Skidmore College, all of whom offered insightful critiques of the Cultural Perspectives.

The team assembled to prepare the ancillary materials accompanying this edition is exceptional; it includes our "webmaster," Russell Murray of the University of Delaware; Irene Girton of California State University, Los Angeles, author of the Electronic Listening Guides; David Hamilton of New

York City and Tom Laskey of Sony Special Products, who assembled, licensed, and mastered the recording packages; Mark McFarland of the University of Texas, El Paso, author of the Instructor's Manual; Roger Hickman of California State University, Long Beach, who has updated and edited the Test-Item File; our research assistant, Jeanne Scheppach; and our Computerized Test-Item File preparer, Susan Hughes.

We owe profound thanks to the very competent individuals with whom we work at W. W. Norton: first and foremost, to our editor, Michael Ochs, for his experienced counsel and dedicated work on this edition; to Susan Gaustad, for her excellent copyediting and her service as project coordinator; to Steve Hoge, for expertly coordinating the technology portions of this package; to Antonina Krass, who merged function and beauty to create the book's stunning design; to Neil Ryder-Hoos, for his very capable illustration research; and to Martha Graedel, for handling more details than we could possibly enumerate. We wish finally to express our deep appreciation to two former music editors at Norton, Claire Brook and David Hamilton, who over the years have guided and inspired *The Enjoyment of Music* to its continued success.

Joseph Machlis
Kristine Forney

Prelude: Listening to Music Today

"There is no such thing as music divorced from the listener. Music as such is unfulfilled until it has penetrated our ears."
—YEHUDI MENUHIN

Our lives are constantly changing, with new avenues of the supertechnology highway opening to us every day. This technological revolution significantly influences our work and our leisure activities; it further conditions how, when, and where we listen to music. From the moment we are awakened by our clock radios, our days unfold against a musical background. We listen to music while on the move—in our cars, on planes, or at the gym—and at home for relaxation. We can hardly avoid it in grocery and department stores, in restaurants and elevators, at the dentist's office or at work. We experience music at live concerts—outdoor festivals, rock concerts, jazz clubs, the symphony hall, the opera stage—and we hear it on television, at the movies, and even on the Internet. MTV (Music Television) has forever changed the way we "listen" to popular music; it is now a visual experience as well as an aural one. This increased dependency on our eyes makes our ears work less actively, a factor we will attempt to counteract in this book.

Music media too are rapidly changing. With the LP record all but obsolete and cassettes quickly falling into disuse in favor of CDs, newer formats are already on the horizon. Video disc players are part of many home stereos, and CD-ROM drives are standard on today's computer systems. In our musical experiences, we have learned to accept new sounds, many produced electronically rather than by traditional instruments. Much of the music we hear on television, at the movies, and in pop music performances is synthetic, produced by instruments that can accurately re-create the familiar sounds of piano, violin, or drums, as well as totally new sounds and noises for special effects.

Composers have welcomed the technological revolution; the basic tools of music composition—formerly, a pen, music paper, and perhaps a piano—

*Listening to a favorite tape
on her Walkman enhances
the outdoors experience
for this roller blader.*

now include a synthesizer, computer, and laser printer. In short, modern technology has placed at our disposal a wider diversity of music from every period in history, from every kind of instrument, and from every corner of the globe than has ever been available before.

Given this diversity, we must choose our path of study. In this book, we will focus on the classics of Western music while paying special attention to the important influences that traditional, popular, and non-Western musics have had on the European and American heritage. Our purpose is to expand the listening experience through a heightened awareness of many styles of music, including those representing various subcultures of the American population. We will hear the uniquely American forms of ragtime, blues, jazz, and musical theater, as well as rock and contemporary world music. The book seeks to place music, whether art, traditional, or popular, within its cultural context, and to highlight the relationships between different styles. To this end, the Cultural Perspectives, informative boxed texts placed throughout the book, open windows onto other cultures and their musics. You can also explore these topics further on the *Enjoyment* web site, which provides links to related sites of interest.

The language of music cannot be translated into the language of words. You cannot deduce the actual sound of a piece from anything written about it; as the great violinist Yehudi Menuhin notes above, the ultimate meaning lies in the sounds themselves and in the ears of the listener. While certain styles are immediately accessible to an audience, without any explanation, the world of music often brings us into contact with sounds and concepts that we grasp more slowly. What, you might wonder, can prepare the nonmusician to understand and appreciate an eighteenth-century symphony, a contemporary opera, or an example of African drumming? A great deal. We can discuss the social and historical context in which a work was born. We can explore the characteristic features of the various styles throughout the history of music, so that we can relate a particular piece or style to parallel developments in literature and the fine arts. We can read about the lives of the composers who left us so rich a heritage, and take note of what they said about their art. (Engaging comments by composers appear throughout the book, labeled "In His/Her Own Words.") We can acquaint ourselves with the elements out of which music is made, and discover how the composer combines these into any one work. All this knowledge—social, historical, biographical, technical, and analytical—can be interrelated. What emerges is a total picture of a work, one that will clarify, in far greater degree that you may have thought possible, the form and meaning of a composition.

There are people who claim they prefer not to know anything technical about the music they hear, that to intellectualize the listening experience de-

The popular dance troop Stomp performing at the Academy Awards in Los Angeles, March 25, 1996.

stroys their enjoyment of the music. Yet most sports fans would hardly suggest that the best way to enjoy football is to avoid learning the rules of the game. A heightened awareness of musical processes and styles brings listeners closer to the sounds and allows them to hear and comprehend more.

Some Practical Suggestions

It takes practice to become good listeners. Most of us "listen" to music as a background to another activity—perhaps reading or studying—or for relaxation. In either case, we are probably not concentrating on the music. The approach set out in this book is intended to develop your listening skills and expand your musical memory. In order to accomplish this, you should listen to the examples repeatedly, focusing solely on what you are hearing. As you play the music, you will also find it helpful to follow the Listening Guides distributed throughout the book. Since they are outlines, they should not divert your attention from the sounds you hear. The music examples printed in the Listening Guides may be useful if you can follow the general line of the music (see Appendix I, "Musical Notation"). Don't worry if you can't read music; the verbal descriptions of each piece and its sections will tell you what to listen for. An explanation of the format for the Listening Guides follows this introduction.

It is also important to hear music in live performance. Why not try something new and unfamiliar? There are many possibilities; if you need help finding out about concerts or are unsure of some of the conventions followed in the concert hall or opera house, consult Appendix III, "Attending Concerts." The goal is to open up a new world of musical experiences for you that you can enjoy the rest of your life.

You will notice that each historical era begins with a general discussion of the culture, its arts, and its ideas. This chapter should help you integrate the knowledge you have gained from other disciplines into the world of music and help you understand that developments in music are closely related to the art, literature, philosophy, religion, and scientific knowledge of the time as well as the social background of the era.

You may be surprised at how technical the study of music can be, and how many new terms you will learn. Studying music is not easier than studying other subjects, but it can be more fun. Make use of the Glossary in Appendix II, and note that the most important terms, when introduced in the book, are printed in italics. Some of these terms may be familiar to you from another context ("texture," for example, is a term commonly used to describe a surface or cloth); we will learn to associate these words with different, often more specific, meanings. Many others, such as the directions for musical expression, tempo, and dynamics, come from foreign languages. We will begin

The Los Angeles Philharmonic Orchestra performing at the Dorothy Chandler Pavilion.

building this vocabulary in the first chapters by breaking music into its constituent parts—its building blocks, or elements. Listening Activities based on the CDs and cassettes accompanying the book appear in each elements chapter, reinforcing the terminology and concepts presented there. We will then analyze how a composer proceeds to shape a melody, how that melody is fitted with accompanying harmony, how music is organized in time, and how it is structured so as to assume logical, recognizable forms. In doing so, we will become aware of the basic principles that apply to all styles of music (classical and popular, Western and non-Western), to music from all eras and countries, and beyond that, to the other arts as well.

"To understand," said the painter Raphael, "is to equal." When we come to understand a musical work, we grasp the "moment of truth" that gave it birth and thus become worthy of keeping company with its creator. We receive the message of the music, we recognize the intention of the composer. In effect, we listen perceptively—and that is the one sure road to the enjoyment of music.

About the Listening Guides

Refer to the sample Listening Guide opposite as you read the following explanations.

1. The red panel at the top contains information to help you locate each work in the various recording sets:

   Chr/Std: *Norton Recordings* (8 CDs or 8 cassettes) for the Chronological and Standard versions

   Sh: *Norton Recordings* (4 enhanced CDs or 4 cassettes) for the Shorter version

   MW: *Norton CD-ROM Masterworks,* vol. 1.

   For CDs: the first number indicates the individual CD within the set; the number or numbers following the diagonal indicate the track or tracks on that CD devoted to the work.

   For cassettes: the first number indicates the individual cassette within the set; the letter A or B represents the side of the cassette; the number following the diagonal indicates the selection number on that cassette side.

2. The title of the work is followed by some basic information about the piece.

3. The total duration of a piece is given in parentheses to the right of the title. (In multimovement works, the duration of each movement is also given to the right of the movement title.)

4. The far left column provides boxed numbers corresponding to the CD tracks. In the Chronological and Standard versions of the book, these relate to the *Norton Recordings,* 8-CD set; in the Shorter version, they relate to the *Norton Recordings,* 4-enhanced-CD set.

5. The second column gives cumulative timings, starting at zero for each movement. Listeners using cassettes may set tape counters to 0:00 at the start of the movement and use these timings for orientation while listening.

6. The Listening Guides often provide musical examples. Even if you cannot read music notation well, the examples will give you some idea of the shape of the line you will hear. If the examples are not helpful, focus on the accompanying descriptions and the timings to identify the musical event in question.

7. For vocal works, the Listening Guides provide texts that are sung and translations for those not in English. Both text and translation are printed between blue vertical bars, to distinguish them from descriptions of the music and commentary.

Note: In cases where the Shorter *Norton Recordings* include less of the work than the 8-CD set, a note appears at the relevant moment in the Listening Guide.

Listening Guide Sample

BRAHMS: *A German Requiem*, Fourth Movement (5:46)

Date of work: 1868

Genre: Requiem, for Protestant church

Medium: 4-part chorus, soloists, and orchestra

Movements: 7

FOURTH MOVEMENT: Mässig bewegt (moderately agitated)

Text: Psalm 84
Form: Rondo (**A-B-A′-C-A′**)
Character: Lilting triple meter, marked *dolce* (sweetly)

Opening melody—clarinets and flutes begin with inversion of first phrase in chorus:

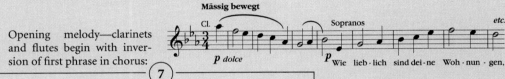

		Text	Translation	Description
15	0:00	Wie lieblich sind deine Wohnungen, Herr Zebaoth!	How lovely is Thy dwelling place, O Lord of Hosts!	**A**—a flowing, arched melody, SATB homophonic setting, answers orchestral opening, in E-flat major; text repeated in tenors, joined by other voices.
16	1:26	Meine Seele verlanget und sehnet sich nach den Vorhöfen des Herrn; mein Leib und Seele freuen sich in dem lebendigen Gott.	My soul longs and even faints for the courts of the Lord; my flesh and soul rejoice in the living God.	**B**—shift to minor, builds fugally with word repetition from lowest to highest voices; sudden accents on first beat of measures, with plucked strings; text is repeated, climax on "lebendigen."
17	2:39	Wie lieblich . . . Wohl denen, die in deinem Hause wohnen,	How lovely . . . Blessed are they that live in Thy house,	**A′**—opening returns in E-flat major, with new text and varied setting.
18	3:51	die loben dich immerdar!	that praise Thee evermore!	**C**—martial quality, faster movement in polyphonic setting.
19	4:44	Wie lieblich . . .	How lovely . . .	**A′**—coda-like return, reminiscent of opening; soft orchestral closing, in E-flat major.

Part 1

1

The Materials of Music

Sonia Delaunay *(1885–1979)*, Electric Prisms *(1914)*. (Musée National d'Art Moderne, Centre Georges Pompidou, Paris)

The Elements of Music

1

Melody: Musical Line

"It is the melody which is the charm of music, and it is that which is most difficult to produce. The invention of a fine melody is a work of genius."—JOSEPH HAYDN

Melody is often the element in music that makes the most direct appeal to the listener. It is usually what we remember and whistle and hum. We know a good melody when we hear it, and we recognize its power to move us, although we may not be able to explain why it does. Millions of melodies have been written around the world, but no matter how different they may sound, all music cultures share the concept of melody as a musical line.

DEFINING MELODY

A *melody* is a coherent succession of single pitches. We perceive the pitches of a melody in relation to each other, in the same way we hear the words of a sentence—not singly but as an entire thought. *Pitch* refers to the highness or lowness of a tone, depending on the rate of vibration (or *frequency*)—the faster the vibration, the higher the pitch. The distance between two different

Pitch

The familiar architectural line of the Pyramid of Cheops at Giza, in Egypt (2680–2258 B.C.E.), relates to the upward and downward turns that shape a melody.

Interval

pitches is called an *interval*. Intervals may be large or small. The intervals of Western music are familiar to us, while certain world musics use intervals so small as to be virtually indistinguishable to our ears.

CHARACTERISTICS OF MELODY

Melodies may rise and fall with bold movement, or change slowly, subtly, almost imperceptibly. The melodies of each music culture have their own distinctive character. In some cultures, melody is closely bound to rhythm, and in others, including Western culture, a melody (more popularly called a *tune*) is nearly inseparable from the sounds that are combined with it. (We will come to know this concept as harmony.)

We can describe some characteristics of any melody: its range, its shape, and the way it moves. A melody goes up and down, one tone being higher or **Range** lower than another; by *range*, we mean the distance between the melody's lowest and highest tones. This span can be very narrow, as in a children's song that is easy to sing, or it can be very wide, which is often true of melodies played on an instrument. The range of a piece is usually described in approximate terms—narrow, medium, or wide.

Shape

Shape is determined by the direction a melody takes as it turns upward or downward or remains static. This movement can be charted on a kind of line graph, resulting in an ascending or descending line, an arch, or a wave.

Conjunct and disjunct movement

A melody can move from pitch to pitch in small intervals, or it can move by leaps to more distant pitches. Melodies that move principally by small intervals in a joined, connected manner are called *conjunct*, while those that move in disjointed or disconnected intervals are described as *disjunct*. Melodies do not necessarily remain the same throughout. A melody may, for example, begin with a small range and conjunct motion and, as it develops, expand its range and become more disjunct.

Melodic Examples

1. Opening of *Shall We Gather at the River* (American hymn):

Range: narrow (4-note span)
Shape: wavelike
Type of movement: conjunct (but with two small leaps in the
    middle and at the end)

2. Opening of *Joy to the World* (Christmas carol):

Range: medium (8-note span)
Shape: descending line
Type of movement: conjunct (no leaps)

3. Opening of *The Star-Spangled Banner* (U.S. national anthem):

Range: wide (10-note span)
Shape: wavelike
Type of movement: disjunct (many leaps)

THE STRUCTURE OF MELODY

Phrase
Cadence

Just as a sentence can be divided into its component units or phrases, so can a melody. A *phrase* in music, as in language, denotes a unit of meaning within a larger structure. The phrase ends in a resting place, or *cadence*, which punctuates the music in the same way that a comma or period punctuates a sentence. The cadence may be inconclusive, leaving the listener with the impression that more is to come, or it may sound final, giving the listener the sense that the melody has reached the end. The cadence is where a singer or instrumentalist pauses to draw a breath.

If the melody is set to words, the text line and the musical phrase will generally coincide. Many folk and popular tunes consist of four musical phrases that are set to a four-line poem. The first and third lines of the poem may rhyme, as do the second and fourth—this symmetrical type of stanza is reflected in the phrase-and-cadence structure of the melody.

Rhyme scheme

An example is the well-known American folk hymn *Amazing Grace*. Its four phrases, in both the poem and the music, are of equal length, and the rhyme scheme is described *a-b-a-b*. (The *rhyme scheme* of a poem describes the similarity in sound of the last syllables in each line—here they are "sound," "me," "found," and "see.") The first three cadences (at the end of

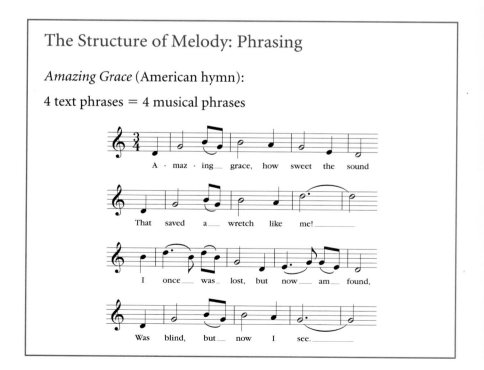

The Structure of Melody: Phrasing

Amazing Grace (American hymn):

4 text phrases = 4 musical phrases

A - maz - ing__ grace, how sweet the sound

That saved a__ wretch like me!_____

I once__ was lost, but now__ am__ found,

Was blind, but__ now I see.__

each of the first three lines) are inconclusive (incomplete), with an upward inflection like a question at the end of the second phrase. The fourth phrase, with its final downward motion, provides the answer; that is, it gives the listener a sense of finality. One pitch serves as home base, around which the melody revolves and to which it ultimately returns.

This same feeling of symmetry and balance can be achieved in melodies that do not rely on words but are played on instruments. Composers can also adapt asymmetrical melodies of irregular phrase length to both vocal and instrumental works. We will hear examples of all these structures in our study of various musical styles.

A world of variety is possible when it comes to forming melodies. In order to maintain the listener's interest, a melody must be shaped carefully, either by the composer who plans it out in advance or by the performer who invents it on the spot. What makes a striking effect is a climax, the high point in a melodic line, which usually represents a peak in intensity as well as in range. (Think of the stirring last phrase of *The Star-Spangled Banner*, when the line rises to the words "O'er the land of the free.")

We will also hear music that features several simultaneous melodies. Sometimes the relative importance of one over the other is clear, and the added tune is called a *countermelody* (literally, "against a melody"). In other styles, each melodic line is of seemingly equal importance.

Countermelody

For much of the music we will study, melody is the most basic element of communication between the composer or performer and the listener. As the twentieth-century composer Aaron Copland aptly put it, "The melody is generally what the piece is about."

Listening Activity: Melody

Tonight, from Bernstein's *West Side Story*

Let's try out your understanding of terms relating to melody with a familiar musical theater song from Leonard Bernstein's ever-popular *West Side Story*. Locate and listen to the beautiful love song *Tonight* on your sound package (on the cassettes, the song begins about 1' 20" into the *Tonight Ensemble*). Notice first that it is built from four symmetrical *phrases* (all the same length), and reaches a prominent *cadence* on a long note at the end of each phrase (on the words "star," "are," "light," and "night"—note too that these words *rhyme*). The overall *range* of the melody is wide, spanning twelve notes, beginning in a lower range and growing higher as the song progresses. This characteristic, coupled with its mostly *disjunct* movement, makes it more challenging to sing. (Note how the line jumps up and then immediately down on the beginning words, "Tonight, tonight.") The third phrase of the song is considerably more *conjunct*, with the notes closer together on the text: "Today the minutes seem like hours, the hours go so slowly, and still the sky is light." Finally, see if you can hear the *countermelody* in this third phrase—after the voice begins, the violins enter with the same melody a few notes behind the vocal part. If you have difficulty with any of these concepts, try listening to an example below. (For the location of each in your sound package, see the table on the front and back inside covers of this book.)

Other Suggested Listening Examples

Conjunct movement, small range—Gregorian chant: *Haec dies*

Mostly conjunct movement, medium range—Mozart: *The Marriage of Figaro* (opening of excerpt)

Disjunct movement, wide range—Schoenberg: *Pierrot lunaire*, No. 18

Symmetrical phrasing—Mozart: *Eine kleine Nachtmusik*, third movement

Countermelody—Haydn: Symphony No. 94 in G major, second movement (countermelody begins about one minute into the piece)

2

Rhythm: Musical Time

"I got rhythm, I got music . . ."
—IRA GERSHWIN

Beat

Music is propelled forward by *rhythm*, the element that organizes movement in time. The term refers to the length, or duration, of individual notes. The basic unit we use to measure time is called the *beat*—the regular pulsation heard in most Western styles of music. Some beats are stronger than others; these are known as *accented*, or strong, beats. In much of the music we hear, these strong beats occur at regular intervals—every other beat, every third beat, every fourth, and so on—and thus we perceive all the beats in groups of two, three, four, or more. These patterns into which rhythmic pulses are or-

Meter and measure

ganized are called *meters* and are marked off in *measures*, each measure containing a fixed number of beats. The first beat of each measure generally receives the strongest accent.

Meter is a broader term. While the term "rhythm" encompasses the overall movement of music in time, meter is the actual measurement of time. It

The principles of symmetry and repetition of elements in architecture are comparable to the regular organization of rhythm into meters. The Temple of the Warriors, *an eleventh-century structure in Chichén Itza, Yucatán.*

refers to the number of beats in a measure, the placement of accents within the measure, and the way each beat in a measure is divided into smaller parts. A parallel may be drawn in the realm of poetry. For example, the following stanza by the American poet Robert Frost is in a meter that alternates a strong and weak beat. A metrical reading of this poem will bring out the regular pattern of accented (´) and unaccented (-) syllables:

Thē wóods āre lóve-lȳ, dárk ānd déep.
Būt Í hāve próm-īs-és tō kéep,
Ānd míles tō gó bē-fóre Ī sléep,
Ānd míles tō gó bē-fóre Ī sléep.

When we read rhythmically, on the other hand, we bring out the natural flow of the language within the basic meter and the meaning of the words.

METRICAL PATTERNS

Much of Western music is based on simple recurring patterns of two, three, or four beats grouped together in a measure. As in poetry, these patterns, or meters, depend on the regular recurrence of an accent. Simplest of all is a succession of beats in which a strong beat alternates with a weak beat: ONE-two, ONE-two, or, in marching, LEFT-right, LEFT-right. This common pattern of two beats to a measure is known as *duple meter*.

Duple meter
Triple meter

Triple meter, another basic pattern, consists of three beats to a measure—one strong beat and two weak—and is traditionally associated with such dances as the waltz and the minuet.

Quadruple meter

Quadruple meter, also known as *common time*, contains four beats to the measure, with a primary accent on the first beat and a secondary accent on the third. Although it is sometimes not easy to tell duple and quadruple meter apart, quadruple meter usually has a broader feeling.

Simple meters
Compound meters

When duple, triple, and quadruple meters subdivide the beat into two or four, they are called *simple meters*. However, meters in which each beat is divided into three are known as *compound meters*. *Sextuple meter*, for example, with six beats to the measure, is usually heard as a duple-compound meter, in which the principal accents fall on one and four (ONE-two-three, FOUR-five-six). Marked by a gently flowing effect, this pattern is often found in lullabies.

The following examples illustrate the four basic patterns.

Examples of Meters

′ = primary accent
˘ = secondary accent
‾ = unaccented beat

SIMPLE METERS

Duple meter: *Twinkle, Twinkle, Little Star* (children's song)

Accents:	Twín-	klē,	twín-	klē,	lít-	tlē	stár,___	
Meter:	1	2	1	2	1	2	1	2
	Hów	Ī	wón-	dēr	whát	yōu	áre,___	
	1	2	1	2	1	2	1	2

Other examples of duple meter:
    Yankee Doodle (American Revolutionary War song)
    Oh, Susanna (19th-century American song by Stephen Foster)
    Dixie (American Civil War song)

Triple meter: *America* (patriotic song)

Mý	cōun-	trȳ	'tís_____	ōf	thēe,
1	2	3	1	2	3
Swéet	lānd	ōf	lí-	-	bēr-tȳ
1	2	3	1	2	3
Óf	thēe	Ī	síng._____		
1	2	3	1	2	3

Other examples of triple meter:
   The Star-Spangled Banner (U.S. national anthem)
   Happy Birthday (traditional American song)
   Amazing Grace (American hymn)
   Cielito lindo (traditional Spanish song)
   Goodbye, Old Paint (American cowboy song)

Quadruple meter: *America, the Beautiful* (patriotic song)

Ōh,	beaú-	-	tī-	fŭl	fōr	spá-	- ciōus skĭes,
4 |	1	2		3	4 |	1	2	3

Fōr	ám-	bēr	wăves	ōf	gráin,_____
4 |	1	2	3	4 |	1	2	3

Fōr	púr-	-	plē	moŭn- tāin	má-	- jēs-tĭes
4 |	1	2		3	4 |	1	2	3

Ā-	bóve	thē	frŭit-	ēd	pláin,_____
4 |	1	2	3	4 |	1	2	3

Other examples of quadruple meter:
   Shall We Gather at the River (19th-century American hymn)
   Battle Hymn of the Republic (American Civil War song)
   Aura Lea (folk song, same tune as *Love Me Tender*)
   Auld Lang Syne (traditional Scottish song)
   O Canada (Canadian national anthem)

COMPOUND METER

Sextuple meter: *Rock-a-bye Baby* (children's lullaby)

Róck- ā-	bȳe	bă-	-	bȳ,	ón	thē	trēe- tŏp,		
1	2	3	4	5	6 |	1	2	3	4	5	6|

Whén thē	wīnd	blŏws,	thē	crá-	dlē	wĭll	rŏck,		
1	2	3	4	5	6 |	1	2	3	4	5	6|

Other examples of sextuple meter:
   Greensleeves (English folk song)
   Silent Night (Christmas carol)
   Scarborough Fair (American folk song)
   When Johnny Comes Marching Home (American Civil War
      song)

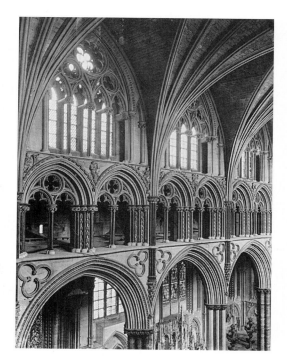

The duple subdivisions of the vaulted arches in the Angel Choir of Lincoln Cathedral (c. 1282), in England, can be compared to simple meters in music.

Upbeat

In some cases, a piece does not begin with an accented beat. For example, *America, the Beautiful,* in quadruple meter, begins with an *upbeat,* or on the last beat of the measure—in this case, on beat 4. (Notice that the Frost poem cited earlier also begins with an upbeat.)

Syncopation

Composers have devised a number of ways to keep the recurrent accent from becoming monotonous. The most common is the use of *syncopation,* a deliberate upsetting of the normal pattern of accentuation. Instead of falling on the strong beat of the measure, the accent is shifted to a weak beat or to an *offbeat* (in between the beats). Syncopation has figured in the music of the masters for centuries, and is characteristic of the African-American dance rhythms out of which jazz developed. The examples on the facing page illustrate the technique.

Syncopation is only one technique that throws off the regular patterns. A composition may change meters during its course. Indeed, certain twentieth-century pieces shift meters nearly every measure. Another technique is the simultaneous use of rhythmic patterns that conflict with the underlying beat, such as "two against three" or "three against four"—in a piano piece, for example, the left hand might play two notes to a beat, while the right hand plays three notes to the same beat. This is called *polyrhythm* (many rhythms), and occurs frequently in the musics of many African cultures as well as in music influenced by those cultures, such as jazz and rock. In some non-Western musics, the rhythmic organization is even more complex, being based on an *additive meter,* or grouping of irregular numbers of beats that add up to a larger overall pattern. For example, a rhythmic pattern of ten beats common

Polyrhythm

Additive meter

Examples of Syncopation

1. Gently syncopated: *Swing Low, Sweet Chariot* (duple meter) (African-American spiritual)

Swing low, _____	sweet		char-	- i- ot, ____	
1	2	|	1	2	|
com-in' for to	car-ry me		home _____		
1	2	|	1	2	|

2. Accented and syncopated: *Hello! Ma Baby* (quadruple meter) (ragtime song)

Hel-lo!	ma' ba-	by,	Hel-lo!	ma' ho-	ney,	
1	2	3	4	1	2	3	4 |
Hel-lo!	ma' rag-	time	gal._____			
1	2	3	4	1	2	3	4 |

in the music of India divides into groupings of 2 + 3 + 2 + 3. We will see that certain folk styles employ similar additive patterns of accents.

Some music moves without any strong sense of beat or meter. We might say that such a work is *nonmetric*, as some early Western music is, or that the pulse is veiled or weak, with the music moving in a floating rhythm that typifies certain non-Western styles.

Nonmetric

Time is a crucial dimension in music, and its first law is rhythm. This is the element that binds together the parts within the whole: the notes within the measure and the measure within the phrase.

Listening Activity: Rhythm

Tonight, from Bernstein's *West Side Story*

Let's return to *Tonight,* the same musical theater song we listened to in Chapter 1, and see what rhythmic and metric characteristics you can hear. Listen to the song again and clap your hands with the beat. (Hint: the main pulse moves at a moderate speed, just a little faster than one beat per second.) The song is in *duple meter,* alternating each *strong beat* with a *weak beat.* The first word of the text ("Tonight") prompted the composer to begin the song with an *upbeat* (or weak beat) that anticipates the accent or strong pulse of a *downbeat,* so that the word is sung as it is spoken—to-**night,** with the accent on the second syllable. Because this is a jazz-inspired piece composed in the mid–twentieth century, the melody is accompanied by complex rhythmic patterns that subdivide the beat and that shift accents to weak beats or *offbeats* (in between the beats), creating *syncopation*. The accompaniment also features *polyrhythm*, two different rhythmic patterns occurring simultaneously. If you have difficulty hearing any of these features, listen to the suggested examples below. (For the location of each in your sound package, see the table on the front and back inside covers of this book.)

Other Suggested Listening Examples
    Nonmetric—Gregorian chant: *Haec dies*
    Duple meter—Haydn: Symphony No. 94 in G major, second movement
    Triple meter—Mozart: *Eine kleine Nachtmusik*, third movement
               Brahms: *A German Requiem*, fourth movement
    Quadruple meter—Mozart: *Eine kleine Nachtmusik*, first movement
    Compound meter—Jacquet de la Guerre: Suite No. 1, 2nd Gigue
    Changing meter—
        Bernstein: *Mambo*, from *West Side Story*
        Bartók: *Interrupted Intermezzo*, from *Concerto for Orchestra*
    Veiled pulse—Debussy: *Prelude to "The Afternoon of a Faun"*
    Syncopation—Joplin: *Maple Leaf Rag*
    Polyrhythm—Ligeti: *Disorder*, from *Etudes for Piano*
               Traditional: Ugandan drumming

3

Harmony: Musical Space

"We have learned to express the more delicate nuances of feeling by penetrating more deeply into the mysteries of harmony."
—ROBERT SCHUMANN

To the linear movement of the melody, harmony adds another dimension: depth, or the simultaneous happenings in music. Harmony is to music what perspective is to painting—it introduces the impression of musical space. Not all musics of the world rely on harmony for interest, but it is central to most Western styles.

Harmony describes the movement and relationship of intervals and chords. We already know that an interval is the distance between any two tones. Intervals can occur melodically—that is, when one note follows another—or simultaneously. When three or more tones are sounded together, a *chord* is produced. The intervals from which melodies and chords are built are chosen from a particular *scale*, or collection of pitches arranged in ascending or descending order. For convenience, the tones of the most frequently used Western scales are assigned syllables, *do-re-mi-fa-sol-la-ti-do*, or numbers, 1-2-3-4-5-6-7-8 (both ascending scales). Thus the interval *do-re* (1-2) is a second, *do-mi* (1-3) is a third, *do-fa* (1-4) is a fourth, *do-sol* (1-5) is a fifth, *do-la* (1-6) is a sixth, *do-ti* (1-7) is a seventh, and *do-do* (1-8) is an *octave*. As you can see from the example on page 16, melody constitutes the horizontal aspect of music, while harmony, comprising blocks of tones (the chords), constitutes the vertical.

Chord
Scale

Syllables

Octave

THE FUNCTION OF HARMONY

Chords have meaning only in relation to other chords—that is, only as each chord leads into the next. Harmony therefore implies movement and progression. And the progression of harmonies in a musical work gives us a feeling of order and unity.

Harmony lends a sense of depth to music, as perspective does to painting. **Meindert Hobbema** *(1638–1709),* The Avenue, Middelharnis. (National Gallery, London)

Triad   The most common chord in Western music is a certain combination of three tones known as a *triad*. Such a chord may be built on any step, or *degree*, of the scale by combining every other note. A triad built on the first degree consists of the first, third, and fifth pitches of the scale (*do-mi-sol*); on the second degree, steps 2-4-6 (*re-fa-la*); on the third degree, steps 3-5-7 (*mi-sol-ti*); and so on. The triad is a basic formation in our music. In the example below, the melody of *Old MacDonald* is harmonized with triads. The supporting role of harmony is apparent when a singer or solo instrument is accompanied by piano. As in *Old MacDonald*, a vocalist sings the melody while an instrument provides the harmonic background. Melody and harmony do not function independently of one another. On the contrary, the melody suggests the harmony that goes with it, and each constantly influences the other.

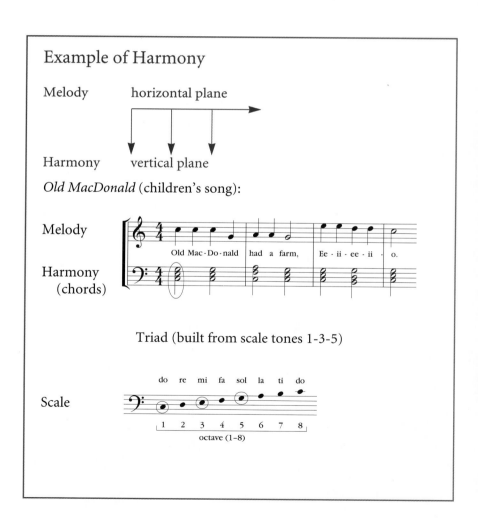

THE ORGANIZATION OF HARMONY

In all musics of the world, certain tones assume greater importance than others. In Western music, the first tone of the scale, *do*, also called the *tonic* or keynote, serves as a home base around which the others revolve and to which they ultimately gravitate. We observed this principle at work earlier with the tune *Amazing Grace* (p. 4). It is this sense of a home base that helps us recognize when a piece of music ends.

The principle of organization around a central tone, the tonic, is called *tonality*. The particular scale chosen as the basis of a piece determines the identity of the tonic and the tonality. Two different types of scales are commonly found in Western music written between about 1650 and 1900: major and minor. What characterizes these two types are the intervals on which they are built. We will learn more about the formulation of scales later (in Chapter 17). For the moment, it is necessary to know only that there are certain perceived differences between scales: music in major is usually thought of as bright, while minor often sounds more subdued. Some people find that minor sounds sadder to them than major. Indeed, a nineteenth-century composer would hardly choose a minor tonality for a triumphal march or for the grand finale of a piece. We will regard major and minor as scale types and as tonalities, each with its own unique quality of sound.

We distinguish between notes that belong to a particular scale and tonality and those that do not. The term *diatonic* describes melodies or harmonies that are built from the tones of a major or minor scale; *chromatic* (from the Greek word *chroma*, meaning "color") describes the full gamut of notes available in the octave.

Tonic

Tonality

Major and minor scales

Diatonic and chromatic

CONSONANCE AND DISSONANCE

Harmonic movement, as we will see, is generated by motion toward a goal or a feeling of resolution. This striving for resolution is the dynamic force in our music. It shapes the forward movement, providing focus and direction. Movement in music receives its maximum impetus from *dissonance*, a combination of tones that sounds discordant, unstable, in need of resolution.

Dissonance introduces the necessary tension into music in the same way suspense and conflict create tension in drama. Dissonance finds its resolution in *consonance*, a concordant (or agreeable) combination of musical tones that provides a sense of relaxation and fulfillment. At their extremes, dissonance

Dissonance

Consonance

can sound harsh, while consonance is more pleasing to the ear. Each complements the other, and each is a necessary part of the artistic whole.

In general, music has grown more dissonant through the ages. It is easy to understand why. A combination of tones that sounded extremely harsh when first introduced begins to seem less so as the sound became increasingly familiar. As a result, each later generation of composers uses ever more dissonant harmonies in order to create the same degree of excitement and tension as its predecessor.

Drone

Historically, harmony appeared much later than melody—about a thousand years ago—and its development took place largely in the West. In many Far Eastern cultures, harmony takes the subsidiary role of a single sustained tone, called a *drone*, against which melodic and rhythmic complexities unfold. This harmonic principle also occurs in certain European folk musics, where, for example, a bagpipe might play one or more accompanying drones to a lively dance tune.

Our harmonic system has advanced steadily over the past millennium, continually responding to new needs. Composers have tested the rules as they have experimented with innovative sounds and procedures. Yet their goal remains the same: to impose order on the raw material of sound, organizing the pitches so that they reveal a unifying idea.

Listening Activity: Harmony

Haydn's Symphony No. 94 in G major (*Surprise*)

Listening to this appealing orchestral work will help us recognize some aspects of *harmony* (the simultaneous happenings in music). We should notice first the simple—and singable—melody that begins the second movement. Its bright, happy nature is a good clue that the work is built on a *major scale*, and it hovers around a central tone, or *tonic* (called *do*), which serves as a kind of home base for the melody and its accompanying harmonies. At first, the harmony is hardly noticeable underneath the tune—that is, until the first loud, crashing *chord* (the simultaneous sounding of three or more notes). This is the composer's "surprise," humorously intended to awake dozing audience members (and students!). A few more loud chords interrupt the cheerful tune, after which Haydn changes the entire mood of the piece with a shift to *minor*, coupled with an increased volume level. (Hint: this happens about two minutes into the piece.) Suddenly, our attention is captured by the dramatic and emotional sound of a new *scale* (sequence of pitches) and its harmonies. We soon return to the familiar light-hearted version of the melody, built once again on a major scale. If you feel as though we have come full circle, then you have perceived the organizational principle of *tonality*, in which a work centers around a single pitch and scale. In general, this piece is *consonant*, or agreeable sounding, with tension built mostly from the volume changes and the shift to minor, and it is *diatonic* rather than *chromatic*, with its notes drawn mostly from the major or minor scale. For more practice hearing these musical principles, try some of the examples suggested below. (For the location of each in your sound package, see the table on the front and back inside covers of this book.)

Other Suggested Listening Examples
Major tonality—Mozart: *Eine kleine Nachtmusik*, third movement
Minor tonality—Beethoven: Symphony No. 5, first movement
Consonance—Handel: "Hallelujah Chorus," from *Messiah*
Dissonance—Ligeti: *Disorder*, from *Etudes for Piano*

4

Musical Texture

"Ours is an age of texture."—GEORGE DYSON

TYPES OF TEXTURE

Another property of music is what we call its texture, or fabric. Melodic lines may be thought of as the various threads that make up the musical fabric. This texture may be one of several distinct types.

The simplest texture is *monophonic*, or single-voiced. ("Voice" refers to an individual part or line, even when we are talking about instrumental music.) Here, the melody is heard without any harmonic accompaniment or other melodic lines. It may be accompanied by rhythm and percussion instruments that embellish it, but interest is focused on the single line rather than on any accompaniment. Up to about a thousand years ago, the Western music we know about was monophonic, as much music of the Far and Middle East is to this day.

Monophonic

One type of texture that is found widely outside the tradition of Western art music is based on two or more voices (parts) simultaneously elaborating the same melody, usually in an improvised performance. Called *heterophony*,

Heterophony

this technique usually results in a melody combined with an ornamented version of itself. It can be heard too in some folk musics as well as in jazz and spirituals, where *improvisation* (in which some of the music is created on the spot) is central to performance.

Polyphony

Counterpoint

Distinct from heterophony is *polyphony* (or many-voiced texture), in which two or more different melodic lines are combined, thus distributing melodic interest among all the parts. Polyphonic texture is based on *counterpoint*. This term comes from the Latin *punctus contra punctum,* "point against point" or "note against note"—that is to say, one musical line set against another. Counterpoint is the art of combining two or more simultaneous melodic lines, usually with rules defined in a particular era.

Homophony

In the fourth type of texture, *homophony,* a single voice takes over the melodic interest, while the accompanying parts take a subordinate role. Normally, they become blocks of harmony, the chords that support, color, and enhance the principal line. Here, the listener's interest is directed to a single melodic line, but this is conceived in relation to a harmonic background. Homophonic texture is heard when a pianist plays a melody in the right hand while the left sounds the chords, or when a singer or violinist carries the tune against a harmonic accompaniment on the piano. Homophonic texture, then, is based on harmony, just as polyphonic texture is based on counterpoint.

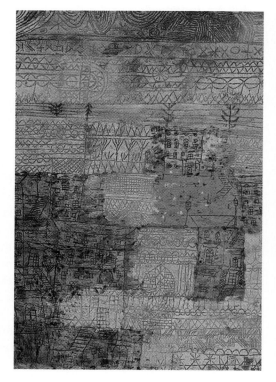

Line and texture are the subject of **Paul Klee's** *(1879–1940) painting* Neighborhood of the Florentine Villas *(1926).* (Musée National d'Art Moderne, Centre Georges Pompidou, Paris)

Examples of Musical Texture

Monophonic—one melodic line, no accompaniment
Gregorian chant: *Alleluia, Emitte spiritum:*

Al - le - lu - ia,_____ al - le - lu - ia,

Polyphonic—several independent melodic lines combined
Bach: Organ chorale prelude, *Jesu, Joy of Man's Desiring:*

Homophonic—one melody with accompaniment (melody on top)
Mozart: Piano Concerto in C major, second movement (piano solo):

A composition need not use one texture or another exclusively. For example, a large-scale work may begin by presenting a melody against a homophonic texture, after which the interaction of the parts becomes increasingly polyphonic as more independent melodies enter. So too in a largely homophonic piece, the composer may enhance the effect of the principal melody through an interesting play of countermelodies and counterrhythms in the accompanying parts.

We have seen that melody is the horizontal aspect of music, while harmony is the vertical. Comparing musical texture to the weave of a fabric consequently has validity. The horizontal threads, the melodies, are held together by the vertical threads, the harmonies. Out of their interaction comes a texture that may be light or heavy, coarse or fine.

CONTRAPUNTAL DEVICES

Imitation

When several independent lines are combined (in polyphony), one method composers use to give unity and shape to the texture is *imitation*, in which a melodic idea is presented in one voice and then restated in another. While the imitating voice restates the melody, the first voice continues with new material. Thus to the vertical and horizontal threads in musical texture imitation adds a third, the diagonal (see the example on facing page).

Canon and round

The length of the imitation may be brief or may last the entire work. In the latter case, we have a strictly imitative type of work known as a *canon*. (The name comes from the Greek word for "law" or "order.") The simplest and most popular form of canon is a *round*, in which each voice enters in succession with the same melody, which can be repeated endlessly; well-known examples include *Row, Row, Row Your Boat* and *Frère Jacques* (*Are You Sleeping?*). In the example below, the round begins with one voice singing "Row, row, row your boat," then another voice joins it in imitation, followed by a third voice and finally a fourth, creating a four-part polyphonic texture.

Retrograde Inversion

Contrapuntal writing is marked by a number of devices that have flourished for centuries. *Retrograde* refers to a statement of the melody backward, beginning with its last note and proceeding to its first. *Inversion* is a technique that turns the melody upside down; that is, it follows the same intervals but in the opposite direction (if the melody originally moved up a third, the

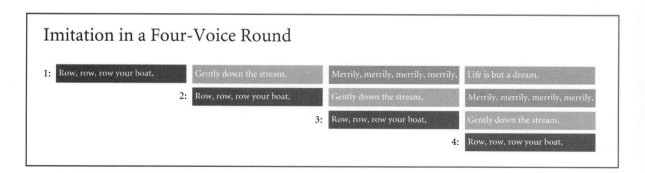

Imitation in a Four-Voice Round

1: Row, row, row your boat,   Gently down the stream,   Merrily, merrily, merrily, merrily,   Life is but a dream.

2: Row, row, row your boat,   Gently down the stream,   Merrily, merrily, merrily, merrily,

3: Row, row, row your boat,   Gently down the stream,

4: Row, row, row your boat,

inverted version moves down a third). These two techniques can be combined in the *retrograde inversion* of a melody: upside down and backward. *Augmentation* calls for the melody to be presented in longer time values, often twice as slow as the original. We can think of this procedure as augmenting or increasing the time it takes to play the melody. The opposite technique is called *diminution*, in which the melody is presented in short time values, thus diminishing the time it takes to be played. These structural devices are often difficult for the ear to pick out.

Retrograde inversion
Augmentation

Diminution

Examples of Contrapuntal Devices*

Imitation at interval of fifth above (not exact):

Other contrapuntal devices:

Original: MELODY

Inversion: ᴍƎ˥OꓒY

Retrograde: YDOLEM

Retrograde inversion: ᴚꓒO˥Ǝᴍ

Augmentation: MELODY

Diminution: MELODY

*Based on *The Art of Fugue*, by Johann Sebastian Bach

MUSICAL TEXTURE AND THE LISTENER

Different textures require different kinds of listening. Monophonic music with its single melodic line is, in principle, the simplest type of music, and we perceive it on a linear time line. Homophonic music is the most familiar texture to most of us today, and we are therefore accustomed to focusing on the main melody and its subordinate harmonies, and following the interrelation of the two. Indeed, much of the music we have heard since childhood—including many traditional and popular styles—consists of melody and accompanying chords.

Polyphony and heterophony present the most challenging textures. Still, in heterophony, we are generally aware of the principal melody, in spite of the linear fabric that surrounds it. In polyphony, we must be attentive to the independent lines as they flow against one another, each in its own rhythm. With practice and repeated hearings, we will learn to follow the individual voices within the contrapuntal web.

Listening Activity: Texture

"Hallelujah Chorus," from Handel's *Messiah*

The famous "Hallelujah Chorus," from *Messiah* (often performed at Christmas- or Eastertime), can help us review the different musical textures we have learned. Throughout, Handel varies the *texture*, or the way the melodic and harmonic threads of the work are interwoven, between homophony, monophony, and polyphony. A short, majestic orchestral introduction leads to choral statements on the word "Hallelujah" in a *homophonic texture* (all the parts move together), supporting the main melody. After ten homophonic statements of "Hallelujah," the text "For the Lord God Omnipotent reigneth" is set in a *monophonic texture* (all the voice parts sing the same notes together). The text is repeated—with "Hallelujah" set homophonically and "For the Lord God Omnipotent reigneth" monophonically. And the composer then increases the complexity of the music by combining these two texts and their melodies into a *polyphonic texture* (two or more different melodic lines played together). Listen for how *imitation* is used to build an intricate polyphonic fabric—with the words "And He shall reign for ever and ever," each of the choral parts (first the basses, then tenors, altos, and sopranos) enters in turn with the same melody, overlapping the previous statement. As the chorus progresses, see if you can recognize the shifts between these three textures and how the composer emphasizes the word "Hallelujah" throughout by returning to a simpler, ho-mophonic setting each time the word recurs. If you need more practice in hearing different textures, try the examples listed below. (For the location of each in your sound package, see the table on the front and back inside covers of this book.)

Other Suggested Listening Examples
    Monophonic texture—Gregorian chant: *Haec dies*
    Polyphonic texture—Bernstein: *Mambo,* from *West Side Story*
    Imitation—Bach: Fugue in C minor
            Josquin: *Ave maria . . . virgo serena*
    Homophonic texture—Handel: "Rejoice greatly," from *Messiah*
    Heterophonic texture—*The Wind That Shakes the Barley,* by The Chieftains

5

Musical Form

"The principal function of form is to advance our understanding. It is the organization of a piece that helps the listener to keep the idea in mind, to follow its development, its growth, its elaboration, its fate."—ARNOLD SCHOENBERG

In all the arts, a balance is required between unity and variety, between symmetry and asymmetry, activity and repose. Nature too has embodied this balance in the forms of plant and animal life and in what is perhaps the supreme achievement—the human form. In music, *form* gives us an impression of conscious choice and rational arrangement. In other words, it is a work's structure or shape, the way the elements of a composition have been combined, or balanced, to make it understandable to the listener.

STRUCTURE AND DESIGN IN MUSIC

Our lives are composed of sameness and difference: certain details occur again and again, others are new. Music, regardless of its cultural origin, mirrors this dualism. Its basic structural elements are *repetition and contrast*—unity and variety. Repetition fixes the material in our minds and satisfies our

Repetition and contrast

need for the familiar. Contrast stimulates our interest and feeds our love for change. From the interaction between the familiar and the new—the repeated elements and the contrasting ones—result the contours of musical form. Every kind of musical work, from the nursery rhyme to the symphony, has a conscious structure.

Variation

One principle of form that falls between repetition and contrast is *variation*, where some aspects of the music are altered but the original is still recognizable. We hear this formal technique when we listen to a new arrangement of a well-known popular song; the tune is recognizable, but many features of the version we know may be changed.

The variety of musical structures reflects procedures worked out by generations of composers. No matter how diverse the structures, they are based in one way or another on repetition and contrast. The forms, however, are not fixed molds into which composers pour their material. What makes a piece of music unique is the way it adapts a general plan to its own requirements. All faces have two eyes, a nose, and a mouth; in each face, though, these features make a wholly individual combination. Similarly, no two symphonies of Haydn or Mozart, no two sonatas of Beethoven, are exactly alike. Each is a fresh and unique solution to the problem of fashioning musical material into a logical and coherent form.

Improvisation

Performers sometimes participate in shaping a composition. In works based primarily on *improvisation* (pieces created in performance as opposed to being precomposed), such as most jazz and rock, and certain non-Western styles, all the elements described above—repetition, contrast, and variation—play a role. Thus, even when a piece is created on the spot, a balance of these structural principles is present.

TWO-PART AND THREE-PART FORM

Binary form

Ternary form

Two of the most basic patterns in Western music are two-part, or *binary*, form, based on a statement and a departure, without a return to the opening section; and three-part, or *ternary*, form, which extends the idea of statement and departure by bringing back the first section. (In our example, opposite, the pattern of chorus-verse-chorus gives us a ternary form.) Formal patterns are generally outlined with letters: binary form as **A-B** and ternary form as **A-B-A** (illustrated in the chart opposite).

Both two-part and three-part forms are common in short pieces such as songs and dances. Ternary form, with its logical symmetry and its balancing of the outer sections against the contrasting middle one, constitutes a simple, clear-cut formation that is favored by architects and painters as well as musicians (see illustration on p. 26).

Binary and Ternary Form

Binary form: *Yankee Doodle*

Statement—**A**

Yan-kee Doo-dle went to town, a - rid-ing on a po - ny,

Stuck a fea-ther in his cap and called it ma-ca - ro - ni.

Departure—**B**

Yan-kee Doo-dle keep it up, Yan-kee Doo-dle dan - dy,

Mind the mu-sic and the step and with the girls be han - dy.

Ternary form: *Goodbye, Old Paint*

Statement—**A**

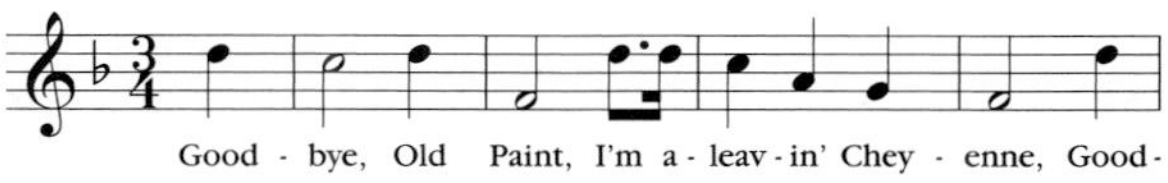

Good - bye, Old Paint, I'm a - leav - in' Chey - enne, Good-

bye, Old Paint, I'm a - leav - in' Chey - enne. My

Contrast
(departure)—**B**

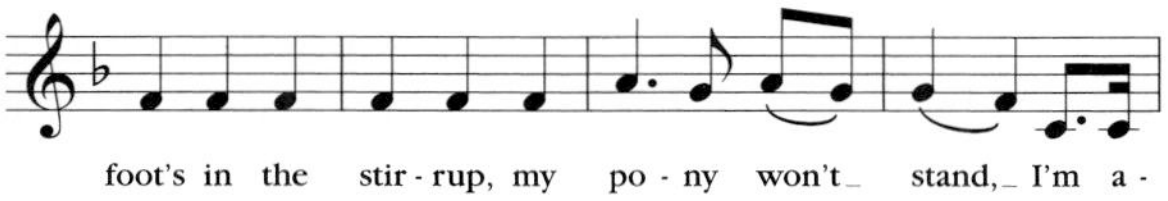

foot's in the stir - rup, my po - ny won't stand, I'm a -

leav - in' Chey - enne and I'm off to Mon - ta - na. Good-

Repetition—**A**

bye, Old Paint, I'm a - leav - in' Chey - enne, Good-

bye, Old Paint, I'm a - leav - in' Chey - enne.

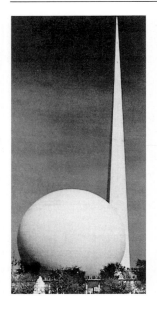

*(Left): the Trylon and Perisphere, symbols of the New York World's Fair of 1939, are a visual realization of binary (**A-B**) form. (Right): the Taj Mahal in Agra, India, one of the world's seven wonders, illustrates that three-part (**A-B-A**) form is as appealing to the eye as it is to the ear.*

THE BUILDING BLOCKS OF FORM

Theme   When a melodic idea is used as a building block in the construction of a musical work, we call it a *theme*. The theme is the first in a series of musical events, all of which must grow out of its basic idea as naturally as the plant does from the seed. Spinning out a theme, weaving and reweaving its lines, is the essence of musical thinking. This process of expansion has its parallel in prose writing, where an idea stated at the beginning of a paragraph is embroidered and enlarged upon until it has been explored as thoroughly as the author desires. Each sentence leads smoothly into the one that follows. In similar fashion, every measure in a musical work takes up where the one before left off and brings us logically to the next.

Thematic development   The most tightly knit kind of expansion in music is known as *thematic development*—elaborating or varying a musical idea, revealing its capacity for growth. One of the most important techniques in musical composition, thematic development requires imagination, craftsmanship, and intellectual power. The principle of extended melodic elaboration is important also to the melody-oriented styles of many Far Eastern and Middle Eastern musics.

In the process of development, certain procedures have proved to be particularly effective. The simplest is repetition, which may be either exact or varied. Or the idea may be restated at a higher or lower pitch level; the restatement is known as a *sequence*.

Another important technique of thematic development entails breaking up a theme into its component parts, or motives. A *motive* is the smallest fragment of a theme that forms a melodic-rhythmic unit. Motives are the cells of musical growth. By breaking themes into fragments, repeating and varying motives, and combining them in new patterns, composers impart to their works the qualities of evolution and growth.

These musical building blocks can be seen in action even in simple songs, such as the popular national tune *America* (see below). In this piece, the opening three-note motive ("My country") is repeated in sequence (at a different pitch level) on the words "Sweet land of." Another example of a sequence occurs later in the piece: the musical motive set to the words "Land where our fathers died" is repeated beginning on a lower note for the words "Land of the pilgrim's pride."

Whatever the length or style of a composition, it will show the principles of repetition and contrast, of unity and variety, that we have traced here. One formal practice linked to repetition that can be found throughout much of the world is *call and response*, or responsorial music. Heard in many African, Native American, and African-American musics, this style of performance is based on a social structure that recognizes a singing leader who is imitated by a chorus of followers. We will study the practice first as it occurs in early styles of Western church music (see p. 329). Yet another widely used structural procedure linked to the principle of repetition is *ostinato*, a short musical pattern—melodic, rhythmic, or harmonic—that is repeated continually

Sequence

Motive

Call and response

Ostinato

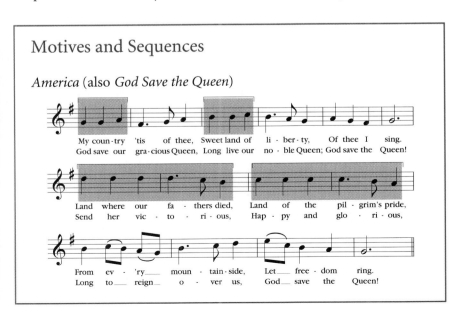

Motives and Sequences

America (also *God Save the Queen*)

My coun-try 'tis of thee, Sweet land of li - ber-ty, Of thee I sing.
God save our gra-cious Queen, Long live our no - ble Queen; God save the Queen!

Land where our fa - thers died, Land of the pil - grim's pride,
Send her vic - to - ri - ous, Hap - py and glo - ri - ous,

From ev - 'ry__ moun - tain-side, Let__ free - dom ring.
Long to__ reign o - ver us, God__ save the Queen!

throughout a work or a major section of a composition. This unifying technique is especially prevalent in many African musics as well as popular styles such as blues, jazz, and rock.

Composed and improvised music displays the striving for organic form that binds together the individual tones within a phrase, the phrases within a section, the sections within a *movement* (a complete, comparatively independent division of a large-scale work), and the movements within the work as a whole—just as a novel binds together the individual words, phrases, sentences, paragraphs, chapters, and parts.

Movement

Listening Activity: Form

March, from Tchaikovsky's *The Nutcracker*

The catchy march from the popular ballet *The Nutcracker* offers us a chance to test our musical memory in listening for the *form*, or structure, of a composition. This selection is in *ternary*, or three-part, form (outlined **A-B-A**), which provides both familiarity, through *repetition* of music, and variety, through *contrast*, or new music. We must pay attention to the opening *theme*, a melodic idea used as a building block in the piece, so that we can recognize it when it returns later in the march. Here, Tchaikovsky has given us a memorable brassy tune (played by the trumpets) that we hear a number of times before the work moves on. The clue that we have arrived at the new, contrasting middle section of the work is the absence of this tune, replaced with a sense of rushing movement in a downward cascading melody played by other instruments. This new idea passes by very quickly, and soon we find ourselves back to the familiar march heard at the opening. This time the melody is heard with some *variation*—although different instruments accompany the theme, we can still recognize it. You may want to practice listening for other musical forms with some of the examples listed below. (For the location of each in your sound package, see the table on the front and back inside covers of this book.)

Other Suggested Listening Examples

Variation and improvisation—Ellington: *Ko-Ko*
Binary form—Jacquet de la Guerre: Suite No. 1, 2nd Gigue
Ternary form—Handel: "Rejoice greatly," from *Messiah*
Motive and thematic development—Beethoven: Symphony No. 5 in
    C minor, first movement
Responsorial music—Gregorian chant: *Haec dies*
Ostinato—Ellington: *Ko-Ko*

6

Tempo and Dynamics

"Any composition must necessarily possess its unique tempo. . . . A piece of mine can survive almost anything but a wrong or uncertain tempo."—IGOR STRAVINSKY

THE PACE OF MUSIC

In our musical system, meter tells us how many beats there are in a measure, but it does not tell us whether these beats occur slowly or rapidly. The *tempo*, or rate of speed, of the music provides the answer to this vital question. Consequently, the flow of music in time involves both meter and tempo.

Tempo

Tempo carries emotional implications. We hurry our speech in moments of agitation or eagerness. Vigor and gaiety are associated with a brisk speed, just as despair usually demands a slow one. In an art that moves in time, as music does, the pace is of prime importance, drawing from listeners responses that are both physical and psychological.

Because of the close connection between tempo and mood, tempo markings indicate the character of the music as well as the pace. The markings, along with other indications of expression, are given by tradition in Italian. This practice reflects the domination of Italian music in Europe during the period from around 1600 to 1750, when such performance directions were established. A list of some of the most common tempo markings follows:

Tempo markings

grave	solemn (very, very slow)
largo	broad (very slow)
adagio	quite slow
andante	a walking pace
moderato	moderate
allegro	fast (cheerful)
vivace	lively
presto	very fast

Frequently, we also encounter modifying adverbs such as *molto* (very), *meno* (less), *poco* (a little), and *non troppo* (not too much). Of great importance are

Dynamic contrasts in music may be compared to light and shade in painting. **Georges de La Tour** *(1593–1652),* Joseph the Carpenter. (The Louvre, Paris)

terms indicating a change of tempo, among them *accelerando* (getting faster), *ritardando* (holding back, getting slower), and *a tempo* (in time, or returning to the original pace).

LOUDNESS AND SOFTNESS

Dynamics

Dynamics denote the volume (degree of loudness or softness) at which music is played. Like tempo, dynamics can affect our emotional response. The main dynamic indications, listed below, are based on the Italian words for soft *(piano)* and loud *(forte).*

pianissimo (***pp***)	very soft
piano (***p***)	soft
mezzo piano (***mp***)	moderately soft
mezzo forte (***mf***)	moderately loud
forte (***f***)	loud
fortissimo (***ff***)	very loud

Directions to change the dynamics, either suddenly or gradually, are indicated by words or signs. Among the most common are the following:

crescendo (◁———): growing louder
decrescendo or *diminuendo* (———▷): growing softer
sforzando (**sf**), "forcing": accent on a single note or chord

TEMPO AND DYNAMICS AS ELEMENTS OF MUSICAL EXPRESSION

The composer adds markings for tempo and dynamics to help shape the expressive content of a work. These expression marks steadily increased in number during the late eighteenth and nineteenth centuries, as composers tried to make their intentions known ever more precisely, until in the early twentieth century few decisions were left to the performer.

If tempo and dynamics are the domain of the composer, what is the role of performers and conductors in interpreting a musical work? Performance directions can be somewhat imprecise—what is loud or fast to one performer may be moderate in volume and tempo to another. Even when composers give precise tempo markings in their scores (using a device known as a *metronome*, which measures the exact number of beats per minute), performers have the final say in choosing a tempo that best delivers the message of the music. And for the many styles of music—non-Western, folk, and popular, among others—that do not rely on composer directions or even printed music, the performer takes full responsibility for interpreting the music.

Metronome

Tempo and Dynamics in a Musical Score

From Beethoven's Piano Sonata in C minor, Op. 13 (*Pathétique*)

Tempo: Very fast and with vigor (Allegro molto e con brio)
Dynamics: Soft (*p*), growing (*cresc.*) to loud (*f*), then soft (*p*)

Listening Activity: Tempo and Dynamics

Haydn's Symphony No. 94 in G major (*Surprise*)

Let's return to the second movement of Haydn's *Surprise* Symphony to consider elements of *expression* in music. Both *tempo*, or rate of speed, and *dynamics*, or level of softness and loudness, can affect our emotional response to music. Haydn wished this piece to have a bouncy, cheerful character, and thus set the tempo at *Andante* (a moderate walking pace). We noted earlier (in Chapter 3) that the composer influences our response to the music by varying dynamics. Listen to how the melody opens softly (with a marking of *piano*), then is repeated even more quietly (*pianissimo*). But then our relaxed state of mind is suddenly jarred by a very loud chord (played *fortissimo*), after which the quiet melody returns with softer dynamics. Several more loud chords (marked *forte*) interrupt the peaceful mood of the work. Soon, however, the entire character changes, when new harmonies (in minor) are introduced at a *fortissimo* dynamic level. This shifting of dynamics is one important way a composer can introduce variety and contrast into a musical work, thereby evoking emotional responses from the listener. The additional listening examples below will be helpful in reviewing other expression markings commonly found in music. (For the location of each in your sound package, see the table on the front and back inside covers of this book.)

Other Suggested Listening Examples

Grave—Purcell: Dido's Lament, from *Dido and Aeneas*

Adagio—Beethoven: Piano Sonata in C minor (*Pathétique*), second movement

Moderato—Brahms: *A German Requiem*, fourth movement

Allegro—Bartók: *Concerto for Orchestra*, fourth movement

Vivace—Stravinsky: *Petrushka*, opening

Piano—Copland: *Street in a Frontier Town*, from *Billy the Kid*, opening

Forte—Stravinsky: *Petrushka*, opening

Crescendo/decrescendo—Brahms: *A German Requiem*, fourth movement, opening

Musical Instruments and Ensembles

7

Musical Instruments I

"Whoever plays an instrument must be conversant with singing."—GEORG PHILIPP TELEMANN

PROPERTIES OF MUSICAL SOUND

Most musical sounds can be described in terms of four qualities, or proper-ties: pitch, duration, volume, and timbre. We have seen that *pitch* refers to the relative position—high or low—of a tone in a scale. Pitch is determined by the rate of vibration, measured in *frequency* (the number of vibrations per second), which depends on the length of the vibrating body. Other condi-tions being equal, the shorter a string or column of air, the more rapidly it vi-brates and the higher the pitch. The longer a string or column of air, the fewer the vibrations per second and the lower the pitch. The width, thickness, density, and tension of the vibrating body also affect the outcome. *Duration* depends on the length of time over which the vibration continues. We hear tones as being not only high or low but also short or long. *Volume* (dynam-ics) depends on the intensity of the vibrations, which determines whether the tone strikes us as being loud or soft.

Pitch

Duration

Volume

Timbre

The fourth property of sound—known as tone color, or *timbre*—best accounts for the striking differences in the sound of instruments. It is what makes a trumpet sound altogether different from a guitar or a drum. Timbre is influenced by a number of factors, such as the size, shape, and proportions of the instrument, the material it is made of, and the manner in which vibration is produced (a string, for example, may be bowed, plucked, or struck).

Instrument

People produce music vocally (by singing or chanting) or by playing a musical instrument. (An *instrument* is a mechanism that generates musical vibrations and launches them into the air.) Each voice type and instrument has a limited melodic range (the distance from the lowest to the highest tone) and dynamics range (the degree of softness or loudness beyond which the voice or instrument cannot go). We describe a specific area in the range of an instrument or voice, such as low, middle, or high, as its *register*. These and a host of similar considerations help determine the composer's and performer's choices.

Register

THE VOICE AS A MODEL FOR INSTRUMENTAL SOUND

The human voice is the most natural of all musical instruments; it is also one of the most widely used—all cultures have some form of vocal music. Each person's voice has a particular quality, or character, and range. Our standard designations for vocal ranges, from highest to lowest, are *soprano, mezzo-soprano,* and *alto* (short for *contralto*) for female voices, *tenor, baritone,* and *bass* for male voices.

Vocal ranges

In earlier eras, Western social and religious customs severely restricted women's participation in public musical events. Thus young boys, and occasionally adult males with soprano- or alto-range voices, sang female roles in church music and on the stage. In the sixteenth century, women singers came into prominence in secular (nonreligious) music. Tenors were most often featured as soloists in early opera; the lower male voices, baritone and bass, became popular soloists in the eighteenth century. In other cultures, the sound of women's voices has always been preferred for certain styles of music; for example, in certain Muslim cultures of northern Africa, wedding songs are traditionally performed by professional women singers.

Throughout the ages, the human voice has served as a model for instrument builders and players who have sought to duplicate its lyric beauty, expressiveness, and ability to produce *vibrato* (a throbbing effect) on their instruments.

THE WORLD OF MUSICAL INSTRUMENTS

The diversity of musical instruments played around the world defies description. Since every conceivable method of sound production is used, and every possible raw material employed, it would be impossible to list them all here. However, specialists have devised a method of classifying instruments that is based solely on the way their sound is generated. There are four basic categories in this system. *Aerophones* produce sound by using air as the primary vibrating means. Common instruments in this grouping are flutes, whistles, bagpipes, and horns—in short, nearly any wind instrument. *Chordophones* are instruments that produce sound from a vibrating string stretched between two points. The string may be set in motion by bowing or plucking, so the instruments are as disparate as the violin, harp, guitar, Japanese koto, Chinese hammered dulcimer (*yangqin*), and Indian sitar.

Aerophones

Chordophones

   Idiophones produce sound from the substance of the instrument itself. They may be struck, blown, shaken, scraped, or rubbed. Examples of idiophones are bells, rattles, xylophones, and cymbals—in other words, a wide variety of percussion instruments, among others. *Membranophones* are drum-type instruments that are sounded from tightly stretched membranes. These instruments can be struck, plucked, rubbed, or even sung into, thus setting the skin in vibration (see illustrations on pp. 35–36).

Idiophones

Membranophones

Aerophone: a European bagpipe, often used in folk music, sounds a sustained drone under the melodic line.

Chordophone: the Japanese koto, a plucked instrument with thirteen strings, is often played with the three-stringed shamisen (right).

Idiophone: the rattles on the African dancers' ankles are one common type of idiophone.

Membranophone: Native Americans playing drums and shaking a gourd rattle (idiophone).

In the next chapter, the instruments used most frequently in Western music will be described and categorized. Throughout the book, however, you will see allusions to other instruments associated with popular and art music cultures around the world that have influenced the Western tradition.

Listening Activity: Voices

Quartet, from Verdi's *Rigoletto*

Let's investigate the musical character (*timbre*, or tone color) and range of the standard voice designations in a quartet from an opera by Verdi. This work allows us to hear four of the vocal ranges, first in quick succession and then singing together. We will study the setting and story of the Italian opera at a later point in the text; for now, we only need to know that each of the four characters—two men and two women—has a different vocal range and sound quality. The principal singer, who begins the work, is a *tenor* with a robust and powerful voice that projects an emotional quality, especially in its high range. Notice how dramatic the voice sounds as he reaches a musical climax on a long note near the top of his range. (This high *pitch* is determined by the rate at which his vocal chords vibrate.) Soon, a dialogue begins between the *alto* (or *contralto*), whose voice is dark and heavy, and the *soprano*, who sings in a higher range and whose vocal quality is brighter. Finally, a deep-voiced *baritone* enters as the supporting and lowest voice in the ensemble. At times, the ear is drawn again to the tenor, with the other voices accompanying him, and at other points, the soprano soars high above the ensemble with her crystal-clear sound. You can listen to additional vocal examples, as listed below (as well as different kinds of instruments), to hear not only the ranges, but the differing qualities of sound that the different singers possess. (For the location of each example in your sound package, see the table on the front and back inside covers of this book.)

Other Suggested Listening Examples

Soprano—Handel: "Rejoice greatly," from *Messiah*

Mezzo-soprano—Purcell: Dido's Lament, from *Dido and Aeneas*

Tenor—Bernstein: *Tonight* (solo in *Tonight Ensemble*), from *West Side Story*

Baritone—Schubert: *Erlking*

Bass—Wagner: Finale, from *Die Walküre*

Ensemble (baritone, tenor, soprano)—Mozart: Act I, scene 7, from *The Marriage of Figaro*

Chordophone—*The Moon Reflected on the Second Springs* (bowed and struck)

Aerophone—*The Wind That Shakes the Barley*, by The Chieftains (wooden flute at beginning; later, bagpipe)

Idiophone (cowbell) and membranophones—Bernstein: *Mambo*, from *West Side Story*

8

Musical Instruments II

"In music, instruments perform the function of the colors employed in painting."—HONORÉ DE BALZAC

The instruments of the Western world—and especially those of the orchestra—may be further categorized into four familiar groups: strings, woodwinds, brass, and percussion. We will see, however, that these categories, or families, of instruments are not entirely homogeneous; that is, all woodwinds are not made of wood, nor do they share a common means of sound production. Also, we will see that certain instruments do not fit neatly into any of these convenient categories (the piano, for example, is both a string and a percussion instrument).

STRING INSTRUMENTS

The string family, like the grouping of chordophones, includes two types of instruments: those that are bowed and those that are plucked. The bowed string family has four principal members: violin, viola, violoncello, and double bass, each with four strings (double basses often have five) that are set vibrating by drawing a bow across them. The hair of the bow is rubbed with *rosin* (a substance made from hardened tree sap) so that it will "grip" the strings. The bow is held in the right hand, while the left hand is used to "stop" the string by pressing a finger down at a particular point, thereby leaving a certain portion of the string free to vibrate. By stopping the string at another point, the performer changes the length of the vibrating portion, and with it the rate of vibration and the pitch.

Violin   The *violin* evolved to its present form at the hands of the brilliant instrument makers who flourished in Italy from around 1600 to 1750. Most famous among them were the Amati and Guarneri families—in these dynasties, the secrets of the craft were transmitted from father to son—and the master builder of them all, Antonio Stradivari (c. 1645–1737). Preeminent as a melody instrument, the violin is capable of brilliance and dramatic effect, subtle nuances from soft to loud, and great agility in rapid passages throughout its extremely wide range.

Viola   The *viola* is somewhat larger than the violin and thus has a lower range. Its strings are longer, thicker, and heavier. The tone is husky in the low register, somber and penetrating in the high. The viola is an effective melody instrument that often balances the more brilliant violin by playing a countermelody. It usually fills in the harmony, or it may double another part. One instrument is said to *double* (reinforce) another when it plays the same notes an octave higher or lower.

Violoncello   The *violoncello*, popularly known as *cello*, is lower in range than the viola and is notable for its singing quality, which takes on a dark resonance in the low register. Cellos often carry the melody, they enrich the sound with their full timbre, and together with the double basses, they supply the foundation for the harmony of the string family.

Double bass   The *double bass*, known also as a *contrabass* or *bass viol*, is the lowest of the string instruments of the orchestra. Accordingly, it plays the bass part—that is, the foundation of the harmony. Its deep tones support the cello part an octave lower.

These four instruments constitute the string section, or what is often called "the heart of the orchestra," a designation that indicates the section's versatility and importance.

Orchestral string instruments can be played in many styles and can produce many special effects. They excel at playing *legato* (smoothly, connecting the notes) as well as the opposite, *staccato* (with notes short and detached). A special effect, *pizzicato* (plucked), is created when a performer plucks the string with a finger instead of using the bow. *Vibrato*, a throbbing effect, is achieved by a rapid wrist-and-finger movement on the string that slightly alters the pitch. For a *glissando*, a finger of the left hand slides along the string while the right hand draws the bow, thereby sounding all the pitches under the left-hand finger, in one swooping sound. *Tremolo*, the rapid repetition of a tone through a quick up-and-down movement of the bow, is associated with suspense and excitement. No less important is the *trill*, a rapid alternation between a tone and one adjacent to it.

Double-stopping means playing two strings simultaneously; playing three or four strings together is called *triple-* or *quadruple-stopping*. Using this technique, the members of the violin family, essentially melodic instruments, become capable of producing harmony all by themselves. Another effect is created by the *mute*, a small attachment that fits over the bridge, muffling (and changing) the sound. *Harmonics* are crystalline tones in a very high register that are produced by lightly touching the string at certain points while the bow is drawn across the string.

Special effects

Violinist Anne-Sophie Mutter.

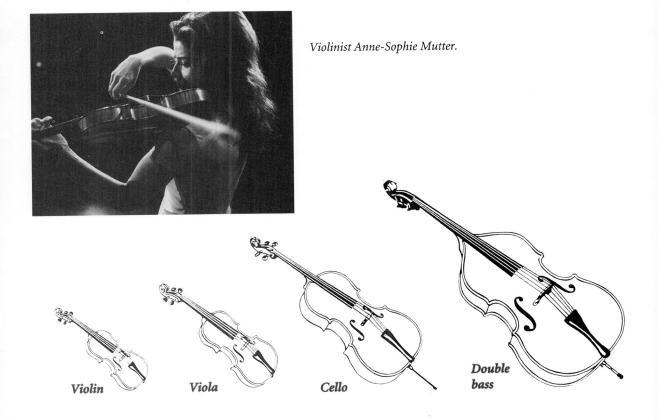

Violin   *Viola*   *Cello*   *Double bass*

Yo-Yo Ma, cellist.   *Milt Hinton playing the double bass.*

Harp

Guitar

Two plucked string instruments, the harp and the guitar, are also widely used. The *harp* is one of the oldest of musical instruments, with a home in many cultures outside Europe. Its plucked strings, whose pitches are changed by means of pedals, produce an ethereal tone. Chords on the harp are frequently played in broken form—that is, the tones are sounded one after another instead of simultaneously. From this technique comes the term *arpeggio*, which means a broken chord (*arpa* is Italian for "harp"). Arpeggios can be created in a variety of ways on many instruments.

The *guitar*, another old instrument, dating back at least to the Middle Ages, probably originated in the Middle East. It has always been a favorite solo instrument, and is associated today with folk and popular music as well as classical styles. The standard acoustical (as opposed to electric) guitar is made of wood and has a fretted fingerboard and six nylon strings, which are plucked with the fingers of the right hand or with a pick. The *electric guitar*, an electronically amplified instrument capable of many specialized techniques, comes in two main types: the hollow-bodied (or electro-acoustic), favored by jazz musicians, and the solid-bodied, used by rock musicians. Related to the guitar are such traditional instruments as the banjo and mandolin.

David Byrne (of the Talking Heads) on the electric guitar.

Narciso Yepes plays the classical guitar.

WOODWIND INSTRUMENTS

The tone of woodwind instruments (aerophones) is produced by a column of air vibrating within a pipe that has little holes along its length. When one or another of these holes is opened or closed, the length of the vibrating air column within the pipe is changed. Woodwind players are capable of remarkable agility on their instruments by means of an intricate mechanism of keys arranged to suit the natural position of the fingers.

This group is less homogeneous than the strings. Nowadays woodwinds are not necessarily made of wood, and they require several different methods of setting up vibration: blowing across a mouth hole (flute family), blowing into a mouthpiece that has a single reed (clarinet and saxophone families), or blowing into a mouthpiece fitted with a double reed (oboe and bassoon families). They do, however, have one important feature in common: the holes in their pipes. In addition, their timbres are such that composers think of them and write for them as a group.

Flute

The *flute* is the soprano voice of the woodwind family. Its tone is cool and velvety in the expressive low register, mellow in the middle, and often brilliant in the upper part of its range. The present-day flute, made of a silver alloy rather than wood, is a cylindrical tube, closed at one end, that is held horizontally. The player blows across a mouth hole cut in the side of the pipe near the closed end. The flute is used frequently as a melody instrument—its timbre stands out against the orchestra—and offers the performer great versatility in playing rapid repeated notes, scales, and trills. The *piccolo* (from the Italian *flauto piccolo*, "little flute") is actually the highest pitched instrument in the orchestra. In its upper register, it takes on a shrillness that is easily heard even when the orchestra is playing *fortissimo*.

Piccolo

Oboe

The *oboe* continues to be made of wood. The oboist blows directly into a double reed, which consists of two thin strips of cane bound together so as to leave between them a very narrow passage for air. The oboe's timbre, generally described as nasal and reedy, is often associated with pastoral effects and nostalgic moods. As the oboe's pitch is reasonably stable, it traditionally sounds the tuning note for the other instruments of the orchestra. The *English horn* is an alto oboe. Its wooden tube is wider and longer than that of the oboe and ends in a pear-shaped opening called a *bell*, which largely accounts for its soft, expressive timbre. The instrument is not well named, for it is neither English nor is it a horn.

English horn

Clarinet

The *clarinet* has a single reed, a small thin piece of cane fastened against its chisel-shaped mouthpiece. The instrument possesses a smooth, liquid tone, as well as a remarkably wide range from low to high and from soft to loud. Almost as agile as the flute, it has an easy command of rapid scales, trills, and repeated notes. The *bass clarinet*, one octave lower in range than the clarinet, has a rich tone, a wide dynamic range, and great flexibility.

Bass clarinet

Bassoon

The *bassoon*, another double-reed instrument, possesses a tone that is weighty and thick in the low register, crisp and sonorous in the middle, and reedy and intense in the upper. Capable of a hollow-sounding staccato and wide leaps that can sound humorous, it is at the same time a highly expressive instrument. The *contrabassoon* produces the lowest tone of the woodwinds. Its function in the woodwind section of supplying a foundation for the harmony may be compared with that of the double bass among the strings.

Contrabassoon

Saxophone

The *saxophone* is of more recent origin than the other woodwind instruments, having been invented by the Belgian Adolphe Sax in 1840. It was created by combining the features of several other instruments—the single reed of the clarinet, the conical tube of the oboe, and the metal body of the brass instruments. The saxophone blends well with either woodwinds or brass. By the 1920s, it had become the characteristic instrument of the jazz band, and has remained a favorite sound in many styles of music today.

Flutist James Galway.

Elaine Duvas, oboist.

Richard Stolzman playing the clarinet in Carnegie Hall.

Bernard Garfield playing the bassoon.

BRASS INSTRUMENTS

The main instruments of the brass family (also aerophones) are the trumpet, French horn (generally referred to simply as horn), trombone, and tuba. All these instruments have cup-shaped mouthpieces (except for the horn, whose mouthpiece is shaped like a funnel) attached to a length of metal tubing that flares at the end into a bell. The column of air within the tube is set vibrating by the tightly stretched lips of the player, which are buzzed like a kind of double reed. Going from one pitch to another involves not only mechanical means, such as a slide or valves, but also enough muscular control to vary the pressure of the lips and breath. Brass and woodwind instrument players often **Embouchure** speak about their *embouchure*, referring to the entire oral mechanism of lips, lower facial muscles, and jaws.

Trumpets and horns were widely used in the ancient world. At that time, they were fashioned from animal horns and tusks, which at a later stage of civilization were reproduced in metal, and were used chiefly for religious ceremonies and military signals. Their tone could be terrifying—remember that in the biblical account, the walls of Jericho came tumbling down to the sound of trumpets.

Trumpet The *trumpet*, highest in pitch of the brass family, possesses a brilliant timbre that lends radiance to the orchestral mass. It is often associated with ceremonial display. The trumpet can also be muted, using a pear-shaped, metal or cardboard device that is inserted in the bell to achieve a bright, buzzy sound. Jazz trumpet players have experimented with various kinds of mutes that produce many different timbres.

French horn The *French horn* is descended from the ancient hunting horn. Its mellow resonance lends itself to a variety of uses: it can be mysteriously remote in soft passages and nobly sonorous in loud ones. The timbre of the horn blends equally well with woodwinds, brasses, and strings. Although capable of considerable agility, the horn is often used in sustained, supportive parts. The muted horn has a distant sound. Horn players often "stop" their instrument by plugging the bell with the right hand, producing a somewhat eerie and rasping quality.

Trombone The *trombone*—the Italian word means "large trumpet"—has a full and rich sound that combines the brilliance of the trumpet with the majesty of the horn, but in a lower range. In place of valves, it features a movable U-shaped slide that alters the length of the vibrating air column in the tube.

Tuba The *tuba* is the bass instrument of the brass family. Like the string bass and contrabassoon, it furnishes the foundation for the harmonic fabric. The tuba adds body to the orchestral tone, and a dark resonance ranging from velvety softness to a rumbling growl.

Wynton Marsalis, trumpeter.

Christian Lindberg, trombonist.

Barry Tuckwell playing the French horn.

Noreen Harris playing the tuba.

Other brass instruments

Other brass instruments are used in concert and marching bands. Among these is the *cornet*, which makes a rounder, less brilliant sound than the trumpet. In the early twentieth century, the cornet was very popular in concert bands; today, however, the trumpet has replaced it in virtually all ensembles. The *bugle*, which evolved from the military (or field) trumpet of early times, has a powerful tone that carries well in the open air. Since it is not equipped with valves, it is able to sound only certain tones of the scale, which accounts for the familiar pattern of duty calls in the army. The *fluegelhorn*, much used in jazz and commercial music, is really a valved bugle with a wide bell. The *euphonium* (also known as the *baritone horn*) is a tenor-range instrument whose shape resembles the tuba. And the *sousaphone*, an adaptation of the tuba designed by the American bandmaster John Philip Sousa, features a forward bell and is coiled to rest over the shoulder of the marching player.

PERCUSSION INSTRUMENTS

The percussion section of the orchestra is sometimes referred to as "the battery." Its members accentuate the rhythm, generate excitement at the climaxes, and inject splashes of color into the orchestral sound.

Pitched percussion instruments

The percussion family (encompassing the vast array of idiophones and membranophones) is divided into two categories: instruments capable of being tuned to definite pitches, and those that produce a single sound in the realm between music and noise (instruments of indefinite pitch). In the former class are the *timpani*, or *kettledrums*, which are generally used in sets of two or four. The timpani is a hemispheric copper shell across which is stretched a "head" of plastic or calfskin held in place by a metal ring. A pedal mechanism enables the player to change the tension of the head, and with it the pitch. The instrument is played with two padded sticks, which may be either soft or hard. Its dynamic range extends from a mysterious rumble to a thunderous roll. The timpani first arrived in western Europe from the Middle East, where Muslims and Turks on horseback used them in combination with trumpets.

Also among the pitched percussion instruments are several members of the *xylophone* family; instruments of this general type are used in Africa, Southeast Asia, and throughout the Americas. The xylophone consists of tuned blocks of wood laid out in the shape of a keyboard. Struck with mallets with hard heads, the instrument produces a dry, crisp sound. The *marimba* is a more mellow xylophone of African origin. The *vibraphone* combines the principle of the xylophone with resonators, each containing revolving disks operated by electric motors. Its highly unusual tone is marked by an exaggerated vibrato, which can be controlled by changing the speed of the motor.

This selection of percussion instruments includes (top, left to right): vibraphone, chimes, xylophone, gong, and marimba. (Center): timbales, suspended cymbal, and various percussion accessories. (Bottom): timpani, jazz drum set, concert tom-toms, marching snare drum, concert snare drums, crash cymbals, and bass drum. Instrument identification by Dr. John J. Papastefan, University of South Alabama.

The vibraphone is often featured in jazz groups, and has been used by a number of contemporary composers.

The *glockenspiel* (German for "set of bells") consists of a series of horizontal tuned steel bars of various sizes, which when struck produce a bright metallic sound. The *celesta*, a kind of glockenspiel that is operated by means of a keyboard, resembles a miniature upright piano. The steel plates are struck by small hammers to produce a sound like a music box. *Chimes,* or *tubular bells*, a set of tuned metal tubes of various lengths suspended from a frame and struck with a hammer, are frequently called on to simulate church bells.

Unpitched percussion instruments

The percussion instruments that do not produce a definite pitch include the *side drum, or snare drum*, a small cylindrical drum with two heads stretched over a shell of metal and played with two drumsticks. This instrument owes its brilliant tone to the vibrations of the lower head against taut snares (strings). The *tenor drum*, larger in size, has a wooden shell and no snares. The *bass drum* is played with a large soft-headed stick and produces a low, heavy sound. The *tom-tom* is a colloquial name given to Native American or African drums of indefinite pitch. The *tambourine* is a round, hand-held drum with "jingles"—little metal plates—inserted in its rim. The player can strike the drum with the fingers or elbow, shake it, or pass a hand over the jingles. Of Middle Eastern origin, it is particularly associated with music of Spain, as are *castanets*, little wooden clappers moved by the player's thumb and forefinger.

The *triangle* is a slender rod of steel bent into a three-cornered shape; when struck with a steel beater, it gives off a bright, tinkling sound. *Cymbals* came to the West from central Asia during the Middle Ages. They consist of two large circular brass plates of equal size, which when struck against each other produce a shattering sound. The *gong*, or *tam-tam*, is a broad circular disk of metal, suspended in a frame so as to hang freely. When struck with a heavy drumstick, it produces a deep roar. The gong has found its widest use in the Far East and Southeast Asia, where it is central to the ensemble known as the *gamelan* (see p. 54).

OTHER INSTRUMENTS

Piano

Aside from the instruments just discussed, several others, especially those of the keyboard family, are frequently heard in solo and ensemble performances. The *piano* was originally known as the *pianoforte*, Italian for "soft-loud," which suggests its wide dynamic range and capacity for nuance. Its strings are struck with hammers controlled by a keyboard mechanism. The piano cannot sustain tone as well as the string and wind instruments, but in the hands of a fine performer, it is capable of producing a singing melody.

Pianist André Watts.

Each string (except in the highest register) is covered by a damper that stops the sound when the finger releases the key. There are generally three pedals. If the one on the right, the damper pedal, is pressed down, all the dampers are raised, so that the strings continue to vibrate, producing a luminous haze of sound. The pedal on the left, known as the soft (or *una corda*) pedal, shifts the hammers to reduce the area of impact on the strings, thereby inhibiting the volume of sound. In between is the sustaining pedal (missing on upright pianos), which sustains only the tones held down at the moment the pedal is depressed.

The piano has a notable capacity for brilliant scales, arpeggios, trills, rapid passages, and octaves. Its range from lowest to highest pitch spans more than seven octaves, or eighty-eight semitones. Closely related is the *electric piano*, an electronically amplified instrument capable of producing piano-like sounds. The more generic electronic keyboard, commonly used in rock groups, can create numerous different sonorities.

The *organ*, once regarded as "the king of instruments," is a wind instru- **Organ** ment. The air flow to each of its many pipes is controlled by the organist from a console containing two or more keyboards and a set of pedals. Grada-tions in the volume of tone are made possible by enclosing some of the pipes in shuttered cabinets called swell boxes. The organ's multicolored sonority can easily fill a huge space. Electrically amplified keyboards, capable of imi-tating pipe organs and other timbres, have become commonplace, and they have been followed by such similar sound-production methods as oscillators, digital waveform synthesizers, and sampling devices. (On early organ types and their music, see pp. 353, 454.)

The instruments described in this and the previous chapter form a vivid and diversified group. To composers, performers, and listeners alike, they offer an endless variety of colors and shades of expression.

Listening Activity: Instruments

Britten's *The Young Person's Guide to the Orchestra*

Let's check your ability to recognize the four groups of instruments that make up the Western orchestra as well as the sound of each individual instrument by listening to a work written expressly for this purpose. Britten's *The Young Person's Guide to the Orchestra* introduces the listener first to the sound of the entire orchestra, then to each of its instrument families in the order *woodwinds, brasses, strings,* and *percussion.* The work then passes the principal melody through each instrument individually, proceeding from the highest-ranged instrument to the lowest. If you turn to Listening Guide 1 (pp. 59–60), you can see the order in which the instruments are heard. If you find this exercise difficult to follow, you might look in your college library for a recording of this piece that is narrated (or watch the narrated video *The Instruments of the Orchestra*). To hear some instruments that are not a regular part of the orchestra, try the additional listening examples below. (For the location of each in your sound package, see the table on the front and back inside covers of this book.)

Other Suggested Listening Examples

Saxophone—Ellington: *Ko-Ko*

Piano—Beethoven: Piano Sonata in C minor (*Pathétique*), second movement

Piano (electronic and sampler)—Reich: *Check It Out,* from *City Life*

Harpsichord—Jacquet de la Guerre: Suite No. 1, 2nd Gigue

9

Musical Ensembles

The great variety in musical instruments is matched by a wide assortment of ensembles, or performance groups. Some are homogeneous—for example, choral groups using only voices or perhaps only men's voices. Others are more heterogeneous—for example, the orchestra, which features instruments from the different families. Across the world, any combination is possible.

CHORAL GROUPS

Choral music—music performed by many voices in a chorus or choir—is sung around the world, both for religious purposes (sacred music) and for secular (nonspiritual) occasions. Loosely defined, a *chorus* is a fairly large body of singers who perform together; their music is usually sung in several voice parts. Most often the group consists of both men and women, but choruses can also be restricted to women's or men's voices only. A *choir* is traditionally a smaller group, often connected with a church or with the performance of sacred music. (Later we will hear an example sung by Ladysmith Black Mambazo, a South African men's choir that often sings religious music.) The standard voice parts in both chorus and choir correspond to the voice ranges described earlier: sopranos, altos, tenors, and basses.

Chorus

Choir

In early times, choral music was often performed without accompaniment, a style of singing known as *a cappella* (meaning "in the church style"). The organ eventually became coupled with the choir in church music, and by the eighteenth century, the orchestra also had established itself as a partner of the chorus.

A cappella

The boy's choir of St. Thomas's Church in Leipzig, Germany, where Johann Sebastian Bach was once choirmaster.

Other choral groups   Smaller, specialized vocal ensembles include the *madrigal choir* and *chamber choir*. The madrigal choir might perform *a cappella* secular works, known as *part songs*. The designation "chamber choir" refers to a small group of up to twenty-four singers, performing either *a cappella* or with piano accompaniment.

INSTRUMENTAL CHAMBER ENSEMBLES

Chamber music is ensemble music for a group of two to about a dozen players, with one player to a part—as distinct from orchestral music, in which a single instrumental part may be performed by as many as eighteen players or more. The essential trait of chamber music is its intimacy.

Many of the standard chamber music ensembles consist of string players.

The Colorado String Quartet (Julie Rosenfeld, violin; Diane Chaplin, cello; Deborah Redding, violin; Francesca Martin Silos, viola) enjoys an international reputation.

A standard combination is the *string quartet*, made up of two violins, viola, and cello. Other popular combinations are the *duo sonata* (soloist with piano); the *piano trio, quartet,* and *quintet*, each made up of a piano and string instruments; the *string quintet*; as well as larger groups—the *sextet, septet,* and *octet*. Winds too form standard combinations, especially *woodwind* and *brass quintets*. Some of these ensembles are listed below.

These chamber music combinations have remained popular well into the twentieth century. We will see that contemporary composers have experimented with new groupings that combine voice with small groups of instruments and electronic elements with live performers. In some cultures, chamber groups mix what might seem to be unlikely timbres to the Western

Standard Chamber Ensembles

DUOS

    Solo instrument
    Piano

TRIOS

String trio
    Violin 1
    Viola or Violin 2
    Cello

Piano trio
    Piano
    Violin
    Cello

QUARTETS

String quartet
    Violin 1
    Violin 2
    Viola
    Cello

Piano quartet
    Piano
    Violin
    Viola
    Cello

QUINTETS

String quintet
    Violin 1
    Violin 2
    Viola 1
    Viola 2
    Cello

Piano quintet
    Piano
    String quartet (Violin 1,
        Violin 2, Viola, Cello)

Woodwind quintet
    Flute
    Oboe
    Clarinet
    Bassoon
    French horn (a brass instrument)

Brass quintet
    Trumpet 1
    Trumpet 2
    French horn
    Trombone
    Tuba

Ravi Shankar (center) in a classical Indian ensemble featuring two sitars (long-necked, fretted chordophone) and tabla (a pair of tuned hand drums).

listener—in India, plucked strings and percussion are standard, and in some styles of Chinese music, plucked and bowed strings are normally combined with flutes.

THE ORCHESTRA

In its most general sense, the term "orchestra" may be applied to any performing body of diverse instruments—the Japanese ensemble used for court entertainments (called *gagaku*) or the gamelan orchestras of Bali and Indonesia, made up largely of gongs, xylophone-like instruments, and drums. (See illustration on p. 490.) In the West, the term is now synonymous with *symphony orchestra*, an ensemble of strings coupled with an assortment of woodwinds, brass, and percussion instruments.

The symphony orchestra has varied in size and makeup throughout its history, but has always featured string instruments as its core. From its origins as a small group of twenty or so members, the orchestra has grown into an ensemble of more than a hundred musicians, approximately two-thirds of whom are string players. The list on page 56 shows the distribution of instruments typical of a large orchestra today.

The instruments of the orchestra are arranged to achieve the best balance of tone. Thus, most of the strings are near the front, as are the gentle woodwinds. The louder brass and percussion are at the back. A characteristic seating plan for the Orchestre Symphonique de Montréal is shown opposite; this arrangement varies somewhat from one orchestra to another.

Above: the Orchestre Symphonique de Montréal, Charles Dutoit, conductor.
Below: the seating plan of the orchestra.

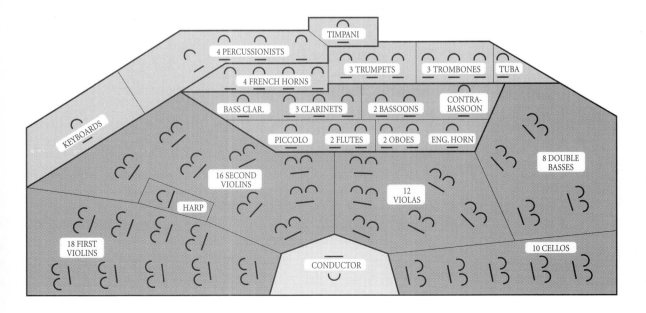

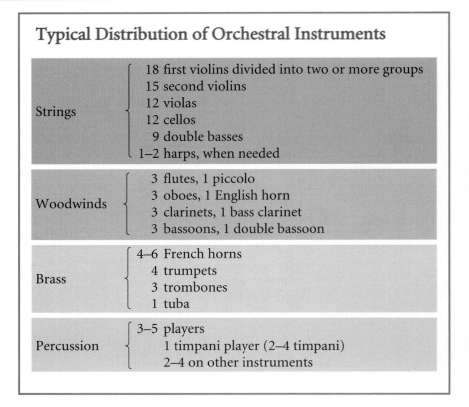

Typical Distribution of Orchestral Instruments

Strings	18 first violins divided into two or more groups 15 second violins 12 violas 12 cellos 9 double basses 1–2 harps, when needed
Woodwinds	3 flutes, 1 piccolo 3 oboes, 1 English horn 3 clarinets, 1 bass clarinet 3 bassoons, 1 double bassoon
Brass	4–6 French horns 4 trumpets 3 trombones 1 tuba
Percussion	3–5 players 1 timpani player (2–4 timpani) 2–4 on other instruments

CONCERT, JAZZ, AND ROCK BANDS

"Band" is a generic name applied to a variety of ensembles, most of which feature winds and percussion at their core. The band is a much-loved American institution, whether it is a concert, marching, or military band or a jazz or rock ensemble. The earliest wind and percussion groups (including Turkish "Janissary" bands—see p. 288) were used for military purposes: musicians accompanied soldiers to war, playing their brass and percussion instruments from horseback and their fifes and drums from among the ranks of the foot soldiers to spur the troops on into battle. Concert wind groups originated in the Middle Ages. In northern Europe, a wind band of three to five musicians played each evening, often from the high tower of a local church or city hall. From these traditions grew the military bands of the French Revolution and American Civil War. One American bandmaster, John Philip Sousa (1854–1932), achieved worldwide fame with his brass band and the repertory of marches he wrote for it.

The Indiana University marching band in formation for a football game.

Today the *concert band* (sometimes called a *wind ensemble*) ranges in size from forty to eighty or so players; it is an established institution in most secondary schools, colleges, and universities, and in many communities as well. Modern composers like to write for this ensemble, since it is usually willing to play new compositions. The *marching band*, well-known today in the United States and Canada, commonly entertains at sports events and parades. Besides its core of winds and percussion, this group often includes a spectacular display of drum majors/majorettes, flag twirlers, and the like.

The precise instrumentation of *jazz bands* depends on the particular music being played, but generally includes a reed section made up of clarinets and saxophones of various sizes, a brass section of trumpets and trombones, and a rhythm section of percussion, piano, and strings, especially double bass and electric guitar. *Rock bands* typically feature amplified strings, percussion, and electronically generated sounds.

Concert band

Marching band

Jazz band

Rock band

THE ROLE OF THE CONDUCTOR

When they are playing, Western musicians in large ensembles such as an orchestra, band, or chorus need to think about meter in order to keep "in time," and a conductor helps them do this. The conductor beats the meter with the right hand in a prescribed pattern that all the musicians in the group understand. These conducting patterns, shown in the diagrams on p. 58, further emphasize the strong and weak beats of the measure: beat 1, the strongest in any meter, is always given a downbeat, or a downward motion of the hand; a secondary accent is shown by a change of direction; and the last beat of the measure, a weak beat, is always an upbeat or upward motion, thereby leaving the right hand ready for the downbeat of the next measure.

American conductor Leonard Bernstein assembled an orchestra and chorus from East and West Germany for a performance of Beethoven's Ninth Symphony at the East Berlin Schauspielhaus, December 23, 1989, one month after the Berlin Wall fell.

Basic Conducting Patterns

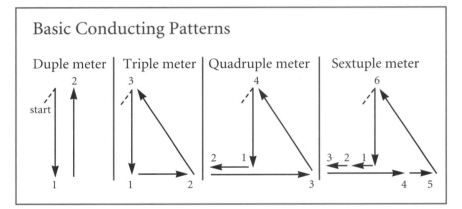

THE ORCHESTRA IN ACTION

A helpful introduction to the modern orchestra is Benjamin Britten's *The Young Person's Guide to the Orchestra*, which was written expressly to illustrate the timbre of each instrument. The work, composed in 1946 and subtitled *Variations and Fugue on a Theme of Purcell*, is based on a dance tune by Henry Purcell (1659–1695), a great seventeenth-century English composer.

Britten introduces the sound of the entire orchestra playing together, then the sonorities of each instrumental family as a group—woodwinds, brasses, strings, percussion—and finally repeats the statement by the full orchestra. Once the listener has the theme, or principal melody, well in mind, every instrument is featured in order from highest to lowest within each family. Next we encounter variations of the theme, each played by a new instrument with different accompanying instruments. (See Listening Guide 1 for the order of instruments.) The work closes with a grand fugue, a polyphonic form popular in the Baroque era (1600–1750), which is also based on Purcell's theme. The fugue, like the variations, presents its subject, or theme, in rapid order in each instrument. (For a discussion of the fugue, see p. 456.)

Listening Guide 1

CD: Chr/Std 1/1–7
Cassette: Chr/Std 1A/1

BRITTEN: *The Young Person's Guide to the Orchestra*
(Variations and Fugue on a Theme of Purcell)   (Total time: 17:24)

Date of work: 1946

Theme: Based on a dance from Henry Purcell's incidental music to the play *Abdelazar*
(*The Moor's Revenge*)

Form: Theme and variations, followed by a fugue

☐1	0:00	**I. Theme:** 8 measures in D minor, stated six times to illustrate the orchestral families: 1. Entire orchestra 2. Woodwinds 3. Brass 4. Strings 5. Percussion 6. Entire orchestra

II. Variations: 13 short variations, each illustrating a different instrument.

		Variation	Family	Solo instrument	Accompanying instruments
☐2	3:01	1	Woodwinds:	flutes, piccolo	violins, harp, and triangle
		2		oboes	strings and timpani
		3		clarinets	strings and tuba
		4		bassoons	strings and snare drum
☐3	6:13	5	Strings:	violins	brass and bass drum
		6		violas	woodwinds and brass
		7		cellos	clarinets, violas, and harp
		8		double basses	woodwinds and tambourine
		9		harp	strings, gong, and cymbal
☐4	10:33	10	Brass:	French horns	strings, harp, and timpani
		11		trumpets	strings and snare drum
		12		trombones, tuba	woodwinds and high brass
☐5	12:50	13	Percussion:	various	strings

(Order of introduction: timpani, bass drum and cymbals, timpani, tambourine and triangle, timpani, snare drum and wood block, timpani, castanets and gong, timpani, whip, whole percussion section)

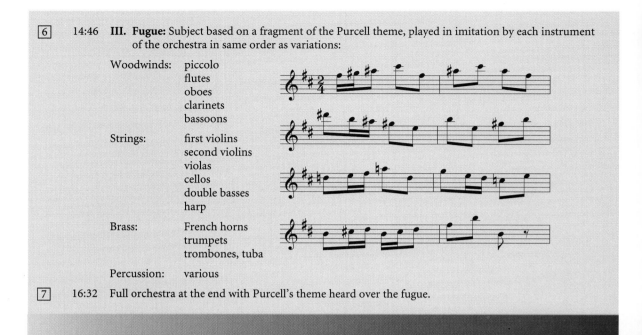

6 14:46 **III. Fugue:** Subject based on a fragment of the Purcell theme, played in imitation by each instrument of the orchestra in same order as variations:

Woodwinds: piccolo
            flutes
            oboes
            clarinets
            bassoons

Strings: first violins
            second violins
            violas
            cellos
            double basses
            harp

Brass: French horns
            trumpets
            trombones, tuba

Percussion: various

7 16:32 Full orchestra at the end with Purcell's theme heard over the fugue.

The modern orchestra, with its amplitude of tonal resources, its range of dynamics, and its infinite variety of color, offers a memorable experience to both the musician and the music lover. It is clearly one of the wonders of Western musical culture.

Suggested Listening Examples

Choral groups
    Chorus—Palestrina: Gloria, from *Pope Marcellus* Mass
    Choir—Josquin: *Ave maria . . . virgo serena*
    Men's choir—Bernstein: *Tonight Ensemble,* from *West Side Story* (opening)
    Madrigal choir—Monteverdi: *A un giro sol*
Chamber music
    String chamber ensemble—Mozart: *Eine kleine Nachtmusik,* first movement
    Voice and chamber ensemble (20th century)—Schoenberg: *Pierrot lunaire,* No. 18
    Instrumental chamber ensemble (20th century)—Ung: *Spiral*

> **Orchestra**
> > Baroque orchestra—Vivaldi: *Spring*, from *The Four Seasons*
> > > > > Handel: Alla hornpipe, from *Water Music*
> > Classical orchestra—Beethoven: Symphony No. 5 in C minor
> > Romantic orchestra—Smetana: *The Moldau*
> > Twentieth-century orchestra—
> > > Stravinsky: *Petrushka*
> > > Larsen: *Fresh Breeze*, from *Symphony: Water Music*
> **Choir with orchestra**—Bach: Cantata No. 80, first movement
> **Jazz band**—Ellington: *Ko-Ko*
> **Traditional Irish band**—*The Wind That Shakes the Barley*, by The Chieftains
>
> (For the location of each in your sound package, see the table on the front and back inside covers of this book.)

10

Style and Function of Music in Society

"A real musical culture should not be a museum culture based on music of past ages. . . . It should be the active embodiment in sound of the life of a community—of the everyday demands of people's work and play and of their deepest spiritual needs."
—WILFRID MELLERS

In every culture, music is intricately interwoven with the lives and beliefs of its people. This is especially true of many non-Western societies where, just as in the West, the "classical" exists alongside the "popular" and both are nourished from the rich store of traditional music that is closely allied with daily living. (Later, we will study *The Moon Reflected on the Second Springs*, a piece written by a Chinese folk musician that is today viewed as "classical" conservatory repertory.) Music serves different functions in different societies, though some basic roles are universal. It accompanies religious and civic ceremonies, it helps workers establish a uniform rhythm to get the job done more efficiently, and it provides entertainment through song and dance. The social organization of any particular culture has much to do with its musical types and styles. In some cultures, such as in the Western classical tradition, only a few people are involved with the actual performance of music; in others, such as that of the African Pygmies, cooperative work is so much a part of society that the people sing as a group, with each person contributing a separate part to build a complex whole.

Genres

There is music for every conceivable occasion, but the specific occasions celebrated vary from one culture to another. Thus musical *genres*, or categories of repertory, do not necessarily transfer from one society to the next, though they may be similar. For example, Japanese *Noh* drama and Peking opera serve essentially the same social role as opera does in the Western world. And we can distinguish in most cultures between *sacred music*, for religious or spiritual functions, and *secular music*, for and about everyday people outside a religious context.

It is important to differentiate between genre and form: a *genre* is a more general term that suggests something of the overall character of the work as well as its function. For example, the term *symphony* is a genre designation for a standard format—usually a four-movement orchestral work. As we will see later, each movement has a specific internal *form*, or structure. "Sym-

Medium

phony" also implies the *medium*, or the specific group that performs the piece—in this case, an orchestra.

Titles for musical compositions occasionally indicate the genre and key, such as Symphony No. 94 in G major, by Joseph Haydn. Another way works are identified is through a cataloguing system, often described by *opus number* (*opus* is Latin for "work"; an example is Polonaise, Opus 53, a piano work by Chopin). Other titles are more descriptive, such as *The Nutcracker* (a ballet by the Russian composer Tchaikovsky), *The Trout* (a song by Schubert, an Austrian composer), and *The Wind That Shakes the Barley* (an Irish dance tune performed by The Chieftains).

Suggested Listening Examples

Sacred music—
    Palestrina: Gloria, from *Pope Marcellus* Mass
    Brahms: *A German Requiem*, fourth movement
Secular music—Farmer: *Fair Phyllis*
               Schubert: *Erlking*
Popular music—Joplin: *Maple Leaf Rag*
Crossover—Bernstein: Excerpts from *West Side Story*
Traditional music—*The Wind That Shakes the Barley*, by The Chieftains
For examples of Western art music styles, see individual chapters.

Just as the context for music—when, why, and by whom a piece is performed—varies from culture to culture, so do aesthetic judgments of what is beautiful and what is appropriate. For example, the Chinese consider a thin, tense vocal tone desirable in their operas, while the Italians prefer a full-throated, robust sound in theirs. Likewise, certain performers and styles gain or lose in popularity as cultural preferences change.

Not all music is written down and learned from books or formal lessons. Music of most cultures of the world, including some styles of Western popular and traditional music, is transmitted by example (through a master-apprentice relationship) or by imitation and is performed from memory. The preservation of music without the aid of written notation is referred to as *oral transmission.*

Oral transmission

We will focus much of our study on Western art music—that is, the notated music of a cultivated and largely urban society. We often label art music as "classical," or serious, for lack of better terms. However, the lines that distinguish art music from other kinds are often blurred. Popular and traditional musics are art forms in their own right: performers of these styles may be as talented as those that present classical music; and both jazz and rock are considered by many to be new art forms, having already stood the test of time. To confuse these categories further, some composers and performing artists *cross over* from one type of music to another—from jazz to rock, from rock to Western classical—or simply borrow elements of one style to use in another, drawing them ever closer. Later we will hear elements of Latin-American dance music in the musical theater work *West Side Story* (Chapter 77) and some elements of Western blues combined with a traditional African singing style in choral music of the South African ensemble Ladysmith Black Mambazo (see Chapter 78).

Actors performing in a Noh play (a Japanese theatrical genre of music and dance).

Transition I

Hearing Musical Styles

"A good style should show no sign of effort. What is written should seem a happy accident."—SOMERSET MAUGHAM

THE CONCEPT OF STYLE

Style may be defined as the characteristic way an artwork is presented. We distinguish between the style of a novel and that of an essay, between the style of a cathedral and that of a palace. The word may also indicate the creator's personal manner of expression—the distinctive flavor that sets one artist apart from all others. Thus we speak of the literary style of Dickens or Shakespeare, the painting style of Picasso or Rembrandt, the musical style of Bach or Mozart. We often identify style with nationality, as when we refer to French, Italian, or German style; or with an entire culture, as when we contrast a Western musical style with one of China, India, or some other region.

Treatment of elements   What makes one musical work sound similar to or different from another? It is the individualized treatment of the elements of music. We have seen that Western music is largely a melody-oriented art based on a particular musical system, from which the underlying harmonies are also built. Musics of other cultures may sound foreign to Western ears, sometimes "out of tune," because they are based on entirely different musical systems, and many do not involve harmony to any great extent. One important factor in these differing languages of music is the way in which the octave is divided and scales are produced, an area we will explore in more detail in Chapter 17. Complex rhythmic procedures and textures set some world musics apart from Western styles, while basic formal considerations—such as repetition, contrast, and variation—bring musics of disparate cultures closer. In short, a style is made up of pitch, time, timbre, and expression, creating a sound that each culture recognizes as its own.

MUSICAL STYLES IN HISTORY

The arts change from one age to the next, and each historical period has its own stylistic characteristics. No matter how greatly the artists, writers, and composers of a particular era may vary in personality and outlook, when seen in the perspective of time, they turn out to have certain qualities in common. Because of this, we can tell at once that a work of art—whether music, poetry, painting, sculpture, or architecture—dates from the Middle Ages or the Renaissance, from the eighteenth century or the nineteenth. The style of a period, then, is the total art language of all its artists as they react to the artistic, political, economic, religious, and philosophical forces that shape their environment. We will find that a knowledge of historical styles will help us place a musical work within the context (time and place) in which it was created.

Scholars will always disagree as to precisely when one style period ends and the next begins. Each period leads by imperceptible degrees into the following one, dates and labels being merely convenient signposts. The outline below shows the generally accepted style periods in the history of Western music. Each represents a conception of form and technique, an ideal of beauty, a manner of expression and performance attuned to the cultural climate of the period—in a word, a style!

Historical periods

400–1450:	Middle Ages
400–600:	Early Christian period
600–850:	Early Middle Ages—Gregorian chant
850–1150:	Romanesque period—development of polyphony
1150–1450:	Late Middle Ages (Gothic period)
1450–1600:	Renaissance
1600–1750:	Baroque period
1725–1775:	Rococo period
1750–1825:	Classical period
1820–1900:	Romantic period
1890–1915:	Post-Romantic and Impressionist period
1900–2000:	Twentieth century

Part 2

2

The Nineteenth Century

Caspar David Friedrich *(1774–1840)*, Journey Above the Clouds. (Kunsthalle, Hamburg)

The Romantic Movement

11

The Spirit of Romanticism

"Music, of all the liberal arts, has the greatest influence over the passions."—NAPOLEON BONAPARTE

Historians observe that style in art moves between two poles, the classical and the romantic. Both the classicist and the romanticist strive to express significant emotions within beautiful forms. Where they differ is in their point of view. The spirit of classicism seeks order, poise, and serenity as surely as the romantic longs for strangeness, wonder, and ecstasy. Classicists are apt to be more objective in their approach; they try to view life sanely and "to see it whole." Romanticists, on the other hand, tend to view the world in terms of their personal feelings. The nineteenth-century German philosopher Friedrich Nietzsche dramatized the contrast between the two through the symbols of Apollo, Greek god of light and measure, and Dionysus, god of passion and intoxication. Classical and romantic ideals have alternated and even existed side by side from the beginning of time, for they correspond to two basic impulses in human nature: the need for moderation and the desire for uninhibited emotional expression.

The "Classical" and "Romantic" labels are also attached to two important periods in European art. The Classical era held the stage in the last half of the eighteenth century and the early decades of the nineteenth. The Romantic era, which grew out of the social and political upheavals that followed the French Revolution, came into full blossom in the second quarter of the nineteenth century.

French Revolution

The French Revolution resulted from the inevitable clash between momentous social forces. It signaled the transfer of power from a hereditary landholding aristocracy to the middle class, firmly rooted in urban commerce and industry. Like the American Revolution, this upheaval ushered in a social order shaped by the technological advances of the Industrial Revolution. The new society, based on free enterprise, emphasized the individual as never before. The slogan of the French Revolution—"Liberty, Equality, Fraternity"—inspired hopes and visions to which artists responded with zeal. Sympathy for the oppressed, interest in simple folk and in children, faith in humankind and its destiny, all formed part of the increasingly democratic character of the Romantic period.

Romantic writers

The Romantic poets rebelled against the conventional concerns of their Classical predecessors; they were drawn to the fanciful, the picturesque, and the passionate. One of the prime traits of all Romantic artists was their emphasis on intensely emotional expression. Another was their sense of uniqueness, their heightened awareness of themselves as individuals apart from all others. "I am different from all the men I have seen," proclaimed Jean Jacques Rousseau. "If I am not better, at least I am different." In Germany, a group of young writers created a new kind of lyric poetry that culminated in the art of Heinrich Heine, who became a favorite poet of

The spirit of the French Revolution is captured in Liberty Leading the People, *by* **Eugène Delacroix** *(1798–1863).* (The Louvre, Paris)

Sympathy for the oppressed underscored the essentially democratic character of the Romantic movement. **Honoré Daumier** *(1808–1879)*, The Third-Class Carriage. (Metropolitan Museum of Art, New York)

Romantic composers. A similar movement in France was led by Victor Hugo, its greatest prose writer, and Alphonse de Lamartine, its greatest poet. In England, the revolt against the formalism of the Classical age produced an outpouring of lyric poetry that reached its peak in the works of Byron, Shelley, and Keats.

The newly won freedom of the artist proved to be a mixed blessing. Confronted by a bourgeois world indifferent to artistic and cultural values, artists felt more and more cut off. A new type emerged—the artist as bohemian, the rejected dreamer who starved in an attic and through peculiarities of dress and behavior "shocked the bourgeois." Eternal longing, regret for the lost happiness of childhood, an indefinable discontent that gnawed at the soul— these were the ingredients of the Romantic mood. Yet the artist's pessimism was not without its basis in reality. It became apparent that the high hopes fostered by the revolution were not to be realized overnight. Despite the brave slogans, all people were not yet equal or free. Inevitably optimism gave way to doubt and disenchantment—"the illness of the century."

This state of mind was reflected in the arts of the time. Hugo dedicated *Les Misérables* "to the unhappy ones of the earth." The nineteenth-century novel found one of its great themes in the conflict between the individual and society. Jean Valjean, the hero of Hugo's novel, Heathcliff in Emily Brontë's *Wuthering Heights,* and Tolstoy's Anna Karenina are among the memorable characters who point up the frustrations and guilts of the nineteenth century.

Some writers sought escape by glamorizing the past, as did Sir Walter Scott in *Ivanhoe* and Alexandre Dumas in *The Three Musketeers.* A longing for far-off lands inspired the exotic scenes that glow on the canvases of J. M. W. Turner and Eugène Delacroix. The Romantic world was one of "strangeness and wonder": the eerie landscape we meet in Coleridge's *Kubla Khan,* Hawthorne's *The Scarlet Letter,* and Poe's *The Raven.*

The artist as bohemian

Romantic world view

69

Romanticism dominated the artistic output of the nineteenth century. It gave its name to a movement and an era, and created a multitude of colorful works that still hold millions in thrall.

12

Romanticism in Music

"Music is the melody whose text is the world."
—ARTHUR SCHOPENHAUER

Art mirrors the great social forces of its time. Thus Romantic music reflected the profound changes that were taking place in the nineteenth century at every level of human existence.

Improved musical instruments

The Industrial Revolution brought with it the means to create cheaper and more responsive musical instruments, with technical improvements that strongly influenced the sound of Romantic music. For example, the addition of valves to brass instruments made them much more maneuverable, so that nineteenth-century composers like Wagner and Tchaikovsky could write melodies for the horn that would have been unplayable in the eighteenth century. Several new wind instruments were developed as well, including the tuba and the saxophone. As a result of improved manufacturing techniques, the piano acquired a cast-iron frame and thicker strings, giving it a deeper and more brilliant tone. If a Romantic piano work by Liszt sounds different from a sonata of the Classical period, it is not only because Liszt's era demanded a different kind of expression, but also because he was writing for a piano capable of effects that were impossible in the earlier period.

The gradual democratization of society resulted in a broadening of educational opportunities. New conservatories were established in the chief cities of Europe to train more and better musicians, so that nineteenth-century composers could count on performers whose skill was considerably more advanced than in former times.

The development of the orchestra

As music moved from palace and church to the public concert hall, orchestras increased in size, giving composers a more varied and colorful means of expression. This naturally had a direct influence on the sound. For example, where most eighteenth-century music ranged in dynamic level only from *piano* (soft) to *forte* (loud), the dynamic range of the orchestra in the nineteenth century was far greater. The heaven-storming *crescendos* and the violent contrasts of loud (*fff*) and soft (*ppp*), which lend such drama to

The nineteenth-century orchestra offered the composer new instruments and a larger ensemble. Engraving of an orchestral concert at the Covent Garden Theater, London, 1846.

the music of the Romantics, had come into fashion. And as orchestral music became more important, the technique of writing for instruments, individually and together—that is, *orchestration*—became an art in itself. At last the musician had a palette comparable to the painter's, and used it as the painter did—to conjure up sensuous beauty, to create mood and atmosphere, to suggest nature scenes and calm or stormy seascapes.

In order to communicate their intentions as precisely as possible, composers developed a vocabulary of highly expressive terms. Among the directions frequently encountered in nineteenth-century musical scores are *dolce* (sweetly), *cantabile* (songful), *dolente* (weeping), *mesto* (sad), *maestoso* (majestic), *gioioso* (joyous), *con amore* (with love, tenderly). These and similar terms suggest not only the character of the music but the frame of mind behind it.

Increased expressiveness

The interest in folklore and the rising tide of nationalism inspired Romantic musicians to make increased use of the folk songs and dances of their native lands. As a result, a number of national idioms—Hungarian, Polish, Russian, Bohemian, Scandinavian, and eventually American—flourished, greatly enriching the melodic, harmonic, and rhythmic language of music.

Use of folklore

Nineteenth-century exoticism manifested itself first in the northern nations' longing for the warmth and color of the south, and second in the West's interest in the fairy-tale splendors of Asia and the Far East. The first impulse

Exoticism

The Royal Pavilion at Brighton, England (1815–18), with its Islamic domes, minarets, and screens, reflects the nineteenth-century fascination with Eastern culture. Designed by **John Nash** *(1752–1835).*

found expression in the works of German, French, and Russian composers who turned for inspiration to Italy and Spain. The long list includes Tchaikovsky's *Capriccio italien*, Mendelssohn's *Italian* Symphony, Ravel's *Spanish Rhapsody*, and Bizet's *Carmen*, the last two of which we will study.

The glamour of the East was brought to international attention by the Russian national school, whose music is pervaded by the fairy-tale background of Asia. Rimsky-Korsakov's orchestrally resplendent *Sheherazade*, Borodin's opera *Prince Igor*, and Ippolitov-Ivanov's *Caucasian Sketches* are among the many Eastern-inspired works that found favor throughout the world. A number of French and Italian opera composers also drew on exotic themes: Saint-Saëns in *Samson and Delilah*, Verdi in *Aida*, and Puccini in *Madame Butterfly* and *Turandot*.

ROMANTIC STYLE TRAITS

Singable melody

The nineteenth century above all was the period when musicians tried to make their instruments "sing." It is no accident that themes from Romantic symphonies, concertos, and other instrumental works have been transformed into popular songs, for Romantic melody was marked by a lyricism that gave it an immediate emotional appeal. This is evidenced by the enduring popularity of the tunes of such Romantic composers as Schubert, Verdi, and Tchaikovsky.

Through innumerable songs and operas as well as instrumental pieces, Romantic melody appealed to a wider audience than music ever had before.

Nineteenth-century music strove for a harmony that was highly emotional and expressive. Composers such as Richard Wagner employed combinations of pitches that were more chromatic and dissonant than those of their predecessors.

Expressive harmony

Romantic composers gradually expanded the instrumental forms they had inherited from the eighteenth century, to give their ideas more time to play out. A Classical symphony by Haydn or Mozart takes about twenty minutes to perform; a Romantic one by Tchaikovsky, Brahms, or Dvořák lasts at least twice that long. As public concert life developed, the symphony became the most important form of orchestral music, comparable to the novel in Romantic literature. As a result, nineteenth-century composers approached the writing of a symphony with greater deliberation than their predecessors did. Where Haydn wrote more than a hundred symphonies and Mozart more than forty, in the nineteenth century Schubert and Dvořák (following the example of Beethoven) wrote nine, Tchaikovsky six, Robert Schumann and Brahms four each. New orchestral forms emerged as well, including the one-movement symphonic poem, the choral symphony, and works for solo voice with orchestra.

Expanded forms

Music in the nineteenth century drew steadily closer to literature and painting—that is, to elements that lay outside the realm of sound. The connection with Romantic poetry and drama is most obvious in the case of music with words. However, even in their purely orchestral music, the Romantic composers responded to the mood of the time and captured with remarkable vividness the emotional atmosphere that surrounded nineteenth-century poetry and painting.

Nineteenth-century music was linked to dreams and passions, to profound meditations on life and death, human destiny, God and nature, pride in one's country, desire for freedom, the political struggles of the age, the ultimate triumph of good over evil. These intellectual and emotional associations, nurtured by the Romantic movement, brought music into a commanding position as a moral force, a vision of human greatness, and a direct link between the artist's inner life and the outside world.

THE MUSICIAN IN SOCIETY

The emergence of a new kind of democratic society strongly affected the lives of composers and performers. Musical life began to center on the public concert hall as well as the salons of the aristocracy and upper middle class. Where eighteenth-century musicians had functioned under the system of aristocratic patronage and had been dependent on the favor of royal courts or the

*A caricature of the virtuoso
Paganini in performance.*

nobility, nineteenth-century musicians were supported by the new middle-class audience. Musicians of the eighteenth century belonged to a glorified servant class that served the needs of a public high above them in social rank. In the nineteenth century, however, musicians met their audience as equals.

The solo performer   Indeed, as solo performers began to dominate the concert hall, whether as pianists, violinists, or conductors, they became "stars" who were idolized by the public. The Romantic virtuosos Mendelssohn, Liszt, and Paganini were welcomed into the great homes of their time as celebrities, unlike Haydn and Mozart half a century earlier.

Music thrived both in private homes and in the public life of most cities and towns. Permanent orchestras and singing societies abounded, printed music was readily available at a cost that many could afford, and music journals kept the public informed about musical activities and new works.

With this expansion of musical life, composers and performing artists were called on to assume new roles as educators. Felix Mendelssohn, active as composer, pianist, and conductor, used his immense prestige to found and direct the Leipzig Conservatory, whose curriculum became a model for music schools all over Europe and America. Later in the era, the Russian composer-pianist Anton Rubinstein performed a similar role as founder of the St. Petersburg Conservatory. Robert Schumann became a widely read critic. Franz Liszt, a composer, conductor, and considered to be the greatest pianist of his time, taught extensively and trained a generation of great concert pianists. And Richard Wagner directed his own theater at Bayreuth, thus helping the newly interested public understand his music dramas.

Women in Music

We will consider the prevailing social attitudes that strongly influenced the role women played in music in each historical era. The society of the nineteenth century, for example, saw women make great strides in establishing careers as professional musicians. This path was now possible through the broadening of educational opportunities; in public conservatories, women could receive training as singers, instrumentalists, and even composers. Likewise, the rise of the piano as the favored chamber instrument—both solo and with voice or instruments—provided women of the middle and upper classes with a performance outlet that was socially acceptable. Women's talents received full expression on the stage, where as opera singers they performed major roles.

Although composition remained largely a man's province, some women broke away from tradition and overcame societal stereotypes to become successful composers: among them were Fanny Mendelssohn Hensel, known for her Lieder, piano music, and chamber works; Clara Schumann, a talented performer and composer of piano and chamber music; and the American

An evening of string quartet music at the Berlin house of the composer and poet Bettina von Arnim, one of the most accomplished women of German Romanticism. Watercolor by **Johann Carl Arnold**, *c. 1855.* (Freies Deutsches Hochstift-Goethemuseum, Frankfurt)

Amy Cheney Beach, one of the first women composers to be recognized in the field of orchestral music. We will study all three. (The issues and attitudes surrounding nineteenth-century women composers are discussed further in CP 3 on p. 154.)

Women also exerted a significant influence as patrons of music or through their friendships with composers. We will see that George Sand played an important part in the career of Chopin, as did Carolyne Sayn-Wittgenstein in that of Liszt. Nadezhda von Meck is remembered as the woman who supported Tchaikovsky in the early years of his career and made it possible for him to compose. Several women of the upper class presided over musical salons where composers could gather to perform and discuss their music. One such musical center was the home of the Mendelssohn family, where Fanny Mendelssohn organized concerts that featured works by her more famous brother, Felix.

All in all, women musicians made steady strides in the direction of professional equality throughout the nineteenth century, and thereby laid the foundation for their even greater achievements in the twentieth.

Unit IV

The Nineteenth-Century Art Song

13

The Romantic Song

"Out of my great sorrows I make my little songs."
—HEINRICH HEINE

The art song met the nineteenth-century need for intimate personal expression. The form came into prominence in the early decades of the century and emerged as a favored example of the new lyricism.

TYPES OF SONG STRUCTURE

In the nineteenth century, two main types of song structure prevailed. In *strophic form*, the same melody is repeated with every stanza, or strophe, of the poem—hymns, carols, and many folk and popular songs are strophic. Although the form permits no real closeness between words and music, it sets up a general atmosphere that accommodates itself equally well to all the stanzas. The first may tell of a lover's expectancy, the second of his joy at seeing his beloved, the third of her father's harshness in separating them, and the fourth of her sad death, all sung to the same tune.

Strophic form

Through-composed form

The other song type, what the Germans call *durchkomponiert*, or *through-composed*, proceeds from beginning to end, without repetitions of whole sections. Here the music follows the story line, changing according to the text. This makes it possible for the composer to mirror every shade of meaning in the words.

Modified strophic form

There is also an intermediate type that combines features of the other two. The same melody may be repeated for two or three stanzas, with new material introduced when the poem requires it, generally at the climax. This is a *modified strophic form*, of which we will hear several examples.

THE LIED

Though songs have been sung throughout the ages, the art song as we know it today was a product of the Romantic era. Among the great Romantic masters of the art song were Franz Schubert, Robert Schumann, Johannes Brahms, and Hugo Wolf. Women composers who contributed significantly to the genre include Fanny Mendelssohn Hensel, Clara Schumann, and Amy

The immense popularity of the Romantic art song was due in part to the emergence of the piano as the universal household instrument. A lithograph by **Achille Devéria** *(1800–1857), In the Salon. (Germänische Nationalmuseum, Nuremberg)*

Cheney Beach. The *Lied* (plural, *Lieder*), as the new genre came to be known, is a German-texted solo vocal song with piano accompaniment. Some composers wrote groups of Lieder that were unified by a narrative thread or a descriptive theme. Such a group is known as a *song cycle*; an example is Robert Schumann's *A Poet's Love*, which we will study in Chapter 15.

Song cycle

The Lied depended for its flowering on the outpouring of lyric poetry that marked the rise of German Romanticism. Johann Wolfgang von Goethe (1749–1832) and Heinrich Heine (1797–1856) are the two leading figures among a group of poets who, like Wordsworth, Byron, Shelley, and Keats in English literature, favored short, personal lyric poems. The texts of the Lied range from tender sentiment to dramatic balladry; its favorite themes are love, longing, and the beauty of nature.

Another circumstance that made the Romantic art song popular was the emergence of the piano as the universal household instrument of the nineteenth century. The piano accompaniment translated the poetic images into music. Voice and piano together infused the short lyric form with feeling, and made it suitable for amateurs and artists alike, for the home and the concert hall.

14

Schubert and the Lied

"When I wished to sing of love, it turned to sorrow. And when I wished to sing of sorrow, it was transformed for me into love."

Franz Schubert's life has become a romantic symbol of the artist's fate. He was not properly appreciated during his lifetime, and he died very young, leaving the world a musical legacy of some 900 works.

Franz Schubert

HIS LIFE

Franz Schubert (1797–1828) was born in a suburb of Vienna, the son of a schoolmaster. The boy learned the violin from his father and piano from an elder brother; his beautiful soprano voice gained him admittance to the imperial chapel (he was one of the Vienna Choir Boys) and school where the court singers were trained. His teachers were astonished at the musicality of the shy, dreamy lad. One of them remarked that Franz "had learned everything from God."

When his schooldays were over, young Schubert tried to follow in his fa-

Early years

ther's footsteps, but he was not cut out for the routine of the classroom. He found escape by immersing himself in the lyric poets, the first voices of German Romanticism. As one of his friends said, "Everything he touched turned to song." The music came to him with miraculous spontaneity. *Erlking*, set to a poem by Goethe, was written when Schubert was still a teenager. The song, one of his greatest, drew him immediate public recognition yet, incredibly, he had difficulty finding a publisher willing to issue the work.

Schubert's talent for friendship attracted a band of writers, artists, and musicians, who organized a series of evenings at which his newest works were performed. The spirit of these convivial gatherings, known as "Schubertiads," was captured on canvas by the painter Moritz von Schwind (see below). With the encouragement of his friends, Schubert, not yet twenty, left his father's school. In the twelve years left to him, he composed feverishly, producing one masterpiece after another.

Schubert was not as well-known as some composers of his era (the virtuoso Paganini, for example, received much critical attention), but he was appreciated by the Viennese public and his reputation grew steadily. Still, his musical world was centered in the home, in salon concerts amid a select circle of friends and acquaintances.

Later years   Schubert endured much suffering in his later years, largely owing to his progressive debilitation from syphilis. At times, he was pressed for money, and sold his music for much less than it was worth. Gradually, his youthful exuberance gave way to the maturity of a deeply emotional Romantic artist.

*In his unfinished oil sketch of a "Schubertiad," Romantic artist **Moritz von Schwind** (1804–1871) shows Schubert seated at the piano. Next to him is the singer Johann Michael Vogl, who introduced many of Schubert's songs to the Viennese public.* (Schubert-Museum, Vienna)

Principal Works

More than 600 Lieder, including *Erlkönig* (*Erlking*, 1815) and 3 song cycles, among them *Die schöne Müllerin* (*The Lovely Maid of the Mill*, 1823) and *Winterreise* (*Winter's Journey*, 1827)

9 symphonies, including the *Unfinished* (No. 8, 1822)

Chamber music, including 15 string quartets; 1 string quintet; 2 piano trios and the *Trout* Quintet; 1 octet; various sonatas

Piano sonatas, dances, and character pieces

Choral music, including 7 Masses, other liturgical pieces, and part songs

Operas and incidental music for dramas

Eventually he perceived that the struggle had been decided against him. "It seems to me at times that I no longer belong to this world," he wrote. This emotional climate also pervades the magnificent song cycle *Winter's Journey*, in which the composer introduced a somber lyricism new to music. Overcoming his discouragement, he embarked on his last efforts. To the earlier masterpieces he added, in the final year of his life, a group of profound works that includes the Mass in E-flat, the String Quintet in C, the three posthumous piano sonatas, and thirteen of his finest songs.

Even with these outstanding achievements to his credit, Schubert made arrangements to study counterpoint: "I see now how much I still have to learn." When he was already terminally ill, he managed to correct the proofs of the final part of *Winter's Journey*. His dying wish was to be buried near the master he worshipped above all others—Beethoven. Schubert was thirty-one years old when he died in 1828. His wish was granted.

HIS MUSIC

Schubert's music marks the confluence of the Classical and Romantic eras. His symphonies look back to the eighteenth century in their clear form; but in his Lieder and piano pieces, he was wholly the Romantic. The melodies have a tenderness and a quality of longing that match the Romantic quality of the poetry they set. This magical lyricism prompted the composer Franz Liszt to call him "the most poetic musician that ever was."

In his chamber music, Schubert revealed himself as a direct descendant of the Classical masters. His string quartets, the two piano trios, the String Quintet in C, and the familiar *Trout* Quintet, all masterworks, end the line of Viennese Classicism.

Chamber music

Piano works

In the impromptus and other short piano pieces, the piano sings with a new lyricism. Here spontaneity and the charm of the unexpected take their place as elements of Romantic art. Schubert's piano sonatas, neglected for years, are now firmly situated in the repertory. His lyric imagination needed room in which to unfold, so he expanded the form he inherited from his predecessors.

Songs

Finally, there are the songs, more than six hundred of them. Many were written down at white heat, sometimes five, six, seven in a single morning. Of special interest are the accompaniments: a measure or two conjures up images of the rustling brook (in *The Trout*) or a horse riding through the night (in *Erlking*). Certain of his melodies achieve the universality of folk song. Their eloquence and fresh feeling have never been surpassed. The two superb song cycles, *The Lovely Maid of the Mill* and *Winter's Journey*, both on poems of Wilhelm Müller, convey the deepest feelings of love and despair.

Erlking

This masterpiece of Schubert's youth captures the Romantic "strangeness and wonder" of Goethe's celebrated ballad. *Erlking* is based on the legend that whoever is touched by the king of the elves must die.

The eerie atmosphere of the poem is immediately established by the piano. Galloping triplets are heard against a rumbling figure in the bass. This motive pervades the song, helping to unify it. The poem's four characters—the narrator, the father, the child, and the seductive elf—are vividly differentiated through changes in the melody, harmony, rhythm, and accompaniment. The child's terror is suggested by clashing dissonance and a high vocal range. The

The legend of The Erlking *(c. 1860), as portrayed by Moritz von Schwind.* (Schack-Galerie, Munich)

father, calming his son's fears, has a more rounded vocal line, sung in a low range. And the Erlking cajoles in suavely melodious phrases.

The song is through-composed; the music follows the action of the narrative with a steady rise in tension—and pitch—that builds almost to the end. The obsessive triplet rhythm slows down as horse and rider reach home, then drops out altogether on the last line: "In his arms the child"—a dramatic pause precedes the two final words—"was dead." The work of an eighteen-year-old, *Erlking* was a milestone in the history of Romanticism.

Listening Guide 2

MW
CD: Chr/Std 5/1–8, Sh 3/6–13
Cassette: Chr/Std 5A/1, Sh 3A/2

SCHUBERT: *Erlking (Erlkönig)*

(4:06)

Date of work: 1815
Form: Through-composed Lied
Text: Narrative poem by Johann Wolfgang von Goethe
Medium: Solo voice and piano
Tempo: Schnell (Fast)

Characters (performed by one vocalist):
Narrator: middle range, minor mode
Father: low range, minor mode; reassuring
Son: high range, minor mode; frightened
Erlking: medium range, major mode, coaxing, then insistent

Piano introduction—minor key and rapid repeated octaves in triplets set mood, simulating horse's hooves:

Melody of son's dissonant outcry on "My father, my father":

Mein Va - ter, mein Va - ter,

Text	Translation
NARRATOR (*minor mode, middle range*)	
Wer reitet so spät durch Nacht und Wind?	Who rides so late through night and wind?
Es ist der Vater mit seinem Kind;	It is a father with his child;
Er hat den Knaben wohl in dem Arm,	he has the boy close in his arm,
Er fasst ihn sicher, er hält ihn warm.	he holds him tight, he keeps him warm.
FATHER (*low range*)	
"Mein Sohn, was birgst du so bang dein Gesicht?"	"My son, why do you hide your face in fear?"

1 0:00

"Siehst, Vater, du den Erlkönig nicht?
Den Erlenkönig mit Kron' und Schweif?"

"Father, don't you see the Erlking?
The Erlking with his crown and train?"

FATHER (*low range*)

"Mein Sohn, es ist ein Nebelstreif."

"My son, it is a streak of mist."

ERLKING (*major mode, melodic*)

2   1:29

"Du liebes Kind, komm, geh mit mir!
Gar schöne Spiele spiel' ich mit dir;
Manch' bunte Blumen sind an dem Strand;
Meine Mutter hat manch' gülden Gewand."

"You dear child, come with me!
I'll play very lovely games with you.
There are lots of colorful flowers by the shore;
my mother has some golden robes."

SON (*high range, frightened*)

3   1:53

"Mein Vater, mein Vater, und hörest du nicht,
Was Erlenkönig mir leise verspricht?"

"My father, my father, don't you hear
the Erlking whispering promises to me?"

FATHER (*low range, calming*)

"Sei ruhig, bleibe ruhig, mein Kind;
In dürren Blättern säuselt der Wind."

"Be still, stay calm, my child;
it's the wind rustling in the dry leaves."

ERLKING (*major mode, cajoling*)

4   2:16

"Willst, feiner Knabe, du mit mir geh'n?
Meine Töchter sollen dich warten schön;
Meine Töchter führen den nächtlichen Reih'n
Und wiegen und tanzen und singen dich ein."

"My fine lad, do you want to come with me?
My daughters will take care of you;
my daughters lead the nightly dance,
and they'll rock and dance and sing you to
sleep."

SON (*high range, dissonant outcry*)

5   2:33

"Mein Vater, mein Vater, und siehst du nicht dort,
Erlkönigs Töchter am düstern Ort?"

"My father, my father, don't you see
the Erlking's daughters over there in the
shadows?"

FATHER (*low range, reassuring*)

"Mein Sohn, mein Sohn, ich seh' es genau,
Es scheinen die alten Weiden so grau."

"My son, my son, I see it clearly,
it's the gray sheen of the old willows."

ERLKING (*loving, then insistent*)

6   3:02

"Ich liebe dich, mich reizt deine schöne Gestalt,
Und bist du nicht willig, so brauch' ich Gewalt."

"I love you, your beautiful form delights me!
And if you're not willing, then I'll use force."

SON (*high range, terrified*)

7   3:14

"Mein Vater, mein Vater, jetzt fasst er mich an!
Erlkönig hat mir ein Leids gethan!"

"My father, my father, now he's grasping me!
The Erlking has hurt me!"

NARRATOR (*middle register, speechlike*)

8   3:27

Dem Vater grauset's, er reitet geschwind,
Er hält in Armen das ächzende Kind,
Erreicht den Hof mit Müh und Noth:

In seinen Armen das Kind war todt.

The father shudders, he rides swiftly,
he holds the moaning child in his arms;
with effort and urgency he reaches the court-
yard:

in his arms the child was dead.

15

Robert Schumann and the Song Cycle

"Music is to me the perfect expression of the soul."

The turbulence of German Romanticism, its fantasy and subjective emotion, found its voice in Robert Schumann. His music is German to the core, yet transcends nationalism to belong to the world.

HIS LIFE

Robert Schumann (1810–1856) was born in Zwickau, a town in southeastern Germany, the son of a bookseller whose love of literature was passed on to the boy. At his mother's insistence, he undertook the study of law, first at the University of Leipzig, then at Heidelberg. The youth daydreamed at the piano, immersed himself in the poetry of Goethe and Byron, and attended an occasional lecture. More and more he surrendered to his passion for music; it was his ambition to become a pianist. At last he won his mother's consent and returned to Leipzig to study with Friedrich Wieck, one of the foremost teachers of the day.

The young man practiced intensively to make up for his late start. Unfortunately, physical difficulties with the fingers of his right hand ended his hopes as a pianist. He then turned his interest to composing, and in a burst of creative energy produced, while still in his twenties, his most important works for piano. At the same time, Schumann's literary bent found expression in an important publication, *Die neue Zeitschrift für Musik* (The New Journal for Music), which he established and which, under his direction, became one of the most important music journals in Europe.

The critic

The hectic quality of the 1830s was intensified by Schumann's courtship of the gifted pianist and composer Clara Wieck (see Chapter 20). When he first came to study with her father, Clara was an eleven-year-old prodigy. Five years later, Robert realized he loved her, but her father opposed their marriage, with a vehemence that bordered on the psychopathic: Clara was

Marriage to Clara

Robert Schumann

the supreme achievement of Wieck's life, and he refused to surrender her to another. At length, since she was not yet of age, the couple were forced to appeal to the courts against Wieck. The marriage took place in 1840, when Clara was twenty-one and Robert thirty. This was his "year of song," when he produced over a hundred of the Lieder that represent his lyric gift at its purest.

The two musicians settled in Leipzig, pursuing their careers side by side. Clara became the foremost interpreter of Robert's piano works and in the ensuing decade contributed substantially to the spread of his fame. Yet neither her love nor that of their children could ward off an increasing withdrawal from the world that plagued her husband. Moodiness and nervous exhaustion culminated, in 1844, in a severe breakdown. The couple moved to Dresden, where Robert seemed to recover, but then the periods of depression returned ever more frequently.

Mental illness

In 1850, Schumann was appointed music director at Düsseldorf. But he was ill-suited for public life and was forced to relinquish the post. During a tour of Holland, where he and Clara were warmly received, he began to complain of "unnatural noises" in his head. His last letter to the violinist Joseph Joachim, two weeks before the final breakdown, is a farewell to his art. "The music is silent now . . . I will close. Already it grows dark."

Schumann continued to experience auditory hallucinations. Once he rose in the middle of the night to write down a theme that he imagined had been brought him by the spirits of Schubert and Mendelssohn. It was his last melody. A week later, in a fit of depression, he threw himself into the Rhine River. He was rescued by fishermen, and Clara had no choice then but to place him in a private asylum near Bonn. He died two years later at the age of forty-six.

HIS MUSIC

Piano pieces

In the emotional exuberance of his music, Schumann is the true Romantic. His piano pieces brim over with impassioned melody, novel changes of harmony, and driving rhythms. The titles are characteristic: *Fantasiestücke (Fantasy Pieces), Romances, Scenes from Childhood.* He often attached literary meanings to his music, and was especially fond of cycles of short pieces connected by a literary theme or musical motto.

Lieder

As a composer of Lieder, Schumann ranks second only to Schubert. A common theme in his songs is love, particularly from a woman's point of view. His favored poet was Heine, for whom he had an affinity like Schubert's for Goethe. Especially notable are his several song cycles, the best-known of

Principal Works

More than 300 Lieder, including song cycles *Frauenliebe und Leben* (*A Woman's Love and Life*, 1840) and *Dichterliebe* (*A Poet's Love*, 1840)

Orchestral music, including 4 symphonies and 1 piano concerto (A minor, 1841–45)

Chamber music, including 3 string quartets, 1 piano quintet, 1 piano quartet, piano trios, and sonatas

Piano music, including 3 sonatas; numerous miniatures and collections, among them *Papillons* (*Butterflies*, 1831), *Carnaval* (1835), and *Kinderszenen* (*Scenes from Childhood*, 1838); large works, including *Symphonic Etudes* (1835–37) and Fantasy in C (1836–38)

1 opera; incidental music; choral music

which are *A Poet's Love*, on poems of Heine, and *A Woman's Love and Life*, on poems of Chamisso.

The four symphonies are thoroughly Romantic in feeling. These works, especially the first and fourth, communicate a lyric freshness that has preserved their appeal. Typical of the essence of German Romanticism is the opening of the *Spring* Symphony, his first. "Could you infuse into the orchestra," he wrote the conductor, "a kind of longing for spring? At the entrance of the trumpets I should like them to sound as from on high, like a call to awakening."

Symphonies

A Poet's Love

Schumann wrote his great song cycle *A Poet's Love* (*Dichterliebe*) in 1840, his "year of song," at lightning-fast speed. For the texts, he chose sixteen poems from the *Lyriches Intermezzo* of Heinrich Heine, who wrote some of the Romantic era's most poignant works. Heine's poetry is full of irony and barbed or cynical remarks that reflect disillusioned hopes. The tone of Schumann's music for the cycle is more neutral. The songs tell no real story; rather, they follow a psychological progression that spirals downward from the freshness of love through a growing disappointment to complete despair.

In the eighth song in the cycle, "And if the flowers knew," the first three

In His Own Words

The singing voice is hardly sufficient in itself; it cannot carry the whole task of interpretation unaided. In addition to its overall expression, the finer shadings of the poem must be represented as well—provided that the melody does not suffer in the process.

verses offer comfort—through the flowers, the nightingales, and the stars—
to the poet's lovesick grief, while the last verse echoes the hopelessness of his
suffering: only she who has broken his heart knows its depths. The melody, in
quick-paced, declamatory style, is delivered in four short phrases for each
verse. Schumann sets the first three verses to the same music, which he then
reshapes for the emotional climax in the closing verse. The piano's active accompaniment suits the breathless character of the voice, and its closing measures confirm the angry frustration heard in the last lines of the poem.

Clearly, Schumann was able to achieve the desired unity of expression in
this perfect fusion of dramatic and lyric elements. *A Poet's Love* is universally
regarded as a masterpiece of Romanticism.

Listening Guide 3

CD: Chr/Std 5/50–53, Sh 3/14–17
Cassette: Chr/Std 5A/8, Sh 3A/3

R O B E R T   S C H U M A N N : "A n d   i f   t h e   f l o w e r s   k n e w ,"
f r o m *A P o e t ' s L o v e* (*D i c h t e r l i e b e*), N o . 8   (1:14)

Date of work: 1840

Genre: Lied, from a song cycle

Form: Modified strophic form

Text: Lyric poem by Heinrich Heine
4 verses (rhyme: *a-b-a-b c-d-c-d e-f-e-f g-b-g-b*)

Medium: Solo voice and piano

Tempo: Unmarked, but hurried, in quick and uneven rhythms

Opening vocal line, showing rushed, uneven rhythms:

Und wüs - sten's die Blu - men, die klei - nen, wie tief ver - wun - det mein Herz,

		Text	*Translation*
50	0:00	Und wüssten's die Blumen, die kleinen,	And if the flowers, the little ones, knew
		Wie tief verwundet mein Herz,	how deeply my heart is wounded,
		Sie würden mit mir weinen,	they would weep with me
		Zu heilen meinen Schmerz.	to heal my pain.

51	0:15	Und wüssten's die Nachtigallen, Wie ich so traurig und krank, Sie liessen fröhlich erschallen Erquickenden Gesang.	And if the nightingales knew how sad and sick I am, they would happily sound out their life-affirming song.
52	0:30	Und wüssten sie mein Wehe, Die goldenen Sternelein, Sie kämen aus ihrer Höhe, Und sprächen Trost mir ein.	And if the little golden stars knew my hurt, they would descend from their heights and speak words of comfort to me.
53	0:45	Sie alle können's nicht wissen, Nur Eine kennt meinen Schmerz; Sie hat ja selbst zerrissen, Zerrissen mir das Herz.	All of these cannot know, only one understands my pain; because she herself has torn— has torn my heart in two.
	1:00	Piano postlude	

16

Fanny Mendelssohn Hensel and Romantic Song

Although the talents of Fanny Mendelssohn Hensel (1805–1847) have been overshadowed by those of her more famous brother, Felix Mendelssohn (see Chapter 27), she was a first-rate musician in her own right. Her Lieder and piano pieces in particular claim her legacy among Romantic composers.

HER LIFE

Fanny Mendelssohn Hensel

Fanny Mendelssohn, the eldest of four children, was born into a highly cultured family (her grandfather, Moses Mendelssohn, was a leading Jewish scholar/philosopher). An important element of her background was the close relationship she maintained throughout her life with her younger brother Felix. Raised in Berlin, Fanny received her earliest piano instruction from her mother, Lea, who claimed that the young girl was born with "Bach's fingers." She later studied theory and composition with the well-known composer and conductor Carl Friedrich Zelter. Her first surviving work is a Lied, written in 1819 for her father's birthday. The following year, she enrolled in the Berlin Singakademie.

Because of her sex, however, Fanny was actively discouraged from pursuing music as a career. Her father cautioned her to focus on "the only calling for a young woman—that of a housewife," and her brother Felix echoed the sentiment, claiming that "Fanny possesses neither the inclination nor the calling for authorship. She is too much a woman for that, as is proper, and looks after her house and thinks neither about the public nor the musical world unless that primary occupation is accomplished." Still, her creative talents were recognized by some: the poet Goethe wrote to Felix in 1825, asking that he "give my regards to your equally talented sister," and Felix even published several of her songs among his collections.

Marriage

In 1829, Fanny Mendelssohn married the court artist Wilhelm Hensel, with whom she had a son, Sebastian. She remained active during the following years as a composer, pianist, and participant in the regular salon concerts held each Sunday at the Mendelssohn residence. In 1838, she made one prominent public appearance as a piano soloist, in a benefit performance of her brother's Piano Concerto No. 1 in G minor. The years 1839–40 were especially formative to her creative life: during this time, she traveled in Italy with her family and wrote *The Year (Das Jahr)* for piano, a musical diary of her trip in twelve character pieces (one for each month). With the death of her mother in 1842, Fanny took over the organization of the famous Sunday concerts.

Fanny died suddenly of an apoplectic stroke on May 13, 1847, while preparing to conduct a cantata written by her brother. Her family, devastated by her unexpected death, found one last composition on her writing table: the song *Mountain Yearning (Bergeslust)*, which we will study. Felix, having lost his dearest companion, died just six months later after a series of strokes.

In Her Own Words

I'm beginning to publish . . . and if I've done it of my own free will and cannot blame anyone in my family if aggravation results from it . . . then I can console myself with the knowledge that in no way did I seek or induce the kind of musical reputation that might have brought me such offers. I hope I shall not disgrace you all, for I am no femme libre. . . . If it [my publication] succeeds, that is, if people like the pieces and I receive further offers, I know it will be a great stimulus to me, which I have always needed in order to create. If not, I shall be at the same point where I have always been.

HER MUSIC

Although her output is dominated by Lieder and piano music, Fanny Mendelssohn Hensel also wrote some large-scale works. Important among these are her Piano Trio, Op. 11, a string quartet, several cantatas, and an oratorio. Most of her compositions were intended for performance at the family's Sunday musical gatherings. Although she was intelligent, witty, and confident in daily life, as a composer she lacked self-esteem. It was not until 1846 that she found the courage to publish her first set of songs, Opus 1.

Lieder

Fanny Mendelssohn Hensel's keyboard music is well crafted, reflecting her strong interest in Baroque contrapuntal procedures. Here and in her Lieder, her highly lyrical style displays a wide range of tonal, harmonic, and formal variety. Her complex piano accompaniments and her choice of German Romantic poets place her in the mainstream of the Lieder tradition. Throughout her creative life, she set texts by Goethe, her favorite poet and a family

The beauty of nature provided rich artistic subjects for Romantic poets and artists alike. The English landscape painter **John Constable** *(1776–1837) achieves striking contrasts of light and shade in* Branch Hill Pond, Hampstead Heath. *(The Cleveland Museum of Art)*

friend. She was influenced as well by the Romantic era's love of nature and was thus drawn to texts by Joseph von Eichendorff. Her song *Mountain Yearning* sets one of Eichendorff's folk-inspired poems.

Mountain Yearning

It is ironic that *Mountain Yearning*, her final composition, is one of Fanny Mendelssohn Hensel's most joyful works. She reportedly remarked to her husband on the day she wrote this Lied: "I am happier than I deserve to be." The song's three verses are set in a modified strophic form, with a short piano interlude between each (see Listening Guide 4). The first verse opens with folklike simplicity over a rollicking 6/8 accompaniment. The second is more dramatic, set in the minor mode and extended by the repetition, with varied contours, of its last text lines. The final verse brings back the joyous music of the song's opening, but again the thought is extended, with a slowing down of the pace and some inspired text painting, as the voice and then the piano ascend in a "reach to the realm of heaven."

The music of Fanny Mendelssohn Hensel has been unduly neglected over the years. The recent revival of her works, both in the concert hall and on recordings, has revealed her genuine talents and greatly enriched our modern-day understanding of the challenges faced by women musicians in the Romantic era.

Fanny Mendelssohn Hensel playing the piano in Rome. Drawing by **August Kaselowsky**, *a student of Wilhelm Hensel.*

Listening Guide 4

CD: Chr/Std 5/19–21
Cassette: Chr/Std 5A/4

FANNY MENDELSSOHN HENSEL: *Mountain Yearning (Bergeslust), Op. 10, No. 5*

(1:34)

Date of work: 1847

Genre: Lied

Text: Lyric nature poem by Joseph von Eichendorff
    3 verses (*a-b-a-b c-d-c-d e-f-e-f*), set **A-B-A'**

Medium: Solo voice and piano

Tempo: Allegro molto vivace e leggiaro (Very fast and light)

Opening vocal melody of verse 1, in A major:

Vocal melody of verse 2 (similar but varied from verse 1), in A minor:

		Text	*Translation*
19	0:00	O Lust, vom Berg zu schauen Weit über Wald und Strom, Hoch über sich den blauen, den klaren Himmelsdom.	What longing to gaze from the mountaintop far across forest and stream, with, high above, the blue, clear dome of heaven.
20	0:25	Vom Berge Vögel fliegen, Und Wolken so geschwind, Gedanken überfliegen Die Vögel und den Wind.	From the mountain, birds fly and clouds speed away, thoughts soar over the birds and the wind.
21	0:54	Die Wolken zieh'n hernieder, Das Vöglein senkt sich gleich, Gedanken geh'n und Lieder Bis in das Himmelreich.	The clouds drift downward, the little bird will soon alight, but thoughts and songs reach to the realm of heaven.

Unit V

The Nineteenth-Century Piano Piece

17

The Piano and Its Literature

"I have called my piano pieces after the names of my favorite haunts . . . they will form a delightful souvenir, a kind of second diary."—FANNY MENDELSSOHN HENSEL

The rise in popularity of the piano helped shape the musical culture of the Romantic era. All over Europe and America, the instrument became a mainstay of music in the home. It proved especially attractive to amateurs because, unlike the string and wind instruments, it enabled them to play melody and harmony together. Also popular was *four-hand piano music,* a chamber music form for two performers at one piano or occasionally at two; many works were arranged for this genre, which allowed for home and salon performances of orchestral and other large-ensemble music. The piano thus played a crucial role in the taste and experience of the new mass public.

Four-hand piano music

Hardly less important was the rise of the virtuoso pianist. At first the performer was, as a rule, also the composer; Mozart and Beethoven introduced their own piano concertos to the public, and Franz Liszt was the first to present his *Hungarian Rhapsodies.* With the developing concert industry, however, a class of virtuoso performers arose in the nineteenth century whose only function it was to dazzle audiences by playing music others had written.

This beautiful, ornate grand piano was made for the Baroness of Kidderminster by Erard, c. 1840. (Metropolitan Museum of Art, New York)

At the same time, a series of crucial technical improvements led to the development of the modern concert grand piano. By the opening of the twentieth century, the piano recital had come to occupy a central position on the musical scene.

THE SHORT LYRIC PIANO PIECE

The song found an instrumental equivalent in the short lyric piano piece, with its ability to project melodious and dramatic moods within a compact form. Composers adopted new and sometimes fanciful terms for such works. Some titles—"Prelude," "Intermezzo" (interlude), "Impromptu" (on the spur of the moment), for example—suggest free, almost improvisational forms. Many composers turned to dance music, and produced keyboard versions of the Polish mazurka and polonaise, the Viennese waltz, and the lively scherzo. Composers sometimes chose more descriptive titles, such as *Wild Hunt, The Little Bell,* and *Forest Murmurs* (all by Franz Liszt).

The nineteenth-century masters of the short piano piece—Schubert, Chopin, Liszt, Felix Mendelssohn, Fanny Mendelssohn Hensel, Robert and Clara Schumann, Brahms—showed inexhaustible ingenuity in exploring the technical resources of the instrument and its potential for expression.

18

Chopin and Piano Music

"My life [is] an episode without a beginning and with a sad end."

Frédéric François Chopin (1810–1849) has been called the "poet of the piano." The title is a valid one. His music, rooted in the heart of Romanticism, made this era the piano's golden age.

HIS LIFE

Frédéric Chopin

Chopin, considered the national composer of Poland, was half French. His father had emigrated to Warsaw, where he married a lady-in-waiting to a countess and taught French to the sons of the nobility. Frédéric, who proved to be musically gifted as a child, was educated at the newly founded Conservatory of Warsaw. At the age of twenty-one, he left for Paris, where he spent the rest of his career. Paris in the 1830s was the center of the new Romanticism. The circle in which Chopin moved included musicians such as Liszt and Berlioz, and literary figures such as Victor Hugo, George Sand, and Alexandre Dumas (the father). The poet Heinrich Heine became his friend, as did the painter Eugène Delacroix. A man ruled by his emotions, Chopin was much influenced by these leading intellectuals of France.

George Sand

Through the virtuoso pianist Liszt, Chopin met Aurore Dudevant, "the lady with the somber eye," known to the world as the novelist George Sand. She was thirty-four, he twenty-eight when their famous friendship began. Madame Sand was brilliant and domineering; her need to dominate found its counterpart in Chopin's need to be ruled. She left a memorable account of the composer at work:

> His creative power was spontaneous, miraculous. It came to him without effort or warning. . . . But then began the most heartrending labor I have ever witnessed. It was a series of attempts, of fits of irresolution and impatience to recover certain details. He would shut himself in his room for days, pacing up and down, breaking his pens, repeating and modifying one bar a hundred times.

For the next eight years, Chopin spent his summers at Sand's estate at No-

George Sand (Aurore Dudevant)

hant, where she entertained many of France's prominent artists and writers. These were productive years for the composer, although his health grew progressively worse and his relationship with Sand ran its course from love to conflict, from jealousy to hostility. They parted in bitterness.

According to his friend Liszt, "Chopin felt and often repeated that in breaking this long affection, this powerful bond, he had broken his life." The lonely despair of the Romantic artist pervades Chopin's last letters. "What has become of my art?" he wrote during a visit to Scotland. "And my heart, where have I wasted it?"

Chopin died of tuberculosis in Paris at the age of thirty-nine. Thousands joined together at his funeral to pay him homage. The artistic world bid its farewell to the strains of the composer's own funeral march, from his B-flat-minor Piano Sonata.

HIS MUSIC

Chopin was one of the most original artists of the nineteenth century. His style is so entirely his own that there is no mistaking it for any other. He was the only master of the first rank whose creative life centered about the piano, and he is credited with originating the modern piano style. From the first, his imagination was wedded to the keyboard, and he created a universe within that narrow frame. His genius transformed even the limitations of the instrument—its inability to sustain tone for any length of time—into sources of beauty. For example, widely spaced chords in the bass, sustained by pedal, set up masses of tone that encircle the melody. The delicate ornaments in his music—trills, grace notes, runs—seem magically to prolong the single tones. And all this generally lies so well for the trained hand that the music seems almost to play itself. "Everything must be made to sing," he told his pupils.

> **In His Own Words**
>
> *One needs only to study a certain positioning of the hand in relation to the keys to obtain with ease the most beautiful sound, to know how to play long notes and short notes and to [attain] certain unlimited dexterity. . . . A well-formed technique, it seems to me, [is one] that can control and vary a beautiful sound quality.*

Modern piano style

Works for piano and orchestra, including 2 piano concertos
Piano music, including 4 ballades, Fantasy in F minor (1841),
Berceuse (1844), *Barcarolle* (1846), 3 sonatas, preludes, études,
mazurkas, nocturnes, waltzes, polonaises, impromptus, scherzos,
rondos, marches, and variations
Chamber music, all including piano; songs

Small forms

It is remarkable that so many of Chopin's works have remained in the standard repertory. His nocturnes—night songs, as the name implies—are melancholic. The preludes are visionary fragments; some are only a page in length, several consist of two or three lines. In the études, which crown the literature of the study piece, piano technique is transformed into poetry. The impromptus are fanciful and capricious, and the waltzes capture the brilliance and coquetry of the salon. The mazurkas, derived from a Polish peasant dance, evoke the idealized landscape of his youth.

Larger forms

Among the larger forms are the four ballades, epic works of spacious proportions. The polonaises revive the stately processional dance in which Poland's nobles hailed their kings. The Fantasy in F minor and the dramatic scherzos reveal the composer at the peak of his art. The Sonatas in B minor and in B-flat minor are thoroughly Romantic in spirit, as are the Piano Concertos in E minor and F minor.

Polonaise in A-flat

The heroic side of Chopin's style shows itself in the most popular of his polonaises, the A-flat, Op. 53 (1842). The introduction establishes a dramatic mood

Chopin giving a piano lesson to the renowned opera singer Pauline Viardot (see p. 171). A caricature (1844) by **Maurice Sand**.

against which is set the opening dance theme, a proud melody in a stately triple meter. The octaves for the left hand in the following **B** section approach the limits of what the piano can do. After this episode, the emotional temperature drops perceptibly; this is Chopin's way of building up tension against the return of the theme, which rounds off the ternary form (a three-part, or **A-B-A,** structure). A *coda* (Italian for "tail," a concluding section) closes the work. In the hands of a virtuoso, this polonaise assumes a dazzling brilliance; it is the epitome of the grand style. (See the outline in Listening Guide 5.)

Important in this piece, as in all of Chopin's music, is the *tempo rubato*—the "robbed time," or "borrowed time," that is so characteristic of Romantic style. In tempo rubato, certain liberties are taken with the rhythm without upsetting the basic beat. As Chopin taught it, the accompaniment—usually the left hand—was played in strict time, while above it the right-hand melody might hesitate a little here or hurry forward there. In either case, the borrowing had to be repaid before the end of the phrase. Rubato, like any seasoning, must be used sparingly. But when it is done well, it imparts to the music a quality of caprice. And it remains an essential ingredient of Chopin's style.

Tempo rubato

Listening Guide 5

MW

CD: Chr/Std 5/44–47, Sh 3/18–21
Cassette: Chr/Std 5A/6, Sh 3A/4

CHOPIN: Polonaise in A-flat, Op. 53   (6:16)

Date of work: 1842

Form: **A-B-A′**, with introduction

Genre: Polonaise, a stately triple-meter Polish dance

Medium: Solo piano

Tempo: Alla Polacca e maestoso (Like a polonaise and majestic); use of rubato

| 44 | 0:00 | Introduction—dramatic mood established, fast ascending lines build into main theme of **A**. |
| 45 | 0:28 | **A** section—stately, dancelike theme, in tonic key (A-flat major): |

Repeated in louder statement, in octaves.

1:57   Brief diversion, features typical polonaise rhythm:

2:13   Main theme stated again; closing cadence chords.

46   2:48   **B** section—rolled chords introduce rapid descending octaves in bass, played staccato (dots); introduces theme in E major (in right hand):

3:52   Lyrical melody, leads back to repeat of **A**.

47   5:17   **A′** section—abridged repeat of first section; main theme heard once in loud, dramatic statement.

5:55   Coda—animated repetition of opening motive of main theme; dramatic closing chords.

Prelude in E minor

Chopin's set of twenty-four preludes was clearly inspired by an earlier work: the great *Well-Tempered Clavier* (containing forty-eight preludes and fugues) of the Baroque master Johann Sebastian Bach. Like Bach's preludes, Chopin's display an infinite variety of form and texture but, unlike Bach's, do not serve to introduce anything. The works of Chopin's set are arranged to be played as a cycle, offering contrast, tension, and release; they are, however, frequently played individually as well.

The Prelude in E minor, Op. 28, No. 4 (1839), reveals Chopin's uncanny power to achieve the utmost expressiveness with the simplest means (see Listening Guide 6). The melody hardly moves, unfolding in sustained tones over a succession of chords that change very subtly, usually one note at a time.

The music creates a gently mournful mood that is the essence of Romanticism. Tension builds slowly; there is something inevitable about the climax, where the melody, now advancing in bold leaps, takes on the character of a passionate outcry that subsides to a sorrowful *pianissimo* ending. Rarely has so much been said in a single page.

His countrymen have enshrined Chopin as the national composer of Poland. Yet in his music, he is the embodiment of European culture. The poet Heinrich Heine claimed, "His true country was the land of poetry."

Listening Guide 6

CD: Chr/Std 5/48–49
Cassette: Chr/Std 5A/7

CHOPIN: Prelude in E minor, Op. 28, No. 4   (1:49)

Date of work: 1839

Genre: Prelude (from set of 24)

Medium: Solo piano

Tempo: Largo

Character:
  Melody: simple, conjunct, in right hand only
  Rhythm: regular pulse kept by left-hand chords; much use of rubato
  Harmony: centered on E minor, constantly shifting chords with much chromaticism
  Texture: homophonic, melody with accompaniment
  Form: free, opening repeated with variations

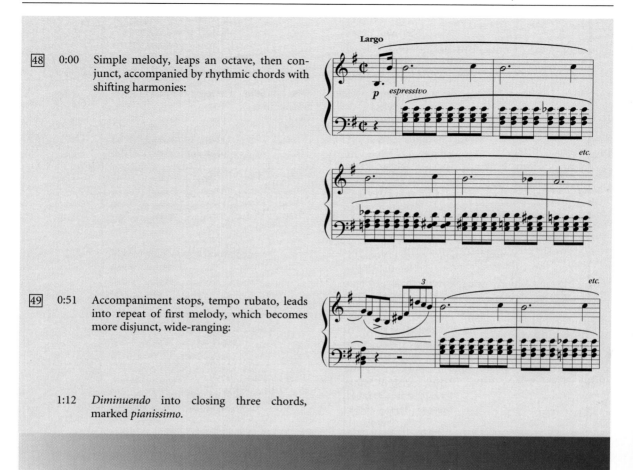

48   0:00   Simple melody, leaps an octave, then con-junct, accompanied by rhythmic chords with shifting harmonies:

49   0:51   Accompaniment stops, tempo rubato, leads into repeat of first melody, which becomes more disjunct, wide-ranging:

1:12   *Diminuendo* into closing three chords, marked *pianissimo*.

19

Liszt and the Rise of the Performer/Composer

"Sorrowful and great is the artist's destiny."

As composer, conductor, teacher, and organizer of musical events, Franz Liszt occupied a central position in the artistic life of the nineteenth century. Yet this fabulously successful artist did not escape the Romantic melancholy. "To die and die young," he once exclaimed, "—what happiness!"

His Life

Franz Liszt (1811–1886) was born in Hungary, the son of a steward in the employ of a wealthy family. A stipend from a group of Hungarian noblemen enabled him to pursue his musical studies in Paris. There he came under the spell of French Romanticism, with whose leaders he, like Chopin, formed close friendships.

Franz Liszt

The virtuoso

The new concertgoing public favored spectacular soloists. Like the sensational violinist Paganini, who appeared in Paris in 1831, Liszt met this need. He was one of the greatest of pianists—and showmen. An actor to his fingertips, he possessed the personal magnetism of which legends are made. Instead of sitting at the piano with his back to the audience or facing it, as had been the custom previously, he introduced the more effective arrangement that prevails today, which showed off his chiseled profile as he crouched over the instrument, thundering and caressing the keys. Countesses swooned, while less exalted ladies fought for his snuffbox and tore his handkerchief to shreds. Liszt encouraged these antics as a necessary part of the legend. But behind the facade was a true musician.

The lover

Inseparable from the legend of the pianist was that of the lover. Liszt never married, yet his personal life for the better part of fifty years was marked by unhappy endings to relationships. One woman who played an important role in his career was Countess Marie d'Agoult, who wrote novels under the pen name of Daniel Stern. The two shared an idyllic relationship in Switzerland that lasted for a number of years, and one of their three children, Cosima, subsequently became the wife of composer Richard Wagner. After their bitter parting, the countess satirized Liszt in her novels.

The composer

Liszt withdrew from the concert stage at the height of his fame in order to devote himself to composing. In 1848, he settled in Weimar, Germany, where he became court conductor to the grand duke. The Weimar period (1848–61) saw the production of his chief orchestral works. As director of the ducal opera house, he was in a position to influence public taste, and he used this power to further the "music of the future," the type of music that he and composers Richard Wagner and Hector Berlioz advocated. At Weimar, Liszt directed the first performances of operas by Wagner and Berlioz and many other nineteenth-century works.

The Weimar period also saw his association with the woman who most decisively influenced his life. Princess Carolyne Sayn-Wittgenstein, wife of a powerful nobleman at the court of the czar, fell in love with Liszt during his final concert tour of Russia; shortly thereafter, she came to Weimar to be with him. For years, their home was a center of artistic activity. A woman of strong will and intellect, the princess assisted Liszt in his later literary efforts. These include a book on Gypsy music and his *Life of Chopin*, both of which are eloquent but inaccurate.

An imaginary gathering painted by **Joseph Dannhauser** *in 1840 shows Liszt at the piano with Marie d'Agoult at his feet; seated behind him are George Sand and Alexandre Dumas (the elder); standing are Victor Hugo, Paganini, and Rossini. Looking out on this improbable assemblage is a marble bust of Beethoven.*

The cleric

In his last years, Liszt sought peace by entering the church. In this period, Abbé Liszt, as he was known, composed his major religious works. At seventy-five, he was received with enthusiasm in England, which had always been reluctant to recognize him as a composer. After journeying to Bayreuth to visit his daughter Cosima, now a widow, he died during the festival of Richard Wagner's works, naming with his last breath the masterpiece of the "music of the future"—Wagner's opera *Tristan and Isolde*.

HIS MUSIC

Symphonic poem

Thematic transformation

Liszt's goal was pure lyric expression—projecting a state of soul through the language of music. To give his lyricism free rein, Liszt created a new genre: the *symphonic poem*, a one-movement orchestral work with a literary or pictorial program. Here, as in his symphonies and concertos, he based his music on the technique of *thematic transformation*. By varying the melodic outline, harmony, or rhythm of a theme, by shifting it from soft to loud, from slow to fast, from low to high register, from strings to woodwinds or brass, he found it possible to transform its character so that it might suggest romantic love in one section, a pastoral scene in another, tension and conflict in a third, and triumph in the last.

Ladies swoon at a performance by Liszt in Berlin.

Liszt was one of the creators of modern piano technique. The best of his piano pieces, like his songs, are fine examples of Romanticism. Characteristic are the colorful *Hungarian Rhapsodies* and the vastly popular *Liebestraum* (*Love Dream*, c. 1850). The one-movement Sonata in B minor (1853) and the two concertos have long been favorites of virtuoso pianists.

Piano pieces

The Little Bell

From the beginning of his career, Liszt was fascinated by the technical possibilities of the piano. Like Chopin, he was drawn to the étude, or study piece, in which the composer confronted a particular technical problem. Liszt also fell under the spell of the great violin virtuoso Paganini, whose playing he heard in Paris: "What a man, what a violin, what an artist! O God, what pain and suffering, what torment in those four strings!" The pianist paid musical homage to the virtuoso in his *Transcendental Etudes after Paganini* (1838–39; revised 1851), a set of six technical masterpieces for piano based largely on Paganini's *Caprices* for solo violin.

The third étude, *The Little Bell* (*La campanella*), was inspired by the finale of Paganini's Second Violin Concerto, from which Liszt drew two musical sections and alternated them in continually varied figurations (the **A** section in minor, the **B** section in major; see Listening Guide 7). In the violin concerto, the *campanella* (a small church bell) is evoked with the triangle and the extreme high register of the violin. Liszt sounds the bell in each statement of the lilting **A** theme through a repeated note at high pitch that alternates with the main line of the melody (thus using a technique known as a *pedal point*). The work is physically challenging to play: among other technical difficulties, the distance between the principal melody and the bell notes exceeds the natural span of the hand, forcing the pianist to pivot the right hand back and

Principal Works

Orchestral music, including symphonic poems (*Les préludes*, 1848); *Dante* Symphony (1856), *Faust* Symphony (1857); 2 piano concertos; and *Totentanz* (for piano and orchestra, 1849)

Piano music, including *Transcendental Etudes* (1851), Sonata (B minor, 1853), *Hungarian Rhapsodies*, nocturnes, waltzes, ballades, polonaises, and other character pieces; numerous transcriptions of orchestral and opera works for piano

Choral music, including Masses, oratorios, psalms, cantatas, and secular part songs

1 opera; songs with piano

forth very quickly. With each variation, the passagework becomes more dazzlingly elaborate until the work reaches its dramatic closing, sounded in loud octaves.

Liszt joined Chopin in transforming the étude from a dry exercise into a poetic mood piece. Often regarded as the greatest pianist ever, he transcended the limitations of the keyboard and transformed virtuosic displays into expressions of great tonal beauty.

Listening Guide 7

CD: Chr/Std 5/54–63
Cassette: Chr/Std 5B/3

Liszt: *The Little Bell (La campanella)* (4:20)

Date of work: 1838–39; revised 1851

Genre: Etude, No. 3 from *Transcendental Etudes after Paganini*

Medium: Solo piano

Form: Sectional, with variations (**A-B-A′-B′-A″-B″-A‴**)

Basis: Paganini, Violin Concerto No. 2, Finale

Tempo: Allegretto (Fast and light), in 6/8 meter

Original theme from Paganini violin concerto:

| 54 | 0:00 | Introduction—shifting octaves, hesitant. |
| 55 | 0:09 | **A** section—main theme, with high, bell-like pedal, in minor: |

56	0:24	Main theme repeated, with embellishments.
57	0:41	**B** section—begins after rest, with sequential idea, in major; bridge section leads back to **A**.
58	1:16	**A'** section—variation of main theme, now heard in left hand:

Main theme in faster triplet pattern.

| 59 | 1:45 | **B'** section—rapid repeated notes, followed by chromatic scales. |
| 60 | 2:40 | **A''** section—main theme heard under high, trill-like pattern, with four trill notes heard for each one of melody: |

61	3:10	**B''** section—shifts of octaves with many leaps, in freer tempo, more dynamic contrasts.
62	3:46	**A'''** section—final statement of theme, played in loud, staccato octaves.
63	4:02	Coda—*animato* (animated) closing, in loud octaves, with simpler rhythms.

20

Clara Schumann:
Pianist and Composer

"The practice of [music] is . . . a great part of my inner self. To me, it is the very air I breathe."

Clara Schumann (1819–1896) is universally regarded as one of the most distinguished musicians of the nineteenth century. She was admired throughout Europe as a leading pianist of the era, but the world in which she lived was not prepared to acknowledge that a woman could be an outstanding composer. Hence her considerable creative gifts were not recognized or encouraged during her lifetime.

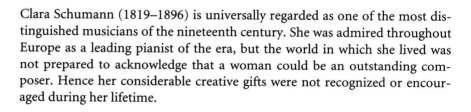

HER LIFE

Clara Schumann

Clara Schumann's close association with two great composers—her husband, Robert Schumann (see Chapter 15), and her lifelong friend Johannes Brahms (see Chapter 30)—put her at the center of musical life in her time. From her earliest years, she had the clearest possible conception of her goals as an artist and the strength of character to realize them. She studied piano from age five, made her first public appearance as a concert artist in Leipzig at age nine, and undertook her first extended concert tour several years later.

Marriage to Robert Schumann

A great crisis in her life came with the violent opposition of Friedrich Wieck, her father and teacher, to her marrying Robert Schumann, but she had the courage to defy him. She then faced the problems of a woman torn between the demands of an exacting career and her responsibilities as a wife and mother. She and Robert had seven children (an eighth died in infancy), yet she managed throughout those years to maintain her position as one of the outstanding concert artists of Europe. Liszt admired her playing for its "complete technical mastery, depth, and sincerity of feeling." Her situation was made more difficult by her being much more famous than her husband during their life together. The disparity in their reputations might have led to serious strains between them, had she not from the first dedicated her talents to advancing Robert's music. She gave first performances of all his important works, also becoming known as a leading interpreter of Brahms and Chopin.

Clara's life was not an easy one. "What will become of my work?" she wrote after learning she was expecting a fifth child. "Yet Robert says 'children are blessings' and he is right . . . so I have decided to face the difficult time that is coming as cheerfully as possible. Whether it will always be like this, I don't know." Although Clara enjoyed a loving relationship with her husband, life became increasingly difficult. Robert suffered from shifting moods and frequent depressions that eventually led to a complete breakdown. After his death, she concertized in order to support herself and her children. Now she in turn was sustained by Brahms's devotion. (See CP 3 on women and music.)

Clara had the talent, training, and background that many composers would envy, but from the beginning of her career she accepted the nineteenth-century attitude toward women composers. At twenty, she confided to her diary, "I once believed that I possessed creative talent, but I have given up this idea; a woman must not desire to compose—there has never yet been one able to do it. Should I expect to be the one? To believe this would be arrogant, something that my father once, in former days, induced me to do."

Called the "priestess" by her colleagues, Clara was devoutly serious about her artistic endeavors. Her husband was sympathetic to her creativity, assisting when he could with the publication of her music. But Robert also accepted the prevailing attitudes. "Clara has composed a series of small pieces," he wrote in their joint diary, "which show a musical and tender ingenuity such as she never attained before. But to have children, and a husband who is

Clara Schumann playing with the virtuoso violinist Joseph Joachim. A chalk drawing by **Adolf von Menzel** *(1854).*

always living in the realm of imagination, does not go together with composing. She cannot work at it regularly, and I am often disturbed to think how many profound ideas are lost because she cannot work them out."

Clara Schumann gave her last public concert at the age of seventy-two, and succumbed to a stroke five years later, in 1896. Her dying wish was to hear her husband's music once more.

HER MUSIC

Clara's output includes many small, intimate works such as songs and piano pieces. There are also two large-scale works, a piano concerto and a trio for piano and strings; a number of virtuoso pieces; and, as a gesture of homage to her husband, a set of Variations on a Theme by Robert Schumann. While her early works leaned toward technical display, which showed off her phenomenal talent, the later ones were more serious and introspective pieces typical of the era in which she lived.

Scherzo, Opus 10

Composed in 1838 when Clara was nineteen, the Scherzo in D minor, Opus 10, exemplifies her virtuoso style. Marked Con passione (with passion), a performance indication typical of the Romantic period, the piece is the kind that allows pianists to dazzle their public. Clara wrote to Robert from Paris, "It is extraordinary to me that my Scherzo is so well liked here. I always have to repeat it."

The structure is altogether clear-cut. A *scherzo* is a quick-paced, triple-meter dance usually paired with a lyrical *trio* in an **A-B-A** form; **A** represents the scherzo, **B** the trio. This impetuous scherzo has two trios, or contrasting sections, which are more relaxed in character. (See Listening Guide 8.) Sudden dissonances and *sforzando*s (accents) add to the drama; trills and extended arpeggio figures keep the pianist's fingers busy. The main theme, an exuberant rising figure, builds steadily to the *fortissimo* ending, while the two trios, with their flowing melodic lines, offer the necessary release of tension.

This scherzo displays Clara's creative gift in a most attractive way. It further attests to her extraordinary talents as a virtuoso performer. Forgotten for decades, Clara Schumann is finally receiving the world recognition long due her.

Listening Guide 8

CD: Chr/Std 5/69–76, Sh 3/22–29
Cassette: Chr/Std 5B/5, Sh 3A/5

CLARA SCHUMANN: Scherzo, Op. 10   (4:57)

Date of work: c. 1838

Form: Scherzo with 2 trios

Medium: Solo piano

Tempo: Presto, Scherzo con passione

Key: D minor

Meter: 3/4

69 0:00 Introduction—14 measures; trill-like, arpeggiated figures lead to main theme:

70 0:08 Scherzo—very rhythmic, unison rising line; soft, punctuated by *sf* chord, alternates with arpeggiated figure, key of D minor:

Opening theme restated in G minor; return of trill-like figure from introduction followed by loud, dissonant chords.

71   0:36   Scherzo repeated in D minor.

72   1:04   Scherzo varied, opens in D minor; trill figures in left hand, then both hands; becomes more chromatic—*diminuendo* into trio.

73   1:30   Trio I—marked *doloroso* (sorrowful), slower; smooth descending melodic lines:

Alternates with rhythmic, accented theme from opening scherzo (4-note rhythm); returns to conjunct line, more chromatic; *crescendo* into opening tempo, based on 4-note rhythm.

74   2:12   Scherzo returns—*fortissimo*, arpeggiated figures increasingly chromatic and slower, leading to second trio.

75   2:41   Trio 2—arched *marcato* (stressed) melody—begins in E-flat major:

Lower-pitched melody played rubato, then in middle range with rolled chord and 4-note rhythm accompaniment; trill and arpeggio figures lead back to scherzo.

76   4:13   Scherzo returns in D minor, builds to loud, fiery close with descending arpeggio and two *fortissimo* chords.

Unit VI

Romantic Program Music

21

The Nature of Program Music

"The painter turns a poem into a painting; the musician sets a picture to music."—ROBERT SCHUMANN

Program music is instrumental music that has literary or pictorial associations; the nature of these associations is indicated by the title of the piece or by an explanatory note—the "program"—supplied by the composer. A title such as *King Lear* (by Berlioz) suggests specific characters and events, while the title *Pièces fugitives* (*Fleeting Pieces*, by Clara Schumann) merely labels the mood or character of the work. Program music is distinguished from *absolute music* (or pure music), which consists of musical patterns that have no literary or pictorial meanings.

Absolute music

This genre was of special importance in the nineteenth century, when musicians became sharply conscious of the connection between their art and the world about them. It helped them to bring music closer to poetry and painting, and to relate their work to the moral and political issues of their time.

VARIETIES OF PROGRAM MUSIC

One impulse toward program music came from the opera house, where the *overture* was a rousing orchestral piece in one movement designed to serve as an introduction to an opera (or a play). Many operatic overtures achieved independent popularity as separate concert pieces. This pointed the way to a new type of overture not associated with an opera: a single-movement concert piece for orchestra based on a literary idea, such as Tchaikovsky's *Romeo and Juliet.* Such a composition, the *concert overture*, might evoke a land- or seascape or embody a poetic or patriotic idea.

The concert overture

Incidental music

Another species of program music, *incidental music*, usually consists of an overture and a series of pieces to be performed between the acts of a play and during important scenes. The most successful pieces of incidental music were arranged into suites (Mendelssohn's music for Shakespeare's *A Midsummer Night's Dream* is one of the best-known). Incidental music is still important today, in the form of film music and background music for television.

Shakespeare's play A Midsummer Night's Dream *inspired Felix Mendelssohn's incidental music as well as this fanciful canvas by* **Henry Fuseli,** Titania and Bottom *(c. 1790). (Tate Gallery, London)*

The passion for program music was so strong that it invaded even the most hallowed form of absolute music, the symphony. Thus came into being the *program symphony*, a multimovement orchestral work. Important examples are the program symphonies of Berlioz—including *Symphonie fantastique*, which we will study—and two by Liszt, the *Faust* and *Dante* Symphonies.

Program symphony

Eventually, the need was felt for a large form of orchestral music that would serve the Romantic era. Franz Liszt filled this need with the creation of the *symphonic poem* (he first used the term in 1848), the nineteenth century's one original contribution to the large forms. Liszt's *Les Préludes* is among the best-known examples of this genre.

Symphonic poem

A symphonic poem is a piece of program music for orchestra, in one movement, which in the course of contrasting sections develops a poetic idea, suggests a scene, or creates a mood. It differs from the concert overture, which usually retains one of the traditional Classical forms, by being much freer in its structure. The symphonic poem (also called *tone poem*) gave composers the flexibility they needed for a big single-movement form. It became the most widely cultivated type of orchestral program music through the second half of the century. We will study two examples: *The Moldau*, by the Bohemian composer Bedřich Smetana, and *Prelude to "The Afternoon of a Faun,"* by Claude Debussy.

Program music is one of the most striking manifestations of nineteenth-century Romanticism. This new, descriptive genre impelled composers to try to express specific feelings; it proclaimed the direct relationship of music to life.

22

Berlioz and the Program Symphony

"To render my works properly requires a combination of extreme precision and irresistible verve, a regulated vehemence, a dreamy tenderness, and an almost morbid melancholy."

The flamboyance of Victor Hugo's poetry and the dramatic intensity of Eugène Delacroix's painting found their counterpart in the works of Hector Berlioz, who described the prevailing characteristics of his music as passionate expression, intense ardor, rhythmic animation, and unexpected turns. He was the first great exponent of musical Romanticism in France.

His Life

Hector Berlioz

Harriet Smithson

Hector Berlioz (1803–1869) was born in France in a small town near Grenoble. His father, a well-to-do physician, expected the boy to follow in his footsteps, and at eighteen Hector was sent away to attend medical school in Paris. The conservatory and the opera, however, intrigued Berlioz much more than the dissecting room. The following year, the fiery youth made a decision that horrified his upper-middle-class family: he gave up medicine for music.

The Romantic revolution was brewing in Paris, and Berlioz, along with Hugo and Delacroix, found himself in the camp of "young France." Having been cut off by his parents, he gave music lessons and sang in a theater chorus to make ends meet. He became a huge fan of Beethoven and of Shakespeare, to whose plays he was introduced by a visiting English troupe. Berlioz fell madly in love with an actress in this troupe, whose portrayals of Ophelia and Juliet excited the admiration of the Parisians. In his *Memoirs*, which read like a Romantic novel, he describes his infatuation with Harriet Smithson: "I became obsessed by an intense, overpowering sense of sadness. I could not sleep, I could not work, and I spent my time wandering aimlessly about Paris and its environs."

In 1830, Berlioz was awarded the coveted Prix de Rome, which gave him an opportunity to live and work in Italy. That same year he composed the *Symphonie fantastique*, to this day his most celebrated work. Upon his return from Rome, he commenced a hectic courtship of Harriet Smithson. There were strenuous objections from both their families, and violent scenes, during one of which the excitable Hector attempted suicide. But he recovered, and the two were married.

Harriet Smithson

Now that the unattainable ideal had become his wife, Berlioz's passion cooled. It was Shakespeare he had loved rather than Harriet, and in time he sought the ideal elsewhere. All the same, the first years of his marriage were the most fruitful of his life. By age forty, he had produced most of the works on which his fame would rest.

In the latter part of his life, Berlioz conducted his music in all the capitals of Europe. Paris, however, resisted him to the end. For his last major work, the opera *Béatrice et Bénédict*, he wrote his own libretto after Shakespeare's *Much Ado About Nothing*. Following this effort, the embittered composer wrote no more. He died seven years later, at sixty-six.

His Music

Berlioz was one of the boldest innovators of the nineteenth century. His approach to music was wholly individual, his sense of sound unique. From the start, he had an affinity in his orchestral music for the vividly dramatic or pictorial program.

His works show the favorite literary influences of the Romantic period. *The Damnation of Faust*, for example, was inspired by Goethe; *Harold in Italy* (a program symphony with viola solo) and *The Corsair* (an overture) are based on works by the English poet Byron. Shakespeare is the source for the overture *King Lear* and for the dramatic symphony *Romeo and Juliet*.

Orchestral works

Principal Works

Orchestral music, including overtures *Waverley* (1828), *Rob Roy* (1831), *Le roi Lear (King Lear,* 1831); and program symphonies *Symphonie fantastique* (1830), *Harold en Italie (Harold in Italy,* 1834), *Romeo et Juliette* (1839)

Choral music, including a Requiem Mass (1837), Te Deum (Hymn of Praise, 1849), *La damnation de Faust (The Damnation of Faust,* 1846), and the oratorio *L'enfance du Christ (The Childhood of Christ,* 1854)

3 operas, including *Les Troyens (The Trojans,* 1858) and *Béatrice et Bénédict* (1862)

9 solo vocal works with orchestra

Writings on music, including an orchestration treatise (1843/55)

Francisco Goya *(1746–1828) anticipated the passionate intensity of Berlioz's music in this painting of the* Witches' Sabbath, *c. 1819–23.* (Museo del Prado, Madrid)

Vocal works   Berlioz's most important opera, *The Trojans,* on his own libretto after the ancient Roman poet Virgil, has been successfully revived in recent years. His sacred vocal works, including the Requiem Mass (Mass for the Dead) and the Te Deum, are conceived on a similarly grandiose scale. But this love of huge orchestral and choral forces represents only one aspect of Berlioz's personality. No less characteristic is the tenderness that finds expression in the oratorio *The Childhood of Christ,* the fine-spun lyricism that wells up in his songs, and the sensibility that fills his orchestra with French clarity and grace.

It was in the domain of orchestration that Berlioz's genius asserted itself most fully. His daring originality in handling the instruments opened up a new world of Romantic sound. His scores, calling for the largest orchestra that had ever been used, abound in novel effects and discoveries that would serve as models for all who came after him. Indeed, the conductor Felix Weingartner called Berlioz "the creator of the modern orchestra."

Symphonie fantastique

Berlioz wrote his best-known program symphony when he was twenty-seven years old, drawing its story from his personal life. "A young musician of morbid sensibility and ardent imagination, in . . . lovesick despair, has poisoned himself with opium. The drug, too weak to kill, plunges him into a heavy sleep accompanied by strange visions. . . . The beloved one herself becomes for him a melody, a recurrent theme that haunts him everywhere."

Idée fixe   The symphony's recurrent theme, called an *idée fixe* (fixed idea), symbolizes the beloved; it becomes a musical thread unifying the five diverse movements, though its appearances are varied in harmony, rhythm, meter, tempo, dynamics, register, and instrumental color. (See Listening Guide 9 for theme and analysis.) These transformations take on literary as well as musical significance, as the following description by Berlioz shows.

I. *Reveries, Passions.* "[The musician] remembers the weariness of soul, the indefinable yearning he knew before meeting his beloved. Then, the volcanic love with which she at once inspired him, his delirious suffering . . . his religious consolation." The Allegro section introduces a soaring melody—the fixed idea.

First movement

II. *A Ball.* "Amid the tumult and excitement of a brilliant ball he glimpses the loved one again." This dance movement is in ternary, or three-part, form. In the middle section, the fixed idea reappears in waltz time (a lilting triple meter).

Second movement

III. *Scene in the Fields.* "On a summer evening in the country he hears two shepherds piping. The pastoral duet, the quiet surroundings . . . all unite to fill his heart with a long absent calm. But she appears again. His heart contracts. Painful forebodings fill his soul." The composer said that his aim in this pastoral movement was to establish a mood "of sorrowful loneliness."

Third movement

IV. *March to the Scaffold.* "He dreams that he has killed his beloved, that he has been condemned to die and is being led to the scaffold. . . . At the very end the fixed idea reappears for an instant, like a last thought of love interrupted by the fall of the axe."

Fourth movement

V. *Dream of a Witches' Sabbath.* "He sees himself at a witches' sabbath surrounded by a host of fearsome spirits who have gathered for his funeral. Unearthly sounds, groans, shrieks of laughter. The melody of his beloved is heard, but it has lost its noble and reserved character. It has become a vulgar tune, trivial and grotesque. It is she who comes to the infernal orgy. A howl of joy greets her arrival. She joins the diabolical dance. Bells toll for the dead. A burlesque of the *Dies irae*. Dance of the witches. The dance and the *Dies irae* combined."

Fifth movement

The fourth movement, a diabolical march in minor, exemplifies the nineteenth-century love of the fantastic. The theme of the beloved appears at the very end, on the clarinet, and is cut off by a grim *fortissimo* chord.

The final movement opens with a Larghetto (not quite as slow as Largo). Berlioz here enters into a kind of infernal spirit that nourished a century of satanic operas, ballets, and symphonic poems. The mood is heightened with the introduction of the traditional religious chant *Dies irae* (Day of Wrath) from the ancient Mass for the Dead, heard in the bassoons and tubas (originally written for *ophicleide*, a nineteenth-century brass instrument that is now obsolete). The movement reaches its climax when this well-known melody, now in shorter note values, is combined with the Witches' Dance.

There is a grandeur of line and gesture in the music of Berlioz, and an abundance of vitality and invention. He is one of the major prophets of the era.

Listening Guide 9

CD: Chr/Std 5/31–43, Sh 3/30–35
Cassette: Chr/Std 5B/1–2, Sh 3B/1

BERLIOZ: *Symphonie fantastique*, Fourth and Fifth Movements   (14:27)

Date of work: 1830

Genre: Program symphony, 5 movements

Program: A lovesick artist in an opium trance is haunted by a vision of his beloved, which becomes an *idée fixe* (fixed idea).

I. Reveries, Passions
Largo, Allegro agitato e appassionato assai (Lively, agitated, and very impassioned); introduces the main theme, the fixed idea:

II. A Ball
Valse, Allegro non troppo (Waltz, not too fast); **A-B-A** form, triple-meter dance.

III. Scene in the Fields
Adagio; A-B-A form, 6/8 meter.

IV. March to the Scaffold   (4:46)
Allegretto non troppo; duple-meter march, in minor mode.

|31| 0:00 Opening motive: muted horns, timpani, and pizzicato low strings, forecasts syncopated rhythm of march (theme **B**):

|32| 0:27 Theme **A**—an energetic, downward minor scale, played by low strings, then violins:

33	1:39	Theme **B**—diabolical march tune, played by brass and woodwinds:	

Opening section repeated.

34	2:04	Developmental section:

    Theme **B**—in brass, accompanied by strings and woodwinds.

    Theme **A**—soft, with pizzicato strings.

    Theme **B**—brass, with woodwinds added.

    Theme **A**—soft, pizzicato strings, then loud in brass.

35	3:15	Theme **A**—full orchestra statement in original form, then inverted (now an ascending scale).

36	4:15	*Idée fixe* (fixed idea) melody in clarinet ("a last thought of love"), marked "dolce assai e appassionato" (as sweetly and passionately as possible), followed by loud chord that cuts off melody ("the fall of the axe"):	

Loud forceful chords close movement.

(Shorter recordings end here.)

V. *Dream of a Witches' Sabbath* (9:41)

37	0:00	Larghetto—very soft muted strings evoke infernal atmosphere; chromatic scales in strings, low brass, and high woodwinds depict "unearthly sounds, groans, shrieks of laughter."

38	1:18	Allegro—fixed idea in high clarinet in transformed version with trills and grace notes ("a vulgar tune, trivial and grotesque"):	

Orchestral *fortissimo* signals "howl of joy" at the beloved's arrival.

	1:35	Fixed idea continues in woodwinds, with bassoons in grotesque accompanying figure.

39	2:53	"Bells toll for the dead."

Dance tune forecast by its opening motive in violas, followed by foreboding sounds in low brass:

40	3:19	Chant tune *Dies irae* sounded in bassoons and tubas, first slow, then twice as fast in brass:

41	3:51	"Burlesque of the *Dies irae*" in strings and woodwinds in altered rhythm; alternates with brass and bells.

121

| 42 | 5:12 | "Dance of the Witches" ("Ronde du Sabbat")—begins in low strings, builds in fugal setting: |  |

Dance dies out, followed by strange sounds in low strings with fragment of *Dies irae* tune; builds to *fortissimo*.

| 43 | 7:57 | "The dance and the *Dies irae* combined"; strings play dance tune with wood of bows alternating with loud brass statements of *Dies irae*; builds to final cadence. |

23

Musical Nationalism

"I grew up in a quiet spot and was saturated from earliest childhood with the wonderful beauty of Russian popular song. I am therefore passionately devoted to every expression of the Russian spirit. In short, I am a Russian through and through!"
—PETER ILYICH TCHAIKOVSKY

In nineteenth-century Europe, political conditions encouraged the growth of nationalism to such a degree that it became a decisive force within the Romantic movement. The pride of conquering nations and the struggle for freedom of suppressed ones gave rise to strong emotions that inspired the works of many creative artists.

The Romantic composers expressed their nationalism in a number of ways. Some based their music on the songs and dances of their people: Chopin in his mazurkas, Liszt in his *Hungarian Rhapsodies*, Dvořák in the *Slavonic Dances*. A number wrote dramatic works based on folklore or peasant life, such as the German folk opera *Der Freischütz* by Carl Maria von Weber and the Russian fairy-tale operas and ballets of Tchaikovsky and Rimsky-Korsakov. Others wrote symphonic poems and operas celebrating the exploits of a national hero, a historic event, or the scenic beauty of their country; Tchaikovsky's *1812 Overture* and Smetana's *The Moldau* exemplify this trend.

In associating music with the love of homeland, composers were able to give expression to the hopes and dreams of millions of people. And the political implications of this musical nationalism were not lost on the authorities.

Many of Verdi's operas, for example, had to be altered again and again to suit the Austrian censor. During the Second World War, the Nazis forbade the playing of Smetana's descriptive symphonic poems in Prague and Chopin's polonaises in Warsaw because of the powerful symbolism behind these works.

A CZECH NATIONALIST: BEDŘICH SMETANA

"My compositions do not belong to the realm of absolute music, where one can get along well enough with musical signs and a metronome."

Bedřich Smetana (1824–1884) was the first Bohemian composer to achieve international prominence. He was born in a small village in eastern Bohemia (now the Czech Republic), the son of a master brewer. In his teens, he was sent to school in Prague, where his love for music was kindled by the city's active cultural life. Smetana's career, like those of other nationalist composers, played out against a background of political agitation. Bohemia stirred restlessly under Austrian rule, caught up in a surge of nationalist fervor that culminated in a series of uprisings in 1848. The young Smetana joined the patriotic cause. After the revolution was crushed, the atmosphere in Prague was oppressive for those suspected of sympathy with the nationalists, so in 1856, he accepted a conducting position in Sweden.

Bedřich Smetana

On his return to Prague several years later, Smetana resumed his musical career by writing operas for the National Theater, where performances were given in his native tongue. Of his eight operas, *The Bartered Bride* won him worldwide fame. Today he is best-known for *My Country* (*Má vlast*), a vast cycle of six symphonic poems whose composition occupied his time from 1874 to 1879. These works were inspired by the beauty of Bohemia's countryside, the rhythm of its folk songs and dances, and the pomp and pageantry of its legends. While writing the cycle, Smetana's health declined as a result of advanced syphilis, and, like Beethoven, he grew deaf. His diary reveals his deep suffering: "If my illness is incurable," he wrote, "then I should prefer to be delivered from this miserable existence."

The Moldau

The Moldau, the second of the programmatic poems from *My Country*, represents Smetana's finest achievement in the field of orchestral music. In this work, the Bohemian river Moldau (Vltava in Czech) becomes a poetic

Cultural Perspective 1

MUSIC AND NATIONALISM

We have noted that musical nationalism can take a number of different forms: it can conjure up images of a particular scene, it can portray a folk hero, or it can retell a legend from folklore. In *My Country*, a cycle of six symphonic poems, Bedřich Smetana aims to present images of the scenery, the history, and the folk legends of his native land.

Each culture has a value system that lies at the heart of its folklore: children learn right from wrong and prepare for adulthood through folktales, which are transmitted, like folk music, through oral tradition. The characters we find in these folk legends are often rascals whose wrongdoings prove the moral of the story. Such is the case with Peer Gynt, a peasant figure from Norwegian history whose adventures are recounted musically by Edvard Grieg in incidental music to a drama by Henrik Ibsen. Peer Gynt abandons his wife to seek other pleasures, then returns to her forty years later to find her still faithful to him. His wanderings take him to Africa, where he incurs the wrath of the Mountain King for seducing a local maiden. Another famous musical rogue, this one from medieval German legend, is portrayed in Richard Strauss's popular tone poem *Till Eulenspiegel's Merry Pranks* (1895). Till's adventures include riding through a marketplace and upsetting all the goods, disguising himself as a priest, mocking a group of professors, and finally paying the penalty for his pranks: he is tried and hanged, though his spirit cannot be suppressed.

Folk material also inspired the Russian composer Modest Musorgsky in composing his programmatic suite *Pictures at an Exhibition*, written for piano and made famous in an orchestral version by Maurice Ravel. The suite is based on an art show commemorating the life and works of Victor Hartmann. One movement, *The Hut on Fowl's Legs*, describes Hartmann's design for a clock shaped like the house of the witch Baba-Yaga. According to Russian legend, Baba-Yaga lured small children to her hut in the woods, where she ate them and ground their bones in her giant mortar. An equally frightening episode occurs in the famous tale of "Hansel and Gretel," collected and retold by Jakob and Wilhelm Grimm; here, the witch's hut is a gingerbread house to which the children are attracted, only to be fattened up for her to eat. This German legend inspired an opera by the nineteenth-century composer Engelbert Humperdinck (whose name was adopted by a twentieth-century pop singer) and was later included as one of a pastiche of tales in the popular Stephen Sondheim musical *Into the Woods* (1988).

In addition to Musorgsky, other Russian composers have turned to their native folk traditions for inspiration: the early-twentieth-century master Igor Stravinsky brought life to the Russian fable of *The Firebird* in an exquisite ballet (1910); and his contemporary Sergei Prokofiev immortalized the well-known story of *Peter and the Wolf* in a symphonic fairy tale of the same name (1936).

Folklore often transcends national boundaries. The French tales "Sleeping Beauty" and "Cinderella" (both from the 1697 collection of Charles Perrault) were set as Russian ballets (*The Sleeping Beauty* by Tchaikovsky in 1890 and *Cinderella* by Prokofiev in 1945); and a fanciful story by the German writer E. T. A. Hoffmann, in an expanded version by French writer Alexandre Dumas, served as the basis for Tchaikovsky's most famous ballet, *The Nut-*cracker (1892), which we will study in a later chapter.

The theater has traditionally offered an enjoyable means through which to retell these stories, in the form of operas and musicals, as well as ballets. Today, Perrault's "Sleeping Beauty," the Grimms' "Beauty and the Beast," Hans Christian Andersen's "The Little Mermaid," the ancient Greek myth of "Hercules," and the Arabian folktale of "Aladdin" from *The Thousand and One Nights* are brought to life in Disney animated films, whose images and songs keep these cultural expressions alive for a younger generation.

Suggested Listening:

Grieg: Incidental music from *Peer Gynt*
Musorgsky: *The Hut on Fowl's Legs*, from
  Pictures at an Exhibition
Tchaikovsky: *The Sleeping Beauty* or *The
  Nutcracker*
Prokofiev: *Peter and the Wolf*
Sondheim: *Into the Woods*

Bernadette Peters as the witch and Pamela Winslow as Rapunzel in the 1987 Broadway production of Stephen Sondheim's musical Into the Woods.

Principal Works

8 operas, including *The Bartered Bride* (1866)

Orchestral music, including *Má vlast* (*My Country*), cycle of 6 symphonic poems (No. 2 is *The Moldau*, 1874–79)

Chamber and keyboard works, choral music, and songs

symbol of the beloved homeland. (For the text of Smetana's program, see Listening Guide 10.) The music suggests first the rippling streams that flow through the forest to form the mighty river. Smetana then evokes a hunting scene with French horns and trumpets, followed by a peasant wedding in a lilting folk dance. The mood changes to one of enchantment as nymphs emerge from their fairy-tale haunts to hold their nightly revels under the moonlight; here, the melody is heard in muted strings over a bubbling accompaniment. The portrayal of the St. John Rapids musters all the brass and percussion, which announce the broad river theme in major mode. Finally, as the Moldau approaches the capital city of Prague, it flows past castles and fortresses that remind the composer of his country's proud history. The river then flows out to sea, as the music fades to a *pianissimo*, closing a work that has captured the imagination of listeners for over a century.

The Moldau River flows in majestic peace through the Czech capital city of Prague.

Listening Guide 10

CD: Chr/Std 6/7–14, Sh 3/36–43
Cassette: Chr/Std 6A/2, Sh 3A/6

SMETANA: *The Moldau*   (11:36)

Date: 1874–79

Genre: Symphonic poem, from cycle *My Country* (*Má vlast*)

Tempo: Allegro commodo non agitato (Fast, not agitated)

Program: Scenes along the river Moldau in Bohemia

Smetana's program: "Two springs pour forth in the shade of the Bohemian forest, one warm and gushing, the other cold and peaceful. Coming through Bohemia's valleys, they grow into a mighty stream. Through the thick woods it flows as the merry sounds of a hunt and the notes of the hunter's horn are heard ever closer. It flows through grass-grown pastures and lowlands where a wedding feast is being celebrated with song and dance. At night, wood and water nymphs revel in its sparkling waves. Reflected on its surface are fortresses and castles—witnesses of bygone days of knightly splendor and the vanished glory of martial times. The Moldau swirls through the St. John Rapids, finally flowing on in majestic peace toward Prague to be welcomed by historic Vyšehrad. Then it vanishes far beyond the poet's gaze."

		Program	Description
7	0:00	Source of river, two springs	Rippling figures in flute, then added clarinets; plucked string accompaniment.
		Stream broadens	Rippling figure moves to low strings.
8	1:11	River theme	Stepwise melody in violins, minor mode, rippling in low strings; repeated:

| 9 | 3:01 | Hunting scene | Fanfare in French horns and trumpets: |

Rippling continues (in strings); dies down to gently rocking motion.

| 10 | 3:58 | Peasant dance | Repeated notes in strings lead to rustic folk tune, staccato in strings and woodwinds: |

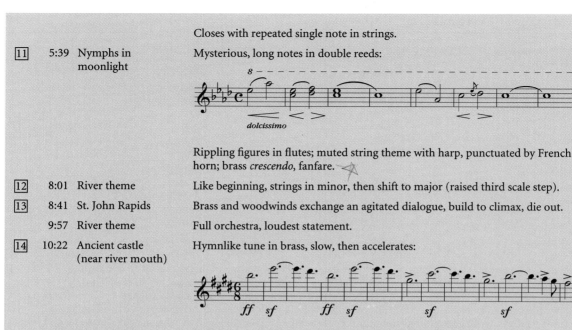

			Closes with repeated single note in strings.
11	5:39	Nymphs in moonlight	Mysterious, long notes in double reeds:

			Rippling figures in flutes; muted string theme with harp, punctuated by French horn; brass *crescendo*, fanfare.
12	8:01	River theme	Like beginning, strings in minor, then shift to major (raised third scale step).
13	8:41	St. John Rapids	Brass and woodwinds exchange an agitated dialogue, build to climax, die out.
	9:57	River theme	Full orchestra, loudest statement.
14	10:22	Ancient castle (near river mouth)	Hymnlike tune in brass, slow, then accelerates:

	11:06	River dies away	Strings slow down, lose momentum; two forceful closing chords.

OTHER NATIONALISTS

Antonín Dvořák (1841–1904) stands alongside Smetana as a founder of the Czech national school. We will consider his music, which drew inspiration not only from the songs and dances of his native land but also from America, in a later chapter.

Edvard Grieg   To the international music public, Edvard Grieg (1843–1907) came to represent "the voice of Norway." The nationalist movement was especially resonant in Norway, owing to the country's struggle for independence from Sweden. This cause, to which Grieg was devoted with all his heart, was successful not long before his death. His songs and piano pieces attained enormous popularity during his lifetime, and they still speak to audiences today. To the concertgoing public, he is known best for his Piano Concerto and the incidental music for *Peer Gynt*.

Jean Sibelius   In the final decades of the nineteenth century, Finland tried to free itself from czarist Russia. Out of this turmoil flowered the art of Jean Sibelius (1865–1957), which announced to the world that his country had come of age musically. During the 1890s, Sibelius produced a series of symphonic poems that captured the spirit of Finnish legends and myths. The most popular of these is *Finlandia* (1899), which occupies the same position in Finland as *The Moldau* does in the Czech Republic.

The foundation for a Russian national school was laid by Mikhail Ivanovich Glinka (1804–1857), whose dream of a Russian music was taken over by a group of young musicians who were called "The Mighty Five" or "The Mighty Handful." Their leader was Mily Balakirev (1837–1910), a self-taught composer who persuaded his four disciples—Alexander Borodin (1833–1887), César Cui (1835–1918), Nikolai Rimsky-Korsakov (1844–1908), and Modest Musorgsky (1839–1881)—that they would have to free themselves from the influence of German symphony, Italian opera, and French ballet if they wanted to express the Russian soul. Their colleague Peter Ilyich Tchaikovsky (1840–1893) was more receptive to European influences. Of these musicians, Musorgsky and Tchaikovsky are now recognized as Russia's greatest composers.

Russian national school

Late in the century, musical nationalism came to England in the works of Edward Elgar (1857–1934) and Frederick Delius (1862–1934). Spain produced three important nationalists in Isaac Albéniz (1860–1909), Enrique Granados (1867–1916), and Manuel de Falla (1876–1946). America's musical nationalism, relatively late in flowering, will be discussed in Chapter 28.

Absolute Forms in the Nineteenth Century

24

The Romantic Symphony

"A great symphony is a man-made Mississippi down which we irresistibly flow from the instant of our leave-taking to a long foreseen destination."—AARON COPLAND

Earlier we noted that in contrast to program music, absolute music has no nonmusical associations provided by the composer, whether of story, scene, or mood. Rather, the musical ideas are organized in such a way that without any aid from external images, they give the listener a satisfying sense of order and continuity. The larger forms of absolute music range from a sonata for solo instrument to the full-scale symphony.

A *symphony* is a large work for orchestra in several parts, or movements. (You may remember that a *movement* is a complete, self-contained part within a larger work.) The movements are contrasted in character, mood, and tempo. Taken together, they form a structural as well as musical entity. During the Classical period, the symphony became the most exalted form of absolute orchestral music. The three Viennese masters—Haydn, Mozart, and Beethoven—carried it to its highest level of significance and formal beauty. They passed on to composers of the Romantic era a flexible art form that could be adapted to meet the emotional needs of the new age.

In the course of its development, the symphony steadily gained greater weight and importance. Nineteenth-century composers found the symphony a suitable framework for their lyrical themes, harmonic experiments, and individual expressions. By the Romantic era, music had moved from palace to public concert hall, the orchestra had vastly increased in size, and symphonies were growing steadily longer and more expansive. The nineteenth-century symphonists were thus not as prolific as their predecessors had been. Felix Mendelssohn, Robert Schumann, Brahms, and Tchaikovsky each wrote fewer than seven symphonies. These were in the domain of absolute music, while Liszt and Berlioz cultivated the program symphony.

The Nature of the Symphony

Chapter 45 gives a detailed discussion of symphonic structure. Here, we look at the four-movement form that was standard at the turn of the nineteenth century.

First movement

The first movement is generally the most dramatic of the cycle, written in what is known as *sonata-allegro* (because the tempo of this movement is almost always Allegro), or first-movement, form. This is a three-part structure: the *exposition,* or statement; the *development;* and the *recapitulation,* or restatement. Sometimes a slow introduction leads into the movement proper. The exposition usually presents two contrasting themes—one strongly rhythmic, one lyrical. There is a *transition,* or bridge, that leads from the first theme (or theme group) to the second, usually modulating to another key. A *codetta* completes the exposition.

The development is marked by a tremendous increase in tension. Here, the composer may break the theme into fragments, recombining them in fresh patterns and revealing them in a new light. In the recapitulation, we hear again the themes of the exposition, more or less in their original guise but with a wealth of new meaning that they have taken on in the course of the movement. There follows the *coda,* whose function is to round off the action and to bring the movement to a close.

Second movement

The second movement, in contrast with the first, is generally lyrical (melodious), set in a slow tempo. It may, however, vary in mood from whimsical, even playful, to tragic and passionate. The tempo marking in most cases is Andante, Adagio, or Largo. This movement may be in three-part (**A-B-A**) or theme and variations form. Other possibilities are indicated in later chapters.

Third movement

Third in the cycle, in the symphonies of the Romantic period, is the strongly rhythmic and excited scherzo, with overtones of humor, surprise, whimsy, or folk dance. "Scherzo" is the Italian word for "jest," but the mood may range from elfin lightness to demonic energy. The tempo marking indicates a lively pace—Allegro molto, Vivace, or the like, in a triple meter. The form is usually a large **A-B-A;** the middle section, known as the trio, is somewhat quieter. In some symphonies, the scherzo falls second in the cycle.

Fourth movement   The fourth and final movement of the Romantic symphony has a dimension and character designed to balance the first. Frequently, this movement is a spirited Allegro in sonata-allegro form, and may close the symphony on a note of triumph or pathos. Some composers experimented with the form: in his Fourth Symphony, for example, Brahms turned to the noble Baroque passacaglia (a work based on a melodic or harmonic ostinato) for its closing movement, while the finale of Mendelssohn's *Italian* Symphony is based on a popular Italian "jumping dance" known as the saltarello. The chart opposite reviews the standard form of the symphony.

Such is the barest outline of symphonic form; we will not get a complete picture until after we have heard several representative works. What is important to understand at this point is that the symphony's several movements present abstract musical ideas, which unfold in such a way as to give the successive movements a quality of logical continuity. The essence of nineteenth-century symphonic style is dramatic contrast and development. It arouses emotion in the listener, but emotion not directed toward any specific image.

Themes and motives, discussed in Chapter 5, figure prominently in the symphony, as they do in any major musical form. A theme may be a fully rounded melody, or it may be a compact melodic-harmonic-rhythmic kernel that is capable of further growth. It may also be broken down into its constituent fragments, or motives. In the playing out of a symphony, the theme and its motives might undergo continual development, as their capacity for growth is explored.

The nineteenth-century symphony holds a place of honor in the works of the era. It retains its hold on the public today, and remains one of the most striking manifestations of the spirit of musical Romanticism.

BRAHMS's SYMPHONY NO. 3 IN F MAJOR

Johannes Brahms did not attempt to write a symphony until he was past forty. He was fond of saying that it was no laughing matter to compose a symphony after Beethoven. "You have no idea," he told a friend, "how the likes of us feel when we hear the tramp of a giant like him behind us." (A discussion of Brahms's life and music appears in Chapter 30.)

The Third Symphony, which Brahms wrote in 1883 when he was fifty years old, is the shortest of his four symphonies and the most Romantic in tone. In

A Typical Romantic Symphony

First movement	Sonata-allegro form Home key	Allegro; optional slow introduction
	Exposition —Theme 1 (home key) —Theme 2 (contrasting key) —Closing theme (same contrasting key) Development (free modulation) Recapitulation —Theme 1 (home key) —Theme 2 (home key) —Closing theme (home key) —Coda	Rhythmic character Lyrical character Fragmentation or expansion of themes
Second movement	Sonata-allegro form, A-B-A form, or theme and variations Different key	Slow, lyrical
Third movement	Minuet and trio or scherzo and trio, A-B-A Home key	Triple meter
	Minuet or scherzo, 2 sections Trio, 2 sections Minuet or scherzo returns	Sections repeated
Fourth movement	Sonata-allegro form, rondo form, or some other form Home key	Allegro or presto; shorter and lighter than first movement

form, however, the work looks back to the Classical structures of the eighteenth century. The first movement, a conventional sonata-allegro, opens with a dramatic figure: a three-note motive (F-A♭-F) that is often related to the composer's personal motto, "Frei aber froh" (Free but happy). This motive permeates the entire symphony. The commanding gesture of the first theme eventually gives way to a lyrical, pastoral theme in the woodwinds, projecting a mood of warm contentment. The two themes are then subjected to a brief but intense development, which is unified by the motto theme. The recapitulation, which features the mellow timbre of the French horn, leads to an ample coda and a quiet close.

The slow movement, a haunting Andante, evokes the peacefulness of nature with its simple, hymnlike theme in the woodwinds. Clara Schumann poetically summed up her impression of this movement in a letter to Brahms: "I feel as though I were watching the worshippers at a woodland shrine, with a babbling brook and the joyous play of beetles and insects. There is a bustle and a whispering around me—I feel safely at home in the joys of nature."

Rather than following with a scherzo, Brahms wrote a tuneful, moderately paced third movement in a three-part, or **A-B-A,** form. It is an impassioned orchestral song richly colored with exotic harmonies. The sentimental and highly memorable opening theme for the cello makes this one of Brahms's most popular symphonic movements.

The finale, a dramatic movement in sonata-allegro form, features concise themes and abrupt changes of mood. The first idea is a quiet, searching melody, narrow in range, played in unison by bassoons and strings. The low register, minor key, and instrumental color all project a somber mood. Contrast is provided by a chantlike theme, which is transformed into a triumphant second theme in C major. A long and vivacious closing theme leads into a development that is chopped up, making it difficult to pinpoint just where the recapitulation begins. The opening theme is now heard in a fragmented state and later, in the extended, fantasy-like coda, as a broad, flowing melody. The dark, brooding mood finally gives way to the major mode, and in a final brilliant stroke, the violins hint at the opening theme of the first movement. (This unifying procedure, used in Berlioz's *Symphonie fantastique*, is called *cyclical structure*.) Thus the monumental work concludes with a nostalgic touch. Throughout, the listener is challenged by shifting moods, timbres, and melodies that affirm the technical command and the creative invention of a great Romantic master.

Listening Guide 11

CD: Chr/Std 6/20–31
Cassette: Chr/Std 6A/4

BRAHMS: Symphony No. 3 in F major, Fourth Movement (8:35)

Date of work: 1883

Movements:
  I. Allegro con brio; sonata-allegro form
  II. Andante; sonata-allegro form
  III. Allegretto; **A-B-A** form (Intermezzo)
  IV. Allegro; sonata-allegro form

FOURTH MOVEMENT: Allegro; sonata-allegro form, duple (cut time), F minor/F major

EXPOSITION

20 0:00 Theme 1a; haunting running melody (marked *sotto voce*, "in an undertone"), in unison strings and bassoon, F minor (answered by clarinets and flutes):

21 0:28 Theme 1b; majestic melody heard in low strings and woodwinds; homophonic texture:

22 0:49 Stormy transitional theme in full orchestra—uneven rhythms, polyphonic texture.

23 1:21 Theme 2 introduced by cellos; cheerful C-major melody, with disjunct triplet movement; answered by violins and woodwinds:

24 1:52 Closing theme; climaxes in C minor, with accented *fortissimo* theme in full orchestra:

DEVELOPMENT/RECAPITULATION
(combined)

25 3:17 Theme 1a, running theme, fragmented and developed, in various keys:

26 3:40 Marchlike mutation of theme 1b.

27 4:06 Triumphant statement, based on theme 1b, establishes return to F major, then minor.

28 4:12 Transition theme from exposition, leads to theme 2.

29	4:43	Theme 2, in F major, first in cellos and horns.
30	5:14	Closing theme, *fortissimo*, with accents on offbeats.
		Coda; an extended, fantasy-like section; theme la broken up into short motives in key of B♭ minor; violas with triplet melody.
31	6:31	Broad F-major melody in augmentation:

Theme 1b heard in brass accompanied by sixteenth-note string movement; ascending 3-note motive (F-A♭-F) from opening of first movement heard near closing; ends tranquilly in F major.

25

Dvořák as a Symphonist

"In the Negro melodies of America I discover all that is needed for a great and noble school of music. These beautiful and varied themes are the product of the soil. . . . They are the folk songs of America, and your composers must turn to them."

Antonín Dvořák is one of numerous late-Romantic composers who found inspiration in the traditional music of their native land. He stands alongside Bedřich Smetana as a founder of the Czech national school.

HIS LIFE

Antonín Dvořák

Dvořák (1841–1904) was born in Bohemia (now part of the Czech Republic) and grew up in a village near Prague, where his father kept an inn. For a time, poverty threatened to rule out a musical career. However, at sixteen the boy managed to get to Prague, where he mastered his craft and secured a position playing the viola in the Czech National Theater under the baton of Smetana.

Inspired by the older master, Dvořák wrote his earliest works during this period; these included several symphonies and a song cycle dedicated to one of his students, Anna Čermáková, whom he eventually married.

In 1874, the Austrian government awarded him a stipend that allowed him to resign his orchestra post and devote himself to composing. He was much encouraged by Brahms, who helped the younger composer find a publisher for his works. By the time he was forty, Dvořák had left behind the financial cares that had plagued his early career, and as professor of composition at the Conservatory of Prague, he was able to exert an important influence on the musical life of his country.

The spontaneity and melodious character of his music assured its popularity; by the last decade of the century, Dvořák was known throughout Europe and the United States. In 1891, Jeanette Thurber, who ran the National Conservatory of Music in New York City, invited him to become its director. There he received $15,000 a year (a fabulous sum in those days), as compared with the annual $600 he had earned in Prague. His stay in the United States was eminently fruitful, resulting in what has remained his most successful symphony, *From the New World*, a number of chamber music works, including the *American* Quartet, and the highly lyrical Cello Concerto. Mrs. Thurber wanted him to write an opera on *The Song of Hiawatha;* but al-

American visit

Dvořák's family shortly after their arrival in America in 1892.

though Dvořák already knew and admired Longfellow's poem, the project never materialized. The operas he did complete—fourteen in all—were based on European themes.

Dvořák spent a summer at the Czech colony in Spillville, Iowa, in an atmosphere that suited his simple tastes. Although every effort was made to persuade him to continue at the New York conservatory, homesickness overrode all other considerations. After three years, he returned to his beloved Bohemia and spent his remaining years in Prague, in the happy circle of his wife and children, students and friends. He died at the age of sixty-three, revered throughout his native land as a national artist.

His Music

Dvořák was a natural musician with a great gift for melody. His style reveals the strong influence of native folk melodies, coupled with a solid craftsmanship that enabled him to shape musical ideas into large forms notable for their clarity. His expressive harmonies and instrumental combinations further evoke the traditional music of his homeland.

Principal Works

Orchestral music, including 9 symphonies (No. 9, *From the New World*, 1893); symphonic poems; other symphonic works, including *Slavonic Rhapsodies* (1878) and *Slavonic Dances* (orchestrated 1886)

Concertos, including 1 cello concerto (1895)

14 operas, including *Rusalka* (1901); incidental music

Choral music, including a cantata (*The Spectre's Bride*, 1884) and a Requiem (1890); Masses; oratorio; other sacred choral music, including Stabat mater (1877); part songs and choral arrangements of Czech folk songs

Chamber music, including 14 string quartets (*American*, 1893), 3 string quintets, 6 piano trios (*Dumky*, 1891), 2 piano quartets, and duo sonatas

Keyboard music, including dances and character pieces; music for 2 pianos (*Slavonic Dances*, 1878); organ music

Dvořák's large output included all genres of music. His operas, highly influenced by Smetana, have achieved a preeminence as the most strongly national of his country. His symphonies reflect a mastery of Classical procedures, and the *Slavonic Dances* and *Rhapsodies* are filled with orchestral color. The Cello Concerto is a crowning achievement in that instrument's repertory. Landmarks among his chamber works include the *Dumky* Piano Trio and the *American* Quartet, so-called for its use of a *pentatonic* (five-note) scale often associated with Native American music.

Having arrived in the United States with an established reputation as a nationalist composer, Dvořák tried to steer his American pupils toward their native heritage. One of his students was Henry T. Burleigh, an African-American baritone and arranger of spirituals. The melodies Dvořák heard from Burleigh appealed to the folk poet in him, and strengthened his conviction that American composers would find their true path only when they had thrown off the influence of Europe and sought their inspiration in the Native American, African-American, and traditional folk songs of their own country. This doctrine helped prepare the way for the rich harvest of American works by composers of the next generations.

The *New World* Symphony

Dvořák wrote his Symphony No. 9, subtitled *From the New World*, during his stay in the United States, and it received its first performance in New York in 1893. The whole symphony may be seen as a descriptive landscape, evoking the openness of the American prairie as well as the composer's longing for his homeland. It is set in a standard four-movement framework, the middle movements of which can be directly linked to the influence of Longfellow's *Song of Hiawatha*. The clearest association is in the third movement, a scherzo, which portrays *Hiawatha's Wedding Feast* (beginning with the *Dance of the Pa-Puk-Keewis*); the trio depicts a group of natives who are turned into birds.

We will study the slow movement, a Largo set in a ternary (**A-B-A**) form, which the composer associated with a section of the poem called *Hiawatha's Wooing* (see Listening Guide 12). The movement's outer sections loosely portray the travel homeward of Hiawatha and Minnehaha; the mournful middle section, set in an emotion-charged minor key, is supposed to represent Minnehaha's death. The deeply felt English-horn tune that opens the Largo was made famous when sung as a kind of spiritual, set to the words "Goin' Home."

Although Dvořák himself said of the symphony that "the influence of America can be felt to anyone who has 'a nose,'" the listener unacquainted with the composer's intention is as likely to associate this tune with a typically Czech folk song.

In His Own Words

My own duty as a teacher . . . is not so much to interpret Beethoven, Wagner, or other masters of the past, but to give what encouragement I can to the young musicians of America. I . . . hope that just as this nation has already surpassed so many others in marvelous inventions and feats of engineering and commerce, and has made an honorable place for itself in literature in one short century, so it must assert itself in the . . . art of music. . . . To bring about this result, we must trust to the very youthful enthusiasm and patriotism of this country.

Dvořák's Influence on African-American Art Music

The Bohemian composer Antonín Dvořák was inspired by traditional music of America (as well as of his native Bohemia)—specifically, spirituals, Creole tunes and dances, and what he perceived as music of Native Americans. Yet there is little in the *New World* Symphony that is reminiscent of actual Native American music, although, as we have learned, the two middle movements can be linked with Henry Wadsworth Longfellow's epic poem *The Song of Hiawatha*.

What, then, of Dvořák's professed interest in the traditional music of African Americans? We know that the composer came to love the spirituals sung to him by his student Henry Burleigh (1866–1949), and he supposedly had a particular fondness for *Swing Low, Sweet Chariot* (a variant of this spiritual can be heard in the first movement of the symphony). The rhythmic syncopations and the particular scale formations used in the *New World* Symphony (the minor mode with a lowered, or flatted, seventh degree; see p. 214) have often been cited as evidence of borrowings from African-American musical styles.

But Dvořák gave much more to American music than he took from it. As a respected teacher, he issued a challenge to American composers to throw off the domination of European music and forge a path of their own, using the "beautiful and varied themes . . . the folk songs of America." Some followed his suggestion, including two of his African-American students. Burleigh published a landmark collection of spirituals arranged in an art music style (*Jubilee Songs of the U.S.A.*, 1916, which included *Deep River*); his goal was to bring the genre to the concert stage. Will Marion Cook (1869–1944), while a student in Dvořák's composition class, began an opera on *Uncle Tom's Cabin* (Harriet Beecher Stowe's novel about life under slavery), but then turned his efforts to musical theater.

Florence Price (1888–1953), the first African-American woman to be recognized as a distinguished composer, is believed to have drawn inspiration for her Symphony in E minor (1932) directly from Dvořák's *New World* Symphony. Price's work parallels Dvořák's in a number of ways, including original themes that allude to characteristic African-American rhythms and melodies.

The composer who best rose to Dvořák's challenge was William Grant Still (1895–1978), whose output exceeds one hundred concert works in a wide variety of genres—symphonies, symphonic poems, suites, operas, ballets, chamber music, choral music, and songs. A nationalist, Still drew musical inspiration from African-American work songs, spirituals, ragtime, blues, and jazz. For his *Afro-American* Symphony (1930), his best-known work today, Still stated his goal clearly: "I knew I wanted to write a symphony, I knew that it had to be an American work; and I wanted to demonstrate how the blues, so often considered a lowly expression, could be elevated to the highest musical level." Although not the first symphonic work written in a jazz or blues style (George Gershwin's *Rhapsody in Blue* was premiered in 1924), Still's symphony was firmly rooted in the music of his African-American heritage.

Dvořák would surely have welcomed these examples of musical nationalism, which were products of an early-twentieth-century movement often referred to as the Black, or Harlem, Renaissance. Today, the "validation" of a vernacular music by art music standards described by William Grant Still is no longer necessary, since all musics are coming to be accepted as valuable products of the culture and people who created them.

Suggested Listening:

Dvořák: *New World* Symphony, Second Movement
Still: *Afro-American* Symphony, First Movement
Spiritual (*Swing Low, Sweet Chariot*)

Left: William Grant Still, composer of the Afro-American Symphony. Right: Henry T. Burleigh, one of Dvořák's students, noted for his collections of spirituals in art-music style.

Listening Guide 12

CD: Chr/Std 6/49–51
Cassette: Chr/Std 6B/2

Dvořák: Symphony No. 9 in E minor, *From the New World*, Second Movement

(12:07)

Date of work: 1893

Basis: Loosely connected to Longfellow's poem *The Song of Hiawatha*

Movements:
  I.   Adagio, Allegro molto; duple meter, E minor
  II. Largo; 4/4 meter, D-flat major
  III. Molto vivace (scherzo and trio, very lively); 3/4 meter, E minor
  IV. Allegro con fuoco (Fast, with fire); 4/4 meter, E minor

---

SECOND MOVEMENT: Largo; A-B-A form, 4/4 meter, D-flat major

A SECTION

[49] 0:00   Opens with slow, chromatic chords in brass.

0:37   Theme 1—songful and pensive, English-horn solo:

2:06   Brass and woodwind chords introduce string variation of first theme, followed by English horn, then French horns.

B SECTION (un poco più mosso, moving a little more)

[50] 4:27   New theme—wavering line in flutes and oboes, C-sharp minor.

4:59   Sustained woodwind theme over plucked "walking" bass line, then heard in strings:

8:01   More animated, staccato woodwinds lead to orchestral climax; theme from first movement is heard.

A SECTION (Tempo I)

[51] 8:57   Theme 1 returns—English horn answered by strings, D-flat major, broken up by fermatas.

11:10 Ends with brass chords, followed by soft, high strings.

26

The Romantic Concerto

"We are so made that we can derive intense enjoyment only from a contrast."—SIGMUND FREUD

THE NATURE OF THE CONCERTO

A *concerto* is a large-scale work in several movements for solo instrument (or instruments) and orchestra. Here, our attention is focused on the solo performer as, for example, the massive sonorities of the piano, the sweetness of the violin, or the dark resonance of the cello is pitted against the orchestra. This opposition of forces constitutes the essential nature of the concerto.

In its dimensions, the concerto is comparable to the symphony. Most concertos are in three movements: a dramatic Allegro, usually in sonata-allegro form, is followed by a lyrical slow movement and a brilliant finale. In the opening movement, as in the first movement of the symphony, contrasting themes are stated, developed, and restated. In this case, however, the tension is twofold: not only between the contrasting ideas but also between the opposing forces—between the solo instrument and the group. Each of the basic themes may be announced by the *tutti* (literally, "all"— that is, the orchestra as a whole) and then taken up by the solo part. Or the soloist may introduce ideas and the orchestra elaborate on them. In any case, there is usually a twofold statement of the themes by the orchestra and the soloist, producing a double exposition within the first-movement form.

A characteristic feature of the concerto is the *cadenza*, a fanciful solo passage in the manner of an improvisation that interrupts the movement. The cadenza came out of a time when improvisation was an important element in art music, as it is today in jazz. The cadenza produces a dramatic effect, as the orchestra falls silent and the soloist launches into a free play of fantasy on one or more themes of the movement. Before the nineteenth century, the performer was usually the composer. With the rise of a class of professional performers who interpreted the music of others but did not invent their own,

Tutti

Cadenza

the art of improvisation declined. Thus the cadenza came to be composed beforehand, by either the composer or the performer.

Second movements present lyrical melodies, often in a loosely structured three-part form. The finales of the Romantic concerto bring to a head the dramatic tension between soloist and orchestra. The soloist is often featured again in a brilliant cadenza that closes the concerto cycle.

VIRTUOSITY AND THE CONCERTO

The origins of the Romantic concerto reach back to earlier eras. Mozart and Beethoven, both formidable pianists, performed their concertos in public, delighting and dazzling their audiences. This element of virtuosic display, combined with appealing melodies, helped make the concerto one of the most widely appreciated types of concert music. As the concert industry developed, technical brilliance became a more and more important element of

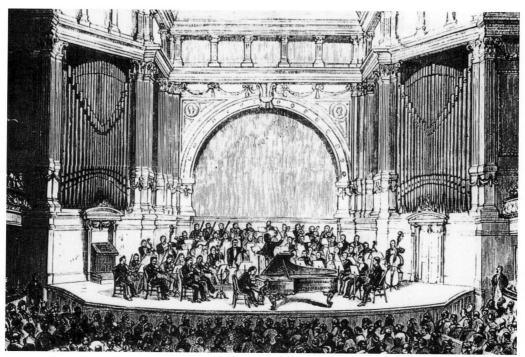

In this woodcut from the 1870s, the noted virtuoso Hans von Bülow performs a piano concerto with orchestra in New York City.

concerto style. We have seen that nineteenth-century composer-performers such as Paganini and Liszt carried virtuosity to new heights. This development kept pace with the increase in the size and resources of the symphony orchestra. The Romantic concerto took shape as one of the most favored genres of the age. Felix Mendelssohn, Chopin, Liszt, Robert and Clara Schumann, Brahms, Tchaikovsky, and Dvořák all contributed to its literature.

Composers of the concerto often write with particular artists in mind, and may even consult them about what is possible given their own technique and that of their instrument. We will see that Mozart wrote piano concertos not only for himself but for several noted women performers of his time, including one of his students. The Violin Concerto of Felix Mendelssohn, which we will study, was written for the virtuoso Ferdinand David, concertmaster of the Leipzig Gewandhaus Orchestra, which the composer conducted. Brahms consulted Joseph Joachim, the leading violinist of the day, when he wrote his Violin Concerto. And Tchaikovsky wrote his with the virtuoso Leopold Auer in mind; when Auer found the work unplayable, the composer turned to another extraordinary violinist, Adolf Brodsky, who gave the premiere performance.

A Typical Romantic Concerto

First movement	Concerto form (double exposition) Home key	Allegro
	Orchestral exposition —Several themes Solo exposition —Same themes and others Development Recapitulation Cadenza (solo instrument alone) Coda, or closing	
Second movement	A-B-A form Contrasting key	Slow, lyrical
Third movement	Rondo form or sonata-allegro form Home key	Allegro or presto

27

Felix Mendelssohn and the Concerto

"People often complain that music is too ambiguous, that what they should think when they hear it is so unclear, whereas everyone understands words. With me it is exactly the opposite, and not only with regard to an entire speech but also with individual words. These too seem to me so ambiguous, so vague, so easily misunderstood in comparison to genuine music, which fills the soul with a thousand things better than words."

Felix Mendelssohn, whose music is a blend of meticulous craftsmanship and serene, elegant expression, represents the classicist trend within the Romantic movement. The works of this man of culture, education, and creative gifts hold a prominent place in the repertory.

HIS LIFE

Felix Mendelssohn

Felix Mendelssohn (1809–1847) was the son of a music-loving banker and grandson of a famous Jewish philosopher, Moses Mendelssohn (his family converted to Protestantism when Felix was still a child). The Mendelssohn home was a meeting place for Berlin intellectuals, their garden house the scene of memorable concerts. Here an orchestra under the direction of the seventeen-year-old Felix performed his Overture to *A Midsummer Night's Dream* for a captivated audience. As we have seen, Felix was not the only musician in the household. His sister Fanny was a gifted pianist and composer as well. (Some of her works were published under her brother's name.)

The youth's education was thorough and well rounded. He visited the venerable poet Goethe at Weimar and attended the philospher Hegel's lectures at the University of Berlin. Meanwhile, he worshipped the music of earlier mas-

Bach revival

ters—Bach, Mozart, and Beethoven. In 1829, at the age of twenty, Felix organized a performance of Bach's *St. Matthew Passion*, which had been neglected since the death of its composer. The event proved to be a turning point in the nineteenth-century revival of Bach's choral music.

Mendelssohn excelled in a number of roles—as pianist, conductor, organizer of music festivals, and educator. At twenty-six, he was named conductor of the Gewandhaus Orchestra in Leipzig and went on to transform the orchestra into the finest in Europe. Later he founded the Conservatory of Leipzig, which raised the standards for the training of musicians. His ten visits to England elicited a frenzy of enthusiasm. All this in addition to directing one or another of the provincial festivals that formed the backbone of musical life in Germany.

Mendelssohn's happy life was shattered in 1847 by the death of his sister Fanny, to whom he was deeply attached. This blow, along with his very demanding musical career, brought on a stroke, from which he died at age thirty-eight.

His Music

Mendelssohn was dedicated to preserving the tradition of the Classical forms in an age that was turning from them. His fastidious craftsmanship links him to that great tradition. But it should not be supposed that he was untouched by Romanticism. In his early works, he is the ardent poet of nature, a landscape painter of gossamer brush. Tenderness and melancholy breathe from his music.

Mendelssohn composed with a speed and facility that invite comparison with Mozart or Schubert, but he seldom allowed himself the inner repose

Principal Works

Orchestral music, including 5 symphonies (No. 3, *Scottish*, 1842; No. 4, *Italian*, 1833; No. 5, *Reformation*, 1830); concert overtures (*A Midsummer Night's Dream*, 1826; *The Hebrides, or Fingal's Cave*, 1830); 2 piano concertos, Violin Concerto in E minor (1844)

Dramatic music, including 1 opera and incidental music for 6 plays (*A Midsummer Night's Dream*, 1843)

Choral music, including 2 oratorios (*St. Paul*, 1836; *Elijah*, 1846); cantatas, anthems, and part songs

Chamber music, including 6 string quartets, 2 string quintets, piano quartets, 1 octet, and various sonatas

Piano music, including *Songs Without Words* (8 sets, 1829–45); sonatas, fugues, and fantasias

Organ music; solo vocal music, transcriptions and arrangements of Bach, Handel, Mozart, and Beethoven

that might have imparted profundity to much of his music. Of his symphonies, the best-known are the Third (the *Scottish*) and the Fourth (the *Italian*)—mementos of his youthful travels. Both works were begun in 1830, when he was twenty-one. The Concerto for Violin and Orchestra, which we will study, is one of the most popular of all time. The Octet for Strings, written when the composer was sixteen, is much admired, as are the *Songs Without Words*, eight sets of short piano pieces. Mendelssohn was a prolific writer for the voice; the oratorio *Elijah*, one of his best-loved works, represents the peak of his achievement in this category.

Violin Concerto in E minor

Written three years before the composer's death, the Violin Concerto in E minor (1844) was Mendelssohn's last orchestral work. He was already planning it in 1838, when he wrote to the virtuoso Ferdinand David: "I should like to write a violin concerto for you next winter. One in E minor is running through my head, and the beginning does not leave me in peace." This work reveals the composer's special gifts: clarity of form, subtlety of orchestration, and a reserved, sentimental expression. The concerto's three-movement structure conforms to the classical ideals, although new ideas of unity have been imposed. For example, the three movements are to be played without pause, and a reference back to the first movement occurs in the second, hinting at cyclical form.

The first movement, an Allegro molto appassionato (very fast and impassioned), does away with the customary orchestral introduction in concerto form; rather, the solo violin announces the main theme almost immediately in a dramatic and expansive melody that forms a broad arch with balanced, symmetrical phrases. The continuation of this idea gives the soloist plenty of opportunity for brilliant display, in triplets and double stops (playing two notes simultaneously). The narrow-ranged, stepwise second theme is quietly introduced by the clarinets and flutes over a sustained low pitch (G) on the solo instrument. (A sustained tone over which harmonies change is called a **Pedal point** *pedal point*.) The solo violin then takes over the tranquil theme, eventually picking up the pace to close the exposition.

The development section explores motives from the principal theme and the transitional idea. The momentum culminates in the cadenza, which instead of coming at the end of the movement serves as a link between the development and a shortened recapitulation. Written out by the composer, the cadenza is here an integral part of the piece. The recapitulation brings back the main themes, as the movement gains steadily in pace and in power.

The Andante follows with no interruption, linked by a solo bassoon holding a note from the previous movement. The opening theme, in 6/8 meter, is calm and meditative. The developmental middle section is more animated as the orchestra and soloist carry on a dialogue, after which the serene opening melody returns. An interlude leads into the third movement, an Allegro molto vivace (very fast and lively) in sonata-allegro form. The first theme is light and breezy, demanding agile fingers, brilliance of tone, and high-spirited playing. The second theme is a light-hearted march. As with the first movement, the recapitulation is short, as excitement builds to the dazzling virtuosity of the coda. With its appealing melodies and formal clarity, this concerto displays the tender sentiment and classical moderation that are so typical of Mendelssohn's music.

Listening Guide 13

CD: Chr/Std 5/22–30
Cassette: Chr/Std 5A/5

MENDELSSOHN: Violin Concerto in E minor, First Movement

(13:22)

Date of work: 1844

Movements (played without pauses):
I. Allegro molto appassionato; first-movement concerto form
II. Andante; **A-B-A′** form
III. Allegro molto vivace; sonata-allegro form

FIRST MOVEMENT: Allegro molto appassionato; 2/2 meter (cut time), E minor, first-movement concerto form

EXPOSITION

22 | 0:00 | Theme 1, broad melody in solo violin, played in high register, in E minor:

Continuation of theme 1 in solo violin, in running triplet figures, punctuated by chords in orchestra.

1:00 | Full orchestral statement of theme 1.

23 | 1:32 | Transitional melody, in first violins, then long solo violin passage:

24 2:59   Theme 2, in G major, conjunct, with narrow range, played by clarinet and flutes, over sustained pitch G in solo violin:

pp *tranquillo*

          3:15   Solo violin with theme 2.

25   4:20   Closing idea based on theme 1; solo violin with brilliant passage work.

            DEVELOPMENT

26   5:36   Fragmentation of themes 1 and 2; varied moods and dynamics; cadence in B major (dominant key) to prepare for cadenza.

            CADENZA

27   7:20   Unaccompanied solo violin, with fragments of principal melody and broken chords, use of trills, double stops, and extreme registers of violin.

            RECAPITULATION

28   8:54   Theme 1 in E minor heard in orchestra, under virtuosic arpeggios in solo violin.

          9:13   Transition theme, *fortissimo*, in full orchestra, then extended in solo violin, growing softer.

29   9:50   Theme 2 played softly in woodwinds over violin pedal point, in E major; then in solo violin.

            Closing idea, in rapid triplet motion, leads to coda.

            CODA

30   12:32   Faster tempo (Più presto), transitional theme in solo violin; then in full orchestra, fast-paced to end; solo bassoon holds single note over into next movement.

28

Amy Beach and Classical Composition in America

"I hear America singing, the varied carols I hear."
—WALT WHITMAN

By 1850, a vibrant musical life had grown up in major U.S. and Canadian cities, dominated by European composers and musicians. (We will explore aspects of earlier American concert life and genres unique to North America in later Cultural Perspectives, pp. 240, 392.) Young Americans who were attracted to careers as performers or composers went abroad to complete their studies. When they returned home, they brought the European traditions with them. Virtuosity was admired by American audiences, who thronged to hear the "Swedish nightingale" Jenny Lind on her extended concert tour. One of America's first native virtuoso musicians was Louis Moreau Gottschalk (1829–1869), a charismatic pianist and composer of mixed racial heritage who was born in New Orleans and trained in Paris. Gottschalk pioneered the use of American song and dance in his works; his original keyboard compositions, such as *The Banjo* and *Bamboula*, incorporated elements from African-American and Creole music idioms that he had absorbed growing up in New Orleans. He left the United States permanently in 1865 when a minor incident involving an encounter with a young woman in San Francisco was blown into a scandal; he died in Brazil at the age of forty.

The European musical tradition prevailed in the Americas for several more generations. The German-born conductor Theodore Thomas devoted his energies to cultivating a public taste for orchestral music in America by setting up a concert series across the continent and establishing, in 1864, New York City's second professional orchestra (the Philharmonic Society had been formed in 1842). Among American educators, Lowell Mason (1792–1872) was single-handedly responsible for establishing music as a part of the public school curriculum, a contribution still valued today.

Among the first American composers to write music comparable in quality to that of European musicians was the New Englander John Knowles Paine (1839–1906), whose Mass in D, modeled on Beethoven's *Missa solemnis*, was the first large-scale classical work by an American to be performed in Europe. Paine's First Symphony in C minor, premiered by Theodore Thomas, is also indebted to Beethoven. From 1876 until his death thirty years later, Paine held the country's first professorship in music, at Harvard University.

One of Paine's students at Harvard was Arthur Foote (1853–1937), a Boston-based composer remembered today for his orchestral and chamber music, conceived in the Brahmsian tradition. Foote held a teaching position for some years at the New England Conservatory of Music. George Whitefield Chadwick (1854–1931), born into a musical New England family, was influential in giving an American flavor to music based on European models. His symphonic works, most of which were premiered by the Boston Symphony Orchestra, and his five string quartets were well received. Chadwick left his mark on students both as a teacher and as director of the New England Conservatory in Boston.

Another composer who made important strides in turning the national path away from the Germanic style was Edward MacDowell (1860–1908), a New Yorker who studied piano and composition in Europe. His very popular

Woodland Sketches, for piano, and his Second Orchestral Suite both incorporate Native American tunes. In 1896, MacDowell became the first professor of music at Columbia University (where Mozart's librettist Lorenzo da Ponte had taught Italian in the 1820s and masterminded New York opera productions). Amy Cheney Beach, a contemporary of these influential musicians, was widely recognized in her lifetime as the leading American woman composer. Renewed interest in her work has shown her to be in the forefront of the so-called New England School of composition.

Beach: Her Life and Music

Amy Cheney Beach

"Remember that technique is valuable only as a means to an end. You must first have something to say—something which demands expression from the depths of your soul. If you feel deeply and know how to express what you feel, you make others feel."

Amy Cheney (1867–1944) was born in Henniker, New Hampshire, the only child of a wealthy industrialist, Charles Abbott Cheney, and a gifted amateur singer and pianist, Clara Imogene Cheney. A child prodigy, Amy had a keen ear for music: by the age of one, she could sing some forty songs, always in the same key; by age four, she could play four-part hymns by ear at the piano. She studied piano with her mother, and at the tender age of seven gave her first public recital, playing works by Chopin and Beethoven as well as some pieces of her own. In 1875, the family moved to Boston, where Amy studied piano and composition, and taught herself the art of orchestration, translating into English Berlioz's renowned treatise on the subject. She published her first composition, a song set to a Longfellow poem, in 1883.

Amy concertized regularly and in 1885 performed Chopin's F-minor Piano Concerto in the first of several concerts she played with the Boston Symphony

Marriage

Orchestra. In the same year, she married Henry Harris Aubrey Beach, a forty-three-year-old physician and amateur singer. Out of respect for his wishes, she limited her performances, focusing her energies on composition.

Between 1885 and 1910, Amy Cheney Beach (or Mrs. H. H. A. Beach, as she chose to be known) produced a number of her major works. These include the Mass in E-flat, the concert aria *Racing Clouds*, the *Gaelic* Symphony, and the Piano Concerto in C-sharp minor—all performed by prestigious musical groups such as the Boston Symphony Orchestra, the Symphony Society of New York, and the Handel and Haydn Society of Boston. Her *Festival Jubilate*, commissioned for the dedication of the Women's Building of the Chicago World Exposition of 1893, provided her with the international venue she needed to gain wide visibility and recognition as a composer.

After the death of her husband in 1910, she embarked on an extended and highly successful European tour. One reviewer described her as "a virtuoso pianist" with "a musical nature tinged with genius." With the onset of World War I, she returned home to a demanding U.S. tour. From 1915 until the mid-1930s, she gave annual winter concert tours, leaving her summers free for composing and practicing.

In her later years, Beach helped shape the careers of many young musicians. She held leadership positions in the Music Educators National Conference and the Music Teachers National Association; she also served as cofounder and first president of the Society of American Women Composers. At her death in 1944, she left her royalties to the MacDowell Colony, a retreat for artists, writers, and composers in Peterborough, New Hampshire, where she spent a portion of each summer from 1921 on.

Beach's early works show the influence of the German Romantic School, especially Brahms and Wagner, but her later compositions reflect an assimilation of the new French Impressionism. Her Symphony in E minor, the first symphony composed by an American woman, is a masterpiece that is thought to have been inspired by Dvořák's *New World* Symphony, also in E minor. Aware of Dvořák's suggestion that American composers look to their own folk music

Musical influences

In Her Own Words

The women composers of today have advanced in technique, resourcefulness, and force, and even the younger composers have achieved some effects which the great masters themselves would never have dared to attempt. The present composers are getting away more and more from the idea that they must cater to the popular taste, and in expressing their individual ideas, are giving us music of real worth and beauty.

Principal Works

Orchestral music, including *Gaelic* Symphony (1896) and Piano Concerto (1899)

1 opera, *Cabildo* (1932)

Chamber music, including a violin sonata (1896), piano quintet (1907), string quartet (1929), and piano trio (1938)

Choral music, including the Mass in E-flat (1890), *Festival Jubilate* (1891), and many sacred works (anthems and hymns); secular choral works, including *The Song of Welcome* (1898) and *The Chambered Nautilus* (1907)

More than 120 songs for voice and piano, including *Five Songs to Words by Robert Burns* (1899) and *Three Browning Songs* (1900); concert aria *Eilende Wolken* (*Racing Clouds*), for voice and orchestra (1892)

Keyboard music, including character pieces (*The Hermit Thrush at Morn* and *The Hermit Thrush at Eve*, 1921); *Suite for Two Pianos on Old Irish Melodies* (1924); sets of variations

Numerous articles on composition and pedagogical topics

Cultural Perspective 3

WOMEN AND MUSIC: A FEMINIST ISSUE

Have you wondered why we study so few works by women composers? We will see that in earlier eras, upper-class women frequently studied music, especially keyboard playing and singing—indeed, such study was a near necessity in proper society. Some, like the medieval abbess Hildegard of Bingen, were inspired to compose music, but exclusively for the needs of the church; others, like the French Baroque composer Elisabeth-Claude Jacquet de la Guerre, worked as musicians and composers, but strictly within the confines of aristocratic court society. One Baroque-era musician, Lavinia della Pietà, composed in secret; as she confided to her diary, "I could not do otherwise. They would not take me seriously, they would never let me compose. The music of others is like words addressed to me; I must answer and hear the sound of my own voice. . . . Woe betide me should they find out."

Although the gender barrier began to break down in the later nineteenth century, many still held the view that women lacked creativity in the arts. This attitude drove some women to pursue literary careers under male pseudonyms: George Eliot (alias Mary Ann Evans), George Sand (alias Baronne Aurore Dudevant), and Daniel Stern (alias Comtesse Marie d'Agoult), to name just three. Despite the social attitudes of the era, Clara Schumann and Fanny Mendelssohn Hensel, among others, saw their compositions published and critically acclaimed. But the odds were against them in this endeavor. George Upton, writing in 1880, claimed, "Not only are women too emotional and lacking in stamina to write music, but a woman's mind simply cannot grasp the scientific logic of music making," and even Clara Schumann herself remarked that "women always betray themselves in their compositions." Still, women made their musical mark, especially in songs, piano music, and chamber works.

Repression of women became an important social issue at the beginning of the twentieth century. A women's movement arose to bring about social reform: some worked against societal problems such as alcoholism, some fought for improved education, and many rallied for suffrage, or the right to vote. (It was not until 1920, with the passage of the Twentieth Amendment to the Constitution, that women won legal equality in the political arena.) By the turn of the century, some female musicians had adopted militant feminist perspectives.

One activist was the English composer Ethel Smyth, a prominent suffragist who fought against sexual discrimination in music. Her *March of the Women* became the anthem of a feminist organization called the Women's Social and Political Union. It was sung at meetings, in the streets, and even in prison. (Smyth herself was imprisoned for two months, for breaking the window of a cabinet minister.) She also led a campaign to secure positions in all professional orchestras for women performers. (This crusade was not altogether successful in her lifetime—the Vienna Philharmonic Orchestra reluctantly admitted its first permanent woman member, a harpist, in 1997!) In her later years, Smyth was viewed as somewhat eccentric when she began wearing manly tweed suits and smoking a pipe.

Not all women composers followed her courageous path. As we have seen, the American composer Amy Beach was more conservative, choosing to be known professionally as Mrs. H. H. A. Beach in deference to her married status; however, in later life, she headed several important educational organizations that reached out to both sexes.

Feminists today have posed some interesting questions regarding women composers. For example, do women and men speak differently through music? Is there a woman's "voice" in music, and if so, what characterizes it? More scientifically, does biology play a role in the creative process? Reviewers, mostly male, have criticized musical works by nineteenth-century women that failed to conform to traditional structural procedures. Did women base their choice of forms on their concert settings (which were mostly salons instead of public halls), on the makeup of their audiences, or on their musical training, which usually occurred at home? Or did they avoid the common procedures of composition because of the "masculine" implications of the forms—which were, after all, designed and defined exclusively by men? Critics have not always applied the same standards to compositions by both sexes: while a woman might be criticized for writing music that was too "feminine," a man who writes music considered "feminine" (Chopin, for example) is credited with having a full range of emotional expression.

Society has clearly come a long way in accepting women and their creative musical expressions. And while we have not fully resolved the intriguing questions raised above, differences between the sexes include the ideas men and women express through music. One of the major contributions of the feminist perspective in modern times has been the recognition of women's own experiences, as distinct from men's perception of women's experiences. Thus, the multimedia artist Meredith Monk often composes works about women and their views of life. Her 1988 film *Book of Days*, for example, tells the tale of a fourteenth-century Jewish girl who is troubled with baffling visions of the future, and her operas *Education of the Girlchild* (1975) and *Atlas* (1991), the latter commissioned by the Houston Grand Opera, both focus on women and their lifetime quests. The composer Libby Larsen (b. 1950), whom we will meet later, frequently sets women's writings to music. Her *Songs from Letters: Calamity Jane to her Daughter Janey* (1989) is a song cycle based on excerpts from the famous frontierwoman's diary; her opera *Frankenstein, the Modern Prometheus* (1990) reinterprets Mary Shelley's famous novel; and she has also set poems by Emily Dickinson and short stories by Willa Cather, among others.

Popular music has opened up to a new woman's voice and to improved perceptions of women. While many rock songs have made demeaning references to women and expressed violent attitudes toward them, modern artists such as Salt 'N Pepa, the first successful female rap group, and Queen Latifah have sounded a strong voice against female bashing through their own artistic creations. As society gradually moves not only to accept the creative contributions of women, but to welcome and understand them, there is no doubt that more female musicians and composers will achieve success and inspire others in their chosen professions.

Suggested Listening:

Works by Hildegard, Clara Schumann, Fanny Mendelssohn, Ethel Smyth, Meredith Monk, Libby Larsen, Salt 'N Pepa, Queen Latifah (*All Hail the Queen*), Alanis Morissette (*Jagged Little Pill*)

The title page to English composer Ethel Smyth's March of the Women, *a work that became the rallying cry of the early feminist movement.*

for inspiration (see CP 2), Beach noted that New Englanders were likely to be of Irish, Scottish, or English ancestry, and thus drew on these musical traditions in her *Gaelic* Symphony. This work, along with the Piano Concerto in C-sharp minor and the Mass in E-flat mentioned previously, show her abilities in large-scale compositional forms.

In the realm of chamber music, Beach contributed, in addition to the Violin Sonata we will study, the Piano Quintet in F-sharp minor, the Piano Trio, and the Quartet for Strings, Op. 89, which sets Inuit (Eskimo) themes. Forming the heart of her output are highly lyrical songs (which also provided themes for instrumental works, including her Symphony, Piano Trio, and Piano Concerto), with texts by American, English, French, and German poets as well as poems written in Scottish dialect by Robert Burns. Her choral works, especially the anthems and hymns, have held an important place in the Protestant church music repertory. In two piano works written during her first summer at the MacDowell Colony, *The Hermit Thrush at Morn* and *The Hermit Thrush at Eve*, she set the calls of a bird she heard daily outside her studio. This practice predates works of the twentieth-century French composer Olivier Messiaen, who also used birdcalls as the basis for many compositions.

Violin Sonata in A minor

A mature work, the Violin Sonata in A minor demonstrates Beach's natural gift for melody and her rich harmonic vocabulary. Written just after her impressive *Gaelic* Symphony in 1896, the duo sonata received its premiere in Boston with violinist Franz Kneisel, concertmaster of the Boston Symphony Orchestra, and Beach herself at the piano in a program that included Beethoven and Mozart quartets. The reviews were positive, one critic noting that the sonata was "not crushed" by the two masterworks but was rather a "notable feature of the program," another writing that it "fairly teems with musical ideas, all fine and fresh . . . it bears the stamp of originality as well as scholarship of surpassing merit." The European premiere was given in Berlin several years later by the Spanish violinist Carl Halir and the great Venezuelan pianist Teresa Carreño, to whom Beach dedicated her Piano Concerto in C-sharp minor. The sonata "met with a decided success," wrote Carreño, herself a composer, "and this is said to the credit of the public."

The Violin Sonata, impressive in scale, looks to the Germanic tradition in its developmental procedures. The first movement, an Allegro moderato in sonata-allegro form, makes extensive use of variation as well as shifting major-minor tonality. Beach inverted the inner movements of the classical sonata structure, writing a bouncy G-major scherzo and trio set in duple rather than triple meter as the second movement. The violin's dancelike opening theme sets up a syncopated rhythm that quickly becomes the developmental idea for the movement. The violin and piano toss short imitative motives back and forth with all the energy of a *perpetuum mobile* (perpetual motion work). The pace is slowed in the more melodious trio, which is rich with chromatic color. The return of the scherzo, in abridged form, brings a new version of the energetic theme. The third movement, a brooding Largo con dolore (Very slow, with sorrow) in E minor, is followed by a driving finale, marked Allegro con fuoco (Fast, with fire), a sonata-allegro form with a fugal development section.

This well-constructed, appealing work, along with the *Gaelic* Symphony, signaled the final strains of American Romanticism. It also marks Beach's significant contribution to classical composition in North America.

Listening Guide 14

CD: Chr/Std 7/8–10
Cassette: Chr/Std 7A/3

BEACH: Violin Sonata in A minor, Second Movement   (4:10)

Date: 1896

Movements:
  I.   Allegro moderato; sonata-allegro form
  II. Scherzo: Molto vivace; scherzo and trio form
  III. Largo con dolore
  IV. Allegro con fuoco

SECOND MOVEMENT: Scherzo; scherzo and trio form (A-B-A'), 2/4 meter, G major

A Scherzo

[8] 0:00 Opening buoyant scherzo theme in violin; 8-bar phrase repeated up an octave:

Melody continues with rhythmic syncopation across bar lines, ends with high-pitched tremolo in violin.

First section repeated literally.

B Trio

☐9 1:34 Slower (marked Più lento); in G minor; piano with conjunct introduction to chromatic theme (shown), accompanied by pedal G on violin:

2:25 Violin plays tranquil trio theme over sustained, low-pitched pedal G in piano:

3:08 Rhythmic pace picks up; leads into scherzo rhythm.

A′ Scherzo

☐10 3:16 Opening theme in violin, then repeated an octave higher; new, lush chromaticism introduced in continuation of theme; closing marked Vivo (Very fast), with sustained trill in violin over active piano chords.

Choral and Dramatic Music in the Nineteenth Century

29

Romantic Choral Music

"God sent his singers upon earth with songs of sadness and of mirth."—HENRY WADSWORTH LONGFELLOW

Amateur choral groups

The nineteenth century witnessed a spreading of the democratic ideal and an enormous expansion of the audience for music. This climate was uniquely favorable to choral singing, a group activity enjoyed by increasing numbers of amateur music lovers that played an important role in the musical life of the Romantic era.

Since singing in a chorus required less skill than playing in an orchestra, it attracted many people who had never learned to play an instrument or who could not afford to buy one. With a modest amount of rehearsal (and modest vocal quality), they could take part in the performance of great choral works. The members of the chorus not only enjoyed a pleasant social evening once or twice a week but also, if their group was good enough, became a source of pride to their community.

Choral music offered the masses an ideal outlet for their artistic energies. It served to relieve, for example, the drabness of life in the English factory towns of the early Victorian period. And it had the solid support of the authorities, who felt that an interest in music would protect ordinary citizens from the dangerous new ideas that were floating around.

The repertory centered about the great choral heritage of the past. Never-

In the nineteenth century, enormous choral and orchestral forces were a common sight, as in this engraving depicting the opening concert at St. Martin's Hall, London, 1850.

theless, if choral music was to remain a vital force, its literature had to be enriched by new works that would reflect the spirit of the time. The list of composers active in this area includes some of the most important names of the nineteenth century: Schubert, Berlioz, Felix and Fanny Mendelssohn, Clara and Robert Schumann, Liszt, Verdi, Brahms, Dvořák. These composers produced a body of choral music that represents some of the best creative efforts of the Romantic period.

Among the large-scale genres of choral music in the nineteenth century were the Mass, the Requiem Mass, and the oratorio. We will study these in detail in later chapters. For now, here are some brief definitions. A *Mass* is a musical setting of the most solemn service of the Roman Catholic Church. A *Requiem* is a setting of the Mass for the Dead. It takes its name from the opening text: "Requiem aeternam dona eis, Domine" (Give them eternal rest, O Lord). An *oratorio* is a dramatic composition based on a text of religious or serious character, performed by solo voices, chorus, and orchestra. All three forms were originally intended to be performed in church. By the nineteenth century, they had found a wider audience in the concert hall.

Choral forms

In addition, a vast literature of secular choral pieces appeared. These works, settings for chorus of lyric poems in a variety of moods and styles, were known as *part songs*—that is, songs with three or four voice parts. Most of them were short melodious works, easy enough for amateurs. They gave pleasure both to the singers and to their listeners, and played an important role in developing the new audience of the nineteenth century.

Part songs

Words are not as easy for the listener to grasp when a multitude of voices project them as they are in a solo song. In addition, the four voice parts in the cho-

Choral texts

rus (soprano, alto, tenor, and bass) may be singing different words at the same time. Most important, music needs more time to establish a mood than words do. For these reasons, the practice arose of repeating a line, a phrase, or an individual word over and over again instead of introducing new words all the time.

30

Brahms and Choral Music

"It is not hard to compose, but it is wonderfully hard to let the superfluous notes fall under the table."

Johannes Brahms created a Romantic art in the purest Classical style. His veneration for the past and his mastery of musical architecture brought him closer to the spirit of Beethoven than any of his contemporaries.

HIS LIFE

Johannes Brahms

Johannes Brahms (1833–1897) was born in Hamburg, the son of a double-bass player. As a youth of ten, Johannes helped increase the family income by playing the piano in the dance halls of the slum district where he grew up. By the time he was twenty, he had acquired sufficient reputation as a pianist to accompany the Hungarian violinist Eduard Reményi on a concert tour.

His first compositions greatly impressed Joseph Joachim, the leading violinist of the day, who arranged for Brahms to visit Robert Schumann at Düsseldorf. Schumann recognized in the shy young composer a future leader of the circle dedicated to absolute music. In his role as music critic, Schumann published in his journal a famous essay, "New Paths," in which he named the twenty-year-old "young eagle" as one who "was called forth to give us the highest ideal expression of our time." Brahms was suddenly famous.

Friendship with Schumanns

Robert and Clara Schumann took the fair-haired youth into their home, and their friendship opened up new horizons for him. But then came the tragedy of Schumann's mental collapse. With tenderness and strength, Brahms supported Clara through the ordeal of Robert's illness. (On Robert Schumann as a composer, see Chapter 15.)

Robert Schumann lingered for two years while Brahms was shaken by the great love of his life. Fourteen years his senior and the mother of seven children, Clara Schumann, herself a fine pianist and composer, appeared to young

Brahms as the ideal of womanly and artistic achievement. (On Clara Schumann, see Chapter 20.) What had begun as filial devotion ripened into romantic passion. "You have taught me," he wrote her, "to marvel at the nature of love, affection, and self-denial. I can do nothing but think of you." At the same time, he was torn by feelings of guilt, for he loved and revered Robert Schumann, his friend and benefactor, above all others. He thought of suicide and spoke of himself, at the youthful age of twenty-two, as "a man for whom nothing is left."

This conflict was resolved the following year by Robert's death, but another conflict took its place. Now that Clara was no longer the unattainable ideal, Brahms was faced with the choice between love and freedom. Time and again in the course of his life, he was torn between the two, with the decision always going to freedom. His ardor subsided into a lifelong friendship, although two decades later he could still write her, "I love you more than myself and more than anybody and anything on earth."

Ultimately, Brahms settled in Vienna, where he remained for the next thirty-five years. During this time, he became enormously successful, the acknowledged heir of the Viennese masters.

This exacting artist had a curiously two-sided nature. He could be morose and withdrawn, yet he loved coarse humor. A bohemian at heart, he craved bourgeois respectability. Behind a rough exterior he hid the tenderness that found expression in his music. Although he complained of loneliness and on oc-

A famous caricature of Brahms in his later years; the composer was a familiar sight in Vienna as he made his way to The Red Hedgehog, his favorite tavern.

casion fell in love, he was unable to accept the responsibility of a sustained relationship. "It would be as difficult for me to marry," he explained, "as to write an opera. But after the first experience I should probably undertake a second!"

In 1896, Clara Schumann's declining health gave rise to the *Four Serious Songs.* Her death profoundly affected the composer, already ill with cancer. He died ten months later, at the age of sixty-four, and was buried in Vienna not far from Beethoven and Schubert.

His Music

Brahms was a traditionalist; his aim was to show that new and important things could still be said in the tradition of the Classical masters. In this he differed from avowed innovators such as Berlioz, Liszt, and Wagner.

Orchestral music   Brahms's four symphonies are unsurpassed in the late Romantic period in breadth of conception and design, yet their forms draw upon those of earlier eras. We saw this Classical approach in his Third Symphony (in Chapter 24). Among his other orchestral works, the *Variations on a Theme by Haydn* and his two concert overtures are frequently heard today. In his two piano concertos and his violin concerto, the solo instrument is integrated into a full-scale symphonic structure.

Principal Works

Orchestral music, including 4 symphonies (1876, 1877, 1883, 1884–85); *Variations on a Theme by Haydn* (1873); 2 overtures (*Academic Festival,* 1880; *Tragic,* 1886); 4 concertos (2 for piano, 1858, 1881; 1 for violin, 1878; 1 double concerto for violin and cello, 1887)

Chamber music, including string quartets, quintets, sextets; piano trios, quartets, and 1 quintet; 1 clarinet quintet; sonatas (violin, cello, clarinet/viola)

Piano music, including sonatas, character pieces, dances, and variation sets (on a theme by Handel, 1861; on a theme by Paganini, 1862–63)

Choral music, including *A German Requiem* (1868), *Alto Rhapsody* (1869), and part songs

Lieder, including *Vergebliches Ständchen* (*Futile Serenade,* 1881), *Four Serious Songs* (1896), and folk song arrangements

To a greater degree than any of his contemporaries, Brahms captured the tone of intimacy that is the essence of chamber music style. He is an important figure in piano music as well. His two variation sets, on themes by Handel and Paganini, represent his top achievement in that field. The Romantic in Brahms also found expression in short lyric piano pieces: the rhapsodies, ballades, capriccios, and intermezzi are among the treasures of the literature. On a more popular level are the *Hungarian Dances* and the set of sixteen waltzes for piano duet.

Chamber and solo music

As a song writer, Brahms stands in the direct line of succession to Schubert and Robert Schumann. His output includes about two hundred solo songs and an almost equal number for two, three, or four voices. The favorite themes are love, nature, and death. We will study his finest choral work, *A German Requiem*, written to biblical texts he selected himself. This work more than any other spread his fame during his lifetime.

Vocal music

A German Requiem

A German Requiem was rooted in the Protestant tradition into which Brahms was born. Its aim was to console the living and lead them to a serene acceptance of death as an inevitable part of life, hence its gentle lyricism. Rather than using the traditional Latin text of the Roman Catholic Church, Brahms chose his text from the Old and New Testaments: from the Psalms, Proverbs, Isaiah, and Ecclesiastes as well as from Paul, Matthew, Peter, John, and Revelation. Brahms was not religious in the conventional sense, nor was he affiliated with any particular church. He was moved to compose his Requiem by the death first of his teacher and friend Robert Schumann, then of his mother, whom he idolized; but the piece transcends personal emotions and endures as a song of mourning for all humanity.

Written for soloists, four-part chorus, and orchestra, *A German Requiem* is in seven movements arranged in a formation resembling an arch. There are connections between the first and last movements, between the second and sixth, and between the third and fifth; that leaves the fourth movement, the widely sung chorus *How Lovely Is Thy Dwelling Place*, as the centerpiece.

This movement is based on a verse from Psalm 84 (see Listening Guide 15). The first two lines of the psalm are heard three times, separated by two contrasting sections that present the other lines. The form can be outlined as **A-B-A'-C-A'**. (This structure is a kind of rondo form, about which we will learn later.) The first two sections for the most part move in quarter notes, but the third section (**C**) moves more quickly in a vigorous rhythm, better suiting the line "that praise Thee evermore," with much expansion on "evermore." With the final reappearance of the **A** section, the slower tempo returns. Marked *piano* and *dolce* (soft and sweet), this passage serves as a coda that brings the piece to its gentle and serene close.

BRAHMS: *A German Requiem*, Fourth Movement (5:46)

Date of work: 1868

Genre: Requiem, for Protestant church

Medium: 4-part chorus, soloists, and orchestra

Movements: 7

FOURTH MOVEMENT: Mässig bewegt (moderately agitated)

Text: Psalm 84
Form: Rondo (**A-B-A'-C-A'**)
Character: Lilting triple meter, marked *dolce* (sweetly)

Opening melody—clarinets and flutes begin with inversion of first phrase in chorus:

		Text	Translation	Description
15	0:00	Wie lieblich sind deine Wohnungen, Herr Zebaoth!	How lovely is Thy dwelling place, O Lord of Hosts!	**A**—a flowing, arched melody, SATB homophonic setting, answers orchestral opening, in E-flat major; text repeated in tenors, joined by other voices.
16	1:26	Meine Seele verlanget und sehnet sich nach den Vorhöfen des Herrn; mein Leib und Seele freuen sich in dem lebendigen Gott.	My soul longs and even faints for the courts of the Lord; my flesh and soul rejoice in the living God.	**B**—shift to minor, builds fugally with word repetition from lowest to highest voices; sudden accents on first beat of measures, with plucked strings; text is repeated, climax on "lebendigen."
17	2:39	Wie lieblich . . . Wohl denen, die in deinem Hause wohnen,	How lovely . . . Blessed are they that live in Thy house,	**A'**—opening returns in E-flat major, with new text and varied setting.
18	3:51	die loben dich immerdar!	that praise Thee evermore!	**C**—martial quality, faster movement in polyphonic setting.
19	4:44	Wie lieblich . . .	How lovely . . .	**A'**—coda-like return, reminiscent of opening; soft orchestral closing, in E-flat major.

31

Romantic Opera

*"Opera is free from any servile imitation of nature. By the power
of music it attunes the soul to a beautiful receptiveness."*
—FRIEDRICH VON SCHILLER

For well over three hundred years, opera has been one of the most alluring
forms of musical entertainment. A special glamour is attached to everything
connected with it—its superstar performers, extravagant scenic designs, even
the glitter and excitement of opening nights.

At first glance, opera seems to demand that the spectator believe the unbe-
lievable. It presents us with human beings caught up in dramatic situations,
who sing to each other instead of speaking, even after they've been strangled
or stabbed or shot. The reasonable question is: how can an art form based on
so unnatural a procedure be convincing?

True enough, people in real life do not sing to each other. Neither do they
converse in blank verse, as Shakespeare's characters do, nor live in rooms of
which one wall is conveniently missing so that the audience may look in. All the
arts employ conventions that are accepted by both the artist and the audience.
The conventions of opera are just, perhaps, more evident. In any case, the fundamental goal of art is not to copy nature but to heighten our awareness of it.

Opera uses the human voice to project basic emotions—love, hate, jealousy, joy, grief—with an elemental force. The logic of reality gives way on the
operatic stage to the power of music and the imagination.

THE COMPONENTS OF OPERA

An opera is a drama that is sung. It combines the resources of vocal and instrumental music—soloists, ensembles, chorus, orchestra, and sometimes
ballet—with poetry and drama, acting and pantomime, scenery and costumes. To weld the diverse elements into a unity is a challenge that has attracted some of the most creative minds in the history of music.

Explanations necessary to advance the plot and action are generally presented in a kind of musical declamation known as *recitative*. This disjunct
vocal style imitates the natural inflections of speech; its rhythm is shaped to

Recitative

the rhythm of the language. Rarely presenting a purely musical line, recitative is often characterized by a fast-paced patter and "talky" repetition of the same note, as well as rapid question-and-answer dialogue that builds dramatic tension in the theater. In time, two styles of recitative became standard: *secco*, which is accompanied only by continuo instruments (a bass melody instrument, such as a cello, and a keyboard instrument, such as a harpsichord or organ) and moves with great freedom, and *accompagnato*, which is accompanied by the orchestra and thus moves more evenly.

Aria

Recitative gives way at lyric moments to the *aria* (Italian for "air"), which releases through melody the emotional tension accumulated in the course of the action. The aria is a song, usually of a highly emotional kind. It is what audiences wait for, what they cheer, what they remember. An aria, because of its tunefulness, can be effective even when removed from its context. Indeed, many arias are familiar to people who have never heard the operas from which they are excerpted. One formal convention that developed early in the genre's history is the *da capo aria*, a ternary, or **A-B-A,** form that brings back the first section with embellishments improvised by the soloist.

Ensembles

An opera may contain ensemble numbers—duets, trios, quartets, quintets, sextets, septets—in which the characters pour out their respective feelings. The chorus may be used to back up the solo voices, or it may function independently. It may comment and reflect on the action like the chorus in Greek tragedy, or it may be integrated into the action.

Overture

The orchestra supports the action of the opera as well, setting the appropriate mood for the different scenes. It also performs the *overture*, an instrumental number heard at the beginning of most operas, which may introduce melodies from the arias to come. Each act of the opera normally opens with an orchestral introduction, and between scenes we may find interludes, or *sinfonias*, as they were called in Baroque opera.

Libretto

The opera composer works with a *librettist*, who writes the text of the work, using dramatic insight to create characters and plot and to fashion situations that justify the use of music. The *libretto*, the text or script of the opera, must be devised so as to give the composer an opportunity to write music for the diverse numbers—recitatives and arias, ensembles, choruses, interludes—that have become the traditional features of this art form.

THE DEVELOPMENT OF NATIONAL STYLES

As one of the most important and best-loved theatrical genres of the nineteenth century, opera fostered different national styles in three of Europe's leading musical countries—France, Germany, and Italy.

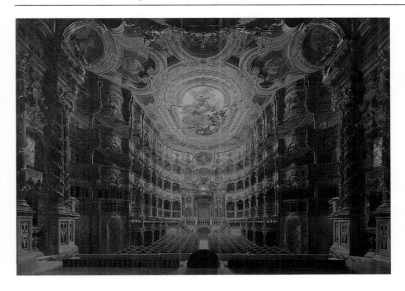

Margrave's Opera House in Bayreuth, 1879. A painting by **Gustav Bauernfeind.** (Deutsches Theatermuseum, Munich)

France
Grand opera

In Paris, the opera center of all Europe in the late eighteenth and early nineteenth centuries, *grand opera* was all the rage. This new genre, which focused on serious, historical themes and was nourished by the propagandist purposes of France's new leaders, suited the bourgeoisie's taste for the big and the spectacular very well. Complete with huge choruses, crowd scenes, ornate costumes and scenery, and elaborate dance episodes, grand opera was as much a spectacle as a musical event. Giacomo Meyerbeer (1791–1864), a German composer who studied in Italy, was primarily responsible for bringing grand opera to Paris. His best-known works in the style are *Robert le diable* (*Robert the Devil*, 1831) and *Les Huguenots* (1836), both of which reveal careful attention to the drama as a whole—a blend of social statement, history, and spectacle with memorable melodies and rich orchestration.

Opéra comique

Less pretentious than French grand opera was *opéra comique*, which required smaller performance forces, featured a simpler compositional style, and included spoken dialogue rather than recitatives. One of the lighter works that delighted Parisian audiences was Jacques Offenbach's (1819–1880) *Orphée aux enfers* (*Orpheus in the Underworld*, 1858), which blended wit and satire into the popular model. Eventually the spectacle of grand opera and the simplicity of opéra comique merged, to produce *lyric opera*. This hybrid type featured appealing melodies and romantic drama, and found its greatest proponent in Georges Bizet, whose *Carmen* is a masterpiece of the French lyric stage (see Chapter 34).

Lyric opera

Nineteenth-century Germany had no long-established opera tradition, as France and Italy did. The immediate predecessor of German Romantic opera was the *Singspiel*, a light or comic drama with spoken dialogue. The first

Germany
Singspiel

composer to express the German Romantic spirit in opera was Carl Maria von Weber (1786–1826), whose best-known work is *Der Freischütz* (*The Freeshooter*, 1821). In this opera, supernatural beings and mysterious forces of nature intertwine with heros and heroines to produce drama featuring simple and direct melodies that are almost folklike, accompanied by expressive timbres and harmonies. The greatest figure in German opera—and one of the most significant in the history of the Romantic era—was Richard Wagner, who created the music drama, a genre that integrated theater and music completely (see Chapter 33).

Italy

Italy in the early nineteenth century still recognized the opposing genres of *opera seria* (serious opera) and *opera buffa* (the Italian version of comic opera), legacies of an earlier period. Important composers of these styles include Gioachino Rossini (1792–1868), whose masterpiece was *Il barbiere di Siviglia* (*The Barber of Seville*, 1816); Gaetano Donizetti (1797–1848), composer of some seventy operas, including *Lucia di Lammermoor* (*Lucy of Lammermore*, 1835); and Vincenzo Bellini (1801–1835), whose *Norma* (1831) is preeminent for its lovely melodies. These operas marked the high point of a

Bel canto style

bel canto (beautiful singing) style, characterized by florid melodic lines and delivered by voices of great agility and purity of tone. The consummate master of nineteenth-century Italian opera was Giuseppe Verdi, who sought to develop a uniquely national style (see Chapter 32).

WOMEN IN OPERA

Opera was one medium that allowed women musicians a good deal of visibility. Only a few tried their hand at composing full-scale operas, but those who did were able to see a number of their works produced. The French composer

Louise Bertin

Louise Bertin (1805–1877) had several produced at the exclusive Opéra-Comique in Paris, including *La Esmeralda* (1836), on a libretto based on Victor Hugo's well-known novel about the hunchback of Notre Dame.

Women opera singers were among the most prominent performers of their day, idolized and in demand throughout Europe and the Americas. One

Jenny Lind

such international star was Jenny Lind (1820–1887), known as the "Swedish nightingale" and famous for her roles in operas by Meyerbeer, Donizetti, Weber, and Bellini. A concert artist as well, Lind made her American debut in 1850 in a tour managed with immense hoopla by circus impresario P. T. Barnum.

Professional singing was often a family tradition: the offspring of the celebrated Spanish tenor Manuel Garcia provide a case in point. A brilliant

Maria Malibran

teacher, Garcia coached two of his daughters to stardom. His eldest, Maria Malibran (1808–1836), became renowned as an interpreter of Rossini, whose

The famous singer Jenny Lind during a recital at Exeter Hall, London, 1855.

works she sang in London, Paris, Milan, Naples, and New York. A riding accident brought her very successful career to a tragic close. Her youngest sister, Pauline Viardot (1821–1910), was highly acclaimed for her great musical and dramatic gifts. Viardot did much to further the careers of Charles Gounod, Jules Massenet, and Gabriel Fauré (French composers of operas and songs), and sang the premieres of vocal works by Brahms, Robert Schumann, and Berlioz. In 1849, her Paris performance in Meyerbeer's *Le prophète (The Prophet)*, in a role created specially for her, prompted Berlioz to write: "Madame Viardot is one of the greatest artists . . . in the past and present history of music." A composer herself, Viardot's intellectual approach to her art did much to raise the status of women singers (see illustration on p. 98).

Pauline Viardot

32

Verdi and Italian Opera

"Success is impossible for me if I cannot write as my heart dictates!"

In the case of Giuseppe Verdi, the most widely loved of operatic composers, time, place, and personality were happily merged. He inherited a rich musical tradition, his capacity for growth was matched by extraordinary energy and will, and he was granted a long span of life in which to fully exploit his creative gift.

Giuseppe Verdi

His Life

Born in a small town in northern Italy where his father kept an inn, Giuseppe Verdi (1813–1901) grew up amid the poverty of village life. His talent attracted the attention of a prosperous merchant and music lover in the neighboring town of Busseto who made it possible for the youth to pursue his studies. After two years in Milan, Verdi returned to Busseto to take a position as an organist. When he fell in love with his benefactor's daughter, the merchant in wholly untraditional fashion accepted the penniless young musician as his son-in-law. Verdi was twenty-three, Margherita sixteen.

Early years

Three years later, he returned to Milan with the manuscript of an opera, which was produced at the opera house of La Scala in 1839. The work brought him a commission to write three others. At this time, Verdi faced a string of crises in his life. His first child, a daughter, had died before he left for Milan. The second, a baby boy, was carried off by fever in 1839, a catastrophe followed several months later by the death of his young wife. "In a sudden moment of despondency I despaired of finding any comfort in my art and resolved to give up composing," he wrote.

As the months passed, the distraught young composer held to his decision. Then one night he happened to meet the director of La Scala, who insisted that he take home a libretto about Nebuchadnezzar, King of Babylon. Verdi returned to work, and the resulting opera, *Nabucco*, presented at La Scala in 1842, was a triumph for the twenty-nine-year-old composer and launched him on a spectacular career.

Verdi the nationalist

Italy at the time was liberating itself from Austrian Hapsburg rule. Verdi from the beginning identified himself with the national cause: "I am first of all an Italian!" he declared. In this charged atmosphere, his works took on special meaning for his compatriots. Whatever the time or place in which an opera was set, it was interpreted as a symbol of their cause. The chorus of exiled Jews from *Nabucco* became an Italian patriotic song that is still sung today.

Although he became a world-renowned figure, Verdi retained the simplicity that was at the core of both the artist and the man. He returned to his roots, to an estate at Busseto, where he settled with his second wife, the singer Giuseppina Strepponi. She was a sensitive and intelligent woman who had created the leading roles in his early operas and who was his devoted companion for half a century. After Italy won independence, Verdi was urged to run for election to parliament because of the prestige his name would bring the new state. Although the task conformed to neither his talents nor his inclinations, he accepted and sat in the Chamber of Deputies for some years.

During his time in public life, he was somehow able to produce one mas-

The singer Giuseppina Strepponi, Verdi's second wife, with a score of his opera Nabucco. (Museo Teatrale alla Scala, Milan)

Late years

terpiece after another. He was fifty-seven when he wrote *Aida*. At seventy-three, he completed *Otello*, his greatest lyric tragedy. And in 1893, on the threshold of eighty, he astonished the world with *Falstaff*.

Verdi's death at eighty-seven was mourned throughout the world. He left the bulk of his fortune to a home for aged musicians he had founded in Milan (still in operation today). Italy accorded him the rites reserved for a national hero. From the voices of thousands who marched in his funeral procession there arose the haunting melody of "Va pensiero sull' ali dorate" ("Go, thought, on gilded wings"), the chorus from *Nabucco*, with which he had inspired his fellow Italians sixty years earlier.

His Music

Verdi's music stands as the epitome of Romantic drama and passion. Endowed with an imagination that saw all emotion in terms of action and conflict, Verdi was able to communicate a dramatic situation with shattering expressiveness. True Italian that he was, he prized melody above all; to him this was the most immediate expression of human feeling. "Art without spontaneity, naturalness, and simplicity," he maintained, "is no art."

Early works

Of his fifteen early operas, the most important is *Macbeth*, his first work based on story material from Shakespeare. Following in close succession came *Rigoletto* (which we will study), on a play by Victor Hugo; *Il trovatore* (*The Troubador*), derived from a fanciful Spanish play; and *La traviata*, based on *La dame aux camélias* (*The Lady of the Camellias*), by the younger Alexandre Dumas. In these works, the mature musical dramatist was revealed.

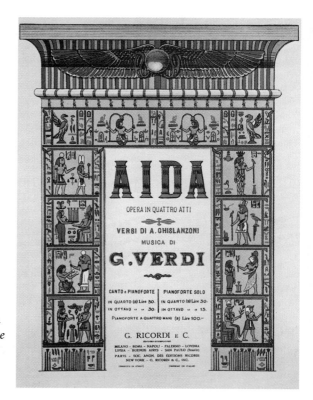

The Egyptian theme of Verdi's opera Aida *is graphically illustrated on the cover of the score published by G. Ricordi in Milan.*

Middle period

The operas of the middle period show Verdi writing on a more ambitious scale and incorporating elements of the French grand opera. The three most important are *A Masked Ball, The Force of Destiny*, and *Don Carlos*. "After *La traviata*," he declared, "I could have taken things easy and written an opera every year on the tried and true model. But I had other artistic aims."

Final period

These aims were carried even further in *Aida*, the work that ushers in his final period (1870–93). *Aida* was commissioned in 1870 by the ruler of Egypt to mark the opening of the Suez Canal. After being delayed by the outbreak of the Franco-Prussian War, the production was mounted with great splendor in Cairo the following year. The year 1874 saw composed the Requiem, in memory of Alessandro Manzoni, a novelist and patriot whom Verdi had revered.

Verdi and Boito

For his last two operas, Verdi found an ideal librettist in Arrigo Boito (1842–1918), who brilliantly adapted two plays by Shakespeare. *Otello*, their first collaboration, is the high point of three hundred years of Italian lyric tragedy. After its opening night, the seventy-four-year-old composer declared, "I feel as if I had fired my last cartridge. Music needs youthfulness of the senses, impetuous blood, fullness of life." But he disproved his words when six years later (1893) he completed *Falstaff*, based on Shakespeare's *Merry Wives of Windsor*. Fitting crown to the labors of a lifetime, this luminous work ranks with the greatest comic operas.

174

Rigoletto

The writer Victor Hugo, an acknowledged leader of French Romanticism, was Verdi's source of inspiration for *Rigoletto*. Hugo's play *Le roi s'amuse* (*The King Is Amused*, 1832) was banned in France but achieved universal popularity through its adaptation in Verdi's opera. The plot, featuring lechery, deformity, irony, and assassination, revolves around a hunchbacked jester, Rigoletto, who is a fascinating study in opposites. (You will remember that Hugo wrote of another hunchback, in his historical novel *Notre-Dame de Paris*, or *The Hunchback of Notre Dame;* the intriguing bell-ringer Quasimodo has inspired several well-known movies, including the recent Disney animated musical.) With a libretto by Francesco Piave, *Rigoletto* was Verdi's first great success.

The story is set in the Renaissance era at the ducal court of Mantua, a small city in northern Italy. The first scene takes place in a great hall of the ducal palace, where a ball is in progress. The Duke, a notorious womanizer, woos the wife of one of his courtiers, the Count of Ceprano. The court jester, Rigoletto, mocks the unlucky husband to all who will listen, and then suggests to the Duke that the Count of Ceprano be disposed of. Meanwhile, gossiping courtiers spread a rumor that the hunchbacked jester has a mistress. An elderly nobleman, Monterone, interrupts the scene and accuses the Duke of having seduced his daughter. The Duke promptly has the aging father arrested; Rigoletto taunts the man, who returns his gibes with a curse.

In a dark alley, Rigoletto meets up with the assassin Sparafucile, who warns the jester that he has enemies and offers him his services. Arriving home, Rigoletto's spirits are raised when he sees his daughter, Gilda, whom he keeps in seclusion. He warns Gilda and her nurse to stay in the house and not admit anyone. As Rigoletto leaves, the Duke enters the garden, realizing then that the beautiful young woman he had noticed in church is the jester's daughter; she, however, did not tell her father of the attractive young man

In His Own Words

For dramatic effectiveness, it seems to me that the best material I have yet put to music is Rigoletto. *It has the most powerful situations, it has variety, vitality, pathos; all the dramatic developments result from the frivolous, licentious character of the Duke. Hence Rigoletto's fears, Gilda's passion, etc., which give rise to many dramatic situations, including the scene of the quartet, which, so far as effect is concerned, will always be one of the finest our theater can boast.*

Principal Works

28 operas, including *Macbeth* (1847), *Rigoletto* (1851), *Il trovatore* (*The Troubadour*, 1853), *La traviata* (*The Lost One*, 1853), *Un ballo in maschera* (*A Masked Ball*, 1859), *La forza del destino* (*The Force of Destiny*, 1862), *Don Carlos* (1867), *Aida* (1871), *Otello* (1887), and *Falstaff* (1893)

Vocal music, including a Requiem Mass (1874)

The quartet scene from Verdi's Rigoletto *in the London premiere (1853) at Covent Garden. Rigoletto and his daughter, Gilda (on the right), are watching the Duke and Maddalena inside the tavern.*

who had caught her eye. The Duke, claiming to be a poor student, professes his love to Gilda. As courtiers approach the house, he escapes. Believing that Gilda is the deformed jester's mistress, the courtiers plan to abduct her in retribution for Rigoletto's cruel taunting. When the father returns, he is tricked into being blindfolded, and Gilda is carried off as Rigoletto recalls Monterone's curse.

In Act II, the Duke realizes that his new love has vanished, and Rigoletto bemoans his own loss while striving to convince everyone that Gilda was indeed his daughter. Gilda is brought out and throws herself in her father's arms, ashamed at her behavior. Rigoletto vows vengeance on the abductors.

The final act takes place on a stormy night at a tavern near the river. Sparafucile's sister, Maddalena, has lured the Duke to the lonely tavern, and Rigoletto forces Gilda to watch through a window as the Duke pursues Maddalena. Planning to send her away, Rigoletto then instructs his daughter to dress as a man for her escape. Meanwhile, it has been arranged that Sparafucile will kill the Duke and return his body to Rigoletto in a bag to be thrown in the river. However, Maddalena succumbs to the Duke's charms and begs her brother to spare the handsome nobleman. Sparafucile agrees, only if a substitute shows up at the tavern. Gilda, now in male attire, overhears the plan, and enters the tavern to sacrifice herself for the unworthy man she loves. Sparafucile returns the sack to Rigoletto, as arranged, but just as the hunchback is about to dispose of the body, he hears the Duke singing from an upstairs window. Horrified, he opens the sack to find a dying Gilda, who begs forgiveness for herself and the Duke. Rigoletto recalls the curse one last time, as Gilda dies in his arms.

Two of the most popular operatic moments of all time occur in Act III. The Duke sings the best-known of Verdi's tunes, "La donna è mobile" (Woman is fickle), a simple but rousing song accompanied by a guitar-like orchestral strumming. The orchestra previews the catchy melody, which is heard numerous times in a strophic setting that brings back the opening text as a refrain.

The quartet that follows shortly is a masterpiece of operatic ensemble writing, as Verdi himself noted in the quote above. Each of the four characters presents a different point of view: the Duke woos Maddalena in a lovely bel canto–style melody, calling her "beautiful daughter of love"; Maddalena answers with a laughing line in short notes, "Ha! Ha! I laugh heartily"; Gilda, watching from outside, is heartbroken as she laments her lost love; and Rigoletto hushes her, swearing vengeance for such treatment of his beloved daughter. Although the text becomes increasingly more difficult to follow as the characters sing together, the emotions of each soar through clearly (see Listening Guide 16 for text and form).

These two show-stopping numbers ensured the immediate success of *Rigoletto*. It remains one of the most frequently performed operas of the international repertory.

Listening Guide 16

CD: Chr/Std 6/1–6, Sh 3/49–54
Cassette: Chr/Std 6A/1, Sh 3B/3

VERDI: *Rigoletto*, Act III, excerpt

(8:30)

First performance: 1851, Venice
Librettist: Francesco Maria Piave
Basis: Play, *Le roi s'amuse*, by Victor Hugo

Major characters:
The Duke of Mantua (tenor)
Rigoletto, the Duke's jester, a hunchback (baritone)
Gilda, Rigoletto's daughter (soprano)
Sparafucile, an assassin (bass)
Maddalena, Sparafucile's sister (contralto)

Aria: "La donna è mobile" (Duke)

Form: Strophic, with refrain

Orchestral introduction previews the Duke's solo, also appears in middle and at the closing; opening melody of aria:

La don · na è mo · bi · le qual pium · a al ven · to, mut · a d'ac · cen · to

The Duke, in a simple cavalry officer's uniform, sings in the inn; Sparafucile, Gilda, and Rigoletto listen outside.

DUKE

La donna è mobile	Woman is fickle
Qual piuma al vento,	like a feather in the wind,
Muta d'accento,	she changes her words
E di pensiero.	and her thoughts.
Sempre un amabile	Always lovable,
Leggiadro viso,	and a lovely face,
In pianto o in riso,	weeping or laughing,
È menzognero.	is lying.
La donna è mobile, etc.	Woman is fickle, etc.

È sempre misero	The man's always wretched
Chi a le s'affida,	who believes in her,
Chi lei confida	who recklessly entrusts
Mal cauto il core!	his heart to her!
Pur mai non sentesi	And yet one who never
Felice appieno	drinks love on that breast
Chi su quel seno	never feels
Non liba amore!	entirely happy!
La donna è mobile, etc.	Woman is fickle, etc.

Sparafucile comes back in with a bottle of wine and two glasses, which he sets on the table; then he strikes the ceiling twice with the hilt of his long sword. At this signal, a laughing young woman in gypsy dress leaps down the stairs: the Duke runs to embrace her, but she escapes him. Meanwhile Sparafucile has gone into the street, where he speaks softly to Rigoletto.

SPARAFUCILE

È là il vostr'uomo . . .	Your man is there . . .
Viver dee o morire?	Must he live or die?

RIGOLETTO

Più tardi tornerò l'opra a compire.	I'll return later to complete the deed.

Sparafucile goes off behind the house toward the river. Gilda and Rigoletto remain in the street, the Duke and Maddalena on the ground floor.

Quartet: "Un dì" (Duke, Maddalena, Gilda, Rigoletto)

DUKE

Un dì, se ben rammentomi,	One day, if I remember right,
O bella, t'incontrai . . .	I met you, O beauty . . .
Mi piacque di te chiedere,	I was pleased to ask about you,
E intesi che qui stai.	and I learned that you live here.
Or sappi, che d'allora	Know then, that since that time
Sol te quest'alma adora!	my soul adores only you!

GILDA

Iniquo!	Villain!

MADDALENA

Ah, ah! . . . e vent'altre appresso	Ha, ha! . . . And does it now perhaps
Le scorda forse adesso?	forget twenty others?
Ha un'aria il signorino	The young gentleman looks like
Da vero libertino . . .	a true libertine . . .

DUKE (*starting to embrace her*)

Sì . . . un mostro son . . .   Yes . . . I'm a monster . . .

GILDA

Ah padre mio!   Ah, Father!

MADDALENA

Lasciatemi, stordito.   Let me go, foolish man!

DUKE

Ih che fracasso!   Ah, what a fuss!

MADDALENA

Stia saggio.   Be good.

DUKE

E tu sii docile,   And you, be yielding,
Non fare tanto chiasso.   don't make so much noise.
Ogni saggezza chiudesi   All wisdom concludes
Nel gaudio e nell'amore.   in pleasure and in love.

(*He takes her hand.*)

La bella mano candida!   What a lovely, white hand!

MADDALENA

Scherzate voi, signore.   You're joking, sir.

DUKE

No, no.   No, no.

MADDALENA

Son brutta.   I'm ugly.

DUKE

Abbracciami.   Embrace me.

GILDA

Iniquo!   Villain!

MADDALENA

Ebro!   You're drunk!

DUKE

D'amor ardente.   With ardent love.

MADDALENA

Signor l'indifferente,   My indifferent sir,
Vi piace canzonar?   would you like to sing?

DUKE

No, no, ti vo' sposar.   No, no, I want to marry you.

MADDALENA

Ne voglio la parola.   I want your word.

DUKE (*ironic*)

Amabile figliuola!   Lovable maiden!

RIGOLETTO (*to Gilda, who has seen and heard all*)

È non ti basta ancor?   Isn't that enough for you yet?

GILDA

Iniquo traditor!   Villainous betrayer!

MADDALENA	
Ne voglio la parola.	I want your word.
DUKE	
Amabile figliuola!	Lovable maiden!
RIGOLETTO	
È non ti basta ancor?	Isn't that enough for you yet?

Quartet (2nd part): "Bella figlia" (Duke, Maddalena, Gilda, Rigoletto)

Overall form: **A-B-A′-C**

Diagram showing how characters interact in the ensemble and how they fit into the musical structure:

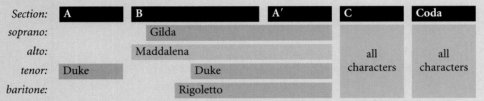

Opening melody of "Bella figlia," sung by Duke:

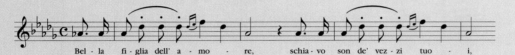

		DUKE		
4	4:32	Bella figlia dell'amore,	Beautiful daughter of love,	**A**
		Schiavo son de' vezzi tuoi;	I am the slave of your charms;	(Many lines of text
		Con un detto sol tu puoi	with a single word you can	throughout the quartet
		Le mie pene consolar.	console my sufferings.	are repeated.)
		Vieni, e senti del mio core	Come, and feel the quick beating	
		Il frequente palpitar . . .	of my heart . . .	
		Con un detto sol tuo puoi	With a single word you can	
		Le mie pene consolar.	console my sufferings.	
		MADDALENA		
5	5:36	Ah! ah! rido ben di core,	Ha! Ha! I laugh heartily,	**B**
		Chè tai baie costan poco.	for such tales cost little.	
		GILDA		
		Ah! così parlar d'amore . . .	Ah! To speak thus of love . . .	
		MADDALENA		
		Quanto valga il vostro gioco,	Believe me, I can judge	
		Mel credete, sò apprezzar.	how much your game is worth.	
		GILDA		
		. . . a me pur l'infame ho udito!	. . . I too have heard the villain so!	
		RIGOLETTO (*to Gilda*)		
		Taci, il piangere non vale.	Hush, weeping is of no avail.	

	GILDA	
	Infelice cor tradito,	Unhappy, betrayed heart,
	Per angoscia non scoppiar. No, no!	do not burst with anguish. Ah, no!
	MADDALENA	
	Son avvezza, bel signore,	I'm accustomed, handsome sir,
	Ad un simile scherzare.	to similar joking.
	Mio bel signor!	My handsome sir!
	DUKE	
6 6:19	Bella figlia dell'amore, etc.	Beautiful daughter of love, etc. **A'**
	Vieni!	Come!
	RIGOLETTO	
	Ch'ei mentiva sei sicura.	You are sure that he was lying.
	Taci, e mia sarà la cura	Hush, and I will take care
	La vendetta d'affrettar.	to hasten vengeance.
	Sì, pronta fia, sarà fatale,	Yes, it will be swift and fatal,
	Io saprollo fulminar.	I will know how to strike him down.
	Taci, taci . . .	Hush, hush . . .

33

Wagner and the Music Drama

"The error in the art genre of opera consists in the fact that a means of expression—music—has been made the object, while the object of expression—the drama—has been made the means."

Richard Wagner looms as the single most important phenomenon in the artistic life of the later nineteenth century. Historians often divide the period into "before" and "after" Wagner. The course of post-Romantic music is unimaginable without the impact of this complex and fascinating figure.

Richard Wagner

HIS LIFE

Richard Wagner (1813–1883) was born in Leipzig, the son of a minor police official who died when Richard was still an infant. The future composer was almost entirely self-taught; he received in all about six months of instruction in music theory. At twenty, he abandoned his academic studies at the Univer-

Early years

sity of Leipzig and obtained a position as chorus master in a small opera house. Over the next six years, he gained practical experience conducting in provincial theaters. He married the actress Minna Planer when he was twenty-three, and produced his first operas at this time. He wrote the librettos himself, as he did for all his later works; in this way, he was able to unify the music and drama more than anyone had before.

Wagner was thirty when his grand opera *Rienzi* won a huge success in Dresden. As a result, he found himself appointed conductor to the King of Saxony. With his next three works, *The Flying Dutchman, Tannhäuser,* and *Lohengrin,* Wagner took an important step from the drama of historical intrigue to the idealized folk legend. He chose subjects derived from medieval German epics, displayed a profound feeling for nature, employed the supernatural as an element of the drama, and glorified the German land and people. But the Dresden public was not prepared for *Tannhäuser.* They had come to see another *Rienzi* and were disappointed.

Wagner the revolutionary

The Zurich years

A revolution broke out in Dresden in 1849. Wagner not only sympathized openly with the revolutionaries but took part in their activities. When the revolt failed, he fled to Weimar, where his friend Liszt helped him cross the border into Switzerland. In Zurich, he commenced the most productive period of his career. First, Wagner produced his most important literary works, *Art and Revolution, The Art Work of the Future,* and the two-volume *Opera and Drama,* which sets forth his theories of the *music drama,* as he named his concept of opera. He next proceeded to put theory into practice in the cycle of four music dramas called *The Ring of the Nibelung.* But when he reached the second act of *Siegfried* (the third opera in the cycle), he grew tired "of heaping one silent score upon the other," and laid aside the gigantic task. He turned to writing two of his finest works—*Tristan and Isolde* and *Die Meistersinger von Nürnberg.* (In English-speaking countries, many operas are commonly known by their original rather than translated titles. Just as Verdi's *La traviata* is seldom referred to as *The Lost One,* Wagner's *Die Meistersinger* is rarely called *The Mastersingers of Nuremberg,* and his *Götterdämmerung* is not known by its English title, *The Twilight of the Gods.*)

The years following the completion of *Tristan* were the darkest of his life. The musical scores accumulated in his drawer without hope of performance; Europe contained neither singers nor a theater capable of presenting them. At this point, a miraculous turn of events intervened. In 1864, an eighteen-year-old boy who was a passionate admirer of Wagner's music ascended the throne of Bavaria as Ludwig II. In one of his most artistically important acts, the young monarch summoned the composer to Munich, where *Tristan* and *Die Meistersinger* were performed at last. The king then commissioned him to complete the *Ring,* and Wagner took up where he had left off a number of years earlier.

A theater was planned specifically for the presentation of Wagner's music

Richard Wagner at Home in Bayreuth: *a painting by* **W. Beckmann,** *1882. To Wagner's left is his wife, Cosima; to his right, Franz Liszt and Hans von Wolzogen.*

dramas, which ultimately resulted in the Festival Theater at Bayreuth. And to crown his happiness, the composer found a woman he considered his equal in will and courage—Cosima, the daughter of his old friend Liszt. She left her husband and children in order to join Wagner; they were married some years later, after Minna's death.

Bayreuth

The Wagnerian gospel spread across Europe as a new art-religion. Wagner societies throughout the world gathered funds to raise the theater at Bayreuth. The *Ring* cycle was completed in 1874, and the four dramas were presented to worshipful audiences at the first Bayreuth Festival two years later.

One task remained: to make good the financial deficit of the festival, Wagner undertook *Parsifal* (1877–82), a "consecrational festival drama" based on the legend of the Holy Grail. He finished the opera as he reached seventy. In every sense a conqueror, Wagner died shortly thereafter and was buried at Bayreuth.

His Music

Wagner did away with the old "number" opera with its separate arias, duets, ensembles, choruses, and ballets. His aim was to create a continuous fabric of melody that would never allow the emotions to cool. He therefore evolved an

Endless melody

"endless melody" that was molded to the natural inflections of the German language, more melodious than the traditional recitative, more flexible and free than the traditional aria. Wagner's concept was that of a total artwork (in German, *Gesamtkunstwerk*), in which all the arts—music, poetry, drama, visual spectacle—were fused.

The orchestra is in fact the focal point and unifying element in Wagnerian music drama. It floods the characters and the audience in a torrent of sound that embodies the sensuous ideal of the Romantic era. The composer thus developed a type of symphonic opera as native to the German genius as bel canto opera is to the Italian.

Leitmotifs

The orchestral tissue is fashioned out of concise themes, the *leitmotifs*, or "leading motives"—Wagner called them basic themes—that recur throughout a work, undergoing variation and development as do the themes and motives of a symphony. The leitmotifs carry specific meanings, like the "fixed idea" of Berlioz's *Symphonie fantastique*. They have an uncanny power to suggest in a few notes a person, an emotion, an idea, an object (the gold, the ring, the sword) or a landscape (the Rhine, Valhalla, the lonely shore of Tristan's home). Through a process of continual transformation, the leitmotifs trace the course of the drama, the changes in the characters, their experiences and memories, their thoughts and hidden desires. As the leitmotifs accumulate layer upon layer of meaning, they themselves become characters in the drama, symbols of the relentless process of growth and decay that rules the destinies of gods and heroes.

Chromatic harmony

Wagner based his musical language on chromatic harmony, which he pushed to its then farthermost limits. Chromatic dissonance gives Wagner's

---

Principal Works

13 music dramas (operas), including *Rienzi* (1842); *Der fliegende Holländer* (*The Flying Dutchman*, 1843); *Tannhäuser* (1845); *Lohengrin* (1850); *Tristan und Isolde* (1865); *Die Meistersinger von Nürnberg* (*The Mastersingers of Nuremberg*, 1868); *Der Ring des Nibelungen* (*The Ring of the Nibelung*), consisting of *Das Rheingold* (*The Rhine Gold*, 1869), *Die Walküre* (*The Valkyrie*, 1870), *Siegfried* (1876), and *Götterdämmerung* (*The Twilight of the Gods*, 1876); and *Parsifal* (1882)

Orchestral music, including *Siegfried Idyll* (1870)

Piano music; vocal music; choral music

music its restless, intensely emotional quality. Never before had unstable pitch combinations been used so eloquently to portray states of soul.

Die Walküre

The story of *The Ring of the Nibelung* centers on the treasure of gold that lies hidden in the depths of the Rhine River, guarded by three Rhine Maidens. The world is young and does not know the power of gold. Only someone who renounces love can gain that power. Alberich the Nibelung, of a hideous race of dwarfs that inhabits the dark regions below the earth, tries to make love to each of the maidens. When they repulse him, he renounces love, steals the treasure, and makes it into a ring that brings unlimited power to its owner. Wotan, father of the gods (for whom our Wednesday, or Wotan's Day, is named), compromises his honor by obtaining the ring through trickery, whereupon Alberich pronounces a terrible curse: may the ring destroy the peace of mind of all who gain possession of it, may it bring them misfortune and death.

Thus begins the cycle of four dramas—the Tetralogy, as it is known—that ends only when the curse-bearing ring is returned to the Rhine Maidens. Gods and heroes, mortals and Nibelungs, intermingle freely in this tale of betrayed love, broken promises, magic spells, and general corruption brought on by the lust for power. Wagner freely adapted the story from the myths of the Norse sagas and the legends associated with a medieval German epic poem, the *Nibelungenlied*.

He wrote the four librettos in reverse order. First came his poem on the

> ### In His Own Words
>
> *True drama can be conceived only as resulting from the collective impulse of all the arts to communicate in the most immediate way with a collective public. . . . Thus especially the art of tone, developed with such singular diversity in instrumental music, will realize in the collective artwork its richest potential—will indeed incite the pantomimic art of dancing in turn to wholly new discoveries and inspire the breath of poetry no less to an undreamed-of fullness. For in its isolation music has formed itself an organ capable of the most immeasurable expression—the orchestra.*

The Ride of the Valkyries, *from Wagner's opera* Die Walküre, *in a design by* **Carl Emil Doepler** *(c. 1876).* (Richard Wagner Museum, Bayreuth)

death of the hero Siegfried. This became the final opera, *Götterdämmerung*, in the course of which Siegfried, now possessor of the ring, betrays Brünnhilde, to whom he has sworn his love, and is in turn betrayed by her. Wagner then realized that the events in Siegfried's life resulted from what had happened to him in his youth; the poem of *Siegfried* explains the forces that shaped the young hero. Aware that these in turn were determined by events set in motion before the hero was born, Wagner next wrote the poem about Siegfried's parents, Siegmund and Sieglinde, that became *Die Walküre*. Finally, this trilogy was prefaced by *Das Rheingold*, the drama that unleashes the workings of fate and the curse of gold out of which the entire action stems.

Act I   First performed in Munich in 1870, *Die Walküre* revolves around the twin brother and sister who are the offspring of Wotan by a mortal. (In Norse as in Greek and Roman mythology, kings and heroes were the children of gods.) The ill-fated love of Siegmund and Sieglinde is not only incestuous but also adulterous, for she has been forced into a loveless marriage with the grim chieftain Hunding, who challenges Siegmund to battle.

Act II   The second act opens with a scene between Wotan and Brünnhilde. She is one of the Valkyries, the nine daughters of Wotan, whose perpetual task is to circle the battlefield on their winged horses and swoop down to gather up the fallen heroes, whom they bear away to Valhalla, where they will sit forever feasting with the gods. Wotan first tells Brünnhilde, his favorite daughter, that in the ensuing combat between Siegmund and Hunding, she must see to it that Siegmund is the victor. But Wotan's wife, Fricka, the goddess of marriage, insists that Siegmund has violated the holiest law of the universe, and that he must die. Although he argues with her, Wotan sadly realizes that even he must obey the law. When Brünnhilde comes to Siegmund to tell him of his fate, she yields to pity and decides to disobey her father. The two heroes fight, and Brünnhilde tries to shield Siegmund. At the decisive moment, Wotan appears and holds out his spear, upon which Siegmund's sword is shattered. Hunding then buries his own spear in Siegmund's breast. Wotan, overcome by his son's death, turns a ferocious look upon Hunding, who falls dead. Then the god rouses himself and hurries off in pursuit of the daughter who dared to defy his command.

Act III   The prelude to Act III is the famous "Ride of the Valkyries," a vivid orchestral picture of the Amazon-like goddesses whirling through a storm on their chargers. Brünnhilde rushes in to carry off Siegmund's body from the scene of battle. His lover, Sieglinde, wants to die, but Brünnhilde hands her the two fragments of Siegmund's sword and tells her she must live to bear his son, who will become the world's mightiest hero. Sieglinde takes refuge in the forest, while Brünnhilde remains to face her father's wrath. Her punishment is severe. She is to be deprived of her godhood, Wotan tells her, to become a mortal woman. No more will she sit with the gods, nor will she carry heroes to Valhalla. He will put her to sleep on a rock, and she will fall prey to the first mortal who finds her. Brünnhilde defends herself. In trying to protect Siegmund, was she not carrying out her father's innermost desire? She begs him to soften her punishment: let him at least surround the rock with flames, so that only a fearless hero will be able to penetrate the wall of fire. Wotan relents and grants her request. He kisses her on both eyes, which close at once.

Striking the rock three times, he invokes Loge, the god of fire. Flames spring up around the rock—and in the music—as the tall figure of the god in his black cloak is silhouetted against the red sky. "Whosoever fears the tip of my spear shall never pass through the fire," he sings, as the orchestra announces the theme of Siegfried, the fearless hero who in the next music drama will force his way through the flames and awaken Brünnhilde with a kiss. (See Listening Guide 17 for text and an analysis.) The curtain falls on a version of the Sleeping Beauty legend as poetic as any artist ever created.

Listening Guide 17

CD: Chr/Std 5/64–68, Sh 3/55–57
Cassette: Chr/Std 5B/4, Sh 3B/4

WAGNER: *Die Walküre*, Act III, Finale   (10:55)

Date of work: 1856; first performed 1870, Munich

Genre: Music drama, second in a cycle of 4, *The Ring of the Nibelung*

Characters:
   Wotan, father of the gods (bass-baritone)
   Brünnhilde, one of the Valkyries, the favorite of the 9 daughters of Wotan (soprano)

(Shorter recordings begin with trombone passage, bottom of p. 188.)

  0:00   Orchestra with "slumber" motive, Langsam (Slow):

Opening melody of Wotan's farewell:

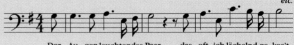

Der Au - gen leuchtendes Paar,   das oft ich lächelnd ge - kos't

Text	Translation
WOTAN	
Der Augen leuchtendes Paar,	That bright pair of eyes
das oft ich lächelnd gekos't,	that often I fondled with smiles
wenn Kampfes lust ein Kuss dir lohnte,	when lust of battle won you a kiss,

wenn kindisch lallend der Helden Lob	when childlike chatter in praise of heroes
von holden Lippen dir floss:	flowed from your dear lips:
dieser Augen strahlendes Paar,	that radiant pair of eyes,
das oft im Sturm mir geglänzt,	that often in tempests blazed at me,
wenn Hoffnungssehnen das Herz mir sengte,	when hopeful yearning burned up my heart,
nach Welten wonne mein Wunsch verlangte	when for worldly joy my desires longed
aus wild webendem Bangen:	amid wild weaving fear:
zum letzten Mal	for the last time
letz' es mich heut'	let them delight me today
mit des Lebewohles letztem Kuss!	with farewell's last kiss!
Dem glücklicher'n Manne	May their star shine
glänze sein Stern:	for that happier man:
dem unseligen Ew'gen	for the luckless immortal
muss es scheidend sich schliessen.	they must close in parting.

(He clasps her head in his hands.)

| Denn so kehrt der Gott sich dir ab, | For thus the god departs from you, |
| so küsst er die Gottheit von dir! | thus he kisses your godhead away! |

(He kisses her long on the eyes.)

65 3:36 "Magic sleep" motive in woodwinds and harp:

(She sinks back with closed eyes, unconscious, in his arms. He gently bears her to a low mossy mound, which is overshadowed by a wide-spreading fir tree, and lays her upon it. He looks upon her and closes her helmet; his eyes then rest on the form of the sleeper, which he now completely covers with the great steel shield of the Valkyrie. He turns slowly away, then again turns around with a sorrowful look.)

"Slumber" motive is heard again, in brass, then in strings.

(He strides with solemn decision to the middle of the stage and directs the point of his spear toward a large rock.)

66 6:34 Forceful trombone passage precedes invo-
cation to Loge:

WOTAN

Loge, hör'! Lausche hieher!	Loge, listen! Harken here!
Wie zuerst ich dich fand, als feurige Gluth,	As I found you first, a fiery blaze,
wie dann einst du mir schwandest,	as once you vanished from me,
als schweifende Lohe;	a random fire;
wie ich dich band, bann' ich dich heut'!	as I allied with you, so today I conjure you!
Herauf, wabernde Lohe,	Arise, magic flame,
umlod're mir feurig den Fels!	girdle the rock with fire for me!

(He strikes the rock thrice with his spear.)

Loge! Loge! Hieher!	Loge! Loge! Come here!

(A flash of flames issue from the rock, which swell to an ever-brightening fiery glow. Bright shooting flames surround Wotan. With his spear he directs the sea of fire to encircle the rock; it presently spreads toward the background, where it encloses the mountain in flames.)

67   7:35   "Magic fire" music is heard in full orchestra:

"Magic sleep" music is heard, followed by "slumber" motive in orchestra.

WOTAN

68   8:34

Wer meines Speeres Spitze fürchtet,	Whosoever fears the tip of my spear
durchschreite das Feuer nie!	shall never pass through the fire!

(He stretches out the spear as a spell. He gazes sorrowfully back on Brünnhilde. Slowly he turns to depart. He turns his head again and looks back. He disappears through the fire.)

Wotan sings "Siegfried" motive to text above, followed by brass, announcing the hero to come:

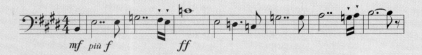

Orchestral closing with "magic fire" music and "slumber" motive.

34

Exoticism in Opera

"The composer gives the best of himself to the making of a work. He believes, doubts, enthuses, despairs, rejoices, and suffers in turn."—GEORGES BIZET

We saw that a yearning for far-off lands was an important component of the Romantic imagination. This tendency found a perfect outlet in opera, whose action could take place anywhere in the world. Composers of such works were not terribly interested in authenticity; their primary concern was to create a picturesque atmosphere that would appeal to audiences. In other words, an exotic setting reflected the imagination of the composer rather than firsthand knowledge of a culture. If the action took place in Asia or Africa, the work was still in the musical language of the West, but that language was flavored with melodies, harmonies, and rhythms suggestive of the faraway locale.

A prime example is Verdi's *Aida*, which manages within the traditional idiom of Italian opera to evoke ancient Egypt under the pharaohs. The French composer Camille Saint-Saëns (1835–1921) turned to the Bible for the story of *Samson and Delilah*. Another biblical story inspired the German composer Richard Strauss to write *Salome*; although the opera is set in ancient Judea, Salome's "Dance of the Seven Veils" centers around a tune reminiscent of a langorous Viennese waltz. The turn-of-the-century Italian master Giacomo Puccini (1858–1924) produced two well-known operas with Asian settings: *Madame Butterfly*, a romantic drama set in late-nineteenth-century Japan, and *Turandot*, based on a legend of ancient China.

French composers have always been fascinated by Spain. Thus a number of French orchestral classics describe the colorful peninsula, as Bizet does in his wonderful opera *Carmen*, which we will study.

GEORGES BIZET: HIS LIFE AND MUSIC

Georges Bizet (1838–1875) was born and raised in Paris. As a student at the conservatory there, he won its highest award, the Prix de Rome, which made possible a three-year stay in the Italian capital. He passed the rest of his career in his native city. The works of his youth were followed by three operas that display the composer's power of evoking exotic atmosphere: *The Pearl Fishers*, a drama of love and ritual in Ceylon (modern-day Sri Lanka); *The Fair Maid of Perth* (after Walter Scott's novel), which takes place in a romanticized Scotland; and *Djamileh*, set in Cairo, Egypt. Although these operas were not overwhelmingly successful, they established Bizet's reputation as a composer to be reckoned with.

When Bizet was offered a libretto that Henri Meilhac and Ludovic Halévy had fashioned from Prosper Mérimée's celebrated story of Spanish Gypsy (today called Romany) life and love, he was ready for the task. The result was the greatest French opera of the century. Mérimée's tale belonged to a new type of literature, which tried to portray the realities of life more accurately. His characters—many of them smugglers and bandits—were depicted with an honesty that proclaimed the new realism. Although Bizet's opera softened the naked fury of the original story, enough remained to disturb the audience that assembled for the opening night on March 3, 1875. The Opéra-Comique was a "family theater" where the bourgeois of Paris brought their wives and marriageable daughters. Passion on the stage was acceptable if it concerned kings and duchesses long dead; Carmen and her unsavory companions were too close for comfort.

The opera failed to conquer its first audience. But the rumor that the piece was not quite respectable secured it a run of thirty-seven performances in the next three months, an average of three a week. In addition, the manager offered the composer and his librettists a contract for their next work. But Bizet had put every ounce of his genius into *Carmen*, and its lukewarm reception was a bitter disappointment. His delicate constitution, worn out by months of rehearsals and by the emotional tension surrounding the production, was ill prepared to take the blow. Exactly three months after the premiere, he died of a heart attack, at the age of thirty-seven. His death came just when he had found his mature style.

Carmen was immediately dropped by the Opéra-Comique. Yet within three years, it had made its way to Vienna and Brussels, London and New York. Five years later, it returned to Paris, where it was received rapturously and launched on its fabulously successful career. Today it is one of the world's best-loved operas.

Georges Bizet

Carmen

The power of this lyric drama stems from the impact with which it projects strong emotions—love, hate, desire—and from its compelling theme: the disintegration of a personality. The action is swift and unfaltering as the characters are carried step by step to their doom. The story centers around Carmen, a beautiful, tempestuous Gypsy girl who works in a cigarette factory in

Acts I and II

Cultural Perspective 4

THE LURE OF SPAIN

The French composer Georges Bizet's opera *Carmen* is described in the text as an example of exoticism. But what exactly did Bizet find exotic about this story (based on a tale by French writer Prosper Mérimée) and its Spanish setting? And how does his music for this opera fire the listener's imagination with thoughts of far-off lands?

In *Carmen*, Bizet romanticized Gypsy (or Romany) culture, which he presents through a title character whose moral values—or lack of them—shocked nineteenth-century audiences. The libretto echoes the theme of naturalism, a movement led by the French novelist Émile Zola (1840–1902) that focused on the life of the lower classes and their suffering. Carmen and her friends, a band of Gypsy smugglers, fall far short of the standards of middle-class virtue. But they are seen against the exotic allure of Spain, and Bizet's music invests them with a certain human dignity. The music for *Carmen* imitates the songs and dances of the Spanish Gypsies, a style often referred to as flamenco. Typical of southern Spain, fla-

menco music is actually a variety of different dance songs, most performed to the accompaniment of a strummed guitar, with hand clapping, foot stomping, and finger snapping. One type of flamenco music heard in *Carmen* is the seguidilla, a dance in moderate triple meter that is sung to a fixed poetic verse form. Flamenco performances often begin with shouts of encouragement from the audience, followed by a rhapsodic guitar introduction that sets the mood for the dancers. Distinctive features include a hoarse, nasal vocal quality and a freely melismatic style of singing, both influences of Arab music in southern Spain. Some styles of flamenco also make use of castanets, a percussion instrument consisting of two shell-shaped pieces of wood clapped together in one hand. Today, flamenco remains a vibrant and spectacular entertainment that reflects the interpenetration of other folk and popular genres.

But Bizet also looked to a more distant locale in his music. Carmen's famous aria—the *Habanera*, which we will study—is based

Seville, and Don José, the simple soldier who falls in love with her. Don José had been planning to marry his childhood sweetheart Micaela, but his desire for Carmen grips him with obsessive force. She tries to lure him into her band of smugglers, but he cannot possibly abandon the respectable life he has known. However, when his superior officer, Lieutenant Zuniga, tries to make love to Carmen, José, mad with jealousy, attacks him. Now he can no longer return to the barracks. The band of smugglers welcomes the deserter into their midst with a rousing chorus that hails the freedom of their lawless life.

on a Cuban dance form. A habanera is a slow dance in duple meter whose name reflects its origin in Havana. It gained popularity in nineteenth-century Europe and Latin America, and greatly influenced the Argentine tango, a dance with sudden rhythmic movements performed by couples in a tight embrace. The tango has enjoyed popularity for some years as a ballroom dance, and was recently revived in a new Broadway show, *Forever Tango* (1997), which chronicles the colorful history of the dance.

Terms to Note:

flamenco   habanera
seguidilla   tango
castanets

Suggested Listening:

Bizet: *Habanera,* from *Carmen*
Spanish dance music (flamenco)
Tango music

The American expatriate painter **John Singer Sargent** *(1856–1925) was drawn to the exoticism of Spain, as illustrated here in* El Jaleo: Spanish Dancer with Guitarists. (Isabella Stewart Gardner Museum, Boston)

In a deserted mountain pass that serves as the hideout of the smugglers, José gloomily reflects on his life. His happiness with Carmen was short-lived. As fickle as she is willful, she has tired of him and transferred her affection to the handsome bullfighter Escamillo. She suggests to José that he had perhaps better return to his village. They quarrel. Carmen's friends, Frasquita and Mercédès, open a deck of cards and tell their fortunes. The cards promise to each what her heart desires—to Frasquita a handsome young lover, to Mercédès a rich old husband who will die and leave her his money. Carmen cuts

Act III

The Habanera, *from Act I of the Virginia Opera's 1992 production of Bizet's* Carmen. *Carol Sparrow appears in the title role.*

the cards and draws the ace of spades. "Death! I've read it well. First I, then he," she says. Micaela comes looking for José, hoping still to rescue him from his madness. Then the bullfighter arrives, eager to join Carmen. He fights with the jealous José, but they are separated. José learns from Micaela that his mother is dying and is persuaded to leave with her. "We will meet again!" he warns Carmen, as the orchestra sounds the motive of fate that runs like a dark thread through the score.

Act IV   The final act takes place outside the bullring in Seville. A festive crowd hails the bullfighters; finally Escamillo enters, with a radiant Carmen on his arm. The crowd accompanies him into the bullring; Carmen remains to face José. Their encounter is tense and volcanic. Each is driven by a basic instinct: José cannot relinquish his love, she cannot surrender her freedom. He begs her to go with him; there is still time to begin again. She refuses.

"Then you love me no more?" he asks.

"No, I love you no more."

"But I, Carmen, I still love you!" He reaches the breaking point against the jubilant strains of the chorus in the arena. He stabs her as the *Toreador Song* rises from the crowd pouring out of the arena. José, dazed, kneels beside her body. The orchestra again sounds the motive of fate.

The libretto is a tightly knit text revolving around a few key words— "l'amour" (love), "le sort" (fate), "jamais" (never), "la mort" (death), all highly singable. Bizet's brilliant orchestration and rhythmic vitality evoke the warmth and color of Spain (which the composer never experienced first-hand). The work remains one of the great examples of nineteenth-century exoticism, its picturesque atmosphere inescapably romantic. With its spoken

Principal Works

Orchestral music, including incidental music for *L'arlésienne* (*The Woman of Arles*, 1872) and the Symphony in C (1855)

Operas, including *Les pêcheurs de perles* (*The Pearl Fishers*, 1863), *La jolie fille de Perth* (*The Fair Maid of Perth*, 1867), *Djamileh* (1872), and *Carmen* (1875)

Piano music; vocal music

dialogue, set to music after Bizet's death by his friend Ernest Guiraud, *Carmen* was conceived in the tradition of popular opéra comique. But it expanded that tradition with its realism, sensuality, and tragic ending, in the same way that a century later *West Side Story* expanded the conventions of the Broadway musical. (We will study Bernstein's *West Side Story* in Chapter 77.)

Our excerpt from Act I is set in a square in Seville in front of the cigarette factory (see Listening Guide 18). Soldiers loiter before the guard house. A trumpet offstage announces the changing of the guard; the relieving troop arrives, led by bugle and fife. The newcomers are hailed by a crowd of street boys who strut beside them, pretending to be soldiers too. They sing a snappy march tune in high register, their "Ta ra ta ta" imitating a bugle call. The retiring squad marches offstage, followed by the youngsters, and the march tune dies away in the distance.

The factory bell rings at noon, and the young men of the town gather to flirt with the girls who are about to come out. They express their anticipation in a short chorus sung in unison. The girls enter smoking cigarettes, which was quite a daring thing for women to do back in 1875. They blow smoke rings as they sing their chorus to a gentle melody that is in Bizet's suavest manner.

The mood changes as a few agitated measures prepare us for the entrance of Carmen. The scene is set for her aria in the graceful dotted rhythm of a *habanera*, a Cuban dance-song that originated in Havana and was popular in the early nineteenth century. Based on a descending chromatic scale, the *Habanera* follows a "verse and chorus" form; at the choral verse, Carmen sings a seductive countermelody on the key word "l'amour." Carmen's song establishes her character—capricious, tough, and dangerous. "The bird you thought to surprise has spread its wings and flown; love is far away, you may wait for it; when you've given up waiting, it is there!" She throws Don José a flower. He doesn't know it yet, but she has already settled his fate.

Habanera

BIZET: *Carmen*, Act I, excerpt   (13:49)

Date of work: 1875, Paris

Libretto: Henri Meilhac and Ludovic Halévy

Basis: Short story by Prosper Mérimée

Principal characters:

Carmen, seductive cigarette girl (mezzo-soprano)

Don José, a corporal obsessed with Carmen (tenor)

Escamillo, vain bullfighter who wins Carmen's love (bass-baritone)

Micaela, childhood sweetheart of Don José (soprano)

Lieutenant Zuniga, Don José's superior officer, who also desires Carmen (bass)

---

32   0:00   The relieving guard arrives, signaled by a trumpet fanfare, followed by a staccato march tune:

A group of street children follow, singing the march:

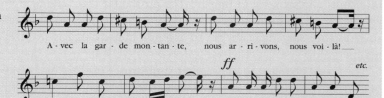

A - vec la gar - de mon - tan - te, nous ar - ri - vons, nous voi - là!

Son - ne, trom - pette é - cla - tan - te! Ta ra ta ta, ta ra ta ta.

Text	Translation
	CHORUS OF BOYS

1:15

Text	Translation
Avec la garde montante,	Along with the relief guard,
nous arrivons, nous violà!	here we come, here we are!
Sonne, trompette éclatante!	Let the shrill trumpet sound!
Ta ra ta ta, ta ra ta ta.	Ta ra ta ta, ta ra ta ta.
Nous marchons la tête haute	We come marching, head held high,

		comme de petits soldats,		like little soldiers

comme de petits soldats,
marquant sans faire de faute,
une, deux, marquant le pas.
Les épaules en arrière
et la poitrine en dehors,
les bras de cette manière,
tombant tout le long du corps.
Avec la garde montante,
Nous arrivons, nous violà!
Sonne, trompette éclatante!
Ta ra ta ta, ta ra ta ta, *etc.*

like little soldiers
marching all in step,
one, two, marching time.
Shoulders back
and chest thrown out,
arms like this, held
straight down next to the body.
Along with the relief guard,
here we come, here we are!
Let the shrill trumpet sound!
Ta ra ta ta, ta ra ta ta, *etc.*

(They continue in the same strain.)

Recitative:

MORALES (*to José*)

33 2:23

Une jeune fille charmante
vient de nous demander
si tu n'étais pas là!
Jupe bleue et natte tombante.

A pretty girl
has just been asking us.
if you were here!
Blue skirt and long braids!

DON JOSÉ

Ce doit être Micaela.

It must be Micaela.

(The retiring guard departs, accompanied by the children.)

CHORUS OF BOYS

34 2:43

Et la garde descendante
rentre chez elle et s'en va.
Sonne, trompette éclatante!
Ta ra ta ta, ta ra ta ta.
Nous marchons la tête haute, *etc.*

And the retiring guard
is returning to barracks and going off duty.
Let the shrill trumpet sound!
Ta ra ta ta, ta ra ta ta.
We come marching, head held high, *etc.*

ZUNIGA (*to Don José, who is occupied with his equipment*)

35 3:50

C'est bien là, n'est-ce pas,
dans ce grand bâtiment
que travaillent les cigarières?

It's right there, isn't it,
in that big building
that the cigarette girls work?

DON JOSÉ

C'est là, mon officier, et
bien certainement on ne vit
nulle part filles aussi légères.

It is, sir, and
you certainly won't find a more
flighty bunch of females anywhere.

ZUNIGA

Mais au moins sont-elles jolies?

But are they pretty, at least?

DON JOSÉ

Mon officier, je n'en sais rien,
et m'occupe assez peu de ces
galanteries.

I couldn't say, sir,
I'm not much interested in goings-on
of that sort.

ZUNIGA

Ce qui t'occupe, ami,
je le sais bien,
une jeune fille charmante
qu'on appelle Micaela—
jupe bleue et natte tombante.
Tu ne réponds rien à cela?

I know very well what you are
interested in, my friend,
a charming girl
called Micaela—
blue skirt and long braids!
Have you nothing to say to that?

DON JOSÉ

Je réponds que c'est vrai,　　　　　　I say it's true,
Je réponds que je l'aime!　　　　　　I say I love her!
Quant aux ouvrières d'ici　　　　　　As for the local factory girls
quant à leur beauté, les voici!　　　and their looks, here they come!
Et vous pouvez juger vous-même.　　You can judge for yourself.

(José resumes what he is doing and remains completely indifferent to everything that goes on around him. The factory bell rings.)

CHORUS OF MEN (*Tenors*)

| 36 | 5:09 |

La cloche a sonné, nous,　　　　　　The bell has rung, and we
des ouvrières nous venons　　　　　　are on the look-out here
ici guetter le retour;　　　　　　　for the factory girls' return.
et nous vous suivrons,　　　　　　　And we shall follow you
brunes cigarières,　　　　　　　　　dusky cigarette girls
En vous murmurant　　　　　　　　　murmuring protestations of love,
des propos d'amour!　　　　　　　　and making loving proposals.

(*Basses*)

| 37 | 6:30 |

Voyez-les! Regards impudents,　　　Just look at them! Impudent glances
mine coquettes!　　　　　　　　　　and flirtatious airs,
fumant toutes, du bout des dents　each with a cigarette dangling
la cigarette.　　　　　　　　　　　from her lips.

CIGARETTE GIRLS

Dans l'air nous suivons des yeux　In the air we follow with our eyes
la fumée, qui vers les cieux　　　the fragrant smoke as it
monte, monte parfumée.　　　　　　rises to the skies.
Cela monte gentiment à la tête　Sweetly it rises to our heads,
tout doucement,　　　　　　　　　　gently, imperceptibly,
Cela vous met l'âme en fête!　　　it makes you feel good!
Le doux parler des amants　　　　　Lovers' pretty speeches
c'est fumée!　　　　　　　　　　　are smoke!
Leurs transports et leurs serments　Their transports and their vows
c'est fumée! *etc.*　　　　　　　　are smoke! *etc.*
Oui, c'est fumée, c'est fumée!　　Yes, it's smoke, so much smoke!
Dans l'air nous suivons des yeux,　In the air we follow with our eyes,
dans l'air nous suivons la fumée　In the air, we watch the smoke,
qui monte en tournant vers les cieux!　which rises in spirals to the skies!
La fumée, la fumée!　　　　　　　　The smoke! The smoke!

CHORUS OF YOUNG MEN

| 38 | 8:41 |

Mais nous ne voyons pas　　　　　　But we don't see
la Carmencita!　　　　　　　　　　Carmencita!
La voilà! La voilà!　　　　　　　Ah! there she is! Here she comes!

ALL

La voilà! Voilà la Carmencita!　There she is! Here's Carmencita!

CHORUS OF YOUNG MEN

Carmen! sur tes pas nous nous pressons tous!　Carmen, we all crowd around you.
Carmen! sois gentille,　　　　　　Carmen, be kind,
au moins réponds-nous　　　　　　　at least answer us
et dis-nous quel jour　　　　　　　and say when you will
tu nous aimeras!　　　　　　　　　love us!

CARMEN

(having cast a swift glance in the direction of the oblivious José)

Quand je vous aimerai?	When I shall love you?
Ma foi, je ne sais pas!	Upon my word, I don't know!
Peut-être jamais, peut-être demain!	Perhaps never, perhaps tomorrow!
Mais pas aujourd'hui, c'est certain.	But not today, that's certain.

Opening of Carmen's *Habanera*, with dancelike rhythmic ostinato in bass:

Habanera:

[39] 9:52

L'amour est un oiseau rebelle	Love is a rebellious bird
que nul ne peut apprivoiser,	that nobody can tame,
et c'est bien en vain qu'on l'appelle	and it's simply no good calling it
s'il lui convient de refuser.	if it suits it to refuse;
Rien n'y fait, menace ou prière,	neither threat nor prayer will prevail.
l'un parle bien, l'autre se tait;	One of them talks, the other holds his peace.
et c'est l'autre que je préfère;	and I prefer the other one!
il n'a rien dit, mais il me plaît.	He hasn't said a word, but I like him!

CHORUS

L'amour est un oiseau . . .	Love is a rebellious bird . . .

CARMEN

L'amour! L'amour! L'amour!	Love! Love! Love!
L'amour est enfant de Bohème,	Love is a Gypsy,
il n'a jamais connu de loi,	it has never been subject to any law.
si tu m'aimes pas, je t'aime;	If you do not love me, I love you;
si je t'aime, prends garde à toi!	if I love you, take care!

CHORUS

Prends garde à toi! . . .	Take care! . . .

CARMEN

11:53 L'oiseau que tu croyais surprendre	The bird you thought to surprise
battit de l'aile et s'envola;	has spread its wings and flown;
l'armour est loin, tu peux l'attendre;	love is far away, you may wait for it;
tu ne l'attends plus, il est là!	when you've given up waiting, it is there!

Tout autour de toi vite, vite,	All around you, quickly, quickly
il vient, s'en va, puis il revient;	it comes, goes, and comes again.
Tu crois le tenir, il t'évite;	You think you've caught it, it escapes you;
Tu crois l'éviter, il te tient!	you think to escape it, you are caught!

CHORUS

| Tout autour de toi . . . | All around you . . . |

CARMEN

| L'amour! L'amour! . . . | Love! Love! . . . |

CHORUS OF GIRLS

| L'amour est enfant de Bohème . . . | Love is a Gypsy . . . |

(The factory bell rings a second time. Chattering noisily, the girls enter the premises, while the townsfolk disperse and the soldiers, all save José, enter the guard house.)

35

Late Romantic Opera

Verismo

The Italian operatic tradition was carried on in the post-Romantic era by a group of composers that included Giacomo Puccini, Pietro Mascagni (1863–1945), and Ruggero Leoncavallo, whom we will study. These Italians were associated with a movement known as *verismo* (realism), whose advocates tried to bring into the lyric theater the naturalism of such writers as Émile Zola, Henrik Ibsen, and their contemporaries. Instead of choosing historical or mythological themes, they picked subjects from everyday life and treated them in down-to-earth fashion. The most famous operas in this tradition include *La bohème (Bohemian Life,* 1896) and *Tosca* (1900), both by Puccini; *Cavalleria rusticana* (Rustic Chivalry, 1890), by Mascagni; and *Pagliacci* (The Clowns, 1892), by Leoncavallo. Although a short-lived movement, verismo had counterparts in Germany and France, and it produced some of the best-loved works in the operatic repertory.

RUGGERO LEONCAVALLO: HIS LIFE AND MUSIC

Leoncavallo (1857–1919) was born in the southern Italian city of Naples, the son of a police magistrate. He studied composition at the Naples Conservatory, and then completed a degree in literature at the University of Bologna.

His first opera, *I Medici* (first performed in 1893), about the famous historical family of Florence, was not a success, and Leoncavallo was forced to earn
his living for a time as a café pianist. His second opera, *Pagliacci* (1892)—for
which he wrote the libretto himself, drawing the plot from one of his father's
murder cases—made him famous overnight. The premiere took place in
Milan, under the baton of the great conductor Arturo Toscanini.

Leoncavallo wrote several additional operas, which met with only marginal
success. He was one of the first composers to become involved with a new
medium—the phonograph record—and *Pagliacci* had the honor of being the
first opera recorded in Italy (1907).

Leoncavallo belongs to the category of artists who with a single work
achieve a huge success that they never again duplicate. To the world, he
is the composer of *Pagliacci*; his twenty other stage works are more or less
forgotten.

Ruggero Leoncavallo

Pagliacci

Although the action of *Pagliacci* is drawn from a real-life scenario, its characters—a troupe of traveling actors, or "clowns"—look back to the earlier Italian tradition of the *commedia dell'arte* (comedy of the arts), a comic theatrical entertainment that parodied aristocratic society through improvised
singing, dancing, and acrobatics. Its stock characters included the bumbling
doctor (Dottore Graziano), the innocent girl (Columbina), the lecherous old
man (Pantalone), the clowns (Harlequin and Pierrot, or Pagliaccio), the
hook-nosed scoundrel (Pulcinella, who evolved into Punch, of the Punch
and Judy puppet shows), and the proud captain (Capitano), each with his or
her own costume, mask, and accessories. These lovable characters have
served as models for comic figures throughout history in pantomime, in
plays (Shakespeare and Molière), and in opera (Pergolesi and Mozart). We
will see too that the clown of the *commedia dell'arte* tradition inspired two
notable works from the early twentieth century: *Petrushka*, a ballet by the

Commedia dell'arte

Principal Works

10 operas, including *Pagliacci* (*The Clowns*, 1892), *I Medici*
(1893), *La bohème* (1897), and *Zazà* (1900)
Other vocal works, including 10 operettas (in French, Italian, and
English); songs and choruses, including a Requiem
Orchestral works, including a symphonic poem and a ballet
Piano works, including short character pieces and dances

Luciano Pavarotti in full costume as
Canio for a performance of Pagliacci.

Act I   Russian composer Igor Stravinsky, and *Pierrot lunaire*, a song cycle by the Viennese composer Arnold Schoenberg.

    Pagliacci opens with the arrival of the actors in Calabria, a region in southern Italy. The troupe immediately sets about drumming up an audience for the evening performance. Canio is the middle-aged head of the group. Tonio, a clown, lusts after Canio's beautiful young wife, Nedda, and tries to make love to her. But he fills her with disgust, and she drives him off with a whip. Tonio, rejected, overhears Nedda planning to elope with a handsome young villager, Silvio. Eager for revenge, he reveals the plan to the husband. Canio surprises the lovers and tries to catch Silvio, who escapes. He then beats Nedda to make her name her lover, but she refuses to do so. Heartbroken, Canio puts on his greasepaint and prepares for the evening show.

Act II   With Act II, a play within the play begins, presenting the stereotyped characters of the *commedia dell'arte*. Harlequin (Beppe) and Colombina (Nedda) plan to elope. Her husband, Pagliaccio (Canio), suspects them and catches them in their lovemaking, but Harlequin escapes. Pagliaccio tries to force Colombina into revealing who her lover is. At this point, the fine line in Canio's mind between reality and make-believe snaps, and he can no longer control his feelings. With mounting urgency, he demands the name of her lover. At first the audience thinks Canio is a marvelous actor, but they soon begin to suspect that something is amiss. Beside himself with rage, Canio draws out a knife and chases the frightened Nedda across the stage. As he stabs her to death, Silvio rushes upon him, only to be stabbed as well. Canio, dazed, holds up the dagger and cries, "The comedy is finished!"

    We will hear Canio's great tenor solo "Vesti la giubba" (Put on your costume) from the end of Act I. He's only a clown, he tells himself. The audience comes for amusement; the show must go on no matter what he feels inside. (See Listening Guide 19 for text.) This poignant area, preceded by a short recitative, is colored with the rich harmonic language that marks it distinctly as a late-nineteenth-century work. Leoncavallo originally planned *Pagliacci* as a one-act opera. But on opening night, the wild applause after "Vesti la giubba" made him realize that the aria created a perfect ending for an act, and that the play within the play could form a new, second act.

Canio's shattering aria has become a staple of the operatic repertory. It was sung and recorded by several generations of famous singers, including three of the foremost tenors of our time—José Carreras, Plácido Domingo, and Luciano Pavarotti.

Listening Guide 19   MW   CD: Chr/Std 6/52–53
Cassette: Chr/Std 6B/3

LEONCAVALLO: *Pagliacci*, Act I, Canio's Aria   (3:34)

Date of work: 1892

Librettist: The composer

Setting: Calabria, in southern Italy

Characters:
Canio, head of the troupe (tenor)
Nedda, his wife (soprano)
Tonio, a clown (baritone)
Beppe, a clown (tenor)
Silvio, a handsome villager (baritone)

Recitative

		Text	*Translation*
		CANIO	
52	0:00	Recitar! Mentre preso dal delirio	Perform! When my head's whirling with
		non so più quel che dico e quel che faccio!	anguish, not knowing what I'm saying or what
		Eppurè d'uopo . . . sforzati!	I'm doing! And yet I'll have to force myself!
		Bah, sei tu forse un om? Tu se' Pagliaccio!	Bah, can't you be a man? You're a clown!

Opening of recitative, introduced by timpani and sustained chord in strings:

Re - ci - tar!   Men - tre   pre - so dal de - li - rio

Aria: two sections and postlude, with 4-measure phrases

A section—four 4-measure phrases

53	0:49	Vesti la giubba e la faccia infarina.	Put on your costume and paint your face.
		La gente paga e rider vuole qua.	Your public pays you and they must be amused.
		E se Arlecchin t'invola Colombina,	Even if Harlequin and Colombina betray you,
		Ridi, Pagliaccio . . . e ognun applaudirà!dgs	laugh, clown, be merry . . . and they will all applaud!

Transition—two 4-measure phrases

Tramuta in lazzi lo spasmo ed il pianto;	You must transform your despair into laughter;
in una smorfia il singhiozzo e'l dolor . . .	and make a joke of your sobbing, your pain . . .
Ah!	Ah!

B section—two 4-measure phrases

1:46

Ridi, Pagliaccio, sul tuo amore infranto!	Laugh and be merry, though your love betrayed
Ridi del duol che t'avvelena il cor!	you! Laugh through the torment that poisons
	your heart!

Climax of aria (**B** section), marked "in full voice, heartrending":

Postlude—shifts to triple meter, lush, chromatic chords.

36

Tchaikovsky and the Ballet

"Dancing is the lustiest, the most moving, the most beautiful of the arts, because it is no mere translation or abstraction from life; it is life itself."—HAVELOCK ELLIS

BALLET—PAST AND PRESENT

Ballet has been an adornment of European culture for centuries. Ever since the Renaissance, it has been central to lavish festivals and theatrical entertainments presented at the courts of kings and dukes. Royal weddings and similar celebrations were accompanied by spectacles with scenery, costumes, and staged dancing known as an *intermedio* in Italy, a *masque* in England, and a *ballet de cour* in France. Louis XIV himself took part in one as the Sun King. Elaborate ballets were also featured in the operas of Lully and Rameau.

The eighteenth century saw the rise of ballet as an independent art form. French ballet achieved preeminence in the early nineteenth century. Then Russian ballet came into its own, fostered by the patronage of the czar's court and helped along considerably by the arrival in 1847 of the great choreographer Marius Petipa at St. Petersburg. Petipa created the dances for more than

Marius Petipa

a hundred works, invented the structure of the classic *pas de deux* (dance for two), and brought the art of staging ballets to unprecedented heights.

The history of early-twentieth-century ballet is closely identified with the career of Serge Diaghilev (1872–1929), an impresario whose genius lay in his ability to recognize the genius of others. Diaghilev's dance company, the Ballets Russes, which he brought to Paris in the years before the First World War, opened up a new chapter in the cultural life of Europe. He surrounded his dancers—the greatest were Vaslav Nijinsky and Tamara Karsavina—with productions worthy of their talents. He invited such artists as Picasso and Braque to paint the scenery, and commissioned the three ballets—*The Firebird*, *Petrushka*, and *The Rite of Spring*—that catapulted the composer Igor Stravinsky to fame. (We will study Stravinsky's ballet *Petrushka* in Chapter 70.) His ballets have served as models for the composers and choreographers who followed.

Serge Diaghilev

Ballet is the most physical of the arts, depending as it does on the leaps and turns of the human body. Out of these movements it weaves an enchantment all its own. We watch with amazement as the ballerinas perform pirouettes and intricate footwork with the utmost grace, and their partners make leaps that seem to triumph over the laws of gravity. A special glamour attaches to the great dancers—Nureyev, Baryshnikov, and their peers—yet theirs is an art based on an inhumanly demanding discipline. Their bodies are their instruments, which they must keep in excellent shape in order to perform the gymnastics required of them. They create moments of elusive beauty, made possible only by total control of their muscles. It is this combination of physical and emotional factors that marks the distinctive power of ballet.

These days, ballet is becoming more and more popular in the United States. Regional groups thrive throughout the country, their activities supplemented by visits from the famous European companies—the Bolshoi from Moscow, the Royal Ballet from London, the Paris Opéra Ballet, the Stuttgart and Danish Ballets, among others. This is a many-faceted art, and the number of its devotees is steadily growing.

PETER ILYICH TCHAIKOVSKY: HIS LIFE AND MUSIC

"Truly there would be reason to go mad were it not for music."

Few composers typify the end-of-the-century mood as does Peter Ilyich Tchaikovsky (1840–1893), who belonged to a generation that saw its truths crumbling and found none to replace them. This composer expressed above all the pessimism that engulfed the late Romantic movement.

Peter Ilyich Tchaikovsky

Nadezhda von Meck

Tchaikovsky was born at Votinsk in a distant province of Russia, the son of a government official. His family intended him for a career in the government; he graduated at nineteen from the aristocratic School of Jurisprudence in St. Petersburg and obtained a minor post in the Ministry of Justice. But at twenty-three, he decided to resign his position and enter the newly founded Conservatory of St. Petersburg. He completed the music course there in three years and was immediately recommended by Anton Rubinstein, director of the school, for a teaching post in the new Moscow Conservatory. His twelve years in Moscow saw the production of some of his most successful works.

Extremely sensitive by nature, Tchaikovsky was subject to attacks of depression aggravated by guilt over his homosexuality. In the hope of achieving some degree of stability, he married a student of the conservatory, Antonina Milyukova, who was hopelessly in love with him. But his sympathy for her soon turned into uncontrollable revulsion, and, on the verge of a serious breakdown, he fled to his brothers in St. Petersburg.

In this desperate hour, Nadezhda von Meck, the wealthy widow of an industrialist, sent him money to go abroad and recover his health, and launched him on the most productive period of his career. Overbearing and emotional, von Meck lived the life of a recluse in a Moscow mansion from which she ran her railroads, her estates, and the lives of her eleven children. Her passion was music, especially Tchaikovsky's. Bound by the rigid conventions of her time and her class, she had to be certain that her enthusiasm was for the artist, not the man; hence she stipulated that she was never to meet the recipient of her patronage.

Their correspondence gives us an insight into Tchaikovsky's method of work. "You ask me how I manage the instrumentation," he wrote. "I never compose in the abstract. I invent the musical idea and its instrumentation si-

Principal Works

8 operas, including *Eugene Onegin* (1879) and *Pique Dame* (*The Queen of Spades*, 1890)

3 ballets: *Swan Lake* (1877), *The Sleeping Beauty* (1890), and *The Nutcracker* (1892)

Orchestral music, including 7 symphonies (No. 1, 1866; No. 2, 1872; No. 3, 1875; No. 4, 1878; No. 5, 1888; No. 6, *Pathétique*, 1893; *Manfred*, 1885); 3 piano concertos, 1 violin concerto; and symphonic poems and overtures (*Romeo and Juliet*, 1870)

Chamber and keyboard music; choral music and songs

multaneously." The years covered by the correspondence saw the spread of Tchaikovsky's fame. He was the first Russian whose music appealed to Western tastes, and in 1891 he was invited to participate in the ceremonies for the opening of Carnegie Hall in New York. From America, he wrote,

American visit

> These Americans strike me as very remarkable. In this country the honesty, sincerity, generosity, cordiality, and readiness to help you without a second thought are extremely pleasant. . . . The houses downtown are simply colossal. I cannot understand how anyone can live on the thirteenth floor. I went out on the roof of one such house. The view was splendid, but I felt quite giddy when I looked down on Broadway. . . . I am convinced that I am ten times more famous in America than in Europe.

In 1893, immediately after finishing his Sixth Symphony, the *Pathétique*, he went to St. Petersburg to conduct it. The work met with a lukewarm reception, in part because Tchaikovsky, painfully shy in public, conducted his music without conviction. He died within several weeks, at the age of fifty-three. The suddenness of his death and the tragic tone of his last work led to rumors that he had committed suicide.

Final year

In the eyes of Russians, Tchaikovsky is a national artist. He himself laid great weight on the national element in his music: "I am Russian through and through!" At the same time, Tchaikovsky was a cosmopolitan who came under the spell of Italian opera, French ballet, German symphony and song. These he joined to the strain of folk melody that was his heritage as a Russian, imposing on this mixture his sharply defined personality.

The Nutcracker

Tchaikovsky had a natural affinity for the ballet. Dances, especially waltzes, are scattered throughout his works. His three ballets—*Swan Lake*, *The Sleeping Beauty*, and *The Nutcracker*—were not immediately popular with the dancers, who complained that the rhythms were too complicated to be danced to. Within a few years, however, they had changed their view, and these three ballets established themselves as basic works of the Russian repertory.

The Nutcracker was based on a fanciful story by E. T. A. Hoffmann. An expanded version by Alexandre Dumas served as the basis for choreographer Petipa's scenario, which was offered to Tchaikovsky when he returned from his visit to the United States in 1891.

Act I takes place at a Christmas party during which two children, Clara and Fritz, help decorate the tree. Their godfather arrives with gifts, among them a nutcracker. The children go to bed but Clara returns to gaze at her gift, falls asleep, and begins to dream. (Russian nutcrackers are often shaped like a

Act I

> **In His Own Words**
>
> *How can one express the indefinable sensations that one experiences while writing an instrumental composition that has no definite subject? It is a purely lyrical process. It is a musical confession of the soul, which unburdens itself through sounds just as a lyric poet expresses himself through poetry. . . . As the poet Heine said, "Where words leave off, music begins."*

Mikhail Baryshnikov in an American Ballet Theater production of The Nutcracker.

human head or a whole person, which makes it quite logical for Clara to dream, as she does, that this one was transformed into a handsome prince.) First, she is terrified to see mice scampering around the tree. Then the dolls she has received come alive and fight a battle with the mice, which reaches a climax in the combat between the Nutcracker and the Mouse King. Clara helps her beloved Nutcracker by throwing a slipper at the Mouse King, who is vanquished. The Nutcracker then becomes the Prince, who takes Clara away with him.

Act II   Act II takes place in Confiturembourg, the land of sweets, which is ruled by the Sugar Plum Fairy. The Prince presents Clara to his family, and a celebration follows, with a series of dances that reveal all the attractions of this magic realm.

The mood of the ballet is set by the Overture, whose light, airy effect Tchaikovsky achieved by omitting most of the brass instruments. The peppy *March* is played as the guests arrive for the party (see Listening Guide 20). "I have discovered a new instrument in Paris," Tchaikovsky wrote his publisher, "something between a piano and a glockenspiel, with a divinely beautiful tone, and I want to introduce it into the ballet." The instrument was the *celesta*, whose timbre perfectly suits the Sugar Plum Fairy and her veils. In the *Trepak* (Russian Dance, with the famous Cossack squat-kick), the orchestral sound is enlivened by a tambourine. The muted *Arab Dance* is followed by the *Chinese Dance*, in which bassoons set up an ostinato that bobs up and down against the shrill melody of flute and piccolo. *The Dance of the Toy Flutes* is extraordinarily graceful. Finally, the climax of the ballet comes with the *Waltz of the Flowers*, which has delighted audiences for more than a century. With its suggestion of swirling ballerinas, this finale conjures up everything we have come to associate with the Romantic ballet.

Listening Guide 20

CD: Chr/Std 6/40–48, Sh 4/1–3
Cassette: Chr/Std 6A/5–7, Sh 4A/1

TCHAIKOVSKY: *The Nutcracker*, Three Dances from Act II

(5:09)

Date of work: 1892

Genre: Ballet (from which an orchestral suite was made)

Basis: E. T. A. Hoffmann story, expanded by Alexandre Dumas

Choreographer: Marius Petipa

Sequence of dances in orchestral suite:

March	Chinese Dance
Dance of the Sugar Plum Fairy	Dance of the Toy Flutes
Trepak	Waltz of the Flowers
Arab Dance	

March: **Tempo di marcia viva (lively march); A-B-A form, 2/4 meter, G major** (2:13)

A SECTION

40   0:00   Brass announce march theme:

0:06   Answered by strings in irregular rhythms:

Alternation of two ideas.

B SECTION

41   0:59   Short section, featuring staccato runs in woodwinds and strings.

A SECTION

42   1:11   Brass march theme returns, answered by strings.

(Shorter recordings end here.)

Dance of the Sugar Plum Fairy: Andante non troppo; A-B-A form, 2/4 meter   (1:44)

A SECTION

43   0:00   Short introduction (4 measures) of pizzicato
            strings.

     0:08   Main theme introduced by celesta, staccato
            in high range (heard in dialogue with bass
            clarinet):

B SECTION

44   0:39   Brief section with arched lines in wood-
            winds, answered by strings.

A SECTION

45   1:11   Solo celesta leads back to main theme, ac-
            companied by plucked strings.

            Closes with loud pizzicato chord.

Trepak (**Russian Dance**): Tempo di trepak, molto vivace (very lively); A-B-A form,
2/4 meter   (1:12)

A SECTION

46   0:00   Lively dance tune in strings, repeated in full
            orchestra:

B SECTION

47   0:27   Brief diversion in same rhythmic style,
            melody in low strings.

A SECTION

48   0:47   Return of dance tune, quickens at end, with
            trumpet fanfare and syncopations.

Part 3

3

More
Materials
of Music

Romare Bearden *(1912–1988),* Mary Lou Williams: The Piano Lesson, *lithograph, c. 1984.* (Hampton University Museum, Virginia; ©Romare Bearden Foundation/licensed by VAGA, New York)

Unit IX

The Organization of Musical Sounds

37

Musical Systems

"Composing is like driving down a foggy road toward a house. Slowly you see more details of the house, the color and slates and bricks, the shape of the windows. The notes are the bricks and mortar of the house."—BENJAMIN BRITTEN

At the beginning of this book, we learned the various elements, or building blocks, of music. Now that we have heard how these are combined in a number of works, we are ready to consider the materials of music on a more advanced level: specifically, how musical systems are built—in the West and elsewhere.

THE MIRACLE OF THE OCTAVE

To understand the concept of an octave, we need to review some basic principles of physics. A string that is set in motion vibrates at a certain rate per second and produces a certain pitch. Given the same conditions, a string half as long will vibrate twice as fast and sound an octave higher. A string twice as long will vibrate half as fast and sound an octave lower. When we sound two tones other than the octave simultaneously, such as C-D or C-F, we hear two distinctly different tones. But when we strike an octave—two notes with the same name, such as a C and another C—we recognize a very strong similarity between the two tones. Indeed, if we were not listening carefully, we might believe that a single tone was being sounded. This "miracle of the octave" was observed thousands of years ago in many musical cultures, with the result that the octave became the basic interval in music. (An interval, remember, is the distance and relationship between two tones.)

Half steps   One important variable in the different languages of music around the world is the way the octave is divided. In Western music, it is divided into twelve equal semitones, or *half steps*; from these are built the major and minor scales (each with seven notes), which have constituted the basis of this musical language for nearly four hundred years.

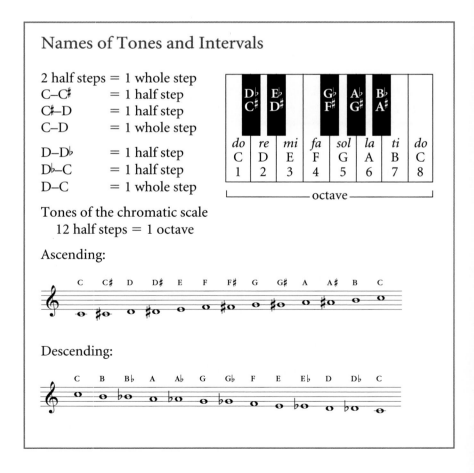

Names of Tones and Intervals

2 half steps = 1 whole step
C–C♯   = 1 half step
C♯–D   = 1 half step
C–D   = 1 whole step

D–D♭   = 1 half step
D♭–C   = 1 half step
D–C   = 1 whole step

Tones of the chromatic scale
   12 half steps = 1 octave

Ascending:

Descending:

THE FORMATION OF MAJOR AND MINOR SCALES

The twelve semitones described above constitute what is known as the *chromatic scale*. (You can see these twelve half steps on the piano keyboard, counting all the white and black keys from any tone to its octave.) No matter how vast and intricate a musical work, it is made up of the same twelve tones and their higher and lower duplications. The composer Paul Hindemith once reminded his fellow musicians: "There are only twelve tones. You must treat them carefully."

Just as in fractions two halves make a whole, so do two half steps equal a whole step. The chart opposite gives the names of the notes on a piano keyboard. You can see that the black keys are named in relation to their white-key neighbors. When the black key between C and D is thought of as a half step higher than C, it is know as C-sharp (♯). When the same key is thought of as a half step lower than D, it is called D-flat (♭). Thus, a *sharp* raises a tone by a half step, and a *flat* lowers a tone a half step. Note that the distance between C and D is a whole step, made up of two half steps. Similarly, D-sharp is the same tone as E-flat, F-sharp is the same tone as G-flat, and G-sharp is the same tone as A-flat. Which of these names is used depends on the scale and key in which a sharp or flat appears.

Both major and minor scales function within *tonality*, a principle of organization whereby we hear a piece of music in relation to a central tone, the tonic. When we listen to a composition in the key of C major, we hear a piece built around the central tone C, using the harmonies formed from the C-major scale. Tonality is the basic harmonic principle at work in most Western music written from around 1600 to 1900.

By a *key*, then, we mean a group of related tones that revolve around the central tone, the tonic, or keynote, to which they ultimately gravitate. This perceived "loyalty to the tonic" is fostered by much of the music we hear. It underlies our whole system of relationships between the tones that form scales, harmonies, and keys.

Chromatic scale

Sharp
Flat

Key

The Major Scale

The major scale is probably very familiar to our ears. If you play the white keys on the piano from C to C (the C-major scale), you will hear the *do-re-mi-fa-sol-la-ti-do* pattern already mentioned. Let us examine it a little more closely.

Looking at the piano keyboard illustrated opposite, we notice that there is no black key on the piano between E and F (*mi-fa*) or between B and C (*ti-do*). These tones, therefore, are a half step apart, while the other white keys are a whole step apart. Consequently, when we sing the *do-re-mi-fa-sol-la-ti-do* sequence, we are measuring off a pattern of eight tones that are each a whole step apart except tones 3-4 (*mi-fa*) and 7-8 (*ti-do*). (The succession of intervals that form a major scale is summarized in the table opposite.) You may find it helpful to sing this scale, trying to distinguish between the half- and whole-step distances as you sing.

Mode

Whether the major scale begins on C, D, E-flat, or any other tone, it follows the same pattern of whole and half steps. Such a pattern is known as a *mode*. Thus all the major scales have the same arrangement of whole and half steps and are in the major mode.

Within each major scale are certain relationships based on tension and resolution. One of the most important is the thrust of the seventh tone to the eighth (*ti* seeking to be resolved to *do*). Similarly, if we sing *do-re*, we are left with a sense of incompleteness that is resolved when *re* moves back to *do*; *fa* gravitates to *mi*; and *la* descends to *sol*.

1	2	3	4	5	6	7	8

Most important of all, the major scale defines two poles of traditional harmony: the tonic (*do*), the point of ultimate rest; and the fifth note, the dominant (*sol*), which represents the active harmony. Tonic going to dominant and returning to tonic is a basic progression of harmony in Western music. It also serves, we will find, as a basic principle of form.

The Minor Scale

The minor scale complements and serves as a contrast to the major. It differs from the major primarily in that its third degree is lowered a half step—hence the name "minor" (Latin for "smaller"). For example, the scale of C minor has an E-flat where the scale of C major has an E-natural (white key E); the interval C-E-flat is smaller than the interval C-E in the major ("larger") scale. The minor is pronouncedly different from the major in mood and coloring.

Like the major, the pattern of the minor scale (or mode), given in the table opposite, may begin on any of the twelve tones of the octave. Each of the twelve major and minor scales is made up of its own particular group of seven tones; that is, each scale includes a different number of sharps or flats. The scales thus generate twelve keys in the major mode and twelve keys in the minor mode.

Pattern of Major and Minor Scales

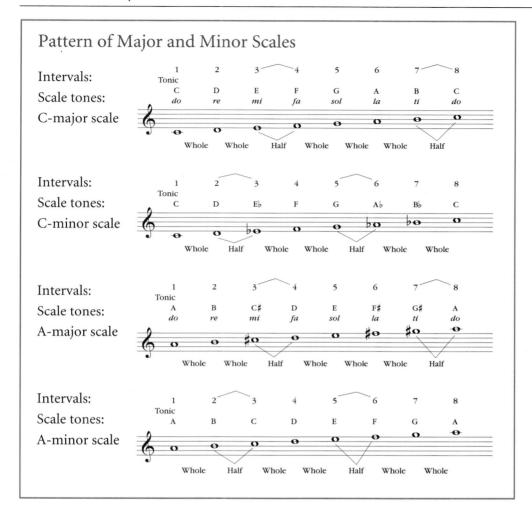

CHROMATICISM

In order for a piece to sound firmly rooted in a key, the seven notes of its scale should prevail. If the five additional foreign tones become too prominent in the melody and harmony, the relationship to the key center is weakened, and the key feeling becomes ambiguous. The distinction between the tones that do not belong within the key area and those that do is expressed in the contrasting terms "chromatic" and "diatonic." *Chromatic*, we have noted, refers to the twelve-tone scale, including all the semitones of the octave, whereas *diatonic* refers to music based on the seven tones of a major or minor

Chromatic

Diatonic

scale, and to harmonies that are firmly rooted in the corresponding key. We have seen that Romantic-era composers such as Liszt and Wagner explored the possibilities of chromaticism to charge their music with emotion. In contrast, music of the Baroque and Classical eras tended to be largely diatonic, centering more closely around a keynote and its related harmonies.

OTHER SCALE TYPES

Pentatonic scale

The Western musical system affords one way to structure music. The musical languages of other cultures often divide the octave differently, producing different scale patterns. Among the most common is the *pentatonic*, or five-note, scale, used in some African, Far Eastern, and Native American musics. Pentatonic scales can be formed in a number of patterns, each with its own unique quality of sound. Thus the scales heard in Japan and China, although both pentatonic, sound quite different from each other. (Later we will hear two forms of the pentatonic scale: one by an Asian-American composer and another from a traditional Chinese work.) Other scale types include *tritonic*, a three-note pattern found in the music of some African cultures, and a number of other seven-note, or *heptatonic*, scales fashioned from interval combinations other than those found in major and minor scales.

Tritonic and heptatonic scales

Microtones

Some scales are not playable on Western instruments because they employ intervals smaller than our half step. Such intervals, known as *microtones*, may sound "off-key" to Western ears. One way of producing microtonal music is by *inflecting* a pitch, or making a brief microtonal dip or rise from the original pitch; this technique, similar to that of the "blue note" in jazz (see Chapter 76), makes possible a host of subtle pitch changes unknown in Western melody. Microtonal inflections can be sung, and played on a wide variety of string and wind instruments (as in the example of Japanese koto music on p. 224).

Ragas

In some cultures, the ascending and descending orders of a scale are more complex, and melodic formulas can even be built in to scales. In music of India, for example, the scale formations—called *ragas*—contain certain pitches that are heard in only one direction (see example on facing page). These "scales" also have extra-musical associations connected with certain emotions, colors, seasons, times of day, or magical properties. The following example, entitled *Bhimpalasi*, is pentatonic (B♭-C-E♭-F-G) as it ascends (with gaps between its notes) and heptatonic (seven-note) as it descends—its downward pattern also turns back up for one note. This raga, performed in the afternoon, is meant to evoke a mood of tenderness and longing in the listener.

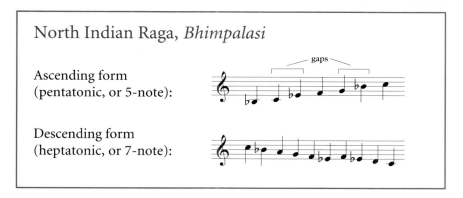

North Indian Raga, *Bhimpalasi*

Ascending form
(pentatonic, or 5-note):

Descending form
(heptatonic, or 7-note):

Thus it is the musical system and the tones chosen in that system that determine the sound and character of each work, whether classical, popular, or traditional. They are what make Western music sound familiar to us and musics of some cultures sound foreign.

38

Aspects of the Major-Minor System

"All music is nothing more than a succession of impulses that converge towards a definite point of repose."—IGOR STRAVINSKY

There are several other aspects of the harmonic system that make it both flexible and practical. For example, composers can set an entire work in a new key altogether or shift the tonal center within a work temporarily to another key. These principles are known as transposition and modulation.

TRANSPOSITION

Suppose a certain melody usually begins on the pitch G. If you felt that the song lay a little too high for your voice, you might begin on F instead of G and shift all the tones of the melody one step lower. Someone else, who found the song too low, could begin on A and sing each tone of the melody one step higher. The act of shifting all the tones of a musical composition a uniform distance to a different pitch level is called *transposition*.

When we transpose a piece, we shift it to another key. We change the keynote and the corresponding notes of the scale. But the melody line remains the same because the pattern of its whole and half steps does not change in the new key. That is why the same song can be published in various keys for soprano, alto, tenor, or bass.

Choice of key   Why does a composer choose one key rather than another? In former times, external factors strongly influenced this choice. Up to around the year 1815, for example, brass instruments were not able to change keys as readily as they are now, since they had no valves. In writing for string instruments, composers considered the fact that certain effects, such as playing on the open strings, could be achieved in one key but not in another. Composers have even associated an emotional atmosphere or a color with certain keys, a concept not too far removed from the extra-musical meaning found in the ragas of India.

MODULATION

The contrast between keys and the movement from one key to another is an essential element of musical structure. We have seen that the pitches belonging to a key form a group of seven out of twelve, which provides coherence and focus to the music. But this closed group may be opened up, in which case we are shifted, either gently or abruptly, to another area centering on another keynote. The process of passing from one key to another is known as *modulation*. There is no way to describe in words something that can only be heard. Suffice it to say that composers can "lift" us from one tonal area to another. As the composer Arnold Schoenberg put it, "Modulation is like a change of scenery."

The twelve major and twelve minor keys may be compared to rooms in a house, with the modulations equivalent to corridors leading from one to the other. (See illustration on p. 398 of the terraced levels in the Residenz, home of the Prince-Bishop of Wurzburg.) We shall see that modulation was a common practice of the Baroque period and was refined as a formal procedure in the Classical era. The eighteenth-century composer as a rule established the home key, shaped the passage of modulation—the "corridor"—in a clear-cut manner, and usually passed to a key area that was not too far away from the starting point. These procedures resulted in a spaciousness of structure that can be thought of as the musical counterpart to the balanced facades of eighteenth-century architecture.

Nineteenth-century Romanticism, on the other hand, demanded a whipping-up of emotions, an intensifying of all musical processes. In the Romantic era, modulations were more frequent and abrupt, leading to an emotion-charged music that wandered restlessly from key to key and fulfilled the Romantic artist's need for excitement.

ACTIVE AND REST CHORDS

Just as melodies have inherent active and rest poles, so do the harmonies supporting these tones. The three-note chord, or *triad*, built on the first scale tone is known as the I chord, or the *tonic*, and serves as a point of rest. But rest only has meaning in relation to activity. The chord of rest is counterposed to other chords, which are active. The active chords in turn seek to be completed, or resolved, in the rest chord. This striving for resolution is the dynamic force in our music, providing a forward direction and goal.

Triad
Tonic

The fifth scale step, the *dominant*, is the chief active chord, which seeks to resolve to the tonic. The triad built on the fourth scale step (*fa*) is known as the *subdominant*. The movement from the subdominant to the tonic (IV to I) is familiar from the chords accompanying the "Amen" sung at the close of many hymns.

Dominant

Subdominant

These three triads, the basic ones of our system, suffice to harmonize many a tune. The Civil War song *The Battle Hymn of the Republic* (also known as *John Brown's Body*) is a good example.

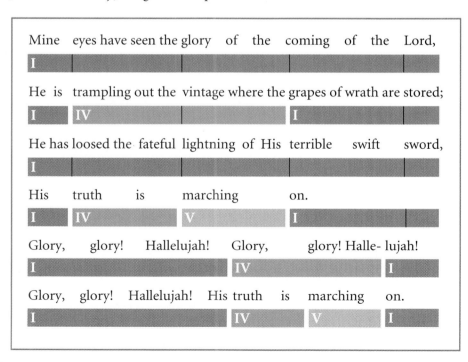

THE KEY AS A FORM-BUILDING ELEMENT

The three main chords of a musical work—tonic (I), dominant (V), and subdominant (IV)—are the focal points over which melodies and harmonic progressions unfold. Thus the key becomes a prime factor for musical unity.

Key contrast
At the same time, the contrast between keys adds welcome variety. Composers can pit one key against another, thereby achieving a dramatic opposition between them. They begin by establishing the home key, then modulate to a related key, generally that of the dominant (for example, from C major to G major, or from G major to D major). In so doing, they create a tension, since the dominant key is unstable compared with the tonic. This tension requires resolution, which is provided by the return to the home key.

The progression, or movement, from home key to contrasting key and back outlines the basic musical pattern of statement-departure-return. The home key is the anchor, the safe harbor; the foreign key represents adventure. The home key provides unity; the foreign key ensures variety and contrast.

Listening Activity: Key

Haydn's Symphony No. 94 in G major (*Surprise*)

In an earlier chapter, we listened to the second movement from this Haydn symphony movement to distinguish the sounds of major and minor harmonies (see p. 18). Let's return to the work again to enrich your understanding of these important musical principles. As noted above, this movement is in the *key* of C major—thus the melody and the accompanying chords will center around the pitch C (which is the tonic, or *do*), and the most important chord, the *tonic* (I) chord, will be built on C. Two other important chords are the *dominant* (V) chord, built on the fifth note of the C-major scale, G (or *sol*), and the *subdominant* (IV) chord, built on the fourth note, F. The dominant and subdominant are *active chords*, needing resolution, while the tonic serves as a point of *rest*. To understand how these chords work, try singing through the tune of this movement yourself, using the note *syllables* of the C scale (given below) as a kind of text.

Do do mi mi sol sol mi	*fa fa re re*	*ti ti sol*
I (tonic)	IV (subdom.)	V (dom.)
do do mi mi sol sol mi	*do do fa(♯)fa(♯)*	*sol*
I (tonic)	II⁷ (new)	V (dom.)

Now let's consider the implied harmonies. The *tonic triad* (a three-note chord) is spelled *do-mi-sol*; these are the precise notes that occur in the tune, so the tonic triad sounds consonant and very appropriate as an accompaniment. Continuing on, the tune calls for the *subdominant triad* (spelled *fa-la-do*), then the *dominant* (spelled *sol-ti-re*), followed by a return of the opening tune and its tonic harmony. Near the end of this brief example, we hear a new chord, built on the second scale tone (*re*)—this harmony introduces a *chromatic* tone, F-sharp, into the melody, which is otherwise *diatonic*, falling within the notes of the C-major scale.

Note that we have stopped this example on the dominant harmony, leaving us dangling and the music unresolved. This short introductory passage provides us with an idea of how a melody generates accompanying harmonies. As you continue listening to this movement, notice how the composer changes the harmonic basis from major to minor, at which point the music sounds very ponderous and serious. If you wish to practice listening for shifts between major and minor tonalities, try one of the examples below. (For the location of each in your sound package, see the table on the front and back inside covers of this book.)

Other Suggested Listening Examples
  Major tonality—Mozart: *Eine kleine Nachtmusik*, first movement
  Minor tonality—Bach: Prelude and Fugue in C minor
  Major/minor tonality—Smetana: *The Moldau*
  Chromaticism—Purcell: Dido's Lament, from *Dido and Aeneas*

Unit X

Focus on Form

39

The Development of Musical Ideas

"I alter some things, eliminate and try again until I am satisfied. Then begins the mental working out of this material in its breadth, its narrowness, its height and depth."
—LUDWIG VAN BEETHOVEN

Thinking, whether in words or tones, demands continuity and sequence. Every thought should flow from the one before and lead logically into the next. In this way, we feel a sense of steady progression toward a goal. Uniting the first phrase of one melody and the second phrase of another would not make any more sense than joining the beginning of one sentence to the end of another. On the contrary, an impression of cause and effect, of natural flow, must pervade an entire musical work.

This desired impression is achieved in a variety of ways, depending on the piece's style. In Western music, as we saw, a musical idea that is used as a building block in the construction of a composition is called a *theme*, and its expansion is known as *thematic development*. Conversely, a theme can be fragmented by dividing it into its constituent motives, a *motive* being its smallest melodic unit. A motive can grow, as a germ cell multiplies, into an expansive melody, or it can be treated in sequence, that is, repeated at a higher or lower level. A short, repeated musical pattern—called an *ostinato*—can also be an important organizing feature of a work.

Thematic development is generally too complex a technique to use in short pieces; in these, a simple contrast between sections and a modest expansion of material supply the necessary continuity. But thematic development is necessary in larger forms of music, where it provides clarity, coherence, and logic.

All the ways of developing thematic material—extension, contraction, repetition—are as typical of musics around the world as they are of Western art music. We have already seen that much music is improvised, or created spontaneously, by performers. Although it might seem that structure and logic would be alien to this process, this is rarely the case. In jazz, for example, musicians organize their improvised melodies within a highly structured, preestablished harmonic pattern, time frame, and melodic outline that is understood by all the performers. In India and the Middle East, improvisation is a refined and classical art, where the seemingly free and rhapsodic spinning out of the music is tied to a prescribed musical process that results in a lacework of variations.

Let's compare the way themes are developed in music from two very different cultures. The first example, from the opening of Beethoven's Symphony No. 5, which we will study later, illustrates the thematic development of a four-note motive that is repeated in sequence one step lower and then grows into a theme. Here the composer has developed and expanded his short idea to realize all its possibilities.

The second example comes from the opening of *Fuki*, a Japanese work written for voice and *koto* (a long wooden instrument with thirteen strings and movable frets, played by plucking the strings; see illustration on p. 35). While this instrumental excerpt appears to have the regular four-measure phrase structure common in much Western music, its style is more freely conceived and lacks metrical accents. Each phrase of sixteen beats is based on the opening four measures, but no two are identical; rather, a kind of variation form is at work, with each repetition subtly shifting pitches and rhythms, then dividing beats in dotted figures and adding octave leaps. Note too the use of sequence and the widely disjunct movement of the melody. (We have already observed variation form in Britten's *The Young Person's Guide to the Orchestra*, and we will study it as a major structural procedure in the Classical era; see p. 262.) One unique element of the koto selection is the use of *pitch inflections*—small dips or rises on a note—to ornament the melody. Since these inflections are difficult to notate precisely in our Western system (the Japanese system is quite different), they are indicated with up or down arrows. Thus musical processes from distant cultures can sometimes be compared, even when their contexts and resulting sounds differ greatly.

Pitch inflections

Beethoven: Symphony No. 5 in C minor

Opening of first movement:

Theme based on repetitions of motive:

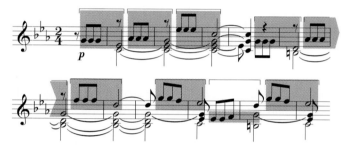

Theme based on extension of motive:

Fuki, Japanese koto piece

Beethoven's Symphony No. 5 in C minor

The familiar opening of Beethoven's Fifth Symphony allows us a chance to hear how a small musical idea, or *motive*, grows and develops into a full-blown *theme*, one of the building blocks of large musical works. We will study the symphony in detail in a later chapter; for now, note how the opening motive (dah-dah-dah-DAH), played by the strings, is repeated immediately at a lower pitch, or in *sequence*. The idea is then propelled forward with rising sequences grouped in threes, expanded through *thematic development*. We have already lost the melodic shape of the original motive, but its insistent rhythm remains familiar. Even as the work progresses to new, more lyrical musical ideas (introduced by French horns and woodwinds), we are subtly aware of that unrelenting rhythm of the four-note motive throbbing underneath. If you continue listening, you will hear the idea come back again and again throughout all the movements of this symphony. It is remarkable that this tiny germ can generate so profound a musical work. If you wish to hear other types of thematic development, some written down and others improvised, try some of the suggested examples below. (For the location of each in your sound package, see the table on the front and back inside covers of this book.)

Other Suggested Listening Examples

Thematic development (variation)—Haydn: Symphony No. 94 in G major, second movement

Improvisation—Ellington: *Ko-Ko*

The Wind That Shakes the Barley, by The Chieftains

Ostinato—Purcell: Dido's Lament, from *Dido and Aeneas*

Ellington: *Ko-Ko*

40

The Sonata Cycle

"Great art likes chains. The greater artists have created art within bounds. Or else they created their own chains."
—NADIA BOULANGER

Every musical work has a certain form; sometimes it is simple, other times complex. In some cases, the form is dictated by considerations outside music, such as a text or an accompanying program, as we observed in Berlioz's *Symphonie fantastique.*

Absolute music   In *absolute* (or *pure*) *music*, however, form is especially important, since there is no prescribed story or text to hold the music together. The story is the music itself, so its shape is of primary concern for the composer, the performer, and the listener. Large-scale works have an overall form that determines the relations between the several movements and the tempos at which they proceed. In addition, each movement has an internal form that binds its different sections into one artistic whole. We have already learned two of the simplest forms: two-part, or binary (**A-B**), and three-part, or ternary (**A-B-A**).

Now we will examine one of the most important structural procedures of Western art music—sonata cycle, used from around 1750 well into the twentieth century. The term *sonata* (from the Italian *suonare*, "to sound") refers to an instrumental genre for one or two players (a solo or duo sonata), consisting of three or four contrasting movements. *Sonata cycle* refers to the structural plan of a sonata and other multimovement genres, such as the concerto, symphony, and string quartet. The following discussion describes the standard form for each movement of these large-scale works.

The First Movement

The most highly organized and characteristic movement of the sonata cycle is the opening one, which is usually in a fast tempo such as Allegro and is writ-

Sonata-allegro form   ten in *sonata-allegro form* (also known as first-movement form, or simply sonata form). A movement in sonata-allegro form is based on two assumptions. The first is that the music establishes a home key, moves or modulates to another area, and ultimately returns to the home key. We may therefore regard sonata-allegro form as a drama between two contrasting key areas. The "plot"—that is, the action and the tension—derives from this contrast.

The second assumption is that a theme or its components may have the potential for development (we saw an example in the previous chapter). Most useful for this purpose is a brief, incisive theme, one that has momentum and tension and lends itself well to creative manipulation. The themes are stated, or "exposed," in the first section; developed in the second; and restated, or "recapitulated," in the third.

Exposition   The opening section of sonata-allegro form, the *exposition*, or statement, generally presents the two opposing keys and their respective themes. (A theme may consist of several related ideas, in which case we speak of a *theme group*.) The first theme and its expansion establish the home key, or tonic. A *transition*, or *bridge*, leads into a contrasting key; in other words, the function of the bridge is to modulate. The second theme and its expansion establish the contrasting key. A closing section rounds off the exposition in the con-

trasting key. In eighteenth-century sonata-allegro form, the exposition is repeated.

Conflict and action, the essence of drama, find their place in the *development*, where the conflict erupts, and the action reaches maximum intensity.
This section may wander further through a series of foreign keys, building up
tension against the inevitable return home. The frequent modulations contribute to a sense of activity and restlessness. At the same time, the composer
seeks to reveal the potential of the themes by varying, expanding, or contracting them, breaking them into their component motives, or combining them
with other motives or with new material. If the work is written for orchestra,
a fragment of the theme may be presented by one group of instruments and
imitated by another, thereby changing register and timbre.

Development

When the development has run its course, the tension lets up. A bridge
passage leads back to the key of the tonic. The beginning of the third section,
the *recapitulation*, or restatement, is in a sense the psychological climax of
sonata-allegro form. The first theme appears as we first heard it, in the tonic,
satisfying the listener's need for unity.

Recapitulation

The recapitulation follows the general path of the exposition, restating the
first and second themes more or less in their original form, but with new and
varied twists. Most important of all, in the recapitulation the opposing elements are reconciled, the home key is triumphant. For this reason, the third
section differs in one important detail from the exposition: it now remains in
the tonic for the second theme, which was originally heard in a contrasting
key. In other words, although the second theme and its expansion play out in
substantially the same way as before, we now hear this material transposed
into the home key.

The movement often ends with a *coda*, fashioned from material previously
heard in the closing section, to which new matter is sometimes added. The
coda leads us to the final cadence in the home key.

Coda

The features of sonata-allegro form, summed up in the chart on page 228
(which is color-coded to show keys), are present in one shape or another in
many movements, yet no two are exactly alike. Each movement exhibits a
unique character, mood, and relation of forces. Thus what looks on paper
like a fixed plan followed by the composer becomes, when transformed into
living sound, a supple framework for infinite variety.

THE SECOND MOVEMENT

The second is usually the slow movement of the sonata cycle, offering a contrast to the Allegro that preceded it; it can be an Andante or Adagio in **A-B-A**
form, a shortened sonata form, or a theme and variations. Here, composers
can give prominence to lyrical, songful melody.

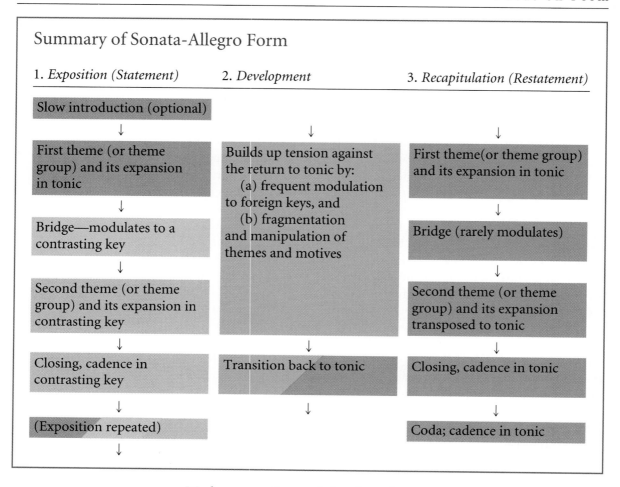

Summary of Sonata-Allegro Form

1. *Exposition (Statement)*	2. *Development*	3. *Recapitulation (Restatement)*
Slow introduction (optional)		
↓	↓	↓

First theme (or theme group) and its expansion in tonic	Builds up tension against the return to tonic by:
	    (a) frequent modulation to foreign keys, and
	    (b) fragmentation and manipulation of themes and motives
		First theme(or theme group) and its expansion in tonic

↓		↓
Bridge—modulates to a contrasting key		Bridge (rarely modulates)
↓		↓
Second theme (or theme group) and its expansion in contrasting key		Second theme (or theme group) and its expansion transposed to tonic
↓	↓	↓
Closing, cadence in contrasting key	Transition back to tonic	Closing, cadence in tonic
↓	↓	↓
(Exposition repeated)		Coda; cadence in tonic
↓		

Theme and variations

We have seen that variation is an important procedure found in every species of music, but in one form—*theme and variations*—it is the ruling principle. There, the theme is stated at the outset, so that the audience learns the basic idea that serves as the point of departure. The melody may be newly invented or borrowed (like the theme in Britten's *The Young Person's Guide to the Orchestra*). The theme is apt to be a small two- or three-part idea, simple in character to allow room for elaboration. The statement of the theme is followed by a series of variations in which certain features of the original idea are retained while others are altered. Each variation sets forth the idea with some new modification—one might say in a new disguise—through which the listener glimpses something of the original theme.

Any musical element may be drawn in to the variation process. The melody may be varied by adding or omitting notes or by shifting the melody **Melodic variation** to another key. *Melodic variation* is a favorite procedure in a jazz group, where the solo player embellishes a popular tune with a series of decorative flourishes. In *harmonic variation*, the chords that accompany a melody are replaced by others, perhaps shifting from major to minor mode. The type of accompaniment may be changed, or the melody may be shifted to a lower register with new harmonies sounding above it. So too the rhythm, meter, and tempo may be varied—*rhythmic variation*—leading to interesting changes in the nature of the tune. The texture may be enriched by interweaving the melody with new themes or countermelodies. By combining these methods with changes in dynamics and tone color, composers can also alter the expressive content of the theme; this type of character variation was especially favored in the nineteenth century.

Harmonic variation

Rhythmic variation

THE THIRD MOVEMENT

In the Classical symphony, the third movement is almost invariably a *minuet and trio*. The minuet was actually a Baroque court dance whose stately 3/4 time embodied the ideal of an aristocratic age. In the eighteenth century, the minuet was taken over into absolute music, where it served as the third movement of some sonata cycle works.

Minuet and trio

Since dance music lends itself to symmetrical construction, we often find in a minuet a clear-cut structure based on phrases of four and eight measures. (All the same, we will see that the minuets of Haydn and Mozart reveal an abundance of nonsymmetrical phrases.) In tempo, the minuet ranges from stateliness to a lively pace and whimsical character. Indeed, certain of Haydn's minuets are closer in spirit to folk dance than to the palace ballroom.

It was customary to present two dances as a group, the first repeated at the end of the second (**A-B-A**). The dance in the middle was originally arranged for only three instruments; hence the name "trio," which persisted even after the customary setting for three had long been abandoned. The trio as a rule is thinner in texture and more subdued in mood. Frequently in a symphony, woodwinds figure prominently in this section, creating an out-of-doors atmosphere that lends it a special charm. At the end of the trio, we find the words *da capo* ("from the beginning," often abbreviated *D.C.*), signifying that the first section is to be played over again.

Minuet-trio-minuet is a symmetrical three-part structure in which each part in turn is a small two-part, or binary, form. The second section of the minuet or trio may bring back the theme of the first at its close, making a *rounded binary form*. (See chart on the next page.) The composer indicates the repetition of the subsections within repeat signs (‖: :‖). However, when the minuet returns after the trio, it is customarily played straight through, without repeats. A *codetta* may round off each section.

Rounded binary form

Minuet and Trio

Minuet (**A**)	Trio (**B**)	Minuet (**A**)
‖: **a** :‖: **b-a** :‖	‖: **c** :‖: **d-c** :‖	**a-b-a**
or	or	or
‖: **a** :‖: **b** :‖	‖: **c** :‖: **d** :‖	**a-b**

Scherzo   In the nineteenth-century symphony, the minuet was replaced by the *scherzo*, generally the third movement but occasionally appearing as the second; it is usually in 3/4 time. Like the minuet, it is a three-part form (scherzo-trio-scherzo), the first section being repeated after the middle part. But it differs from the minuet in its faster pace and vigorous rhythm. The scherzo—Italian for "jest"—is marked by abrupt changes of mood, from the humorous or the whimsical to the mysterious and even demonic. In Beethoven's hands, the scherzo became a movement of great rhythmic drive.

THE FOURTH MOVEMENT

Rondo   The Classical sonata and symphony often ended with a *rondo*, a lively movement filled with the spirit of the dance. Its distinguishing characteristic is the recurrence of a musical idea, the rondo theme, in alternation with contrasting episodes. Its symmetrical sections create a balanced architecture that is satisfying aesthetically and easy to hear. In its simplest form, **A-B-A-B-A**, the rondo is an extension of three-part form. If there are two contrasting themes, the sections may follow an **A-B-A-C-A** or similar pattern.

The rondo as developed by the Classical masters was more ambitious in scope, typically taking the arched form **A-B-A-C-A-B-A**. It featured a catchy theme that lent itself to being heard over and over again. The rondo figured in eighteenth- and nineteenth-century music both as an independent piece and as a member of the sonata cycle. We will see, however, that symphonists in the nineteenth century frequently set the finale as a sonata-allegro, whose spacious dimensions served to balance the first movement.

THE SONATA CYCLE AS A WHOLE

The four-movement cycle of the Classical masters, as found in their symphonies, sonatas, string quartets, and other types of chamber music, became the vehicle for their most important instrumental music. The following out-

Sonata Cycle: General Scheme

Movement	Character	Form	Tempo
First	Long and dramatic	Sonata-allegro	Allegro
Second	Slow and lyrical	Theme and variations, sonata form, or **A-B-A**	Andante, Adagio, Largo
Third	Dancelike Minuet (18th century) Scherzo (19th century)	 Minuet and trio Scherzo and trio	 Allegretto Allegro
Fourth	Lively, "happy ending" (18th century) Epic-dramatic with triumphal ending (19th century)	Sonata-allegro Sonata-rondo Theme and variations	Allegro, Vivace, Presto

line sums up the common practice of the Classical-Romantic era. It will be helpful provided you remember that it is no more than a general scheme and does not necessarily apply to all works of this kind.

Eighteenth-century composers thought of the four movements of the cycle as self-contained entities connected by key. First, third, and fourth movements were in the home key, the second movement in a contrasting key. The nineteenth century sought a more obvious connection between movements—a thematic link. This need was met by a *cyclical structure*, in which a theme from earlier movements reappears in the later ones as a kind of motto or unifying thread. We will see that Beethoven's famous Fifth Symphony displays elements of cyclical structure, with each movement making reference to the famous opening idea.

The sonata cycle satisfied composers' need for an extended instrumental work of an abstract nature, and showcased the contrasts of key and mode inherent in the major-minor system. With its fusion of emotional and intellectual elements, its intermingling of lyricism and action, the sonata cycle may justly claim to be one of the most ingenious art forms ever devised.

Listening Activity: Sonata Cycle

Mozart's *Eine kleine Nachtmusik*

Let's see how your musical memory is progressing. In earlier listening activities, we worked on hearing musical phrases and their repetitions (in Bernstein's *Tonight*, from *West Side Story*, p. 5) and on identifying sections of a short, three-part work (in the *March*, from Tchaikovsky's ballet *The Nutcracker*, p. 28). If you are feeling confident about these exercises, we can proceed to a more structured work from the four-movement *sonata cycle* so loved by Classical masters. The third-movement triple-meter dance, a *minuet and trio*, from Mozart's charming *Eine kleine Nachtmusik* will help us practice hearing on two levels: the big picture of its structure, and the small, detailed view of one of its parts. We know that a minuet and trio has an overall three-part shape: a rhythmic, strongly accented minuet, followed by a more lyrical, flowing trio, and then a return to the original minuet. Listen to the third movement of *Eine kleine Nachtmusik* first for this large-scale form; you need only know when something new happens (the trio) and recognize the return of the first part (the minuet). Since this is a short piece, you do not have to extend your musical memory for terribly long. Now listen again, this time for the smaller picture in just the minuet. It has two short sections, each of which is repeated. Furthermore, each of its sections is the same length (eight measures), so that its phrasing becomes predictable. (Hint: you might count out eight statements of the triple meter—1-2-3, 2-2-3, 3-2-3, etc.) This dance gives a feeling of closure because its second section ends with a smattering of the first, making the minuet alone a kind of *rounded binary form* (the second section is "rounded" off with a hint of the first idea). This listening activity is a good warm-up for some of the other forms to come and will help you understand what lies within the great instrumental works of such masters as Mozart, Haydn, and Beethoven. (For the location of the examples below in your sound package, see the table on the front and back inside covers of this book.)

Other Suggested Listening Examples

Sonata-allegro form—
   Mozart: *Eine kleine Nachtmusik*, first movement
   Beethoven: Symphony No. 5 in C minor, first movement
Theme and variations—Haydn: Symphony No. 94 in G major,
   second movement
Scherzo and trio—Beethoven: Symphony No. 5 in C minor, third
   movement
Rondo—Beethoven: Piano Sonata in C minor (*Pathétique*), second
   movement
Sonata cycle—
   Mozart: *Eine kleine Nachtmusik* (4 movements)
   Beethoven: Symphony No. 5 in C minor (4 movements)

Part 4

Eighteenth-Century Classicism

Jacques Louis David *(1748–1825),* Mars Disarmed by Venus and the Graces, *1824.* (Musée Royaux des Beaux-Arts, Brussels)

Unit XI

The Classical Spirit

41

Classicism in the Arts

"Music [is] the favorite passion of my soul."
—THOMAS JEFFERSON

Classicism can be defined in two ways: in general terms, it pertains to the highest order of excellence in literature and art, specifically the culture of the ancient Greeks and Romans. The Classical attitude suggests that supreme excellence has been reached in the past and can be attained again through adherence to tradition.

Classicists stress the power of their art as a means of communication rather than as a means of self-expression. For them, a work exists in its own right, not as an extension of their own egos. This disciplined view encourages the qualities of order, stability, and harmonious proportion that we have come to associate with the Classical style.

The art of the eighteenth century bears the imprint of the spacious palaces and formal gardens—with their balanced proportions and finely wrought detail—that formed the setting for the era's great courts. In the middle of the century, Louis XV presided over extravagant celebrations in Versailles, Frederick the Great ruled in Prussia, Maria Theresa in Austria, and Catherine the Great in Russia. In such societies, the ruling class enjoyed its power through hereditary right. The past was revered and tradition was prized, no matter what the cost.

European rulers

The Parthenon, Athens (448–432 B.C.E.). The architecture of ancient Greece embodied the ideals of order and harmonious proportions.

French Revolution   Before the end of the eighteenth century, Europe was convulsed by the French Revolution (1789–99). The Classical era therefore witnessed both the twilight of the old regime and the dawn of a new political-economic alignment in Europe—specifically, the transfer of power from the aristocracy to the middle class, whose wealth was based on a rapidly expanding capitalism.

Industrial Revolution   Such a drastic shift was made possible by the Industrial Revolution, which gathered momentum in the mid–eighteenth century with a series of important inventions, from James Watt's steam engine and James Hargreaves's spinning jenny in the 1760s to Eli Whitney's cotton gin in the 1790s.

These decades saw significant advances in science. Benjamin Franklin harnessed electricity, Joseph Priestley discovered oxygen, and Edward Jenner perfected vaccination. There were important events in intellectual life as well, such as the publication of the French *Encyclopédie* (1751–52) and the first edition of the *Encyclopaedia Britannica* (1771).

The American Revolution (1775–83) broke out more than fourteen years before the French. Its immediate cause was the anger of the colonists at the economic injustices imposed on them by King George III. Beyond that, however, was a larger vision of human equality and freedom, a vision that impelled Thomas Jefferson, principal author of the Declaration of Independence, to incorporate into that epoch-making document the idea that all people have the right to life, liberty, and the pursuit of happiness. These words became fundamental to the democratic faith that has resonated throughout the course of American history.

The intellectual climate of the Classical era, then, was nourished by two opposing streams. While Classical art captured the exquisite refinement of a way of life that was drawing to a close, it also caught the first intimations of a new social structure that was struggling to be born. The eighteenth century has been called the Age of Reason; but the philosophers who created the French *Encyclopédie* and the Enlightenment—Voltaire, Rousseau, and others—also invoked reason to attack the existing order. Thus these advocates for the rising middle class became prophets of the approaching upheaval.

Intellectual climate

Eighteenth-century thinkers idealized the civilization of ancient Greece and Rome. They viewed the Greek temple as a thing of beauty, unity, proportion, and grace. And to the leaders of the middle class, Greece and Rome represented city-states that had rebelled against tyrants and absolute power. It was in this spirit that the foremost painter of revolutionary France, Jacques-Louis David, filled his canvases with symbols of Greek and Roman democracy. In this spirit too, Thomas Jefferson patterned the nation's Capitol, the University of Virginia, and his home at Monticello after Greek and Roman temples. His example gave strength to the classical revival in the United States, which made Ionic, Doric, and Corinthian columns indispensable features of public buildings well into the twentieth century.

Classical ideals

By the 1760s, though, a number of works had already appeared that clearly indicated the new interest in a romantic point of view. In the same decade, the French philospher Jean-Jacques Rousseau (1712–1778), the "father of

Literature

Thomas Jefferson's design for the Rotunda of the University of Virginia at Charlottesville reflects his admiration for classical architecture.

Sir Joshua Reynolds *(1723–1792)*
captured the era's idealization of antiquity
in his portrait Mrs. Siddons as the Tragic
Muse. (Henry E. Huntington Library and
Art Gallery, San Marino, California)

Romanticism," produced some of his most significant writings. His celebrated declaration "Man is born free, and everywhere he is in chains" epito-
mizes the temper of the time. The first manifestation of the Romantic spirit
in Germany, the movement known as *Sturm und Drang* (storm and stress),
took shape in the 1770s, when it produced two characteristic works by its
most significant young writers: the *Sorrows of Young Werther*, by Johann
Wolfgang von Goethe, and *The Robbers*, by Friedrich von Schiller. (Goethe,
we have seen, became the favorite lyric poet of the Romantic composers.) By
the end of the century, the atmosphere had completely changed.

Eighteenth-century Classicism, then, mirrored the unique moment in history when the old world was dying and the new was in the process of being
born. From the meeting of two historic forces emerged an art of noble simplicity that constitutes one of the pinnacles of Western culture.

42

Classicism in Music

"Passions, whether violent or not, must never be expressed in such a way as to disgust, and [music] must never offend the ear."
—W. A. MOZART

The Classical period in music (c. 1750–1825) is characterized best by the achievements of the masters of the Viennese School—Haydn, Mozart, Beethoven, and their successor Franz Schubert. These composers practiced their art in a time of great musical experimentation and discovery, when musicians took on three challenges: first, to explore fully the possibilities offered by the major-minor system; second, to perfect a large form of absolute instrumental music that would mobilize those possibilities to the fullest degree; and third, having found this ideal form in the sonata, to differentiate between its various types—the solo and duo sonata, trio, quartet, other kinds of chamber music, the concerto, and the symphony.

If by "Classicism" we mean strict adherence to traditional forms, we certainly cannot apply the term to the composers of the Viennese School, who experimented boldly and ceaselessly with the materials at their disposal. It should not surprise us to find that Romantic elements abound in the music of Haydn, Mozart, and Beethoven, especially their late works. These composers dealt with musical challenges so brilliantly that their symphonies and concertos, piano sonatas, duo sonatas, trios, string quartets, and similar works remained unsurpassable as models for all who came after.

ELEMENTS OF CLASSICAL STYLE

The music of the Viennese masters is notable for its elegant, lyrical melodies. Classical melodies "sing," even those intended for instruments. They are usually based on symmetrical four-bar phrases marked off by clear-cut cadences, and they move stepwise or by narrow leaps within a narrow range. Clarity is further provided by repetition and the frequent use of sequence (the repeti-

Map of Europe, 1763–1789, showing major musical centers.

tion of a pattern at a higher or lower pitch). These devices make for balanced structures that are readily accessible to the listener.

Equally clear are the harmonies that sustain these melodies. The chords are firmly rooted in the key and do not change so rapidly as to be confusing. They underline the balanced symmetry of phrases and cadences, and they form vertical columns of sound over which the melody unfolds freely and easily, generally in a homophonic texture.

Diatonic harmony

The harmony of the Classical period is based on the seven tones of the major or minor scale; in other words, it is largely *diatonic*. This diatonic harmony gives the music of Haydn, Mozart, and Beethoven its directness and its feeling of being rooted in the key.

Rhythmic regularity

Melody and harmony are powered by strong rhythms that move at a steady tempo. Much of the music is in one of the four basic meters—2/4, 3/4, 4/4, or 6/8. If a piece or movement begins in a certain meter, it is apt to stay there until the end. Classical rhythm works closely with melody and harmony to make clear the symmetrical phrase-and-cadence structure of the piece. Clearly shaped sections establish the home key, move to contrasting but closely related keys, and return to the home key. The result is the beautifully molded architectural forms of the Classical style, fulfilling the listener's need for both unity and variety.

Despite its aristocratic elegance, music of the Classical era absorbed a variety of folk and popular elements. This influence made itself felt not only in the German dances and waltzes of the Viennese masters but also in their songs, symphonies, concertos, string quartets, and sonatas.

Folk elements

THE PATRONAGE SYSTEM

The culture of the eighteenth century thrived under the patronage of an aristocracy who adopted the arts as a necessary adornment of life. Music was part of the elaborate ritual that surrounded the nobility, and the center of musical life was the palace.

The social events at court created a steady demand for new works that composers had to supply. While musicians ranked little better than servants, their situation was not quite as depressing as it sounds, for in that society virtually everybody was a servant of the ruler. The patronage system actually gave musicians economic security and provided a social framework within which they could function. It offered important advantages to the great masters who successfully adjusted to its requirements, as the career of Haydn clearly shows. On the other hand, Mozart's tragic end illustrates how heavy the penalty could be for those unable to make that adjustment.

Women too found a place as musicians under the patronage system. In Italy and France, professional female singers achieved prominence in opera and in court ballets. Others found a place within aristocratic circles as court instrumentalists and music teachers, offering private lessons to members of the nobility. As we will see, a number of women pianists and violinists also made their mark as solo performers. With the growth of the music trades, especially music printing and publishing, women found more professional opportunities open to them. And as more amateurs participated in music making, women of the middle as well as upper classes found an outlet for their talents.

Women under patronage

At this time, musical performances were beginning to move from the palace to the concert hall. The rise of the public concert gave composers a new venue (site) in which to perform their works. Haydn and Beethoven conducted their own symphonies at concerts, and Mozart and Beethoven played their own piano concertos. The public flocked to hear the latest works—unlike modern concertgoers, who are interested mainly in the music of the past. The eagerness of eighteenth-century audiences for new music surely stimulated composers to greater productivity.

Concert venues

Cultural Perspective 5

CONCERT LIFE IN THE AMERICAS: THEN AND NOW

What kind of music did people hear in eighteenth-century America and Canada? It should not surprise us that British musical tastes and traditions were highly influential. By the 1760s, European-style benefit and subscription concert series were flourishing in major Eastern cities, notably Boston, Charleston, and New York. Typically, a concert was a long affair, lasting three hours or more and featuring a wide variety of music and performers—quite different from modern events focused on a soloist, an orchestra, or a string quartet. Concerts were organized into acts, as we have in theatrical works, and frequently closed with a ball at which the latest fashionable dances were played. The concert repertory centered on English composers and others popular in England (such as Handel and Haydn).

Other types of entertainment aimed at a wider spectrum of the North American public. Opera was immensely popular in eighteenth-century America. But an evening at the theater then differed from what it is today: the performance of an English stage work might well include spoken drama, dance, mime, and even acrobatics. Songs were sometimes borrowed from other operas, and requests might be shouted from the audience, resulting in inserted numbers and encores. (An encore, from the French word for "again," is an extra piece or the repetition of a piece performed in response to audience applause.) The theater public sometimes became rowdy—in the gallery, the section farthest from the stage, there was even drunkenness, gambling, and prostitution going on during the performance—which caused some controversy over the morality of theatrical productions.

Public concert life slackened during the years of the American Revolution (1775–83), but music making continued in the home. Many of America's great patriots were amateur musicians: George Washington played the flute, Thomas Jefferson and Patrick Henry were both violinists, and Benjamin Franklin performed on the guitar, harp, and an instrument of his own invention called the glass harmonica (not a harmonica as we know it, but a set of glass bowls played by running a wet finger around the rim). This instrument became fashionable in Europe as well as America in the late eighteenth century. The literature even includes a quintet for flute, oboe, viola, cello, and glass harmonica composed by none other than Mozart.

Women too were active in amateur music making. The diary of Philip Fithian, an eighteenth-century teacher, describes talents then considered desirable in the educated woman: "She plays well on the Harpsichord, & Spinet; understands the principles of Musick, & therefore performs her Tunes in perfect time . . . she sings likewise to her instrument, has a full, strong voice, & a well-judging Ear."

After the revolution, musical societies, which sponsored professional and amateur concerts alike, sprang up around the country. Typical among these was the Boston Handel and Haydn Society, founded in 1815 and one of the earliest still in existence. As more North American composers were trained, their works were eventually included in the concert repertory along with those of the European masters. Theatrical spectacles with music were especially popular in the eastern Canadian provinces, and it was Montreal that saw the premiere of Joseph Quesnel's *Colas et Colinette* (1790), possibly the first opera written in North America.

The United States and Canada have sustained a vibrant musical life throughout their history, thanks to such major institutions as the Philharmonic Society of New York (established 1842), the Metropolitan Opera Company (1883), the Chicago Symphony Orchestra (1891), the Toronto Symphony Orchestra (1906), and the San Francisco Symphony Orchestra (1911). Today, symphony concerts and opera performances abound in large and small cities alike, on college campuses and in community forums, alongside rock concerts, Broadway musicals, and a myriad of other programs. Our musical palette continually widens, beckoning new audiences to sample its varied sounds.

Terms to Note:

encore
subscription concert
glass harmonica

A scene from an American performance of the dialogue opera The Padlock *(1768), by the British composer Charles Dibdin (1745–1814).* (New York Public Library)

Unit XII

Classical Chamber Music

43

Eighteenth-Century Chamber Music Style

"No other form of music can delight our senses with such exquisite beauty of sound, or display so clearly to our intelligence the intricacies and adventures of its design."
—SIR WILLIAM HENRY HADOW

Chamber music, as we have seen, is music for a small ensemble—two to eight (or more) players—with one player to a part. In this intimate genre, each instrument is expected to assert itself fully, but the style of playing differs from that of the solo virtuoso. Virtuosos are encouraged to display their own personalities; chamber music players function as part of a team.

The Classical era was the golden age of chamber music. Haydn and Mozart, Beethoven and Schubert established the true chamber music style, which is in the nature of a friendly conversation among equals. The central position in Classical chamber music was held by the string quartet, which, we have seen, consists of two violins (a first and a second), viola, and cello. Other favored combinations were the duo sonata—violin and piano, or cello and piano; the trio—violin, cello, and piano; and the quintet, usually a combination of string or wind instruments, or a string quartet and solo instrument such as the piano or clarinet. (See chart on p. 53.) Composers of the era also produced some memorable examples of chamber music for larger groups—sextets, septets, and octets.

Some types of compositions stood midway between chamber music and the symphony, their chief purpose being entertainment. Most popular among these were the *divertimento* and the *serenade*.

Divertimento and serenade

THE STRING QUARTET

The string quartet soon became the most influential chamber music genre of the Classical period. Although its four-line texture was viewed as ideal by composers, its focused string timbre posed a special challenge to both composer and listener. In its general structure, the string quartet follows the four-movement scheme of the sonata cycle. The first movement is usually an Allegro in sonata-allegro form. The second is a slow, lyrical movement, often in **A-B-A** or theme and variations form. Third is a moderate dance in minuet and trio form. And the fourth is a fast movement in either sonata-allegro or rondo form. This pattern applies equally to chamber music other than string quartets; the composer adjusts the material to the particular combination of instruments, but the underlying structure is more or less the same.

The movements

The musical texture is woven out of the movements' themes and motives, which the composer distributes among the four instruments. Haydn favored a dense musical texture based on the continual expansion and development of motives, while Mozart was more lyrical and relaxed. Beethoven and Schubert further expanded the architecture of the quartet, the former through

Quartet style

A vignette of amateur music making from the title page of Joseph Haydn's Trio for Piano or Harpsichord, Violin, and Cello (1798).

This eighteenth-century representation depicts a performance of a string quartet, the most influential chamber music genre of the era.

motivic development and the latter through song, which was his special gift. Folk elements abound in Haydn's quartets, while Mozart's exude the elegance of court dances. Beethoven's rousing scherzos replaced the graceful minuet movement.

Because the string quartet was addressed to a small group of cultivated music lovers, composers did not need expansive gestures here. They could present in the quartet their most private thoughts, and indeed, the final string quartets of Haydn, Mozart, and Beethoven contain some of their most profound expressions.

Haydn's String Quartet, Op. 76, No. 2 (*Quinten*)

Franz Joseph Haydn, with his sixty-eight string quartets, played a central role in the evolution of this genre. His late quartets show fanciful harmonic relationships, wanderings from one key to the next, a greater demand of virtuosity from the players, and a texture in which the four instruments are equal members.

The six string quartets making up Haydn's Opus 76 were composed in 1797 and published two years later. They date from a period when Haydn was producing one masterpiece after another, all of them marked by freedom and diversity of style. (We will study Haydn's life and works in detail in Chapter 46.) The slow movement of the third quartet (Opus 76, No. 3) consists of a set of variations on a melody Haydn wrote for the emperor's birthday, *Gott erhalte Franz den Kaiser* (*God Save the Emperor*), which became the national anthem of the Hapsburg Empire.

The quartets of this set owe much to the style of Mozart. Indeed, Haydn and Mozart continually learned from and influenced each other. Mozart so esteemed the older composer that he dedicated a set of six quartets to him in the mid-1780s, now called the "Haydn" quartets.

The *Quinten* Quartet

The second string quartet of Haydn's Opus 76, in D minor, is known as the *Quinten*—a term meaning the interval of a fifth—because its opening theme, played by the first violin, features a repeated motive marked by a descending fifth. The first movement is written in a tight, economic style with much imitation between the four instruments. The second movement, a graceful theme and variations, is in D major but switches to D minor in the middle. Third is the minuet, set in a canonic, or strictly imitative, texture. On account of its harsh harmonies, this movement is called the "Witches' Minuet"; even the trio section, which usually relaxes tension, in this instance maintains it.

Fourth movement

The fourth movement is a folklike finale in quick tempo and sonata-allegro form (see Listening Guide 21). The first theme, with its strong syncopations, smacks of a Hungarian dance tune. Like Baroque dances, it is stated in two sections, each of which is repeated. The second theme is a gentle duet between the two violins, quickly followed by a disjunct idea building to a cadence at the end of the exposition. The movement begins in the home key of D minor, but changes to D major in the recapitulation and remains there until the end. Notable is Haydn's introduction of a triplet rhythm (three notes to the beat instead of two), which gives the closing section, or coda, a sense of climax that leads naturally to the *fortissimo* ending.

Listening Guide 21

CD: Chr/Std 2/66–71
Cassette: Chr/Std 2B/9

HAYDN: String Quartet, Op. 76, No. 2 (*Quinten*), Fourth Movement

(3:52)

Date of work: 1797

Key: D minor

Movements:
  I.   Allegro; sonata-allegro form
  II. Andante o più tosto allegretto; theme and variations form
  III. Menuetto, Allegro ma non troppo; minuet and trio form
  IV. Vivace assai; sonata-allegro form

FOURTH MOVEMENT: Vivace assai (Very lively); 2/4 meter, D minor/major

EXPOSITION

66 0:00 Theme 1

       a—8 measures, first violin ends with upward sweep, which is held; section is repeated:

       b—12 measures, tune in first violin, repeated.

    0:32 Transition—denser texture; pedal sustained in cello, 2nd violin has tune; unison writing leads to theme 2.

67 0:55 Theme 2—gentle tune in violins, F major:

    1:06 Closing—more animated, disjunct rhythm builds to close over pedal in cello.

DEVELOPMENT

68 1:31 Based on theme 2.

RECAPITULATION

69 2:12 Theme 1—heard first in D minor, as in exposition.

70 2:40 Theme 1—in D major, now in first violin:

71 3:03 Theme 2—heard in D major.

       Closing—disjunct theme, D major.

       Coda—quick triplet figures in first violin build to *fortissimo* chords at end.

44

Mozart and Chamber Music

"People make a mistake who think that my art has come easily to me. Nobody has devoted so much time and thought to composition as I. There is not a famous master whose music I have not studied over and over."

Something of the miraculous hovers about the music of Mozart. His masterful melodic writing, his elegance of style, and his rich orchestral colors sound effortless. This deceptive simplicity is indeed the art that conceals art.

HIS LIFE

Wolfgang Amadeus Mozart (1756–1791) was born in Salzburg, Austria, the son of Leopold Mozart, an esteemed composer-violinist at the court of the Archbishop of Salzburg. Wolfgang began his career as the most extraordinarily gifted child in the history of music. He first started to compose before he was five, and, with his sister Nannerl, performed at the court of Empress Maria Theresa at the age of six. The following year, his ambitious father organized a concert tour that included Paris, London, and Munich. By the time he was thirteen, the boy had written sonatas, concertos, symphonies, religious works, and several operas.

Mozart reached adulthood having attained a mastery of all musical forms. The speed and sureness of his creative power, unrivaled by any other composer, is best described by Mozart himself: "Though it be long, the work is complete and finished in my mind. I take out of the bag of my memory what has previously been collected into it. For this reason the committing to paper is done quickly enough."

The high-spirited young artist rebelled against the social restrictions imposed by the patronage system, and relations with his patron, the Archbishop of Salzburg, were strained. Mozart was finally dismissed after quarreling with the archbishop and at twenty-five established himself in Vienna to pursue the career of a free-lance musician. His remaining ten years were spent in a struggle to achieve financial security, which meant winning the backing of the court. But Emperor Joseph II either passed him by in favor of lesser composers such as Antonio Salieri or assigned him to tasks unworthy of his ge-

Wolfgang Amadeus Mozart

From patronage to free artist

nius, such as composing dances for the court balls. On his pay for this work Mozart remarked with bitterness, "Too much for what I do, too little for what I could do."

Marriage to Constanze

In 1782, he married Constanze Weber, against his father's wishes. This step signaled Mozart's liberation from the very close ties that had bound him to his father, a well-meaning but domineering man who strove to ensure his son's success.

The da Ponte operas

With the opera *The Marriage of Figaro*, written in 1786 on a libretto by Lorenzo da Ponte, Mozart reached the peak of his career. The following year, he was commissioned to do another work for the Prague Opera; the result, with da Ponte again as librettist, was *Don Giovanni*. A success in Prague, this opera baffled the Viennese public. Joseph II declared, "The opera is heavenly, perhaps more beautiful than *Figaro*, but no food for the teeth of my Viennese." Upon which Mozart commented, "Then give them time to chew it."

Last years

Though his final years were spent in poor health, in the last year of his life he still managed to produce the Clarinet Concerto and, for the Viennese theater, *The Magic Flute*. With a kind of fevered desperation, he then turned to the Requiem Mass, which had been commissioned by a music-loving count who fancied himself a composer and intended to pass off the work as his own. Mozart became obsessed with the notion that this Mass for the Dead was intended for himself and that he would not live to finish it. A tragic race with time began.

Mozart was cheered in his last days by the growing popularity of *The Magic Flute*. One afternoon, singers from the theater visited the gravely ill composer to sing through a completed movement of his Requiem. He died that same night, December 4, 1791, shortly before his thirty-sixth birthday. His favorite pupil, Franz Xavier Süssmayr, completed the work from the master's sketches, making some additions of his own.

Mozart Family Portrait *(1780–81), by* **Johann Nepomuk della Croce.** *Child prodigies Wolfgang and his sister Nannerl are at the keyboard, while Leopold observes them, violin in hand. The portrait of the late Frau Mozart hangs on the wall.* (Mozarteum, Salzburg)

This performing group has all the features of the pre-Classical orchestra, with the leader at a large rectangular harpsichord and the string players and singers distributed on both sides of the garden. Open-Air Orchestra, c. 1790. *Engraving by* **Giuseppe Servellini.**

HIS MUSIC

Mozart is preeminent among composers for the inexhaustible wealth of his simple, elegant, and songful melodies. His fondness for moderately chromatic harmonies is revealed especially in the development sections of his sonata forms. In all his instrumental music, Mozart infused a sense of drama, with contrasts of mood ranging from lively and playful to solemn and tragic. His orchestration is richly colorful, his part writing notable for its careful interweaving of the lines.

The Salzburg years saw the completion of a quantity of social music—divertimentos and serenades of great variety, the most famous of which is *Eine kleine Nachtmusik* (1787), the work we will study. In chamber music, Mozart, like Haydn, favored the string quartet. His last ten quartets are some of the finest in the literature, among them the set of six dedicated to Haydn, his "most celebrated and very dear friend." Worthy companions to these are the string quintets (for two violins, two violas, and cello) and the enchanting Quintet for Clarinet and Strings.

Chamber music

One of the outstanding pianists of his time, Mozart wrote many works for his favorite instrument. The Fantasia in C minor, K. 475, and the Sonata in C minor, K. 457, are among his finest solo piano works. (The K followed by a number refers to the catalogue of Mozart's works by Ludwig Köchel, who numbered them all in what he determined to be the order of their composition.) And his twenty-seven concertos for piano and orchestra elevated this genre to one of the most important positions in the Classical era.

Piano works

Mozart's symphonies, which extended across his career, are characterized by a richness of orchestration, a freedom in part writing, and a remarkable depth of emotion. The exact number of them is difficult to determine. Al-

Symphonies

though four of the forty-one numbered symphonies are probably not by Mozart, newly discovered and reworked compositions still bring the number to over fifty. The most important are the six written in the final decade of his life. With these works, the symphony achieved its position as the most significant form of abstract music in this period.

Operas   But the genre most central to Mozart's art was opera. He wrote in the three dramatic styles of his day: *opera buffa*, or comic Italian opera (including *The Marriage of Figaro* and *Don Giovanni); opera seria*, or serious Italian opera (including *Idomeneo*); and *Singspiel*, a lighter form of German opera with spoken dialogue (*The Magic Flute*). No one has ever surpassed his power to delineate character in music or his lyric gift, so delicately molded to the human voice. His orchestra, never obtruding upon the voice, becomes the magical framework within which the action takes place.

Eine kleine Nachtmusik

Mozartean elegance is embodied in *Eine kleine Nachtmusik*, a serenade for strings whose title means "A Little Night Music." Probably the work was written for a double string quartet supported by a bass and was meant for public entertainment, in outdoor performance. The four movements of the version we know (originally there were five) are compact, intimate, and beautifully proportioned.

The first movement, a sonata-allegro form in 4/4 time in G major, opens in a marchlike manner. The first theme ascends rapidly to its peak, then turns downward at the same rate. The second theme, with the downward curve of its opening measure, presents a graceful contrast to the upward-leaping character of the first. A delightful closing theme then rounds off the exposition. As befits the character of a serenade, which is less serious than a symphony or a concerto, the development section is brief. The recapitulation follows the course of the exposition but expands the closing theme into a vigorous coda. (See Listening Guide 22 for themes and an analysis of all four movements.)

First movement

Second is the Romanza, an eighteenth-century Andante that maintains the balance between lyricism and restraint. In this movement, symmetrical sections are arranged in a rondo-like structure. The main theme (**A**) is gracious, a quality that is maintained by the faster-moving **B** section. The **C** section, darker in tone, centers about C minor and is heard against a restless background of quick notes. The movement is brought to a close with a return to the **A** section.

Second movement

The minuet and trio is an Allegretto in G major, marked by regular four-bar phrases set in a rounded binary form. The minuet opens brightly and decisively. The trio, with its soaring Mozartian melody, presents a lyrical contrast. The opening music then returns, satisfying the Classical desire for balance and symmetry.

Third movement

The last movement, a sprightly Allegro in the home key of G, alternates with an idea in the key of the dominant, D major. We have here a prime example of the Classical sonata-rondo finale, bright, jovial, and stamped with an aristocratic refinement.

Fourth movement

Listening Guide 22 MW

CD: Chr/Std 3/52–71, Sh 1/50–69
Cassette: Chr/Std 3B/3–6, Sh 1B/5–8

MOZART: *Eine kleine Nachtmusik*, K. 525   (17:35)

Date of work: 1787

Medium: Double string quartet with double bass, or chamber orchestra

Movements: 4

FIRST MOVEMENT: Allegro; sonata-allegro form, 4/4 meter, G major (5:30)

EXPOSITION

| 52 | 0:00 | Theme 1—aggressive, ascending "rocket" theme, symmetrical phrasing, in G major: |

Transitional passage, modulating.

| 53 | 0:46 | Theme 2—graceful, contrasting theme, less hurried, in key of dominant, D major: |

| | 0:58 | Closing theme—insistent, repetitive, ends in D major: |

Repeat of exposition.

DEVELOPMENT

| 54 | 3:07 | Short, begins in D major, manipulates theme 1 and closing theme; modulates, and prepares for recapitulation in G major. |

RECAPITULATION

55	3:40	Theme 1, in G major.
56	4:22	Theme 2, in G major.
	4:34	Closing theme, in G major.
	5:05	Coda—extends closing, in G major.

SECOND MOVEMENT: Romanza, Andante; sectional rondo form, duple meter, C major (5:50)

| 57 | 0:00 | A section—lyrical, serene melody in 2 parts, each repeated (‖: a :‖: b a :‖): |

| 58 | 0:55 | First violin with faster movement at beginning of second part of A: |

| 59 | 1:54 | B section—more rhythmic movement, varies idea of a, brings a back at end; in 2 sections, each repeated (‖: c :‖: d a :‖): |

| 60 | 2:55 | Return of a theme (first time). |

252

61	3:23	C section—in C minor, active rhythmic accompaniment; exchanges between violins and cellos; in 2 sections (‖:e:‖f).
62	4:13	A section—return of first section in tonic, without repeats (**a-b-a**).
		Coda—3 loud chords extend the idea of **a**.

THIRD MOVEMENT: Allegretto; minuet and trio form, 3/4 meter, regular 4-measure phrases, G major   (2:09)

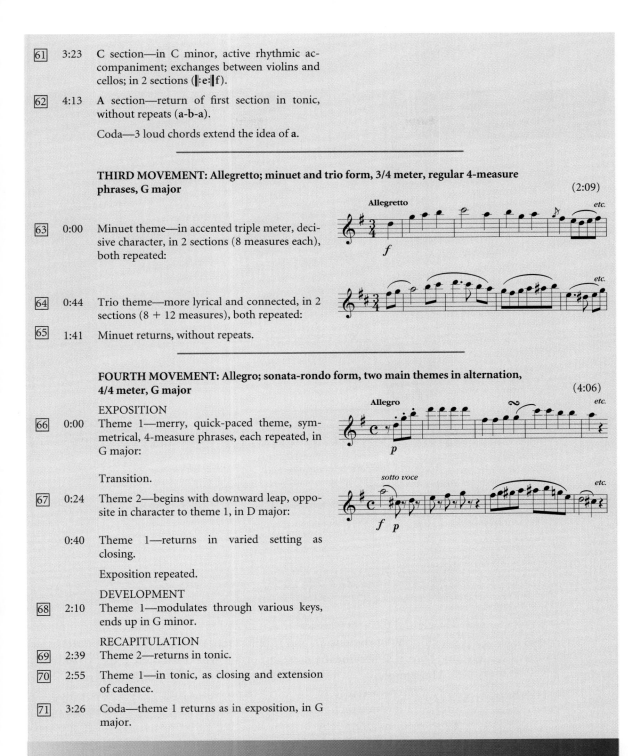

63	0:00	Minuet theme—in accented triple meter, decisive character, in 2 sections (8 measures each), both repeated:
64	0:44	Trio theme—more lyrical and connected, in 2 sections (8 + 12 measures), both repeated:
65	1:41	Minuet returns, without repeats.

FOURTH MOVEMENT: Allegro; sonata-rondo form, two main themes in alternation, 4/4 meter, G major   (4:06)

EXPOSITION

66	0:00	Theme 1—merry, quick-paced theme, symmetrical, 4-measure phrases, each repeated, in G major:
		Transition.
67	0:24	Theme 2—begins with downward leap, opposite in character to theme 1, in D major:
	0:40	Theme 1—returns in varied setting as closing.
		Exposition repeated.

DEVELOPMENT

| 68 | 2:10 | Theme 1—modulates through various keys, ends up in G minor. |

RECAPITULATION

69	2:39	Theme 2—returns in tonic.
70	2:55	Theme 1—in tonic, as closing and extension of cadence.
71	3:26	Coda—theme 1 returns as in exposition, in G major.

The Classical Symphony

45

The Nature of the Symphony

"I frequently compare a symphony with a novel in which the themes are characters. After we have made their acquaintance, we follow their evolution, the unfolding of their psychology."
—ARTHUR HONEGGER

HISTORICAL BACKGROUND

The central place in Classical instrumental music was held by the symphony, which grew in dimension and significance. With the final works of Mozart and Haydn, it became the most important type of absolute music of the era.

The symphony as it developed in the Classical period had its roots in the Italian opera overture of the early eighteenth century. This was a piece for orchestra in three sections: fast-slow-fast. First played to introduce an opera, these sections eventually became separate movements, to which the early German symphonists added a number of effects that were later taken over by Haydn and Mozart. One innovation was the use of a quick, aggressively rhythmic theme rising from low to high register with such speed that it came to be known as a *rocket theme* (as in the opening of Mozart's *Eine kleine Nachtmusik*). Equally important was the use of drawn-out *crescendos* slowly gathering force as they rose to a climax. Both these effects are generally credited to composers active at Mannheim, a German city along the Rhine River. With the addition of the minuet and trio, also a Mannheim contribution, the symphony paralleled the string quartet in following the four-movement sonata cycle.

THE CLASSICAL ORCHESTRA

The Classical masters established the orchestra as we know it today: an ensemble of the four instrumental families. The heart of the orchestra was the string choir. Woodwinds, used with great imagination, ably assisted the strings. The brass sustained the harmonies and contributed body to the sound mass, while the timpani supplied rhythmic life and vitality. The eighteenth-century orchestra numbered from thirty to forty players; thus the vol-

In this eighteenth-century performance scene, the orchestra is at the rear of the hall, arranged in two tiers, one seated and one standing. Concert in the Shoemakers' Hall. *Anonymous engraving, 1753.* (Zentralbibliothek, Zurich)

ume of sound was still more appropriate for the salon than the concert hall. (We have noted that it was near the end of the Classical period that musical life began its move toward the public concert.)

Haydn and Mozart created a dynamic style of orchestral writing in which all the instruments participated actively and each timbre could be heard. The interchange and imitation of themes among the various instrumental groups assumed the excitement of a witty conversation. The Classical orchestra also brought effects to absolute music that had long been familiar in the opera house, such as abrupt alternations of soft and loud, sudden accents, dramatic pauses, and the use of tremolo and pizzicato, all of which added drama and tension.

THE MOVEMENTS OF THE SYMPHONY

First movement

The first movement of a Classical symphony is an Allegro in sonata-allegro form, sometimes preceded by a slow introduction (especially in the symphonies of Haydn). Sonata-allegro form, we saw, is based on the opposition of two keys, made clearly audible by the contrast between two themes. However, Haydn sometimes based a sonata-allegro movement on a single theme, which was first heard in the tonic key and then in the contrasting key. Such a movement is referred to as *monothematic*. Mozart, on the other hand, preferred two themes with maximum contrast between them, which was frequently achieved through varied instrumentation; for example, the first theme might be played by the strings and the lyrical second theme by the woodwinds.

Second movement

The slow movement of a symphony is often a three-part form (**A-B-A**), a theme and variations, or a modified sonata-allegro (without a development section). Generally a Largo, Adagio, or Andante, this movement is in a key other than the tonic, with colorful orchestration that often emphasizes the woodwinds. The mood is essentially lyrical, and there is less development of themes here than in the opening movement.

Third movement

Third is the minuet and trio in triple meter, a graceful **A-B-A** form in the tonic key; as in the string quartet, its tempo is moderate. The trio is gentler in mood, with a moderately flowing melody and a prominent wind timbre. Beethoven's scherzo (a replacement for the minuet and trio), also in 3/4 time, is taken at a swifter pace.

Fourth movement

The fourth movement (finale), normally a vivacious Allegro molto or Presto in rondo or sonata-allegro form, is not only faster but also lighter than the first movement, and brings the cycle to a spirited ending. It often features themes with a folk-dance character, especially in Haydn's works. (We observed this characteristic in the last movement of his String Quartet Op. 76, No. 2.) We will see that with Beethoven's Fifth Symphony, however, the fourth movement was transformed into a triumphant finale in sonata-allegro form. (Remember too the drama that Brahms infused into the finale of his Third Symphony.)

Mozart's Symphony No. 40

Using Mozart's Symphony No. 40 in G minor as a model, we can observe how the movements of a particular composition conform to the description given above. Symphony No. 40 represents the mingling of Classical and Romantic elements that marked the final decades of the eighteenth century. The symphony is especially moving with its setting in the minor mode. (In Vienna, it is known as the *Romantic.*)

The first movement, in sonata-allegro form, opens with an intense theme for the violins that establishes the home key of G minor. This theme flowers out of a three-note motive that is genuinely symphonic in its capacity for growth. A vigorous transitional passage that sustains tension through a steady *crescendo* leads into the contrasting key: the relative major, B-flat. The second theme provides an area of comparative relaxation in the fast-paced drive of the movement. The codetta, in which we hear echoes of the basic motive, establishes the cadence in the contrasting key. (See Listening Guide 23.) *First movement*

The development, which modulates rapidly from one key to the next, concentrates on the three-note motive from the exposition. Mozart develops his material in a number of ways: by changing the melody, putting it in the bass with a new melody above it, combining motives, expanding them through a descending sequence, or turning them upside down (inversion). This section is crowned by the transition back to the home key, one of those extraordinary passages that only Mozart could have written.

The recapitulation follows the course of the exposition. The transition is expanded and circles about the home key, and the second theme is shifted to G minor rather than major, taking on a more tender tone. The coda energetically confirms the home key.

The second movement, an Andante in E-flat, is also in sonata-allegro form. With its graceful embellishments, this movement reflects the courtly refinement of the era. The third movement, a minuet and trio in G minor, recaptures the emotional tension and vigor of the first. The finale, Allegro assai (Very fast), is a compact sonata-allegro form, abrupt and commanding, with a first subject that represents the kind of rocket theme much favored in the Classical era. In all, this symphony is the work of a great artist functioning at the height of his powers. *Other movements*

Listening Guide 23

CD: Chr/Std 4/4–8
Cassette: Chr/Std 4A/1

MOZART: Symphony No. 40 in G minor,
First Movement   (8:12)

Date of work: 1788

Movements:

    I.   Allegro molto; sonata-allegro form, G minor
   II.   Andante; sonata-allegro form, E-flat major
  III.   Allegro moderato; minuet and trio form, G minor
  IV.   Allegro assai; sonata-allegro form, G minor

FIRST MOVEMENT: Allegro molto; sonata-allegro form, 2/4 meter, G minor

EXPOSITION

[4] 0:00   Theme 1—in G minor, vigorous melody, develops from 3-note motive (shaded), presented in violins:

       0:33   Bridge—vigorous passage, building in a
crescendo; modulation to key of relative
major (B-flat).

[5] 0:52   Theme 2—in B-flat major; lyrical, relaxed
melody in woodwinds and strings:

       1:28   Codetta—based on 3-note motive from
theme 1, leads to cadence in B-flat major
that closes exposition.

Exposition repeated.

DEVELOPMENT

[6] 4:04   Short, compact section built on 3-note motive in various guises; in new keys, in the bass
part (bassoon and low strings), and as focus
of string and woodwind dialogue, in inversion; then returns to tonic of G minor.

46

Haydn and the Symphony

"Can you see the notes behave like waves? Up and down they go!
Look, you can also see the mountains. You have to amuse yourself
sometimes after being serious so long."

The long career of Haydn spanned the decades when the Classical style was being formed. The contribution he made to his art—especially to the symphony and string quartet—was second to none.

HIS LIFE

Joseph Haydn (1732–1809) was born in Rohrau, a village in lower Austria, the son of a wheelwright. Folk song and dance were his natural heritage. The beauty of his voice secured him a place as a choirboy at St. Stephen's Cathedral in Vienna, where he remained until he was sixteen and his voice had broken (the natural change that occurs in an adolescent boy's voice). Haydn then settled himself in an attic in Vienna, managed to obtain a dilapidated harpsichord, and went about mastering the art of music. He made his living through teaching and accompanying, and often joined the bands of musicians who performed in the streets. In this way, the popular Viennese idiom entered his style along with the folk music he had absorbed in childhood.

Before long, Haydn attracted the notice of the music-loving aristocracy of Vienna. In 1761, when he was twenty-nine, he entered the service of the Esterházys, a family of enormously wealthy Hungarian princes famous for their patronage of the arts. He remained with this family for almost thirty years, the greater part of his creative career. Eszterháza, the palace of the Esterházys, was one of the most splendid in Europe, even boasting its own opera house,

Joseph Haydn

Esterházy patronage

259

A modern-day photograph of the Eszterháza Palace in Fertöd, Hungary.

and music played a central part in the constant round of festivities there. The musical establishment under the composer's direction included an orchestra, an opera company, a marionette theater, and a chapel. Haydn's life exemplifies the patronage system at its best.

By the time Haydn reached middle age, his music had brought him much fame. After the prince's death, he made two visits to England (1791–92 and 1794–95), where he conducted his works with phenomenal success. He died in 1809, revered by his countrymen and acknowledged throughout Europe as the premier musician of his time.

His Music

It was Haydn's historic role to help perfect the new instrumental music of the late eighteenth century. His terse, angular themes lent themselves readily to motivic development. Significant too, in his late symphonies, was his expansion of the orchestra's size and resources through greater emphasis on the brass, clarinets (new to the orchestra), and percussion (on the new percussion instruments, see CP 7). In his expressive harmony, structural logic, and endlessly varied moods, the mature Classical style seemed to be fully realized for the first time.

Principal Works

Orchestral music, including over 100 symphonies (6 *Paris* Symphonies, Nos. 82–87, 1785–86; 12 *London*, or *Salomon*, Symphonies, Nos. 93–104, 1791–95); concertos for violin, cello, harpsichord, and trumpet; divertimentos

Chamber music, including some 68 string quartets, piano trios, and divertimentos

Sacred vocal music, including 14 Masses (*Mass in Time of War*, 1796; *Lord Nelson* Mass, 1798); oratorios, including *Die sieben letzten Worte* (*The Seven Last Words of Christ*, 1796), *Die Schöpfung* (*The Creation*, 1798), and *Die Jahreszeiten* (*The Seasons*, 1801)

Dramatic music, including 14 operas

Keyboard music, including about 40 sonatas; songs, including folk song arrangements; secular choral music

As mentioned earlier, the string quartet occupied a central position in Haydn's output; his works in that genre are today among the best loved and most frequently performed in the repertory. We can understand why Mozart claimed, "It was from Haydn that I first learned the true way to compose quartets." **String quartets**

Like the quartets, the symphonies—over a hundred in number—extend across Haydn's entire career. Especially popular are the twelve written in the 1790s for his appearances in England. Known as the *London* Symphonies (or *Salomon* Symphonies, after the London impresario who commissioned them), they abound in effects generally associated with later composers: syncopation, sudden *crescendos* and accents, dramatic contrasts of soft and loud, daring modulations, and an imaginative plan in which each choir of instruments plays its allotted part. Haydn's symphonies, like his quartets, are the spiritual birthplace of Beethoven's style. **Symphonies**

Haydn was also a prolific composer of church music; fourteen Masses form the core of his output in this repertory. "At the thought of God," he said, "my heart leaps for joy and I cannot help my music doing the same." Among his oratorios, *The Creation* (which we will study), based on the biblical book of Genesis and John Milton's epic poem *Paradise Lost*, attained a popularity second only to that of Handel's *Messiah*. Haydn followed it with another work based on English literature—*The Seasons*, with a text drawn from the Scottish writer James Thomson's celebrated poem of the same name. Completed when the composer was approaching seventy, it was his last major work. **Church music**

Symphony No. 94 (*Surprise*)

The best-known of Haydn's symphonies, the *Surprise*, in G major, is one of the twelve works composed for his concerts in London. The orchestra that presented these compositions to the world consisted of about forty members: a full string section; two each of flutes, oboes, bassoons, French horns, and trumpets; and harpsichord and timpani. The work is subtitled *Surprise* because of a sudden *fortissimo* crashing chord in the slow movement, purposely intended to startle a dozing audience.

First movement

The work opens with a reflective slow introduction, followed by a forceful Vivace assai (very fast) in sonata-allegro form. The abrupt changes from *piano* to *forte* impart a dramatic quality to the movement and look ahead to Beethoven's emotion-charged style.

Second movement

The second movement, a great favorite in the symphonic literature, presents a theme and four variations. This memorable theme, with all the allure of a folk song, is set in two repeated sections of eight measures each (a *binary form*). The opening melody, in C major, is announced by the violins playing staccato (short, detached notes); the phrase is repeated *pianissimo* and ends abruptly in a loud crash—the "surprise" chord of the work's nickname. The end of the **B** section of the tune refers back to the opening phrase; the section is then repeated with flute and oboe accompanying the melody.

The variations that follow display Haydn's workmanship and wit. The first variation opens at a *forte* level, then retreats to *piano*, with violin arabesques and flutes entering in dialogue with the tune. The second variation, with its dramatic shift to C minor, is played *fortissimo* by all the woodwinds and strings. A solo violin leads into the third variation, which presents the melody in quick, repeated sixteenth notes. In the **B** section of this variation, the theme is heard beneath countermelodies woven by the solo flute and oboe. The final variation is marked by changes in dynamics (now at *fortissimo*); in register (a shift to high range); in orchestration (woodwinds, brass, and timpani take the melody); and in Haydn's employment of a new triplet rhythm in the first violins, heard against offbeat chords in the other strings. The **B** section introduces a new version of the melody based on an uneven, dotted rhythm. The coda brings a return to the opening theme with new harmonies below, quietly summing up the movement.

Third and fourth movements

The third movement, a minuet in G major, is a rollicking Allegro molto that leaves the elegant, courtly dance far behind in favor of a high-spirited, folklike romp. The finale, an energetic Allegro molto in sonata-allegro form, captures for its aristocratic listeners all the charm and humor of a traditional peasant dance. This work radiates the precise qualities that made the London symphonies so successful—innocent, appealing melodies within a masterful treatment of forms. One London critic summed up the symphony as "simple, profound, and sublime."

Listening Guide 24

CD: Chr/Std 3/1–7, Sh 2/9–15
Cassette: Chr/Std 3A/1, Sh 2A/3

HAYDN: Symphony No. 94 in G major (*Surprise*), Second Movement

(6:15)

Date of work: First performed 1792

Medium: Orchestra, with pairs of flutes, oboes, bassoons, French horns, and trumpets, along with strings and timpani

Movements:
I.   Adagio cantabile/Vivace assai; sonata-allegro form with slow introduction, G major
II. Andante; theme and variations form, C major
III. Menueto: Allegro molto; minuet and trio form, G major
IV. Allegro molto; sonata-allegro form, G major

SECOND MOVEMENT: Andante; theme and variations form, 2/4 meter, C major

1   0:00   Theme—folklike melody; in 2 parts, each repeated (binary)

A section—melody outlines triad, played staccato in strings; 8 measures:

A section repeated, *pianissimo*, followed by *fortissimo* chord.

2   0:35   B section—disjunct theme, ending in style of A, 8 measures:

B section repeated, with flutes and oboes.

3   1:08   Variation 1

A section begins with loud chord, has violin countermelody:

A repeated.

B, with decorated violin line.

B repeated.

4 2:13   Variation 2

A heard *fortissimo*, in C minor, (later shifts to major):

A repeated.

Development of A, with fast passages in strings, remains in minor.

Solo violins lead into Variation 3.

5 3:21   Variation 3

A in fast rhythm, heard in oboes:

A repeated in violins, with woodwind countermelody; low strings drop out:

B continues with violins and woodwinds alone.

B repeated.

6   4:25   Variation 4

> A heard in full orchestra, loud statement, includes trumpets and timpani; violins with fast passagework; accents on offbeats:

> A heard in violins in uneven, dotted rhythm, with accompaniment playing off-beats.
>
> B continues in uneven rhythms in strings.
>
> B repeated in loud statement by full orchestra.

     5:29   Bridge to coda; staccato pattern, followed by sustained chord.

7   5:42   Coda returns to A melody, with varied harmony underneath; ends quietly in C major.

47

Beethoven and the Symphony in Transition

"Freedom above all!"

Beethoven belonged to the generation that felt the full impact of the French Revolution. He created the music of a heroic age and, in sounds never to be forgotten, proclaimed a faith in the power of people to shape their own destinies.

Ludwig van Beethoven

Early years in Vienna

HIS LIFE

Ludwig van Beethoven (1770–1827) was born in Bonn, Germany, where his father and grandfather were singers at the court of the local prince, the elector Max Friedrich. The family situation was unhappy; his father was an alcoholic, and Ludwig at an early age was forced to support his mother and two younger brothers. At eleven and a half, he was assistant organist in the court chapel, and a year later he became harpsichordist in the court orchestra. A visit to Vienna in his seventeenth year provided him with an opportunity to play for Mozart. The youth improvised so brilliantly on a theme given to him that Mozart remarked to his friends, "Keep an eye on him—he will make a noise in the world some day."

Beethoven's talents as a pianist took the music-loving aristocracy by storm. He was welcomed in the great houses of Vienna by the powerful patrons whose names appear in the dedications of his works, such as Prince Lichnowsky, Prince Lobkowitz, and Count Razumovsky. In an era of revolution, this young genius forced the "princely rabble," as he called them, to receive him as an equal and friend. "It is good to move among the aristocracy," he observed, "but it is first necessary to make them respect you."

Beethoven functioned under a modified form of the patronage system. Though he was not attached to the court of a prince, the music-loving aristocrats of Vienna helped him in various ways—by paying him handsomely for lessons or presenting him with gifts. He was also aided by the emergence of a middle-class public and the growth of concert life and music publishing. At the age of thirty-one, he was able to write, "I have six or seven publishers for each of my works and could have more if I chose. No more bargaining. I name my terms, and they pay." A youthful exuberance pervades the first decade of his career, an almost arrogant consciousness of his strength. "Power is the morality of men who stand out from the mass, and it is also mine!" Thus spoke the individualist in the new era of individualism.

The onset of deafness

Then, fate struck in a vulnerable spot: Beethoven began to lose his hearing. His helplessness in the face of this affliction dealt a shattering blow to his pride: "Ah, how could I possibly admit an infirmity in the one sense that should have been more perfect in me than in others. A sense I once possessed in highest perfection. Oh, I cannot do it!" As deafness closed in on him—the first symptoms appeared when he was in his late twenties—it brought a sense of apartness from other people. On the advice of his doctors, he retired in 1802 to a summer resort outside Vienna called Heiligenstadt. There he was torn between the destructive forces in his soul and his desire to live and create: "But little more and I would have put an end to my life. Only art ... withheld me. Ah, it seemed impossible to leave the world until I had produced all that I felt called upon to produce, and so I endured this wretched existence." Beethoven slowly realized that art must give him the happiness that life withheld. The will to struggle reasserted itself; he fought his way back to health. The remainder of his career was spent in ceaseless effort to achieve his artistic goals. Biographers and painters have made familiar the image of the squat, sturdy figure (he was five foot four, the same height as that other conqueror of the age, Napoleon) walking hatless through Vienna, the bulging brow wrinkled in thought, stopping to jot down an idea in his sketchbook— an idea that, because he could not hear its sonorous beauty, he envisioned all the more vividly in his mind. A ride in an open carriage during severe weather brought on an attack of edema that proved fatal. Beethoven died in his fifty-seventh year, famous and revered.

Final years

His Music

Beethoven is the supreme architect in music. His genius found expression in the structural type of thinking embodied in the sonata and the symphony. The sketchbooks in which he worked out his ideas show how they gradually reached their final shape.

Beethoven's compositional activity fell into three periods. The first reflected the Classical elements he had inherited from Haydn and Mozart. The middle period saw the appearance of characteristics more closely associated with the nineteenth century: strong dynamic contrasts, explosive accents, and longer movements. Beethoven expanded the dimensions of the first movement, especially the coda, and like Haydn and Mozart, he made the development section the dynamic center of sonata-allegro form. In his hands, the slow movement acquired a hymnlike character, the essence of Beethovenian pathos. The scherzo became a movement of rhythmic energy spanning many moods; his goal here was powerful expression rather than elegance. And he enlarged the finale into a movement comparable in size and scope to the first, ending the symphony on a triumphant note.

Three compositional periods

In his third period—the years of the final piano sonatas and string quartets—Beethoven used more chromatic harmonies and developed a skeletal language from which all nonessentials were rigidly pared away. It was a language that transcended his time. To a listener who asked him if one of his more advanced quartets could even be considered music, he replied, "Not for you. For a later time."

The symphony provided Beethoven with the ideal medium through which to address his public. His nine symphonies are conceived on a scale too large for the aristocratic salon; they demand the concert hall.

Symphonies

The first two symphonies stand closest to the two Classical masters who preceded him, but with his Third Symphony, the *Eroica*, Beethoven achieved

In His Own Words

I carry my thoughts about with me for a long time . . . before writing them down. . . . once I have grasped a theme, I shall not forget it even years later. I change many things, discard others, and try again and again until I am satisfied; then, in my head . . . [the work] rises, it grows, I hear and see the image in front of me from every angle . . . and only the labor of writing it down remains. . . . I turn my ideas into tones that resound, roar, and rage until at last they stand before me in the form of notes.

his own mature style. The work was originally dedicated to Napoleon, who seemed at first to represent the spirit of revolution and freedom. When the news came that Napoleon had proclaimed himself emperor, Beethoven became disenchanted. "He too is just like any other! Now he will trample on the rights of man and serve nothing but his own ambition." The embittered composer tore up the dedicatory page of the just-completed work and renamed it "Heroic Symphony to celebrate the memory of a great man."

The Fifth Symphony is popularly viewed as the archetype of the genre, and the Seventh rivals it in universal appeal. The finale of the Ninth, or *Choral* Symphony, in which vocal soloists and chorus join the orchestra, is a setting of Schiller's *Ode to Joy*, a ringing prophecy of the time when "all people will be brothers."

Concertos and piano sonatas

The concerto offered Beethoven an ideal form in which to combine virtuosity with symphonic structure. His Violin Concerto displays the technical abilities of the soloist within a much enlarged form, and his five piano concertos both coincided with and encouraged the rising popularity of the instrument. The piano itself occupied a central position in Beethoven's art. His thirty-two sonatas form an indispensable part of its literature, whether for the amateur pianist or the concert artist. The are aptly called the pianist's New Testament (the Old being *The Well-Tempered Clavier* of Bach).

Beethoven wrote a great deal of chamber music, the string quartet lying closest to his heart. The six quartets of Opus 18 are the first in a series that extended throughout his entire career. His supreme achievements in this genre are the last five quartets, which, together with the Grand Fugue, Op. 133, occupied the final years of his life. In these works, as in the last five piano sonatas, the master employs a searching, introspective style, far from the exuberance of his youth.

String quartets

Beethoven also made significant contributions to vocal music. His one opera, *Fidelio*, centers on wifely devotion, human freedom, and the defeat of those who would destroy that freedom. The *Missa solemnis* (*Solemn Mass*), which transcends the limits of any specific creed or faith, ranks in importance with the Ninth Symphony and the final quartets. In his manuscript for the Kyrie of the Mass, the composer wrote a sentence that applies to the whole of his music: "From the heart . . . may it find its way to the heart."

Vocal music

The Fifth Symphony

Perhaps the best-known of all symphonies, Beethoven's Symphony No. 5 in C minor, Op. 67, is also the most concentrated expression of what we have come to call Beethovenian. The first movement, in a sonata-allegro form marked Allegro con brio (lively, with vigor), springs out of the rhythmic idea of "three shorts and a long" that dominates the entire symphony. This idea, the most compact and commanding gesture in the whole symphonic litera-

First movement

Facsimile of Beethoven's Fifth Symphony.

Cultural Perspective 6

THE COMPOSER HEARD 'ROUND THE WORLD

Ludwig van Beethoven stands today as the most popular composer of art music in the world. What accounts for the universality of this master? Clearly, his wide acceptance results from more than the powerful influence that Western culture has exerted globally.

Beethoven's Fifth Symphony was recognized in its day as a masterpiece. Premiered in Vienna (December 2, 1808) at a four-hour concert of his music, the work was immediately hailed by one reviewer, the German composer Johann Friedrich Reichardt, as "a great symphony"—not a typical critic's reaction to new music. Although the general public might not have fully understood the master's works, they revered him nevertheless—some twenty thousand people turned out for his funeral in Vienna!

Beethoven represented the newly emerging "free artist," who lived from the sale of his works rather than the bounty of a single prince. In his lifetime, his music was published widely, from Russia to the United States, and emerging music societies around the globe performed his orchestral and choral compositions. The Philharmonic Society of New York (the oldest continuing orchestra in the United States, founded in 1842) opened its first public program with the "Grand Symphony in C minor (the 5th)" by Beethoven. The nineteenth-century composer Hector Berlioz, on first hearing the master's symphonies in 1828, claimed that "Beethoven opened before me a new world of music, as Shakespeare had revealed a new universe of poetry." Berlioz then convinced his teacher, Jean-François Lesueur, to attend a performance of the Fifth Symphony at the Paris Conservatory. Lesueur's reaction was immediate: "Let me get out. I must have some air. It's amazing! Wonderful! I was so moved and disturbed that when I emerged from the box and attempted to put on my hat, I couldn't find my head."

The famous opening motive of the Fifth Symphony—three shorts and a long—has inspired a variety of interpretations, the most popular being "fate knocking at the door." During the Second World War, the rhythm was associated with its Morse code meaning of "V" for victory, and transmitted via radio waves over thousands of miles.

Perhaps even more popular is Beethoven's great Ninth Symphony, with its famous choral finale—commonly known as the *Ode to Joy*—set to inspirational words of unity among peoples by the German poet Friedrich von Schiller. This musical work has exerted such strong appeal that it has been used as a rallying cry for widely divergent philosophies, including democracy, totalitarianism, and fascism. In Japan, the piece is traditionally performed each December 31 with a colossal choir, to bring the year to a close.

The youth of the early rock era first rejected this style of art music, as Chuck Berry's 1956 hit *Roll Over, Beethoven* demonstrated, but even this vernacular music has succumbed to the timelessness of Beethoven: several disco settings of the Fifth Symphony have been produced, including the popular *Hooked on Classics*, and a karaoke version of the Ninth Symphony finale is now available in Japan. (*Karaoke*, a Japanese word meaning "empty orchestra," is a popular nightclub entertainment in which customers sing the melody to an accompanying soundtrack.) Today, Beethoven's music can be heard in commercials and movie soundtracks including the entertaining video *Beethoven Lives Upstairs* (1992) and the recent art film *Immortal Beloved* (1994). These are further testament to the continued popularity of this ageless musician.

Terms to Note:

Philharmonic
karaoke

Suggested Listening:

Beethoven: Symphony No. 9, Fourth
    Movement
Hooked on Classics

Beethoven's death, unlike Haydn's and Mozart's, did not pass unnoticed. Thousands of people from all walks of life followed his funeral procession to the cemetery. A watercolor by **Franz Stöber.** (Beethoven-Haus, Bonn)

ture, is pursued with an almost terrifying single-mindedness in this dramatic movement. In an extended coda, the basic rhythm reveals yet a new fund of explosive energy. (See Listening Guide 25.)

Second movement   The second movement is a serene theme and variations, with two melodic ideas. In the course of the movement, Beethoven exploits his two themes with all the procedures of variation—changes in melodic outline, harmony, rhythm, tempo, dynamics, register, key, mode, and type of accompaniment.

Third movement   Third in the cycle of movements is the scherzo, which opens with a rocket theme introduced by cellos and double basses. After the gruff, humorous trio in C major, the scherzo returns in a modified version, followed by a transitional passage to the final movement in which the memorable four-note motive of the first movement is sounded by the timpani.

Fourth movement   In the monumental fourth movement, composed in sonata-allegro form, Beethoven once again brings back three shorts and a long, making this symphony an example of *cyclical form* (a unifying procedure in which material from earlier movements returns). At the end of the extended coda, the tonic chord is proclaimed triumphantly by the orchestra again and again.

Beethoven's career bridged the transition from the old society to the new. His music is the expression of a titanic force, the affirmation of an all-conquering will.

Listening Guide 25   MW   CD: Chr/Std 4/35–59, Sh 2/16–40
Cassette: Chr/Std 4B/2–4, Sh 2B/1–3

BEETHOVEN: Symphony No. 5 in C minor, Op. 67   (32:02)

Date of work: 1807–8

Movements: 4

FIRST MOVEMENT: Allegro con brio; sonata-allegro form, 2/4 meter, C minor   (7:31)

EXPOSITION

[35] 0:00 Theme 1—based on famous
4-note motive, in C minor:

0:06 Motive treated sequentially:

| | 0:43 | Expansion from 4-note motive; horns modulate to key of second theme: |  |

| 36 | 0:46 | Theme 2—more lyrical, in woodwinds, in E-flat major; heard against rhythm of 4-note motive: |  |

| | 1:07 | Closing theme—descending staccato passage, then 4-note motive. | |

Repeat of exposition.

DEVELOPMENT

| 37 | 2:54 | Beginning of development, announced by horns. | |

| | 3:05 | Manipulation of 4-note motive through a descending sequence: | 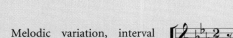 |

| | 3:16 | Melodic variation, interval filled in and inverted: |  |

| | 4:13 | Expansion through repetition; leads into recapitulation: | 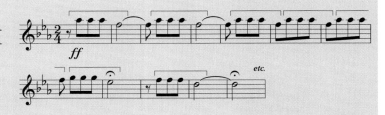 |

RECAPITULATION

| 38 | 4:18 | Theme 1—in C minor, followed by brief oboe solo in cadenza style. | |

39	5:15	Theme 2—returns in C major.
	5:51	Closing theme.
40	5:58	Coda—extended treatment of 4-note motive.

SECOND MOVEMENT: Andante con moto; theme and variations form, with two themes, 3/8, meter, A-flat major

(10:13)

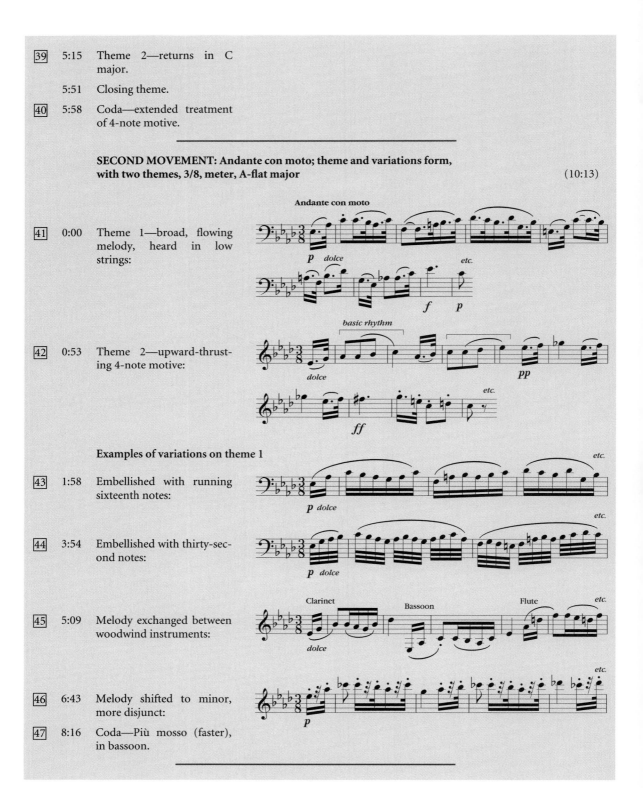

| 41 | 0:00 | Theme 1—broad, flowing melody, heard in low strings: |
| 42 | 0:53 | Theme 2—upward-thrusting 4-note motive: |

Examples of variations on theme 1

43	1:58	Embellished with running sixteenth notes:
44	3:54	Embellished with thirty-second notes:
45	5:09	Melody exchanged between woodwind instruments:
46	6:43	Melody shifted to minor, more disjunct:
47	8:16	Coda—Più mosso (faster), in bassoon.

THIRD MOVEMENT: Allegro; scherzo and trio form, 3/4 meter, C minor (5:33)

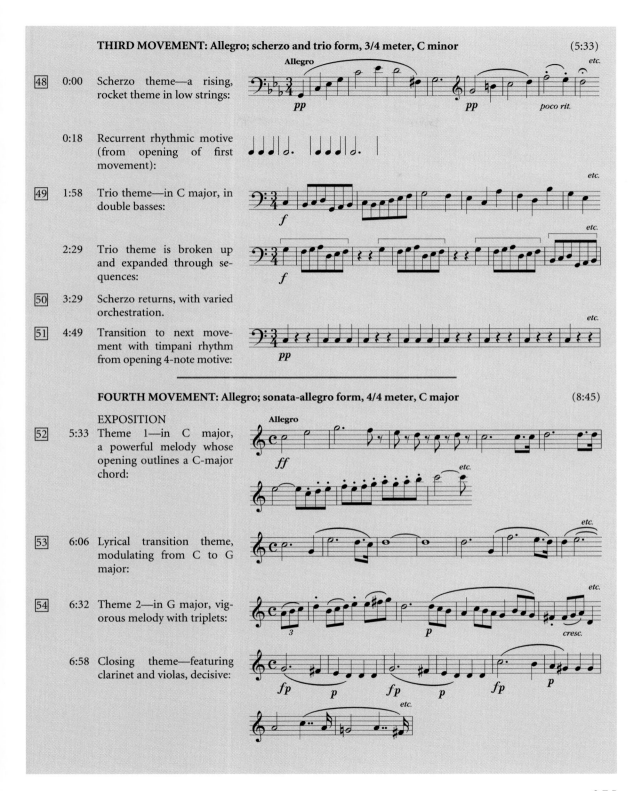

48	0:00	Scherzo theme—a rising, rocket theme in low strings:
	0:18	Recurrent rhythmic motive (from opening of first movement):
49	1:58	Trio theme—in C major, in double basses:
	2:29	Trio theme is broken up and expanded through sequences:
50	3:29	Scherzo returns, with varied orchestration.
51	4:49	Transition to next movement with timpani rhythm from opening 4-note motive:

FOURTH MOVEMENT: Allegro; sonata-allegro form, 4/4 meter, C major (8:45)

EXPOSITION

52	5:33	Theme 1—in C major, a powerful melody whose opening outlines a C-major chord:
53	6:06	Lyrical transition theme, modulating from C to G major:
54	6:32	Theme 2—in G major, vigorous melody with triplets:
	6:58	Closing theme—featuring clarinet and violas, decisive:

DEVELOPMENT

55 7:29 Much modulation and free rhythmic treatment; brings back 4-note motive (3 short and a long) from first movement.

56 9:10 Brief recurrence of scherzo.

RECAPITULATION

57 9:43 Theme 1, in C major.

58 10:50 Theme 2, in C major.

Closing theme.

59 11:47 Coda—long extension.

The Eighteenth-Century Concerto and Sonata

48

The Classical Concerto

"Give me the best instrument in Europe, but listeners who under-stand nothing or do not wish to understand and who do not feel with me in what I am playing, and all my pleasure is spoilt."
—W. A. MOZART

THE MOVEMENTS OF THE CONCERTO

In the early eighteenth century, the word "concerto" implied a mixing to-gether of contrasting forces, and could refer to a solo group and orchestra or to a solo instrument and orchestra. The Classical era shifted the emphasis to the latter combination, with the piano and violin the most common solo in-struments.

The three movements of the Classical concerto follow the fast-slow-fast pattern already established (see Chapter 26). You will recall that one charac-teristic feature of the concerto is the *cadenza*, a fanciful solo passage in the manner of an improvisation that interrupts the movement toward the end.

Cadenza

The cadenza came out of a time when improvisation was an important element in art music, as it still is in jazz. In the solo concerto, the cadenza has a dramatic effect: the orchestra falls silent, and the soloist launches into a free play of fantasy on one or more themes of the movement.

First movement   The Classical concerto begins with a first-movement form that adapts the principles of ritornello procedure (a *ritornello,* developed in the Baroque era, is a recurring musical passage, or theme) to those of sonata-allegro form. The movement usually opens with an orchestral exposition, or ritornello, in the tonic key, often presenting several themes. A second exposition, for the solo instrument and orchestra, now makes the necessary key change to the dominant. The soloist often plays elaborated versions of the themes first heard in the orchestra, and can add new material as well. The development section offers ample opportunity for solo virtuosic display, in dialogue with the orchestra. In the recapitulation, the soloist and orchestra bring back the themes in the tonic. The solo cadenza, a brilliant improvisation, appears near the end of the movement, and a coda brings the movement to a close with a strong affirmation of the home key. First-movement concerto form is sometimes described as a sonata-allegro form with a double exposition.

Second movement   The slow and lyrical second movement, generally an Andante, Adagio, or Largo, features the soloist in songlike melody. This movement is often composed in a key that lies close to the tonic. Thus, if the first movement is in C major, the second might well be in F major (the subdominant), four steps above.

Finale   A typical finale is an Allegro molto or Presto (very fast) that is shorter than the first movement and in rondo form, which could be modified to adopt some developmental features of sonata-allegro form. This movement may contain its own cadenza that calls for virtuoso playing and brings the piece to an exciting end.

Mozart's Piano Concerto in G major, K. 453

Mozart played a crucial role in the development of the piano concerto. His concertos, written primarily as display pieces for his own public performances, abound in the brilliant flourishes and ceremonious gestures characteristic of eighteenth-century music.

During 1784, Mozart, who was in great demand as a pianist, wrote six piano concertos. One of these works, the Concerto in G major, K. 453, was composed for a nineteen-year-old student of his, Barbara von Ployer.

First movement   The first movement, marked Allegro, opens with an orchestral ritornello; the piano then ushers in its own exposition, which includes a new theme. An orchestral tutti leads to the development section, and the ritornello is heard again in the recapitulation. This concerto, notable for its graceful writing for

Mozart's piano, now housed in the Mozarteum in Salzburg. Notice how the white and black keys are reversed in color.

piano and woodwinds, is usually performed today with a cadenza that Mozart wrote for this work. (For analysis, see Listening Guide 26.)

The ensuing slow movement features a kind of double exposition format that is more typical of concerto first movements. This highly lyrical Andante in 3/4, remarkable for its variety of woodwind color, is marked by true Mozartean sentiment.

Second movement

The closing movement, an Allegretto in 2/2, or cut time, is in theme and variations form. The theme is a graceful, dancelike tune made up of two short phrases, each of which is repeated. This clear-cut, highly symmetrical formation makes the binary structure easy to hear. The five variations that follow set the piano and orchestra in a dialogue of melodic, rhythmic, and harmonic elaborations on the highly appealing theme. (Mozart was so fond of this tune that he taught it to his pet starling, who consistently missed one note and got the rhythm wrong.) The movement ends with a Presto coda that introduces new material and displays dazzling piano writing.

Third movement

Listening Guide 26

CD: Chr/Std 3/15–38, Sh 2/41–51
Cassette: Chr/Std 3A/3–5, Sh 2A/4

MOZART: Piano Concerto in G major, K. 453   (29:41)

Date of work: 1784

Movements: 3

FIRST MOVEMENT: Allegro; first-movement concerto form, 4/4 meter, G major   (11:28)

ORCHESTRAL RITORNELLO, in G major

[15] 0:00   Theme 1—refined theme in violins, with woodwind figurations:

0:27   Transitional theme—forceful, in full orchestra.

[16] 1:00   Theme 2—gently undulating theme in violins, answered in woodwinds:

1:40   Closing theme—in full orchestra.

SOLO EXPOSITION

[17] 2:08   Theme 1—piano enters with sweep into main theme, decorated, in G major; woodwind accompaniment; scales and arpeggio figurations in piano.

2:42   Transition theme—orchestral ritornello; piano with decorative part; modulates to key of dominant.

[18] 3:10   Piano theme—introduced by piano alone in D major, then presented in woodwinds:

[19] 4:00   Theme 2—in piano, with string accompaniment.

4:55   Closing—decisive, in D major.

DEVELOPMENT

[20] 5:15   Virtuosic piano part, references to piano theme, runs and arpeggios against woodwinds; various modulations, leading back to tonic.

RECAPITULATION

21   6:35   Theme 1—returns in strings, with woodwind accompaniment; piano joins in with decorated version of theme.

       7:02   Transition theme—forceful, in full orchestra.

22   7:35   Piano theme, solo, in G major, more decorated, with light orchestral accompaniment.

23   8:25   Theme 2—in piano, then in woodwinds, now in G major.

24   9:32   Cadenza—solo piano, variations on earlier themes; ends on dominant.

25   10:47   Closing—final ritornello, in G major.

(Shorter recordings stop here.)

SECOND MOVEMENT: Andante; first-movement concerto form, 3/4 meter, C major   (10:30)

ORCHESTRAL EXPOSITION

26   0:00   Theme 1—gentle, quiet idea in strings, ends with fermata (hold):

Answer by woodwinds in lyrical dialogue:

27   1:16   Theme 2—alternates *forte* in strings with *piano* in woodwinds, in G major.

       1:39   Closing—chromatic line, in strings and woodwinds.

SOLO EXPOSITION

28   2:00   Theme 1—solo piano, in C major; answer in dramatic statement in G minor:

Idea of theme 2 in alternation of soft and loud statements; woodwind dialogue heard near opening, extended by piano.

Closing—chromatic line, extended by piano with cadential trill.

281

DEVELOPMENT

29   4:11   Theme 1 in G major—in woodwinds; answered by dramatic piano statement reminiscent of solo exposition; short modulatory section, with virtuosic piano line; orchestral *crescendo* brings return to C major.

RECAPITULATION

30   5:49   Theme 1—opening in solo piano; answer with *forte,* disjunct theme, E-flat major; woodwind dialogue returns; loud/soft alternating theme returns.

31   7:57   Cadenza—solo piano, ends with cadential trill.

           Coda—woodwinds play theme 1, which is then decorated in solo piano, followed by soft statement of closing theme.

THIRD MOVEMENT: Allegretto, Presto; theme and variations form, 2/2 meter, G major   (7:43)

32   0:00   Theme 1—elegant, dancelike tune in full orchestra; theme in 2 sections (8 measures each), each repeated (‖:a:‖:b:‖)

        a section:

        0:23   **b section:**

33   0:46   Variation 1—solo piano, with melodic ornamentation, each part of theme repeated:

34   1:32   Variation 2—woodwinds introduce each part of theme, repeated by orchestra over piano figurations in triplets.

| | 35 | 2:17 | Variation 3—solo woodwind instruments in dialogue, answered by piano; more lyrical than opening. |

35 | 2:17 | Variation 3—solo woodwind instruments in dialogue, answered by piano; more lyrical than opening.

36 | 3:10 | Variation 4—strings introduce theme, now in mysterious mood in minor key; answered by syncopated, chromatic piano line:

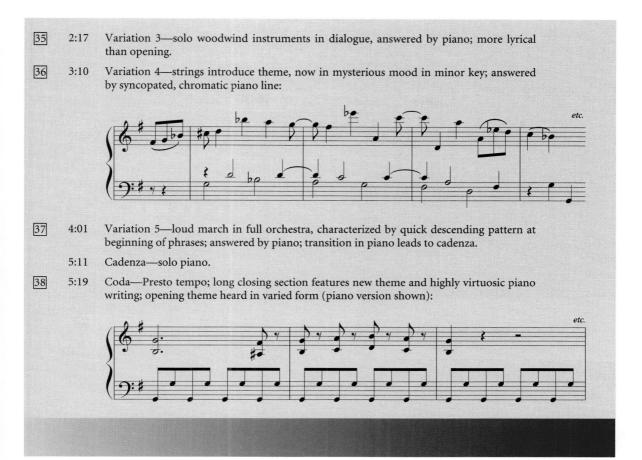

37 | 4:01 | Variation 5—loud march in full orchestra, characterized by quick descending pattern at beginning of phrases; answered by piano; transition in piano leads to cadenza.

5:11 | Cadenza—solo piano.

38 | 5:19 | Coda—Presto tempo; long closing section features new theme and highly virtuosic piano writing; opening theme heard in varied form (piano version shown):

Beethoven's Violin Concerto

As a great public form of musical communication, the concerto interested Beethoven throughout the first and second periods of his creative career. In the third period, his most introspective, it disappeared from his output.

The Violin Concerto in D major, dating from 1806, is one of his most lyrical works. In this highly demanding piece, which shows off the violin's resources brilliantly, Beethoven greatly expanded the proportions of the form and displayed the rich, colorful orchestral writing typical of his middle period. At its first performance in 1806, one Viennese critic reported that the concerto "was received with exceptionally great applause."

The opening Allegro ma non troppo (fast, but not too fast) is a huge first-movement concerto form built on a five-note motive announced by the timpani in the very first measure. Characteristic are the abrupt shifts from major to minor, the lyrical use of the violin's upper register, and Beethoven's inter-

First movement

weaving of the solo part with the orchestra. The songful second theme, which moves stepwise up the scale, has been aptly described as heavenly.

Second movement   The second movement, a Larghetto in G major, is set in a theme and variations form. Muted strings establish a serene stillness, with the solo violin weaving a fanciful embroidery over the orchestral part. A short cadenza leads directly into the finale.

Third movement   The last movement is an energetic rondo, growing out of another five-note motive. This main idea, alternating with two secondary themes, drives the movement forward with endless gusto. Here we can see that rondo form, with its repetition of themes (outlined **A-B-A-C-A-B-A**), is really an outgrowth of the ritornello procedure of the Baroque. This rondo never lets up; on the contrary, it builds tension steadily to its breathtaking coda. (See Listening Guide 27.)

Listening Guide 27

CD: Chr/Std 4/27–34
Cassette: Chr/Std 4A/5

BEETHOVEN: Violin Concerto in D major, Op. 61, Third Movement   (9:14)

Date of work: 1806

Movements:
   I.   Allegro ma non troppo; first-movement concerto form, 4/4 meter, D major
   II. Larghetto; theme and variations form, 4/4 meter, G major
   III. Allegro; rondo form, 6/8 meter, D major

THIRD MOVEMENT: Allegro; rondo (A-B-A-C-A-B-A)

| 27 | 0:00 | A section—lilting theme in solo violin, D major: |

Last motive answered by orchestra, repeated 2 octaves higher by violin; full orchestra with theme, now ponderous.

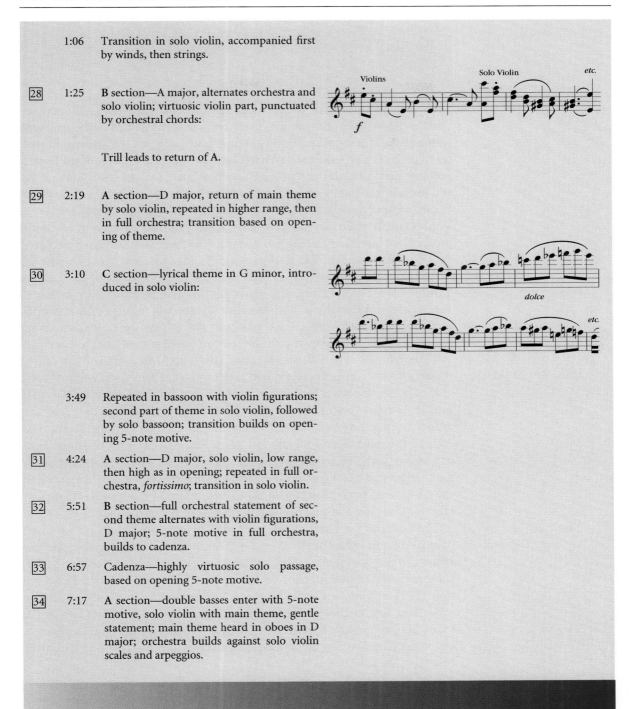

1:06   Transition in solo violin, accompanied first by winds, then strings.

28   1:25   **B section**—A major, alternates orchestra and solo violin; virtuosic violin part, punctuated by orchestral chords:

Trill leads to return of A.

29   2:19   **A section**—D major, return of main theme by solo violin, repeated in higher range, then in full orchestra; transition based on opening of theme.

30   3:10   **C section**—lyrical theme in G minor, introduced in solo violin:

3:49   Repeated in bassoon with violin figurations; second part of theme in solo violin, followed by solo bassoon; transition builds on opening 5-note motive.

31   4:24   **A section**—D major, solo violin, low range, then high as in opening; repeated in full orchestra, *fortissimo*; transition in solo violin.

32   5:51   **B section**—full orchestral statement of second theme alternates with violin figurations, D major; 5-note motive in full orchestra, builds to cadenza.

33   6:57   **Cadenza**—highly virtuosic solo passage, based on opening 5-note motive.

34   7:17   **A section**—double basses enter with 5-note motive, solo violin with main theme, gentle statement; main theme heard in oboes in D major; orchestra builds against solo violin scales and arpeggios.

FAMOUS WOMEN VIRTUOSOS OF THE EIGHTEENTH CENTURY

Since eighteenth-century society deemed it proper that noble and upper-middle-class women study music, many became highly skilled amateurs. Some women were able to make a living as music teachers, and a few attained the status of professional performers. We will later encounter the career of the French Baroque harpsichordist/composer Elisabeth-Claude Jacquet de la Guerre, and will learn of the highly acclaimed performances of the all-female orchestra at Venice's Ospedale della Pietà, where the eighteenth-century composer Antonio Vivaldi taught violin. Several Venetian-trained violinists went on to successful professional careers, including Anna Maria della Pietà, who became a teacher at the Ospedale, where she had studied as a girl, and Maddalena Lombardini, who toured extensively as a soloist. A student of the great violin virtuoso Giuseppe Tartini (1692–1770), Lombardini played his demanding works "with such perfection it is said that she is his descendant," according to one critic. Her technique was so excellent that she was sought out to play the newest, most demanding pieces of her day, and she herself composed several violin concertos.

Maria Anna Mozart

Three women in particular—all associated with Mozart—stand out as impressive keyboard players of the late eighteenth century. Maria Anna Mozart (1751–1829), known as Nannerl, was an accomplished pianist who as a child toured extensively with her brother Wolfgang, performing concertos and four-hand piano works. Her father noted that Nannerl, at age twelve, was "one of the most skillful players in Europe," able to perform the most difficult works with "incredible precision," and that she played "so beautifully that everyone is talking about her and admiring her execution." Later, when she had retired from professional life to raise a family, her brother wrote several works for her and sent his piano cadenzas to her to try out.

Maria Theresa von Paradis

The career of the blind musician Maria Theresa von Paradis (1759–1808) parallels that of her friend Mozart. An excellent pianist and organist, she was renowned for her remarkable musical memory, which was able to retain some sixty different concertos that she prepared for an extended European tour (1783–86). Mozart wrote his Piano Concerto in B-flat, K. 456, for her in 1784, and her teacher, the court composer Antonio Salieri (1750–1825), wrote his only organ concerto in her honor. Paradis was a composer herself, but many of her works, including two concertos, a piano trio, and a number of sonatas, have been lost.

Barbara von Ployer

The third gifted pianist was Barbara von Ployer, a young student of Mozart's for whom he wrote two concertos, including the G-major work we just studied. Mozart was so proud of his talented student that he invited the composer Giovanni Paisiello (1740–1816) to the premiere of the concerto.

He wrote to his father, "I am fetching Paisiello in my carriage, as I want him to hear both my pupil and my compositions."

The public prominence achieved by these women performers was unusual for the era. However, the many engravings and paintings of the time illustrating music-making scenes make it clear that women participated frequently in performances at home, in aristocratic salons, and at court.

49

The Classical Sonata

THE MOVEMENTS OF THE SONATA

The sonata, as Haydn, Mozart, and their successors understood the term, was an instrumental work for one or two instruments, consisting of three or four contrasting movements. The movements followed the basic sonata cycle described earlier in the discussions of string quartet, symphony, and concerto.

In the Classical era, the sonata—for piano solo or for two instruments—became an important genre for amateurs in the home, as well as for composers performing their own music at concerts. In duo sonatas for violin or cello and piano, the piano initially took the leading role, with the string instrument acting as accompaniment. Mozart and Beethoven, however, began to treat the two instruments as equal partners. And the solo piano sonatas of these two composers are the most significant in the literature.

Mozart's Piano Sonata in A major, K. 331

One of Mozart's most delightful piano works is the Sonata in A major, K. 331 (1783). This unusual sonata is set in three movements, but resembles a four-movement structure that is lacking its first movement. Rather than beginning with a sonata-allegro form, the work opens with a lilting set of variations in 6/8 meter on a Czech folk song (*Hořela, líps, hořela*). The second movement is a minuet and trio that sounds anything but dancelike. Highly lyrical with a broken chord accompaniment, it explores new realms of chromatic harmonies. In style, this movement looks forward to the nocturne, a solo piano mood piece popular in the early Romantic era.

The sonata closes with a rondo labeled "alla turca" that evokes the percussive sound of the Turkish Janissary band then popular in Vienna. (See CP 7 for a discussion of Turkish influences on Western music.) A brassy quick-time march in

EAST MEETS WEST: TURKISH INFLUENCES ON THE VIENNESE CLASSICS

We are all attracted and excited by the new and the mysterious. The public of eighteenth-century Vienna turned to the East to satisfy its appetite for the unusual. Over the centuries, there had been ample opportunities, most of them military, for cultural interaction between the Austrian Hapsburg Empire and the large and powerful Ottoman Empire, of which Turkey was a part. When the dust from their hostile skirmishes had settled, more civil relations were established. Viennese cuisine smacked increasingly of Eastern spices, fashions hinted at an Eastern look, and the city's music took on a distinctly martial sound, derived from the Turkish Janissary, or military, bands.

The Janissary band originated in Turkey in the fourteenth century as an elite corps of mounted musicians composed of players of the shawm and bass drum. (We will see later that these instruments were introduced into western Europe as a result of the Crusades and the establishment of early trade routes.) In the seventeenth century, the trumpet, small kettledrums, cymbals, and bell trees were added to this ceremonial ensemble, producing a loud and highly percussive effect. The Turkish sound captured the imagination of the Viennese masters, who attempted to re-create it in their orchestral and theatrical works. Haydn wrote three "military" symphonies, Beethoven composed three orchestral works with

Turkish percussion (including his monumental Symphony No. 9), and Mozart and Haydn, among others, used this military sound in their operas. The influence was felt even in piano music—notably in Mozart's appealing Rondo alla turca from his Sonata in A major, which we studied. So popular was this style that some nineteenth-century pianos featured a "Janissary pedal" to add percussive effects.

Although the fascination with Turkish music proved to be a passing fancy, it nevertheless affected the makeup of the Western orchestra by leading to the establishment of percussion instruments of Turkish origin (bass drum, cymbals, bells) as permanent members of the ensemble. It's hard to imagine an orchestra today without them! The Turkish Janissary ensemble also had a significant impact on the development of the military band in the West and is the direct antecedent of the modern Shriners' band (Ancient Arabic Order of Nobles of the Mystic Shrine), frequently seen in parades today.

Beethoven was fascinated by another Turkish musical tradition—this one a mystical religious ceremony to which he alluded in his incidental music for the stage work *The Ruins of Athens* (1811). The ceremony derives from one of the sects of Islam, that of the Mevlevis, who were famous for their whirling dervish ritual: dancing in a circle with a slow, controlled spinning motion as a part of their religious experience. This ceremony was sung to the accompaniment of flute, lute, and percussion, including kettledrum and cymbals. Beethoven's *Chorus of Whirling Dervishes*, a pale imitation of the original, is an example of exoticism that has been filtered through Western culture. Both the Janissary band and the whirling dervish ceremony are obsolete in modern-day Turkey, except as tourist attractions. The term "whirling dervish"—implying one who twists and turns, like a restless child—has, however, endured in the West.

Terms to Note:

Janissary band
whirling dervish

Suggested Listening:

Turkish music (Janissary ensemble)
Mozart: Rondo alla turca, from Piano Sonata in A, K. 331
Haydn: Symphony No. 100, *Military*, Second Movement
Beethoven: Symphony No. 9, Fourth Movement
Mozart: *The Abduction from the Seraglio*, Overture
Beethoven, *The Ruins of Athens*, Turkish March

A Turkish Janissary band featuring mounted players of trumpets (boru), cymbals (zil), cylindrical drums (davul), and kettledrums (kös). Miniature from The Festival Book of Vehbi, *written and illuminated for Ahmed III (r. 1703–30).* (Topkapi Sarayi Museum, Istanbul)

An eighteenth-century engraving dated 1773 showing a typical violin-piano duo. (Bibliothèque Nationale, Paris)

A minor, this movement features swirling sixteenth-note figurations, a leaping melody, a drone bass with repeated chords, and exaggerated beats—all meant to suggest the jangling of bell trees, cymbals, and triangles that accompanied Turkish soldiers on parade. The minor mode also gives a foreign flavor to the work, whose refrain returns in A major (see Listening Guide 28 for an analysis).

Mozart employed this "Turkish" color in several other works. His Violin Concerto No. 5 is known as the "Turkish" because of the character of the rondo-finale, and his comic opera *The Abduction from the Seraglio* features a plot dealing with Europeans held captive by a Turkish general, offering many opportunities for "exotic" musical color.

Listening Guide 28

CD: Chr/Std 3/8–14
Cassette: Chr/Std 3A/2

MOZART: Piano Sonata in A major, K. 331, Third Movement

(3:27)

Date of work: 1783

Movements: 3
  I. Andante grazioso; theme and variations form, 6/8 meter, A major
 II. Menuetto; minuet and trio form, 3/4 meter, A major
III. Allegretto, Alla turca; rondo form, 2/4 meter, A minor/major

THIRD MOVEMENT: Rondo alla turca (A-B-C-B-A-B; B as refrain)

8   0:00   A section—2-part theme, each phrase repeated, in A minor

         (a) Rising sequential melody in sixteenth notes, ends on dominant:

     0:14   **(b)** Descending sequential line, with return to opening idea, ends in A minor:

9   0:43   B section—marchlike theme in octaves, in 2 parts (each repeated); arpeggiated (rolled) chords emphasize beats; serves as refrain, in A major:

10   0:58   C section—episode in F-sharp minor, in 2 parts (each repeated); a simple variation of A theme, with same accompaniment.

11   1:41   B section—A-major refrain returns, repeated.

12	1:56	**A section**—opening 2 phrases (a and b) return in A minor, each repeated.
13	2:40	**B section**—A-major refrain, with broken chords in right hand, repeated.
14	2:55	**Coda**—long extension of A-major refrain, with arpeggiated chord and grace notes to give jingling quality:

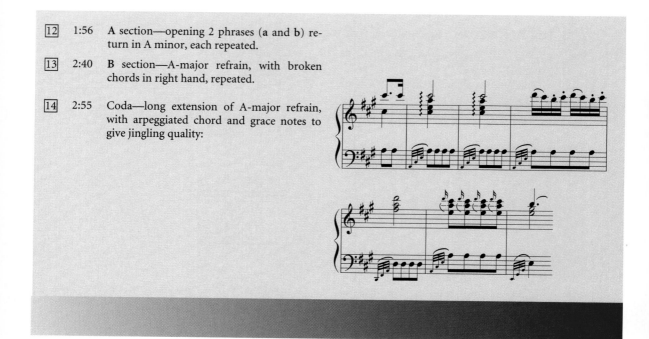

Beethoven's *Pathétique* Sonata

Beethoven himself dubbed the Piano Sonata in C minor, Op. 13, the *Pathétique*. Certainly the Beethovenian pathos is apparent from the first chords of the slow introduction (see Listening Guide 29). Marked Grave (solemn), this celebrated opening has something fantasy-like about it, as if Beethoven had captured here the passionate intensity of his own keyboard improvisations.

First movement In the movement proper, marked Allegro di molto e con brio (Very fast and with vigor), Beethoven uses the resources of the piano most imaginatively: there are contrasts in dynamics and register, brilliant scale passages, and exciting uses of tremolo and a slowly gathering *crescendo*. One very dramatic moment comes near the end, when Beethoven introduces a brief reminder of the slow introduction, then follows this with a swift cadence in the home key.

Second movement The second movement is a famous Adagio cantabile (Slow and songful), which shows off the piano's ability to sing. The opening theme of this melodious rondo (in **A-B-A-C-A** form) is stated in A-flat major, then repeated an octave higher. After a brief contrasting episode, the opening theme returns, followed by a new section in which insistent triplets increase the tension in a dialogue between the pianist's right and left hands. The animation continues through the last statement of the memorable theme and a short coda. This hymnlike Adagio combines an introspective character with the quality of strength that Beethoven made his own.

The final movement is a rondo, whose principal theme is darkened by the **Third movement**
C-minor tonality, setting it apart from the usually cheerful rondo finales of
Haydn and Mozart. Within its spacious structure, lyric episodes alternate
with dramatic ones. The *Pathétique* has been a favorite for generations. In the
hands of a great performing artist, it stands as one of Beethoven's most personal sonatas.

Listening Guide 29

CD: Chr/Std 4/9–26, Sh 3/1–5
Cassette: Chr/Std 4A/2–4, Sh 3A/1

BEETHOVEN: Piano Sonata in C minor, Op. 13 (*Pathétique*)

(19:31)

Date of work: 1798

Movements: 3

(Shorter recordings begin with second movement.)

FIRST MOVEMENT: Grave, Allegro di molto e con brio; sonata-allegro form, 4/4 meter, C minor

(9:24)

EXPOSITION
9 0:00 Grave—free, impassioned chords, in homophonic setting:

10 1:31 Allegro; theme 1—climbing, aggres-sive theme, accompanied by constant rhythmic octaves in left hand:

| 11 | 2:00 | Theme 2—lyrical, in E-flat minor, with grace notes and crossed hands: |

	2:27	Theme 3—in E-flat major, builds to *crescendo*.
	2:45	Codetta—closes exposition with ideas from opening Allegro.
		Exposition repeated.
		DEVELOPMENT
12	6:03	Return of Grave.
		Combines opening Allegro and Grave themes:

		RECAPITULATION
13	7:23	Themes 1, 2, and 3 return in C minor.
14	8:42	Grave returns, leading to coda (Allegro), like opening.

SECOND MOVEMENT: Adagio cantabile; rondo form (A-B-A-C-A), 2/4 meter, A-flat major   (5:53)

| 15 | 0:00 | **A section**—lyrical melody, first in middle range, then repeated up an octave: |

| 16 | 1:17 | **B section**—a contrasting lyrical melody, modulating, more disjunct: |

17 2:15 A section—returns in A-flat major.

18 2:53 C section—more dramatic episode, with triplet figures, accents, and arpeggios:

19 3:52 A section—returns in A-flat major, more rhythmically animated, in triplets.

Coda

(Shorter recordings stop here.)

THIRD MOVEMENT: Allegro; rondo form (A-B-A-C-A-B-A), duple meter, C minor (4:14)

20 0:00 A section—quick-paced melody in C minor; its recurrence is the basis for the movement:

21 0:20 B section—modulates to E-flat major, melody moves up and down in arpeggios, then scales:

Slower, chordal section follows, leading to exchange of motive between right and left hands.

22 1:13 A section—in C minor.

23   1:33   C section—modulates to A-flat major, with disjunct theme and syncopated rhythms, motivic exchange between hands:

etc.

24   2:23   A section—in C minor.

25   2:39   B section—in C major.

26   3:23   A section—in C minor, final statement.

Choral Music and Opera in the Classical Era

50

Sacred Choral Music

"Make a joyful noise to the Lord, all the earth; break forth into joyous song and sing praises."—PSALM 98

MASS, REQUIEM, AND ORATORIO

The late eighteenth century inherited a rich tradition of choral music from earlier eras. Among the principal genres were the Mass, a musical setting of the most solemn service of the Roman Catholic Church, and the *Requiem,* a musical setting of the Mass for the Dead. Both types were originally intended to be performed in church. By the nineteenth century, they had found a much larger audience in the concert hall.

The blending of many voices in a large space such as a church or cathedral could not fail to be an uplifting experience. For this reason, both the Catholic and Protestant churches were patrons of choral music throughout the ages. Haydn and Mozart made significant contributions to the Mass repertory. Haydn's Mass in D minor (*Lord Nelson*) remains one of his most frequently performed works, and Mozart's Requiem, his last composition, quickly established itself as one of the masterpieces of the Classical Viennese School.

A performance of Haydn's oratorio The Creation *in the Great Hall of the University of Vienna in 1808, as painted by* **Balthasar Wigand.** (Vienna Historical Museum)

Another important genre was the oratorio, made popular in the early eighteenth century by Handel in such works as *Messiah* (which we will study in Chapter 62). We will consider the origins of this vocal genre later; for now, it is important to know that the oratorio is a large-scale musical work for solo voices, chorus, and orchestra generally based on a biblical story and performed without scenery, costumes, or acting. As in opera, the action takes place by means of a series of recitatives, arias, ensemble numbers, and choruses. Haydn wrote two oratorios—*The Creation* (which we will study) and *The Seasons*, which attained enormous popularity and helped build a new audience for these genres.

Haydn's *Creation*

While in London, Haydn came to know the Handelian oratorios so loved by English audiences. In a concert of *Messiah* at Westminster Abbey in 1791, he was so moved by the "Hallelujah Chorus" that he tearfully exclaimed of Handel: "He is the master of us all!" When Haydn expressed his interest in writing an oratorio to his friend Barthélemon, the latter picked up a Bible and said: "There! Take that, and begin at the beginning." And so Haydn began work on *The Creation*, with a libretto (originally intended for Handel) that was drawn from the biblical book of Genesis and from Milton's *Paradise Lost*. The work was completed in 1798 and received its first public performance the following year.

In this oratorio, the recitatives, solos, and ensemble numbers are assigned to three archangels—Gabriel (a soprano), Uriel (a tenor), and Raphael (a bass)—and to Adam and Eve. The archangels' voices, whether singing alone or together, contrast with the chorus, which represents the heavenly Host.

The overture, marked Largo, is a "Representation of Chaos" that begins with the emptiness of the octave, a sustained pitch of C held by the full orchestra. Haydn's attempt to depict the void of pre-Creation led him to use ambiguous tonality, dissonance, and chromatic harmonies. **Overture**

The recitatives and the chorus that follow are based on the opening lines of Genesis. Raphael's recitatives set out from C minor ("In the beginning God created the heaven and the earth"), then the chorus begins *pianissimo* ("And the Spirit of God moved upon the face of the waters"). An unforgettable moment occurs at the sudden shift from C minor to C major at the joyous cry "Let there be light." Here and throughout the oratorio, Haydn proves himself to be a master of text painting. **Part I**

A high point of the work is reached in the recitative and chorus that bring Part I to a close. Uriel's recitative—both *secco* and *accompagnato* are heard—describes the creation of the sun, moon, and stars on the fourth day. It is followed by one of Haydn's most noble choruses, "The Heavens Are Telling," with a text adapted from Psalm 19. Here, the choral passages are contrasted with interjections by the trio of archangels (see Listening Guide 30). As the music unfolds in symmetrical four-measure phrases, the four voice parts of the chorus sometimes sing the same words together and in other sections enter in imitation. The climax is achieved through a *crescendo* and *accelerando* toward the end. In the final phrase, all the voices unite in massive chords to produce a majestic cadence.

The second part of the oratorio begins with the fifth day of Creation, when the animals are formed. Here, Haydn illuminates the description of the birds and beasts through humorous examples of text painting. The chorus "Achieved Is the Glorious Work," with its grand double fugue (a polyphonic composition based on imitation of a theme), closes this section, making way for the entrance of Adam and Eve in Part III. The brilliant final chorus is a triumph of contrapuntal writing. **Parts II and III**

The oratorio was a tremendous success, as this description of one of its first performances, by writer Josef Richter, attests:

> In my whole life, I won't hear another piece of music as beautiful; and even if it had lasted three hours longer, and even if the stink and sweat-bath [in the

theater] had been much worse, I wouldn't have minded. For the life of me, I wouldn't have believed that human lungs and sheep gut and calf's skin could create such miracles. The music all by itself described thunder and lightning, and then you'd have heard the rain falling and the water rushing and the birds really singing and the lion roaring, and you could even hear the worms crawling along the ground. In short, . . . I never left a theater more contented, and all night I dreamed of the creation of the world.

Listening Guide 30

CD: Chr/Std 4/1–3
Cassette: Chr/Std 4B/1

HAYDN: *The Creation (Die Schöpfung)*, Part I, excerpts   (6:51)

Date of work: First performed 1799

Genre: Oratorio, in 3 parts

Libretto: English—author unknown
       German—Baron Gottfried van Swieten

Medium: Chorus, orchestra, and vocal soloists
       Adam, bass
       Eve, soprano
       3 archangels:
         Raphael, bass
         Uriel, tenor
         Gabriel, soprano

PART I, SCENE 3, closing

No. 12. Recitative (Uriel)

		Text	Description
1	0:00	And God said: Let there be lights in the firmament of heaven, to divide the day from the night and to give light upon the earth; and let them be for signs and seasons and for days and for years. He made the stars also.	*Secco* (dry) recitative, with little accompaniment; free rhythmic style.
2	0:35		Orchestral interlude, begins *pianissimo* and builds to climax; ascending line in violins; jubilant brass chords lead to recitative.

No. 13. Recitative (Uriel)

In splendor bright is rising now the sun and darts his rays; an amorous joyful happy spouse, a giant, proud and glad to run his measured course.

Accompanied recitative; loud chords punctuate phrases of text; voice has free rhythm.

With softer beams and milder light steps on the silver moon thro' silent night. The space immense of the azure sky in numerous hosts of radiant orbs adorns, and the sons of God announced the fourth day in song divine, proclaiming thus His power.

Adagio, with quiet, sustained low strings; voice soft and slow-moving with strings, suggestive of text.

Allegro, marked *forte*; voice punctuated by dotted rhythmic pattern, freer delivery.

No. 14. Chorus and trio

3   3:13   The heavens are telling the glory of God. The wonder of His works displays the firmament.

Chorus, with homophonic text declamation and full orchestra; exchange of melodic ideas.

Four-part chordal declamation of text:

Today that is coming speaks it the day; the night, that is gone, to following night.

Trio of archangel soloists; C major; trio alternates with orchestra; shift to C minor signals "night."

Repeat of chorus above.

More polyphonic opening; tenors and basses begin, answered by sopranos and altos; loud and triumphant.

In all the lands resounds the word, never unperceived, ever understood.	Trio of archangel soloists; imitative, overlapping entries, accompanied by strings and woodwinds; text repetition.
	Overlapping entries of soloists:

Repeat of chorus.	*Forte* statement; fugal treatment on "The wonder of His works"; extended through word repetition; grandiose closing with brass and timpani.

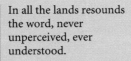

Classical Opera

"Opera is free from any servile imitation of nature. By the power of music, it attunes the soul to a beautiful receptiveness."
—FRIEDRICH VON SCHILLER

The opera house was a center of experimentation in the Classical era. Opera was the most important branch of musical entertainment, the one that reached the widest public. The point of departure was the music, which imposed its forms on the drama.

OPERA TYPES

Opera seria

The opera of the early eighteenth century accurately reflected the society out of which it sprang. The prevalent form was *opera seria*, "serious," or tragic, Italian opera, a highly formalized genre inherited from earlier eras consisting mainly of recitatives and arias specifically designed to display the virtuosity of star singers to the aristocracy. Its rigid conventions were shaped largely by the poet Pietro Metastasio (1698–1782), whose librettos, featuring stories of kings and heroes drawn from the legends of antiquity, were set again and again throughout the century.

Increasingly, however, the need was felt for simplicity and naturalness, for a style of opera that reflected human emotions more realistically. One impulse toward reform came from the operas of Christoph Willibald Gluck, whose achievement in this regard will be discussed later (see p. 466). Another resulted in the popular comic opera that flourished in every country of Europe. Known in England as *ballad* or *dialogue opera*, in Germany as *Singspiel*, in France as *opéra comique*, and in Italy as *opera buffa*, this lighter genre was the response of the rising middle class to the aristocratic form it would inevitably supplant.

Comic opera

Comic opera differed from opera seria in several basic ways. It was sung in the language of the audience rather than in Italian, which was the standard language of international opera. It presented lively, down-to-earth plots rather than dealing with the remote concerns of gods and mythological heroes. It featured an exciting ensemble at the end of each act in which all the characters participated, instead of an unbroken succession of solo arias, as the older style did. And it abounded in farcical situations, humorous dia-

An opera performance at Eszterháza. The musician at the harpsichord (far left, bottom) is thought to be Haydn. Anonymous eighteenth-century watercolor. (Deutsches Theatermuseum, Munich)

logue, popular tunes, and the impertinent remarks of the *buffo*, the traditional character derived from the theater of buffoons, who spoke to the audience in a bass voice, with a wink and a nod—a new sound in theaters previously dominated by the artificial soprano voice of the castrato (a male singer who was castrated in his youth to preserve the high register of his voice; on castrato singers, see p. 399).

As the Age of Revolution approached, comic opera became an important social force whose lively wit delighted even the aristocrats it satirized. Classical opera buffa spread quickly, steadily expanding its scope until it culminated in the works of Mozart, the greatest dramatist of the eighteenth century.

Mozart's Comic Opera *The Marriage of Figaro*

Mozart found his ideal librettist in Lorenzo da Ponte (1749–1838), an Italian-Jewish adventurer and poet whose dramatic vitality matched the composer's own. Their collaboration produced three great operas: *The Marriage of Figaro, Don Giovanni*, and *Così fan tutte (Women Are Like That)*.

Da Ponte adapted his libretto for *The Marriage of Figaro* from a play by Pierre-Augustin Caron de Beaumarchais (1732–1799), a truly revolutionary work in that it satirized the upper classes and allowed a servant—Figaro, the clever and cocky valet of Count Almaviva—to outwit his master. When Louis XVI read the manuscript, he pronounced it detestable and unfit to be seen. It was the liberal friends of the queen, Marie Antoinette, who persuaded the king to allow the play to be produced. Vienna was even more conservative than Paris: the play was forbidden there. But what could not be spoken could be sung. Mozart's opera was produced at Vienna's Imperial Court Theater in May 1786, and brought him the greatest success of his life.

Da Ponte employed all the traditional devices of bedroom farce: characters are disguised as one another, led into all sorts of misunderstandings, and caught in compromising situations they just barely wriggle out of. He cut out some of Beaumarchais's complications, and as court poet to Emperor Joseph II, da Ponte was clever enough to know that he must soften the political satire.

Although *The Marriage of Figaro* came out of the rich tradition of popular comic opera, Mozart's genius lifted the genre to another dimension. In place of the stereotyped characters of opera buffa, he created real human beings who come alive through his music. The Count is a likable ladies' man; the Countess is noble in her suffering. Her maid, Susanna, is pert and endlessly resourceful in resisting the advances of her master. Figaro is equally resourceful in foiling the schemes of the Count. And the Countess's page, Cherubino, is irresistible in his boyish innocence and ardor.

The orchestral overture, in an abridged sonata-allegro form, sets the mood

Overture

In His Own Words

In an opera the poetry must be altogether the obedient daughter. . . . An opera is sure of success when the plot is well worked out, and when the words are written solely for the music, not shoved in here and there to suit some miserable rhyme. . . . The best of all is when a good composer, who understands the stage and is talented enough to make sound suggestions, meets a true phoenix, an able poet.

"The Count discovers the Page." Detail of an illustration from the first Paris edition of Beaumarchais's comedy Le Mariage de Figaro, *engraved by* **Jean-Baptiste Liénard,** *1785.*

for the opera to follow. The lively D-major opening theme of the exposition anticipates the bustling preparations for a wedding. This first theme, played *pianissimo* in the strings, gives way to a broad melody in the winds that quickly builds to a dramatic climax. Scalar passages then transport us to the key of the dominant, A major, for the introduction of the second theme, a more static melody with uneven rhythms and gentle accents (produced by markings of *fp*, or *fortepiano*). The closing theme, a two-part idea, leads into a transition from which the recapitulation immediately follows, with no trace of a development section. An energetic coda hints at the first theme amid a downpour of descending scales. The powerful closing cadences of the overture lead *attaca* (without pause) into the first scene of the opera, where we meet Figaro measuring the room for his marital bed.

The action weaves a complex web: the Count has designs on Figaro's bride, Susanna; the housekeeper is interested in Figaro; and Cherubino is smitten with the Countess. We first hear Cherubino's aria from Act I, "Non so più," which establishes his character as a young man in love with love. "I no longer know who I am or what I'm doing," he sings. "Every woman I see makes me blush and tremble." In Classical opera, the part of a young man was often sung by a soprano or alto wearing trousers. In Mozart's opera, the mezzo-so-

Act I

prano voice is ideally suited to Cherubino's romantic idealism. (For the Italian and English text and an analysis of the aria, see Listening Guide 31.)

Cherubino's aria is followed by recitative, the rapid-fire, talky kind of singing whose main function is to advance the plot. Eighteenth-century audiences accepted this change of texture and orchestration just as today we accept, in a Broadway musical, the change from song to spoken dialogue.

The action moves rapidly, with overtones of farce. Cherubino has sung his love song to the Countess in Susanna's room. When the Count arrives to ask Susanna to meet him that night in the garden, Cherubino hides behind a huge armchair. At this point, the music master Basilio, a gossip if ever there was one, arrives looking for the Count, who also tries to hide behind the chair. Susanna cleverly places herself between the Count and Cherubino, so that the page is able to slip in front of the chair and curl up in it, where she covers him with a throw. With both the front and back of the armchair occupied, Susanna scolds Basilio as a busybody. At this point, the Count reveals his presence (see illustration on p. 305).

Susanna is aghast that the Count has been discovered in her room. The Count, having overheard Basilio say that Cherubino adores the Countess, is angry with the young man. And Basilio thoroughly enjoys the rumpus he has stirred up. The action stops as Susanna, the Count, and Basilio join in a trio in which they express their individual emotions, with quick exchanges between the three voices and much repetition of text. No one has ever equaled Mozart's ability to reconcile the demands of a dramatic situation with the requirements of absolute musical form, and this trio ("Cosa sento! Tosto andate"), which is related to sonata form, is a good example.

When the Count finally pulls the cloth from the chair and discovers Cherubino, he vows to banish him from the estate. At this point, Figaro arrives with a group of peasants whom he has told that the Count has decided to abolish the "right of the first night," the hated feudal privilege that gave the lord of the manor the right to deflower every young woman in his domain. In their gratitude, the peasants have come to serenade their master, singing, "His great kindness preserves the purity of a bride for the one she loves." Figaro, delighted to have forced the Count's hand, announces his impending marriage to Susanna, and the Count plays along by accepting the tributes of the crowd.

Figaro then intercedes for Cherubino with his master, whereupon the Count relents, appoints the page to a captain's post in his regiment, and leaves with Basilio. The complications in the next three acts (and there are many) lead to a happy ending: the Count is reconciled with his wife, and Figaro wins his beloved Susanna.

Two centuries have passed since Mozart's characters first strutted across the stage. They live on today in every major opera house in the world, lifted above time and fashion by the genius of their creator.

Listening Guide 31

CD: Chr/Std 3/39–51, Sh 2/52–59
Cassette: Chr/Std 3B/1–2, Sh 2A/5

MOZART: *The Marriage of Figaro (Le nozze di Figaro)*,
Overture and Act I, Scenes 6 and 7   (14:06)

Date of work: 1786

Genre: Opera buffa (comic opera)

Librettist: Lorenzo da Ponte

Basis: Play by Beaumarchais

Principal characters:
    Figaro, servant to Count Almaviva (bass)
    Susanna, maid to Countess Almaviva (soprano)
    Cherubino, page (trouser role, sung by mezzo-soprano)
    Count Almaviva (baritone)
    Countess Almaviva (soprano)
    Basilio, music master (tenor)
    Doctor Bartolo (bass)
    Marcellina, his housekeeper (soprano)

OVERTURE   (3:52)

    Form: Abridged sonata-allegro (lacking development)

    EXPOSITION

39 0:00 Theme 1a—agitated theme, played *pianissimo* in strings, in D major:

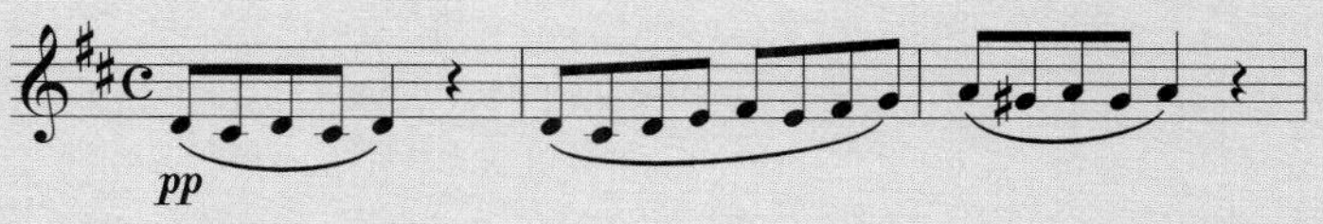

0:05 Theme 1b—a broad wind melody; oboes and flutes build to climax:

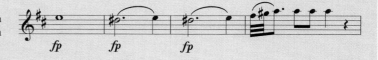

Transitional passage, modulating.

40 0:45 Theme 2—static melody with accented, uneven rhythms; in key of dominant (A major):

1:06 Closing theme (first part); a rising motive that turns downward:

	1:13	Closing theme (second part); lyrical melody in A major:	

ACT I, SCENE 6: Aria, Cherubino (10:14)

Form: **A-B-A-C**, followed by recitative
A—quick rhythms (in E-flat):

B—more lyrical (in B-flat):

A—return (in E-flat).

C—begins quietly, then builds in E-flat, modulates:

CHERUBINO

44	0:00	**A**	Non so più cosa son, cosa faccio, or di foco, ora sono di ghiaccio, ogni donna cangiar di colore, ogni donna mi fa palpitar.	I don't know what I am, what I'm doing; first I seem to be burning, then freezing; every woman makes me change color, every woman I see makes me shake.
45	0:18	**B**	Solo ai nomi d'amor, di diletto, mi si turba, mi s'altera il petto, e a parlare mi sforza d'amore un desio ch'io non posso spiegar.	Just the words "love" and "pleasure" bring confusion; my breast swells in terror, yet I am compelled to speak of love by a force which I cannot explain.
46	0:44	**A**	Non so più cosa son, . . .	
47	1:04	**C**	Parlo d'amor vegliando, parlo d'amor sognando, all'acqua, all'ombra, ai monti, ai fiori, all'erbe, ai fonti, all'eco, all'aria, ai venti,	I speak of love while waking, I speak of love while dreaming, to the water, to shadows, to mountains, to the flowers, the grass, and the fountains, to the echo, to the air, to the winds

che il suon de'vani accenti,	which carry the idle words
portano via con se.	away with them.

C   Parlo d'amor . . .

E se non ho chi m'oda,	And if there is no one to listen,
parlo d'amor con me!	I'll speak of love to myself!

(Seeing the Count in the distance, Cherubino hides behind the chair.)

Recitative: Susanna, Count, Basilio

CHERUBINO

Ah! Son perduto!	I'm done for!

48   2:50

SUSANNA

Che timor . . . il Conte! Misera me!	I'm afraid . . . the Count! Poor me!

(tries to conceal Cherubino)

COUNT ALMAVIVA *(entering)*

Susanna, tu mi sembri agitata e confusa.	Susanna, you seem to be agitated and confused.

SUSANNA

Signor, io chiedo scusa,	My lord, I beg your pardon,
ma, se mai, qui sorpresa,	but . . . indeed . . . the surprise . . .
par carità, partite.	I implore you, please go.

COUNT

(sits down on the chair and takes Susanna's hand; she draws it forcibly away)

Un momento, e ti lascio. Odi.	One moment, then I'll leave. Listen.

SUSANNA

Non odo nulla.	I don't want to hear anything.

COUNT

Due parole: tu sai che ambasciatore	Just a word; you know that the king
a Londra il Re mi dichiarò;	has named me ambassador to London;
di condur meco Figaro destinai.	I had intended to take Figaro with me.

SUSANNA

Signor, se osassi—	My lord, if I dare—

COUNT *(rising)*

Parla, parla, mia cara,	Speak, speak, my dear,
e con quel dritto ch'oggi prendi su me,	and with that right you have of me today,
finchè tu vivi chiedi, imponi, prescrivi.	as long as you live, you may ask, demand,
	prescribe.

SUSANNA

Lasciatemi, signor,	Let go of me, my lord,
dritti non prendo,	I have no rights,
non ne vò, non ne intendo.	I do not want them, nor claim them.
Oh me infelice!	Oh, what misery!

COUNT

Ah no, Susanna, io ti vò far felice!	Ah no, Susanna, I want to make you happy!
Tu ben sai quanto io t'amo;	You well know how much I love you;
a te Basilio tutto già disse.	Basilio has told you that already.
Or senti, se per pochi momenti meco	Now listen, if you would meet me
in giardin, sull'imbrunir del giorno,	briefly in the garden at dusk,
ah, per questo favore io pagherei . . .	ah, for this favor I would pay . . .

BASILIO *(outside the door)*

E uscito poco fa.   He went out just now.

COUNT

Chi parla?   Whose voice is that?

SUSANNA

O Dei!   Oh, heavens!

COUNT

Esci, ed alcun non entri.   Go, and let no one come in.

SUSANNA

Ch'io vi lasci qui solo?   And leave you here alone?

BASILIO *(outside)*

Da madama sarà, vado a cercarlo.   He'll be with my lady, I'll go and find him.

COUNT

Qui dietro mi porrò.   I'll get behind here.

(points to the chair)

SUSANNA

Non vi celate.   No, don't hide.

COUNT

Taci, e cerca ch'ei parta.   Hush, and try to make him go.

SUSANNA

Ohimè! che fate?   Oh dear! What are you doing?

(The Count is about to hide behind the chair; Susanna steps between him and the page. The count pushes her gently away. She draws back; meanwhile the page slips round to the front of the chair and hops in with his feet drawn up. Susanna rearranges the dress to cover him.)

BASILIO

Susanna, il ciel vi salvi!   Heaven bless you, Susanna!
Avreste a caso veduto il Conte?   Have you seen his lordship by any chance?

SUSANNA

E cosa deve far meco il Conte?   And what should his lordship be doing here
Animo, uscite.   with me? Come now, be gone!

BASILIO

Aspettate, sentite, Figaro di lui cerca.   But listen, Figaro is looking for him.

SUSANNA *(aside)*

Oh cielo!   Oh dear! Then he's looking for the one
Ei cerca chi, dopo voi, più l'odia.   man who, after you, hates him most!

COUNT *(aside)*

Vediam come mi serve.   Now we'll see how he serves me.

BASILIO

Io non ho mai nella moral sentito   I have never heard it preached that
ch'uno ch'ama la moglie odi il marito,   one who loves the wife should hate the husband;
per dir che il Conte v'ama.   that's a way of saying the Count loves you.

SUSANNA

Sortite, vil ministro dell'altrui sfrenatezza: Get out, vile minister of others' lechery!
io non ho d'uopo della vostra morale,   I have no need of your preaching
del Conte, del suo amor!   nor of the Count or his lovemaking!

Non c'è alcun male.
Ha ciascun i suoi gusti.
Io mi credea che preferir
doveste per amante,
come fan tutte quante,
un signor liberal, prudente, e saggio,
a un giovinastro, a un paggio.

No offense meant.
Everyone to their own taste.
I thought you would have preferred
as your lover,
as all other women would,
a lord who's liberal, prudent, and wise,
to a raw youth, a mere page.

SUSANNA

A Cherubino?

To Cherubino?

BASILIO

A Cherubino! Cherubin d'amore,
ch'oggi sul far del giorno
passeggiava qui intorno per entrar.

To Cherubino! Love's little cherub
who early today
was hanging about here waiting to come in.

SUSANNA

Uom maligno, un'impostura è questa.

You insinuating wretch, that's a lie.

BASILIO

È un maligno con voi
chi ha gli occhi in testa?
E quella canzonetta,
ditemi in confidenza,
io sono amico,
ed altrui nulla dico,
è per voi, per madama?

Do you call it an insinuation
to have eyes in one's head?
And that little ditty,
tell me confidentially
as a friend,
and I will tell no one else,
was it written for you or my lady?

SUSANNA (*aside*)

Chi diavol gliel'ha detto?

Who the devil told him about that?

BASILIO

A proposito, figlia, istruitelo meglio.
Egli la guarda a tavola sì spesso,
e con tale immodestia,
che s'il Conte s'accorge—
e sul tal punto sapete, egli è una bestia—

By the way, my child, you must teach him
better. At table he gazes at her so often
and so wantonly,
that if the Count noticed it—
on that subject, as you know, he's quite wild—

SUSANNA

Scellerato! e perchè andate voi
tai menzogne spargendo?

You wretch! Why do you go around
spreading such lies?

BASILIO

Io! che ingiustizia!
Quel che compro io vendo,
a quel che tutti dicono,
io non ci aggiungo un pelo.

I! How unfair!
That which I buy I sell,
and to what is common knowledge
I add not a tittle.

COUNT (*emerging from his hiding place*)

Come! che dicon tutti?

Indeed! And what is common knowledge?

BASILIO (*aside*)

Oh bella!

How wonderful!

SUSANNA

Oh cielo!

Oh heavens!

ACT I, SCENE 7: Terzetto (Trio), Count, Basilio, Susanna

Form: Sonata-type structure, with development and recapitulation
Style: Quick exchange between voices; much text repetition; each character with own emotional commentary

The Count—angry:

Basilio and the Count—comforting
Susanna, who has fainted:

|49| 5:59

COUNT

Cosa sento! Tosto andate,
e scacciate il seduttor!

I heard it all! Go at once,
throw the seducer out!

BASILIO

In mal punto son qui giunto;
perdonate, o mio signor.

I have come at an unfortunate moment;
forgive me, o my lord.

SUSANNA

Che ruina! me meschina!
Son' oppressa dal dolor!

What a catastrophe! I am ruined!
Terror grips my heart!

COUNT

Tosta andate, andate . . .

Go at once, go . . .

BASILIO

In mal punto . . .

I have come . . .

SUSANNA

Che ruina!

What a catastrophe!

BASILIO

. . . son qui giunto;

. . . at an unfortunate moment;

COUNT

. . . e scacciate il seduttor.

. . . and throw the seducer out.

BASILIO

. . . perdonate, o mio signor.

. . . forgive me, o my lord.

SUSANNA

Me meschina!
Me meschina!
Son' oppressa dal dolor.

I am ruined!
I am ruined!
Terror grips my heart.

BASILIO, COUNT *(supporting Susanna)*

Ah! già svien la poverina!
Come, oh Dio! le batte il cor.

Ah! The poor girl's fainted!
O God, how her heart is beating.

BASILIO

Pian, pianin, su questo seggio—
(taking her to the chair)

Gently, gently on to the chair—

312

SUSANNA (*coming to*)	
Dove sono? Cosa veggio?	Where am I? What's this I see?
Che insolenza! andate fuor.	What insolence! Leave this room.
BASILIO, COUNT	
Siamo qui per aiutarvi, . . .	We're here to help you, . . .
BASILIO	
. . . è sicuro il vostro onor.	. . . your virtue is safe.
COUNT	
. . . non turbarti, o mio tesor.	. . . do not worry, sweetheart.
BASILIO	
Ah, del paggio, quel che ho detto,	What I was saying about the page
era solo un mio sospetto.	was only my own suspicion.
SUSANNA	
È un'insidia, una perfidia,	It was a nasty insinuation,
non credete all'impostor.	do not believe the liar.
COUNT	
Parta, parta il damerino, . . .	The young fop must go, . . .
SUSANNA, BASILIO	
Poverino!	Poor boy!
COUNT	
. . . parta, parta il damerino.	. . . the young fop must go.
SUSANNA, BASILIO	
Poverino!	Poor boy!
COUNT	
Poverino! poverino!	Poor boy! Poor boy!
ma da me sorpreso ancor!	But I caught him yet again!
SUSANNA	
Come?	How?
BASILIO	
Che?	What?
SUSANNA	
Che?	What?
BASILIO	
Come?	How?
SUSANNA, BASILIO	
Come? che?	How? What?
COUNT	
Da tua cugina,	At your cousin's house
l'uscio jer trovai rinchiuso,	I found the door shut yesterday.
picchio, m'apre Barbarina	I knocked and Barbarina opened it
paurosa fuor dell'uso.	much more timidly than usual.
Io, dal muso insospettito,	My suspicions aroused by her expression,
guardo, cerco in ogni sito,	I had a good look around,
ed alzando pian, pianino,	and very gently lifting
il tappeto al tavolino,	the cloth upon the table,
vedo il paggio.	I found the page.

(imitating his own action with the dress over the chair, he reveals the page)

Ah, cosa veggio?	Ah, what do I see?

SUSANNA

Ah! crude stelle!	Ah! wicked fate!

BASILIO

Ah! meglio ancora!	Ah! better still!

COUNT

[51] 8:54

Onestissima signora, . . .	Most virtuous lady, . . .

SUSANNA

Accader non può di peggio.	Nothing worse could happen!

COUNT

. . . or capisco come va!	. . . now I see what's happening!

SUSANNA

Giusti Dei, che mai sarà!	Merciful heaven, whatever will happen?

BASILIO

Così fan tutte . . .	They're all the same . . .

SUSANNA

Giusti Dei! che mai sarà	Merciful heaven! Whatever will happen?
Accader non può di peggio,	Nothing worse could happen!
ah no! ah no!	ah no! ah no!

BASILIO

. . . le belle,	. . . the fair sex,
non c'è alcuna novità,	there's nothing new about it,
così fan tutte.	they're all the same.

COUNT

Or capisco come va,	Now I see what's happening,
onestissima signora!	most virtuous lady!
or capisco, *ecc.*	Now I see, *etc.*

BASILIO

Ah, del paggio, quel che ho detto,	What I was saying about the page
era solo un mio sospetto.	was only my own suspicion.

SUSANNA

Accader non può di peggio, *ecc.*	Nothing worse could happen, *etc.*

COUNT

Onestissima signora, *ecc.*	Most virtuous lady, *etc.*

BASILIO

Così fan tutte, *ecc.*	They're all the same, *etc.*

Transition II

From Classicism to Romanticism

"I am in the world only for the purpose of composing. What I feel in my heart, I give to the world."—FRANZ SCHUBERT

We have studied three great masters of the Viennese Classical School: Haydn, Mozart, and Beethoven. And we have seen that certain traits of Beethoven's music—his striking dynamic contrasts, his explosive accents, his expansion of strict Classical forms, his hymnlike slow movements, and the overall dramatic intensity of his music—clearly foreshadow the Romantic style.

The music of another Viennese master, Franz Schubert, reveals him to be heir to the Classical tradition. In his approach to chamber music and the symphony, Schubert followed in a direct line of development from Haydn, Mozart, and Beethoven. But we know that Schubert's life coincided with the first upsurge of Romanticism, and in his songs we can hear many of the prime interests of this new Romanticism, especially a fascination with nature. We will observe this happy marriage of Classical form and Romantic content in two related works: a song entitled *The Trout (Die Forelle,* composed in 1817), and a movement from a chamber work for piano and strings based on this song.

Schubert's *The Trout*

Schubert's songs display the composer's supreme gift for melody. Unlike the dramatic *Erlking,* which we heard earlier, *The Trout* is folklike in its simplicity; at the same time, it typifies Schubert's interest in nature. The text, by the German poet Christian Schubart (1739–1791), spins a fishing tale of a trout

The Irish landscape painter **Joseph Wright** *captures a serene fishing scene in* Outlet of Wyburn Lake *(1796), demonstrating the early Romantic artist's love of nature.* (The Nelson-Atkins Museum of Art, Kansas City)

that is sought after and finally caught. Schubert beautifully captures the imagery of the trout darting about in a stream with a bubbling piano accompaniment to an innocent, diatonic melody. The song is modified strophic in form; that is, the first two stanzas are sung to the same music, while the last displays much more agitation and chromatic color. This verse ends, however, with the same music that ended the first two.

Two years after he wrote *The Trout*, Schubert used the music as the basis for a movement of his popular Piano Quintet in A major (the *Trout*). The instrumentation of this chamber work—for violin, viola, cello, string bass, and piano—is unusual, in that it gives extra weight to the bass line. (For the standard instrumentation of a piano quintet, see p. 53.) The quintet is modeled on the Classical chamber works of Haydn and Mozart, except that it has five movements instead of the usual four.

The fourth movement, inserted between the traditional scherzo and the finale, is a theme with six variations on the charming melody of *The Trout*.

Here we see Schubert the true Classicist. From the music of the song's first two stanzas he forms a theme in two parts, (**A** and **B**), each of which is repeated. Then each of the instruments takes a turn with the melody in the variations that follow: the piano, in variation 1, decorates the tune; the viola, in variation 2, is set against a violin countermelody; the double bass, in variation 3, is accompanied by virtuosic passagework in the piano; the violin and piano engage in a dialogue in variation 4, which begins with a dramatic shift to D minor; the cello, in variation 5, reshapes the tune with exaggerated dotted rhythms; and finally, in the last variation, the violin and cello return us solidly to the tonic key in a bright, quickened Allegretto. A gentle closing passes the familiar "bubbling" figure to the low strings.

The *Trout* Quintet remains one of Schubert's most beloved compositions. The elegant workmanship, melodious charm, and refinement of feeling embodied in this chamber piece ensures its permanent place in the repertory.

Listening Guide 32

CD: Chr/Std 5/9–18
Cassette: Chr/Std 5A/2–3

SCHUBERT: *The Trout* (*Die Forelle*) and the *Trout* Quintet, Fourth Movement   (9:58)

THE TROUT (DIE FORELLE)   (2:17)

Date: 1817

Genre: Lied

Poem: C. F. Schubart

Form: Modified strophic (3 verses; 1 and 2 identical, 3 varied)

Tempo: Etwas lebhaft (Rather lively)

Bubbling piano accompaniment introduces folklike melody at opening:

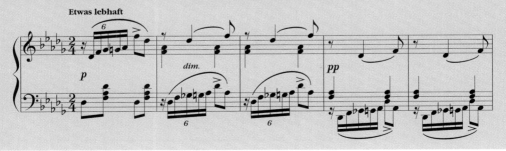

		Text	Translation
9	0:00	In einem Bächlein helle, Da schoss in froher Eil' Die launische Forelle Vorüber wie ein Pfeil. Ich stand an dem Gestade Und sah in süsser Ruh' Des muntern Fischleins Bade Im klaren Bächlein zu. [last two lines repeated]	In a bright little stream the good-natured trout darted about in joyous haste like an arrow. I stood on the bank and watched in sweet repose the bath of the lively little fish in the clear water.
10	0:46	Ein Fischer mit der Rute Wohl an dem Ufer stand, Und sah's mit kaltem Blute, Wie sich das Fischlein wand. So lang' dem Wasser Helle, So dacht, ich, nicht gebricht, So fängt er die Forelle Mit seiner Angel nicht. [last two lines repeated]	A fisherman with his rod also stood on the bank and cold-bloodedly watched the little fish swimming to and fro. As long as the water stays clear, I thought, he won't catch the trout with his rod.
11	1:23	Doch endlich ward dem Diebe Die zeit zu lang. Er macht Das Bächlein tückisch trübe, Und eh' ich es gedacht, So zuckte seine Rute, Das Fischlein zappelt dran, Und ich mit regem Blute Sah die Betrog'ne an. [two last lines repeated]	Bur finally the wait grew too long for the thief. He made the brook all muddy, and before I knew it, his rod quivered, the little fish wriggled at its end, and I, my blood boiling, gazed at the betrayed one.

PIANO QUINTET IN A MAJOR (THE *TROUT*), Fourth Movement   (7:41)

Date: 1819

Medium: Violin, viola, cello, double bass, and piano

Form: 5-movement sonata cycle
    I. Allegro vivace; sonata-allegro form, A major
   II. Andante; F major
  III. Scherzo; scherzo and trio, A major
  IV. Andantino; theme and variations, D major
   V. Allegro giusto; sonata-allegro form, A major

IV. Andantino; theme and variations, 2/4 meter, D major

| 12 | 0:00 | Theme: Strings alone, with melody in violin, D major; in 2 parts (**A** and **B**) |

A section (8 measures):

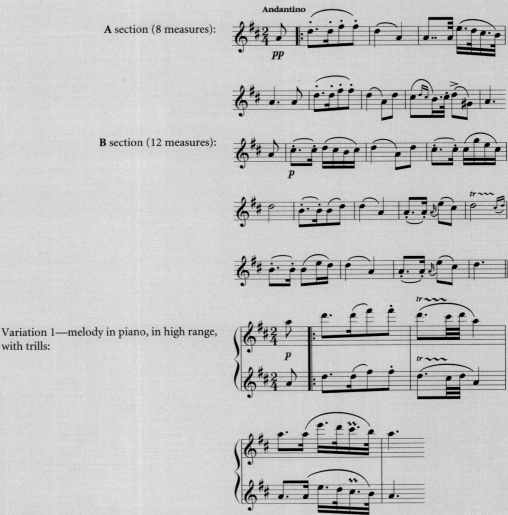

B section (12 measures):

| 13 | 1:04 | Variation 1—melody in piano, in high range, with trills: |

Low strings play pizzicato, upper strings have fluttering figure; trills in violin in **B** section.

| 14 | 1:59 | Variation 2—melody in viola, with counter-melody in violin: |

Piano imitates brief phrases of melody.

15 2:59   Variation 3—melody in double bass, accompanied by very fast, virtuosic piano part (not shown below) and rhythmic strings:

16 3:49   Variation 4—dramatic shift to D minor with sudden dynamic changes; begins *fortissimo*, then *piano*; dialogue between piano and strings; shifts from major to minor.

17 4:48   Variation 5—melody in cello with exaggerated dotted rhythm; sparse accompaniment; begins in B-flat major; **B** section extended.

18 6:26   Variation 6—quicker tempo (Allegretto); melody in violin accompanied by piano figuration from song:

Repeat of **A** section with cello melody; violin has melody in **B** section, repeated with cello; closes with quiet postlude, as in song.

A Comparison of Classical and Romantic Styles

	Classical (c. 1750–1825)	Romantic (c. 1820–1900)
Composers	Haydn, Mozart, Beethoven, Schubert	Beethoven, Schubert, Fanny Mendelssohn Hensel, Felix Mendelssohn, Clara Schumann, Robert Schumann, Chopin, Liszt, Berlioz, Brahms, Tchaikovsky, Verdi, Wagner
Melody	Symmetrical melody in balanced phrases and cadences; tuneful; diatonic, with narrow leaps	Expansive, singing melodies; wide ranging; more varied, with chromatic inflections
Rhythm	Clear rhythmically, with regularly recurring accents; dance rhythms favored	Rhythmic diversity and elasticity; tempo rubato
Harmony	Diatonic harmony favored; tonic-dominant relationships expanded, became basis for large-scale forms	Increasing chromaticism; expanded concepts of tonality
Texture	Homophonic textures; horizontal perspective	Homophony, turning to increased polyphony in later years of era
Instrumental genres	Symphony, solo concerto, solo sonata, string quartet	Same large genres, adding one-movement symphonic poem; solo piano works
Vocal genres	Opera, Mass, solo song	Same vocal forms, adding works for solo voice and piano/orchestra
Form	Ternary form predominant; sonata-allegro form developed; absolute forms preferred	Expansion of forms and interest in continuous as well as miniature programmatic forms
Audience	Secular music predominant; aristocratic audience	Secular music predominant; middle-class audience
Dynamics	Continuously changing dynamics through *crescendo* and *decrescendo*	Widely ranging dynamics for expressive purposes
Timbre	Changing tone colors between sections of works	Continual change and blend of tone colors; experiments with new instruments and unusual ranges
Performing forces	String orchestra with woodwinds and some brass; 30-to-40-member orchestra; rise of piano to prominence	Introduction of new instruments (tuba, English horn, saxophone); much larger orchestras; piano predominant as solo instrument
Virtuosity	Improvisation largely limited to cadenzas in concertos	Increased virtuosity; composers specified more in scores
Expression	Emotional restraint and balance	Emotions, mood, atmosphere emphasized; interest in the bizarre and macabre

Part 5

5

Medieval and Renaissance Music

Raphael *(1483–1520)*, Galatea (Villa Farnesina, Rome).

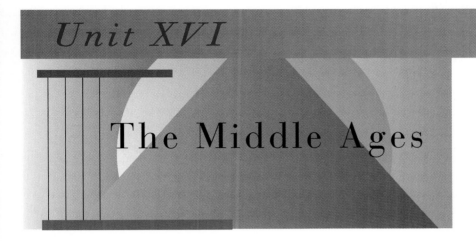

Unit XVI

The Middle Ages

52

The Culture
of the Middle Ages

*"Nothing is more characteristic of human nature than to be
soothed by sweet modes and disturbed by their opposites. Infants,
youths, and old people as well are so naturally attuned to musical
modes by a kind of spontaneous feeling that no one of any age is
without delight in sweet song."*—BOETHIUS

The relics of the ancient civilizations—Sumer, Babylonia, Egypt, Greece—
bear witness to a flourishing musical art. Only a few fragments of the music
of antiquity have survived, however. The centuries have forever silenced the
sounds that echoed through the Athenian amphitheater and the Roman circus. Those sounds and the attitudes they reflected, in Greece and throughout
the Mediterranean world, were the foundation on which the music of later
ages was based. They became part of the Western heritage (see CP 8).

The Middle Ages extended over the thousand-year period between the fall
of Rome, commonly set in the year 476, and the cultural flowering of the Renaissance. The first half of this millennium, lasting from around 500 to 1000 **Early Middle Ages**
and once referred to as the Dark Ages, should be viewed as a period not of

Cultural Perspective 8

MUSIC OF THE MUSES

How old is the art of music, and what role did it play in ancient societies? Archeologists have unearthed flutes and drums that date back 30,000 years and Neolithic cave paintings that provide pictorial evidence of a musical tradition among early humans. Looking back five or six millennia to Mesopotamia, the so-called cradle of civilization (modern-day Syria and Iraq; see world map), we find the first threads of a musical culture that can be traced directly to modern times. By around 2500 B.C.E. (before the common era), the Sumerians had developed several types of plucked string instruments: the harp and its relative the lyre. A small-sized lyre favored by the Babylonians in the second millennium was exported first to Egypt and later to Greece and Rome. Hand drums and clappers developed to accompany dancing, as did the earliest wind instrument: a double-reed pipe that was adopted by the Egyptians and later became a standard in Greek culture, known there as the aulos.

Music pervaded the lives of the Jews, as the Hebrew Bible, or Old Testament, vividly describes. The Israelites' escape from slavery in Egypt was celebrated in Miriam's dance with timbrels (percussion instruments related to the tambourine; Exodus 15:20); David's harp soothed Saul's distemper (1 Samuel 16:14–23); and the sounds of military music felled the walls of Jericho (Joshua 11:4).

Our word "music" derives from the Greek *mousike*, which refers to the art of the Muses of Greek mythology. Each of the Muses, who were the nine daughters of Zeus, father of the gods, presided over an art: for example, Calliope was the Muse of epic poetry, Terpsichore guided dancing and choral singing, and Euterpe inspired lyric poetry and music. Text and music were linked, because most poetry was sung or recited to an instrumental accompaniment. The Greek philosopher Plato, in his dialogue the *Republic*, advised young people to develop skills in both gymnastics and music so they could be strong in war and express themselves through song. Thus, music was woven into all aspects of Greek life. It played a role in ceremonial rites—marriages, funerals, the harvest—and it served as the focus of singing competitions.

The study of music was a serious endeavor, taken up by philosophers such as Pythagoras, who discovered the mathematical ratios of musical intervals, and Aristotle, who recognized the influence of music's harmonies on the soul. In later antiquity, music was grouped with three mathematical arts—arithmetic, geometry, and astronomy—into what was called the quadrivium; these subjects held an elevated status among the seven liberal arts well into the Middle Ages.

A link between theater and music that was established by the Greeks carried over to the culture of ancient Rome, where musical preludes and interludes were interspersed throughout theatrical comedies, and pantomime (in which an actor silently played all the parts in a show) was accompanied by singing. The Roman world produced both professional and amateur musicians. Among the gifted amateurs was the notorious Emperor Nero (r. 54–68; see pp. 403–5), who, according to legend, "fiddled while Rome burned" in a fire he claimed to have set himself.

The ancient sounds of music have their direct descendants in today's world. The value we place on music and the emotional response we have to its appealing melodies, rhythms, and harmonies have also come down to us from early times, as part of our heritage. And the inclusion of music in school and college curricula, as both an applied art and an academic study, rests on a cultural tradition that is literally thousands of years old.

Terms to Note:

lyre   Muses
aulos   quadrivium
timbrel   pantomime

Apollo sings of his triumph over the python, accompanying himself on the lyre. Fresco (c. 65–70) from the House of the Vettii at Pompeii.

decline but rather of ascent and development. In this society, all power flowed from the king, with the approval of the Roman Catholic Church and its bishops. The two centers of power, church and state, were bound to clash, and the struggle between them shaped the next chapter of European history. The modern concept of a strong, centralized government as the guardian of law and order is generally credited to Charlemagne (742–814), the legendary emperor of the Franks. This progressive monarch, who regretted until his dying day that he did not know how to write (he regarded writing as an inborn talent he simply did not possess), encouraged education and left behind him an ideal of social justice that illuminated the perceived "darkness" of the early medieval world.

The church as patron

The culture of this period was largely shaped by the rise of monasteries. It was the members of these religious communities who preserved the learning of the ancient world and transmitted it, through their manuscripts, to European scholars. In their desire to enhance the church service, they supported music extensively, and because of their efforts as patrons, the art music of the Middle Ages was largely religious. Women as well as men played a role in preserving knowledge and cultivating music for the church, as nuns figured prominently in church society. One woman who stands out in particular is Hildegard of Bingen, head of a monastery in a small town in western Germany. She is remembered today for her writings on natural history and medicine and for her poetry and music for special church services. We will study a religious drama with music by Hildegard in Chapter 53.

Late Middle Ages

The late Middle Ages, from around 1000 to 1400, witnessed the construction of the great cathedrals and the founding of universities throughout Europe. Cities emerged as centers of art and culture, and within them the townspeople—the bourgeoisie—played an ever expanding role in civic life. Developing national literatures helped shape the languages of Europe. Literary landmarks, such as the *Chanson de Roland* (c. 1100) in France, Dante's *Divine Comedy* (1307) in Italy, and Chaucer's *Canterbury Tales* (1386) in England, find their counterparts in painting: Lorenzetti's frescoes for the Town Hall in Siena (1338–40), for example, and Orcagna's *Last Judgment* for Florence (c. 1355).

The age of knighthood

In an era of violence brought on by deep-set religious beliefs, knights embarked on holy—and bloody—Crusades to conquer the Holy Land. Although feudal society was male-dominated, idealizing as it did the figure of the fearless warrior, women's status was raised by the universal cult of Mary, mother of Christ, and by the concepts of chivalry that arose among the knights. In the songs of the court minstrels, women were adored with a fervor that laid the foundation for our concept of romantic love. This poetic attitude found its perfect symbol in the image of the faithful knight who worshipped his lady from afar and was inspired by her to deeds of great daring and self-sacrifice.

Music is a part of civic life as shown in a detail of **Ambrogio Lorenzetti's** *(d. 1348?) fresco* Good Government in the City. (Palazzo Pubblico, Siena)

The Middle Ages, in brief, encompassed a period of enormous ferment and change. Out of its stirrings, faint at first but with increasing clarity and strength, emerged a profile of what we know today as Western civilization.

53

Sacred Music in the Middle Ages

"When God saw that many men were lazy, and gave themselves only with difficulty to spiritual reading, He wished to make it easy for them, and added the melody to the Prophet's words, that all being rejoiced by the charm of the music, should sing hymns to Him with gladness."—ST. JOHN CHRYSOSTOM

The early music of the Christian church was shaped in part by Greek, Hebrew, and Syrian influences. In time, it became necessary to assemble the ever growing body of music into an organized liturgy. The task extended over several generations, though tradition credits Pope Gregory the Great (reigned 590–604).

Like the music of the Greeks and Hebrews, *Gregorian chant* (also known as *plainchant* or *plainsong*) consists of a single-line melody; in other words, it is monophonic in texture, lacking harmony and counterpoint. Its freely flowing vocal line is subtly attuned to the inflections of the Latin text and is generally free from regular accent. Its unmeasured flow expresses what may be called

Gregorian chant

prose rhythm in music, or free-verse rhythm, as distinguished from the metrical-poetry rhythm we find in the regularly accented measures of duple or triple meter.

The Gregorian melodies, numbering more than three thousand, form an immense body of music, nearly all of it anonymous. Gregorian chant avoids wide leaps and dynamic contrasts, allowing its gentle contours to create a kind of musical speech. Free from regular phrase structure, the continuous, undulating vocal line is the counterpart in sound of the lacy ornamentation typical of Romanesque art and architecture.

Neumes

At first the chants were handed down orally from one generation to the next. As the number of chants increased, singers needed help in remembering the general outlines of the different melodies. Thus *neumes*, little ascending and descending signs, were written above the words to suggest the contours of the melody. Neumes eventually developed into a musical notation consisting of square notes on a four-line staff (see facing page).

Text settings

The melodies fall into three main classes, according to the way they are set to the text: *syllabic*, with one note sung to each syllable of text; *neumatic*, generally with groups of two to four notes sung to a syllable; and *melismatic*, with long groups of notes set to a single syllable of text. The melismatic style, descended from the elaborate improvisations heard in Middle Eastern music, became a prominent feature of Gregorian chant and exerted a strong influence on subsequent Western music.

Modes

From Gregorian chant through Renaissance polyphony, Western music used a variety of scale patterns, or *modes*. In addition to major and minor modes, which possess a strong sense of gravitation to a tonic note, there were others that lacked this sense. The modes served as the basis for European art music for a thousand years. With the development of polyphony—music for several independent lines—a harmonic system based on these scale patterns evolved. The adjective *modal* thus refers to the type of melody and harmony that prevailed in the early and later Middle Ages. It is frequently used in opposition to *tonal*, which refers to the harmony based on major-minor tonality of later eras.

THE MASS

The Mass, a reenactment of the sacrifice of Christ, is the most solemn ritual of the Roman Catholic Church. The name is derived from the Latin words *ite, missa est* (go, the Mass is ended; or, more literally, [the congregation] is dismissed), recited at the end of the service. The collection of prayers that

Proper and Ordinary

make up the Mass fall into two categories: the *Proper*, texts that vary from day to day throughout the church year, depending on the feast being celebrated; and the *Ordinary*, texts that remain the same in every Mass. (A chart showing the organization of the Mass with the individual movements of the Proper and Ordinary appears in Chapter 56, p. 364.) There are Gregorian melodies for each section of the ceremony. In this way, Gregorian chant has been central to the celebration of the Mass, which was and remains the primary service in the Catholic Church.

A GREGORIAN MELODY: *HAEC DIES*

Haec dies, from the Mass for Easter Day, serves as a fine example of Gregorian chant. It is a *Gradual*, which comes as the fourth item of the Proper, or variable part of the Mass, and takes its name from the Latin word for "steps" (the melody may have been sung from the steps of the altar). The term was applied to the singing of certain portions of a psalm (a prayer from the Old Testament Book of Psalms) in a musically elaborate, melismatic style. The Gradual is performed in a *responsorial* manner—as a series of exchanges between a soloist singing what is known as a *verse* and the chorus answering with the *response*. Despite the resulting contrast between two dissimilar bodies of sound, its texture remains monophonic.

Gradual

Responsorial singing

Haec dies opens with the soloist singing an introductory passage. The choral response makes up the first half of the melody. The second half is the soloist's verse, which is followed by a brief choral conclusion on the last word. (See Listening Guide 33 for the text, which is drawn from two psalms.) The melody is conjunct (moving stepwise or in small leaps), has a narrow range, and consists of a series of tiny motives that grow like cells and expand in a natural process of variation. Certain key words are drawn out over a series of notes; this striking melismatic treatment emphasizes such important words as "Dominus" (Lord) and "exsultemus" (we will rejoice), setting them apart from the others.

Melismatic setting

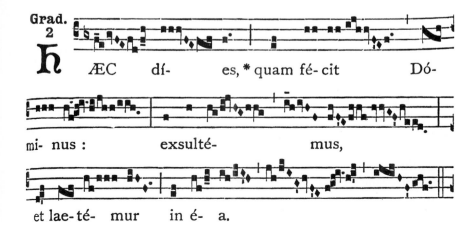

The opening of the chant *Haec dies* in Gregorian notation.

THE RISE OF POLYPHONY: THE NOTRE DAME SCHOOL

Polyphony, the single most important development in the history of Western music, began to emerge toward the end of the Romanesque period (c. 850–1150). (*Polyphony*, you will remember, combines two or more simultaneous melodic lines.)

Once several melodic lines were sung or played at the same time, the flexible prose rhythms found in single-line music disappeared. Polyphony helped bring about the use of regular meters, which was needed if the different voices were to keep together. Because this music had to be written down in a way that would indicate the precise rhythm and pitch, a more exact notational system was worked out, not unlike the one in use today. (For an explanation of our modern notational system, see Appendix I, "Musical Notation," p. A-1.)

Development of notation

With the development of a more precise notation, music progressed from being an art of improvisation and oral tradition to one that was carefully planned and preserved. During the Gothic era (c. 1150–1450), which saw the rise of cathedrals with their choirs and organs, the period of anonymous creation drew to a close, and the individual composer came to be recognized. The learned musicians, mostly clerics in religious communities, mastered the art of writing extended musical works that used the various devices of counterpoint discussed earlier (Chapter 4, pp. 20–21). The prime interest of these musicians was in creating a structure through the combination of musical elements (which explains the derivation of the word "composer" from the Latin *componere*, "to put together").

Organum

The earliest polyphonic music, called *organum*, developed from the custom of adding a second voice that ran above or below the Gregorian melody at the interval of a fifth or fourth. Soon a polyphonic art blossomed in which the individual voices moved with ever greater independence, not only in parallel but also in contrary motion. In the forefront of this evolution were the composers centered at the Cathedral of Notre Dame in Paris during the twelfth and thirteenth centuries. Their leader, Léonin (fl. third quarter of twelfth century), is the first composer of polyphonic music whose name is known to us.

Notre Dame School
Léonin

To the medieval mind, the new had to be founded on the old. Therefore composers of organum based their pieces on preexisting Gregorian chants. While the lower voice sang the fixed melody in extremely long notes, the upper voice sang a freely composed part that moved rapidly above it. In such a setting, the chant was no longer recognizable as a melody. Its presence was symbolic, anchoring the new in the old.

In both architecture and music, the Gothic period saw great advances in the techniques of construction. The Cathedral of Notre Dame, Paris (1163–1235).

In the organum *Haec dies* (see Listening Guide 33), solo polyphonic sections feature the faster-moving top voice singing in a *rhythmic mode*—a fixed pattern of long and short notes that is repeated or varied. Already European music was on its way to finding the metrical patterns familiar to modern listeners.

Rhythmic mode

THE EARLY MEDIEVAL MOTET

While Léonin limited himself to polyphony in two parts, his successor, Pérotin (fl. early thirteenth century), extended the technique by writing for three and four different voices. Toward the end of Pérotin's life, musicians began writing new texts for the previously textless upper voices of organum. The addition of these texts resulted in the *motet*, the most important form of early polyphonic music. The term "motet" derives from *mot* (French for "word"), referring to the words that were added to the vocal lines. Sometimes two different Latin texts went on at the same time, or one voice might sing in Latin, another in French. The medieval motet, then, is a *polytextual* (more than one text) vocal composition, either sacred or secular; it may or may not have had instrumental accompaniment.

Pérotin

Motet

Polytextual

The early motet illustrates how medieval composers based their own works on what had been handed down from the past. A composer selected a fragment of Gregorian chant (such as the *Haec dies*) for a particular voice part, and, keeping the pitches intact, gave them precise rhythmic values, usually of very long notes. This stretched-out chant served as the structural skeleton of the piece, to which the composer added one, two, or three freely composed, rhythmically active countermelodies. (A *countermelody*, as noted earlier, is a melody heard against another.) In the motet, a sacred text might be combined with one that is quite secular, even racy. The basic Gregorian tune, hidden among the voices, fused these disparate elements into a unity—if not in the listener's ear, at least in the composer's mind.

Countermelody

The anonymous thirteenth-century motet *O mitissima / Virgo / Haec dies* displays three-part polyphony built on a bottom voice, the *Tenor* (from the Latin *tenere*, meaning "to hold"). The Tenor, which was performed either vocally or instrumentally, sounds the notes of the chant *Haec dies* in a repeated rhythmic pattern, long-long-short-long, forming the structural basis for the piece. Such a repetition of a short musical pattern—whether melodic, rhythmic, or harmonic—is known as an *ostinato*. Above the Tenor, musical interest is focused in the two upper parts, which present different Latin poems in praise of the Virgin Mary. These voices are set in a similar rhythm of long and short notes, with the two lines frequently crossing each other in a lively exchange. (See Listening Guide 33.) This structural procedure developed into the later medieval *isorhythmic motet* (*iso* means "the same"), which features more elaborate rhythmic and melodic ostinatos.

Tenor

Isorhythmic motet

The motet is in triple meter, which to medieval listeners symbolized the perfection of the Trinity (the Father, the Son, and the Holy Ghost).

Listening Guide 33   MW   CD: Chr/Std 1/8–11, Sh 1/1–4
Cassette: Chr/Std 1A/2–4, Sh 1A/1–3

GREGORIAN CHANT, ORGANUM, AND MOTET   (4:23)

GREGORIAN CHANT: *Haec dies*   (2:27)

Text: Psalms 118:24 and 106:1

Chant type: Gradual, from the Proper of the Mass

Occasion: Easter Sunday

Performance: Responsorial (solo and chorus)

Style: Elaborate and melismatic

		Text	Translation	Performance
8	0:00	Haec dies,	This is the day	Solo intonation
	0:09	quam fecit Dominus exsultemus et laetemur in ea.	which the Lord hath made; we will rejoice and be glad of it.	Choral response
9	1:14	Confitemini Domino, quoniam bonus: quoniam in saeculum misericordia	O give thanks to the Lord, for He is good: for His mercy endureth	Solo verse
	2:05	ejus.	forever.	Chorus

Solo verse, with syllabic setting on "Confitemini" and melisma on "Domino":

---

10   **ORGANUM:** *Haec dies* (excerpt)   (1:25)

Date of work: c. 1175

Composer: Notre Dame School of Paris, in style of Léonin

Voices: 2 voices, both singing *Haec dies* text, polyphonic

Upper voice—freely composed, rhythmic, fast moving, sung melismatically:

Lower voice—*Haec dies* chant in long notes:

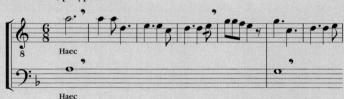

---

11   **MOTET:** *O mitissima / Virgo / Haec dies*   (0:31)

Date of work: 13th century

Composer: Anonymous

Voices/Text: 3 voices, each with different text (polytextual)

Characteristics: Polyphonic, all voices rhythmically active

Basis: Lowest voice (Tenor) with chant notes, on 2 words only ("Haec dies")

Text	Translation

Top voice

O mitissima Virgo Maria,	O sweetest Virgin Mary,
Posce tuum filium,	beg thy son
Ut nobis auxilium	to give us help
Det et remedium	and resources
Contra demonum	against the deceptions
Fallibiles astucias	of the demons
Et horum nequicias.	and their iniquities.

Middle voice

Virgo virginum,	Virgin of virgins,
Lumen luminum,	light of lights,
Reformatrix hominum,	reformer of men,
Que portasti Dominum,	who bore the Lord,
Per te Maria,	through thee, Mary,
Detur venia,	let grace be given
Angelo nunciante,	as the Angel announced:
Virgo es post et ante.	Thou art a Virgin before and after.

Tenor voice
(performed instrumentally on the Norton recording)

Haec dies	This is the day . . .

Motet opening—ostinato pattern shaded (long-long-short-long):

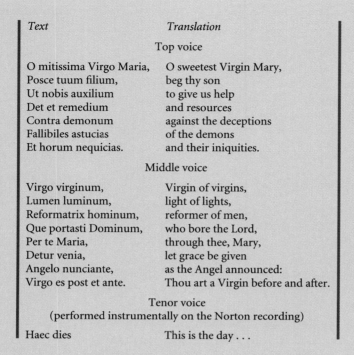

The opening and closing sounds and those at the *cadences*—resting places that punctuate the music—are based on open fifths and octaves, which have a hollow ring to our ears. We will see that these open sounds intrigued later composers such as Claude Debussy, who tried centuries later to recapture the essence of medieval music.

LIFE IN THE MEDIEVAL CLOISTER

One lifestyle available to men and women in the Middle Ages centered around the church. Life in a cloister (a place for religious seclusion) allowed people to withdraw from secular society to the shelter of monasteries and convents, where they devoted themselves to prayer, scholarship, preaching, charity, or healing the sick, depending on the religious order they joined. Some adopted a freer form of spirituality: men joined orders of wandering friars who preached to the masses, and women joined lay religious groups devoted to teaching or hospital work. Individuals from all levels of society chose the religious life—members of the aristocracy and the middle class who sought a quiet, contemplative existence, younger sons of the gentry who failed to inherit land, and young women who lacked marriage prospects.

A life devoted to the church was not an easy one. Some religious orders, such as the Franciscans, required vows of poverty; each new member discarded all worldly possessions upon joining. The discipline was arduous. A typical day began at 2:00 or 3:00 A.M. with the celebration of daily services, the reading of lessons, and the singing of psalms. Each day in the church calendar had its own ritual and its own order of prayers. The members of the community interspersed their religious duties with work in the fields, in the library, in the workshop. Some produced items that could be sold—wine, beer, or cheese, for example—thus bringing in revenue to the order.

In this fourteenth-century manuscript illumination, the monks sing during the celebration of Mass and an altar boy (left) pulls a bell rope.

Cultural Perspective 9

INFLUENCES ON THE EARLY CHRISTIAN CHURCH

How did the early Christians first establish the rituals of their church, and where did their musical practices come from? Since Christianity descended directly from Judaism—Jesus and his followers were, after all, Jews—the early Christians naturally retained some familiar Judaic traditions in defining their religious beliefs and practices. For example, they affirmed the concept of one God (many religions of the world worship more than one deity) and the general code of moral behavior that governs us today. Christianity also borrowed from Judaism the practice of congregational prayer, an appreciation of books, especially the biblical texts of the Hebrew Scriptures (Old Testament), and the practice of reading and discussing sacred texts in a public meeting house—the Jewish synagogue or Christian church. Some Hebrew words, such as *amen* (in truth) and *hallelujah* (praise God), are still used in Christian prayer.

Judaism and Christianity are linked musically by the 150 texts from the Old Testament Book of Psalms. Many of these mention singing; "O come, let us sing to the Lord," "O sing to the Lord a new song," and "I will sing of loyalty and justice" are a few opening lines. The psalms eventually gained a respected place in both religions; they were sung during services, at ceremonial meals, and in the home. The psalm texts lent themselves especially well to responsorial singing by the synagogue cantor (a soloist and singing leader) and the congregation. In the Roman Catholic Church, the recitation of psalms, more like speaking than singing, became the core of many religious services. We will see later that the practice of singing psalms was adopted in the services of the Protestant churches during the Reformation and after (see CP 12 on music and religion in the Americas).

Other practices in the early Roman Catholic Church were borrowed from the East—the church of Byzantium (or Constantinople, now Istanbul in Turkey), another branch of the Christian church. The influence of Byzantium can be seen as well in the architecture of some Roman Catholic churches: perhaps the most famous example is St. Mark's in the great seaport of Venice (see p. 386). Features of Greek music and other Mediterranean cultures were also absorbed into the liturgy of the early Christian church.

You may wonder why the music of the early Christian church—Gregorian chant, as we call it today—was sung *a cappella*, without instrumental accompaniment. Early Christians believed that instrumental music did not serve religion and that music lacking a spiritual text might arouse erotic passions in the listener; hence, most instruments were banned from use in the Roman Catholic

Church for many years. The organ, an invention of the Greeks, is often associated with church music and was the first instrument to be generally accepted for use in Christian worship.

Today, texts for devotional music tend to be in the vernacular (the language of the particular region) rather than in the older languages of Hebrew or Latin, so everyone can understand them. Many styles of music now serve religion, and generally, whatever moves people spiritually is acceptable, whether it be instrumental or vocal, electronic or acoustic, popular or art, new or old.

Terms to Note:

synagogue	Mass
Book of Psalms	responsorial
cantor	Gregorian chant
Divine Offices	*a cappella*

Suggested Listening:

Gregorian chant (*Haec dies*)
Jewish chant or synagogue music

Illuminated initial from Psalm 114 in Hebrew, depicting the exodus from Egypt in which Moses led the Israelites. (From the Kaufmann Haggadah)

Despite the grueling schedule, many men and women in religious life dedicated themselves to writing and preserving knowledge from earlier times. Such a person was Hildegard of Bingen, one of the most remarkable women of the Middle Ages, who was renowned in her day as a poet and prophet and is immensely popular today for her serenely beautiful music.

HILDEGARD OF BINGEN AND MEDIEVAL RELIGIOUS DRAMA

"The words of the musical performance stand for the body, and the musical performance itself stands for the spirit. The celestial harmony announces the divinity, and the words truly uncover the humanity of the Word of God."

Hildegard of Bingen (1098–1171) was the daughter of a noble couple who promised her, as their tenth child, to the service of the church as a *tithe* (giving to the church one-tenth of what one owns). She was raised by a religious recluse and took her vows at the age of fifteen. From childhood, Hildegard experienced visions, which intensified in later life. She was reportedly able to see hidden things and to foretell the future.

With the death of her teacher, Hildegard became head of the order, and in 1152 founded her own convent in Rupertsberg, on the Rhine River near Bingen. As her influence grew, she was able to found yet another house of her followers. Her miracles and prophecies made her famous throughout Europe; popes, kings, and priests sought her advice on political and religious issues. She was also known for her scientific and medical writings. Although never officially canonized, Hildegard is regarded as a saint by the church.

Moved to record her visions and prophecies, Hildegard completed three collections in manuscript. After a particular vision she had in 1141, when "the heavens were opened and a blinding light of exceptional brilliance flowed through my flame," she claimed to fully understand the meaning of the Scriptures.

Hildegard also wrote religious poetry with music, which she collected in a volume entitled *Symphony of the Harmony of Celestial Revelations* (*Symphonia armonie celestium revelationum*). These works form a liturgical cycle appropriate for singing at different religious feasts throughout the year. Best-known of her works is a drama with music called *The Play of the Virtues* (*Ordo virtutum*), which may have been written for the founding of her convent in 1152. Her musical style is highly original; it resembles Gregorian chant, but unlike most other new music of the time, it does not draw on the existing repertory.

In Her Own Words

The words I speak come from no human mouth; I saw and heard them in visions sent to me. . . . I have no confidence in my own capacities—I reach out my hand to God that He may carry me along as a feather borne weightlessly by the wind.

The Play of the Virtues

The Play of the Virtues is a religious drama sung in verse. It is the earliest known example of a *morality play*, a drama meant to teach righteous and up-right values. Written in Latin poetry full of brilliant imagery and mysticism, this play presents the battle between the Virtues and the Devil for Anima, the soul. Many of the characters personify virtues—among them, Faith, Hope, Charity, Patience, Humility, Chastity, Obedience, Discipline, and Victory. Anima falls to the temptations of the Devil but is saved by the Virtues. In a lively debate with the Devil, each Virtue introduces herself with appropriate music and is answered by the others as a group. Having saved another soul, the Virtues rejoice as Victory swoops down on the Devil and ties him up.

Morality play

The music for *The Play of the Virtues* consists of eighty-two monophonic, chantlike melodies organized by the formulaic repetition of certain musical phrases and motives (see Listening Guide 34). The style is largely neumatic—several notes are sung to each syllable of text—except where a word is em-phasized in a melisma. All the parts were sung by women (presumably nuns) except that of the Devil, who was played by a local priest. Hildegard herself appears at the beginning to explain how she came to record her experiences.

Set in a prologue and four scenes, the play reaches its musical high point in the last scene, with the salvation of the soul. The Devil speaks harshly to Anima, who vows to fight him with the help of Victory, Humility, and the other Virtues. Victory sings with a commanding tone in a high range, while

An abbot, head of a monastery, preaches to a group of Flemish nuns in this manuscript miniature (1351).

Humility's voice soars heavenward, anticipating the salvation of the lost soul. The chorus of Virtues responds in a simpler unison line of angelic voices, resounding the celestial triumph in a style unique to Hildegard.

Listening Guide 34

MW **CD: Chr/Std 1/12–14**
    Cassette: Chr/Std 1A/5

HILDEGARD: *The Play of the Virtues (Ordo virtutum),* Scene 4

(4:30)

Date of work: Mid–12th century

Genre: Religious drama (morality play) with music

Principal characters:
  Anima, a soul
  The Devil
  The sixteen Virtues (Humility, Knowledge of God, World Rejection, Charity, Celestial Love, Modesty, Hope, Patience, Obedience, Innocence, Discretion, Faith, Discipline, Chastity, Victory, Compassion)
  Hildegard
  Church Elders and Prophets

SCENE 4, beginning

		Text	Translation	Description
		DEVIL		
12	0:00	Quae es, aut unde venis? Tu amplexata es me, et ego foras eduxi te. Sed nunc in reversione tua confundis me—ego autem pugna mea deiciam te!	Who are you? Where are you coming from? You were in my embrace, and I led you out. Yet now you are going back, defying me—but I will fight you and bring you down!	Spoken rather than sung.
		ANIMA		
13	0:22	Ego omnes vias tuas malas esse cognovi, et ideo fugi a te; modo autem, o illusor, pugno contra te. Inde tu, o regina Humilitas, tuo medicamine adiuva me.	I knew that all your ways were wicked, so I fled you; but now, you deceiver, I'll fight you face to face. Queen Humility, come with your medicine, give me aid.	Sung in neumatic, conjunct style; climaxes on words "regina Humilitas"; with instrumental accompaniment.
		HUMILITY *(to Victory)*		
	1:30	O Victoria, quae istum in caelo superasti, curre cum militibus tuis, et omnes ligate diabolum hunc.	Victory, who once conquered this creature in the heavens, run now, with all your warriors, and all of you, bind this devil.	Line opens with two rising leaps; more animated style.

		VICTORY (*to the Virtues*)		
	2:00	O fortissimi et gloriosissimi milites, venite et adiuvate me istum fallacem vincere.	Bravest and most glorious warriors, come, help me vanquish this deceitful one!	Middle range, forceful delivery, with organ accompaniment.
		VIRTUES		
14	2:32	O dulcissima bellatrix, in torrente fonte qui absorbuit, lupum rapacem! O gloriosa coronata, nos libenter militamus tecum contra illusorem hunc.	O sweetest warrior, in the scorching torrent that swallowed up the voracious wolf! O glorious, crowned one, we'll gladly fight against that deceiver, at your side.	Chorus sings conjunct line, simpler style.
		HUMILITY		
	3:11	Ligate ergo istum, o virtutes praeclarae!	Bind him, then, you shining virtues!	More neumatic style, with short melismas.
		VIRTUES		
	3:27	O regina nostra, tibi parebimus, et praecepta tua in omnibus adimplebimus.	Queen of us all, we obey— we'll carry out your orders in all things.	Chorus, nearly syllabic.
		VICTORY		
	3:48	Gaudate, o socii, quia antiquus serpens ligatus est.	Rejoice, comrades; the old snake is bound.	High range, more dramatic and melismatic; accompanied by bells.
		VIRTUES		
	4:17	Laus tibi Christe, rex angelorum!	Praise be to you, Christ, king of angels!	Chorus, with melismatic ending on "angelorum."

Expressive leaps open Humility's soaring line:

Victory's joyful line, set in high range:

54

Secular Music in the Middle Ages

"A verse without music is a mill without water."—ANONYMOUS TROUBADOUR

Alongside the learned (or art) music of the cathedrals and choir schools, a popular literature sprang up of songs and dances that reflected every aspect of medieval life. The earliest secular songs that have been preserved were set to Latin texts, which suggests that they originated in university towns rather than in villages. Typical are the *Goliard*, or student, songs—many with lewd texts—which express the *carpe diem* (seize the day) philosophy that has always inspired youthful poets. Both poetry and music celebrate the impermanence of love, the beauty of springtime, and the cruelty of fate. Seven hundred years later, the German composer Carl Orff admirably resurrected their spirit in *Carmina burana,* a popular twentieth-century choral work based on racy medieval texts.

Goliard songs

MEDIEVAL MINSTRELS

Minstrels emerged as a class of musicians who wandered among the courts and towns. Some were versatile entertainers who played instruments, sang and danced, juggled and showed tricks, presented animal acts, and performed plays. In an age that had no newspapers, they regaled their audience with gossip and news. These itinerant actor-singers—called *jongleurs* (male) and *jongleuresses* (female)—lived on the fringe of society.

Jongleurs and jongleuresses

On a different social level were the poet-musicians who flourished at the various courts of Europe. Those who lived in the southern region of France known as Provence were called *troubadours,* a term applied to both men and women (women were also called *trobairitz*). In northern France, these musicians were called *trouvères.* Both terms mean the same thing—finders or inventors (in musical terms, composers). Troubadours and trouvères num-

Troubadours

Trouvères

bered among their ranks members of the aristocracy and even some royalty. They either sang their music and poetry themselves or entrusted its performance to other musicians. In Germany, they were known as *minnesingers*, or singers of courtly love.

Minnesingers

Secular music became an integral part of medieval court life, supplying the necessary accompaniment for dancing, dinner, and after-dinner entertainment. It was central to court ceremonies, to tournaments, and to civic processions. Military music supported campaigns, inspired warriors departing on the Crusades, and greeted them on their return. Among the royal musicians were Richard the Lion-Hearted of England—whose mother, the legendary Eleanor of Aquitaine, presided over a famous court of poet-musicians—and Alfonso the Wise of Spain. Whether in France, Germany, Italy, or Spain, the aristocratic singers were creating a literature that would exert a profound influence on European culture.

Roles of secular music

Heinrich von Meissen, called "Frauenlob" (champion of ladies), is exalted by musicians playing drum, flute, shawm, fiddles, psaltery, and bagpipe. Frauenlob was a Minnesinger (singer of courtly love), the German counterpart of the troubadour. (Heidelberg University Library)

OPENING DOORS TO THE EAST

The Middle Ages was an era of religious wars and exploration, both of which opened doors to the East. Between 1096 and 1217, there were five organized Crusades, military expeditions undertaken by European Christians in an attempt to conquer the Holy Land of Palestine. Along the way, crusaders massacred local people, plundered their riches, and destroyed their artworks. Yet out of these violent episodes came a significant meeting of cultures. The crusading knights learned from the expert military skills and weapons of the Turkish and Moorish warriors. The advanced medical and scientific knowledge of the Arab world was imported to Europe, and the Arab number system was adopted in Western commerce and banking. (Until then, Europeans had used Roman numerals—I, II, III, IV, V; today, we primarily use Arabic numerals—1, 2, 3, 4, 5.)

What of the musical interaction of these cultures? Instruments of all kinds as well as music and theoretical ideas were brought back to western Europe. For example, the medieval rebec, a small, violin-like instrument, was derived from the Arab rabab, and the loud, double-reed shawm used for outdoor events was closely related to the Turkish zurna. We have already noted that Turkish percussion instruments found their way into Western ensembles in the eighteenth century. Crusaders heard the sounds of the Saracen military trumpets and drums and soon adopted these as their call to battle. The foundations of our Western system of modes (or scale forms) also felt the influence of Eastern theoretical systems.

In 1271, the Venetian merchant and explorer Marco Polo (1254–1324) made a historic journey to China. Polo was welcomed by the great Kublai Khan, a Mongol ruler who had conquered northern China and further modernized the already highly sophisticated civilization there. The Khan encouraged literature, the arts, and medical research, and established Buddhism as the official state religion. Polo and his entourage were much impressed by this society's technical advances; many, such as the making of gunpowder and the art of printing from movable type, were still unknown in western Europe. Polo's diary describes the importance of music to the Chinese military campaigns: "The Tartars never attack until they hear their commander's drums, but while waiting for the battle to begin, they always play and sing."

The information Marco Polo recorded throughout his travels helped open routes for the exchange of commerce (especially silks and spices), arts, and ideas from East to West. Although these early encounters were isolated, they helped immeasurably in the centuries that followed to encourage communication between different nations and cultures. We see the results of this process today in the unprecedented freedom of exchange between different societies, making it possible for students from all regions of the globe to attend schools in foreign countries, and enabling audiences everywhere to enjoy performing artists from distant lands, in person or via the Internet.

Terms to Note:

rebec
shawm
mode

Suggested Listening:

Turkish music (Janissary ensemble; see p. 288)
Medieval dance with shawm (estampie; see p. 355)

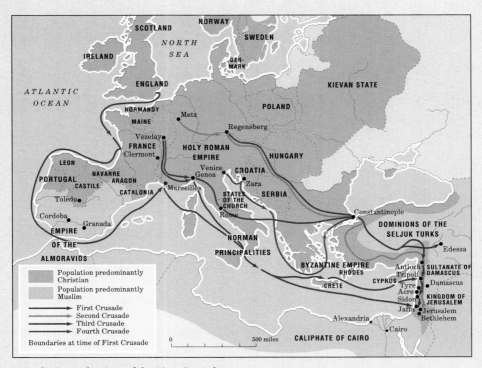

Boundaries at the time of the First Crusade.

Courtly poetry

The poems of the troubadour and trouvère repertory ranged from simple ballads to love songs, political and moral ditties, war songs, chronicles of the Crusades, laments, and dance songs. They praised the virtues recognized in the age of chivalry: valor, honor, nobility of character, devotion to an ideal, and the quest for perfect love. Like so many of our popular songs today, many of the medieval lyrics dealt with the subject of unrequited—or unconsummated—passion. The object of the poet's desire was generally unattainable, either because of rank or because the beloved was already wed to another. This poetry, in short, dealt with love in its most idealized form. The subjects of poems by women were similar to those by men, ranging from the sorrow of being rejected by a lover to the joy of true love, but they were approached from a feminine point of view. The songs in praise of the Virgin Mary were cast in the same style and language, sometimes even set to the same melodies, as those that expressed a more worldly kind of love.

MONIOT D'ARRAS AND THE TROUVÈRE TRADITION

Moniot d'Arras (fl. 1213–39), a monk in the abbey of St. Vaast, wrote both secular and sacred songs. His work in his native Arras marked the end of the trouvère tradition. We will study his love song *Ce fut en mai* (It Happened in May), which tells of an unhappy lover who finds comfort in the joys of another couple. (See Listening Guide 35.) The music is folklike and charming, and it makes no attempt to express the unhappiness described in the text. The song is monophonic in texture, consisting of a single line of melody heard against an accompaniment that was improvised.

Medieval instruments

In our recording, the accompaniment is played on three early string instruments: a psaltery, a dulcimer, and a vielle. The *psaltery*, a medieval folk instrument, consisted of a sound box over which were stretched four or five strings that were plucked to produce the melody and a larger number of strings for supplying accompaniments. The *dulcimer* resembled the psaltery, but its strings, instead of being plucked, were struck with little hammers. The *vielle* was an ancestor of the violin.

The poem consists of five stanzas, with an elaborate rhyme scheme (as the Listening Guide makes clear). The melody unfolds in two short sections, each of which is repeated. The overall musical form is strophic, in which the same melody is repeated with every stanza of the poem. A brief instrumental interlude is improvised between the stanzas. The timeless theme expressed in this appealing trouvère chanson—the longing for lost love—would find a new voice in the polyphonic music of the next century.

Listening Guide 35

CD: Chr/Std 1/15–19
Cassette: Chr/Std 1A/6

MONIOT D'ARRAS: *Ce fut en mai* (Trouvère Song)   (2:36)

Date of work: Mid–13th century

Genre: Chanson, strophic setting of 5 stanzas, each containing 12 lines

Musical form: **A-A-B-B** (2 short sections, each repeated, for every stanza)

Rhyme scheme: *a-a-b-a-a-b-c-c-b-c-c-b* (for each stanza)

Melody of song, with 2 sections shown:

		Text	Rhyme scheme	Musical form	Translation
		I			
15	0:00	Ce fut en mai	*a*	**A**	In early May
		Au douz tens gai	*a*		When skies are gay
		Que la saisons est bele;	*b*		And green the plains and mountains,
		Main me levai	*a*	**A**	At break of day
		Joer m'alai	*a*		I rose to play
		Lez une fontenele.	*b*		Beside a little fountain.
		En un vergier	*c*	**B**	In garden close
		Clos d'aiglentier	*c*		Where shone the rose
		Oi une viele;	*b*		I heard a fiddle played, then
		La vi dancier	*c*	**B**	A handsome knight
		Un chevalier	*c*		That charmed my sight
		Et une damoisele.	*b*		Was dancing with a maiden.
		II			
16	0:35	Cors orent gent	*a*	**A**	Both fair of face,
		Et avenant,	*a*		They turned with grace
		Et molt très bien dançoient;	*b*		To tread their Maytime measure;

		En acolant	a	A	The flowering place,
		Et en baisant	a		Their close embrace,
		Molt biau se deduisoient.	b		Their kisses, brought them pleasure.
		Au chief du tor,	c	B	Yet shortly they
		En un destor,	c		Had slipped away
		Doi et doi s'en aloient;	b		And strolled among the bowers;
		Le jeu d'amor	c	B	To ease their heart
		Desus la flor	c		Each played the part
		A lor plaisir faisoient.	b		In love's games on the flowers.

III

17	1:04	J'alai avant,	a	A	I crept ahead
		Molt redoutant,	a		All chill with dread
		Que nus d'aus ne me voie,	b		Lest someone there should see me,
		Maz et pensant	a	A	Bemused and sad
		Et desirrant	a		Because I had
		D'avoir ausi grant joie.	b		No joy like theirs to please me.
		Lors vi lever	c	B	Then one of those
		Un de lor per	c		I'd seen there, rose
		De si loing com j'estoie	b		And from afar off speaking,
		Por apeler	c	B	He questioned me
		Et demander	c		Who I might be
		Qui sui ni que queroie.	b		And what I came there seeking.

IV

18	1:33	J'alai vers aus	a	A	I stepped their way
		Dis lor mes maus,	a		To sadly say
		Que une dame amoie,	b		How long I'd loved a lady
		A cui loiaus	a	A	Whom all my days
		Sans estre faus	a		My heart obeys
		Tot mon vivant seroie,	b		Full faithfully and steady,
		Por cui plus trai	c	B	Though still I bore
		Paine et esmai	c		A grief so sore
		Que dire ne porroie.	b		In losing one so lovely
		Et bien le sai,	c	B	That surely I
		Que je morrai,	c		Would come to die
		S'ele ne mi ravoie.	b		Unless she deigned to love me.

V

19	2:02	Tot belement	a	A	With wisdom rare,
		Et doucement	a		With tactful air,
		Chascuns d'aus me ravoie.	b		They counseled and relieved me.
		Et dient tant	a	A	They said their prayer
		Que Dieus briement	a		That God might spare
		M'envoit de celi joie	b		Some joy in love that grieved me,
		Por qui je sent	c	B	Where all my gain
		Paine et torment:	c		Was loss and pain,
		Et je lor en rendoie	b		So I, in turn, extended
		Merci molt grant	c	B	My thanks sincere
		Et en plorant	c		With many a tear
		A Dé les comandoie.	b		And them to God commended.

Guillaume de Machaut and the French *Ars nova*

"Music is a science that would have us laugh, sing, and dance."

The breakup of the feudal social structure brought with it new concepts of life, art, and beauty. These changes were reflected in the musical style known as *Ars nova* (new art), which made its appearance at the beginning of the fourteenth century in France and somewhat later in Italy. The music of the French *Ars nova* shows greater refinement than music of the *Ars antiqua* (old art), which it displaced. Writers such as Petrarch, Boccaccio, and Chaucer were turning from the "divine comedy" of the world beyond to human subjects; painters would soon begin to discover the beauties of nature and the attractiveness of the human form. Similarly, composers turned increasingly from religious to secular themes. The *Ars nova* ushered in developments in rhythm, meter, harmony, and counterpoint that transformed the art of music.

Its outstanding figure was the French composer-poet Guillaume de Machaut (c. 1300–1377). His name—William from Machaut, a small town in northern France—was typical for the era. He took holy orders at an early age, became secretary to John of Luxembourg, King of Bohemia, and was active at the court of Charles, Duke of Normandy, who subsequently became King of France. Machaut spent his old age as a canon at the Cathedral of Rheims, admired as the greatest musician of the time.

Machaut's double career as cleric and courtier inspired him to write both religious and secular music. His output includes more than twenty motets, many secular *chansons* (French for "songs"), and an important polyphonic setting of the complete Ordinary of the Mass. His own poetry reveals him as a proponent of the ideals of medieval chivalry. One of his writings, a long autobiographical poem of more than nine thousand lines in rhymed couplets, tells the love story of the aging Machaut and a young girl named Peronne. The two exchanged poems and letters, some of which the composer set to music.

The Chanson *Puis qu'en oubli*

Machaut's music introduced a new freedom of rhythm, characterized by gentle syncopations and the interplay of duple and triple meters. Among secular genres, Machaut favored the chanson, which was generally set to courtly love poems written in one of several fixed text forms. These poetic forms—the *rondeau, ballade,* and *virelai*—established the musical repetition scheme of

Fixed forms

A polyphonic chanson is performed with voice and lute in this miniature representing the Garden of Love, from a Flemish manuscript of Le Roman de la Rose *(c. 1500).*

the chansons. We will study his love song *Puis qu'en oubli*, a rondeau for three voices with a refrain echoing the pain of unrequited love ("Since I am forgotten by you, sweet friend, I bid farewell to a life of love and joy"; see Listening Guide 36 for complete text and translation). In Machaut's elegant chanson, whose low melodic range makes it appropriate for three men's voices or a solo male voice accompanied by instruments, the two musical sections alternate in a pattern dictated by the poetry. This may be the very work referred to by Machaut in a letter to his beloved Peronne: "I am sending you a rondel with music of which I made the tune and the text some time ago, but I've newly made the tenor and contratenor [the two lower parts]; should you like to get to know it, it seems to me good." The influence of this last great poet-composer was far-reaching, his music and poetry admired long after his death.

Listening Guide 36

CD: Chr/Std 1/20–24, Sh 1/5–9
Cassette: Chr/Std 1A/7, Sh 1A/4

MACHAUT: *Puis qu'en oubli* (1:46)

Date of work: Mid–14th century

Genre: Polyphonic chanson, 3 voices

Poem: Rondeau (with 2-line refrain)

Musical form: 2 short musical sections, **A** and **B**, repeated as follows: **A-B-a-A-a-b-A-B**
(capital letters indicate refrain text)

Top-line melody of **A** section, with refrain text:

Top-line melody of **B** section, with refrain text:

			Text	Musical form	Translation
20	0:00	Refrain	Puis qu'en oubli sui de vous, dous amis,	**A**	Since I am forgotten by you,
			Vie amoureuse et joie a Dieu commant.	**B**	sweet friend, I bid farewell to a life of love and joy.
21	0:25	Verse	Mar vi le jour que m'amour en vous mis;	**a**	Unlucky was the day I placed my love in you;
22	0:38	Partial refrain	Puis qu'en oubli sui de vous, dous amis.	**A**	Since I am forgotten by you, sweet friend.
23	0:52	Verse	Mais ce tenray que je vous ay promis:	**a**	But what was promised you I will sustain: That I shall never have any other love.
			C'est que jamais n'aray nul autre amant.	**b**	
24	1:17	Refrain	Puis qu'en oubli sui de vous, dous amis,	**A**	Since I am forgotten by you, sweet friend, I bid farewell to a life of love and joy.
			Vie amoureuse et joie a Dieu commant.	**B**	

EARLY INSTRUMENTAL MUSIC

The fourteenth century witnessed a steady growth in the scope and importance of instrumental music. Though the central role in art music was still reserved for vocal works, instruments were put to more and more uses. As we have seen, they could play a supporting role in vocal music, doubling or accompanying the singers. Instrumental arrangements of vocal works grew increasingly popular. And instruments found their earliest prominence in dance music, where rhythm was the prime consideration.

Improvised music   Unlike the sophisticated vocal music of church and court, instrumental music was rarely written down; rather, it was improvised, much as jazz would be six centuries later. We can therefore only estimate the extent and variety of the instrumental repertory during the late Middle Ages. But our speculation can be guided by an ever growing body of knowledge. Some of the instruments themselves survive, in museums and private collections. While not always reliable in details, the many paintings and sculptures that portray instruments provide much information about their use and playing technique. Historical documents such as court payrolls tell us about the size and makeup of musical establishments. From these, and from the written instrumental music that has survived, scholars have reconstructed a remarkable body of knowledge about early instruments.

Although these old instruments were more limited in range and volume than their modern counterparts, they were well suited to the purposes of the societies that devised them. Thus, while early instruments fell into the same general families as modern ones—strings, woodwinds, brass, percussion, and keyboard—they were also divided into *soft* (*bas*), or indoor, and *loud* (*haut*), or outdoor, categories according to their use.

Soft instruments   Among the most commonly used soft instruments were the *recorder*, an end-blown flute with a breathy tone; the *lute*, a plucked string instrument of Middle Eastern origin with a rounded back; the *harp* and *psaltery*, plucked string instruments of biblical fame; and the *rebec* and *vielle*, the two principal bowed string instruments of the Middle Ages.

Loud instruments   The loud category of instruments, used mainly for outdoor occasions such as tournaments and processions, included the *shawm*, an ancestor of the oboe with a loud, nasal tone, and the *slide trumpet*, which developed into the early trombone known as the *sackbut*. Two wind instruments that became increasingly popular in the late Middle Ages do not fit neatly into the categories of loud and soft. The *crumhorn* (crooked horn) is a woodwind instrument shaped like the letter J with a cap over its double reed, making it considerably less raucous than the shawm. The *cornetto* developed from the traditional cow horn but was made of wood; it had a cup-shaped mouthpiece like a brass

Three shawms and a slide trumpet accompany dancers in this detail from the Adimiri wedding chest, c. 1450. (Galleria dell'Accademia, Florence)

instrument's, with fingerholes like a woodwind's. Percussion instruments of the time included a large cylindrical drum called the *tabor* and small drums known as *nakers*, usually played in pairs. Several of these instruments had their origins in the Middle East, and nakers are mentioned in Marco Polo's account of his travels in Asia.

Organs

Several types and sizes of organ were already in use in the Middle Ages. There were large ones, requiring a team of men to pump their giant bellows and often several more to manipulate the cumbersome slider mechanisms that opened and closed the pipes. At the other extreme were *portative* and *positive* organs—smaller instruments with keyboards and a few ranks of pipes. One type of small organ, the *regal*, took its name from one of the reed stops of the larger organs.

The revival of early music has grown in recent decades, as scholars and performers have worked to reconstruct some of the conditions under which the music was originally performed. Most of the ensembles that now specialize in this repertory boast players who have mastered the old instruments. Their concerts and recordings have made the public aware of the sound of these instruments to a degree that was undreamed of fifty years ago.

Dancers, some bearing torches, performing at a feast to the accompaniment of a flute, drum, and a partly visible string instrument. Book of Hours, Flemish, ca. 1500. (British Library)

Royal estampie No. 4: An Anonymous Medieval Dance

Professional instrumentalists of the Middle Ages must have been both skilled and sophisticated, since their earnings were often quite high. Even so, many of them did not read or write musical notation—they had no need to, because most of their music was improvised—and consequently, little of their music has survived. The particular dance we will study is one of eight found in a late-thirteenth-century French manuscript called the *Chansonnier du Roy* (*Song-book of the King*), which contains trouvère and troubadour songs. The dances in this collection are of the type known as *estampie*, a stately dance, probably for couples, characterized by elaborate body movements. The music for *Royal estampie* No. 4 is a monophonic melody with seven different short sections, each of which is repeated with first and second endings (called *open* and *closed endings*) that serve as a kind of refrain (see Listening Guide 37). Notice that the triple-meter melody is in asymmetrical sections of varying lengths, lending complexity to the musical structure. In our performance, we will hear the estampie played by a mixture of loud and soft instruments, with improvised percussion and other accompaniment (sustained tones called drones and harmony produced by mirroring the melody line a fifth above or below). *Embellishments*, or improvised musical decoration, are added to the basic melodic line. One important literary source of this era, *The Remedy of Fortune*, by the composer Machaut, attests to the use of all kinds of instruments for the dance; in it, Machaut provides a detailed description of a day's entertainment—both indoors and out—and the musical performance of an estampie:

Embellishments

> You should have seen after the meal the minstrels who entered in generous number, with shining hair and simple dress! They played many varied har-

monies ... certainly it seems to me that never was such a melody seen nor heard, for each of them, according to the tone of his instrument, without discord, plays on vielle, gittern, citole, harp, trumpet, flageolet, pipe bellows, bagpipe, nakers, or tabor, and every sound that one can make with fingers, quill, and bow I heard and saw in that park.

Listening Guide 37

CD: Chr/Std 1/25–31
Cassette: Chr/Std 1A/8

ANONYMOUS: *Royal estampie* No. 4   (2:29)

Date of work: Late thirteenth century (France)

Form: Monophonic dance in seven sections, each repeated; open (x) and closed (y) endings repeat as refrains: 1x1y 2x2y 3x3y 4x4y 5x5y 6x6y 7x7y

Character:
Tempo and meter—moderate, stately triple-meter dance
Melody—narrow range, built from short motives; asymmetrical phrase lengths
Harmony—improvised as drone (sustained tone) and in parallel fifths with melody

Instruments used in Norton recording: 2 shawms, 3-holed pipe (similar to a recorder), rebec, 2 vielles, tambourine, and drum

		Section (each repeated)	Solo instrument	Refrain (x and y endings)
25	0:00	1	Shawm	Ensemble (x and y), monophonic
26	0:19	2	Vielle	Ensemble (x and y), monophonic
27	0:38	3	Pipe	Ensemble (x and y), monophonic
28	1:00	4	Shawm	Ensemble (x), monophonic; ensemble (y), in parallel fifths
29	1:19	5	Vielle (with drone)	Ensemble (x and y), in parallel fifths
30	1:42	6	Vielle (with drone)	Ensemble (x and y), in parallel fifths
31	2:04	7	Ensemble (heterophonic)	Ensemble (x and y), in parallel fifths

Melody for section 1, with repeat written out showing open (x) and closed (y) endings:

The Renaissance

55

The Renaissance Spirit

*"I am not pleased with the Courtier if he be not also a musician,
and besides his understanding and cunning [in singing] upon the
book, have skill in like manner on sundry instruments."*
—BALDASSARE CASTIGLIONE

The Renaissance (c. 1450–1600) is one of the most beautiful if misleading
names in the history of culture: beautiful because it implies an awakening of
intellectual awareness, misleading because it suggests a sudden rebirth of
learning and art after the presumed stagnation of the Middle Ages. History
moves continuously rather than by leaps and bounds. The Renaissance was
the next phase in a cultural process that, under the leadership of the church,
universities, and princely courts, had long been under way.

THE ARTS IN THE RENAISSANCE

**Philosophical
developments**

The Renaissance marks the passing of European society from an exclusively
religious orientation to a more secular one, and from an age of unquestion-
ing faith and mysticism to one of belief in reason and scientific inquiry. The
focus of human destiny was seen to be life on earth rather than the hereafter.

People began to rely more on the evidence of the senses rather than on tradition and authority, and they gained new confidence in their ability to solve their own problems and rationally order their world. This awakening found its symbol in the culture of Greek and Roman antiquity. Renaissance society, led by the humanists, discovered the summit of human wisdom not only in the Church Fathers and saints, as their ancestors had done, but also in the ancient philosophers and writers, including Homer and Virgil.

Historical developments

Historians used to date the onset of the Renaissance from the fall of Constantinople to the Turks in 1453 and the emigration of Greek scholars to the West. Today, we recognize that there are no such clear demarcations in history, though a series of momentous circumstances around that time help to set off the new era from the old. The introduction of gunpowder signaled the eventual end of the age of knighthood. The development of the compass made possible the voyages of discovery that opened up a new world and demolished old superstitions. Although the great European explorers of this age—Christopher Columbus, Amerigo Vespucci, and Ponce de León, among others—were in search of a new trade route to the riches of China and the Indies, they stumbled on the unknown (to them) continents of North and South America. During the course of the sixteenth and seventeenth centuries, these new lands became increasingly important to European treasuries and society.

Artistic developments

The revival of ancient writings mentioned earlier, spurred by the introduction of printing, had its counterpart in architecture, painting, and sculpture. If the Romanesque found its grand architectural form in the monastery and the Gothic in the cathedral, the Renaissance lavished its constructive energy on palace and château. The gloomy fortified castles of the medieval princes gave way to spacious villas that displayed the harmonious proportions of the classical style. (The term "classical" in this context refers to the culture of the ancient Greeks and Romans, whose art was thought to embody the ideals of order, stability, and balanced proportions.)

So too the elongated saints and martyrs of medieval painting and sculpture were replaced by the David of Donatello and the gentle Madonnas of Leonardo. Even where artists retained a religious theme, the Mother of Sorrows and the symbols of grief gave way to smiling Madonnas—often posed for by very secular ladies—and dimpled cherubs. The nude human form, denied or covered for centuries, was revealed as a thing of beauty and used as an object of anatomical study. Nature entered painting as well, and with it an intense preoccupation with the laws of perspective and composition.

Medieval painting had presented life through symbolism; the Renaissance preferred realism. The medieval painters posed their figures frontally, impersonally; the Renaissance developed the art of portraiture and humanized its subjects. Medieval painting dealt in stereotypes; the Renaissance concerned itself with individuals. Space in medieval painting was organized in a succes-

Cultural Perspective 11

WHEN THE OLD WORLD MEETS THE NEW WORLD

Can you imagine the reaction of European explorers to the Native American peoples and cultures they encountered on first reaching the New World? And vice versa? Christopher Columbus recorded his impressions in his diary, remarking that the first locals he met were "so peaceful . . . they love their neighbors as themselves; and their discourse is ever sweet and gentle, and accompanied by a smile."

Europeans found the music of the Native Americans quite foreign to their ears, noting the highly repetitive nature of the songs, the use of vocables (sung syllables that lack literal meaning), and the sometimes high, piercing vocal quality (sung by males in falsetto, a technique by which they can sing above their normal vocal range). The English explorer Captain John Smith (1580–1631) described the instruments he saw among the locals of eastern Virginia.

> For their musicke, they use a thicke cane, on which they pipe as on a Recorder. For their warres, they have a great deepe platter of wood. They cover the mouth thereof with a skin . . . that they may beat upon it as upon a drumme. But their chiefe instruments are Rattels made of small gourds or Pumpion [pumpkin] shels. Of these they have Base, Tenor, Countertenor, Meane and Trible.

Thus this particular tribe had flute- or whistle-like instruments (of the aerophone category) fashioned from cane, drums made from hollowed trees over which animal skins were stretched (membranophones), and rattles of widely varying sizes made from gourds or animal horns (idiophones). The use of the latter two categories of instruments typified the musics of many Native American nations.

There were frequent occasions for music making among the Native Americans. Their songs told of love and war, the harvest and the hunt, deities, birth, marriage, and death. For example, the music of the Iroquoian tribes (of southeastern Canada and the northeastern United States) was organized around their agricultural year; one song, the *Corn Dance*, was sung to the female corn spirit to encourage the growth of their most important crop. The Plains tribes welcomed the summer crops with the Sun Dance, while the Pacific Coast tribes performed a Mystery Dance to honor the regeneration of nature in spring.

Smith had the opportunity to observe ceremonial rituals of one tribe in Virginia: "Their devotion was most in songs in which the chiefe Priest beginneth and the rest followed him." This call-and-response exchange, much like the responsorial singing we have noted in early church music, is a style that has developed in the musics of many world cultures.

Unlike some encounters we will observe, relatively little cross influence of styles took place between Native Americans and Europeans during the seventeenth century, perhaps because the two cultures were so profoundly different. The music of Native Americans has been preserved largely through oral tradition within their individual cultures. In our own century, there has been a lot of stylistic cross-fertilization. Young Native Americans listen to the same rock and country/western music as youths of European, African, or Asian heritage, while a few Native Americans have brought their music to a wider audience. For example, flutist R. Carlos Nakai (of Navaho-Ute heritage) has combined his native musical traditions with those of European art music and has made haunting recordings that have captured the imagination of many listeners.

Terms to Note:

vocable	idiophone
falsetto	call and response
aerophone	responsorial singing
membranophone	oral tradition

Suggested Listening:

Native American ceremonial music
Modern Native American music
    (R. Carlos Nakai)

Powatans of Virginia in a ceremonial dance, as depicted by the English artist **John White** *in 1585.* (The British Museum, London)

sion of planes that the eye perceived as a series of episodes. Renaissance painters made it possible to see the whole simultaneously. They discovered the landscape, created the illusion of distance, and focused on the physical loveliness of the world.

The Renaissance came to flower in Italy, the nation that stood closest to the classical Roman culture; as a result, the great names we associate with its painting and sculpture are predominantly Italian: Donatello (c. 1386–1466), Botticelli (1444–1510), Leonardo da Vinci (1452–1519), Michelangelo (1475–1564), Raphael (1483–1520), and Titian (c. 1488–1576). With masters who lived in the second half of the sixteenth century, such as Tintoretto (1518–1594) and Veronese (1528–1588), we approach the world of the early Baroque.

From the colorful tapestry of Renaissance life emerges a galaxy of great names. The list includes the Dutch scholar-philosopher Erasmus (c. 1466–1536), the German religious reformer Martin Luther (1483–1546), the Italian statesman Machiavelli (1469–1527) and his compatriot the scientist Galileo (1564–1642), the French writer Rabelais (c. 1494–c. 1553), the Spanish author Cervantes (1547–1616), and the English playwrights Marlowe (1564–1593) and Shakespeare (1564–1616).

The Renaissance marks the birth of the modern European spirit and of Western society as we have come to know it. That turbulent time shaped the moral and cultural climate we live in today.

The Renaissance painter preferred realism to allegory and psychological characterizations to stylized stereotypes. These attributes are exemplified in the famous portrait of Mona Lisa, *by* **Leonardo da Vinci** *(1452–1519).* (The Louvre, Paris)

The human form, denied for centuries, was revealed in the Renaissance as an object of beauty. David, *by* **Donatello** *(c. 1386–1466).* (Museo Nazionale del Bargello, Florence)

MUSICIANS IN RENAISSANCE SOCIETY

Musicians as professionals

Musicians of the sixteenth century were supported by the chief institutions of their society—the church, city, and state, as well as royal and aristocratic courts. Musicians could find employment as choirmasters, singers, organists, instrumentalists, copyists, composers, teachers, instrument builders, and music printers and publishers. There was a corresponding growth in a number of supporting musical institutions: church choirs and schools, publishing houses, civic wind bands. And there were increased opportunities for apprentices to study with master singers, players, and instrument builders. A few women can be identified as professional musicians in this era, earning their living as court instrumentalists and singers. In Chapter 57, we will learn more about a famous ensemble of vocalists known as the Singing Ladies of Ferrara.

The rise of the merchant class brought with it a new group of music patrons. This development was paralleled by the emergence, among the cultivated middle and upper classes, of the amateur musician. When the system for printing from movable type was successfully adapted to music in the early sixteenth century, printed music books became available and affordable, making possible the rise of great publishing houses in Venice, Paris, and Antwerp. As a result, musical literacy spread dramatically.

RENAISSANCE MUSICAL STYLE

A cappella music

Continuous imitation

The vocal forms of the Renaissance were marked by smoothly gliding melodies conceived for the voice. In fact, the sixteenth century has come to be regarded as the golden age of the *a cappella* style (the term, you will recall, refers to a vocal work without instrumental accompaniment). Polyphony in such works was based on a principle called *continuous imitation*. In this procedure, the motives are exchanged between vocal lines, the voices imitating one another so that the same theme or motive is heard now in the soprano or alto, now in the tenor or bass, resulting in a close-knit musical fabric capable of the most subtle and varied effects. (See Listening Guide 39 for examples.)

Word painting

Most church music was written in *a cappella* style. Secular music, on the other hand, was divided between purely vocal works and those in which the singers were supported by instruments. The period also saw the growth of solo instrumental music, especially for lute and for keyboard instruments. In the matter of harmony, composers of the Renaissance leaned toward fuller chords. They turned away from the parallel fifths and octaves preferred in medieval times to the more pleasing thirds and sixths. The expressive device of *word painting*—that is, making the music reflect the meaning of the words—was much favored in secular music. An unexpected, harsh dissonance might coincide with the word "death," or an ascending line might lead up to the word "heavens" or "stars." (The use of dissonance in sacred music was more carefully controlled.)

In the sixteenth century, women played an active role in music making in the bourgeois home. The Van Berchem Family, *credited to* **Frans Floris**, *1561.* (Musea Wuyts–Van Campen en Baron Caroly, Lier)

Polyphonic writing offered the composer many possibilities, such as the use of a *cantus firmus* (fixed melody) as the basis for elaborate ornamentation in the other voices. As we have seen, triple meter had been especially attractive to the medieval mind because it symbolized the perfection of the Trinity. The new era, much less preoccupied with religious symbolism, showed a greater interest in duple meter.

Cantus firmus

The composers of the Burgundian, or Franco-Flemish, School were preeminent in European music from around 1450 to the end of the sixteenth century. They came from the southern Lowlands (present-day Belgium) and from the adjoining provinces of northern France and Burgundy. Among them, Du Fay and Josquin created some of the masterpieces of the epoch.

56

Renaissance Sacred Music

"He who does honor and reverence to music is commonly a man of worth, sound of soul, by nature loving things lofty."
—PIERRE DE RONSARD

Music played a prominent part in the ritual of the church. In addition to the monophonic Gregorian chant, music for church services included polyphonic settings of the Mass, motets, and hymns. These were normally contrapuntal and, especially in the early sixteenth century, based on preexistent music. Such works were sung by professional singers, trained from childhood in the various cathedral choir schools.

THE EARLY RENAISSANCE MASS

With the rise of Renaissance polyphony, composers concentrated their musical settings on the Ordinary, the fixed portion of the Mass that was sung daily. This practice brought into prominence the five main sections of the Mass: Kyrie, Gloria, Credo, Sanctus, and Agnus Dei. (Today, these sections of the Mass are recited or sung in the *vernacular*, that is, the language of the country.) The first of these sections, the Kyrie, is a prayer for mercy that dates from the early centuries of Christianity, as its Greek text attests. It takes an **A-B-A** form that consists of nine invocations: three of "Kyrie eleison" (Lord,

Sections of the Mass

have mercy), three of "Christe eleison" (Christ, have mercy), and again three of "Kyrie eleison." The Kyrie is followed by the Gloria ("Glory be to God on high"), a joyful hymn of praise that is omitted in the penitential seasons of Advent and Lent.

The third movement, the Credo ("I believe in one God, the Father Almighty"), is the confession of faith and the longest of the Mass texts. Fourth is the Sanctus ("Holy, holy, holy"), which concludes with the "Hosanna" ("Hosanna in the highest"). The fifth and last part, the Agnus Dei ("Lamb of God, Who takes away the sins of the world"), is sung three times.

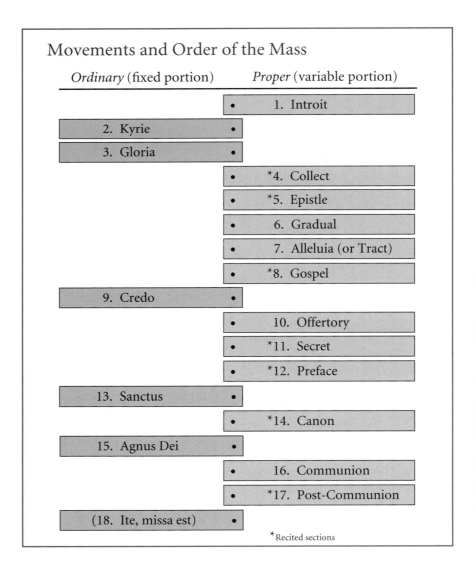

Movements and Order of the Mass

Ordinary (fixed portion)   *Proper* (variable portion)

Ordinary (fixed portion)	Proper (variable portion)
	1. Introit
2. Kyrie	
3. Gloria	
	*4. Collect
	*5. Epistle
	6. Gradual
	7. Alleluia (or Tract)
	*8. Gospel
9. Credo	
	10. Offertory
	*11. Secret
	*12. Preface
13. Sanctus	
	*14. Canon
15. Agnus Dei	
	16. Communion
	*17. Post-Communion
(18. Ite, missa est)	

*Recited sections

Twice it concludes with "miserere nobis" (have mercy on us), and the third time with the prayer "dona nobis pacem" (grant us peace). A summary of the order of the Mass, with its Proper and Ordinary movements, may be found opposite. (Remember that we studied an example of a Gradual for Easter Sunday, *Haec dies*, in Chapter 53.)

Early polyphonic settings of the Mass were usually based on a fragment of Gregorian chant, which became the *cantus firmus* (fixed melody). The cantus firmus thus served as the foundation of the work, supporting the florid patterns that the other voices wove around it. It provided composers with a fixed element that they could embellish with all the resources of their artistry, and when used in all the movements, it helped unify the Mass as well.

Of the Masses for special services, the most important is the *Requiem*, or Mass for the Dead, sung at funerals and memorial services. The name comes from the opening verse, "Requiem aeternam dona eis, Domine" (Grant them eternal rest, O Lord). Included are prayers in keeping with the solemnity of the occasion, among them the awesome evocation of the Last Judgment, "Dies irae" (Day of Wrath). (You may recall that we heard a Protestant Requiem by Brahms, written in German rather than Latin.)

Requiem

The Mass as an art form extends over some eight hundred years of history, and has inspired some of the greatest music ever written.

Du Fay and the Cantus Firmus Mass

Guillaume Du Fay (c. 1397–1474) was one of the earliest composers of the Burgundian School to make a career in Italy, where he spent his formative years. He was also active in southeastern France at the court of Savoy, which was noted for the brilliance of its artistic life. He spent his last years in his native Cambrai in northern France, where he continued to compose until his death.

Du Fay and his Burgundian colleagues abandoned the rhythmic complexities of fourteenth-century music in favor of a less uncomplicated, more accessible style. The meandering vocal lines of the past were replaced in their music by well-defined melodies and clear-cut rhythms. Harmony grew simpler and more consonant, foreshadowing a language based on triads and a sense of key. Eventually, Du Fay expanded the standard musical texture from three voices to four. He wrote polyphonic music in all the genres current during his lifetime, including Masses, motets, hymns, and secular songs in French and Italian. His output included at least nine complete settings of the Ordinary of the Mass as well as many individual Mass movements. Some of his Masses are built on a cantus firmus taken from a Gregorian chant or from a popular song.

The *L'homme armé* Mass uses a catchy, popular tune as its basis. Although

Guillaume Du Fay (left) stands next to a portative organ, while fellow composer Gilles Binchois holds a harp. Miniature from Le Champion des dames, *by* **Martin Le Franc,** *dated 1441–42. (Bibliothèque Nationale, Paris)*

often concealed in a web of polyphony, the melody provides the structural framework for each section of the Mass and is usually sounded in long notes by the tenors. Du Fay divides the opening movement, the Kyrie, into three sections according to its text (see Listening Guide 38). He begins each of these sections with a reduced number of voices, then adds the tenor singing different parts of the fixed tune (cantus firmus) and filling out the harmonies. In this Mass, we can hear at times the hollow-sounding octaves and fifths of medieval music and also the sonorous thirds and sixths that were growing in popularity.

Listening Guide 38

CD: Chr/Std 1/32–35
Cassette: Chr/Std 1B/1–2

Du Fay: *L'homme armé* Mass, Kyrie   (5:21)

Date of work: 1460s

Basis: Cantus firmus, based on the tune *L'homme armé (The Armed Man)*

Medium: 4 voices, nonimitative polyphony

Movements from the Ordinary of the Mass:

Kyrie   Sanctus
Gloria   Agnus Dei
Credo

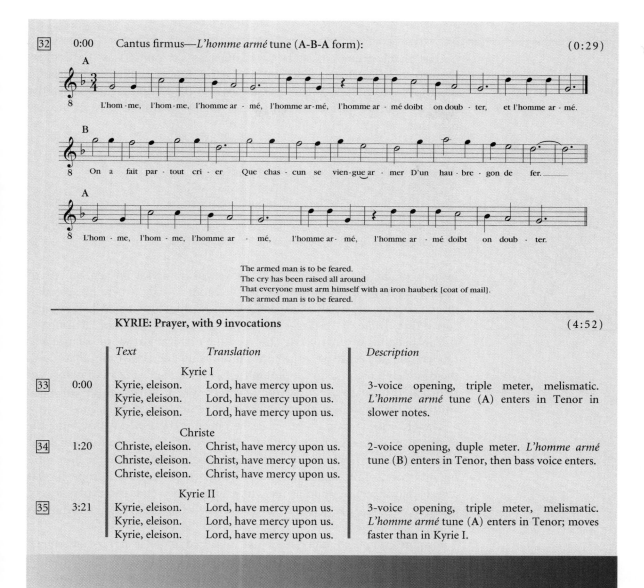

32   0:00   Cantus firmus—*L'homme armé* tune (**A-B-A** form):   (0:29)

A

L'hom - me, l'hom - me, l'homme ar - mé, l'homme ar-mé, l'homme ar - mé doibt on doub - ter, et l'homme ar - mé.

B

On a fait par - tout cri - er   Que chas - cun se vien-gue ar - mer D'un hau - bre - gon de fer._____

A

L'hom - me, l'hom - me, l'homme ar - mé,   l'homme ar - mé,   l'homme ar - mé doibt   on doub - ter.

> The armed man is to be feared.
> The cry has been raised all around
> That everyone must arm himself with an iron hauberk [coat of mail].
> The armed man is to be feared.

KYRIE: Prayer, with 9 invocations   (4:52)

		Text	Translation	Description
		Kyrie I		
33	0:00	Kyrie, eleison.	Lord, have mercy upon us.	3-voice opening, triple meter, melismatic.
		Kyrie, eleison.	Lord, have mercy upon us.	*L'homme armé* tune (**A**) enters in Tenor in
		Kyrie, eleison.	Lord, have mercy upon us.	slower notes.
		Christe		
34	1:20	Christe, eleison.	Christ, have mercy upon us.	2-voice opening, duple meter. *L'homme armé*
		Christe, eleison.	Christ, have mercy upon us.	tune (**B**) enters in Tenor, then bass voice enters.
		Christe, eleison.	Christ, have mercy upon us.	
		Kyrie II		
35	3:21	Kyrie, eleison.	Lord, have mercy upon us.	3-voice opening, triple meter, melismatic.
		Kyrie, eleison.	Lord, have mercy upon us.	*L'homme armé* tune (**A**) enters in Tenor; moves
		Kyrie, eleison.	Lord, have mercy upon us.	faster than in Kyrie I.

THE MOTET IN THE RENAISSANCE

In the Renaissance, the motet became a sacred form with a single Latin text, for use in the Mass and other religious services. Motets in praise of the Virgin Mary were extremely popular because of the many religious groups all over Europe devoted to Marian worship. These works, written for three or four voices, were sometimes based on a chant or other cantus firmus.

One of the greatest masters of the Renaissance motet was the Franco-Flemish composer Josquin Desprez (c. 1440–1521). With him, the transition is complete from the anonymous composer of the Middle Ages through the shadowy figures of the late Gothic to the highly individual artist of the Renaissance.

Josquin Desprez

JOSQUIN DESPREZ AND THE MOTET

"He is the master of the notes. They have to do as he bids them; other composers have to do as the notes will."—MARTIN LUTHER

Josquin (as he is known) exerted a powerful influence on generations of composers to follow. His varied career led him to Italy, where he served at several courts—especially those of Cardinal Ascanio Sforza of Milan and Ercole d'Este, Duke of Ferrara—and in the papal choir in Rome. During his stay in Italy, his northern style absorbed the classical virtues of balance and moderation, the sense of harmonious proportion and clear form, that found their model in the radiant art of Raphael. Toward the end of his life, Josquin returned to his native France, where he served as a provost at the collegiate church of Condé; he was buried in the choir of the church.

The older generation of musicians had been preoccupied with solving the technical problems of counterpoint, an interest that fit the intellectual climate of the late Middle Ages. Josquin appeared at a time when the humanizing influences of the Renaissance were being felt throughout Europe; he was able to harness contrapuntal ingenuity to a higher end: the expression of emotion. His music is rich in feeling, in serenely beautiful melody, and in expressive harmony.

Josquin composed more than one hundred motets, at least seventeen Masses, and numerous secular pieces, making use of a variety of techniques. Some works were based on preexistent monophonic or polyphonic models, others were original throughout.

Ave Maria . . . virgo serena is a prime example of how Josquin used the motet to experiment with different combinations of voices and textures (see Listening Guide 39). In this four-voice composition, which sets a rhymed poem to the Virgin Mary, high voices are set in dialogue with low ones and imitative textures alternate with homophonic settings. Josquin opens the piece with a musical reference to a chant for the Virgin, but soon drops this melody in favor of a freely composed form that is highly sensitive to the text. The final couplet, a personal plea to the Virgin ("O Mother of God, remember me"), is set in a simple texture that emphasizes the words, proclaiming the emotional spirit of a new age—the humanism of the High Renaissance.

JOSQUIN: *Ave Maria . . . virgo serena*

(4:38)

Date of work: 1470s

Genre: 4-voice motet

Basis: Chant to Virgin Mary (opening only)

Poem: Rhymed poem (a couplet, 5 quatrains, and a closing couplet)

Opening of soprano line, based on Gregorian chant:

		Text	Translation	Description
41	0:00	Ave Maria, gratia plena, Dominus tecum, virgo serena.	Hail Mary, full of grace, The Lord is with you, gentle Virgin.	4 voices in imitation (SATB); chant used; duple meter.
42	0:45	Ave cujus conceptio Solemni plena gaudio Coelestia, terrestria, Nova replet laetitia.	Hail, whose conception, Full of solemn joy, Fills the heaven, the earth, With new rejoicing.	2 and 3 voices, later 4 voices; more homophonic texture.
43	1:21	Ave cujus nativitas Nostra fuit solemnitas, Ut lucifer lux oriens, Verum solem praeveniens.	Hail, whose birth Was our festival, As our luminous rising light Coming before the true sun.	Voice pairs (SA/TB) in close imitation, then 4 voices in imitation.
44	1:59	Ave pia humilitas, Sine viro fecunditas, Cujus annuntiatio, Nostra fuit salvatio.	Hail, pious humility, Fertility without a man, Whose annunciation Was our salvation.	Voice pairs (SA/TB); a more homophonic texture.
45	2:27	Ave vera virginitas, Immaculata castitas, Cujus purificatio Nostra fuit purgatio.	Hail, true virginity, Unspotted chastity, Whose purification Was our cleansing.	Triple meter; clear text declamation; homophonic texture.
46	3:04	Ave praeclara omnibus Angelicis virtutibus, Cujus fuit assumptio Nostra glorificatio.	Hail, famous with all Angelic virtues, Whose assumption was Our glorification.	Imitative voice pairs; return to duple meter.

O Mater Dei,	O Mother of God,	Completely homophonic; text
Memento mei.	Remember me.	declaration in long notes, sepa-
Amen.	Amen.	rated by simultaneous rests.

Continuous imitation, with voice entries at regular intervals:

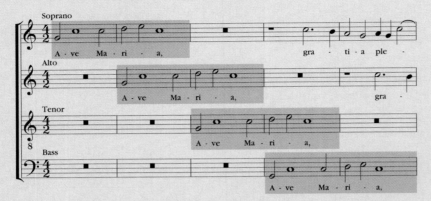

Imitation with paired voices (top two voices answered by bottom two):

THE HIGH RENAISSANCE MASS

Counter-Reformation

After the Protestant revolt led by Martin Luther (1483–1546), the Catholic Church responded with a reform movement focused on a return to true Christian piety. This movement became part of the Counter-Reformation, whereby the church strove to recapture the loyalty of its people. The Counter-Reformation, which extended from the 1530s to the end of the sixteenth century, saw work with the poor, undertaken by the religious orders of Franciscans and Dominicans, the founding of the Society of Jesus (Jesuits) by St. Ignatius Loyola (1491–1556), and the deliberations of the Council of Trent, which extended—with some interruptions—from 1545 to 1563.

In its desire to regulate every aspect of religious discipline, the Council of Trent took up the matter of church music. The attending cardinals were concerned about corruption of the traditional chant by the singers, who added extravagant embellishments to the Gregorian melodies. The council members objected to the use of certain instruments in religious services, to the practice of incorporating popular songs in Masses, to the secular spirit that had invaded sacred music, and to the generally irreverent attitude of church musicians. In polyphonic settings of the Mass, the cardinals claimed, the sacred text was made unintelligible by the overelaborate contrapuntal texture. Some advocated abolishing counterpoint altogether and returning to Gregorian chant, but there were many music lovers among the cardinals who opposed so drastic a step.

Council of Trent

The committee assigned to deal with the problem contented itself with issuing general recommendations in favor of a pure vocal style that would respect the integrity of the sacred texts, that would avoid virtuosity and encourage piety. One composer who answered the demands for a reformed church music was Giovanni Pierluigi da Palestrina.

A choir and instruments participate in the celebration of Mass in this engraving by **Philip Galle,** *after* **J. Stradanus,** *from* Encomium musices *of 1595.*

Palestrina presents his earliest printed work to Pope Julius III, in this sixteenth-century engraving.

PALESTRINA AND THE POPE MARCELLUS MASS

"I have held nothing more desirable than what is sung throughout the year, according to the season, should be more agreeable to the ear by virtue of its vocal beauty."

Giovanni Pierluigi da Palestrina (c. 1525–1594), called Palestrina after his birthplace, worked as an organist and choirmaster at various churches, including St. Peter's in Rome. His patron, Pope Julius III (r. 1550–55), appointed him to the Sistine Chapel Choir even though, as a married man, he was ineligible for the semi-ecclesiastical post. He was dismissed by a later pope but ultimately returned to direct another choir at St. Peter's, where he spent the last twenty-three years of his life. The beauty of Palestrina's music is a contemplative one; it stems from emotion directed to an act of faith.

Palestrina wrote over a hundred Masses, of which the most famous is the Mass for Pope Marcellus, successor to Julius III. It is popularly believed that this Mass was written to satisfy the new, strict demands placed on polyphonic church music by the Council of Trent. Since the papal choir at the time sang without instrumental accompaniment, the *Pope Marcellus* Mass was probably performed *a cappella*. It was written for six voice parts—soprano, alto, two tenors, and two basses, a typical setting for the all-male church choirs of the era. The highest voice was sung by boy sopranos or male falsettists, the alto part by male altos, or countertenors (tenors with very high voices), and the lower parts were distributed among the normal ranges of the male voice.

The Gloria from the *Pope Marcellus* Mass exhibits Palestrina's conservative style. The work begins with a monophonic intonation of the opening line, "Gloria in excelsis Deo" (Glory be to God on high), which, according to church practice, is chanted by the celebrant (or officiating priest). Palestrina carefully constructed a polyphonic setting for the remaining text, balancing the harmonic and polyphonic elements of his art so that the words of the sacred text are clear and audible, an effect desired by the Council of Trent. Changes in register and in the number of voices singing at any one time vary the musical texture throughout. (See Listening Guide 40 for the text and analysis.)

Palestrina's music is representative of the pure *a cappella* style of vocal polyphony. *A cappella*, meaning "in the church style," indicates a vocal performance without instruments, hence a manner of writing that is focused above all on the beauty and capacity of the human voice. This was Palestrina's ideal of sound—pure, serene, and celestial.

Listening Guide 40

CD: Chr/Std 1/48–49, Sh 1/17–18
Cassette: Chr/Std 1B/5, Sh 1A/6

PALESTRINA: *Pope Marcellus* Mass, Gloria

(6:15)

Date of work: Published 1567

Genre: Mass; Gloria, from a setting of the Ordinary

Voices: 6 (SATTBB)

Characteristics: Frequent textural changes, reduction of voices

Opening of Gloria, showing 6 voice parts (4 singing at one time), in clear word declamation:

		Text	No. of voices	Translation
48	0:00	Gloria in excelsis Deo	1	Glory be to God on high,
		et in terra pax hominibus	4	and on earth peace to men
		bonae voluntatis.	4	of good will.
		Laudamus te. Benedicimus te.	4	We praise Thee. We bless Thee.
		Adoramus te.	3	We adore Thee.
		Glorificamus te.	4	We glorify Thee.
		Gratias agimus tibi propter	5/4	We give Thee thanks for
		magnam gloriam tuam.	3/4	Thy great glory.
		Domine Deus, Rex caelestis,	4	Lord God, heavenly King,
		Deus Pater omnipotens.	3	God, the Father Almighty
		Domine Fili	4	O Lord, the only-begotten Son,
		unigenite, Jesu Christe.	6/5	Jesus Christ.
		Domine Deus, Agnus Dei,	3/4	Lord God, Lamb of God,
		Filius Patris.	6	Son of the Father.
49	2:43	Qui tollis peccata mundi,	4	Thou that takest away the sins of the world,
		miserere nobis.	4	have mercy on us.
		Qui tollis peccata mundi,	4/5	Thou that takest away the sins of the world,
		suscipe deprecationem nostram.	6/4	receive our prayer.
		Qui sedes ad dexteram Patris,	3	Thou that sittest at the right hand of the Father,
		miserere nobis.	3	have mercy on us.
		Quoniam tu solus sanctus.	4	For Thou alone art holy.
		Tu solus Dominus.	4	Thou only art the Lord.
		Tu solus Altissimus.	4	Thou alone art most high.
		Jesu Christe, cum Sancto Spiritu	6/3/4	Jesus Christ, along with the Holy Spirit
		in gloria Dei Patris.	4/5	in the glory of God the Father.
		Amen.	6	Amen.

57

Renaissance Secular Music

"Come sing to me a bawdy song, make me merry."—Falstaff, in
WILLIAM SHAKESPEARE's *Henry IV, Part 1*

MUSIC IN COURT AND CITY LIFE

In the Renaissance, both professionals and amateurs took part in music making. Professionals entertained noble guests at court and civic festivities, and

Amateur music making   with the rise of the merchant class, music making in the home became increasingly popular. Most prosperous homes had a lute (a plucked-string in-

Courtly musicians perform a polyphonic chanson with voice, flute, and lute in this detail from The Prodigal Son Among the Courtesans *(sixteenth century, artist unknown).* (Musée Carnavalet, Paris)

strument with a rounded body) or a keyboard instrument, and the study of music was considered part of the proper upbringing for a young girl or, to a lesser degree, boy. Women began to play a prominent part in the performance of music both in the home and at court. During the later sixteenth century in Italy, a number of professional women singers achieved great fame (see p. 381).

From the union of poetry and music arose two important secular genres: the chanson and the madrigal. In both of these song forms, music was used to enhance the poetry of such major literary figures as Francesco Petrarch (1304–1374) and Pierre de Ronsard (1524–1585). The intricate verse structures of French and Italian poetry in turn helped to shape the resulting musical forms.

THE CHANSON

In the fifteenth century, the chanson was the favored genre at the courts of the dukes of Burgundy and the kings of France, all great patrons of the arts. Chansons were usually written for three voices, with one or both lower parts meant to be played on instruments. They were set to the courtly love poetry of the French Renaissance, much of which remained in the fixed forms of the Middle Ages: the rondeau, the ballade, and the virelai (see p. 349). We saw in the case of a Machaut chanson that the text established the type of setting and the musical repetition of sections. The preeminent composers of this northern genre were Johannes Ockeghem, Gilles Binchois, and Guillaume Du Fay.

A Burgundian Chanson:
Il sera pour vous / L'homme armé

Il sera pour vous / L'homme armé is an unusual chanson in that it combines two texts: the top voice sings a rondeau that mockingly praises the victories over the Turks of Symon le Breton, a singer in the Burgundian court chapel of Philip the Good, while the two lower voices sing bits of the familiar popular tune *L'homme armé*. (Remember that this tune, which is sung monophonically before the chanson begins, also served as the basis for Du Fay's *L'homme armé* Mass, described earlier.) Although the work clearly was written by a musician associated with the court of Duke Philip the Good, scholars have not agreed on who composed it—possibly the Englishman Robert Morton or perhaps even Du Fay. Despite its double text, the chanson is performed as a rondeau, one of the most widespread poetic forms of the fifteenth century. It opens with a four-line refrain, which returns in part in the middle of the poem and in full at the end. (See Listening Guide 41 for the text and musical structure.)

The Renaissance chanson continued to be a favorite secular form throughout the sixteenth century, culminating in the works of the towering figure of Roland de Lassus (c. 1532–1594). This North European master wrote about 150 chansons, many of them setting the verses of such famous French poets as Pierre de Ronsard and Clément Marot. These texts, freed from the fixed forms of the previous century, cover a wide range of emotions, from amorous to lusting to religious. Sixteenth-century chansons were most often set for four voices, generally in a chordal, or homophonic, style.

Listening Guide 41

CD: Chr/Std 1/32, 36–40
Cassette: Chr/Std 1B/1, 3

BURGUNDIAN CHANSON: *Il sera pour vous / L'homme armé*

(1:46)

Composer: Musician associated with Burgundian chapel (Robert Morton? Guillaume Du Fay?)

Date of work: c. 1458

Genre: Polyphonic chanson, 3 voices

Text: 2 poems
   Top voice: *Il sera pour vous*, rondeau with 4-line refrain
   Lower voices: *L'homme armé*, popular song in A-B-A form

Musical form: 2 musical sections, A and B, repeated as follows: A-B-a-A-a-b-A-B
   (capital letters = refrain text)

32 0:00 *L'homme armé* tune, sung monophonically (for text and music, see Listening Guide 38, p. 367)

Rondeau text:

	Text	Musical form	Translation
36 0:00 **Refrain**	Il sera pour vous conbatu Le doubté Turcq, Maistre Symon; Certainement ce sera mon, Et de crocq de ache abatu.	A B	He will be fought for you, the dreaded Turk, Master Symon —there's no doubt about it— and be struck down with an axe spur.
37 0:27 Verse	Son orqueil tenons a batu S'il chiét en voz mains, le felon.	a	We hold his pride to have been beaten if he falls into your hands, the felon.
38 0:38 Partial refrain	Il sera pour vous conbatu Le doubté Turcq, Maistre Symon.	A	He will be fought for you, the dreaded Turk, Master Symon.
39 0:49 Verse	En peu d' heure l'arés batu Au plaisire Dieu. Puis dira-on, "Vive Symonet le Breton Que sur le Turcq s'est enbatu!"	a b	In a short time you will have beaten him to God's pleasure. Then they will say, "Long live little Symon le Breton because he has fallen on the Turk!"
40 1:16 Refrain	Il sera pour vous conbatu Le doubté Turcq, Maistre Symon; Certainement ce sera mon, Et de crocq de ache abatu.	A B	He will be fought for you, the dreaded Turk, Master Symon —there's no doubt about it— and be struck down with an axe spur.

L'homme armé text:

Text	Translation
L'homme, l'homme, l'homme armé, L'homme armé doibt on doubter. On a fait par tout crier "A l'assault! et a l'assault!" Que chescun se doibt armer D'un haubregon de fer. L'homme, l'homme, l'homme armé L'homme armé doibt on doubter.	The armed man, The armed man is to be feared. The cry has been raised all around, "Attack! Attack!" that everyone must arm himself with an iron hauberk [coat of mail]. The armed man, The armed man is to be feared.

Opening of chanson, showing both texts and popular tune:

INSTRUMENTAL DANCE MUSIC

The sixteenth century witnessed a remarkable blossoming of instrumental dance music. With the advent of music publishing, printed dance music became readily available for solo instruments as well as small ensembles. Venice, Paris, and Antwerp took the lead as centers of the new publishing industry. The dances were often fashioned from vocal works such as madrigals and chansons, which were published in simplified versions that were played instead of sung.

Instruments   The instruments to be used in these dance arrangements were left unspecified. As in medieval performances, they were determined by the particular occasion. Outdoor performances called for loud instruments such as the shawm and sackbut (medieval oboe and trombone); for certain civic occasions, on the other hand, soft instruments such as recorders and bowed strings were preferred. Although percussion parts were not written out in Renaissance music, the evidence suggests that they were improvised.

Dance types   A number of dance types became popular during the sixteenth century. The stately court dance known as the *pavane* often served as the first number of a set that included one or more quicker dances, especially the Italian *saltarello* (jumping dance) and the French *galliard* (a more vigorous version of the saltarello). The *allemande*, or German dance, in moderate duple time, retained its popularity throughout the time of Bach and was adapted into the Baroque dance suite. Less courtly was the *ronde*, or round dance, a lively romp associated with the outdoors and performed in a circle.

THE ITALIAN MADRIGAL

In the madrigal, Renaissance composers found one of their chief forms for secular music. The sixteenth-century *madrigal* was an aristocratic form of poetry-and-music that flourished at the small Italian courts, where it was a favorite diversion of cultivated amateurs. The text consisted of a short poem of lyric or reflective character, often including the emotional words for weeping, sighing, trembling, and dying, which the Italian madrigalists learned to set with a wealth of expression. Love and unsatisfied desire were popular topics of the madrigal but by no means the only ones. Included too were humor and satire, political themes, and scenes and incidents of city and country life, with the result that the Italian madrigal literature of the sixteenth century presents a vivid panorama of Renaissance thought and feeling.

Instruments participated, duplicating or even substituting for the voices. Sometimes only the top part was sung while the other lines were played on

instruments. During the first period of the Renaissance madrigal—the second quarter of the sixteenth century—the composer's chief concern was to give pleasure to the performers, often amateurs, without much thought to virtuosic display. In the middle phase (c. 1550–80), the madrigal became an art form in which words and music were clearly linked.

The final phase of the Italian madrigal (1580–1620) extended beyond the late Renaissance into the world of the Baroque. The form became the direct expression of the composer's personality and feelings. Certain traits were carried to an extreme: rich chromatic harmony, dramatic declamation, vocal virtuosity, and vivid depiction of emotional words in music. We will hear some of these qualities in a work by the greatest of the Italian madrigalists, Claudio Monteverdi.

MONTEVERDI AND THE MADRIGAL

The late Renaissance madrigal came to full flower in the music of Claudio Monteverdi (1567–1643). In 1613, having spent twelve fruitful years at the court of the Duke of Mantua in northern Italy, Monteverdi was appointed choirmaster of St. Mark's in Venice and retained that prestigious post until his death thirty years later. We will look at his dramatic music in more detail in connection with early Baroque opera. What is important to know here is that between 1587 and 1643, he published eight books of madrigals that span the transition from Renaissance to Baroque styles.

Monteverdi's five-voice *A un giro sol*, from the *Fourth Book of Madrigals* (1603), represents a superb example of the composer's style. The poem, by Giovanni Guarini, is written in the courtly manner of much madrigal poetry,

Claudio Monteverdi

This sixteenth-century Venetian painting may have been an homage to the famous women singers from Ferrara. A Concert.

with exaggerated contrasts of delight and despair and rich examples of word painting. Notice how melodic turns depict such words as "giro sol" (turning glance), "ride l'aria d'intorno" (the breeze laughs all about), and "venti" (wind); how the lulling motion of the sea is heard, followed by a calm ("E'l mar s'acqueta") under which the winds ("i venti") begin to pick up with quick notes; and how poignant dissonances accentuate the word "crudele" (cruel).

Monteverdi had intended to present some of the madrigals in this collection to the Duke of Ferrara (in northern Italy), but the duke died before they were published. *A un giro sol* exhibits the passagework typical of a new

Principal Works

Operas, including *Orfeo* (1607), *Arianna* (1608, music lost), *Il ritorno d'Ulisse* (*The Return of Ulysses*, 1640), and *L'incoronazione di Poppea* (*The Coronation of Poppea*, 1642); other dramatic music, including *Combattimento di Tancredi e Clorinda* (*The Combat of Tancredi and Clorinda*, 1624)

Secular vocal music, including 9 books of madrigals (1587–1651; Book 9 posthumous), scherzi musicali, and canzonettas

Sacred vocal music, including Vespers (1610), Masses, Magnificats, madrigali spirituali, motets, and psalms

singing style developed at Ferrara, which featured a famous ensemble of professional women singers known as the Concerto delle donne (Ensemble of the Ladies). The theorist Vincenzo Giustiniani, a frequent visitor to Ferrara, described their brilliant florid singing in some detail:

> The ladies vied with each other . . . in the design of exquisite passages. . . . They moderated their voices, loud or soft, heavy or light, according to the demands of the piece they were singing; now slow, breaking off sometimes with a gentle sigh, now singing long passages legato or detached, now turns, now leaps, now with long trills, now short, or again with sweet running passages sung softly to which one sometimes heard an echo answer unexpectedly. They accompanied the music and the sentiment with appropriate facial expressions, glances, and gesture. . . . They made the words clear in such a way that one could hear even the last syllable of every word.

Monteverdi was one of many composers who wrote music for these famous singers in a unique style that intermingled their high voices in sweet dissonance and elaborate ornamentation, accompanied by a bass instrument and a harpsichord or lute. The contrast of high and low, without the middle range filled in with polyphonic writing, sounded the beginnings of the new Baroque style.

Listening Guide 42

CD: Chr/Std 1/52–54, Sh 1/19–21
Cassette: Chr/Std 1B/7, Sh 1A/7

MONTEVERDI: *A un giro sol*   (2:10)

Date of work: Published 1603, *Fourth Book of Madrigals*

Genre: Italian madrigal, 5 voices (SSATB)

Text: 8-line poem (*a-b-a-b-c-c-d-d*) by Giovanni Guarini

		Text	Translation
52	0:00	A un giro sol de'bell'occhi lucenti,	At a single turning glance from those bright eyes
		Ride l'aria d'intorno	the breeze laughs all about,
53	0:24	E'l mar s'acqueta e i venti	the sea becomes calm, then the wind dies away
		E si fa il ciel d'un altro lumeadorno;	and the sky becomes more radiant.
		Sol io le luci ho lagrimose e meste.	I alone am sad and weeping.
54	1:11	Certo quando nasceste,	Doubtless on the day you were born,
		Cosí crudel e ria,	so cruel and wicked,
		Nacque la morte mia.	my death was also born.

Examples of word painting

Soprano part to "Ride l'aria d'intorno" (the breeze laughs all about), showing melodic turns on "laugh" and "breeze" and a long twisted line on "all about":

Ri - de l'a - ria d'in - tor - - - - - - - no,

Top three parts to "E'l mar s'acqueta" (the sea becomes calm), with wavelike motion followed by a static line:

E'l mar s'ac - que - ta

E'l mar s'ac - que - ta

E'l mar s'ac - que - ta

Two soprano parts with harsh dissonances on "Cosí crudel e ria" (so cruel and wicked):

Co - sí cru - del e ri - - a,

Co - sí cru - del e ri - a,

THE ENGLISH MADRIGAL

Just as Shakespeare and other English poets adopted the Italian sonnet, so the composers of England took the Italian madrigal and developed it into a native art form. All the brilliance of the Elizabethan age is reflected in the school of madrigalists who flourished in the late sixteenth century during the reigns of Elizabeth I (1558–1603) and James I (1603–25). Among the most impor-

In this woodcut from **Edmund Spenser's** The Shepheardes Calendar, *Queen Elizabeth is shown in a pastoral setting, surrounded by her musical ladies-in-waiting.*

tant figures were Thomas Morley (1557–1603), John Wilbye (1574–1638), Thomas Weelkes (c. 1575–1623), and John Farmer, whom we will study.

In the first collection of Italian madrigals published in England, *Musica transalpina* (Music from Beyond the Alps, 1588), the songs were "Englished"—that is, the texts were translated. In their own madrigals, the English composers preferred simpler texts. New, humorous madrigal types were cultivated, some with refrain syllables such as "fa la la."

John Farmer's *Fair Phyllis*

John Farmer (fl. 1591–1601) was active in the 1590s in Dublin, where he was organist and master of the choirboys at Christ Church. In 1599, he moved to London and published his only collection of four-part madrigals. One of these, *Fair Phyllis*, attained great popularity that lasts to this day.

Fair Phyllis is characteristic of the English madrigal in its pastoral text and cheerful mood. Typical are the repeat of sections, the fragments of contrapuntal imitation that overlap and obscure the underlying meter, the changes from homophonic to polyphonic texture, and the cadences on the weaker pulse of the measure. The last line of the poem is set to homophonic chords, with a change to triple meter.

The English composers also adopted the Italian practice of word painting. For example, the opening line, "Fair Phyllis I saw sitting all alone," is sung by a single voice (see Listening Guide 43 for the text). Note too that the statement that Phyllis's lover wandered "up and down" is rendered musically by a downward movement of the notes, which is repeated at various pitch levels and imitated in all the parts.

The Renaissance madrigal inspired composers to develop new techniques of combining music and poetry. In doing so, it prepared the way for one of the most influential forms of Western music—opera.

FARMER: *Fair Phyllis*

(1:21)

Date of work: Published 1599

Genre: English madrigal, 4 voices

Poem: 6 lines (*a-b-a-b-c-c*), 10 or 11 syllables each

Musical style: Polyphonic, with varied textures

Text

60

Fair Phyllis I saw sitting all alone,
Feeding her flock near to the mountain side.
The shepherds knew not whither she was gone,
But after her [her] lover Amyntas hied.
Up and down he wandered, whilst she was missing;
When he found her, oh, then they fell a-kissing.

Examples of word painting

"Fair Phyllis I saw sitting all alone"—sung by soprano alone:

"Up and down"—descending line, repeated in all parts imitatively; shown in soprano and alto (overlapping in same register):

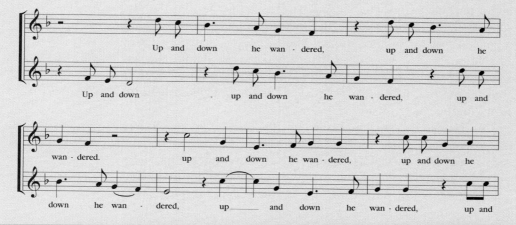

Transition III

From Renaissance to Baroque

"*The [Venetian] church of St. Mark was . . . so full of people that one could not move a step . . . a new platform was built for the singers, adjoining . . . there was a portable organ, in addition to the two famous organs of the church, and the other instruments made the most excellent music, in which the best singers and players that can be found in this region took part.*"
—FRANCESCO SANSOVINO

POLYCHORAL MUSIC IN VENICE

Venice, a major seaport in the sixteenth century, enjoyed a unique position at the crossroads of trade with the East. Its Basilica of St. Mark, famous throughout Europe as a magnificent specimen of Byzantine architecture, became the musical center for an impressive line of choirmasters and organists. The church's balconies and resonant acoustics inspired composers to write *polychoral music*, in which two or three choirs either answered each other in alternation or sang together (a style called *antiphonal* performance). With two organs installed in St. Mark's and a choir placed at each organ and at other points in the church, the element of space became a factor in music, rather like the "surround sound" of today. The result, an interplay of sound that was heightened by the use of strings and winds, finds its counterpart in the dazzling colors and tumultuous scenes of the Venetian painters. Visitors to Venice were amazed by the ceremonial splendor and elaborate music that accompanied religious and secular celebrations, and processions like the one illustrated here by Gentile Bellini were important rituals of Venetian life.

Polychoral music
Antiphonal performance

Venetian painters captured the splendid pageantry of their city on canvas. Above, singers and instrumentalists take part in a religious ceremony. **Gentile Bellini** *(c. 1429–1507),* Procession in Piazza San Marco.

Musicians performing in the singers' gallery of St. Mark's in Venice. Drawing by **Giovanni Antonio Canal** *(1697–1768), called* **Canaletto.** (Kunsthalle, Hamburg)

GIOVANNI GABRIELI AND THE POLYCHORAL MOTET

The Venetian style influenced composers all over Europe but reached its high point in the works of Giovanni Gabrieli (c. 1557–1612), who fully exploited the possibilities of multiple choirs. The use of such large forces drew him away from the subtle complexities of the old contrapuntal tradition to a broad homophonic style in which all the voices unite on the same syllable at the same time, making the words more understandable.

Gabrieli was the first composer to indicate dynamics in music and to take full advantage of the dynamic contrasts possible between a string and wind group, as in his famous *Sonata pian' e forte* (Soft and Loud Sonata). He was also one of the first to specify which instruments were to play a particular piece. Gabrieli achieved a sonorous balance between voices and instruments that was without precedent in his time.

The polychoral motet *O quam suavis* (*O how sweet*), from the second book of *Sacrae Symphoniae* (*Sacred Symphonies*, published posthumously in 1615), is conceived in Gabrieli's grandest manner (see Listening Guide 44). Written for two SATB choirs and instruments, the motet sets a text from the evening service (*Vespers*) for the Feast of Corpus Christi (a celebration of the body of Christ, held on the Thursday after Trinity Sunday). The occasion called for great pageantry in sixteenth-century Venice: a sumptuous procession (similar to the one shown opposite) in which all the fraternal groups and clergy took part was held each year on this day in St. Mark's Square. According to Francesco Sansovino's 1581 guidebook to Venice, the groups were "pompously turned out with decorated robes, wth silver-plate, with relics in their hands, and with [biblical] scenes [performed] on platforms so rare and beautiful that it is a worthy thing to see." *O quam suavis*, undoubtedly sung in the church for this high feast, features poignant chromaticism and intricate rhythmic interaction between the two choirs, which alternate singing antiphonally and together. These traits look toward the dawning of a new era—the opulent and dramatic Baroque period.

Listening Guide 44

CD: Chr/Std 1/50–51
Cassette: Chr/Std 1B/6

GIOVANNI GABRIELI: *O quam suavis*   (3:06)

Date of work: Published 1615

Genre: Polychoral motet

Medium: Two SATB choirs (with instruments)

Text: Evening prayer for Corpus Christi

Meter: Duple, with shifts to triple

		Text	Translation
50	0:00	O quam suavis est, Domine, spiritus;	O how sweet, Lord, is your spirit,
		qui, ut dulcedinem tuam	who demonstrates your sweetness
		in filios demonstrares,	to your sons
		pane suavissimo de caelo praestito,	by providing the sweetest bread from heaven;
		esurientes reples bonis,	you fill the hungry with good things,
51	1:57	fastidiosos divites dimittens inanes.	and send the rich and scornful away empty.

Opening chromatic line (soprano of choir 2):

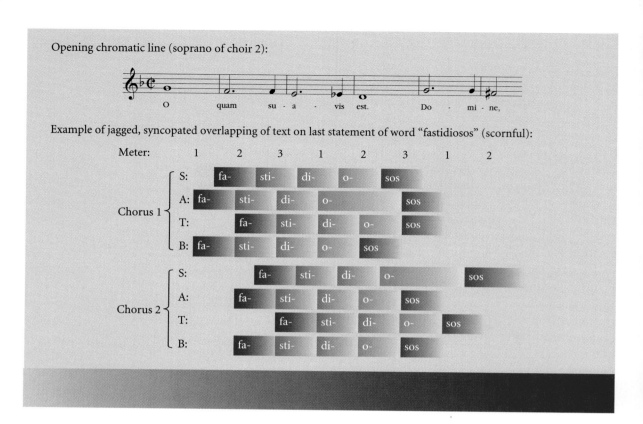

O   quam   su - a - vis est.   Do - mi - ne,

Example of jagged, syncopated overlapping of text on last statement of word "fastidiosos" (scornful):

Meter:	1	2	3	1	2	3	1	2

Chorus 1
- S: fa- sti- di- o- sos
- A: fa- sti- di- o- sos
- T: fa- sti- di- o- sos
- B: fa- sti- di- o- sos

Chorus 2
- S: fa- sti- di- o- sos
- A: fa- sti- di- o- sos
- T: fa- sti- di- o- sos
- B: fa- sti- di- o- sos

A Comparison of Renaissance and Baroque Styles

	Renaissance (1450–1600)	Baroque (1600–1750)
Composers	Du Fay, Ockeghem, Josquin, Palestrina, Monteverdi (early works)	Monteverdi (late works), Purcell, Vivaldi, Handel, Bach, Jacquet de la Guerre
Harmony	Modal harmony	Major and minor tonality
Texture	Imitative polyphony	New monodic or solo style; polyphony in late Baroque
Medium	*A cappella* vocal music	Concerted music (voices and instruments)
Sacred vocal genres	Mass and motet dominant	Oratorio, Lutheran cantata
Secular vocal genres	Chanson, madrigal	Opera, cantata
Instrumental genres	Derived from vocal forms: dance music (instruments not specified)	Sonata, concerto grosso, sinfonia, suite (instruments specified)
Use of preexistent works	Some works built on cantus firmus	Works are freely composed
Performance sites	Church and court	Public theaters

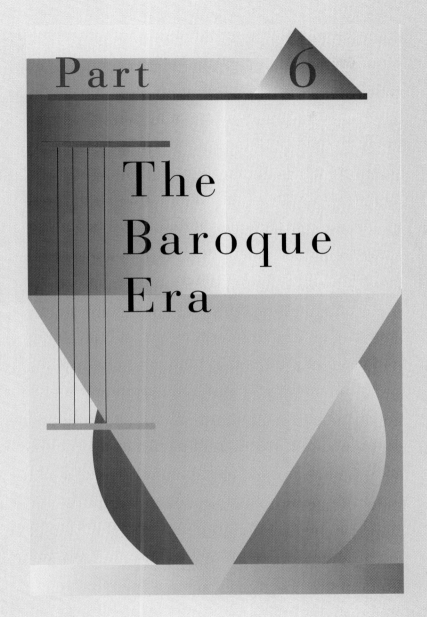

Part 6

The Baroque Era

Hendrik Terbrugghen *(1588–1629),* Duet. (The Louvre, Paris)

Unit XVIII

The Baroque and the Arts

58

The Baroque Spirit

"I do not know what I may appear to the world; but to myself I seem to have been only like a boy playing on the seashore ... whilst the great ocean of truth lay all undiscovered before me."
—SIR ISAAC NEWTON

The period we now call the Baroque stretched across a stormy century and a half of European history. It began shortly before the year 1600, a convenient signpost that need not be taken too literally, and may be regarded as having come to a close with the death of Bach in 1750.

The term "baroque" was probably derived from the Portuguese *barroco*, a pearl of irregular shape much used in the jewelry of the time. The years 1600–1750 encompassed a period of change and adventure. The conquest of the New World stirred the imagination and filled the coffers of western Europe. The middle classes acquired wealth and power in their struggle against the aristocracy. Empires clashed for mastery of the world. Appalling poverty and wasteful luxury, magnificent idealism and savage oppression—against contradictions such as these evolved the pomp and splendor of Baroque art, in all its vigor, elaborate decoration, and grandeur.

The transition from the classically minded Renaissance to the Baroque was foreshadowed in the art of Michelangelo (1475–1564). His turbulent figures, their bodies twisted in struggle, reflect the Baroque love of the dramatic. In

Baroque art

The bold and vigorous Baroque style was foreshadowed in this dramatic drawing by **Michelangelo** *(1474–1564),* Studies for the Libyan Sibyl. (Metropolitan Museum of Art, New York)

like fashion, the Venetian school of painters—Titian, Tintoretto, Veronese—captured the dynamic spirit of the new age: their crowded canvases are ablaze with color and movement.

Politics and culture
The Baroque was an era of absolute monarchy. Rulers throughout Europe took as their model the splendor of the French court at Versailles. Louis XIV's famous "I am the State" summed up a way of life in which all art and culture served the ruler. Courts large and small maintained elaborate musical establishments, including opera troupes, chapel choirs, and orchestras. Baroque opera, the favorite diversion of the aristocracy, told stories of the gods and heroes of antiquity, in whom the occupants of the royal box and their courtiers saw flattering likenesses of themselves.

The middle classes, excluded from the salons of the aristocracy, created a culture of their own. Their music making centered on the home, the church, and the university group known as *collegium musicum* (which functions once again on many campuses today). It was for them that the comic opera and the prose novel, both of which were filled with keen and witty observations of life, came into being. For them, painting abandoned its grandiose themes and turned to intimate scenes of bourgeois life. The Dutch School, embodying the vitality of a new burgher art, reached its high point in Terbrugghen (1588–1629) and especially Rembrandt (1606–1669), masters whose insights penetrated the regions of the soul.

Under the leadership of merchant princes and financiers, the culture of the city came to rival that of the palace. These new art lovers vied with the court in their devotion to splendor; they responded to the beauty of brocade and velvet, marble and jewels. This aspect of the Baroque finds expression in the painting of Peter Paul Rubens (1577–1640), whose canvases exude a driving energy, a celebration of life. His voluptuous nudes established the seventeenth-century ideal of feminine beauty.

The Baroque was an age of reason. The ideas of Kepler, Galileo, and Copernicus in physics and astronomy, of Descartes in mathematics and Spinoza in philosophy, were milestones in the intellectual history of Europe. The English physician William Harvey explained the circulation of the blood, and Sir Isaac Newton formulated the theory of gravity.

Scientific frontiers

The Baroque was also an intensely devout period, and religion was a rallying cry on some of the bloodiest battlefields in history. The Protestants were centered in England, Scandinavia, Holland, and the north German cities, all strongholds of the rising middle class. On the Catholic side were two powerful dynasties, the French Bourbons and the Austrian-Spanish Hapsburgs, who fought one another as fiercely as they did their Protestant foes. After decades of struggle, the great Hapsburg empire was broken in the 1790s, and France emerged as the leading state on the Continent. Germany lay in ruins, England rose to world power, and Europe was ready to advance to the stage of a modern industrial society.

Religion

The Flemish painter **Peter Paul Rubens** *(1577–1640) instills his tribute to the pleasures of life with energy and drama.* The Garden of Love. (The Prado, Madrid)

Cultural Perspective 12

MUSIC AND THE RELIGIOUS SPIRIT IN THE NEW WORLD

Throughout history, music has helped people express and disseminate their beliefs. What role, then, did music play in the establishment of various religions in the Americas? European settlers in the New World brought their faiths with them and, with the aid of music, converted some of the indigenous population. As a result, many people of modern-day Mexico, colonized by the Spanish, and of northeastern Canada, settled by the French, are Roman Catholics.

In the early seventeenth century, the Eastern Seaboard of the present United States and parts of coastal Canada were occupied by various Protestant groups from England, Germany, and the Netherlands. Music, largely the singing of psalms from the Old Testament, played a major part in the religious and social lives of these early colonists. (We learned of the importance of the psalms to Christianity in CP 9.) Some settlers brought psalm books with them from Europe, and in 1640, in Cambridge, Massachusetts, the North American colonies produced their first printed book: *The Whole Booke of Psalms* (commonly known as the *Bay Psalm Book*).

Even though psalm books became increasingly available, not everyone had one, nor were all colonists even literate. Hence, a singing style known as lining out came into practice, characterized by a slow, drawn-out tempo, with a minister or member of the congregation chanting out the text line by line before it was sung by the congregation. Various people embellished the tune, resulting in dissonant heterophony—two or more decorated versions of the melody sung simultaneously—a practice typical of many music cultures around the world.

The lining out style eventually gave way to more sophisticated polyphonic settings of the psalms. The foremost American composer in this genre was the Boston music teacher William Billings (1746–1800), who is remembered today for his fuging tunes—polyphonic settings of psalms or hymns in an overlapping, imitative setting (related to the fugue but not as strict in form). Billings's works were intended for use not in church services but as sacred or devotional music, performed in the singing schools that had sprung up in New England and in the maritime provinces of Canada.

Folklike devotional music was cultivated by African Americans and whites alike in the nineteenth and twentieth centuries in the form of spirituals and gospel hymns, religious songs sung at revivals and prayer meetings. In the twentieth century, gospel music has become an eclectic style of Protestant African-American sacred music, which has supplanted spirituals in popularity for worship and entertainment. In this modern style, vocalists (like Mahalia Jackson), often accompanied by dancing and clapping, embellish simple melodies with complex rhythms, pitch alterations, and added phrases. Yet another devotional style popular among youth today is contemporary Christian music, a kind of sacred country rock exemplified in performances by Amy Grant, among many others.

Terms to Note:

lining out   spiritual
heterophony   gospel music
fuging tune

Suggested Listening:

Early American hymn
Fuging tune (William Billings)
Spiritual (African-American or white)
Gospel music (Mahalia Jackson)
Contemporary Christian music (Amy Grant)

A church service at Reading, Pennsylvania, in the early 1800s. From a drawing by **Lewis Miller.**

At the same time, religion (as well as survival) was an important part of life in the American colonies. Settled largely by Protestant refugees who emigrated from northern Europe during the seventeenth century, the colonies based their new society on religious principles, which some zealots carried to an extreme. (See CP 12.)

With *Paradise Lost,* England's John Milton (1608–1674) produced the poetic epic of Protestantism, as Dante three and a half centuries earlier had expressed the Catholic point of view in *The Divine Comedy.* The Catholic world answered Martin Luther's reforms with the Counter-Reformation, whose rapturous mysticism found expression in the canvases of El Greco (1541–1614). These paintings are the creations of a visionary mind that distorts the real in its search for a reality beyond.

The rapturous mysticism of the Counter-Reformation found expression in this eerie landscape of **El Greco** *(1541–1614),* View of Toledo. (Metropolitan Museum of Art, New York)

Creative artists played a variety of roles in Baroque society. Peter Paul Rubens and Anthony Van Dyck were not only famous painters but also ambassadors and friends of princes. The composer Antonio Vivaldi was also a priest, John Milton a political leader, and George Frideric Handel an opera impresario. Artists usually functioned under royal or princely patronage, or, like Johann Sebastian Bach, they might be employed by a church or city administration. In all cases, artists were in direct contact with their public. Many musical works were created for specific occasions—an opera for a royal wedding, a cantata for a religious service—and for immediate use. Overwhelmingly, composers would write for a particular place and time, and only the great ones created for the ages.

The role of the artist

59

Main Currents in Baroque Music

"The end of all good music is to affect the soul."
—CLAUDIO MONTEVERDI

ORIGINS OF THE MONODIC STYLE

The transition from Renaissance to Baroque brought with it a great change: the shift of interest from a texture of several independent parts to one in which a single melody stood out—that is, from polyphonic music to homophonic. The new style, which originated in vocal music, was named *monody*—literally, "one song," music for one singer with instrumental accompaniment. (Monody is not to be confused with monophony, which is an unaccompanied vocal line; see p. 17.) We associate the year 1600 with the emergence of the monodic style, although the date, like many such milestones, merely indicates the coming to light of a process that developed over time.

Monody

The victory of the monodic style was achieved by a group of Florentine writers, artists, and musicians known as the Camerata, a name derived from the Italian word for "salon." Among them were Vincenzo Galilei, father of the astronomer Galileo Galilei, and the composers Giulio Caccini (c. 1545–1618) and Jacopo Peri (1561–1633). The members of the Camerata

The Camerata

were aristocratic humanists who aimed to resurrect the musical-dramatic art of ancient Greece. Although little was known of ancient music, the Camerata deduced that music must heighten the emotional power of the text. "I endeavored," wrote Caccini in 1602, "the imitation of the conceit of the words, seeking out the chords more or less passionate according to the meaning." Thus came into being what its inventors regarded as the *stile rappresentativo* (representational style), consisting of a melody that moved freely over a foundation of simple chords.

Stile rappresentativo

The Camerata appeared at a time when music had to free itself from the complexities of counterpoint. The year 1600 bristled with discussions about *le nuove musiche*, "the new music," and what its adherents proudly named "the expressive style." They soon realized that this representational style could be applied not only to a poem but to an entire drama. In this way, they were led to what many regard as the single most important achievement of Baroque music: the invention of opera.

Origins of the opera

NEW HARMONIC STRUCTURES

The melody-and-chords of the new music was far removed from the intricate interweaving of voices in the older Renaissance style. Since musicians were familiar with the basic harmonies, it was unnecessary to write the chords out in full. Instead, the composer put a numeral above or below the bass note, indicating the chord required (this kind of notation was called *figured bass*), and the performer filled in the necessary harmony. (See Listening Guide 45 for an example.) This system, known as *basso continuo*, or *continuous bass*, required two instrumentalists for the accompaniment. One played the bass line on a cello or bassoon, and another filled in the harmonies on a chordal instrument, generally harpsichord or organ. Musicians of this period were able to "think with their fingers"; that is, they could read and improvise on these figures with ease. The resulting continuo provided a scaffolding over which a vocal or instrumental melody could unfold.

Figured bass

Basso continuo

As interest shifted from counterpoint to a simpler style based on a single-line melody, the harmonic system grew simpler too, leading to one of the most significant changes in all music history: the establishment of major-minor tonality. With this development, the thrust to the keynote, or tonic, became the most powerful force in music, and each chord could assume its function in relation to the key center. Composers of the Baroque soon learned to exploit the opposition between the chord of rest, the I (tonic), and the active chord, the V (dominant). So too the movement, or modulation, from home key to contrasting key and back became an important element in shaping musical structure. Composers developed forms of instrumental music larger than had ever before been known.

Major-minor tonality

Tonic and dominant

This transition to major-minor tonality was marked by a significant technical advance. Because of a curious quirk of nature, keyboard instruments tuned according to the scientific laws of acoustics (first discovered by the ancient Greek philosopher Pythagoras) give a pure sound in some keys but increasingly out-of-tune intervals in others. As instrumental music acquired greater prominence, it became more and more important to be able to play in any key. Attempts to achieve this goal resulted in a variety of tuning systems. In the seventeenth century, a discovery was made: by slightly adjusting, or tempering, the mathematically "pure" intervals within the octave to equalize the distance between adjacent tones, it became possible to play in every major and minor key without experiencing unpleasant sounds. This tuning adjustment, known as *equal temperament*, greatly increased the range of harmonic possibilities that were available to the composer.

Equal temperament

Although we are uncertain which of the many temperaments, or tuning systems, was preferred by Johann Sebastian Bach, this composer demonstrated that he could write in every one of the twelve major and twelve minor keys. The result, *The Well-Tempered Clavier*, is a two-volume collection, each containing twenty-four preludes and fugues, or one in every possible key. Equal temperament eventually transformed the major-minor system, making it a completely flexible medium of expression.

BAROQUE MUSICAL STYLE

During the Baroque era, the rhythmic freedom of the monodic style eventually gave way to a vigorous rhythm based on regular accent. This new rhythm was carried by the bass part, whose relentless beat is a prime trait of many late Baroque compositions. Once under way, the steady pulsation never slackens, giving Baroque music its unflagging drive—the same effect of restless but controlled motion that we find in Baroque painting, sculpture, and architecture. Rhythm helped capture the drive and movement of a dynamic age.

Vigorous rhythm

The elaborate scrollwork of Baroque architecture found its musical equivalent in the principle of continuous expansion. A movement may start off with a striking musical figure that then spins out ceaselessly. In vocal music, wide leaps and the use of chromatic tones helped create melodies that were highly expressive of the text.

Continuous melody

Baroque musicians used dissonant chords more and more freely, for emotional intensity and color. In setting poetry, for example, a composer might use a dissonant chord to heighten the impact of a particularly expressive word.

Use of dissonance

Baroque music does not know the constant fluctuation of volume that marks later styles. The music moves at a fairly steady level of sonority. A passage uniformly loud will be followed by one uniformly soft, creating the ef-

The grand staircase of the Residenz, home of the Prince-Bishop of Würzburg, is a superb example of Baroque interior design, with its sculptural ornaments and elaborate decorations.

Terraced dynamics

fect of light and shade. For greater volume of tone, composers wrote for a larger number of players rather than directing each instrument to play louder. The shift from one level to the other, known as *terraced dynamics*, is a characteristic feature of the Baroque style. Composers created a major source of expression in the contrast between a soft passage and a loud one, that is, between the two terraces of sound rather than in the *crescendos* of later styles. This conception shapes the structure of the music, lending it a remarkable clarity.

It follows that Baroque composers were much more sparing of expression marks than those who came later. The music of the period carries little else than an occasional *forte* or *piano*, leaving it to the player to supply whatever else may be necessary.

THE RISE OF THE VIRTUOSO MUSICIAN

The heightened interest in instruments during the Baroque era went hand in hand with the need to master their technique. A dramatic rise in the standards of playing paralleled the improvements introduced by the great builders of instruments in Italy and Germany. Composers in turn wrote works that demanded a more advanced playing technique. Out of these developments came the challenging harpsichord sonatas of Domenico Scarlatti and the virtuosic violin works of Antonio Vivaldi, to name only two masters of the period.

The emergence of instrumental virtuosity had its counterpart in the vocal sphere. The rise of opera saw the development of a phenomenal vocal technique, exemplified in the early eighteenth century by the *castrato*, a male singer who was castrated during boyhood in order to preserve the soprano or alto register of his voice for the rest of his life. What resulted, after years of training, was an incredibly agile voice of enormous range, powered by breath control the like of which singers today cannot even begin to approach. The castrato's voice combined the lung power of the male with the brilliance of the female upper register. Strange as it may seem to us, Baroque audiences associated this voice with heroic male roles. (The most famous of Baroque castratos was Farinelli, whose career was depicted in 1994 in the exquisite Belgian movie *Farinelli*.) After the French Revolution, this custom, so offensive to human dignity, was almost universally abolished. When castrato roles are performed today, they are usually sung in lower register by a tenor or baritone, or in the original register by a countertenor, a falsettist, or a woman singer in male costume.

The castrato

Improvisation played a significant role in Baroque music. Singers and players alike added their own embellishments to what was written down (a custom found today in jazz) as their creative contribution to the work. The practice was so widespread that Baroque music sounded quite different in performance from what it looked like on the written page.

Improvisation

Caricature of the famous castrato Farinelli, by **Pier Leone Ghezzi** *(1674–1755).*

THE DOCTRINE OF THE AFFECTIONS

The Baroque inherited from the Renaissance an impressive technique of text painting, in which the music vividly mirrored the words. It was generally accepted that music ought to arouse the emotions, or affections—joy, anger, love, fear, or exaltation. By the late seventeenth century, an entire piece or movement, even of instrumental music, was normally built on a single affection, applying what was known as the *doctrine of the affections*. The opening motive established the mood of the piece, which prevailed until the work's end. The procedure differs markedly from the practice of the Classical and Romantic eras, when music was based on two or more contrasting emotions.

WOMEN IN BAROQUE MUSIC

As they had in the Renaissance, women played an active and expanded role in the music of the Baroque. With the establishment of opera houses throughout Europe, the opportunity for women to enter the ranks of professional musicians greatly increased. Some reached the level of superstars, such as the Italian sopranos Faustina Bordoni and Francesca Cuzzoni, who engaged in a bitter, notorious rivalry. Women also continued their role as patrons of the arts and as hostesses at the salons where music was actively cultivated.

A few women gained renown as composers, principal among them the French composer Elisabeth-Claude Jacquet de la Guerre, who achieved a reputation for both her harpsichord music and her cantatas. She was singled out for praise by no less a master than François Couperin, the leader of the French harpsichord school. We will consider one of her keyboard works in a later chapter.

INTERNATIONALISM

The Baroque was a culturally international period in which national styles existed—but without nationalism. Jean-Baptiste Lully, an Italian, created the French lyric tragedy. George Frideric Handel, a German, wrote Italian operas for English audiences and gave England the oratorio. There was free interchange among national cultures. The sensuous beauty of Italian melody, the pointed precision of French dance rhythm, the luxuriance of German polyphony, the freshness of English choral song—these nourished an all-European art that absorbed the best of each national style.

The great voyages of exploration during the Renaissance had opened up

A performance at the Teatro Argentina in Rome, 1729, as portrayed by **Giovanni Paolo Pannini** *(1697–1765).*

hitherto unknown regions of the globe, sparking a vivid interest among Europeans in remote cultures and far-off locales. As a result, exoticism became a discernible element of Baroque music. A number of operas looked to faraway lands for their settings—Persia, India, Turkey, the Near East, Peru, and the Americas. In one such work, the popular opera-ballet *Les Indes galantes*, by Jean-Philippe Rameau (1683–1764), each act is set in a different corner of the world. These operas offered picturesque scenes, interesting local color, and dances that may not have been authentic but that delighted audiences through their appeal to the imagination. Thus an international spirit combined with an interest in the exotic to produce music that flowed easily across national boundaries.

Exoticism

Vocal Music of the Baroque

60

Baroque Opera

"Opera is the delight of Princes."
—MARCO DA GAGLIANO

Early opera, an outgrowth of Renaissance theatrical traditions and the musical experiments of the Florentine Camerata, lent itself to the lavish spectacles and scenic displays that graced royal weddings and similar ceremonial occasions. Two such operas, *Orfeo* (1607) and *Arianna* (1608), were composed by the first great master of the new genre, Claudio Monteverdi (1567–1643). In Monteverdi's operas, the innovations of the Florentine Camerata reached artistic maturity, and the dramatic spirit of the Baroque found its true representative.

MONTEVERDI AND EARLY BAROQUE OPERA

As noted earlier, the madrigal holds a special place in Monteverdi's output because his eight madrigal collections, published between 1587 and 1638, mark the transition from the older polyphonic style of the Renaissance to the accompanied solo madrigal of the Baroque. Into his operas, ballets, madrigals, and religious works Monteverdi injected an emotional intensity that was new to music. He welded the newborn lyric drama of the Florentines into a coherent musical form and tightened their shapeless recitative into an expressive line filled with drama. He also originated what he called the *stile concitato* (agitated style) to express the hidden tremors of the soul, introducing novel effects, such as the string tremolo and the pizzicato, to portray passion. Monteverdi aspired above all to make his music express the emotional content of the poetry. "The text," he declared, "should be the master of the music, not the servant."

Monteverdi used dissonance and instrumental color to create drama, expressiveness, atmosphere, and suspense. He emphasized the contrast between characters by abrupt changes of key, and used rhythm as a vehicle for dramatic expression. A master of polyphonic writing, Monteverdi retained in his choruses the great contrapuntal tradition of the past. He melded all these elements into a noble and expressive art rooted in human emotions. The characters in his music dramas are neither stereotypes nor abstractions, but men and women who unleash their joy and sorrow through song. When his patron, the Duke of Mantua, suggested a libretto on a mythological subject of the kind fashionable at the time—a dialogue of the winds—the composer protested: "How shall I be able to imitate the speaking of winds that do not speak; and how shall I be able to move the affections by such means? . . . The harmonies imitate human beings, not the noise of winds, the bleating of sheep, the neighing of horses."

The Coronation of Poppea

Although the earliest operas derived their plots from Greek mythology, for *The Coronation of Poppea* (1642), a late work from his Venetian period, Monteverdi turned to history. By this time, the first public opera houses had opened in Venice, as opera was moving out of the palace to become a popular entertainment. In his early court operas, Monteverdi used an orchestra of diverse instruments. But in writing *Poppea*—his last opera—for a theater whose repertory would include works by other composers, he helped develop a more standardized ensemble with strings at its core.

The Coronation of Poppea remained popular after Monteverdi's death; the composer Pietro Francesco Cavalli (1602–1676), who oversaw later productions of the work in Rome, made some revisions to the last act, and it is with his reworkings that the opera is performed today. The librettist, Giovanni Busenello, based his text on an episode in Roman history in which the Emperor Nero plots to depose his wife, Ottavia, in order to marry his mistress, the courtesan Poppea. One of his advisers, the philosopher Seneca, views this decision as an affront to the state and voices his objection, for which he is condemned to death. Once he is out of the way, Poppea triumphs and is crowned Empress of Rome.

The action calls for a varied cast of characters spread across the social spectrum from Emperor to commoners, with vivid characterization of the main personages and dramatic confrontations between them. The opera treats powerful emotions that find expression in recitatives and arias, choruses, and passages in an aria-like style (called *ariosos*). Monteverdi also makes effective use of the "agitated style" in movements interspersed with instrumental sinfonias and ritornellos. A *ritornello*—the term is related to the English "return"—originally denoted an instrumental passage heard at the beginning and end of an aria, but came to mean a passage that returned again and again (within an aria) in the manner of a refrain.

Ritornello

The characters in this historic drama are hardly admirable. Nero (a castrato role) is a spoiled, self-indulgent playboy; Ottavia plots to poison her rival; Poppea is calculating and ambitious; and Seneca, despite his courage in opposing the Emperor, is pompous and aloof. In the final scene, Nero achieves his purpose and leads Poppea to the throne. When the consuls and tribunes arrive to salute Poppea, we hear a number for tenor and bass with much imitation between the two voice parts. (For the complete text, see Listening Guide 45.)

Coronation Scene from The Coronation of Poppea, *New York State Theater at Lincoln Center, March 7, 1973.*

A sinfonia sets the scene for the final love duet between Nero and Poppea, which closes the opera. In the duet, the opening section returns after the middle part, which itself has been repeated; the result is a pattern of **A-B-B-A** that foreshadows the da capo, or **A-B-A,** aria, which was to dominate late Baroque opera. The duet unfolds over a four-note *ground bass* that is carried by various instruments, such as lute, harp, and harpsichord. A ground bass consists of a short phrase repeated over and over in the lower voice while the upper voices pursue their independent lines; with each repetition, some aspect of the melody, harmony, or rhythm is changed. Here, the lovers' voices intermingle in a tender dialogue, with the emotional phrase "pur t'annodo" (I enchain you) highlighted by melismatic treatment. (In a melisma, you will recall, a single syllable of text is extended over a group of notes.) Notable is Monteverdi's affective use of dissonance on such phrases as "più non peno" (no more grieving) and "più non moro" (no more sorrow, or dying): the lovers hope that their union will put an end to all contention.

Ground bass

With Monteverdi, Italian opera took on the basic shape it was to maintain for the next several hundred years. The love duet, established in *The Coronation of Poppea,* became an essential operatic feature, and the powerful musical portrayal of human passions captured here is echoed in the soaring melodies of Giuseppe Verdi's Romantic masterworks two centuries later.

Listening Guide 45

CD: Chr/Std 1/55–59
Cassette: Chr/Std 1B/8

MONTEVERDI: *The Coronation of Poppea (L'incoronazione di Poppea)*, Act III, Scene 7   (6:35)

Date of work: 1642

Genre: Opera, Italian

Basis: Roman history

Characters:
Nero, Emperor of Rome (castrato role, now sung by a mezzo-soprano)
Poppea, his mistress, soon to be Empress (soprano)
Ottavia, wife of Nero, to be deposed (soprano)
Seneca, sage and adviser to Nero (bass)
Consuls and tribunes

Act III, SCENE 7: Coronation Scene

Consuls and tribunes, the crowning of Poppea (sung as a duet on the Norton recording)

		Text	Translation	Description
[55]	0:00	A te, a te sovrana augusta, Con il consenso universal di Roma, Indiademiam la chioma.	O hail to thee, our Empress, our ruler, by our unanimous consent, and that of all Romans, now with this crown, we crown thee.	Two-part writing, imitative, recitative-like.
	0:36	A te l'Asia, a te l'Africa s'atterra; A te l'Europa, e'l mar che cinge e serra Quest'impero felice,	Now shall Asia, now shall Africa be humble before thee. And now let Europe, and all the seas which belong to this most fortunate empire,	Fanfare-like passage.
[56]	0:56	Ora consacra e dona Questa del mondo imperial corona.	offer and consecrate in honor this, the crown of the mighty Roman empire.	Dancelike melody begins with bass, imitated in tenor; closes with tremolo (repeated-note trill) on "imperial."

Example from chorus, with dancelike meter, imitation between two voices, and melisma on "corona" (crown):

[57] 1:46 **Sinfonia**—orchestral section, moving bass line, jubilant in character; sets up love scene between Nero and Poppea

Duet—Nero and Poppea (singing the same text)
Form: **A-B-B-A; A** section with 4-note ground bass

		Text	Translation	Description
[58]	2:22			Instrumental introduction (establishes ground bass).
		A		
	2:37	Pur ti miro, pur ti stringo, pur ti godo, pur t'annodo più non peno, più non moro, O mia vita, o mio tesoro.	I adore you, I embrace you, I desire you, I enchain you, no more grieving, no more sorrow, O my dearest, O my beloved.	4-note ground bass in opening; imitation between 2 voices.
		B		
[59]	3:46	Io son tua, speme mia dillo dì l'idol mio, tu sei pur, si mio ben, sì mio cor, mia vita, sì.	I am yours, O my love, tell me so, you are mine, mine alone, O my love. Feel my heart, see my love, see.	Middle section; free bass; short motives imitated.
		B		
	4:26	Io son tua, etc.	I am yours, etc.	Entire middle section repeated; repeat of opening section.
		A		
	5:16	Pur ti miro, etc.	I adore you, etc.	

Opening of duet (ground bass shaded first time through):

Dissonance on words "moro" (death) and "peno" (grieving):

OPERA IN FRANCE

By the turn of the eighteenth century, Italian opera had gained wide popularity in the rest of western Europe. Only in France was the genre rejected, as French composers set out to fashion a national style, drawn from their strong traditions of court ballet and classical tragedy. The result was the *tragédie lyrique*, which combined colorful, sumptuous dance scenes and spectacular

Tragédie lyrique

Jean-Baptiste Lully

choruses in tales of courtly love and heroic adventure. The most important composer of the tragédie lyrique was Jean-Baptiste Lully (1632–1687), whose operas won him favor with the French royal court under King Louis XIV. Lully was the first to succeed in adapting recitative to the inflections of the French language, and he exerted a major influence in shaping the French overture (see p. 426). With such masterpieces as Lully's *Amadis* (1684) and *Armide* (1686), French opera was born.

OPERA IN ENGLAND

The masque

During the reigns of the first two Stuart kings, James I (r. 1603–25) and Charles I (r. 1625–49), the English *masque*, a type of entertainment that combined vocal and instrumental music with poetry and dance, became popular among the aristocracy. Many masques were presented privately in the homes of the nobility.

In the period of the Commonwealth that followed (1649–60), stage plays were forbidden, because the Puritans regarded the theater as an invention of the devil. A play set to music, though, could be passed off as a "concert." The "semi-operas" that flourished during the rule of Oliver Cromwell (1653–58) were essentially plays with a liberal mixture of solo songs, ensembles, and choral numbers interspersed with instrumental pieces. Since the dramatic tradition in England was much stronger than the operatic, the spoken word inevitably took precedence over the sung. However, in the 1680s, an important step toward opera was taken when John Blow presented his *Venus and Adonis*, which was sung throughout; this work paved the way for the first great English opera, *Dido and Aeneas*, by Blow's pupil Henry Purcell.

Henry Purcell

HENRY PURCELL: HIS LIFE AND MUSIC

"As Poetry is the harmony of Words, so Musick is that of Notes; and as Poetry is a Rise above Prose and Oratory, so is Musick the exaltation of Poetry."

Henry Purcell (1659–1695) occupies a special niche in the annals of his country. He was a leading figure in the illustrious line of composers that stretched back to pre-Tudor times and won England a foremost position in the world of music. Purcell's brief career began at the court of Charles II (r. 1660–85) and extended through the turbulent reign of James II (r. 1685–88) and into the period of William and Mary (r. 1689–1702). At these courts, he held various posts as singer, organist, and composer.

Purcell realized that England's music must be part of the European tradition. It would become his historic role to assimilate the achievements of the Continent—the dynamic instrumental style, the movement toward major-minor tonality, the recitative and aria of Italian opera, and the accentuated rhythms of the French—and to acclimate these to his native land.

Purcell's court odes and religious anthems are solemn ceremonial music of great breadth and power. His instrumental music ranks with the finest achievements of the middle Baroque. His songs display the charm of his lyricism as well as his gift for setting the English language. And in the domain of the theater, Purcell produced, in addition to music for plays, one of the gems of English opera.

Dido and Aeneas

First presented in 1689 "at Mr. Josias Priest's boarding school at Chelsy by young Gentlewomen . . . to a select audience of their parents and friends," *Dido and Aeneas* achieved a level of musical expression for which there was no precedent in England. A school production imposed obvious limitations, to which Purcell's genius adapted itself in extraordinary fashion. Each character in the opera is projected in a few telling strokes. Likewise, the mood of each scene is established with the utmost economy (the opera takes only an hour to perform). Nahum Tate's libretto, despite some inferior rhymes, provided Purcell with a serviceable framework. As in all school productions, this one had to present ample opportunities for choral singing and dancing.

Dido and Aeneas is based on an episode in Virgil's *Aeneid*, the ancient Roman epic that traces the adventures of the hero Aeneas after the fall of Troy. Both Purcell and his librettist could assume that their audience was thoroughly familiar with Virgil's classic; they could therefore compress the plot and suggest rather than fill in the details. Aeneas and his men are shipwrecked at Carthage on the northern shore of Africa. Dido, the Carthaginian

The plot

In His Own Words

Poetry and painting have arrived to their perfection in our own country: music is yet but in its nonage [immaturity], a forward Child, which gives hope of what it may be hereafter in England, when the masters of it shall find more Encouragement.

Principal Works

Dramatic music, including *Dido and Aeneas* (1689) and *The Fairy Queen* (1692); incidental music for plays

Sacred vocal music, including a Magnificat, Te Deum, and anthems

Secular vocal music, including court odes

Instrumental music, including fantasias, sonatas, marches, overtures, and harpsichord suites and dances

Queen, falls in love with him, and he returns her affection. But Aeneas cannot forget that the gods have commanded him to continue his journey until he reaches Italy, as he is destined to be the founder of Rome. Much as he hates to hurt the Queen, he knows that he must depart; she too ultimately realizes that she must let him go.

Dido prepares to meet her fate—death—in the moving recitative "Thy hand, Belinda," and the heart-rending lament that is the culminating point of the opera, "When I am laid in earth." (For the text, see Listening Guide 46.) In Virgil's poem, Dido mounts the funeral pyre, whose flames light the way for Aeneas's ships as they sail out of the harbor. Dido's lament unfolds over a five-measure ground bass, or ostinato (a repeated idea), that descends along the chromatic scale, always symbolic of grief in Baroque music. The opera closes with an emotional chorus mourning Dido's fate.

In *Dido and Aeneas*, Purcell discovered the true tone of lyric drama. Yet this masterpiece did not inspire similar efforts in England until two centuries later. It remained as unique a phenomenon in history as its composer, whom his contemporaries called "the British Orpheus."

Listening Guide 46

CD: Chr/Std 2/9–11, Sh 1/23–25
Cassette: Chr/Std 2A/4, Sh 1A/9

PURCELL: *Dido and Aeneas*, Act III, Dido's Lament   (4:06)

Date of work: 1689

Genre: Opera, English

Basis: Aeneid, by Virgil

Characters:
Dido, Queen of Carthage (soprano)
Aeneas, adventuring hero (baritone)
Belinda, Dido's serving maid (soprano)
Sorceress, Spirit, Witches

Recitative: "Thy hand, Belinda," sung by Dido

Introduces lament aria; accompanied by continuo only

		Text	
9	0:00	Thy hand, Belinda; darkness shades me. On thy bosom let me rest; More I would, but Death invades me; Death is now a welcome guest.	

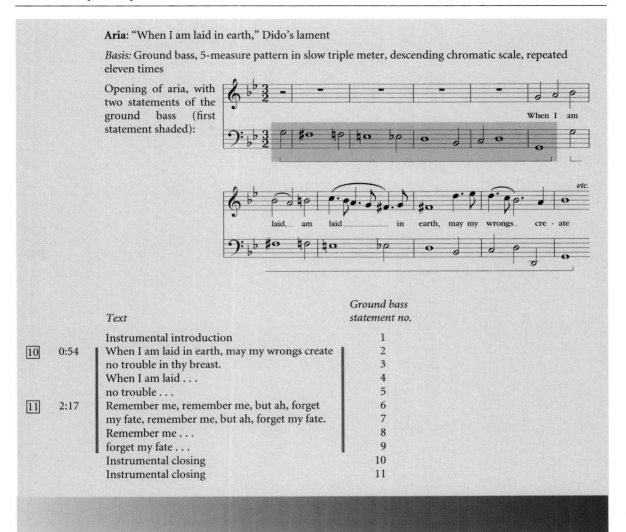

Aria: "When I am laid in earth," Dido's lament

Basis: Ground bass, 5-measure pattern in slow triple meter, descending chromatic scale, repeated eleven times

Opening of aria, with two statements of the ground bass (first statement shaded):

		Text	Ground bass statement no.
		Instrumental introduction	1
10	0:54	When I am laid in earth, may my wrongs create	2
		no trouble in thy breast.	3
		When I am laid . . .	4
		no trouble . . .	5
11	2:17	Remember me, remember me, but ah, forget	6
		my fate, remember me, but ah, forget my fate.	7
		Remember me . . .	8
		forget my fate . . .	9
		Instrumental closing	10
		Instrumental closing	11

HANDEL AND LATE BAROQUE OPERA

Opera in the late Baroque found its master in George Frideric Handel, who, although German by birth, dominated the operatic scene in London during the first decades of the eighteenth century. This was the London of the Hanoverian kings George I (r. 1714–27) and George II (r. 1727–60). It was their taste that Handel managed to please and their aristocrats whom, as an opera impresario, he had to win over.

Handel was in every sense an international figure. His music united the beautiful vocal melody of the Italian School with the stately gestures of the French style and the contrapuntal genius of the Germans. To these elements he added the majestic choral tradition of the English. The result was perfectly suited to the London scene.

Julius Caesar   Handel's dramatic works were in the vein of *opera seria*, or serious Italian opera, which projected heroic or tragic subjects. His opera about Julius Caesar (*Giulio Cesare*, 1724) is one of his finest. In this work, a Cleopatra eager to conquer Caesar with her beauty enchants him with a memorable love song, "V'adoro" (I adore you), establishing at the outset the aria's single affection.

Oratorio   When opera seria declined in popularity, Handel turned his talents toward the *oratorio*, a music drama based on a religious subject, producing his famous masterwork *Messiah* in 1742. (Handel's life and works are discussed in Chapter 62.)

61

Bach and the Cantata

The Baroque inherited the great vocal polyphony of the sixteenth century. At the same time, composers pursued a new interest in solo song accompanied by instruments and in dramatic musical declamation. Out of the fusion of all these styles came a new Baroque form, the cantata.

Cantata   The *cantata* (from the Italian *cantare*, "to sing"—that is, a piece to be sung) is a work for solo vocalists, chorus, and instrumentalists based on a lyric or dramatic poem. It is generally short and intimate, consisting of several movements that include recitatives, arias, and ensemble numbers.

Unlike oratorios, cantatas could be based on either secular or sacred themes. In the Lutheran tradition, to which the late-Baroque composer Johann Sebastian Bach belonged, the sacred cantata was an integral part of the church service, related, along with the sermon and prayers that followed it, to the Gospel for the day. Every Sunday of the church year required its own cantata. With extra works for holidays and special occasions, an annual cycle came to about sixty cantatas. Bach composed four or five such cycles, from which only two hundred works have come down to us. By the second quarter of the eighteenth century, the German cantata had absorbed the recitative, aria, and duet of the opera, the pomp of the French operatic overture, and the dynamic instrumental style of the Italians. These elements were unified by the all-embracing presence of the Lutheran chorale.

THE LUTHERAN CHORALE

A *chorale* is a hymn tune, specifically one associated with German Protestantism. The chorales served as the battle hymns of the Reformation. As one of his reforms, Martin Luther required that the congregation participate in the service. To this end, he inaugurated services in German rather than Latin, and allotted an important role to congregational singing. "I wish," he wrote, "to make German psalms for the people, that is to say sacred hymns, so that the word of God may dwell among the people also by means of song."

Luther and his fellow reformers created the first chorales by adapting tunes from Gregorian chant, from popular sources, and from secular art music. Originally sung in unison, these hymns soon were written in four-part harmony to be sung by the choir. The melody was put in the soprano, where all could hear it and join in the singing. In this way, the chorales greatly strengthened the trend to clear-cut melody supported by chords (homophonic texture).

In the elaborate vocal works that were sung in the Protestant church service, the chorale served as a unifying thread. When at the close of an extended work the chorale sounded in simple four-part harmony, its granitic strength reflected the faith of a nation. The chorale nourished centuries of German music and came to full flower in the art of Bach.

Chorale

Martin Luther

JOHANN SEBASTIAN BACH

"The aim and final reason of all music should be nothing else but the Glory of God and the refreshment of the spirit."

Johann Sebastian Bach (1685–1750) was heir to the polyphonic art of the past. He is the culminating figure of the Baroque style and one of the giants in the history of music.

His Life

Bach was born in Eisenach, Germany, of a family that had supplied musicians to the churches and town bands of the region for several generations. Left an orphan at the age of ten, he was raised by an older brother, an organist who prepared him for the family vocation. From the first, Bach displayed inexhaustible curiosity concerning every aspect of his art. "I had to work hard," he reported in later years, adding with considerably less accuracy, "Anyone who works as hard will get just as far."

Bach held posts as organist at Arnstadt (1703–7) and at Mühlhausen

Johann Sebastian Bach

Early years

An eighteenth-century engraving of St. Thomas's Church in Leipzig, where Bach worked from 1723 until he died, in 1750.

(1707–8), and at the age of twenty-three was appointed to his first important position: court organist and chamber musician to the Duke of Weimar. The Weimar period (1708–17) saw the rise of his fame as an organ virtuoso and the composition of many of his most important works for that instrument. His first six children were born in this period. Bach's two marriages produced at least nineteen offspring, many of whom did not survive infancy. Four of his sons became leading composers of the next generation.

The Cöthen period

Disappointed because the Duke of Weimar had failed to promote him, Bach decided to accept an offer from the Prince of Anhalt-Cöthen, who happened to be partial to chamber music. In his five years at Cöthen (1717–23), Bach produced suites, concertos, sonatas for various instruments, and a wealth of keyboard music; also the six concerti grossi dedicated to the Margrave of Brandenburg. During this period, Bach's wife died, and in late 1721, he married Anna Magdalena Wilcke, a young singer at court. Shortly afterward, Bach's patron married a woman who did not share the prince's love for music. When the composer's position at court gradually declined in importance, he sought employment elsewhere.

The Leipzig years

Bach was thirty-eight when he was appointed to one of the most important music positions in Germany, that of cantor at St. Thomas's Church in

Leipzig. Several candidates were considered before him, among them Georg Philipp Telemann (1681–1767), who was then much more famous than Bach but who declined the offer. One member of the town council reported, "Since the best man could not be obtained, lesser ones would have to be accepted." It was in this spirit that Leipzig received the greatest of its cantors.

Bach's duties at St. Thomas's were formidable. He supervised the music for the city's four main churches, selected and trained their choristers, and wrote music for the church services as well as for special occasions such as weddings and funerals. In 1729, he was appointed to an additional post in Leipzig: director of the collegium musicum, a group of university students and musicians that gave regular concerts. In the midst of all this activity, Bach managed to produce truly magnificent works during his twenty-seven years in Leipzig (1723–50).

The routine of his life was enlivened by frequent professional journeys, when he was asked to test and inaugurate new organs. His last expedition, in 1747, was to the court of Frederick the Great at Potsdam, where Bach's son Carl Philipp Emanuel served as accompanist to the flute-playing monarch.

In His Own Words

Whereas the Honorable and Most Wise Council of this Town of Leipzig have engaged me as Cantor of the St. Thomas School . . . I shall set the boys a shining example . . . , serve the school industriously, . . . bring the music in both the principal churches of this town into good estate, . . . faithfully instruct the boys not only in vocal but also in instrumental music . . . arrange the music so that it shall not last too long, and shall . . . not make an operatic impression, but rather incite the listeners to devotion . . . treat the boys in a friendly manner and with caution, but, in case they do not wish to obey, chastise them with moderation or report them to the proper place.

Principal Works

Sacred vocal works, including over 200 church cantatas; 7 motets; *Magnificat* (1723), *St. John Passion* (1724), *St. Matthew Passion* (1727), *Christmas Oratorio* (1734), Mass in B minor (1749)

Secular vocal works, including over 20 cantatas

Orchestral music, including 4 orchestral suites, 6 *Brandenburg Concertos*, concertos for 1 and 2 violins, and for 1, 2, 3, and 4 harpsichords

Chamber music, including 6 sonatas and partitas for unaccompanied violin, 6 sonatas for violin and harpsichord, 6 suites for cello, *Musical Offering* (1747), flute sonatas, and viola da gamba sonatas

Keyboard music, including 2 volumes of *Das wohltemperirte Clavier (The Well-Tempered Clavier,* 1722, 1742), 6 *English Suites* (c. 1722), 6 *French Suites* (c. 1722), *Chromatic Fantasy and Fugue* (c. 1720), *Italian Concerto* (1735), *Goldberg Variations* (1741–42), and *Die Kunst der Fuge (The Art of Fugue,* c. 1745–50); suites, fugues, capriccios, concertos, inventions, sinfonias

Organ music, including over 150 chorale preludes, toccatas, fantasias, preludes, fugues, and passacaglias

In The Flute Concert, *by the nineteenth-century painter* **Adolf von Menzel**, *Frederick the Great plays to the accompaniment of a chamber ensemble, with J. S. Bach's son Carl Philipp Emanuel at the harpsichord.* (Nationalgalerie, Berlin)

Frederick announced to his courtiers with some excitement, "Gentlemen, old Bach has arrived," then led the composer through the palace, showing him the new pianos that were beginning to replace the harpsichords as the preferred keyboard instruments. At Bach's invitation, the king suggested a theme, on which the composer improvised one of his astonishing fugues. After his return to Leipzig, Bach further elaborated on the royal theme, added a trio sonata based on the same theme, and dispatched the *Musical Offering* to "a Monarch whose greatness and power, as in all the sciences of war and peace, so especially in music, everyone must admire and revere."

The labors of a lifetime took their toll; after an apoplectic stroke and several operations for cataracts, Bach was stricken with blindness. Nevertheless, he persisted in his final task, the revising of eighteen chorale preludes for the organ. The dying master dictated to a son-in-law the last of these, *Before Thy Throne, My God, I Stand.*

His Music

Bach was one of the greatest religious artists in history. He believed that music must serve "the glory of God." Through the Lutheran hymn tunes known as chorales, the most learned composer of the age produced works that spoke for an entire faith.

The prime medium for Bach's talents was the organ, and during his life he was known primarily as a virtuoso organist. Since he was a devout Lutheran, the *chorale prelude* (a short organ piece based on the embellishment of a chorale tune) was central to his output. Chorale preludes are found in his *Little Organ Book* (*Orgelbüchlein*), a collection he compiled in Weimar and Cöthen for his students. One of his most famous organ works is the extended chorale prelude on *A Mighty Fortress Is Our God*, which we will study in Chapter 65.

In the field of keyboard music, Bach's most important work is *The Well-Tempered Clavier*. The forty-eight preludes and fugues in these two volumes have been called the pianist's Old Testament (the New Testament being Beethoven's thirty-two piano sonatas). Of the sonatas for various instruments, the six for unaccompanied violin are central to the repertory. In these, Bach created an intricate polyphonic structure, drawing unheard-of forms and textures from the instrument. The six *Brandenburg Concertos* present various instrumental combinations pitted against one another. (We will study No. 2 of this set in Chapter 63.) The lyricism of the four orchestral suites have made them immensely popular.

The two hundred or so church cantatas that have reached us form the centerpiece of Bach's religious music. They constitute a personal document of spirituality as they project the composer's vision of life and death. The drama of the Crucifixion in particular inspired Bach to eloquence: his Passions are epics of the Protestant faith. (A *Passion* is a musical setting of the account of the Crucifixion according to one of the four Evangelists.) The monumental Mass in B minor, which occupied Bach for a good part of the Leipzig period, was inappropriate for the Catholic service because of its length, but it found its eventual home in the concert hall.

Bach's last works reveal the master at the height of his contrapuntal wizardry; these include the *Musical Offering* and *The Art of Fugue*, which was left unfinished at his death.

Bach's position in history is that of one who raised existing forms to the highest level rather than one who originated new forms. His sheer mastery of contrapuntal composition has never been equaled.

Marginal notes: Organ music · Chorale prelude · Solo and chamber music · Religious music · Passion · Last works

Cantata No. 80: *A Mighty Fortress Is Our God*

Bach's cantatas typically have five to eight movements, of which the first, last, and usually one middle movement are choral numbers—normally fashioned from a chorale tune—ranging from simple hymnlike settings to elaborate choral fugues. Interspersed with the choruses are solo arias and recitatives, some of which may also be based on a chorale melody or its text.

Bach's lyricism found its purest expression in his arias, elaborate movements with ornate vocal lines. The expressive instrumental accompaniments

A German cantata performance with orchestra and organ, as depicted in **J. G. Walther's** Dictionary (1732).

abound in striking motives that combine contrapuntally with the vocal line to create the proper mood for the text and illustrate its meaning. In many cases, the aria is conceived as a kind of duet between the voice and a solo instrument, so that a single instrumental color prevails throughout the piece. This accorded with the doctrine of the single affection.

In the cantata *A Mighty Fortress Is Our God*, Bach set Martin Luther's chorale of that name, for which Luther probably composed the music as well as the words. Luther's words and chorale melody are used in the first, second, fifth, and last movements of this cantata; the rest of the text is by Bach's favorite librettist, Salomo Franck.

Bach could take it for granted that the devout congregation of St. Thomas's knew Luther's chorale by heart. A majestic and inspiring melody, it is today a familiar Protestant hymn tune. Except for an occasional leap, the melody moves stepwise along the scale and is presented in nine phrases that parallel the nine lines of each stanza of Luther's poem (the first two phrases are repeated for lines three and four of the poem; see Listening Guide 47).

The cantata opens with an extended choral movement in D major, in which each line of text receives its own fugal treatment. (A *fugue* is a polyphonic composition based on imitation; the form will be discussed in detail in Chapter 65.) In this movement, each musical phrase is announced by one voice part of the choir, then imitated in turn by the other three. Each phrase is an embellished version of the original chorale tune. The trumpets and drums we hear in this movement were added after Bach's death by his son Wilhelm Friedemann, who strove to enhance the pomp and splendor of the sound.

First movement

The second movement depicts Christ's struggle against the forces of evil. Strings in unison set up a leaping figure over a running bass. (We say that instruments are playing *in unison* when they are all playing the same notes together.) In this duet for soprano and bass soloists in D major, the soprano sings variations on the original tune against the florid counterpoint of the bass voice.

Second movement

The middle movements of the cantata feature freely composed recitatives and arias grouped around an energetic chorus based on Luther's chorale. In this central choral movement, the orchestra creates the framework for the battle between good and evil that is suggested in the tenor recitative and arioso (a short aria-like passage) that follow. In each movement, Bach captures a single affection, a practice typical of the era.

Middle movements

The final number rounds off the cantata, with the chorale sung in D major by full chorus and orchestra. We now hear Luther's melody in a hymnlike, four-part harmonization, with each vocal line doubled by instruments. In this homophonic texture, the great melody of the chorale is sounded in all its simplicity and grandeur.

Final movement

Listening Guide 47

CD: Chr/Std 2/50–62, Sh 1/26–34
Cassette: Chr/Std 2B/4–7, Sh 1A/10–11

BACH: Cantata No. 80, *A Mighty Fortress Is Our God* (*Ein feste Burg ist unser Gott*), Nos. 1, 2, 5, 8   (13:32)

Date of work: 1715/c. 1744; for the Feast of the Reformation (October 31)

Form: 8 movements, for chorus, soloists, and orchestra

Basis: Chorale (hymn) tune (possibly by Martin Luther)

OVERALL STRUCTURE

Movement	Medium	Use of chorale tune
1. Choral fugue	Chorus and orchestra	Embellished fugal chorale
2. Aria, duet	Soprano and bass solo	Soprano line only
3. Recitative/arioso	Bass solo	
4. Aria	Soprano solo	
5. Chorus	Chorus and orchestra	Unison chorale
6. Recitative/arioso	Tenor solo	
7. Aria, duet	Alto and tenor solo	
8. Chorale	Chorus and orchestra	4-part chorale

Original chorale tune:

---

1. Choral fugue, D major, 4/4 meter   (4:51)

		Text	Translation	First sung by
50	0:00	Ein feste Burg ist unser Gott,	A mighty fortress is our God,	Tenors
		ein' gute Wehr und Waffen;	a good defense and weapon:	Sopranos
51	1:15	er hilft uns frei aus aller Not,	He helps free us from all the troubles	Tenors
		die uns jetzt hat betroffen.	that have now befallen us.	Sopranos
52	2:29	Der alte böse Feind,	Our ever evil foe,	Basses
53	2:59	mit Ernst er's jetzt meint,	in earnest plots against us,	Altos
54	3:24	gross Macht und viel List	with great strength and cunning	Tenors
55	3:45	sein grausam Rüstung ist;	he prepares his dreadful plans.	Sopranos
56	4:09	auf Erd' ist nicht seinsgleichen.	Earth holds none like him.	Tenors

Opening melody in tenors (notes of chorale marked with x's):

Instrumental canon, based on chorale tune in augmentation:

(Shorter recordings skip to movement 8.)

2. Duet for soprano and bass, D major, 4/4 meter   (3:52)

Soprano

57	0:00	Mit unsrer Macht ist nichts getan,	With our own strength nothing is achieved,
		wir sind gar bald verloren.	we would soon be lost.
		Es streit't für uns der rechte Mann,	But on our behalf strives the mighty one,
		den Gott selbst hat erkoren.	whom God Himself has chosen.
58	1:48	Fragst du, wer er ist?	Ask you, who is he?
		Er heisst Jesus Christ,	He is called Jesus Christ,
		der Herre Zebaoth,	Lord of Hosts,
		und ist kein andrer Gott,	And there is no other God,
		das Feld muss er behalten.	He must remain master of the field.

Bass

57	0:00	Alles was von Gott geboren,	Everything born of God
		ist zum Siegen auserkoren,	has been chosen for victory.
58	1:48	Wer bei Christi Blutpanier	He who holds to Christ's banner,
		in der Taufe Treu' geschworen,	truly sworn in baptism,
		siegt im Geiste für und für.	his spirit will conquer forever and ever.

Opening of soprano line with second stanza of chorale text (notes of chorale tune marked with x):

5. Chorale for unison chorus, D major, 6/8 meter   (3:30)

		Text	Translation
59	0:00	Und wenn die Welt voll Teufel wär	Though the world were full of devils
		und wollten uns verschlingen,	eager to devour us,
		so fürchten wir uns nicht so sehr,	We need have no fear,
		es soll uns doch gelingen.	as we will still prevail.
60	1:51	Der Fürst dieser Welt,	The arch-fiend of this world,
		wie saur er sich stellt,	no matter how bitter his stand,
		tut er uns doch nicht,	cannot harm us,
		das macht, er ist gericht't,	indeed he faces judgment,
		ein Wörtlein kann ihn fällen.	one Word from God will bring him low.

Orchestral opening, with paraphrase of chorale melody:

Opening of unison chorale (all voices sing same tune):

Und wenn die Welt voll Teu-fel wär

8. Chorale, D major, 4/4 meter, full chorus and orchestra

(1:19)

61	0:00	Das Wort sie sollen lassen stahn	Now let the Word of God abide
		und kein Dank dazu haben.	without further thought.
		Er ist bei uns wohl auf dem Plan	He is firmly on our side
		mit seinem Geist und Gaben.	with His spirit and strength.
62	0:35	Nehmen sie uns den Leib,	Though they deprive us of life,
		Gut, Ehr', Kind, und Weib,	wealth, honor, child, and wife,
		lass fahren dahin,	we will not complain,
		sie haben's kein Gewinn;	it will avail them nothing;
		das Reich muss uns doch bleiben.	for God's kingdom must prevail.

Opening of hymnlike setting of chorale, in 4 voices (instruments doubling voices) and continuo:

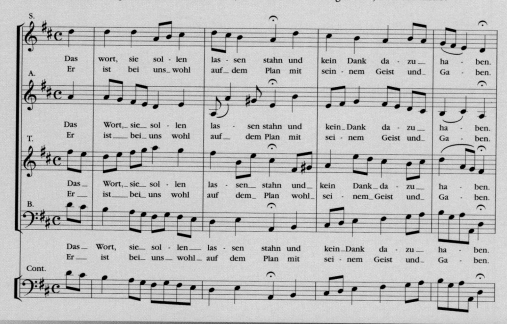

422

62

Handel and the Oratorio

THE ORATORIO

The *oratorio*, one of the great Baroque vocal forms, descended from the religious play-with-music of the Counter-Reformation. It took its name from the Italian word for "a place of prayer." Although the first oratorios were sacred operas, toward the middle of the seventeenth century the genre shed the trappings of the stage and developed its own characteristics as a large-scale musical work for solo voices, chorus, and orchestra. As we saw with Haydn's *The Creation,* its subject was generally biblical and it was performed in a church or hall without scenery, costumes, or acting. The action was usually depicted with the help of a narrator, in a series of recitatives and arias, ensemble numbers such as duets and trios, and choruses. The role of the chorus was often emphasized. Bach's Passions represent a special type of oratorio, focusing on the final events of Christ's life. More typical of the genre are the oratorios of George Frideric Handel, perhaps the consummate master of this vocal form.

GEORGE FRIDERIC HANDEL

"Milord, I should be sorry if I only entertained them. I wished to make them better."

If Bach represents the spirituality of the late Baroque, Handel (1685–1759) embodies its worldliness. Though born in the same year, the two giants of the age never met. As cantor of Leipzig, Bach had little point of contact with a composer who from the first was cut out for an international career.

His Life

Handel was born in Halle, Germany, the son of a prosperous barber-surgeon who did not regard music as a suitable profession for a young man of the

George Frideric Handel

middle class. After spending a year at the University of Halle, the ambitious youth moved to the German city of Hamburg, where he gravitated to the opera house and entered the orchestra as a second violinist. Handel absorbed the Italian operatic style popular in Hamburg so well that his first opera, *Almira*, written when he was twenty, created a sensation. He spent the next three years in Italy, where his operas were received just as enthusiastically.

The early operas

At the age of twenty-five, Handel was appointed conductor to the Elector of Hanover; in this position, he received the equivalent of fifteen hundred dollars a year (Bach at Weimar was being paid only eighty). A visit to London in the autumn of 1710 brought him to the city that was to be his home for nearly fifty years. His opera *Rinaldo* (1711), written in a mere fourteen days, conquered the English public with its fresh, tender melodies. A year later, Handel obtained another leave and returned to London, this time for good.

His great opportunity came with the founding in 1720 of the Royal Academy of Music, launched for the purpose of presenting Italian opera and backed by a group of wealthy peers headed by the king. Handel was appointed one of the musical directors and at thirty-five found himself occupying a key position in the artistic life of England. For the next eight years, he was active in producing and directing his operas as well as writing them. His pace was feverish; he worked in bursts of inspiration, turning out a new opera in two to three weeks. To this period belongs *Julius Caesar*, one of his finest works in the new genre of *opera seria*, or serious opera.

The rise of English opera

Despite Handel's productivity, the Royal Academy failed. The final blow came in 1728 with the sensational success of John Gay's *The Beggar's Opera*. Sung in English and with tunes familiar to the audience, this humorous *ballad*, or *dialogue, opera* was the answer of middle-class England to the gods and heroes of the aristocratic opera seria.

Rather than accept failure, Handel turned from opera to oratorio, quickly realizing the advantages offered by a type of entertainment that dispensed with costly foreign singers and lavish scenery. Among his greatest achievements in this new genre were *Israel in Egypt, Messiah, Judas Maccabaeus*, and *Jephtha*. The British public could not help but respond to the imagery of the Old Testament as set forth in Handel's heroic music.

The final years

Handel suffered the same affliction as Bach—loss of eyesight from cataracts. Like Bach and the English poet John Milton, he dictated his last works, which were mainly revisions of earlier ones. But he continued to appear in public, conducting his oratorios and performing on the organ.

In 1759, shortly after his seventy-fourth birthday, Handel began his usual oratorio season, conducting ten major works in little over a month to packed houses. His most famous oratorio, *Messiah*, closed the series. He collapsed in the theater at the end of the performance and died some days later. The nation he had served for half a century accorded him its highest honor, as a London paper recounted: "Last night about Eight O'clock the remains of the

Principal Works

Operas (over 40), including *Almira* (1705), *Rinaldo* (1711), *Giulio Cesare (Julius Caesar,* 1724), and *Orlando* (1733)

Oratorios, including *Esther* (1718), *Alexander's Feast* (1736), *Israel in Egypt* (1739), *Messiah* (1742), *Samson* (1743), *Belshazzar* (1745), *Judas Maccabaeus* (1747), *Solomon* (1749), and *Jephtha* (1752); other sacred vocal music, including *Ode for the Birthday of Queen Anne* (c. 1713), *Acis and Galatea* (masque, 1718), *Ode for St. Cecilia's Day* (1739), *Utrecht Te Deum* (1713), anthems, and Latin church music

Secular vocal music, including solo and duo cantatas; arias

Orchestral music, including *Water Music* (1717) and *Music for the Royal Fireworks* (1749); concertos for oboe, organ, horn

Chamber music, including solo and trio sonatas

Keyboard music, including harpsichord suites, fugues, preludes, airs, and dances

late great Mr. Handel were deposited . . . in Westminster Abbey. . . . There was almost the greatest Concourse of People of all Ranks ever seen upon such, or indeed upon any other Occasion."

His Music

Handel's rhythm has the powerful drive of the Baroque. You need only hear a Handel chorus to realize what momentum can be achieved with simple 4/4 time. Unlike Bach, who favored chromatic harmony, Handel leaned toward the diatonic. His melody, rich in expression, rises and falls in great majestic arches. His works are based on massive pillars of sound—the chords—within which the voices interweave. And with his roots in the world of the theater, Handel knew how to use tone color for atmosphere and dramatic expression.

Handel's more than forty operas center on stories of heroes and adventurers, in ingenious musical settings that not only appealed to the London public but enjoyed popularity in Germany and Italy as well. His arias run the gamut from brilliant virtuosic displays to poignant love songs.

The oratorios are choral dramas that embody the splendor of the Baroque, with their soaring arias, dramatic recitatives, grandiose fugues, and majestic choruses. With the instinct of the born leader, Handel created in the oratorio an art form steeped in the atmosphere of the Old Testament, ideally suited to the taste of England's middle class.

The oratorios

Handel made the oratorio chorus—the people—the center of the drama.

Freed from the rapid pace imposed by stage action, he expanded the chorus's role in each scene. The chorus at times touches off the action and at other times reflects on it. As in Greek tragedy, it serves as both protagonist and spectator. The characters, among them Saul, Joshua, Deborah, Judas Maccabaeus, and Samson, are creatures of destiny, regal in defeat as in victory.

Handel was prolific as well in composing instrumental music; his most important works are his concertos and his two memorable orchestral suites, the *Water Music* (1717) and *Music for the Royal Fireworks* (1749). (We will consider a movement from the *Water Music* in Chapter 64.)

Messiah

In the spring of 1742, the city of Dublin witnessed the premiere of one of the world's best-loved works, Handel's *Messiah*. Written down in twenty-four days, this oratorio is the product of the composer working as if possessed. His servant found him, after the completion of the "Hallelujah Chorus," with tears in his eyes. "I did think I did see all Heaven before me, and the Great God Himself!" Handel said.

The libretto is a compilation of biblical verses from the Old and New Testaments, set in three parts. The first part (the Christmas section) relates the prophecy of the coming of Christ and his birth; the second (the Easter section), his suffering, death, and the spread of his doctrine; and the third, the redemption of the world through faith. With its impressive choruses, moving recitatives, and broadly flowing arias, the work represents the pinnacle of the Handelian oratorio.

Handel's orchestration of *Messiah* was modest and clear in texture. He wrote mainly for strings and continuo; oboes and bassoons were employed to strengthen the choral parts. Trumpets and drums were reserved for special numbers.

Part I

French overture

The Overture—called "Sinfony" in the score—opens the Christmas section with a Grave (slow, solemn) in a somber E minor. The strings project an affection of intense drama. Handel returned here to the *French overture*, developed a century earlier by Jean-Baptiste Lully, the master of Baroque opera in France. The form consists of two sections: a slow introduction (often repeated) marked by ponderous dotted rhythms, followed by an Allegro in imitative style, based on a short, striking subject. Handel's stately opening section leads into a sturdy fugue in three instrumental voices. The brisk rhythm leads eventually to a brief return of the slow dotted rhythm heard at the opening.

Recitatives

We have noted two kinds of recitative: *secco* ("dry," or unaccompanied), which is supported only by the continuo instruments; and *accompagnato* (accompanied by orchestra). The contrast between the two types is well illustrated by the recitative beginning "There were shepherds abiding in the

A performance of Handel's Messiah *in 1784, from an eighteenth-century engraving.*

field," which is heard in the Christmas section of *Messiah* (No. 14). Listening Guide 48 shows how Handel alternates between these two styles.

This recitative serves to introduce a vigorous four-part chorus, "Glory to God in the highest." Here too we find an interesting contrast: the opening phrase is set to a passage of chords (homophonic texture), but the next phrase, "good-will toward men," is sung by all four voices in imitative counterpoint (polyphonic texture). This jubilant chorus illustrates the pomp and majesty of Handel's music.

The soprano aria "Rejoice greatly, O daughter of Zion" is in three-part, or **A-B-A'**, form. In this type of aria, the composer usually did not write out the third part, since it duplicated the first. Instead we find the words *da capo* at the end of the second section, indicating that the performer was to repeat the first section, freely elaborating it with ornamentation. (*Da capo* is Italian for "from the head," that is, from the beginning.) This kind of structure therefore came to be known as a *da capo aria*. For "Rejoice greatly," Handel did write out the last section, varying it considerably from the first.

Da capo aria

At the beginning of this aria, violins introduce an energetic figure that will soon be taken up by the voice. Notable are the melismatic passages on the word "rejoice." Throughout, the instruments exchange motives with the voice and help provide an element of unity with the ritornellos, or instrumental refrains, that brings back certain passages.

Part II   The climax of *Messiah* comes at the close of the second part, the Easter section, with the familiar "Hallelujah Chorus." In this movement, we hear shifting textures that alternate between overlapping imitative entries of the voice parts and homophonic sections in which all the voices clearly declaim the text together. The musical emphasis given the key word "Hallelujah" is one of those strokes of genius that resound through the ages.

Listening Guide 48

CD: Chr/Std 2/18–29, Sh 1/35–40
Cassette: Chr/Std 2A/7–9, Sh 1B/1–2

HANDEL: *Messiah*, Nos. 1, 14–18, 44   (15:22)

Date of work: 1742

Genre: Oratorio, in 3 parts

Parts:
    I—Christmas Section
    II—Easter Section
    III—Redemption Section

(Shorter recordings include Nos. 18 and 44 only.)

PART I: CHRISTMAS SECTION

1. Overture   (4:04)
Form: French overture, 2 parts (slow-fast), the first part repeated (**A-A-B**)

| 18 | 0:00 | **A** section—Grave, E minor, played twice; stately, dotted rhythms: |  |

| 19 | 1:51 | **B** section—Allegro moderato, E minor, imitative polyphony in 3 voices; opening subject introduced by oboes and first violins: |  |

(1:26)

		Text	*Description*
20	0:00	**14a. Recitative (secco)** There were shepherds abiding in the field, keeping watch over their flock by night.	Sustained chords in harpsichord.
	0:14	**14b. Recitative (accompagnato)** And lo, the angel of the Lord came upon them, and the glory of the Lord shone round about them, and they were sore afraid.	String accompaniment, with arpeggiated chords.

15. Recitative (secco)

| 21 | 0:33 | And the angel said unto them, fear not, for behold, I bring you good tidings of great joy, which shall be to all people. For unto you is born this day in the city of David a Saviour, which is Christ the Lord. | Sustained chords. |

16. Recitative (accompagnato)

| 22 | 1:07 | And suddenly there was with the angels a multitude of the heavenly host, praising God, and saying: | Allegro, with rippling string figure. |

17. Chorus   (1:54)

		Text	Description
23	1:26	Glory to God in the highest	4-voices, homophonic, with moving string accompaniment.
		and peace on earth,	Tenors and basses alone, descending octave leap in basses, homophonic.
		good-will toward men.	Imitative, polyphonic treatment; fugue built from lowest to highest voice; antiphonal exchange of "good-will."
		(All text lines repeated.)	Orchestral closing.

18. Soprano aria (A-B-A')   (4:10)

24	3:20		Instrumental introduction, vocal theme presented in violins in B♭ major.
		A	
		Rejoice greatly, O daughter of Zion shout, O daughter of Jerusalem, behold, thy King cometh unto thee.	Disjunct rising line, melismas on "rejoice"; melody exchanged between soprano and violin.
			Syncopated, choppy melody, ends in F major. Instrumental ritornello.
		B	
25	4:51	He is the righteous Saviour and he shall speak peace unto the heathen.	Begins in G minor, slower and lyrical; modulates to B♭ major.
		A'	
26	5:53	Rejoice greatly . . .	Abridged instrumental ritornello; new melodic elaborations; longer melismas on "rejoice."

Extended melisma on "rejoice" from last section:

PART II: EASTER SECTION

44. Chorus   (3:48)

		Text	*Description*
27	0:00		Short instrumental introduction.
		Hallelujah!	4 voices, homophonic at opening.
28	0:26	For the Lord God omnipotent reigneth.	Textural reductions, leading to imitation and overlapping of text, builds in complexity.
		The kingdom of this world is become the Kingdom of our Lord and of His Christ;	Homophonic treatment, simple accompaniment.
29	1:38	and He shall reign for ever and ever. King of Kings and Lord of Lords. Hallelujah!	Imitative polyphony, voices build from lowest to highest. Women's voices introduce the text, punctuated by "Hallelujah"; closes in homophonic setting with trumpets and timpani.

Opening of chorus, in homophonic style:

Unit XX

Instrumental Music of the Baroque

63

The Baroque Concerto

THE RISE OF INSTRUMENTAL MUSIC

The Baroque was the first period in history in which instrumental music was as important as vocal. New instruments were being developed while old instruments were being perfected. Great virtuosos such as Bach and Handel at the organ, Corelli and Vivaldi on the violin, and Scarlatti and Couperin on the harpsichord raised the technique of playing to new heights.

On the whole, composers still thought in terms of line rather than instrumental color, so that the same line of music might be played by a string, a woodwind, or a brass instrument. (As we have seen, this is different from the practice of the Classical and Romantic periods, when instrumental color was changed frequently.) In the early Baroque, music was often performed by whatever instruments were available. Late Baroque composers tended to choose specific instruments according to their timbre. They also wrote more idiomatically for particular instruments, asking them to do what they could do best. As specifications became more precise, the art of orchestration was born.

BAROQUE INSTRUMENTS

The seventeenth century saw a dramatic improvement in the construction of string instruments. Some of the finest violins ever built came from the workshops of Stradivarius, Guarneri, and Amati. The best of these now fetch sums unimagined even a generation ago. The Stradivarius violin owned by the young concert artist Midori, for example, is now worth more than $3.5 million.

Strings The strings of Baroque instruments were made of gut rather than the steel used today. Gut, produced from animal intestines, yielded a softer yet more penetrating sound. In general, the string instruments of the Baroque resemble their modern descendants except for certain details of construction. Playing techniques, though, have changed somewhat, especially bowing.

Woodwinds The woodwind instruments were used increasingly for color in the late Baroque orchestra. The recorder, flute, and oboe, all made of wood at the time, were especially effective in suggesting pastoral scenes, while the bassoon cast a somber tone. Great improvements in the fingering mechanisms of these instruments were still to come.

Brass The trumpet developed from an instrument used for military signals to one with a solo role in the orchestra. It was still a "natural instrument"—that is, without the valves that would enable it to play in all keys—demanding real virtuosity on the part of the player. Trumpets contributed a bright sonority to the orchestral palette, to which the horns, also natural instruments, added their gentler, outdoor sound.

The three important keyboard instruments of the Baroque were the organ, the harpsichord, and the clavichord. In ensemble music, these provided the continuo (continuous bass), and they were used extensively for solo performance as well. The Baroque *organ*, used both in church and in the home (see **Organ** p. 453), had a pure, transparent timbre. The colors produced by the various sets of pipes contrasted sharply, so that the ear could pick out the separate

A Stradivarius violin.

An evening outdoor concert in 1744 by the Collegium Musicum of Jena, Germany, featuring an orchestra of strings, woodwinds, trumpets, and drums gathered around a harpsichord.

lines of counterpoint. And the use of multiple keyboards made it possible to achieve terraced levels of soft and loud.

Harpsichord

The *harpsichord* differed from the modern piano in two important respects. First, its strings were plucked by quills instead of being struck with hammers, and its tone could not be sustained like that of the piano, a product of the early Classical era. Second, the pressure of the fingers on the keys

A two-manual harpsichord from around 1650, built by **Jan Couchet** *of Antwerp.* (Metropolitan Museum of Art, New York)

The clavichord was favored in home music making for its subtle tone and nuances. This German instrument was built in 1763 by **Christian Kintzing.** (Metropolitan Museum of Art, New York)

varied the tone only slightly, producing subtle dynamic nuances but not the piano's extremes of loud and soft. Rather, in order to obtain different sonorities and levels of sound on the harpsichord, makers often added another set or two of strings, usually with a second keyboard.

Clavichord   The *clavichord* was a favorite instrument for the home. Its very soft, gentle tone was produced by the action of a metal tangent that exerted pressure on the string, allowing for some delicate effects not available on the harpsichord. By the end of the eighteenth century, both the harpsichord and the clavichord had been supplanted in favor of the piano.

In recent years, a new drive for authenticity has made the sounds of eighteenth-century instruments familiar to us. Recorders and wooden flutes, restored violins with gut strings, and mellow-toned, valveless brass instruments are being played again, so that the Baroque orchestra has recovered not only its smaller scale but also its transparent tone quality.

CONCERTO TYPES

Contrast was as basic an element of Baroque music as unity. This twofold principle found expression in the *concerto,* an instrumental form based on the opposition between two dissimilar bodies of sound. (The Latin verb *concertare* means "to contend with," or "to vie with.")

Solo concerto   Baroque composers produced two types: the solo concerto and the concerto grosso. The first type, the concerto for solo instrument and an accompanying instrumental group, lent itself to experiments in sonority and virtuoso playing, especially in the hands of the Italian master Antonio Vivaldi. The violin was the instrument featured most frequently in the solo concerto, which, as we know, usually consisted of three movements, in the sequence Allegro-Adagio-Allegro. This flexible form prepared the way for the solo concerto of the Classical and Romantic periods.

The *concerto grosso* was based on the opposition between a small group of instruments, the *concertino*, and a larger group, the *tutti*, or *ripieno* (Italian for "full"). One of the early contributors to this genre was the Italian composer and violinist Arcangelo Corelli (1653–1713); among his Opus 6 Concerti Grossi, published posthumously in 1714, is the famous *Christmas Concerto*. Giuseppe Torelli (1658–1709), active in the northern Italian musical center of Bologna, contributed significantly to the development of both concerto types. His mature works feature the three-movement structure described above as well as unifying ritornellos (short recurring passages) in individual movements.

The concerto embodied what one writer of the time called "the fire and fury of the Italian style." This Italian style spread all over Europe and strongly influenced the German masters Bach and Handel, among others. Of the many Italian concerto composers, Vivaldi was the most famous and the most prolific.

Concerto grosso

Antonio Vivaldi: His Life and Music

"Above all, he was possessed by music."
—MARC PINCHERLE

Antonio Vivaldi

Antonio Vivaldi (1678–1741), the son of a violinist, grew up in his native Venice. He was ordained in the church while in his twenties and came to be known as "the red priest," a reference to the color of his hair. For the greater part of his career, Vivaldi was *maestro de' concerti*, or music master, at the most important of the four music schools for which Venice was famous, the Conservatorio del'Ospedale della Pietà. These schools were attached to charitable institutions established for the upbringing of orphaned girls, and they played a vital role in the musical life of Venetians. Much of Vivaldi's output was written for concerts at the school, which attracted visitors from all over Europe. One visitor, a French diplomat, recorded his impressions of Vivaldi's all-girl orchestra in 1739:

> The girls are educated at the expense of the state, and they are trained exclusively with the purpose of excelling in music. Thus, they sing like angels and play violin, flute, organ, oboe, cello, and bassoon; in short, no instrument, regardless of its size, frightens them. They live like nuns in a convent. All they do is perform concerts, generally in groups of about forty girls. I swear that there is noth-

In Concert in a Girls' School, **Francesco Guardi** *(1712–1793) depicts a Venetian concert by an orchestra of young women (upper left) similar to the one directed by Vivaldi.* (Alte Pinakothek, Munich)

ing as pleasant as seeing a young and pretty nun, dressed all in white, with a flower over her ear, conducting the orchestra with all the gracefulness and precision imaginable.

While maintaining his position in Venice, Vivaldi found work composing operas for other Italian cities. His life came to a mysterious end: a contemporary Venetian account states that "the Abbé Don Antonio Vivaldi, greatly esteemed for his compositions and concertos, in his day made more than fifty thousand ducats, but as a result of excessive extravagance he died poor in Vienna." He was buried in a pauper's grave, and to save expense, his funeral was given "only a small peal of bells."

Vivaldi was active during a period that was crucially important in the exploration of a new style in which the instruments were liberated from their earlier dependence on vocal music. His novel use of rapid scale passages, extended arpeggios, and contrasting registers contributed decisively to the development of violin style and technique. And he played a leading part in the history of the concerto, effectively exploiting the contrast in sonority between large and small groups of players.

The Four Seasons

Vivaldi's best-known work is *The Four Seasons,* a group of four violin concertos. We have observed the fondness for word painting in Baroque vocal works, where the music is meant to portray the action described by the words. In *The Four Seasons,* Vivaldi applies this principle to instrumental music. Each concerto is accompanied by a poem, presumably written by the composer, describing the joys of that particular season. Each line of the poem is printed above a certain passage in the score; the music at that point mirrors, as graphically as possible, the action described.

Of the four concertos, *Spring (La primavera)* is the least descriptive; it evokes mood and atmosphere rather than specific actions. The solo violin is accompanied by an orchestra consisting of strings—first and second violins, violas, and cellos—with the basso continuo realized (improvised from the figured bass) on harpsichord or organ. The poem is a sonnet whose first two quatrains (making eight lines of text) are distributed throughout the first movement, an Allegro in E major. (See Listening Guide 49 for the text.)

First movement

Both poem and music evoke the birds' joyous welcome to spring and the gentle murmur of streams, followed by thunder and lightning. The image of birdcalls takes shape in staccato notes, trills, and running scales; the storm is portrayed by agitated repeated notes answered by quickly ascending scales. Throughout, an orchestral *ritornello,* or refrain, returns again and again (representing the general mood of spring) in alternation with the episodes, which often feature the solo violin. Ultimately, "the little birds return to their melodious warbling" as we return to the home key of E. A florid passage for the soloist leads to the final ritornello.

Ritornello

In the second movement, a Largo in 3/4, Vivaldi evokes an image from the poem of the goatherd who sleeps "in a pleasant field of flowers" with his faithful dog by his side. Over the bass line played by the violas, which sound an ostinato rhythm, he wrote, "The dog who barks." This dog clearly has a

Second movement

Third movement   sense of rhythm. The solo violin unfolds a tender, melancholy melody in the most lyrical Baroque style. In the finale, an Allegro marked "Rustic Dance," we can visualize nymphs and shepherds cavorting in the fields as the music suggests the drone of bagpipes. Ritornellos and solo passages alternate in bringing the work to a happy conclusion.

Like Bach, Vivaldi was renowned in his day as a performer rather than a composer. Today, he is recognized both as the "father of the concerto," having established ritornello form as its basic procedure, and as a herald of musical Romanticism in his use of pictorial imagery.

Listening Guide 49   MW   CD: Chr/Std 2/1–8, Sh 1/41–46
Cassette: Chr/Std 2A/1–3, Sh 1B/3

VIVALDI: *Spring, from The Four Seasons*
(*La primavera, from Le quattro stagioni*)   (9:35)

Date of work: Published 1725

Genre: Programmatic concerto for solo violin, Op. 8 (*The Contest Between Harmony and Inspiration*), Nos. 1–4, each based on an Italian sonnet:

No. 1: *Spring* (*La primavera*)   No. 3: *Autumn* (*L'autunno*)
No. 2: *Summer* (*L'estate*)   No. 4: *Winter* (*L'inverno*)

OP. 8, NO. 1, *SPRING*

Movements: 3
Basis: Italian sonnet, translated below:

I. Allegro	Joyful spring has arrived, the birds greet it with their cheerful song, and the brooks in the gentle breezes flow with a sweet murmur.
	The sky is covered with a black mantle, and thunder and lightning announce a storm. When they fall silent, the birds take up again their melodious song.
II. Largo	And in the flower-rich meadow, to the gentle murmur of bushes and trees, the goatherd sleeps, his faithful dog at his side.
III. Allegro (*Rustic Dance*)	To the festive sounds of a rustic bagpipe nymphs and shepherds dance in their favorite spot when spring appears in its brilliance.

First movement: Allegro; in ritornello form, E major   (3:33)

Ritornello theme:

		Description	*Program*
1	0:00	Ritornello 1, in E major.	Spring
	0:32	Episode 1; solo violin with birdlike trills and high running scales, accompanied by violins.	Birds
2	1:07	Ritornello 2.	Spring
3	1:15	Episode 2; whispering figures like water flowing, played by orchestra.	Murmuring brooks
	1:39	Ritornello 3.	Spring
4	1:47	Episode 3 modulates; solo violin with repeated notes, fast ascending scales, accompanied by orchestra.	Thunder, lightning
	2:15	Ritornello 4, in relative minor (C-sharp).	Spring
5	2:24	Episode 4; trills and repeated notes in solo violin.	Birds
	2:43	Ritornello 5, returns to E major; brief solo passage interrupts.	
6	3:12	Closing tutti.	

(Shorter recordings stop here.)

7   **Second movement: Largo; 3/4 meter, C-sharp minor, orchestration reduced—for solo violin, two violins, and viola**   (2:32)

Opening of movement, with solo violin, slow and melodious, representing the sleeping goatherd ("Il capraro che dorme") and viola, with insistent rhythm, the dog barking ("Il cane che grida"):

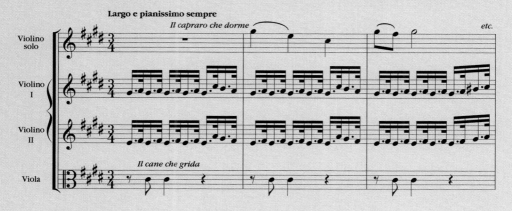

8   **Third movement:** *Danza Pastorale (Rustic Dance)*, **Allegro; in ritornello form, E major**   (3:30)

Opening of movement, with dance tune (ritornello) in upper strings; lilting, compound meter; sustained notes (like bagpipe drone) in lower strings:

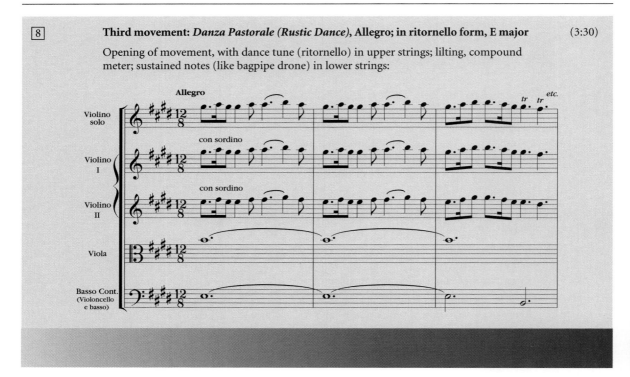

BACH AND THE
LATE BAROQUE CONCERTO

We have already studied Bach as a composer of vocal church music. During the six years he served as court composer at Cöthen (1717–23), Bach produced a large number of instrumental chamber works. In his first year there, he had occasion to perform for a royal visitor, Margrave Christian of Brandenburg. The nobleman was so impressed that he asked the composer to write some works for his orchestra. Several years later, Bach sent him the six *Brandenburg Concertos* pieces that have become known as the *Brandenburg Concertos*, with a dedication to His Royal Highness. It is not known how the margrave responded to the concertos that have immortalized his name.

In these pieces, Bach captured the spirit of the concerto grosso, in which two groups vie with each other. The second of the set, in F major, has long been a favorite, perhaps because of the brilliant trumpet part. The solo group—the *concertino*—consists of trumpet, recorder (sometimes played on a modern flute), oboe, and violin, all of them instruments in the high register. The accompanying group—the *tutti*, or *ripieno*—includes first and second violins, violas, and double basses. The basso continuo is played by cello and harpsichord.

Brandenburg Concerto No. 2

The opening movement of the *Brandenburg Concerto* No. 2 is a sturdy Allegro, bright and assertive. The broad outlines of its form depend on well-defined contrasts in sound—the alternation of the tutti and the solo group. Recorder, oboe, and violin play the recurring, or ritornello, theme in unison with the first violins of the accompanying group, while the trumpet outlines the tonic triad. The contrapuntal lines move in a continuous, seamless texture, powered by a rhythmic drive that never flags from beginning to end. The movement modulates freely from the home key of F major to the neighboring major and minor keys. When its energies have been fully expanded, it returns to F for a vigorous cadence. (See Listening Guide 50.)

First movement

In the slow movement, an Andante in D minor, we hear a soulful dialogue between solo violin, oboe, and recorder (the trumpet is omitted). Each in turn enters with the theme, creating a series of continuous imitations, accompanied only by the continuo group. This moving Andante, with its "sighing" theme, is infused with poignant emotion typical of the Baroque. Third and last comes an Allegro assai (very fast), in which trumpet, oboe, violin, and recorder enter successively with the lively subject of a four-voiced fugue. After interchanges resembling a lively conversation among four equals, the movement reaches its close with one final pronouncement of the subject by the trumpet.

Second and third movements

Listening Guide 50

CD: Chr/Std 2/38–43
Cassette: Chr/Std 2B/1–2

BACH:*Brandenburg Concerto* No. 2 in F major,
First and Second Movements   (8:02)

Date of work: 1717–18

Genre: Concerto grosso

Concertino: Violin, oboe, recorder, trumpet

Movements:
  I. Allegro
  II. Andante
  III. Allegro assai

FIRST MOVEMENT: Allegro; in ritornello form (4:45)

Opening of ritornello theme:

		Section	Description	Key
38	0:00	Ritornello 1	Full ensemble; 8-measure statement.	F major
	0:18	Solo 1	Solo violin; short statement.	F major
	0:23	Ritornello 2	Full ensemble; short statement.	F major
	0:28	Solo 2	Oboe and violin; short statement.	F major
39	0:33	Ritornello 3	Full ensemble; short statement.	C major
	0:37	Solo 3	Recorder and oboe; short statement.	F major
	0:42	Ritornello 4	Full ensemble; short statement.	C major
	0:47	Solo 4	Trumpet and recorder.	F major
	0:52	Ritornello 5	Full ensemble; 6-measure statement.	C major
	1:06	Solo 5	Trumpet, violin, recorder, oboe; short statement.	F major
40	1:11	Ritornello 6	Full ensemble; long statement with entries exchanged between instruments, ending with cellos.	Various
41	2:19	Solo 6	Recorder, violin, oboe, trumpet; each with short statement.	Various
	2:38		Long modulatory tutti section; various exchanges between instruments.	
42	4:00	Ritornello 7	Full ensemble; final statement.	Returns to F major

SECOND MOVEMENT: Andante; continuous imitation and fragmentation, 3/4 meter, D minor

(3:17)

Instrumentation: Violin, oboe, recorder, and continuo (trumpet and strings omitted)

43 "Sighing" theme in imitative entries, over steady bass line in continuo; violin followed by oboe, then recorder:

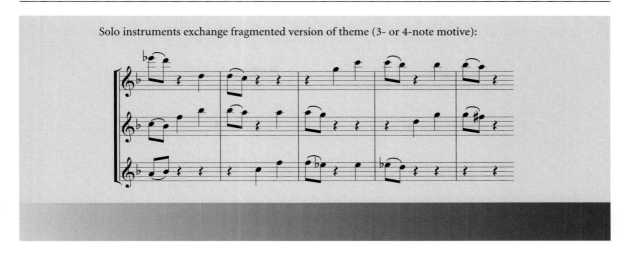

Solo instruments exchange fragmented version of theme (3- or 4-note motive):

64

The Baroque Suite

The suite of the Baroque era was a natural outgrowth of earlier traditions that paired dances of contrasting tempos and character. The suite presented an international galaxy of dance types, all in the same key: the German *allemande*, in quadruple meter at a moderate tempo; the French *courante*, in triple meter at a moderate tempo; the Spanish *sarabande*, a stately dance in triple meter; and the English *jig* (*gigue*), in a lively 6/8 or 6/4. These had begun as popular dances, but by the late Baroque, they had left the ballroom far behind and become abstract types of art music. Between the slow sarabande and fast gigue composers could insert a variety of optional dances—the *minuet*, the *gavotte*, the lively *bourrée*, the *passepied*—that were of peasant origin and that introduced a refreshing earthiness into their more formal surroundings. The suite sometimes opened with an *overture*, and might include other brief pieces with descriptive titles.

Dance types

The standard form of each piece in the suite was a highly developed binary structure (A-B) consisting of two sections of approximately equal length, each rounded off by a cadence. The first part usually moved from the home key (tonic) to a contrasting key (dominant), while the B part made the corresponding move back. The two parts often used closely related melodic material. The form was easy to hear because of the modulation and the full stop at the end of each part. As a rule, each part was repeated, resulting in an A-A-B-B structure (such as we saw in the minuets and trios of the Classical era).

Binary structure

The principle of combining dances into a suite could be applied to cham-

> ## Standard Order of the Baroque Dance Suite
>
> 1. Overture (optional)   4. Sarabande
> 2. Allemande   5. Other dances (optional)
> 3. Courante   6. Gigue (jig)

ber, orchestral, and solo keyboard and lute music as well. In the genre of chamber music, the Italian composer Arcangelo Corelli was noted for his sonatas in suite form, known as *sonatas da camera*, or *chamber sonatas*. (These were distinguished from *sonatas da chiesa*, or *church sonatas*, which were more serious, contrapuntal chamber works.) Bach's French and English suites for harpsichord are splendid examples of solo keyboard suites. In France, dance suites were known as *ordres* (orders), and often contained numerous miniature pieces. Among the composers of solo keyboard suites was François Couperin (1668–1733), the central figure of the French harpsichord school. Notable too was Elisabeth-Claude Jacquet de la Guerre (c. 1666–1729), an extraordinary harpsichordist and composer at the French Royal Court.

Elisabeth-Claude Jacquet de la Guerre

JACQUET DE LA GUERRE: HER LIFE AND MUSIC

A child prodigy whose talents attracted attention in her earliest years, Elisabeth-Claude Jacquet enjoyed the patronage of Louis XIV, the Sun King, who supervised her education at court himself. One reviewer wrote of the young girl's remarkable abilities, "She sings at sight the most difficult music. She accompanies herself, and others who wish to sing, at the harpsichord, which she plays in an inimitable manner. She composes pieces and plays them in all keys asked of her . . . for four years she has been appearing with these extraordinary qualities, and she still is only ten years old."

The daughter of an organ builder, Elisabeth married Marin de la Guerre, organist of the Church of Saint-Chapelle, about 1684; their home became a center of music making in Paris. The French writer Titon du Tillet reported that at these musical gatherings, "all the great musicians and fine connoisseurs went eagerly to hear her." She composed keyboard works, chamber music, cantatas, and a five-act opera, *Cephale and Procris*, which the French Royal Academy presented in 1694.

Principal Works

Keyboard works: 2 books of suites (*Les Pièces de Clavecin*, 1687, and *Pièces de Clavecin qui peuvent se jouer sur le viollon*, 1707)

Instrumental chamber music, including solo sonatas for violin with harpsichord; trio sonatas

Vocal works, including 2 operas (an opera-ballet, 1691, now lost; and *Cephale et Procris*, 1694); 3 collections of cantatas; a Te Deum; songs and airs

---

According to French composer François Couperin, a number of women achieved a high standard of performance as harpsichordists, among them his own daughter, who held a court position as a musician. In his treatise on keyboard playing, Couperin claimed that women such as Jacquet de la Guerre had a natural advantage over men in harpsichord playing because of their smaller hand size and nimble dexterity.

Jacquet de la Guerre retired from public performance in 1717, after the deaths of her husband and son. Following her own death in 1729, a French commemorative medal was struck in her honor (see illustration).

A pioneer in several genres, Jacquet de la Guerre was active in all branches of her art. *Cephale and Procris*, a tragédie lyrique, follows in the operatic tradition of Jean-Baptiste Lully. Her sacred cantatas are based on biblical stories; they are among the few examples of this genre in the French Baroque. In cantatas such as *The Parting of the Red Sea* and *The Deluge*, she led the way in a type of descriptive music that became popular in the nineteenth century.

Vocal music

In 1687, Jacquet de la Guerre produced the first collection of solo harpsichord works ever published by a woman. Two decades later, she published a collection of fourteen pieces representing a new type of chamber music—for harpsichord with an optional violin part—that took us on a path to the duo sonata. These works combine the lyrical Italian style with the decorative and highly ornamented French keyboard style.

Keyboard music

Pieces for Harpsichord

The works in Jacquet de la Guerre's *Pieces for Harpsichord* (1707) form two suites. The first, in D minor, begins with an extended allemande and a variation, called a *double*. The allemande, titled *La Flamande* (*The Flemish Girl*), is followed by a courante and its *double*, a sarabande, and a gigue with *double*. After these come several added movements, including another gigue and a

In The Three Daughters of the Composer Royer, *artist* **Louis Carmontelle** *(1717–1806) shows the young women playing from a ballet score by their father.* (Musée Carnavalet, Paris)

final *chaconne*, an elaborate Baroque form based on a repeated harmonic progression.

The second gigue, a light-hearted dance in 6/8 meter, features many melodic ornaments typical of French harpsichord music. Its disjunct line derives from a French Baroque lute style known as *stile brisé* (broken style). Like the other dances in this suite, this one is written in a standard two part, or binary, form (**A-A-B-B**). The first part moves from D minor to A major (the dominant); the second part moves back to D minor (see Listening Guide 51). Thus the piece traces the movement from tonic to dominant and back to tonic again that we have seen was the basic organizing principle of the Classical style.

Listening Guide 51

CD: Chr/Std 1/61–62, Sh 2/1–2
Cassette: Chr/Std 1B/10, Sh 2A/1

JACQUET DE LA GUERRE: Suite No. 1, 2nd Gigue,
from *Pieces for Harpsichord* (*Pièces de Clavecin*)   (1:40)

Date of work: 1707

Genre: Gigue, 6/8 dance from the Baroque suite

Medium: Solo harpsichord or harpsichord with violin

Form: Binary (A-A-B-B)

Order of movements in Suite No. 1 (D minor):

La Flamande (Allemande)*	Sarabande*	Rigaudon
Double	Gigue*	2nd Rigaudon
Courante*	*Double*	Chaconne
Double	2nd Gigue	
	Double	

*Standard movements of suite

2nd GIGUE

[61] 0:00 A Section—lilting, disjunct theme in D minor, set in 4-measure phrases, with some ornaments; ends in A major:

0:27 A section repeated.

[62] 0:54 B section—more conjunct line, highly ornamented, longer than A section; finally returns to D minor:

(B section not repeated on the Norton recording.)

In this imaginary depiction of Handel's Water Music, *the composer is seen perched on the edge of the front barge, with King George I to the right; in the second barge, musicians seem to be playing Handel's work.*

HANDEL AND THE ORCHESTRAL SUITE

The two orchestral suites by Handel, the *Water Music* and *Music for the Royal Fireworks*, are memorable contributions to the genre. The *Water Music* was surely played (although probably not first composed) for a royal party on the Thames River in London on July 17, 1717. Two days later, the *Daily Courant* reported:

> On Wednesday Evening, at about 8, the King took Water at Whitehall in an open Barge, and went up the River towards Chelsea. Many other Barges with Persons of Quality attended, and so great a Number of Boats, that the whole River in a manner was cover'd; a City Company's Barge was employ'd for the Musick, wherein were 50 Instruments of all sorts, who play'd all the Way from Lambeth (while the Barges drove with the Tide without Rowing, as far as Chelsea) the finest Symphonies, compos'd express for this Occasion, by Mr. Handel; which his Majesty liked so well, that he caus'd it to be plaid over three times in going and returning.

Water Music

The twenty-two numbers of the *Water Music* were performed without continuo instruments, as it was not possible to bring a harpsichord aboard the barge. The conditions of an outdoor performance, in which the music would have to contend with the breeze on the river, birdcalls, and similar noises, prompted Handel to create music that was marked by lively rhythms and catchy melodies.

The *Water Music* opens with a French overture and includes a variety of dance numbers (not in the standard order of the suite), among them minuets in graceful 3/4 time, bourrées in fast 4/4, and hornpipes (an English country dance) in lively triple meter. The occasional echo effects are prime examples of the terraced dynamics of the Baroque. In these varied numbers, Handel combined the Italian string style of Corelli with the songfulness of Purcell and the rhythmic vivacity of French music to produce a style that was imprinted with his own robust personality and was perfectly suited to the taste of an English audience.

The work is divided into three suites. In the opening Allegro of the D-major suite, a fanfare-like theme is sounded by trumpets, then answered by French horns and strings. The lively hornpipe that follows features decorative trills as part of its main theme and a reflective, minor-key middle section. (See Listening Guide 52.)

More than two and a half centuries after it was written, Handel's *Water Music* is still a favorite with the public, indoors or out. We need to hear only a few measures of the work to understand why.

Listening Guide 52

CD: Chr/Std 2/12–17, Sh 1/47–49
Cassette: Chr/Std 2A/5–6, Sh 1B/4

HANDEL: *Water Music*, Suite in D major, excerpts   (4:41)

Date of work: 1717 (first performance)

Genre: Dance suite

Medium: Orchestra (2 trumpets, 2 horns, 2 oboes, bassoon, strings, and continuo; timpani added in Norton recording)

Movements: Allegro
Alla hornpipe
Minuet
Lentement
Bourée

(Shorter recordings include second movement only.)

FIRST MOVEMENT: Allegro; A-B-A' form, 4/4 meter, D major (1:53)

A SECTION

[12] 0:00 Opening fanfare-like theme in trumpets, answered by descending scales in violins, in D major:

B SECTION

[13] 0:29 A dotted-rhythm theme announced by trumpets; begins in A major:

Dotted-rhythm theme taken over by French horns; short motives exchanged between strings and brass.

[14] 1:12 **A SECTION**
Return to opening theme, with varied rhythm; cadence in D major.

1:34 Adagio provides brief link to next movement.

SECOND MOVEMENT: Alla hornpipe; A-B-A form, 3/2 meter, D major (2:48)

A SECTION

[15] 0:00 Disjunct theme in strings and double reeds, with trills, later answered by trumpets and French horns; in D major, at a moderate, spritely tempo:

Continued alternation of motives between brass and strings.

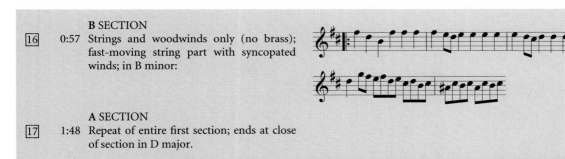

B SECTION		
16	0:57	Strings and woodwinds only (no brass); fast-moving string part with syncopated winds; in B minor:
A SECTION		
17	1:48	Repeat of entire first section; ends at close of section in D major.

65

Other Instrumental Forms

SONATA, PASSACAGLIA, AND OVERTURE

The sonata was widely cultivated throughout the Baroque. In its early stages, it consisted of either a movement in several sections or several movements that contrasted in tempo and texture. We have already noted the distinction that was drawn between the *sonata da camera*, or *chamber sonata*, which was usually a suite of stylized dances, and the *sonata da chiesa*, or *church sonata*, which was more serious in tone and more contrapuntal in texture, its four movements arranged in the sequence slow-fast-slow-fast. The prolific output of the Italian composer Arcangelo Corelli emphasized the distinction between these two types, yet in practice they overlapped. Many church sonatas ended with one or more dancelike movements, while many chamber sonatas opened with an impressive introductory movement in the church-sonata style.

Sonatas were written for one to six or even eight instruments. The favorite combination in the Baroque was two violins and continuo. Because of the three printed staves in the music, such compositions came to be known as *trio sonatas*; yet the title is misleading, because it refers to the number of parts rather than to the number of players. As we saw, the basso continuo needed two performers—a cellist (or bassoonist) to play the bass line and a harpsichordist or organist to realize the harmonies indicated by the figures. Thus it takes four players to perform a trio sonata.

Chamber sonata
Church sonata

Trio sonatas

Sonatas for unaccompanied instruments

Some Baroque composers wrote sonatas for single, unaccompanied instruments. Notable among these was Bach, whose sonatas for unaccompanied violin are centerpieces of the repertory. Domenico Scarlatti (1685–1757) is known for some 550 sonatas for solo harpsichord, characterized by brilliant passagework, hand crossings, and other virtuoso techniques that helped lay the foundation for modern piano technique. Set in one-movement binary form, Scarlatti's works bear the seed that developed into the Classical sonata.

Passacaglia

One of the most majestic forms of Baroque music is the *passacaglia*, which draws on the principle of the ground bass. In this form, a melody, usually four or eight bars long and in a stately triple meter, is introduced alone in the bass. The theme is repeated again and again in the bass, serving as the foundation for a set of continuous variations that exploit all the resources of polyphonic music. (We heard a similar procedure earlier in Dido's lament from Purcell's *Dido and Aeneas.*) A related structure is the *chaconne*, in which the variations are based not on a melody but on a succession of harmonies repeated over and over. The passacaglia and chaconne exemplify the Baroque urge toward abundant variation and embellishment of a musical idea, and that desire to make "much out of little" which is the essence of the creative act.

Chaconne

Overtures: French and Italian

Another important orchestral genre was the operatic overture, of which two types were popular during this period. The *French overture*, an example

A sonata for violin and harpsichord is being performed by Florentine Court Musicians *in a painting by* **Anton Domenico Gabbiani** *(1652–1726).*

of which we heard in Handel's *Messiah* (Listening Guide 48), generally followed the pattern slow-fast, its fast section in the loosely fugal style known as *fugato*. The *Italian overture* consisted of three short, simple sections: fast-slow-fast, with a vivacious, dancelike finale. This pattern, expanded into three separate movements, was later adopted by the concerto grosso and the solo concerto. In addition, the opera overture of the Baroque was one of the ancestors of the symphony of later eras.

KEYBOARD FORMS

The keyboard forms of the Baroque fall into two categories: free forms based on harmony, with a strong element of improvisation, such as the prelude and chorale prelude; and stricter forms based on counterpoint, such as the fugue. Bach's keyboard music shows his mastery of both types.

A *prelude* is a fairly short piece based on the continuous expansion of a   **Prelude**

This two-manual Compenius organ at Frederiksborg Castle, Denmark, dates from the early seventeenth century.

melodic or rhythmic figure. It originated in improvisations performed on the lute and keyboard instruments. In the late Baroque, the prelude was used to introduce a group of dance pieces or a fugue. Since its texture was for the most part homophonic, it made an effective contrast with the contrapuntal texture of the fugue that followed. Later in this chapter, we will study an example of a prelude and fugue from Bach's *Well-Tempered Clavier*.

Church organists, in introducing the chorale to be sung by the congregation, adopted the practice of embellishing the traditional melodies. A body of instrumental works—*chorale preludes* and *chorale variations*—was developed in which organ virtuosity of the highest level was combined with inspired improvisation.

Chorale prelude

Bach and the Chorale Prelude

In his capacity as a church organist, Bach wrote more than 140 organ chorales. Some were short, with the tune stated in its original form. Others presented a longer elaboration of the tune, giving free rein to the imagination. Bach's chorale prelude on *A Mighty Fortress Is Our God*, a melody we heard in Cantata No. 80 (see Chapter 61), was composed in 1709, during his Weimar period. The work features imitation, rearrangements of the tune, and cantus firmus technique (in which the melody is announced clearly in one part, while the other parts move in elaborate counterpoint against it).

The piece is written for an organ with three keyboards and pedals, to allow for different registrations and colors. (By registration, we mean the art of combining various registers, or sets of pipes, through use of the stops that control them.) The texture varies from one to three parts, played by both hands while the feet play the pedals. (See Listening Guide 53 for analysis.)

Listening Guide 53

CD: Chr/Std 2/30–37
Cassette: Chr/Std 2A/10

BACH: Chorale Prelude, *A Mighty Fortress Is Our God* (*Ein feste Burg ist unser Gott*)

(3:33)

Date of work: 1709, Weimar

Genre: Chorale prelude

Medium: Organ

Basis: Lutheran chorale (hymn) tune, *Ein feste Burg ist unser Gott*

Original chorale tune, with 9 phrases:

Basis (chorale phrase)		Description

30	0:00	1	Solo elaboration in *fagotto* (bassoon) stop; higher register elaborates same phrase, now in 2-part texture.
31	0:25	2	2-part texture; tune clearly stated in right hand over moving part.
32	0:37	3	Tune now in lower part, with moving right-hand part above.
33	0:51	4	Tune decorated in dotted notes in lower part; some imitation between parts.
34	1:07	5	2-part imitation on decorated tune, over moving pedal line; 3-part texture.
35	1:22	6, 7	Tune in long notes in pedal, with 2 upper parts in imitation; extension of last note of phrase 7; solo line leads to phrase 8.
36	2:01	8	Tune broken into short motives; imitated between upper parts over ostinato bass; solo line leads to phrase 9.
37	2:26	9	Clear statement of last phrase in high register; 2-part texture; followed by coda featuring imitation and moving pedal line; closes with elaborations over sustained note in pedal.

Opening of work, showing elaborated chorale tune (notes of tune marked with an x):

THE FUGUE AND ITS DEVICES

From the art and science of counterpoint came one of the most exciting forms of Baroque music, the fugue. The name is derived from *fuga*, the Latin word for "flight," implying a flight of fancy, or possibly the flight of the theme from one voice to the other. A *fugue* is a contrapuntal composition in which a theme of strongly marked character pervades the entire fabric, entering in one voice and then in another. The fugue, then, is based on the principle of imitation. Its main theme, the *subject*, constitutes the unifying idea, the focal point of interest in the contrapuntal web.

Fugal voices

We have already encountered the fugue or fugal style in a number of works: at the beginning of the book, in Britten's *The Young Person's Guide to the Orchestra (Variations and Fugue on a Theme of Purcell);* in Handel's overture and choruses of *Messiah;* in the opening movement of Bach's cantata *A Mighty Fortress Is Our God;* and in his organ chorale prelude of the same name. Thus a fugue may be written for a group of instruments, for a solo instrument, or for full chorus. Whether the fugue is vocal or instrumental, its several lines are called voices. In vocal and orchestral fugues, each voice is sounded by a different performer or group of performers. In fugues for keyboard instruments, the ten fingers—and the feet, on the organ, playing the pedals—manage the complex interweaving of the voices.

Subject
Answer
Countersubject

The *subject*, or theme, is stated alone at the beginning in one of the voices—soprano, alto, tenor, or bass. It is then imitated in another voice—this is the *answer*—while the first continues with a *countersubject*, or countertheme. Depending on the number of voices in the fugue, the subject will then appear in a third voice and be answered in the fourth (if any), while the other voices weave a free contrapuntal texture against these. When the theme has been presented in each voice once, the first section of the fugue, the *exposition*, is at an end. From then on, the fugue alternates between sections that feature entrances of the subject and *episodes*—interludes that serve as areas of relaxation—until it reaches its home key.

Exposition

Episodes

The subject of the fugue is stated in the home key, the tonic. The answer is given in a related key, the dominant, which lies five tones above the tonic. There may be modulation to foreign keys in the course of the fugue, which builds up tension before the return home. The Baroque fugue thus embodied the opposition between home and contrasting keys, which was one of the basic principles of the new major-minor system.

As the fugue progresses, the listener experiences a sense of mounting urgency, as in any extended artwork. Each recurrence of the theme reveals new facets of its nature. The composer manipulates the subject's pure musical material as a sculptor might mold clay. Especially effective is the use of *stretto*,

Stretto

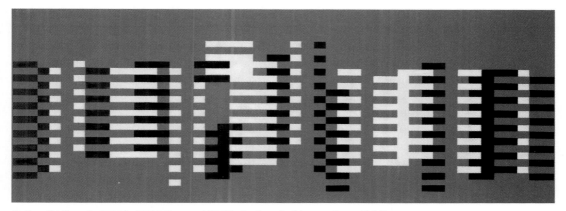

*In **Josef Albers's** (1888–1976)* Fugue *(1925), the interlocking and parallel lines resemble the polyphonic textures produced when several independent melodies are heard simultaneously.* (Öffentliches Kunstmuseum, Basel)

in which the theme is imitated by different voices in close succession. The effect is one of voices crowding upon each other, creating a heightening of tension that brings the fugue to its climax. The final statement of the subject, generally in a decisive manner, closes the fugue.

Fugal composition reached unsurpassed heights at the hands of Bach. In the Baroque and later eras, composers employed some techniques of the fugue in other compositions, in imitative passages known as *fugato*.

Fugato

The Baroque fugue, then, was a form based on imitative counterpoint that combined the composer's technical skill with imagination, feeling, and exuberant ornamentation to produce one of the supreme achievements of the era.

Bach's Prelude and Fugue in C minor

The Well-Tempered Clavier was described in Chapter 59 as the celebrated work that circumnavigated the tonal globe, a journey made possible by the new system of equal temperament for tuning keyboard instruments. It was this system that made it possible to play in all the keys. The first volume of the collection, completed in 1722 during the years Bach worked in Cöthen, contains a prelude and fugue in each of the twelve major and twelve minor keys. The second volume, also containing twenty-four preludes and fugues, appeared twenty years later. The whole collection is thus made up of forty-eight preludes and fugues.

The Prelude and Fugue in C minor is No. 2 in the first volume of *The Well-Tempered Clavier.* The prelude is a "perpetual motion" type of piece based on running sixteenth notes in both hands that seem never to let up, outlining a single chord in each measure. Finally, one hand pauses just long enough to echo the other in strict imitation in a swift *Presto*, which leads into a free, cadenza-like passage. The final cadence, in C major, soon follows.

Prelude

This prelude shows how deeply moving a series of harmonies can be (as did Chopin's Prelude in E minor, which we heard earlier). The music modulates from C minor to the relative major, E-flat major, then returns to the home key. Notable is the unity of mood, the "single affection" that gives this piece its unflagging momentum.

Fugue   The fugue, in three voices, is based on one of those short, incisive themes for which Bach had a special gift. Presented first by the alto voice in the home key of C minor, it is answered by the soprano in G minor, the dominant. The last statement of the subject in the bass line closes the exposition.

There are two countersubjects that play against the subject, whose successive entries are separated by episodes woven out of the basic idea. (See Listening Guide 54.) As in the prelude, the music is characterized by a relentless drive. When the piece finally reaches the C-major chord at the end, we are left with the sense of a journey completed.

Listening Guide 54   MW   CD: Chr/Std 2/44–49, Sh 2/3–8
Cassette: Chr/Std 2B/3, Sh 2A/2

BACH: Prelude and Fugue in C minor, from *The Well-Tempered Clavier*, Book I   (3:22)

Date of work: 1722

Medium: Solo harpsichord

---

44   0:00   **PRELUDE:** Free, improvisatory-style piece; establishes key of C minor; begins with fast, repeated sixteenth-note pattern that moves through various harmonies   (1:47)

Opening of prelude, showing 2 sixteenth-note patterns in top line (in C minor, then F minor), each repeated:

45   1:02   Presto, with left hand in strict imitation of right hand, one measure behind:

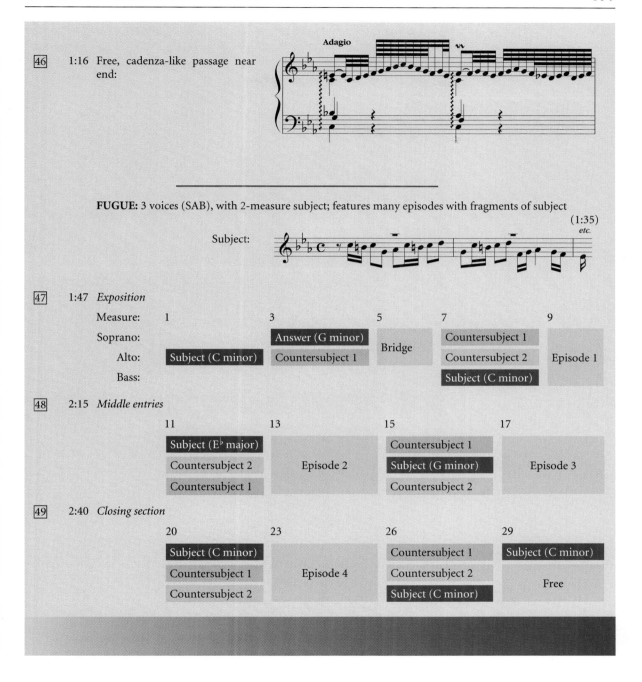

46 1:16 Free, cadenza-like passage near end:

FUGUE: 3 voices (SAB), with 2-measure subject; features many episodes with fragments of subject

(1:35)
etc.

Subject:

47 1:47 *Exposition*

Measure:	1	3	5	7	9
Soprano:		Answer (G minor)		Countersubject 1	
Alto:	Subject (C minor)	Countersubject 1	Bridge	Countersubject 2	Episode 1
Bass:				Subject (C minor)	

48 2:15 *Middle entries*

	11	13	15	17
	Subject (E♭ major)		Countersubject 1	
	Countersubject 2	Episode 2	Subject (G minor)	Episode 3
	Countersubject 1		Countersubject 2	

49 2:40 *Closing section*

	20	23	26	29
	Subject (C minor)		Countersubject 1	Subject (C minor)
	Countersubject 1	Episode 4	Countersubject 2	
	Countersubject 2		Subject (C minor)	Free

Transition IV

To the Age of Enlightenment

"The Italian style and the French style have long divided the Republic of Music in France. For my part, I have always valued those works which have merit, without regard for their composer or country of origin."—FRANÇOIS COUPERIN

THE ROCOCO AND THE AGE OF SENSIBILITY

In the reigns of the French kings Louis XIV (1643–1715) and Louis XV (1715–74), the old regime was waning. With the death of Louis XV, the privileged minority at the top of the social pyramid exchanged their games of power for those of frivolity. Art moved from the monumentality of the Baroque to the caprice and intimacy of the Rococo.

The word derives from the French *rocaille*, "a shell," suggesting the decorative scroll- and shellwork characteristic of the style. The Rococo took shape as a reaction against the grandiose gesture of the Baroque. Out of the disintegrating world of the Baroque came a miniature, ornate art aimed at the enchantment of the senses and asserting a doctrine whose first law was "enjoy yourself."

The greatest painter of the French Rococo was Jean Antoine Watteau (1684–1721). To the dream world of love and gallantry that furnished the themes of his art, Watteau brought the insights and the techniques of the Dutch school of Rubens. Watteau's intimate, pastoral scenes reflected the shift in French society.

Jean Antoine Watteau *(1684–1721), with his dream world of love and gallantry, was the artistic counterpart of François Couperin.* La gamme d'amour (The Gamut of Love). (National Gallery, London)

The musical counterpart to Watteau was François Couperin (1668–1733), referred to earlier as the greatest composer of the French keyboard school. Couperin came from a family of distinguished musicians. His works, along with those of Elisabeth-Claude Jacquet de la Guerre, crystallized the miniature world of the Rococo. Their goal was to charm, to delight, to entertain.

François Couperin

The coming era, the Age of Enlightenment, was characterized by the desire to systematize all knowledge, and this impulse also made itself felt on the musical scene. Jean-Philippe Rameau (1683–1764), the foremost French composer of the era, tried to establish a rational foundation for the harmonic practice of his time. His *Treatise on Harmony* (1722) set forth concepts that served as the point of departure for modern music theory.

Jean-Philippe Rameau

The Rococo witnessed as profound a change in taste as any that has ever occurred in the history of music. In turning to a polished entertainment music, composers adopted a new ideal of beauty. Elaborate polyphonic textures yielded to a single melody line with a simple chordal accompaniment

(Classical homophony), in much the same way that the contrapuntal complexities of late Renaissance music gave way to the early Baroque ideal of monody (it is surely true that history repeats itself). This era desired its music above all to be simple and expressive of natural feeling. Thus was born the "sensitive," or "sentimental," style of the *Empfindsamkeit* and the Age of Sensibility—an age that saw the first stirrings of that direct and natural expression that was to flower fully with Romanticism.

Empfindsamkeit

The new style reached its apex in Germany in the mid–eighteenth century, when Bach's four composer sons—Wilhelm Friedemann, Carl Philipp Emanuel, Johann Christoph, and Johann Christian—were active. Along with their contemporaries, the Bach sons oversaw the revolution in taste that resulted in neglect of their father's music after his death. In this musical revolution, the sonata and the concerto were expanded, and symphonic styles were enriched with elements drawn from the operatic aria and overture and with the tunes and rhythms of Italian comic opera. From these developments was born something new—the Classical sonata cycle, which will be described in Chapter 28 and which we will hear in action in forthcoming examples. This new art form was the collective achievement of several generations of musicians who were active in Italy, France, and Germany throughout the pre-Classical period (c. 1725–75).

C. P. E. Bach

One of the outstanding figures of the pre-Classical era was Carl Philipp Emanuel Bach (1714–1788), the second son of Johann Sebastian. He deepened the emotional content of the abstract instrumental forms and played a decisive role in the creation of the modern piano idiom. His dramatic sonata style exerted a powerful influence on the masters of the Classical era. And his theoretical treatise *Essay on the True Art of Playing Keyboard Instruments* (1753–62) casts much light on the musical practices of the mid–eighteenth century.

THE CHANGING OPERA

"I hope I may be forgiven, that I have not made my opera unnatural, like those in vogue, for I have no recitative."
—JOHN GAY

The vast social changes taking shape in the eighteenth century were bound to be reflected in the lyric theater. Grandiose Baroque opera, geared to an era of absolute monarchy, had no place in the shifting societal structure. Increasingly its pretensions were satirized all over Europe. The defeat of opera seria in London by *The Beggar's Opera* (1728), mentioned earlier, had its counterpart in Paris in 1752, when a troupe of Italian singers in the French capital presented Giovanni Battista Pergolesi's comedy with music *La serva padrona (The Servant Mistress)*. The so-called War of the Buffoons ensued, between those who favored the traditional French court opera and those who saw in the rising Italian comic opera, called *opera buffa*, a new, realistic art. The former camp was headed by the king, Madame de Pompadour (his mistress), and the aristocracy; the latter was led by the queen and such Encyclopedists as Rousseau, who welcomed the comic form for its expressive melody and natural sentiment and for throwing off what they regarded as the outmoded contrapuntal style. In the larger sense, the War of the Buffoons was a contest between the rising bourgeois music and a dying aristocratic art.

"War of the Buffoons"

John Gay's *The Beggar's Opera*

The Beggar's Opera, by John Gay (1685–1732), a satirical play with songs, was presented in London in 1728, where it enjoyed enormous success. The characters—highwaymen, pickpockets, harlots, and their unsavory associates—were a far cry from the gods and heroes of Handel's works for the stage. *The Beggar's Opera* sounded the death knell of opera seria, whose traditions and singers were Italian. It ushered in a vogue of racy pieces in English with popular songs and dances that alternated with spoken dialogue, a trend that has continued in the Broadway musicals of our own time. The new genre, which became known as *ballad*, or *dialogue, opera*, took root throughout Great Britain and in the American colonies. In dialogue opera, the composer is more a compiler or arranger, who adapts familiar tunes to new words.

Ballad (dialogue) opera

The songs for *The Beggar's Opera* were chosen by Gay with the assistance of Johann Christoph Pepusch (1667–1752), who arranged them for performance. Included were some English and Scottish folk songs, along with popular tunes and dances from a variety of sources. Alongside these traditional songs, Gay included tunes borrowed from Handel operas; the public loved this parodying of serious opera.

With Gay's work, opera became a kind of crossover genre, with more widespread appeal than ever. (The term *crossover* applies to a style, artist, or recording that is intended to appeal to a new audience.) Solidly rooted in the eighteenth century, the piece was revived again and again throughout the nineteenth and twentieth centuries. The most famous of these revivals is the *Threepenny Opera* of Bertolt Brecht and Kurt Weill, twentieth-century collaborators who imposed a modern sensibility on the old tale and a few of its tunes. The work was produced in Berlin in 1928, exactly two hundred years after Gay's original was premiered.

Crossover

The Beggar's Opera is introduced by the Beggar—the author—and the Player, who provide satirical commentary on Italian operatic traditions. The

A scene from The Beggar's Opera *of 1728, as drawn by* **William Hogarth** *(1697–1764).*
(Tate Gallery, London)

story involves two women, Polly Peachum and Lucy Lockit, both in love with the criminal Macheath, who has been jailed by their fathers, a bounty hunter and a jailer respectively. The second act ends with what is called the "jealousy scene" between the two women, a parody of a notorious real-life onstage quarrel between two operatic sopranos—Francesca Cuzzoni and Faustina Bordoni. Polly, now married to Macheath, arrives to see her husband and finds Lucy, pregnant by Macheath, visiting at the jail. The women express their jealousy in "Why how now, Madam Flirt," sung to a tune well-known to the London public. This strophic setting alternates verses between the women and is sung in a somewhat operatic style. When Polly's father arrives to take her away, she sings of her love for Macheath in "No pow'r on earth," to a tune by a little-known English composer. Lucy is then persuaded to help Macheath escape, knowing full well that she will lose him. Her lament, "I like the Fox shall grieve," is sung to a moving Scottish air (see Listening Guide 55). It is clear from these attractive tunes why the middle classes preferred this type of popular entertainment to the much more aristocratic opera.

GAY: *The Beggar's Opera*, end of Act II   (5:52)

Date of work: 1728

Genre: Ballad, or dialogue, opera

Characters:
Peachum, a bounty hunter
Mrs. Peachum
Polly Peachum, secretly married to Macheath
Macheath, a highwayman
Lockit, a jailer
Lucy Lockit, in love with Macheath

---

[63] 0:00   **Air 38: "Why how now, Madam Flirt"**—duet, Lucy and Polly

Sung to the tune of *Good-morrow, Gossip Joan*; strophic setting (A-A), in E major; quick tempo, with embellishments in operatic style:

LUCY

A Why how now, Madam Flirt?
   If you thus must chatter;
   And are for flinging Dirt,
   Let's try who best can spatter;
   Madam Flirt!

POLLY

A Why how now, saucy Jade;
   Sure the Wench is Tipsy!
   How can you see me made
   The scoff of such a Gipsy!
   Saucy Jade!

Dialogue: Peachum enters and takes Polly off as she sings of her love for Macheath.

[64] 1:07   **Air 39: "No pow'r on earth"**—solo, Polly

Sung to *Irish Howl*, by George Vanbrughe; A-A-B-C form, in F major, slow tempo:

A No pow'r on earth can e'er divide
   The knot that sacred love hath ty'd.
A No pow'r . . .
B When parents draw against our mind,
   The true-love's knot they faster bind.
C Ho ho ra in ambora
   Ho an ho derry
   Hi an hi derry
   Hoo hoo derry derry
   Derry ambora.

Dialogue: Macheath professes his love to Lucy and convinces her to help him escape by stealing the keys from the sleeping jailer. She knows that freeing him means losing him, and sings of her loss. She fetches the keys, and Macheath escapes.

3:59 **Air 40: "I like the Fox shall grieve"**—solo, Lucy

Sung to the tune of *The Lass of Patie's Mill*; binary form (**A-A-B-B**), D major, slow tempo:

A I like the Fox shall grieve,
   Whose mate hath left her side,
   Whom Hounds, from morn to eve,
   Chase o'er the country wide.
A I like the Fox . . .
B Where can my lover hide?
   Where cheat the weary pack?
   If Love be not his guide,
   He never will come back!
B Where can my lover hide . . .

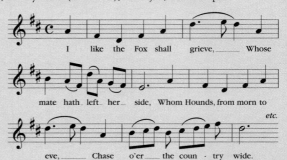

GLUCK AND OPERA REFORM

"There is no musical rule I have not willingly sacrificed to dramatic effect."—CHRISTOPH WILLIBALD GLUCK

It fell to a German-born composer trained in Italy to liberate serious opera from some of its outmoded conventions. Christoph Willibald Gluck (1714–1787) found his way to a style that met the new need for dramatic truth and expressiveness. "I have striven to restrict music to its true office of serving poetry by means of expression and by following the situations of the story, without interrupting the action or stifling it with a useless superfluity of ornaments," he said. How well he realized the aesthetic needs of the new age: "Simplicity, truth, and naturalness are the great principles of beauty in all forms of art."

This conviction was embodied in the works Gluck wrote for the Imperial Court Theater at Vienna, notably *Orpheus and Eurydice* (1762) and *Alceste* (1767), both collaborations with the librettist Raniero Calzabigi. These operas were followed by the lyric dramas with which he conquered the Paris Opera; the most important were based on legends by the ancient Greek writer Homer—*Iphigenia in Aulis* (1774) and *Iphigenia in Taurus* (1778). In these works, Gluck successfully fused a number of elements: the monumental choral scenes and dances that had always been a feature of French lyric tragedy, the animated ensembles of comic opera, the vigor of the new instrumental style in Italy and Germany, and the broadly arching vocal line that was part of Europe's operatic heritage. The result was a music drama whose dramatic truth and expressiveness profoundly affected the course of operatic history.

A Comparison of Baroque and Classical Styles

	Baroque (c. 1600–1750)	Classical (c. 1750–1825)
Composers	Monteverdi, Purcell, Corelli, Vivaldi, Handel, Bach, Jacquet de la Guerre	Haydn, Mozart, Beethoven, Schubert
Melody	Continuous melody with wide leaps, chromatic tones for emotional effect	Symmetrical melody in balanced phrases and cadences; tuneful, diatonic, with narrow leaps
Rhythm	Single rhythm predominant; steady, energetic pulse; freer in vocal music	Dance rhythms favored; regularly recurring accents
Harmony	Chromatic harmony for expressive effect; major-minor system established with brief excursions to other keys	Diatonic harmony favored; tonic-dominant relationship expanded, becomes basis for large-scale form
Texture	Polyphonic texture; linear-horizontal dimension	Homophonic texture; chordal-vertical dimension
Instrumental genres	Fugue, concerto grosso, trio sonata, suite, chaconne, prelude, passacaglia	Symphony, solo concerto, solo sonata, string quartet, other chamber music ensembles
Vocal genres	Opera, Mass, oratorio, cantata	Opera, Mass, oratorio
Form	Binary form predominant	Ternary form becomes important, sonata-allegro form developed
Dynamics	Terraced (contrasting) dynamics	Continuously changing dynamics through crescendo and decrescendo
Timbre	Continuous tone color throughout one movement	Changing tone colors from one section to the next
Performing forces	String orchestra, with added woodwinds; organ and harpsichord in use	Orchestra standardized into four choirs; introduction of clarinet, trombone; rise of piano to prominence
Improvisation	Improvisation expected; harmonies realized from figured bass	Improvisation largely limited to cadenzas in concertos
Emotion	Single affection; emotional exuberance and theatricality	Emotional balance and restraint

Part 7

The Twentieth Century

Pablo Picasso *(1881–1973)*, Harlequin *(1915)*. (Museum of Modern Art, New York)

Transition V

The Post-Romantic Era

"I came into a very young world in a very old time."
—ERIK SATIE

It became apparent toward the end of the nineteenth century that the Romantic impulse had run its course. It fell to the composers who reached artistic maturity in the final years of the century to bridge the gap between a dying Romanticism and the twentieth century.

The post-Romantic era extended from around 1890 to 1910. Some composers of this period continued on the traditional path; others struck out in new directions; and still others tried to steer a middle course between the old and the new.

Two important movements ushered in the twentieth century: Impressionism, heralded by the French composers Claude Debussy and Maurice Ravel, and post-Romanticism. We have already encountered the Italian post-Romantic concept of verismo, exemplified by Leoncavallo's *Pagliacci* and the operas of Giacomo Puccini and Pietro Mascagni. In this chapter, we will explore the German post-Romantic style of Gustav Mahler and Richard Strauss.

GUSTAV MAHLER: HIS LIFE AND MUSIC

"To write a symphony is, for me, to construct a world."

One of the striking phenomena of the later twentieth century has been the increasing popularity of Gustav Mahler's music. For whatever reason, his trou-

Gustav Mahler

Vienna Opera

bled spirit seems to reach out to listeners in a most persuasive way. "My time will come," he used to say. It has.

Gustav Mahler (1860–1911) was born and raised in Bohemia. His parents, quick to recognize the boy's talent, arranged piano lessons for him when he was six. At age fifteen, he entered the conservatory in Vienna, and attended the university there three years later. His professional career began modestly enough: at the age of twenty, he was engaged to conduct operettas at a third-rate summer theater. A dynamic conductor who found his natural habitat in the opera house, Mahler soon achieved a reputation that brought him more important posts; in 1888, he became director of the Royal Opera at Budapest. From Budapest, Mahler went to Hamburg. Then, at thirty-seven, he was offered the most important musical position in the Austrian Empire—the directorship of the Vienna Opera. His ten years there (1897–1907) made operatic history. He brought to his duties a fiery temperament, unwavering devotion to ideals, and an inflexible will. "Humanly I make every concession; artistically—none!" was his creed. When he took over, the current fad was the unpretentious style of the French composer Jules Massenet. By the time his rule ended, he had taught a frivolous public to revere Mozart, Beethoven, and Gluck, and made them listen to uncut versions of Wagner's operas as well.

Conversion to Catholicism

Shortly before he was appointed to Vienna, Mahler converted from Judaism to Catholicism, primarily to ease his way in a city where anti-Semitism was rampant. Beyond that, Mahler belonged to a generation of Jewish intellectuals who had lost identification with their religious heritage and who sought roots in the Austro-German culture of which they felt themselves to be a part. "I am thrice homeless," he remarked. "As a Bohemian born in Austria. As an Austrian among Germans. And as a Jew throughout the world."

Mahler's obstinance in musical matters was bound to create powerful enemies. His final years in Vienna were embittered by various schemes against him, which flourished despite his having transformed the Imperial Opera into the premier lyric theater of Europe. The death of a young daughter left him grief-stricken. A second disaster followed soon after: he was found to have a serious heart ailment. When he finally was forced to resign his post, the blow was not unexpected.

New York Philharmonic

Mahler, now almost forty-eight (he had only three more years to live), accepted an engagement at New York's Metropolitan Opera. He hoped to earn enough to be able to retire at fifty, so that he finally might compose with the peace of mind that had never been granted him. His three years in New York were marked by the storms that his tempestuous personality inevitably provoked. In 1909, he assumed direction of the New York Philharmonic Orchestra. When the ladies of the orchestra's Board once complained to Alma Mahler that her husband had ignored their wishes, she replied, "But in Vienna the Emperor himself did not dare to interfere!"

In the middle of a taxing concert season with the Philharmonic, Mahler fell ill with a streptococcus infection and was taken to Paris, where a new serum had been developed. But he took a turn for the worse, and set forth on his last journey, to the scene of his greatest triumphs—the Vienna that he both loved and detested. He died a few weeks before his fifty-first birthday and was buried, as he had requested, beside his daughter in a cemetery outside Vienna. "The act of creation in me," Mahler said, "is so closely bound up with all my experience that when my mind and spirit are at rest I can compose nothing." In identifying art with emotion, he was entirely the Romantic.

Vocal music

The spirit of song pervades Mahler's art. He followed Schubert and Schumann in cultivating the song cycle, but with orchestral rather than piano accompaniment. *Songs of a Wayfarer*, composed in 1885, is a set of four songs filled with Schubertian longing. Mahler wrote the texts himself, drawing on a theme that appealed to his imagination: the rejected lover wandering alone over the face of the earth. His next cycle was inspired by a famous collection of German folk poetry, *The Youth's Magic Horn*. The moving *Songs on the Death of Children* is a cycle for voice and orchestra to grief-laden poems of Friedrich Rückert. The peak of his vocal writing is *The Song of the Earth*, which we will study.

Symphonies

Mahler was the last in the illustrious line of Viennese symphonists that extended from Haydn, Mozart, Beethoven, and Schubert to Brahms and Bruckner. His tonal imagery is filled with the jovial spirit of Austrian popular song and dance. His nine symphonies abound in long, flowing melodies and richly expressive harmonies. (The Tenth Symphony, left unfinished at his death, was completed in the 1970s from the composer's sketches and drafts.) Mahler's sense of color ranks with that of the great masters of orchestration. He contrasts solo instruments in the manner of chamber music, achieving his bright tonal effects through clarity of line rather than massed sonorities.

It was in the realm of musical texture that Mahler made his most important contribution to contemporary technique. In his orchestral style, which was based on counterpoint, two or more melodies could unfold simultaneously, each setting off the other. Mahler never abandoned the principle of tonality; he used the key as a framework for his vast designs.

In the early 1900s, all of Vienna responded to the vogue for Eastern effects—as did **Gustav Klimt** (1862–1918) in the painting Expectation (1905–9). (Österreichisches Museum für angewandte Kunst, Vienna)

The Song of the Earth

Regarded by many as Mahler's masterpiece, *The Song of the Earth* is an extended cycle of six songs for tenor, contralto (or baritone), and orchestra. It was begun just after his daughter's death, when the composer learned that he had a heart ailment. From initial despair he progressed to a heightened awareness of life: "I see everything in a new light. I thirst for life more than ever before, and find the 'habit of existence' more sweet than it ever was." This mood spurred him to a work in which a fierce joy in the beauty of earthly things mingled with gentle resignation.

Mahler found his text in Hans Bethge's *Chinese Flute*, a translation—more accurately, adaptation—of poems by Li Po, the eighth-century poet considered to be one of China's greatest. In their assertion that youth and happiness are fleeting and a bottle of wine brings the ultimate freedom, these verses are strikingly similar to the *Rubáiyát* of the twelfth-century Persian poet Omar Khayyám. The lyricist in Mahler responded to these eloquent images of joy and despair, while the symphonist painted the images with brilliant orchestral colors. *The Song of the Earth* was completed in 1911, just prior to Mahler's death. It received its premiere in Munich some six months later under the baton of his disciple Bruno Walter.

The third movement of the cycle, *Of Youth (Von der Jugend)*, for tenor and orchestra, delicately evokes its Chinese theme through pentatonic scale patterns, the use of triangle, and haunting woodwind instruments. The text evokes a faraway scene: "In the middle of the little pool stands a pavilion of green and of white porcelain" where friends, beautifully dressed, sit drinking tea, chatting, or writing verses, while watching their reflections in the water below. (For text and analysis, see Listening Guide 56.) Life here is peaceful, and eminently civilized. The bridge of jade that arches like a tiger over the pool has its musical counterpart in the arch form, **A-B-A,** of the movement. The dainty staccato notes of the first and third sections contrast with the smoother pattern of the middle part. The sound is extraordinarily transparent, achieved by a sparse orchestral texture that differs very much from the lush and sumptuous sound of the composer's later symphonies.

Mahler was by no means alone in his fascination with Eastern culture. Earlier, the writer Goethe had fallen under the spell of the evocative texts of Li Po, and had attempted to wed East and West in his German renditions of the Chinese poet. In the Vienna of Mahler's time, the intellectual and artistic climate was ripe for new—even radical—ideas, and East Asian traditions permeated all forms of artistic expression.

Third movement

Listening Guide 56

CD: Chr/Std 6/54–57
Cassette: Chr/Std 6B/4

MAHLER: *The Song of the Earth (Das Lied von der Erde),* Third Movement

(3:10)

Date of work: 1908–9

Basis: The Chinese Flute, by Hans Bethge

Medium: Song cycle for voice (tenor, alto/baritone) and orchestra

Movements:
  I.   *Drinking Song of the Sorrow of the Earth (Das Trinklied vom Jammer der Erde)*
  II. *The Lonely One in Autumn (Der Einsame in Herbst)*
  III. *Of Youth (Von der Jugend)*
  IV. *Of Beauty (Von der Schönheit)*
  V.   *The Drunkard in Spring (Der Trunkene im Frühling)*
  VI. *The Farewell (Der Abschied)*

III. *Of Youth* (*Von der Jugend*), tenor and orchestra (A-B-A form)

Opening woodwind line, based on a pentatonic scale:

Theme 1 (first strophe):

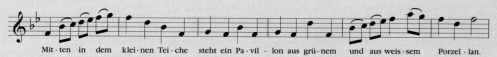

Theme 2 (second strophe):

		Text	Translation	Description
54	0:00			**A** SECTION Introduction — woodwinds, French horn, and triangle; pentatonic theme.
		Mitten in dem kleinen Teiche steht ein Pavillon aus grünem und aus weissem Porzellan.	In the middle of the little pool stands a pavilion of green and of white porcelain.	Strophe 1 — theme 1, in B-flat major, dancelike, with staccato accompaniment.
		Wie der Rücken eines Tigers wölbt die Brücke sich aus Jade zu dem Pavillon hinüber.	Like the back of a tiger the bridge of jade arches over to the pavilion.	Strophe 2 — theme 2, more dramatic.
	0:41			Interlude — woodwinds, with theme 1.
55	0:49	In dem Häuschen sitzen Freunde, schön gekleidet, trinken, plaudern, manche schreiben Verse nieder.	In the little house, friends are sitting, beautifully dressed, drinking, chatting; several are writing verse.	**B** SECTION Strophe 3 — G major, then a G-minor variation of theme 2.
	1:22			Interlude — woodwinds, very brief.
		Ihre seidnen Ärmel gleiten rückwärts, ihre seidnen Mützen	Their silken sleeves slip backwards, their silken caps	Strophe 4 — theme 2.
				Interlude — with varied woodwinds, then strings.
		hocken lustig tief im Nacken.	perch gaily on the back of their necks.	

56	1:39	Auf des kleinen Teiches stiller Wasserfläche zeigt sich alles wunderlich im Spiegelbilde.	On the little pool's still surface everything appears fantastically in a mirror image.	Strophe 5—based on theme 2, slower and more chromatic.
				Interlude—strings, chromatic, based on strophe 5.
57	2:34			A SECTION Introduction—from the beginning, returns to B-flat major.
		Alles auf dem Kopfe stehend	Everything is standing on its head	Strophe 6—theme 1.
		in dem Pavillon aus grünem und aus weissem Porzellan;	in the pavilion of green and of white porcelain;	
		wie ein Halbmond scheint die Brücke umgekehrt der Bogen. Freunde, schön gekleidet, trinken, plaudern.	like a half-moon stands the bridge, upside-down its arch. Friends, beautifully dressed, are drinking, chatting.	Strophe 7—theme 2.

RICHARD STRAUSS: HIS LIFE AND MUSIC

"I work very long on melodies. The important thing is not the beginning of the melody but its continuation, its development into a fully completed artistic form."

Among the German opera composers who followed Wagner, Richard Strauss (1864–1949) was the most prominent. His operas, admired by an international public, remain indispensable works in the repertory.

Strauss's father was a virtuoso horn player who belonged to the court orchestra, and his mother was the daughter of a successful Munich brewer. In this solid middle-class environment, a high value was placed on music and money; these remained Strauss's twin passions throughout his life.

His first works remained in Classical forms. At twenty-one, however, he found his true style in vivid program music, in which he emphasized "the poetic, the expressive in music." *Macbeth*, his first symphonic poem, was followed by *Don Juan*, an extraordinary achievement for a young composer of twenty-four. Then came a series of symphonic poems that trumpeted his name throughout the civilized world: *Death and Transfiguration*, *Till Eulenspiegel's Merry Pranks*, *Don Quixote*, *A Hero's Life*, and *Thus Spake Zarathus-*

Richard Strauss

Symphonic poems

475

tra, whose sensational opening is well-known from the film *2001: A Space Odyssey.*

Operas

In the early years of the twentieth century, Strauss conquered the operatic stage with *Salome, Elektra,* and *Der Rosenkavalier (The Cavalier of the Rose).* The international triumph of the last work on the eve of the First World War marked the summit of his career. Strauss was eager to dispel the romantic notion that the artist is better off starving in an attic. On the contrary, he insisted: "Worry alone is enough to kill a sensitive man, and all thoroughly artistic natures are sensitive." He collected unprecedented fees and royalties for his scores.

Hugo von Hofmannsthal

Strauss's collaboration with poet and playwright Hugo von Hofmannsthal, the librettist of *Elektra* and *Der Rosenkavalier,* continued until the author's death in 1929. By this time, new concepts of modernism had surfaced, and the onetime innovator was now entrenched as a conservative. When the

Involvement with Nazis

Nazis came to power in 1933, Strauss was confronted with a challenge and an opportunity. He was by no means reactionary in his political thinking; his daughter-in-law was Jewish, and the cosmopolitan circles in which he traveled were not susceptible to Hitler's ideology. Hence he faced the challenge to speak out against the Third Reich—or to leave Germany, as many writers, musicians, and other intellectuals were doing. But the new regime was courting writers and artists. Strauss saw an opportunity he could take advantage of. In 1933, on the threshold of seventy, he was elevated to the official hierarchy as president of the Reichsmusikkammer (State Chamber of Music). But his reign was brief and uneasy. For one thing, he declined to support the move to ban Felix Mendelssohn's music. Finally, when his opera *The Silent Woman* was withdrawn after its premiere because the librettist, Stefan Zweig, was Jewish, Strauss resigned.

The war's end found the eighty-one-year-old composer the victim of a curious irony. He was living in near poverty in his villa at Garmisch, in the Bavarian Alps, because the huge sums he was owed for performances of his works in England and America had been impounded as war reparations. To his friends, Strauss explained that he had remained in Nazi Germany because someone had to protect culture from Hitler's barbarians. Perhaps he even believed that. He died shortly after being honored at the Bavarian Academy of Arts on the occasion of his eighty-fifth birthday.

Characteristics of works

Strauss carried to its extreme limit the nineteenth-century appetite for story-and-picture music. His symphonic poems are a treasury of orchestral discoveries. He anticipates modern sound effects—the clatter of pots and pans, the bleating of sheep, the gabble of geese, hoofbeats, wind, thunder, storm. Much more important, these works are packed with movement, with the sound and fury of a fiery temperament.

Salome, from Oscar Wilde's famous play, and *Elektra,* based on Hof-

Principal Works

Orchestral music: symphonic poems, including *Macbeth* (1888), *Don Juan* (1888–89), *Tod und Verklärung (Death and Transfiguration*, 1889), *Till Eulenspiegels lustige Streiche (Till Eulenspiegel's Merry Pranks*, 1895), *Also sprach Zarathustra (Thus Spake Zarathustra*, 1896), *Don Quixote* (1897), and *Ein Heldenleben (A Hero's Life*, 1898); 2 symphonies (*Domestic*, 1903; *Alpine*, 1915); 3 concertos (2 for horn, 1 for oboe)

15 operas, including *Salome* (1905), *Elektra* (1909), *Der Rosenkavalier (The Cavalier of the Rose*, 1911), *Ariadne auf Naxos* (1912), and *Die schweigsame Frau (The Silent Woman*, 1935)

Choral works, with and without orchestra; chamber works

mannsthal's version of the Greek tragedy, are long one-act operas by Strauss that continue to be widely performed. Swiftly paced, moving relentlessly to their climaxes, they make for superb theater. The most popular of his operas, *Der Rosenkavalier*, is notable for its sensuous lyricism and entrancing waltzes.

Der Rosenkavalier

The action takes place in Vienna during the reign of the empress Maria Theresa (r. 1740–80). The Princess of Werdenberg, a great lady of the court, is the wife of the Field Marshall and is therefore known (in German) as the Marschallin. She tries to hold on to her fading youth by having an affair with a handsome young aristocrat, Octavian, who is considerably her junior. Her cousin, Baron Ochs, is a boorish fortune hunter with atrocious manners and morals. Herr von Faninal, a rich merchant of Vienna, is eager to crash high society and is convinced that if the Baron became his son-in-law, all doors would be open. He therefore promises his beautiful young daughter Sophie to the Baron. The opera opens on the day of the betrothal, when Sophie has not yet met her fiancé. When she does, she detests him.

It was customary among the Viennese nobility for a prospective bride-groom to send his lady love a silver rose. Baron Ochs delegates Octavian to deliver the rose to Sophie. Act II opens with the ceremonious scene of the Presentation of the Rose. For the two young people, it is love at first sight. The rest of the action details how the lovers overcome the obstacles that threaten to keep them apart. Sophie defies her father, bringing about a duel in which Octavian wounds the Baron slightly. Octavian then sets in motion a

HUGO·VON·HOFMANNSTHAL━RICHARD·STRAUSS:·OPERA·BUFFA·

BÜHNENBILD·FÜR·DEN·3·AUFZUG·SEPARIERTES·ZIMMER·IN·EINEM·KLEINEN·GASTHOF

Alfred Roller's *stage design for* Der Rosenkavalier, *complete with bedroom suite, helped make the opera an immediate success.*

complicated intrigue to free Sophie from her dreadful engagement. His plot works. At the end of Act III, the Marschallin, realizing that time is against her, relinquishes Octavian to Sophie, and the lovers are united.

This is a glamorous opera about glamorous people, combining comedy, romance, and sentiment. Hofmannsthal's libretto contributed to its spectacular success, as did Strauss's wonderfully lyrical music. *Der Rosenkavalier* was first performed in Dresden, Germany, in 1911 and soon triumphed throughout Europe and America. Strauss had to make some concessions, as parts of the opera were quite risqué for the time. He revised the scenes that took place in the Marschallin's bedroom (in Act I) and toned down the Baron's coarse language, sung in a slang Viennese dialect.

The role of the Marschallin has been associated with some of the greatest sopranos in the history of opera. The Baron's part demands a singing actor of the highest caliber; Sophie is an unforgettable ingenue; and the ardent Octavian is a trouser role—that is, the part of a young man is sung by a woman. (You may remember that Cherubino in Mozart's *Marriage of Figaro* is also a trouser role.)

Trio We will hear the Trio sung toward the end of the third act by the Marschallin, Sophie, and Octavian (see Listening Guide 57). In this ensemble, the three women's voices intermingle in soaring melodies that mark one of the high points of the score. Notable is the sumptuous orchestration that accompanies the characters' outpouring of emotion. Sophie sings of her confused state of mind. Octavian is torn between his love for Sophie and guilt over the pain he is causing the Princess. And the aging Marschallin resigns herself to the inevitable.

Listening Guide 57

CD: Chr/Std 7/6–7
Cassette: Chr/Std 7A/2

STRAUSS: *Der Rosenkavalier (The Cavalier of the Rose),*
Act III, Trio   (5:20)

Date of work: 1909–10

Setting: 18th-century Vienna

Librettist: Hugo von Hofmannsthal

Principal characters:
    Princess von Werdenberg, Marschallin, wife of the Field Marshall (soprano)
    Baron Ochs of Lerchenau, cousin to the Princess (bass)
    Octavian, a young nobleman (trouser role, sung by mezzo-soprano)
    Herr von Faninal, a rich merchant
    Sophie von Faninal, his daughter (soprano)
    Valzacchi and Annina, an Italian couple who specialize in intrigue

---

Act III, Trio

Marschallin's opening motive
(taken from earlier scene):

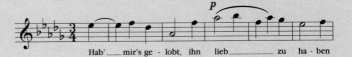

Hab'___ mir's ge - lobt, ihn lieb_____ zu ha - ben

OCTAVIAN *(undecided, as if he wished to follow her)*

| 6 | 0:00 | Marie Theres'! | Maria Theresa! |

MARSCHALLIN *(to herself)*

Hab' mir's gelobt,	I swore I would cherish him
ihn lieb zu haben in der richtigen Weis',	in the right way,
dass ich selbst sein Lieb' zu einer	that I would even love his love
andern noch lieb hab'!	for another!
Hab' mir freilich nicht gedacht,	I certainly did not think
dass es so bald mir aufgelegt sollt werden!	that it would happen so soon.
Es sind die mehreren Dinge auf der Welt,	Most things in the world
so dass sie ein's nicht glauben tät',	would be hard to believe
wenn man sie möcht' erzählen hör'n.	if one were told about them.
Alleinig, wer's erlebt,	Only those who experience it believe it
der glaubt daran und weiss nicht wie—	and do not know how—

OCTAVIAN *(to himself)*

Es ist was kommen	Something has come
und ist was g'scheh'n.	and something has happened.
Ich möcht' sie fragen:	I want to ask her:
darf's denn sein? Und 'grad' die Frag'	can it be? And just that question,
die spür' ich, dass sie mir verboten ist.	I feel, is forbidden.
Ich möcht' sie fragen:	I want to ask her:
warum zittert was in mir?	Why am I trembling?

Ist denn ein grosses Unrecht gescheh'n?	Has there been a great injustice?
Und 'grad' an die	And she is the very one
darf ich die Frag' nicht tun.	I may not question.

SOPHIE *(to herself)*

Mir ist, wie in der Kirch'n,	I feel as if I were in church,
heilig ist mir und so bang	I am awed and so frightened
und doch ist mir unheilig auch!	And yet I also feel profane!
Ich weiss nicht, wie mir ist.	I do not know how I feel.
Ich möcht' mich niederknien dort	I want to kneel down
vor der Frau und möcht' ihr was antun;	before the lady and appeal to her.
denn ich spür', sie gibt mir ihn	Because I sense that she gives him to me,
und nimmt mir was	and takes something of him away
von ihm zugleich.	at the same time.
Weiss garnicht, wie mir ist!	I don't know at all how I feel.

7   3:11   **Tempo primo** *(Return to opening theme)*

MARSCHALLIN

Da steht der Bub, and da steh' ich,	There stands the boy, and here I stand,
und mit dem fremden Mädel dort	and with that strange girl there
wird er so glücklich sein, als wie halt	he will be as happy as men
Männer das Glücklichsein versteh'n.	who understand happiness can be.

OCTAVIAN

Und dann seh' ich dich an,	And then I look at you,
Sophie, und seh' nur dich, und spür'	Sophie, and see only you, sense
nur dich, Sophie, und weiss von	only you, Sophie, and know of nothing
nichts als nur dich hab' ich lieb.	but that I love you.

SOPHIE

Möcht' alles versteh'n	I want to understand everything,
und möcht' auch nichts versteh'n.	and I also do not want to understand.
Möcht' fragen und nicht fragen,	I wish to ask and not to ask,
wird mir heiss und kalt.	I'm getting hot and cold.

(looking into Octavian's eyes)

Und spür' nur dich und weiss nur eins:	And feel only you and know only one thing:
dich hab' ich lieb!	that I love you!

MARSCHALLIN

In Gottes Namen.	In God's name.

66

Debussy and Impressionism

"For we desire above all—nuance,
Not color but half-shades!
Ah! nuance alone unites
Dream with dream and flute with horn."—PAUL VERLAINE

THE IMPRESSIONIST PAINTERS

In 1867, the artist Claude Monet (1840–1926), rebuffed by the academic salons, nevertheless found a place to exhibit his painting *Impression: Sun Rising*. Before long, "Impressionism" had become a term of derision to describe the hazy, luminous paintings of Monet and his followers. A distinctly Parisian style, Impressionism counted among its exponents Camille Pissarro (1830–1903), Edouard Manet (1832–1883), Edgar Degas (1834–1917), and Auguste Renoir (1841–1919). These artists strove to retain on canvas the freshness of their first impressions. What fascinated them was the continuous change in the appearance of things. They ventured out of the studio into the

The Impressionists took painting out of the studio and into the open air; their subject was light. **Claude Monet** *(1840–1926),* Impression: Sun Rising. (Musée Marmottan, Paris)

open air to paint water lilies, a haystack, or a cathedral again and again at different hours of the day. Instead of mixing their pigments on the palette, they juxtaposed brush strokes of pure color on the canvas, leaving it to the eye of the beholder to do the mixing. An iridescent sheen bathes each painting as outlines shimmer and melt in a luminous haze.

The Impressionists abandoned the grandiose subjects of Romanticism. Their focus shifted from the human form to light itself. They showed little interest in the drama-packed themes that had inspired centuries of European art, preferring "unimportant" material: still lifes, dancing girls, nudes; everyday scenes of middle-class life, picnics, boating and café scenes; nature in all its beauty, Paris in all its moods. Ridiculed at first—"Whoever saw grass that's pink and yellow and blue?" grumbled one critic—they eventually succeeded in imposing their vision upon the age.

THE SYMBOLIST POETS

A parallel revolt against tradition took place in poetry under the leadership of the Symbolists, who strove for direct poetic experience unspoiled by intellectual elements. They sought to suggest rather than describe, to present the symbol rather than state the thing. Symbolism as a literary movement gained prominence in the work of French writers Charles Baudelaire (1821–1867), Stéphane Mallarmé (1842–1898), Paul Verlaine (1844–1896), and Arthur Rimbaud (1854–1891), all of whom were strongly influenced by the American Edgar Allan Poe (1809–1849). They were sensitive to the sound of a word as well as its meaning, and tried to evoke poetic images that affected all the senses.

Through their experiments in free verse forms, the Symbolists were able to achieve in language an abstract quality that had once belonged to music alone. Characteristic was Verlaine's pronouncement: "Music above all!" And the essentially musical approach of the Symbolists was not lost on the musicians. According to the composer Paul Dukas (1865–1935), it was the writers, not the musicians, who exerted the strongest influence on Claude Debussy, the greatest of the musical Impressionists.

IMPRESSIONISM IN MUSIC

Impressionism surfaced in France at a crucial moment in the history of European music. The major-minor system had served the art since the seventeenth century, but composers were beginning to feel that its possibilities had

Music and ballet provided **Edgar Degas** *(1834–1917) with many subjects, as in this painting,* The Dance Class. (Metropolitan Museum of Art, New York)

been exhausted. Debussy and his followers were attracted to other scales, such as the church modes of the Middle Ages, which gave their music an archaic sound. They began to emphasize the primary intervals—octaves, fourths, fifths—and the parallel movement of chords in the manner of medieval organum. They also explored scale structures introduced by nationalists such as the Russian composers Alexander Borodin and Modest Musorgsky, and the Norwegian Edvard Grieg. Impressionists responded especially to non-Western music: the Moorish strain in the songs and dances of Spain, and the Javanese and Chinese orchestras that performed in Paris during the World Exposition of 1889. Here they found rhythms, scales, and colors that offered a bewitching contrast to the traditional sounds of Western music.

The major-minor system, as we saw, is based on the pull of the active tones to the tonic, or rest tone. Impressionist composers regarded this as a formula that had become too obvious. In their works, we do not hear the triumphal final cadence of the Classical-Romantic period, in which the dominant chord is resolved to the tonic with the greatest possible emphasis; instead, more subtle harmonic relationships come into play. Classical harmony looked upon dissonance as a momentary disturbance that found its resolution in the consonance. But now, composers began to use dissonance as a value in itself, freeing it from the need to resolve. They taught their contemporaries to accept tone combinations that had formerly been regarded as inadmissible, even as the Impressionist painters taught people to see colors in sky, grass, and water that had never been seen there before.

Use of dissonance

One scale that figures prominently in Impressionist music is the *whole-tone scale*, derived from non-Western sources. This pattern is built entirely of whole-tone intervals: for example, C-D-E-F♯-G♯-A♯-C. The result is a fluid sequence of pitches that lacks the pull toward a tonic, or point of rest.

Whole-tone scale

Several other procedures came to be associated with musical Impressionism as well. One of the most important is the use of parallel, or "gliding," chords, in which a chord built on one tone is duplicated immediately on a higher or lower tone. Such parallel motion was prohibited in the Classical system of harmony, but it was precisely these forbidden progressions that Impressionist composers found fascinating.

Parallel chords

The harmonic innovations identified with Impressionism led to the formation of daring new tone combinations. Characteristic was the use of the five-note combinations known as *ninth chords* (in which the interval between the lowest and highest tones was a ninth). These play so prominent a part in Debussy's opera *Pelléas and Mélisande* that the work came to be known as "the land of ninths." As a result of all these procedures, Impressionist music wavers between major and minor without adhering to either. It hovers in a borderland between keys, creating elusive effects that might be compared to the misty outlines of Impressionist painting.

Ninth chords

In The Boating Party, *by American painter* **Mary Cassatt** *(1845–1926), the eye is drawn toward the relaxed mother and child figures. Inspired by a Monet painting, this work features the strong lines and dramatic colors typical of second-generation Impressionists.* (National Gallery of Art, Washington, D.C.)

Orchestral color

These floating harmonies demanded the most subtle colors. There was no room here for the lush, full sonority of the Romantic orchestra. Instead, we hear a veiled blending of timbres: flutes and clarinets in their dark lower registers, violins in their lustrous upper range, trumpets and horns discreetly muted; and over the whole, a shimmering gossamer of harp, celesta, triangle, glockenspiel, muffled drum, and cymbal brushed with a drumstick. One instrumental color flows into another close by, as from oboe to clarinet to flute, in the same way that Impressionist painting moves from one color to another in the spectrum, as from yellow to green to blue.

Rhythm

Impressionist rhythm too shows the influence of non-Western music. The metrical patterns of the Classical-Romantic era were marked by a recurrent accent on the first beat of the measure. Such emphasis was hardly appropriate for the new dreamlike style. In many works of the Impressionist School, the music glides across the bar line from one measure to the next in a floating rhythm that discreetly obscures the pulse.

Small forms

The Impressionists turned away from the large forms of the Austro-German tradition, such as symphonies and concertos. They preferred short lyric forms—preludes, nocturnes, arabesques—whose titles suggested intimate lyricism or painting, such as Debussy's *Clair de lune* (*Moonlight*), *Nuages* (*Clouds*), and *Jardins sous la pluie* (*Gardens in the Rain*). Without a

Characteristics of Musical Impressionism

1. Whole-tone scale (beginning on C):

2. Example from Debussy's *Pelléas and Mélisande*, illustrating use of whole-tone scales:

3. Parallel movement of chords (octaves and open fifths) in example of 9th-century organum:

4. Parallel movement of chords (fifths and octaves) from Debussy's *Sunken Cathedral:*

5. Structure of a ninth chord built on C:

6. Use of ninth chords in Debussy's *Pelléas and Mélisande:*

doubt, Debussy and his followers rebelled against certain aspects of Romanticism, especially the symphonic tradition of Beethoven and the music drama of Wagner. Yet in a number of ways, Impressionism continued the fundamental tendencies of the Romantic movement in its love of beautiful sound; emphasis on program music, tone painting, and nature worship; addiction to lyricism; attempt to unite music, painting, and poetry; and emphasis on mood and atmosphere. In effect, the Impressionists substituted a thoroughly French brand of Romanticism for the Austro-German variety.

CLAUDE DEBUSSY: HIS LIFE AND MUSIC

"I love music passionately. And because I love it, I try to free it from barren traditions that stifle it. It is a free art gushing forth, an open-air art boundless as the elements, the wind, the sky, the sea. It must never be shut in and become an academic art."

Claude Debussy

The most important French composer of the early twentieth century, Claude Debussy (1862–1918) was born near Paris in the town of St. Germain-en-Laye, where his parents kept a china shop. He entered the Paris Conservatory when he was eleven. Within a few years, he shocked his professors with bizarre harmonies that defied the rules.

"What rules, then, do you observe?" inquired one of his teachers.

"None—only my own pleasure!"

"That's all very well," retorted the professor, "provided you're a genius." It became increasingly apparent that the daring young man was one indeed.

Early years

Debussy was only twenty-two when his cantata *The Prodigal Son* won the coveted Prix de Rome. Like Berlioz before him, he looked upon his stay in the Italian capital as a dreary exile from the boulevards and cafés that made up his world. By this time, he had already realized his future style. "The music I desire," he wrote a friend, "must be supple enough to adapt itself to the lyrical effusions of the soul and the fantasy of dreams."

Pelléas and Mélisande

The 1890s, the most productive decade of Debussy's career, culminated in the opera *Pelléas and Mélisande*. Based on the symbolist drama by the Belgian poet Maurice Maeterlinck, the work occupied him for the better part of ten years. He continued revising the score up to the opening night, which took place at the Opéra-Comique on April 30, 1902. *Pelléas* was attacked as being decadent and lacking in melody, form, and substance. Nevertheless, its quiet intensity and subtlety of nuance had a profound impact on the musical public, and it became an international success.

Pelléas made Debussy famous. He appeared in the capitals of Europe to conduct his works and wrote articles that established his reputation as one of

Later years

the wittiest critics of his time. In the first years of the new century, he exhausted the Impressionist style and found his way to a new and tightly controlled idiom, a kind of distillation of Impressionism.

His energies sapped by the ravages of cancer, Debussy worked on with remarkable fortitude. The outbreak of war in 1914 robbed him of all interest in music. France, he felt, "can neither laugh nor weep while so many of our men heroically face death." But after a year of silence, he realized that he had to contribute to the struggle in the only way he could, "by creating to the best of my ability a little of the beauty that the enemy is attacking with such fury."

Debussy died in March 1918 during the bombardment of Paris. The funeral procession made its way through deserted streets as the shells of the German guns ripped into his beloved city just eight months before victory was celebrated in France. And French culture has ever since celebrated Debussy as one of its most distinguished representatives.

Like the artist Monet and the writer Verlaine, Debussy considered art to be primarily a sensuous experience. The epic themes of Romanticism offended his temperament as both a man and an artist. "French music," he declared, "is clearness, elegance, simple and natural declamation. French music aims first of all to give pleasure."

Debussy turned against sonata-allegro form, the grand structure that the Germans counted as a supreme achievement. He regarded exposition-development-recapitulation as an outmoded formula. (At a concert once, he whispered to a friend, "Let's go—he's beginning to develop!") An even greater threat, he believed, was posed by the Wagnerian music drama, which at the time attracted the intellectuals of France. He found Wagner's grandiose

In His Own Words

A symphony is usually built on a melody heard by the composer as a child. The first section is the customary presentation of a theme on which the composer proposes to work; then begins the necessary dismemberment; the second section seems to take place in an experimental laboratory; the third section cheers up a little in a quite childish way, interspersed with deep sentimental phrases during which the melody recedes, as is more seemly; but it reappears and the dismemberment goes on. . . . I am more and more convinced that music is not, in essence, a thing which can be cast into a traditional and fixed form. It is made up of colors and rhythms.

Principal Works

Orchestral music, including *Prélude à "L'après-midi d'un faune"* (*Prelude to "The Afternoon of a Faun,"* 1894), Nocturnes (1899), *La mer* (*The Sea*, 1905), *Images* (1912), incidental music

Dramatic works, including the opera *Pelléas et Mélisande* (1902) and the ballet *Jeux* (*Games*, 1913)

Chamber music, including a string quartet (1893) and various sonatas (cello, 1915; violin, 1917; flute, viola, and harp, 1915)

Piano music, including *Pour le piano* (*For the Piano*, 1901), *Estampes* (*Prints*, 1903), 2 books of preludes (1909–10, 1912–13)

Songs and choral music; cantatas, including *L'enfant prodigue* (*The Prodigal Son*, 1884)

Debussy chose this Japanese print, The Hollow of the Wave off Kanagawa, *by* **Katsushioka Hokusai** *(1760–1849), for the front cover of his orchestral work* La mer (The Sea). (Metropolitan Museum of Art, New York)

Ring cycle ponderous and tedious. "The idea of spreading one drama over four evenings! Is this admissible, especially when in these four evenings you always hear the same thing? . . . My God! how unbearable these people in skins and helmets become by the fourth night." In the end, however, he paid moving tribute to the master. Wagner "can never quite die," he wrote, and called him "a beautiful sunset that was mistaken for a dawn."

From the Romantic grandeur that left nothing unsaid, Debussy turned toward an art of indirection, subtle and discreet, expressed in short, flexible forms. These mood pieces evoke the favorite images of Impressionist painting: gardens in the rain, sunlight through the leaves, clouds, moonlight, sea, mist.

Because Debussy worked slowly, his fame rests on a comparatively small output; *Pelléas and Mélisande* is viewed by many as his greatest achievement. Among the orchestral compositions, the *Prelude to "The Afternoon of a Faun"* became a favorite with the public early on, as did the three nocturnes (*Clouds, Festivals, Sirens*) and *La mer* (*The Sea*). His handling of the orchestra is thoroughly French, allowing individual instruments to stand out against the ensemble. In his scores, the melodic lines are widely spaced, the texture light and airy.

Orchestral works

Debussy was one of the important piano composers; he created a distinctive new style of writing for the instrument and composed works that form an essential part of the modern repertory. He exploited the piano's resources with maximum finesse—the contrast of low and high registers, the blending of sounds through the use of the pedal, the clash of overtones, and the parallel succession of widely spaced chords. Among his best-known works are

Piano works

Cultural Perspective 13

THE PARIS WORLD EXHIBITION OF 1889: A CULTURAL AWAKENING

How and when did people from distant regions of the world interact before the era of jet travel and electronic communications? One kind of event that has long brought people from various cultures together is a world exposition.

In 1889, France hosted an exposition marking the centenary of the French Revolution. The Eiffel Tower was the French showcase for this world's fair. Musicians from around the world performed for a receptive European public. One of the most popular of the exhibits, from the Indonesian island of Java, featured dancers and gamelan. (You will remember that a gamelan is an ensemble of mainly percussion instruments—including gongs, chimes, and drums, among others.) Many classical composers, including Claude Debussy and Maurice Ravel, heard this gamelan for the first time. Debussy wrote of its unique sound to a friend: "Do you not remember the Javanese music able to express every nuance of meaning, even unmentionable shades, and which makes our tonic and dominant seem like empty phantoms for the use of unwise infants?" He attempted to capture something of this sound—its pentatonic scale, unusual timbre, and texture—in a number of his compositions, including the famous symphonic poem *La mer* (*The Sea*, 1905), the piano work *Pagodas* (from *Estampes*, 1903), and several piano preludes.

Other events sparked the imagination of visitors to the Paris Exhibition. Evening festivities included a parade of musicians representing the African nations of Algeria, Senegal, and the Congo, as well as Java, Anam (now Vietnam), and New Caledonia (a Pacific island off the Australian coast). Performances included belly dancers and whirling dervishes from the Middle East (see p. 288); African-American cakewalk dancers from the southern United States (a cakewalk was a nineteenth-century dance that featured rhythmic strutting and prancing arm in arm in a parody of white plantation owners' behavior); and dancing women from Cambodia.

Folk and popular musics traversed cultural boundaries at the Paris Exhibition. It was there that Debussy was introduced to traditional Russian songs in settings by Rimsky-Korsakov as well as the music of Hungarian and Spanish Gypsies. Like Bizet, Debussy attempted to capture the rhythms of the habanera and the strumming style of flamenco guitars in several of his piano works (*The Interrupted Serenade* and *Evening in Granada*).

The French composer Maurice Ravel (whom we will meet in the next chapter) was even more profoundly influenced by this new world of music. Born in the Basque region of France (where the Pyrénées separate France from Spain), Ravel imbued his *Spanish Rhapsody* (an orchestral suite we will study) with rich Iberian color, his violin work *Tzigane* (*Gypsy*, 1924) with showy, exotic effects, and his song cycle *Don Quixote to Dulcinea* (1933, based on the writings of Miguel de Cervantes) with authentic Spanish dance rhythms. Likewise, his most famous work, the hypnotic *Boléro* for orchestra, is accompanied by the insistent rhythm of a popular Spanish dance form. Nor did the mysteries of Asia escape Ravel: his orchestral song cycle *Sheherazade* (1903) was inspired by the Arabian folktales of *The Thousand and One Nights* (sometimes called *Arabian Nights* and the source for the stories of Aladdin and Ali Baba) and includes what he believed was a Persian melody. A movement from the charming *Mother Goose Suite* (originally for piano), called *Laideronette, Empress of the Pagodas,* is based on a fairy tale about an empress who is serenaded during her bath by whimsical creatures playing fantastic instruments.

Ravel's broad-ranging interests drew him to folk songs from around the world (he arranged Greek, Hebrew, Italian, and French tunes, among others), to the newly popular African-American styles of ragtime, blues, and jazz (the second movement of his Violin Sonata is entitled *Blues*), and to the music of Madagascar (an African island and the subject of his intense song cycle *Songs of Madagascar*, 1925–26).

Today, we do not have to wait for a world exposition to experience music from around the world. We have only to tune in a PBS (Public Broadcasting System) special on Mexican mariachi bands, rent a library video of Japanese Noh drama, or locate a cultural web site on Irish step dancing to stimulate our eyes, ears, and imagination.

Terms to Note:

gamelan
cakewalk

Suggested Listening:

Debussy: *La mer, Pagodas* (from *Estampes*),
    or *Evening in Grenada*
Ravel: *Songs of Madagascar, Boléro,*
    Tzigane, Sheherazade, or *Blues* (from
    Violin Sonata)
Javanese music (gamelan orchestra)

Visible standing in front of this gamelan orchestra from Java are two dancers holding bow and arrow as part of the work they are performing.

Clair de lune (*Moonlight*, the most popular piece he ever wrote), *Evening in Granada, Reflections in the Water,* and *The Sunken Cathedral.* Many of his piano pieces demonstrate an interest in non-Western scales and instruments, which he first heard at the Paris Exhibition in 1889 (discussed in CP 13).

Vocal and chamber music

Debussy helped establish the French song as a national art form independent of the German Lied. His settings of the French Symbolist poets Baudelaire, Verlaine, and Mallarmé are marked by exquisite refinement. In chamber music, he achieved an unqualified success with his String Quartet in G minor. The three sonatas of his last years—for cello and piano; violin and piano; and flute, viola, and harp—reveal him as moving toward a more abstract and concentrated style.

Prelude to "The Afternoon of a Faun"

Debussy's best-known orchestral work was inspired by a pastoral poem of Stéphane Mallarmé that evokes a landscape of antiquity. The text centers on the faun, a mythological creature of the forest that is half man, half goat. This "simple sensuous passionate being" awakes in the woods and tries to remember: was he visited by three lovely nymphs, or was this but a dream? He will never know. The sun is warm, the earth fragrant. He curls himself up and falls into a wine-drugged sleep.

The work is in sections that follow the familiar pattern of statement-departure-return. Yet the movement is fluid and rhapsodic, with almost every fragment of melody repeated immediately. The relaxed rhythm flows across the bar line in a continuous stream. By weakening and even wiping out the accent, Debussy achieved that dreamlike fluidity that is a prime trait of Impressionist music.

We first hear a flute solo in the velvety lower register. The melody glides along the chromatic scale, narrow in range and languorous. (See Listening Guide 58 for themes and an excerpt from the poem.) Glissandos on the harp usher in a brief dialogue in the horns. Such a mixture of colors had never been heard before.

Next, a more decisive motive emerges, marked *en animant* (growing lively). This is followed by a third theme, marked *même movement et très soutenu* (same tempo and very sustained)—an impassioned melody that carries the composition to an emotional climax. The first theme then returns in an altered guise. At the close, antique cymbals play *pianissimo.* (*Antique cymbals* are small disks of brass; the rims are struck together gently and allowed to vibrate.) "Blue" chords (with lowered thirds and sevenths) are heard on the muted horns and violins, sounding infinitely remote. The work finally dissolves into silence, having taken nine minutes to play. Rarely has so much been said in so brief a time.

Listening Guide 58

CD: Chr/Std 7/1–5, Sh 3/58–62
Cassette: Chr/Std 7A/1, Sh 3B/5

DEBUSSY: *Prelude to "The Afternoon of a Faun"*
(Prélude à "L'après-midi d'un faune")   (9:45)

Date of work: 1894

Genre: Symphonic poem

Orchestra: Strings (with 2 harps), flute, oboes, English horn, clarinets, French horns, and antique cymbals

Basis: Symbolist poem by Stéphane Mallarmé

Form: Free ternary (**A-B-A'**)

Style: Impressionist, varied instrumental colors; subtle, floating rhythms; free form

---

Opening of poem:

Text	*Translation*

Ces nymphes, je les veux perpétuer.
    Si clair
Leur incarnat léger, qu'il voltige dans l'air
Assoupi de sommeils touffus.
    Amais-je un rêve?
Mon doute, amas de nuit ancienne, s'achève
En maint rameau subtil, qui, de meuré les vrais
Bois mèmes, prouve, hélas! que bien seul je
    m'offrais
Pour triomphe la faute idéale de roses.
 	
Réfléchissons . . . ou si les femmes dont tu
    gloses
Figurent un souhait de tes sens fabuleux!
	These nymphs I would perpetuate.
	    So light
	their gossamer embodiment, floating on the air
	inert with heavy slumber.
	    Was it a dream I loved?
	My doubting harvest of the bygone night ends
	in countless tiny branches; together remaining
	a whole forest, they prove, alas, that since I am
	    alone,
	my fancied triumph was but the ideal
	    imperfection of roses.
	
	Let us reflect . . . or suppose those women that
	    you idolize
	were but imaginings of your fantastic lust!

1 0:00 **A SECTION**
Opening chromatic melody in flute; passes from one instrument to another, accompanied by muted strings and vague beat:

2 2:48 **B SECTION**
Clarinet introduces more animated idea, answered by rhythmic figure in cellos.

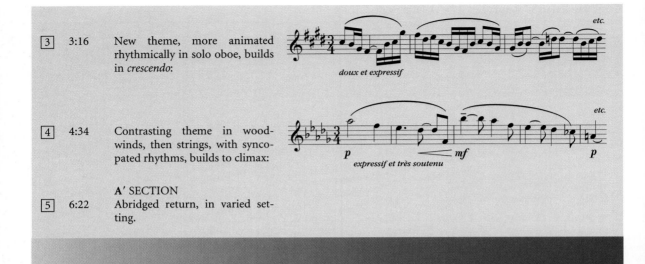

3	3:16	New theme, more animated rhythmically in solo oboe, builds in *crescendo*:	
4	4:34	Contrasting theme in woodwinds, then strings, with syncopated rhythms, builds to climax:	
		A′ SECTION	
5	6:22	Abridged return, in varied setting.	

67

Ravel and Post-Impressionism

"I did my work slowly, drop by drop. I tore it out of me by pieces."

Maurice Ravel was a post-Impressionist whose instinctive need for order and clarity of organization impelled him to return to basic conceptions of form. Thus his music falls between the ideals of Impressionism and Neoclassicism.

HIS LIFE

Maurice Ravel

Early years

Maurice Ravel (1875–1937) was born in Ciboure, a small town in southwestern France, but the family moved to Paris shortly after he was born. His father, a mining engineer who had aspired to be a musician, was sympathetic to the boy's artistic talents. Maurice entered the conservatory when he was fourteen and remained there for sixteen years—an unusually long apprenticeship.

Ravel's artistic development was greatly stimulated by his friendship with a group of avant-garde poets, painters, and musicians who believed in his gifts long before the world took note. Youthful enthusiasts, they called themselves the *apaches* (the French word for "ruffians" or "common criminals"). In this atmosphere, the young composer found the intellectual companionship he needed. Ravel's career followed more or less the same course as that of many Impressionist artists. At first, his music was hissed by the audiences and denounced by the critics. Only a few recognized the special quality of his work, but their number steadily grew.

Ravel came into his own in the years following the First World War. Acknowledged as the foremost composer in France, he was much in demand to conduct his works throughout Europe. In 1928, he was invited to tour the United States. Before he would consider the offer, though, he had to be assured of a steady supply of his favorite French wines and cigarettes. Ravel and America took to one another, although the composer tired first. "I am seeing magnificent cities, enchanting country, but the triumphs are fatiguing," he wrote home, adding an apparent comment on American cuisine: "Besides, I was dying of hunger." *American trip*

Toward the end of his life, Ravel was tormented by restlessness and insomnia. He found comfort in the hectic atmosphere of the Parisian nightclubs, where he would listen for hours to American jazz. As he approached sixty, he fell victim to a rare brain disease that attacked the centers of speech and motor coordination. It gradually became impossible for him to read notes, to remember melodies, or to write. So as not to watch himself "go piece by piece," as he put it, he decided to submit to a risky operation, performed toward the end of 1937. He never regained consciousness. *Last years*

His Music

Like Debussy, Ravel was a national artist to the core. He was drawn, along with Debussy, to the images that fascinated the Impressionist painters: daybreak, the sea, the interplay of water and light. He too exploited Spanish dance rhythms, worshipped the old French harpsichordists, and experimented with the scales of medieval as well as foreign musics. *Comparison with Debussy*

But the musical differences between the two composers are as pronounced as the similarities. Ravel's music glistens with a polished brightness that contrasts with the twilight softness of Debussy's. His rhythms are more incisive and marked by a drive that Debussy rarely strives for. His sense of key is firmer, his harmony is more dissonant, and his melodies are broader in span. Ravel's orchestration, unlike Debussy's, derives from the nineteenth-century masters, in the line of descent from Berlioz, Rimsky-Korsakov, and Richard Strauss. Where Debussy aimed to "decongest" sound, Ravel handled the huge orchestra of the post-Romantic period with brilliant virtuosity. And he was drawn to the Classical forms much earlier in his career than Debussy, who turned to them only toward the end (see CP 13).

Songs

One of the outstanding piano composers of the twentieth century, Ravel extended the heritage of Liszt even as Debussy became the disciple of Chopin. He was a master of the French art song. Among his most impressive works in this genre are two exotic song cycles: *Sheherazade*, loosely connected to the folktales of *The Arabian Nights*, and the powerful *Songs of Madagascar*, whose poetry and music cries out passionately against the evils of French colonialism: the second song of the cycle, for example, opens with a wail—"Aoua"—from the natives of this African island nation, followed by the warning "Do not trust the whites, those who live on these shores."

Orchestral works

It was, however, through his orchestral works that Ravel won the admiration of the international public. The *Spanish Rhapsody*, *Mother Goose*, and the concert versions of the ballets *Daphnis and Chloé*, *La valse*, and *Boléro* have remained among the most frequently performed works of our century. Widely admired too are the Classically oriented Piano Concerto in G and the dramatic Piano Concerto for the Left Hand, a masterpiece written for the brilliant pianist Paul Wittgenstein, who lost his right arm in World War I.

Ravel, like Debussy, has become immensely popular in the United States. His harmonies and orchestration have held a particular attraction for jazz

Principal Works

Orchestral music, including *Rapsodie espagnole* (*Spanish Rhapsody*, 1908), Piano Concerto for the Left Hand (1930), and Piano Concerto in G (1931)

Ballets, including *Ma mère l'oye* (*Mother Goose*, 1911), *Daphnis et Chloé* (1912), *La valse* (1920), and *Boléro* (1928)

2 operas: *L'heure espagnole* (*The Spanish Hour*, 1911) and *L'enfant et les sortilèges* (*The Child and the Enchantments*, 1925)

Chamber music, including a string quartet (1903), sonatas for violin and cello (1922) and violin and piano (1927), and a piano trio (1914)

Piano music, including *Pavane pour une infante défunte* (*Pavane for a Dead Princess*, 1908; orchestrated 1910), *Jeux d'eau* (*Fountains*, 1901), *Gaspard de le nuit* (*Gaspard of the Night*, 1908), *Ma mère l'oye* (4 hands, 1910; later orchestrated), and *Le tombeau de Couperin* (*The Tomb of Couperin*, 1917; orchestrated 1919)

Songs with instruments, including *Sheherazade* (1903) and *Chansons madécasses* (*Songs of Madagascar*, 1925–26); songs with piano

Just as **Henri Rousseau** *(1844–1910) found his subject matter in the images of distant places, so did Ravel seek inspiration in the world's musics.* The Sleeping Gypsy *(1897).* (Museum of Modern Art, New York)

arrangers and Hollywood composers. As a result, his idiom—somewhat altered, to be sure—became part of the daily listening experience of millions of Americans.

Feria, from *Spanish Rhapsody*

In his suite *Spanish Rhapsody,* Ravel paints freely with orchestral color, just as Matisse did with brush strokes on canvas. Throughout, the work radiates a highly Spanish flavor, both in its use of dance rhythms and in its instrumentation, which includes castanets, tambourine, and triangle. The Spanish composer Manuel de Falla, impressed with the brilliance and virtuosity of Ravel's orchestration, pronounced the work "genuinely Spanish."

The first movement, *Prelude at Night,* is mysterious and exotic, with a hypnotic four-note motive heard beneath impressionistic colors and quiet hints of rhythms to come. The *Malagueña* features bold rhythms and vivid orchestral colors. Its climax is cut short by a languorous English horn solo in the style of a flamenco song and a return of the haunting four-note motive from the *Prelude.* The *Habanera,* originally part of an earlier work for two pianos, mesmerizes the listener with its insistent rhythmic alternation of three and two notes to a beat ♫ ♫ . The instruments sprinkle splashes of color about, as in a pointillistic painting. According to de Falla, Ravel turned to the habanera because it was "the song most in fashion among those his mother heard in gatherings in Madrid, in bygone days."

The last movement, *Feria,* is a vigorous Spanish dance song of the type

*In Russian artist **Natalia Goncharova's** Spanish Dancer with a Shawl (1916), the woman's dress is arranged into an elegant, brightly colored composition. This work was a costume design for a Diaghilev ballet production of Rapsodie espagnole. (Musée National d'Art Moderne, Centre Georges Pompidou, Paris)*

known as a *jota*. Typical of northern Spain (near Ravel's birthplace in the Basque region of France), the jota is danced to a quick triple meter, accompanied by castanets and guitars. Ravel's *Feria*, in a loose ternary form, rushes forward with rhythmic energy in its dancelike outer sections, which feature dazzling strokes of instrumental color. A *fortissimo* dissonance ushers in a rhapsodic middle section. The haunting four-note motive of the opening movement recurs, first slowly then more quickly, as the movement builds to its fiery conclusion. This orchestral masterwork would later inspire a ballet production by Serge Diaghilev, with splendid costumes by the Russian designer Natalia Goncharova (see illustration above).

Listening Guide 59

CD: Chr/Std 7/22–27
Cassette: Chr/Std 7A/8

RAVEL: *Feria, from Spanish Rhapsody (Rapsodie espagnole)*

(6:10)

Date: 1907–8

Genre: Suite for orchestra

Movements: Prelude at Night
      Malagueña
      Habanera
      Feria

Form: Free ternary (**A-B-A'**)

Tempo: Assez animé (Very animated), in 6/8 meter

A SECTION

22 | 0:00 Piccolos and harp set up rhythmic, repeated-note accompaniment.

Theme 1, heard first in the solo flute, with grace note ornamentation, written as smaller notes (answered by harp glissando):

Builds from *ppp* in low strings and timpani.

0:21 Theme 1 heard in solo clarinet, followed by harp glissando and string tremolos; orchestral *crescendo* and timpani roll lead to next theme.

23 | 0:42 Spanish dance theme in muted trumpets and tambourine, with triplet rhythm and repeated pitches (answered by woodwinds and xylophone):

0:46 Theme 1 returns in flute; woodwinds in dialogue on theme as orchestra builds in *crescendo*.

24 | 1:03 Full orchestra with rhythmic Spanish dance theme:

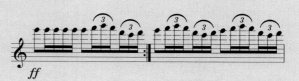

1:08 Low strings introduce more lyrical, arched theme, with triplet rhythms (answered by high strings):

1:21 Wavering lines in flute, answered by trumpet and woodwinds.

1:38 Horns play lyrical theme.

1:45 Builds to *forte* statement of Spanish theme in full orchestra; section ends in *fortissimo* dissonance.

B SECTION

25 | 2:09 Languorous and freer rhythmically; mysterious mood, with two-note string "sighs," followed by English-horn theme, played freely, as in flamenco song:

	2:56	Clarinet with chromatic, descending melody in triplets, against string sighs.
26	3:29	Violins with new version of English-horn theme; accented on first notes.
	3:39	Descending 4-note motive recurs from first movement (*Prelude at Night*) against dissonances; slides heard in strings.
	4:02	Trumpets announce Spanish dance theme.

A' SECTION

	4:16	Flute with theme 1 against Spanish theme in French horns; then wavering melody in woodwinds.
27		
	4:52	French horn with lyrical, arched theme, combined with tambourine.
	5:07	Dance rhythm of theme 2 prevails amid growing chaos; dissonant loud chords.
	5:27	Music builds in tempo and rises in pitch; dies down and builds again; castanets heard prominently in dance rhythm; new syncopated rhythm heard against regular dance rhythm as movement draws to lively and dissonant close.

The Early Twentieth Century

68

Main Currents in Early-Twentieth-Century Music

"The entire history of modern music may be said to be a history of the gradual pull-away from the German musical tradition of the past century."—AARON COPLAND

THE REACTION AGAINST ROMANTICISM

As the quotation from Aaron Copland implies, early-twentieth-century composers had to fight not only the Romantic past but the Romanticism in themselves. The new attitudes took hold just before the outbreak of the First World War. European arts sought to escape their overrefinement and tried to capture the spontaneity and the freedom from inhibition that was associated with primitive life. The fine arts discovered the abstraction of African sculpture, while Paul Gauguin and Henri Rousseau created exotic paintings of monumental simplicity. Some composers turned to the dynamism of non-

The powerful abstraction of African sculpture helped European art resist its overrefinement. A bronze musician from Nigeria.

Western rhythm, seeking fresh concepts in the musics of Africa, Asia, and eastern Europe. Out of the unspoiled, vigorous traditional music in these areas came powerful rhythms of an elemental fury, as reflected in Bartók's *Allegro barbaro* (1911) and Stravinsky's *Rite of Spring* (1913).

NEW TRENDS IN THE ARTS

Dadaism

We have seen that changing currents in art and literature nearly always find parallels in music. In the years immediately preceding the First World War, the influential movement known as Dadaism was founded in Switzerland and spread after 1918 to other major art centers. The Dadaists, principally writers and artists who reacted to the horrors of the bloodbath that had engulfed Europe, rejected the concept of Art with a capital "A"—that is, something to be put on a pedestal and reverently admired. To make their point, they produced works of absolute absurdity. They also reacted against the ex-

Parisian painter **Paul Gauguin** *(1848–1903) was drawn to the simplicity of Tahitian life and the emotional directness of his native subjects. His attention to primitive elements, as seen in* Orana Maria *(1891), has influenced nearly every school of twentieth-century art.* (Metropolitan Museum of Art, New York)

Spanish artist **Joan Miró** *(1893–1983)*
explores the surrealist world of dreams
through the distortion of all the shapes
within the composition. Dutch Interior I.
(Museum of Modern Art, New York)

cessive complexity of Western art by trying to recapture the simplicity of a
child's worldview.

Following their example, the French composer Erik Satie led the way toward a simple, "everyday" music, and exerted an important influence—along
with the writer Jean Cocteau—on the group called *Les Six* (see Chapter 74).
Several decades later, this influence was clearly apparent in the works of the
American composer John Cage, who will be discussed in a later chapter.

The Dada group, which included artists like Hans Arp and Marcel
Duchamp, subsequently merged into the school of Surrealism, as exemplified
by Salvador Dali and Joan Miró, who exploited the world of dreams. Other
styles of modern art included Cubism, the Paris-based style of painting embodied in the works of Pablo Picasso, Georges Braque, and Juan Gris, which
encouraged the painter to construct a visual world in terms of geometric patterns; and Expressionism, which we will see had a significant impact on
music of the early twentieth century.

Subsequent styles

EXPRESSIONISM

Expressionism was the German answer to French Impressionism. Whereas
the French genius rejoiced in radiant impressions of the outer world, the
Germanic temperament preferred digging down to the depths of the soul. As
with Impressionism, the impulse for the movement came from painting.

Expressionist values

The German Expressionist painter **Oskar Kokoschka** *(1886–1980) reveals his feelings about the end of his love affair with Alma Mahler, the composer's widow, and his terror of war in* Knight Errant *(1915).* (Solomon R. Guggenheim Museum, New York)

Wassily Kandinsky (1866–1944), Paul Klee (1879–1940), Oskar Kokoschka (1886–1980), and Edvard Munch (1863–1944)—famous for *The Scream*—influenced the composer Arnold Schoenberg and his followers even as the Impressionist painters influenced Debussy. Expressionism is familiar not only through the paintings of Kandinsky, Klee, and Munch, but also in the writings of Franz Kafka (1883–1924). Expressionism in music triumphed first in central Europe, especially Germany, and reached its full tide in the dramatic works of the Second Viennese School (Arnold Schoenberg and his disciples Alban Berg and Anton Webern).

The language of Expressionism

The musical language of Expressionism favored a hyperexpressive harmonic language marked by extraordinarily wide leaps in the melody and by the use of instruments in their extreme registers. Expressionist music soon reached the boundaries of what was possible within the major-minor system. Inevitably, it had to push beyond.

THE NEW CLASSICISM

One way of rejecting the nineteenth century was to return to the eighteenth. A movement known as "back to Bach" gathered momentum in the early 1920s. There was no question here of duplicating the music of the Baroque master; the slogan implied rather a revival of certain principles that appeared to have been best understood in his time. Instead of revering Beethoven and Wagner, as the Romantics had done, composers began to emulate the great musicians of the early eighteenth century—Bach, Handel, Vivaldi, and Pergolesi—and the detached, objective style that is often associated with their music.

The New Classicism (also called Neoclassicism) tried to rid music of the story-and-picture meanings favored in the nineteenth century. New Classicist composers turned away from the symphonic poem and the Romantic attempt to bring music closer to poetry and painting. They preferred absolute to program music, and they focused attention on craftsmanship and balance, a positive affirmation of the Classical virtues of objectivity and control.

Absolute music

69

New Elements of Musical Style

"To study music, we must learn the rules. To create music, we must break them."—NADIA BOULANGER

THE NEW RHYTHMIC COMPLEXITY

Twentieth-century music discarded the standard rhythmic patterns of duple, triple, and quadruple meter. Rather, composers explored the possibilities of nonsymmetrical patterns based on odd numbers: five, seven, eleven, thirteen beats to the measure. In nineteenth-century music, a single meter customarily prevailed through an entire movement or section. Now the metrical flow shifted constantly, sometimes with each measure. Formerly, one rhythmic pattern was used at a time. Now composers turned to *polyrhythm*—the simultaneous use of several rhythmic patterns. As a result of these innovations, Western music achieved something of the complexity and suppleness of Asian and African rhythms.

Polyrhythm

The new generation of composers preferred freer rhythms of the highest flexibility that gave their works an almost physical power and drive. Indeed, the revitalization of rhythm is one of the major achievements of early-twentieth-century music.

THE NEW MELODY

Rhythm was not the only element in which symmetrical structure was abandoned; melody was affected too. Twentieth-century composers did not develop the neatly balanced phrase repetitions of earlier music. Their ideal was a direct, forward-driving melody from which all nonessentials had been cut away. Their music assumed a quicker perception on the part of the listener than music of the past.

Instrumental melody

Nineteenth-century melody is fundamentally vocal in character; composers tried then to make the instruments "sing." Early twentieth-century melody is neither unvocal nor antivocal; it is simply not conceived in relation to the voice. It abounds in wide leaps and dissonant intervals. Besides, in much twentieth-century music, melody is not even a primary element. In any case, twentieth-century composers have greatly expanded our notion of what a melody is: many patterns are accepted as melodies today that would hardly have been considered as such a century ago.

THE NEW HARMONY

Polychords and polyharmony

No single factor sets off early-twentieth-century music from that of the past more decisively than the new conceptions of harmony. The triads of traditional harmony, we saw, were formed by combining three tones, on every other degree of the scale, or in thirds: 1-3-5 (for example, C-E-G), 2-4-6 (D-F-A), and so on. Traditional harmony also employed four-note combinations, with another third piled on top of the triad, known as seventh chords (1-3-5-7), and (in music of the Impressionists) five-note combinations

In Composition 10: Plus and Minus *(1915), Dutch artist* **Piet Mondrian** *(1872–1944) shows the influence of Cubism in his move toward a geometrically rational art. Music too was undergoing a new formalism and rationalism in the early decades of the twentieth century.* (Rijksmuseum Kröller-Müller, Otterlo)

known as ninth chords (1-3-5-7-9). Twentieth-century composers added more "stories" to such chords, forming highly dissonant *polychords* of six and seven notes. The emergence of these complex "skyscraper" chords brought increased tension to music and allowed the composer to play two or more streams of harmony against each other, creating *polyharmony*.

New Conceptions of Tonality

The new sounds of twentieth-century music necessarily burst the confines of traditional tonality and called for new means of organization, extending or replacing the major-minor system. These approaches, in general, followed four principal paths—expanded tonality, polytonality, atonality, and twelve-tone music.

The widespread use of chromatic harmony in the late nineteenth century led, in the early twentieth, to the free use of all twelve tones around a center. Although this approach retained the basic principle of traditional tonality—gravitation to the tonic—it wiped out the distinction between diatonic and chromatic and between major and minor modes. The expansion of tonality was encouraged by the increased interest in the music of non-Western cultures and in the medieval church modes, as we have already noted.

From the development of polyharmony, a further step followed logically: heightening the contrast of two keys by presenting them simultaneously, which resulted in *polytonality*. Confronting the ear with two keys at the same time meant a radical departure from the basic principle of traditional harmony: centering on a single key. Polytonal pieces still gave the impression of orderly progress toward a central point, though, by permitting one key to assert itself at the end. Polytonality came into prominence with the music of Stravinsky, in such works as the ballet *Petrushka*, which we will study.

Polytonality

The idea of abandoning tonality altogether is associated with the composer Arnold Schoenberg, whom we will meet later. Schoenberg advocated doing away with the tonic by giving the twelve tones of the chromatic scale, in no set order, equal importance—thus creating *atonal* music. (We will study an example of this approach in his song cycle *Pierrot lunaire*.) Atonality was much more of an innovation than polytonality, because it entirely rejected the framework of key. Consonance, according to Schoenberg, was no longer capable of making an impression; atonal music moved from one level of dissonance to another, functioning always at maximum tension, without areas of relaxation.

Atonality

The Twelve-Tone Method

Having accepted the necessity of moving beyond the existing tonal system, Schoenberg sought a unifying principle that would take its place. He found

Serialism
Tone row

this in a strict technique, worked out by the early 1920s, that he called "the method of composing with twelve tones"—that is, with twelve equal tones. Each composition that uses Schoenberg's method, also known as *serialism*, is based on a particular arrangement of the twelve chromatic tones called a *tone row*. (For an example of a tone row, see Listening Guide 63.) This row is the unifying idea for that composition, and serves as the source of all the musical events that take place in it. (The term *dodecaphonic*, the Greek equivalent of *twelve-tone*, is sometimes also used for Schoenberg's method; the term *serial music*, an allusion to the series of twelve tones, has come to refer in more recent decades to the orderly treatment of other elements besides pitches.)

Forms of the row

Once established, a tone row is the basis from which a composer builds themes, harmonies, and counterpoint. Schoenberg provided flexibility and variety in this seemingly confining system through alternative forms of the tone row. A *transposed* row begins on a different note. In its *inversion*, the movement of the notes is in the opposite direction, up instead of down and vice versa, so that the row appears upside down. Its *retrograde* is an arrangement of the pitches in reverse order, so that the row comes out backward, and its *retrograde inversion* turns the row upside down and backward. (You will remember that the same techniques were used in earlier music, especially in the Baroque fugue.)

The Emancipation of Dissonance

The history of music, we have seen, has been the history of a steadily increasing tolerance on the part of listeners. Throughout this long evolution, one factor remained constant: a clear distinction was drawn between dissonance, the element of tension, and consonance, the element of rest. Consonance was the norm, dissonance the temporary disturbance. In many contemporary works, however, tension becomes the norm. Therefore, a dissonance can serve even as a final cadence, provided it is less dissonant than the chord that came before; in relation to the greater dissonance, it is judged to be consonant. Twentieth-century composers emancipated dissonance by freeing it from the obligation to resolve to consonance. Their music taught listeners to accept tone combinations whose like had never been heard before.

TEXTURE: DISSONANT COUNTERPOINT

The nineteenth century was preoccupied with rich, lush harmony; the early twentieth emphasized linear movement, or counterpoint. The new style swept away the sounds of both the Romantic cloudburst and Impressionistic haze. In their place came a sparse linear texture that fit the New Classical ideal of craftsmanship, order, and detachment. Composers began to use dissonance to set off one line against another. Instead of basing their counterpoint on the agreeable intervals of the third and sixth, they turned to astringent seconds and sevenths. Or they might heighten the independence of the voices by putting them in different keys.

ORCHESTRATION

The rich sonorities of nineteenth-century orchestration gave way to a leaner sound, one that was hard and bright, played by a smaller orchestra. The decisive factor in the handling of the orchestra was the change to a linear texture. Color came to be used in the new music not so much for atmosphere as for bringing out the lines of counterpoint and of form. The string section lost its traditional role as the heart of the orchestra; its tone was felt to be too warm. Attention was focused on the more penetrating winds. Composers favored darker instruments—viola, bassoon, trombone. The emphasis on rhythm brought the percussion group into greater prominence than ever before, and the piano, which in the Romantic era was preeminently a solo instrument, found a place in the orchestral ensemble.

NEW CONCEPTIONS OF FORM

The first quarter of the century saw the final expansion of traditional forms in the gigantic symphonies and symphonic poems of Mahler and Strauss. What had been a concise, twenty-five-minute structure in the hands of Haydn and Mozart now could take over an hour and a half to play. As music could hardly go further in this direction, composers began to move toward the Classical ideals of tight organization and succinctness. In addition, they revived a number of older forms such as toccata, fugue, passacaglia and chaconne, concerto grosso, theme and variations, and suite, while retaining the traditional symphony, sonata, and concerto. They tended to value the formal above the expressive, a principle known as *formalism*. The New Classicism, like the old, strove for purity of line and proportion.

Formalism

Composers also vitalized their music through materials drawn from popular styles. Ragtime, with its sprightly syncopations, traveled across the Atlantic to Europe. The rhythmic freedom of jazz captured the ears of many composers, who strove to achieve something of the spontaneity that distinguished the popular style. (We have already noted that Maurice Ravel was influenced by blues and ragtime; we will look into the origins of jazz and its influence on other styles in a later chapter.)

Popular styles

70

Stravinsky and the Revitalization of Rhythm

"I hold that it was a mistake to consider me a revolutionary. If one only need break habit in order to be labeled a revolutionary, then every artist who has something to say and who in order to say it steps outside the bounds of established convention could be considered revolutionary."

Certain artists embody the most significant impulses of their time and affect the cultural life in a most powerful fashion. One such artist was Igor Stravinsky, the Russian composer who for half a century reflected the main currents in twentieth-century music.

HIS LIFE

Igor Stravinsky

Serge Diaghilev

Igor Stravinsky (1882–1971) was born in Oranienbaum, a summer resort not far from St. Petersburg, where his parents lived. He grew up in a musical environment: his father was the leading bass at the Imperial Opera. Although he was taught to play the piano, his musical education was kept on the amateur level because his parents wanted him to study law. Still, while enrolled at the University of St. Petersburg, he continued his musical studies. At twenty, he submitted his compositions to the Russian master Nicolai Rimsky-Korsakov, with whom he subsequently worked for three years.

Success came early to Stravinsky. His music attracted the notice of Serge Diaghilev, the legendary impresario of the Paris-based Russian Ballet, who commissioned Stravinsky to write a score for *The Firebird*. In 1910, the twenty-eight-year-old Stravinsky traveled to Paris to attend the rehearsals. Diaghilev pointed him out to the ballerina Tamara Karsavina with the words "Mark him well—he is a man on the eve of fame."

The Firebird was followed a year later by the ballet *Petrushka*. With dancers Vaslav Nijinsky and Tamara Karsavina in the leading roles, the production secured Stravinsky's position in the forefront of the modern movement. The spring of 1913 saw the staging of the third and most spectacular of the ballets

Stravinsky wrote for Diaghilev, *The Rite of Spring*. On opening night, one of the most scandalous in modern music history, the revolutionary score touched off a near riot. People hooted and screamed, convinced that what they were hearing "constituted a blasphemous attempt to destroy music as an art." However, when the work was presented a year later at a symphony concert under conductor Pierre Monteux, it was received with enthusiasm and established itself as a masterpiece.

The Rite of Spring

The outbreak of war in 1914 ended the way of life that had nurtured Diaghilev's sumptuous dance spectacles. Stravinsky and his family took refuge in Switzerland, their home for the next six years. The difficulty of assembling large performing ensembles during the war worked hand in hand with his evolution as an artist: he moved away from the grand scale of the first three ballets to works more intimate in spirit and modest in dimension.

In 1920, the Russian Revolution having severed Stravinsky's ties with his homeland, he settled in France, where he remained until 1939. During these years, Stravinsky concertized extensively throughout Europe, performing his own music as pianist and conductor. In 1939, he was invited to deliver a lecture series at Harvard University. When the Second World War broke out, he decided to settle in California, outside Los Angeles; in 1945, he became an American citizen. Stravinsky's later concert tours around the world made him the most celebrated figure in twentieth-century music, and the caustically witty books of "conversations" written with his disciple Robert Craft are filled with musical wisdom and footnotes to history. He died in New York on April 6, 1971, at the age of eighty-nine.

American years

HIS MUSIC

Stravinsky's style evolved continuously throughout his career, from the post-Impressionism of *The Firebird* and the primitivism of *The Rite of Spring* to the controlled classicism of his mature style.

Stravinsky was a leader in the revitalization of rhythm in European art music. His first success came as a composer of ballet, where rhythm is allied with body movement and expressive gesture. His was a rhythm of unparalleled dynamic power, furious yet controlled. Stravinsky reacted against the restless chromaticism of the Romantic period, but no matter how daring his harmony, he retained a sense of key. His subtle sense of sound makes him one of the great orchestrators; his sonority is marked by a polished brightness and a texture so clear that, as Diaghilev remarked, "one can see through it with one's ears."

Early works

The national element predominates in such early works as *The Firebird, Petrushka,* and *The Rite of Spring,* the last of which re-creates the rites of an-

Principal Works

Orchestral music, including Symphonies of Wind Instruments (1920), Concerto for Piano and Winds (1924), *Dumbarton Oaks Concerto* (1938), Symphony in C (1940), Symphony in Three Movements (1945), and *Ebony Concerto* (1945)

Ballets, including *L'oiseau de feu* (*The Firebird*, 1910), *Petrushka* (1911), *Le sacre du printemps* (*The Rite of Spring*, 1913), *Les noces* (*The Wedding*, 1923), and *Agon* (1957)

Operas, including *The Rake's Progress* (1951); opera-oratorio *Oedipus Rex* (1927); other dramatic works, including *Histoire du soldat* (*The Soldier's Tale*, 1918)

Choral music, including *Symphony of Psalms* (1930), *Canticum sacrum* (1955), *Threni* (1958), and *Requiem Canticles* (1966)

Chamber music; piano music (solo and for two pianos); songs

cient Russia. In the decade of the First World War, the composer turned to a more economic style: *The Soldier's Tale*, a dance-drama for four characters, is an intimate theater work accompanied by a seven-piece band. The most important work of the years that followed is *The Wedding*, a stylization of a Russian peasant wedding.

Neoclassical period

Stravinsky's Neoclassical period culminated in several major compositions. *Oedipus Rex* is an "opera-oratorio" whose text is a translation into Latin of Jean Cocteau's adaptation of the Greek tragedy by Sophocles. The *Symphony of Psalms*, for chorus and orchestra, regarded by many as the chief work of Stravinsky's maturity, was composed, according to the composer, "for the glory of God." Equally admired is *The Rake's Progress*, an opera on a libretto by W. H. Auden and Chester Kallman, after Hogarth's celebrated series of engravings (see p. 464). Written as the composer was approaching seventy, this radiantly melodious score, which uses the set forms of Mozartean opera, stands as the essence of Neoclassicism.

Twelve-tone works

Stravinsky had yet another surprise in store for his public. In the works written after he was seventy, he showed an increasing receptiveness to the serial procedures of the twelve-tone style, which in earlier years he had opposed. The technique reveals itself in a number of works dating from the middle 1950s, of which the most important are the ballet *Agon* and the choral work *Threni: Lamentations of the Prophet Jeremiah.*

Petrushka

One of the best known of all ballet scores, *Petrushka* presents the ill-fated adventures of a puppet who suddenly comes to life. The clown with the broken heart (we met the type in Leoncavallo's opera) is known in various locales as Pierrot, Pagliaccio, and Petrushka. Stravinsky called him "the immortal and unhappy hero of every fair in all countries."

The setting—a street fair during Carnival week (called Shrovetide) in St. Petersburg in the 1830s—allowed the composer to evoke the colorful atmosphere of the city he loved. His liberal use of folk tunes makes the ballet a work of the Russian national school. *Petrushka* has found an important place in the concert hall as well as in the theater.

The opening tableau, or scene, shows the crowds milling about the booths of the fairgrounds. People of all classes mingle; a group of drunkards pass by as children cluster around a peepshow. A man playing a hurdy-gurdy appears, accompanied by a dancer. Just as she begins her routine, another man, playing a music box, and another dancer set up across the stage. The rivals continue for a short while, then give up and withdraw. Suddenly a drum roll summons the crowd to the little marionette theater in the center of the stage, and the Showman plays his flute. The curtain rises, revealing three puppets— Petrushka, the Ballerina, and the Moor. The Showman touches the dolls with his flute, whereupon they spring to life. At first, they dance on their hooks in the little theater. Then, to the delight of the audience, they step down and break into a tumultuous Russian dance.

First tableau

The second tableau, set in Petrushka's room, focuses on the little clown's unhappy love for the Ballerina, who is put off by his appearance. The third tableau takes place in the Moor's room. He is brutal and stupid, but the Ballerina is charmed by his good looks and his magnificent uniform. Petrushka, mad with jealousy, interrupts their lovemaking. The Moor throws him out.

Second and third tableaux

The original backdrop for the first tableau of Petrushka *established the mood for the entire ballet. Sets and costumes were designed by* **Alexandre Benois,** *who had worked extensively with the Diaghilev company.* (Wadsworth Athenaeum, Hartford, Conn.)

Cultural Perspective 14

PETRUSHKA AND RUSSIAN FOLK TRADITIONS

What are the native folk traditions and songs that attracted the composer Igor Stravinsky when writing his ballets? And what is particularly Russian about them? Stravinsky followed in the footsteps of his friend and mentor Nicolai Rimsky-Korsakov by using Russian folklore and traditional melodies. In his first ballet, *The Firebird*, Stravinsky explored a native folk legend, drawing several memorable themes from his country's rich arsenal of traditional songs.

As in many lands, the festivities celebrated in the Russian countryside combine Christian and older rites. Thus Stravinsky's setting for his second ballet, *Petrushka*, is Shrovetide, or Carnival (known in Russia as Maslenitza, or Butterweek), a pre-Lenten celebration marked by merrymaking and feasting that is celebrated throughout the Christian world in preparation for the penitential Easter season. Among the five traditional songs the composer used in *Petrushka* were one for Easter and one for St. John's Eve (Midsummer Night).

Stravinsky learned several of these songs from *100 Russian Folk Songs*, a collection compiled by Rimsky-Korsakov. One of the songs, the Easter carol *Song of the Volochebniki*, is heard in the first tableau of *Petrushka*. This folk song concerns a group of singing beggars who went from house to house offering Easter greetings. The traditional greeting "For Jesus Christ is arisen" was exchanged not only by beggars but by family and friends as well; the standard reply, "He is indeed risen," was accompanied by a kiss on each cheek. The text details the beggars' demands from a farmer—some eggs, a chicken pie, a hunk of beef.

Like many folk songs, this one is strophic but with every other line repeating the traditional Easter greeting. The tune, spanning a range of only a fifth, is enlivened by occasional shifts from duple to triple meter (shown on facing page).

Another Russian traditional tune heard in the first part of *Petrushka* is the *Song for St. John's Eve*, which evokes the spirit typical of Midsummer Night celebrations. Associated with festivities surrounding the summer solstice (June 21, the longest day of the year by the sun's position), Midsummer Night is, in the Christian cycle of holidays, preparatory to the popular religious feast of St. John the Baptist (June 24). Traditional celebrations included lively dancing around a ritual bonfire coupled with wanton behavior. You may remember tales of this eve from Shakespeare's play *A Midsummer Night's Dream*, in which groups of lovers spend the night in the forest, victims of fairies' pranks and enchantments. Similarly, the *Song for St. John's Eve* is told by a girl who plans to party the whole night with her boyfriend.

Today, both the pre-Lenten Carnival and the summer solstice remain occasions for festivities and music making. Famous carnival celebrations are held in New Orleans and Rio de Janeiro with spectacular parades, masked balls, mock ceremonials, and street dancing. The solstice is observed in the coastal city of Santa Barbara, California, where revelry and a free-spirited, zany parade honor the arrival of summer.

Suggested Listening:

Stravinsky: *The Firebird* and *Petrushka*
Russian folk songs

Song of the Volochebniki:

Ding - a - ling, ding - a - ling, from each one beg an egg, For Je - sus Christ is a - ris - en, God's own Son! Ho - ho! my good mas - ter, is no one at home? For Je - sus Christ is a - ris - en, God's own Son!

Russian village life and customs come alive in The Easter Procession *(1915),* **by Boris Kustodiev** *(1878–1927), a painter known for his colorful, folk-print style.*

Final tableau

In the final tableau, we are back in the festive fairground. Coachmen, grooms, and nursemaids dance merrily. Suddenly there is a commotion in the puppet theater. Petrushka rushes out from behind the curtain, pursued by the Moor, who overtakes him and strikes him with his sword. Petrushka falls and, to the horror of the crowd, dies. The Showman attempts to reassure the bystanders by shaking the little puppet, showing them that it is only a doll stuffed with sawdust. As he begins to drag the puppet to his room, he catches sight of Petrushka's menacing ghost high above him. He had not foreseen that his creation, through suffering, would develop a soul. Stricken with fear, the Showman drops the doll and steals away.

Music of the first tableau

The first tableau consists of three sections, the first and third of which are in rondo form. Between them is a flute cadenza played by the Showman that leads to the rise of the curtain in the puppet theater and the boisterous Russian Dance, which begins the third section. The folk music that surrounded Stravinsky in his childhood is evoked in the opening measures. The orchestra teems with movement and excitement. A solo flute, supported by a second flute, presents a syncopated melody in high register that captures the agitation of the crowd. (See Listening Guide 60.) This tune returns as a unifying element throughout.

The music displays the drive and energy of Stravinsky's rhythm, based on new concepts of irregular meters and polyrhythms. Its complexity presented unprecedented difficulties for the dancers. As the choreographer for the ballet noted, "It was necessary to explain the musical counts to the dancers. At times it was especially difficult to remember the rapid changes of the beats." The ballet's opening passage, for example, alternates 3/4 and 4/4.

Stravinsky drew his melodic inspiration from the folk music of his country. One tune heard in this opening tableau, called the *Song of the Volochebniki* (Singing Beggars), is a Russian Easter carol. It is set in a narrow range and rooted in the key, moving stepwise along the scale (see CP14).

The percussive harmony in *Petrushka* became a hallmark of Stravinsky's style. He used a variety of harmonic devices, including simple diatonic chords to accompany popular tunes, pentatonic, whole-tone, and modal harmonies, and chromatic progressions. And the ballet contains a famous example of polyharmony (two independent chords clashing against each other), called the "Petrushka chord": a C-major arpeggio superimposed on one built on F-sharp major. Sounds like these were absolutely new; they foreshadowed the direction in which harmony would move in the twentieth century and stamped Stravinsky quite early in his career as one of the great innovators.

It was Stravinsky's historic role to sound the spirit of a new era, one that still resounds in our own time. In the closing lines of his autobiography, he wrote: "I live neither in the past nor in the future. I am in the present. I cannot know what tomorrow may bring forth. I can only know what the truth is for me today."

In His Own Words

Consonance, says the dictionary, is the combination of several tones into a harmonic unit. Dissonance results from the deranging of this harmony by the addition of tones foreign to it. One must admit that all this is not clear. Ever since it appeared in our vocabulary, the word "dissonance" has carried with it a certain odor of sinfulness. Let us light our lantern: in textbook language, dissonance is an element of transition, a complex or interval of tones that is not complete in itself and that must be resolved to the ear's satisfaction into a perfect consonance.

Listening Guide 60

MW

CD: Chr/Std 7/35–50, Sh 4/4–12
Cassette: Chr/Std 7B/1, Sh 4A/2

STRAVINSKY: *Petrushka*, First Tableau   (9:54)

Date of work: 1911 (revised in 1947)

Genre: Ballet, often performed as concert piece for orchestra

Setting: Admiralty Square, St. Petersburg, in the 1830s, during Shrovetide (Carnival)

Form: 4 tableaux (scenes)

Characters: 3 puppets (Petrushka, Ballerina, Moor), Showman

FIRST TABLEAU: 3 sections

Scenario: *Crowds of people are strolling about the scene—common people, gentlefolk, a group of drunkards arm-in-arm, children clustering round the peepshow, women round the stalls. A street musician appears with a hurdy-gurdy. He is accompanied by a dancer. Just as she starts to dance, a man with a music box and another dancer turn up on the opposite side of the stage. After performing simultaneously for a short while, the rivals give up the struggle and retire. Suddenly the Showman comes out through the curtains of a little theater on the stage. The curtains are drawn back to reveal three puppets on their stands: Petrushka, the Ballerina, and the Moor. The Showman charms them into life with his flute, and they begin to dance—at first they jig on their hooks on the little stage, but then, to everyone's astonishment, they step down and dance among the public.*

SECTION 1: Vivace; rondo form (**A-B-A-C-A-B-A**)

35	0:00	**A**—crowd scene, syncopated, pentatonic flute melody in shifting meters; portrays agitation:	
		Repeated-note figure dominates:	
36	0:54	**B**—Russian folk song, *Song of the Volochebniki*; full orchestra, homophonic texture, accented:	
37	1:36	**A**—crowd scene music returns from opening, in woodwinds with brass interruptions.	
38	1:44	**C**—hurdy-gurdy player and 2 dancers; dance tune 1, in 3/4, clarinet:	

| 39 | 2:23 | Dance tune 2, in 2/4, flutes and triangle: | 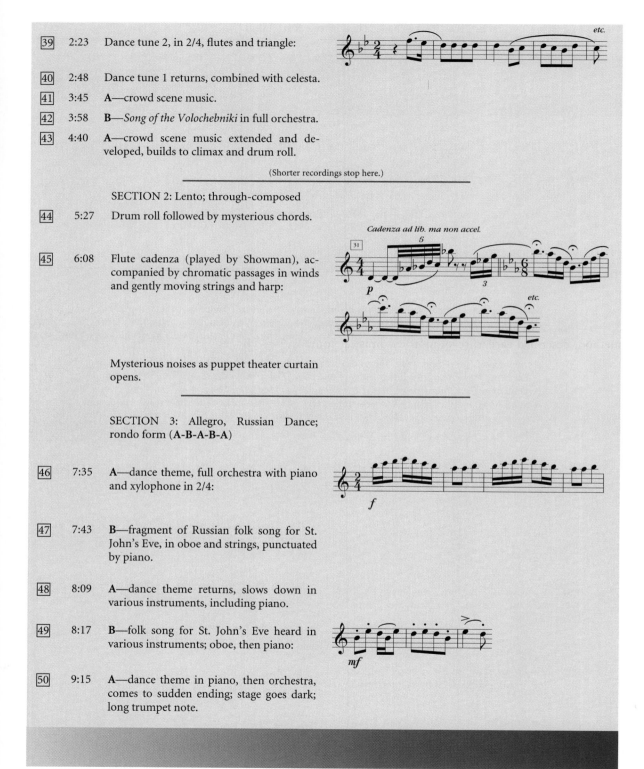 |

| 40 | 2:48 | Dance tune 1 returns, combined with celesta. |

| 41 | 3:45 | **A**—crowd scene music. |

| 42 | 3:58 | **B**—*Song of the Volochebniki* in full orchestra. |

| 43 | 4:40 | **A**—crowd scene music extended and developed, builds to climax and drum roll. |

(Shorter recordings stop here.)

SECTION 2: Lento; through-composed

| 44 | 5:27 | Drum roll followed by mysterious chords. |

| 45 | 6:08 | Flute cadenza (played by Showman), accompanied by chromatic passages in winds and gently moving strings and harp: |

Mysterious noises as puppet theater curtain opens.

SECTION 3: Allegro, Russian Dance; rondo form (**A-B-A-B-A**)

| 46 | 7:35 | **A**—dance theme, full orchestra with piano and xylophone in 2/4: |

| 47 | 7:43 | **B**—fragment of Russian folk song for St. John's Eve, in oboe and strings, punctuated by piano. |

| 48 | 8:09 | **A**—dance theme returns, slows down in various instruments, including piano. |

| 49 | 8:17 | **B**—folk song for St. John's Eve heard in various instruments; oboe, then piano: |

| 50 | 9:15 | **A**—dance theme in piano, then orchestra, comes to sudden ending; stage goes dark; long trumpet note. |

71

Schoenberg and the Second Viennese School

"I personally hate to be called a revolutionist, which I am not. What I did was neither revolution nor anarchy."

The German Expressionist movement was manifested in the music of Arnold Schoenberg and his followers. Schoenberg's pioneering efforts in the breakdown of the traditional tonal system and his development of the twelve-tone method, described earlier, revolutionized musical composition. His innovations were taken further by his most gifted students, Alban Berg and Anton Webern, both of whom we will study. These three composers are often referred to as the Second Viennese School (the first being Haydn, Mozart, and Beethoven).

Arnold Schoenberg

His Life

Arnold Schoenberg (1874–1951) was born in Vienna. He began to study the violin at the age of eight, and soon afterward made his initial attempts at composing. Having decided to devote his life to music, he left school while in his teens. For a time, he earned his living working in a bank, composing in his free hours. Presently he became acquainted with a young musician, Alexander von Zemlinsky, who for a few months gave him lessons in counterpoint. This was the only musical instruction he ever had.

Early years

Through Zemlinsky, young Schoenberg was introduced to the advanced musical circles of Vienna, which at that time were under the spell of Wagner's operas. In 1899, when he was twenty-five, Schoenberg wrote the string sextet *Transfigured Night*. The following year, several of his songs were performed in Vienna and created a scene. "And ever since that day," he once remarked with a smile, "the scandal has not ceased."

In 1901, after his marriage to Zemlinsky's sister, Schoenberg moved to Berlin and obtained a post in a theater, conducting operettas and music-hall songs. The composer's early music already displayed certain traits of his later style. A publisher to whom he offered a quartet observed, "You must think

Arnold Schoenberg *completed this Expressionist painting,* The Red Gaze *(1910), just two years before he wrote* Pierrot lunaire. *It is highly reminiscent of Edvard Munch's* The Scream. *(Arnold Schönberg Center, Vienna)*

that if the second theme is a retrograde inversion of the first theme, that automatically makes it good!"

Return to Vienna

Upon his return to Vienna, Schoenberg became active as a teacher and soon gathered about him a band of disciples that included Alban Berg and Anton Webern. The devotion of these innovative young musicians sustained him in the fierce battle for recognition that still lay ahead. With each new work, Schoenberg moved closer to taking as bold a step as any composer has ever taken—the rejection of tonality.

The First World War interrupted Schoenberg's creative activity. Although he was past forty, he was called up for military duty in the Vienna garrison. His military service was followed by a compositional silence of eight years (1915–23), during which he clarified his position in his own mind and evolved a set of structural procedures to replace tonality. His goal set, Schoenberg pursued it with great determination. His "method of composing with twelve tones" caused much bewilderment in the musical world. All the same, he was now firmly established as a leader of contemporary musical thought.

In 1925, he accepted an appointment at the Prussian Academy of Arts in Berlin, where he taught composition. Then, with the coming to power of Hitler in 1933, he emigrated to America. Like many Austrian-Jewish intellectuals of his generation, he had grown away from his Jewish origins and ultimately converted to Lutheranism. But after he left Germany, he found it spiritually necessary to return to the Hebrew faith. He arrived in the United

Move to the United States

States in the fall of 1933; shortly afterward, he joined the faculty of the University of Southern California, and was later appointed professor of composition at the University of California in Los Angeles. He became an American citizen in 1940, taught until his retirement at the age of seventy, and continued his musical activities until his death seven years later.

Principal Works

Orchestral music, including Five Pieces for Orchestra (1909), Variations for Orchestra (1928), and concertos for violin (1936) and piano (1942)

Operas, including *Die glückliche Hand* (*The Blessed Hand,* 1913) and *Moses und Aron* (incomplete, 1932)

Choral music, including *Gurrelieder* (1911), *Die Jakobsleiter* (*Jacob's Ladder,* 1922), and *A Survivor from Warsaw* (1947); smaller choral works, including *Friede auf Erden* (*Peace on Earth,* 1907)

Chamber music, including 4 string quartets, serenade, wind quintet, string trio, and string sextet *Verklärte Nacht* (*Transfigured Night,* 1899)

Vocal music, including *Pierrot lunaire* (*Moonstruck Peter,* 1912)

Piano music, including Three Piano Pieces, Op. 11 (1909)

HIS MUSIC

Schoenberg's early works are representative of post-Wagnerian Romanticism; they still used key signatures and remained within the boundaries of tonality. The best-known composition of this era is *Transfigured Night.* Schoenberg's second period, the atonal-Expressionist, got under way with the Three Piano Pieces, Opus 11, in which he abolished the distinction between consonance and dissonance and did away with any sense of a home key. The high points of this period are the Five Pieces for Orchestra, Opus 16, and *Pierrot lunaire,* which we will study.

Atonal-Expressionism

Schoenberg's third style period, incorporating the twelve-tone method, reached its climax in the Variations for Orchestra, Opus 31, one of his most powerful works. In the fourth and last part of his career—the American phase—he carried the twelve-tone technique to further stages of refinement. Several of the late works present the twelve-tone style in a manner markedly more accessible than earlier pieces, often with tonal implications. Among these are the brilliant Piano Concerto and the cantata *A Survivor from Warsaw.*

Twelve-tone and American periods

Pierrot lunaire

One of Schoenberg's goals was to bring spoken word and music as close together as possible; he achieved this aim through *Sprechstimme* (spoken

Sprechstimme

In His Own Words

Whether one calls oneself conservative or revolutionary, whether one composes in a conventional or progressive manner, whether one tries to imitate old styles or is destined to express new ideas—whether one is a good composer or not—one must be convinced of the infallibility of one's own fantasy and one must believe in one's own inspiration. The desire for a conscious control of the new means and forms will arise in every artist's mind; and he will wish to follow consciously the laws and rules that govern the forms he has conceived "as in a dream."

Klangfarbenmelodie

The Moonfleck

O Scent of Fabled Yesteryear

voice), a new style in which the vocal melody is spoken rather than sung on exact pitches and in strict rhythm. As Schoenberg explained it, the reciter sounds the written note at first but abandons it by immediately rising or falling in pitch. The result is a weird, strangely effective vocal line, brought to perfection in his most celebrated work, *Pierrot lunaire.*

Schoenberg's song cycle draws its texts from a collection of fifty short poems that the Belgian poet Albert Giraud, a disciple of the Symbolists, published under that title in 1884. Giraud's Pierrot was the poet-rascal-clown whose chalk-white face, passing abruptly from laughter to tears, enlivened every puppet show and pantomime in Europe. (We have already met him in Russia as Petrushka and in Italy as Pagliaccio.) The poems were liberally spiced with elements of the macabre and the bizarre that suited the end-of-century taste for decadence; with their abrupt changes of mood from guilt and depression to atonement and playfulness, they fired Schoenberg's imagination. He picked twenty-one texts (in German translation), arranged them in three groups of seven, and set them for a female reciter and a chamber music ensemble of five players using eight instruments: piano, flute/piccolo, clarinet/bass clarinet, violin/viola, and cello. The work, he explained, was conceived "in a light, ironical, satirical tone."

Giraud's short poems enabled Schoenberg to create a series of miniatures for which Sprechstimme served as a unifying element. This unity was balanced by the utmost variety in structure, texture—from dense to sparse—and instrumentation from one piece to the next. The result was a perfect musical expression of the bizarre images in the text. Schoenberg also experimented with what he called *Klangfarbenmelodie* (tone-color melody), in which each note of a melody is played by a different instrument, creating a shifting effect that evokes the moonbeams mentioned in the poems. Each text is a *rondeau*, a fifteenth-century verse form in which the opening lines return as a refrain in the middle of the poem and at its end (see p. 119).

We will focus on two of the songs from the last group in the cycle. In No. 18, *The Moonfleck* (*Der Mondfleck*; see Listening Guide 61 for the text), Pierrot, out to have fun, is disturbed by a white spot—a patch of moonlight—on the collar of his jet-black jacket. He rubs and rubs but cannot get rid of it. His predicament inspired Schoenberg to contrapuntal complexities of a spectacular kind. The piano introduces a three-voice fugue, while the other instruments unfold such devices as strict canons in diminution (smaller note values) and retrograde (backward). Schoenberg was obviously fascinated by such constructions, which recall the wizardry of the Renaissance contrapuntists.

In No. 21 (the final song of the cycle), *O Scent of Fabled Yesteryear* (*O alter Duft aus Märchenzeit*), Schoenberg employs all eight instruments. Pierrot revels in his memories of old times, looking out serenely on a world bathed in sunlight. This return to an earlier, more innocent time leads Schoenberg to sound the gentle thirds and consonant triads of the harmonic system he had abandoned. Pierrot's Sprechstimme dies away in a *pianissimo*. Thus ends the work that Stravinsky called "the solar plexus as well as the mind of early-twentieth-century music."

Listening Guide 61

MW CD: Chr/Std 7/16–19, Sh 4/13–14
Cassette: Chr/Std 7A/5–6, Sh 4A/3

SCHOENBERG: *Pierrot lunaire*, Nos. 18 and 21 (2:43)

Date of work: 1912

Genre: Song cycle

Medium: Solo voice (mezzo-soprano) and 5 instrumentalists (violin/viola, cello, flute/piccolo, clarinet/bass clarinet, piano)

Text: 21 poems from Albert Giraud's *Pierrot lunaire*, all in rondeau form; cycle organized in 3 parts

Part I: Pierrot, sad clown figure, is obsessed with the moon, having drunk moonwine; his loves, fantasies, and frenzies are exposed.
1. *Moondrunk*
2. *Columbine*
3. *The Dandy*
4. *Pale Washerwoman*
5. *Valse de Chopin*
6. *Madonna*
7. *The Sick Moon*

Part II: Pierrot becomes ridden with guilt and wants to make atonement.
8. *Night*
9. *Prayer to Pierrot*
10. *Theft*
11. *Red Mass*
12. *Gallows Ditty*
13. *Beheading*
14. *The Crosses*

Part III: Pierrot climbs from the depths of depression to a more playful mood, but with fleeting thoughts of guilt; then he becomes sober.
15. *Homesickness*
16. *Vulgar Horseplay*
17. *Parody*
18. *The Moonfleck*
19. *Serenade*
20. *Homeward Journey*
21. *O Scent of Fabled Yesteryear*

---

18. *The Moonfleck (Der Mondfleck)* (0:55)
Medium: Voice, piccolo, clarinet in B♭, violin, cello, piano
Tempo: Sehr rasche (Very quickly)

Voice in Sprechstimme against fast and dissonant accompaniment; canonic treatment veiled in flickering effect of instruments (italics indicate repeated text of rondeau form).

		Text	*Translation*

16 0:00

Einen weissen Fleck des hellen Mondes
Auf dem Rücken seines schwarzen Rockes,
So spaziert Pierrot im lauen Abend,
Aufzusuchen Glück und Abenteuer.

Plötzlich stört ihn was an seinem Anzug,
Er beschaut sich rings und findet richtig—
Einen weissen Fleck des hellen Mondes
Auf dem Rücken seines schwarzen Rockes.

17 0:26

Warte! denkt er: das ist so ein Gipsfleck!
Wischt und wischt, doch—bringt ihn
    nicht herunter!
Und so geht er, giftgeschwollen, weiter,
Reibt und reibt bis an den frühen Morgen—
Einen weissen Fleck des hellen Mondes.

With a fleck of white—from the bright moon—
on the back of his black jacket.
Pierrot strolls about in the mild evening
seeking his fortune and adventure.

Suddenly something strikes him as wrong,
he checks his clothes and sure enough finds
a fleck of white—from the bright moon—
on the back of his black jacket.

Damn! he thinks: that's a spot of plaster!
Wipes and wipes, but—he can't get it off.

And so goes on his way, his pleasure poisoned,
rubs and rubs till the early morning—
a fleck of white—from the bright moon.

Opening, for voice and instruments:

(Shorter recordings stop here.)

21. *O Scent of Fabled Yesteryear (O alter Duft aus Märchenzeit)*   (1:48)

Medium: Voice, flute, piccolo, clarinet in A, bass clarinet in B♭, violin, viola, cello, piano
Tempo: Bewegt (With motion)

Melancholy mood in simpler setting, dissonant, with musical refrain on words "O alter Duft aus Märchenzeit" (shown in italics).

		Text	Translation

18	0:00	*O alter Duft aus Märchenzeit,*	*O scent of fabled yesteryear,*
		Berauschest wieder meine Sinne!	*intoxicating my senses once again!*
		Ein närrisch Heer von Schelmerein	A foolish swarm of idle fancies
		Durchschwirrt die leichte Luft.	pervades the gentle air.

Ein glückhaft Wünschen macht mich froh — A happy desire makes me yearn for

Nach Freuden, die ich lang verachtet: — joys that I have long scorned:

| 19 | 0:44 | *O alter Duft aus Märchenzeit,* | *O scent of fabled yesteryear,* |
| | | *Berauschest wieder mich!* | *intoxicating me again.* |

All meinen Unmut geb ich preis: — All my ill humor is dispelled:

Aus meinem sonnumrahmten Fenster — from my sun-drenched window

Beschau ich frei die liebe Welt — I look out freely on the lovely world

Und träum hinaus in selge Weiten . . . — and dream of beyond the horizon . . .

O alter Duft aus Märchenzeit! — *O scent of fabled yesteryear!*

Opening, for piano and voice in Sprechstimme:

72

Berg and Early-Twentieth-Century Opera

"When I decided to write an opera, my only intention was to give to the theater what belongs to the theater. The music was to be so formed that at each moment it would fulfill its duty of serving the action."

It was the unique achievement of Alban Berg to humanize the abstract procedures of the Schoenbergian technique and to infuse them with feeling. He brought a great lyric imagination to this new, difficult idiom.

Alban Berg

HIS LIFE

Alban Berg (1885–1935) was born in Vienna. He came from a well-to-do family and grew up in an environment that fostered his artistic interests. At nineteen, he made the acquaintance of Arnold Schoenberg, who was sufficiently impressed with the youth's manuscripts to accept him as a pupil. During his six years with the older master (1904–9), Berg acquired the consummate mastery of technique that characterizes his later work. Schoenberg was not only an exacting master, but also a devoted friend and mentor who shaped Berg's whole outlook on art.

The outbreak of war in 1914 hurled Berg into a period of depression. "The urge 'to be in on it,'" he wrote to Schoenberg, "the feeling of helplessness at being unable to serve my country, prevented any concentration on work." A few months later, he was called up for military service despite his uncertain health (he suffered from asthma and a nerve ailment) and was assigned to guard duty and later to the War Ministry in Vienna. At this time, an opera, *Wozzeck*, occupied his thoughts, but he could not begin writing until the war was over. In December 1925, *Wozzeck* was presented at the Berlin State Opera. Suddenly, Berg was lifted from obscurity to international fame.

In the decade that remained to him, he produced only a handful of works, but each was a significant contribution to his total output. During these years, Berg was active as a teacher. He also wrote about music, propagandizing tirelessly on behalf of Schoenberg and his school. With the coming to power of Hitler, the works of the twelve-tone composers were banned in Germany as alien to the spirit of the Third Reich. The resulting loss of income was a source of worry to Berg, as was, to a far greater degree, the rapid spread of Nazism in Austria. Schoenberg's departure for the United States was a bitter blow.

Exhausted and ailing after the completion of his Violin Concerto, Berg went to the country for a short rest before resuming work on his opera *Lulu*. An insect bite brought on an abscess, and the infection spread. He was stricken with blood poisoning on his return to Vienna and died on Christmas Eve 1935, seven weeks before his fifty-first birthday.

HIS MUSIC

Berg's style was rooted in German Romanticism—the world of Schumann, Brahms, Wagner, Richard Strauss, and Mahler. The Romantic streak in his temperament tied him to this heritage even after he had adopted the twelve-

---

Principal Works

2 operas: *Wozzeck* (1917–22) and *Lulu* (unfinished, 1935)

Orchestral music, including Three Orchestral Pieces, Op. 6 (1915), Chamber Concerto (1925), Three Pieces from *Lyric Suite* (1928), and Violin Concerto (1935)

Chamber music, including String Quartet (1910) and *Lyric Suite* (1926)

Piano music, including Piano Sonata, Op. 1 (1908)

Songs, including Four Songs, Op. 2 (1910)

---

tone style. His imagination was that of the musical dramatist: for him, music was bound up with character and action, mood and atmosphere. Yet, like his teacher, he also leaned toward the formal patterns of the past—fugue and invention, passacaglia, variations, sonata, and suite.

After *Wozzeck*, Berg's most widely known composition is the *Lyric Suite*. The work is in six movements, the first and last of which strictly follow "the method of composing with twelve tones." Originally written for string quar-

Atonal Expressionism found its counterpart in the canvases of Expressionist painters who defied notions of beauty in order to define the artist's inner self. **Wassily Kandinsky** *(1886–1944),* Painting No. 199. (Museum of Modern Art, New York)

tet, the *Lyric Suite* achieved such popularity that the composer arranged three of the middle movements for string orchestra.

Lulu

Berg spent the last seven years of his life working on the opera *Lulu*, which is based on a single twelve-tone row. The composer fashioned the libretto himself from two dramas by Frank Wedekind—*Earth Spirit* (1893) and *Pandora's Box* (1901). Lulu is the eternal type of *femme fatale* "who destroys everyone because she is destroyed by everyone." Berg left off orchestrating *Lulu* to write his Violin Concerto, and died shortly thereafter. The opera remained unfinished for many years, but recently the orchestration was completed by the Austrian composer Friedrich Cerha, and now *Lulu* has taken its place alongside *Wozzeck* as one of the challenging works of the modern lyric theater.

Alban Berg is probably the most widely admired master of the twelve-tone school. His premature death at the age of fifty robbed contemporary music of a major figure.

Wozzeck

In 1914, Berg saw the play that inspired him to write *Wozzeck*. The young author, Georg Büchner (1813–1837), belonged to a generation of intellectuals that was stifled by the political repressions imposed on Europe after the defeat of Napoleon. The play is based on real-life events (gruesome as they are). In the title character of Wozzeck, Büchner created an archetype of "the insulted and injured" of the earth.

Berg's libretto organized the play into three acts, each containing five scenes. The scenes are linked by brief orchestral interludes whose motivic structure serves to round off what has preceded and to introduce what follows. As a result, Berg's opera has an astonishing unity of texture and mood.

The action centers on Wozzeck's unhappy love for Marie, by whom he has had an illegitimate child. Wozzeck, a common soldier, is the victim of the sadistic Captain and the coldly scientific Doctor, who uses Wozzeck for his experiments—to which the soldier submits because he needs the money. (Wozzeck is given to hallucinations. The Doctor is bent on proving his theory that mental disorder is related to diet.) Marie is hopelessly infatuated with the handsome Drum Major. Wozzeck slowly realizes that she has been unfaithful to him. Ultimately he cuts her throat, then, driven back to the death scene by guilt and remorse, he drowns himself.

Harmonically, the greater part of the opera is cast in an atonal-Expressionist idiom. Berg anticipates certain twelve-tone procedures; he also looks back to the tonal tradition, writes a number of passages in major and minor keys, and uses leitmotifs in the Wagnerian manner.

Act III, scene 4

We will study the final two scenes of the opera. In scene 4 of Act III, Wozzeck returns to the path near the pond where he has killed Marie, and

In His Own Words

I never entertained the idea of reforming the artistic structure of the opera with Wozzeck. . . . *I wanted to compose good music, to develop musically the contents of Büchner's immortal drama, to translate his poetic language into music; but other than that, when I decided to write an opera, my only intentions, including the technique of composition, were to give the theater what belongs to the theater. In other words, the music was to be so formed as consciously to fulfill its duty of serving the action at every moment.*

stumbles against her body. He asks, "Marie, what's that red cord around your neck?" (See Listening Guide 62 for the text.) He finds the knife with which he committed the murder, throws it into the pond, and, driven by his delusions, follows it into the water. His last words as he drowns—"I am washing myself in blood—the water is blood . . . blood!"—usher in a series of ascending chromatic scales that pass in a ghostly *pianissimo* from strings to woodwinds to brass. The Doctor appears, followed by the Captain. We see the haunted scene through their eyes as, terrified, they run away.

The final scene opens with a symphonic interlude in D minor, a passionate lament for the life and death of Wozzeck. This inspired fantasy indicates how richly Berg's art was influenced by the Romanticism of Mahler. The scene takes place in the morning in front of Marie's house, where children are playing. Marie's little boy rides a hobbyhorse. Other children rush in with news of the murder, but Marie's son does not understand. The children run off as he continues to ride and sing. Then, noticing that he has been left alone, he calls "Hop, hop" and rides off on his hobbyhorse, to the sound of clarinet, drum, xylophone, and strings playing *pianissimo*. For sheer heartbreak, the final curtain has few to equal it in the contemporary lyric theater.

Act III, scene 5

Wozzeck envelops the listener in a hallucinated world in which the hunters are as driven as the hunted. It could only have come from central Europe in the 1920s. But its characters reach out beyond time and place to become eternal symbols of the human condition.

Listening Guide 62

CD: Chr/Std 7/54–57
Cassette: Chr/Std 7B/3

BERG: *Wozzeck*, Act III, Scenes 4 and 5 (9:55)

Date of work: 1922

Genre: Opera, in three acts

Basis: Expressionist play by Georg Büchner

ACT III, SCENE 4: By the pond

Characters: Wozzeck (baritone), Doctor (bass), Captain (tenor)

WOZZECK

54	0:00	Das Messer? Wo ist das Messer? Ich hab's dagelassen. Näher, noch näher. Mir graut's . . . da regt sich was. Still! Alles still und tot.	The knife? Where is the knife? I left it there. Around here somewhere. I'm terrified . . . something's moving. Silence. Everything silent and dead.

(shouting)

Mörder! Mörder!   Murderer! Murderer!

(whispering again)

Ha! Da ruft's. Nein, ich selbst.   Ah! Someone called. No, it was only me.

(Still looking, he staggers a few steps further and stumbles against the corpse.)

Marie! Marie! Was hast du für eine rote   Marie! Marie! What's that red cord around your
Schnur um den Hals? Hast dir das rote   neck? Was the red necklace payment for your
Halsband verdient, wie die Ohrringlein,   sins, like the earrings? Why's your dark hair so
mit deiner Sünde! Was hängen dir die   wild about you? Murderer! Murderer!
schwarzen Haare so wild? Mörder! Mörder!   They will come and look for me. The knife will
Sie werden nach mir suchen. Das Messer   betray me!
verrät mich!

(looks for it in a frenzy)

Da, da ist's.   Here! Here it is!

(at the pond)

So! Da hinunter!   There! Sink to the bottom!

(throws knife into the pond)

Es taucht ins dunkle Wasser wie ein Stein.   It plunges into the dark water like a stone.

(The moon appears, blood-red, from behind the clouds. Wozzeck looks up.)

Aber der Mond verrät mich, der Mond ist   But the moon will betray me: the moon is
blutig. Will denn die ganze Welt es ausplaudern!   bloodstained. Is the whole world going to
Das Messer, es liegt zu weit vorn, sie finden's   incriminate me? The knife is too near the edge:
beim Baden oder wenn sie nach Muscheln   they'll find it when they're swimming or diving
tauchen.   for snails.

(wades into the pond)

Ich find's nicht. Aber ich muss mich   I can't find it. But I must wash myself.
waschen. Ich bin blutig. Da ein Fleck—   There's blood on me. There's a spot here—
und noch einer. Weh! Weh!   and another. Oh, God!
Ich wasche mich mit Blut—   I am washing myself in blood—
das Wasser ist Blut . . . Blut . . .   the water is blood . . . blood . . .

(drowns)

Wozzeck's last words before drowning, accompanied by very soft ascending chromatic scales in
strings:

(The Doctor appears, followed by the Captain.)

CAPTAIN

55   3:03 Halt!   Wait!

DOCTOR *(stops)*

Hören Sie? Dort!   Can you hear? There!

CAPTAIN

Jesus! Das war ein Ton!   Jesus! What a ghastly sound!

(stops as well)

DOCTOR *(pointing to the pond)*	
Ja, dort!	Yes, there!
CAPTAIN	
Es ist das Wasser im Teich. Das Wasser ruft. Es ist schon lange niemand ertrunken. Kommen Sie, Doktor! Es ist nicht gut zu hören.	It's the water in the pond. The water is calling. It's been a long time since anyone drowned. Come away, Doctor. It's not good for us to be hearing it.
(tries to drag the Doctor away)	
DOCTOR *(resisting and continuing to listen)*	
Das stöhnt, als stürbe ein Mensch. Da ertrinkt Jemand!	There's a groan, as though someone were dying. Somebody's drowning!
CAPTAIN	
Unheimlich! Der Mond rot, und die Nebel grau. Hören Sie? . . . Jetzt wieder das Ächzen.	It's eerie! The moon is red, and the mist is gray. Can you hear? . . . That moaning again.
DOCTOR	
Stiller, . . . jetzt ganz still.	It's getting quieter . . . now it's stopped altogether.
CAPTAIN	
Kommen Sie! Kommen Sie schnell!	Come! Come quickly!
(He rushes off, pulling the Doctor along with him.)	

56	4:44	**Orchestral interlude in D minor**

Chromatic, lush strings; Adagio tempo; leads to dissonant climax in brass and woodwinds, with timpani.

ACT III, SCENE 5: Children playing in front of Marie's house

Melody of children's song, distorted:

57	8:29	CHILDREN	
		Ringel, Ringel, Rosenkranz, Ringelreih'n Ringel, Ringel, Rosenkranz, Ring . . .	Ring-a-ring-a-roses, A pocket full of . . .

(Their song and game are interrupted by other children bursting in.)

ONE OF THE NEWCOMERS	
Du, Käthe! Die Marie!	Hey, Katie! Have you heard about Marie?
SECOND CHILD	
Was is?	What's happened?
FIRST CHILD	
Weisst' es nit? Sie sind schon Alle 'naus.	Don't you know? They've all gone out there.
THIRD CHILD *(to Marie's little boy)*	
Du! Dein' Mutter ist tot!	Hey! Your mother's dead!

MARIE'S SON *(still riding)*

Hopp, hopp! Hopp, hopp! Hopp, hopp!	Hop, hop! Hop, hop! Hop, hop!

SECOND CHILD

Wo ist sie denn?	Where is she, then?

FIRST CHILD

Drauss' liegt sie, am Weg, neben dem Teich.	She's lying out there, on the path near the pond.

THIRD CHILD

Kommt, anschaun!	Come and have a look!

(All the children run off.)

MARIE'S SON *(continuing to ride)*

Hopp, hopp! Hopp, hopp! Hopp, hopp!	Hop, hop! Hop, hop! Hop, hop!

(He hesitates for a moment and then rides after the other children.)

Child on hobbyhorse, with *pianissimo* accompaniment:

73

Webern and Serial Technique

"With me, things never turn out as I wish, but only as is ordained for me—as I must."

The works of Anton Webern are brief, subtle, fleeting; yet they hold a firm place in our musical life. They have decisively influenced the thinking of many younger composers of today.

HIS LIFE

Anton Webern (1883–1945) was born in Vienna. His musical gifts were obvious at an early age. He was twenty-one when he met Schoenberg and, with Alban Berg, formed the core of the students who gathered around the master. He also studied musicology and received a doctorate in this field.

After leaving the university, Webern conducted at various German provincial theaters and in Prague. But Vienna was the hub of his world. He became director of the Vienna Workers' Symphony Concerts organized by the authorities of the then socialist city, but as the years passed, he found public activity less and less congenial to his retiring personality. After the First World War, he settled in a suburb of Vienna, where he lived quietly, devoting himself to composition and teaching.

Webern suffered great hardship after Austria became part of the Third Reich. The Nazis, who regarded his music as "cultural Bolshevism," forbade its performance and burned his writings. He was permitted to teach only a few pupils, and had to give his lectures—on the Schoenbergian point of view—in secret. In order to avoid forced labor during the war, he worked as a proofreader for a Viennese publisher. To escape the Allied bombings of Vienna, Webern and his wife sought refuge at the home of their son-in-law in a small town near Salzburg. But fate awaited him there. On September 15, 1945, as he stood outside his daughter's house in the evening to smoke a cigar (the war had ended five months before, but the town was still under a curfew), he was shot to death by an American soldier. "The day of Anton Webern's death," wrote his most celebrated admirer, Igor Stravinsky, "should be a day of mourning for any receptive musician. We must hail not only this great composer but also a real hero. Doomed to total failure in a deaf world of ignorance and indifference, he inexorably kept on cutting his dazzling diamonds, of whose mines he had such a perfect knowledge."

Anton Webern

HIS MUSIC

Webern responded to the radical aspects of Schoenberg's doctrine, just as Berg exploited its more conservative elements. Of the three masters of the modern Viennese School, Webern was the one who cut himself off most completely from the tonal past. The Schoenbergians, we saw, favored short forms. Webern carried this urge for brevity much further than either of his colleagues. His scores call for the most unusual combinations of instruments, which are often used in their extreme registers; they frequently play one at a

---

Principal Works

Orchestral music, including Passacaglia, Op. 1 (1908); Five Pieces for Orchestra, Op. 10 (1913); Symphony, Op. 21 (1928); and Variations, Op. 30 (1940)

Chamber music, including Five Movements for String Quartet (1909) and other string quartets

Choral music, including cantatas; many songs

Piano music, including Variations, Op. 27 (1936)

---

time, and very little. This technique confers on each individual sound an importance never achieved before.

In the works of his maturity, Webern used the twelve-tone technique with unprecedented strictness. Schoenberg had contented himself with an organization based on a fixed series of pitches. Webern extended this concept to include timbres and rhythms, moving toward complete control of all the elements—in other words, *total serialism*. His disciples carried the implications of his music still further. As a result, Webern emerged as the dominant influence on the compositional process of the mid–twentieth century.

Total serialism

Symphony, Opus 21

The Symphony, Opus 21—for clarinet, bass clarinet, two horns, two harps, violins, violas, and cellos—is an excellent introduction to his completely original style. With this work, he became the first of the modern Viennese School to undertake the grand form of the Classical period. (As we saw, neither Schoenberg nor Berg wrote symphonies.) However, Webern's piece is far removed from the expansion-and-development techniques traditionally associated with symphonic style. It is equally far from the tonic-dominant opposition that made the symphony the embodiment of tonal thinking.

Webern's Symphony takes just under ten minutes to play, and shows the same concentration of thought and spareness of writing as do his other scores. In the matter of color, Webern expanded Schoenberg's device of *Klangfarbenmelodie* (tone-color melody), in which each note of a melodic line was played by a different instrument, by assigning two, three, or four notes to each instrument. The result was the exact tonal equivalent of pointillism in painting, in which dots of pure color were juxtaposed to create a shimmering effect.

Klangfarbenmelodie

The symphony abounds in the complex contrapuntal procedures—such as double canon and retrograde (backward) motion—that fascinated com-

In this pointillistic painting, **Georges Seurat** *(1859–1891) uses dots of pure color to create a shimmering effect in the same way Webern and Schoenberg used changing instrumental timbres.* Study for "A Sunday on La Grande Jatte." (Metropolitan Museum of Art, New York)

posers from the late Middle Ages to the Baroque era. The first of its two movements, based on a tone row, is in a sonata form with canonic structures; the second is a theme with seven variations and a coda, all derived from the tone row of the first movement (see Listening Guide 63). The symmetrical organization shows the workings of Webern's mind: Variations 1 and 7 are double canons, 2 and 6 are trios, 3 and 5 are pointillistic in effect, and the 4th serves as the turning point of the movement.

Listening Guide 63

CD: Chr/Std 7/51–53
Cassette: Chr/Std 7B/2

WEBERN: Symphony, Op. 21, Second Movement   (2:54)

Date of work: 1928

Medium: Chamber orchestra

Movements (both 12-tone):
  I. Ruhig schreitend (Moving quietly); sonata form, with double canon for 4 voices
  II. Variationen (Theme and variations)

FIRST MOVEMENT: Sonata form, with double canon

Original form of tone row (note that the second half of the row—the last six pitches—are the retrograde of the first):

SECOND MOVEMENT: Theme and variations

Basis: 11-measure theme, based on the transposed inversion and retrograde inversion of tone row from first movement; inverted tone row heard in harp and French horn; retrograde inversion of same row heard in clarinet and bass clarinet
Character: Pointillistic, disjunct

Forms of tone row used (transposed up one step from original):

51   0:00   **Theme:** Sehr ruhig (Very quiet)
             Gentle statement in clarinets, with muted horns and harps
        Variation 1: Lebhafter (Livelier)
             Muted string; 4-part double canon in contrary motion; alternation of pizzicato
             and bowed notes; second half of variation is retrograde of first half
        Variation 2: Sehr lebhaft (Very lively)
             Clarinet, bass clarinet, and horn, with harp and occasional strings
        Variation 3: Wieder mässiger (Again more moderately)
             Ensemble, in pointillistic style
52   1:06   **Variation 4:** Äusserst ruhig (Extremely quiet)
             Ensemble, in slowest section with dense counterpoint
        Variation 5: Sehr lebhaft (Very lively)
             Strings and harp, in ostinato that builds in volume
        Variation 6: Marschmässig (Marchlike)
             Clarinet, bass clarinet, and horn; canons in woodwinds with sustained horn notes
53   2:08   **Variation 7:** Etwas breiter (Somewhat broader)
             Ensemble, double canon in contrary motion
        Coda:
             Theme and retrograde form in clarinet, harp, violin, and cello; closes with harp
             notes

Unit XXIII

Twentieth-Century Nationalism

74

The European Scene

*"The art of music above all other arts is the expression of the soul
of a nation. The composer must love the tunes of his country and
they must become an integral part of him."*
—RALPH VAUGHAN WILLIAMS

Twentieth-century nationalism differed from its nineteenth-century counterpart in one important respect. Composers approached traditional music with
a scientific spirit, prizing the ancient tunes precisely because they departed
from the conventional mold. By this time, the phonograph had been invented. The new students of folklore took recording equipment into the field
in order to preserve the songs exactly as the village folk sang them, and the
composers who used those songs in their works tried to retain the traditional
flavor of the originals.

NATIONAL SCHOOLS

French composers in the generation after Debussy and Ravel tried to capture   **French school**
the wit and spirit that are part of their national heritage. One group in particular, called *Les Six* (The Six), followed the example of Erik Satie (1866–1925)   *Les Six*

Inspired by the German bombing of the Basque town of Guernica on April 28, 1937, this nationalistic painting was produced by **Pablo Picasso** *for the Spanish Pavilion at the 1938 International Exhibition in Paris.* Guernica. (Museo del Prado, Madrid)

in their efforts to develop a style that combined objectivity and understatement with the New Classicism and the even newer concepts of harmony. Of this group, Darius Milhaud (1892–1974) is remembered today for his ballet *The Creation of the World* (1923) and for being a leader in the development of polytonality. Arthur Honegger (1892–1955), born in France of Swiss parents, shocked the world with *Pacific 231*, a symphonic poem glorifying the locomotive. Germaine Tailleferre (1892–1983), the only woman in this select group of composers, furthered the cause of the New Classicism, writing in most genres with fluency.

Francis Poulenc (1899–1963) has emerged as the most significant figure of *Les Six.* One of the outstanding art song composers of his day, he also wrote thoroughly Parisian piano pieces. Two of his best-known operas—*Dialogues of the Carmelites* (1953–56) and *The Human Voice* (1958), the latter based on a one-act play by Jean Cocteau—have found a wide audience in the United States in English versions by Joseph Machlis, the coauthor of this book.

Russian school

In the post-Romantic period, the Russian school produced two composers of international fame. The piano works of Sergei Rachmaninoff (1873–1943) are enormously popular with the concertgoing public, especially his Second Piano Concerto and his Variations on a Theme of Paganini. (His Third Piano Concerto recently achieved fame through the Academy-Award-winning film *Shine* [1996], about the Australian pianist David Helfgott.) Alexander Scriabin (1872–1915), a visionary artist whose music is wreathed in a subtle lyricism, was one of the leaders in the twentieth-century search for new harmonies. In the next generation, two important figures emerged: Sergei

Prokofiev, whom we will study later in this chapter; and Dmitri Shostakovich (1906–1975), the first Russian composer of international repute who was wholly a product of the musical culture during the period of the Soviet Union (1917–91).

England had produced no major composer for two hundred years until Edward Elgar and Frederick Delius appeared on the scene. They were followed by two figures who were of prime importance in establishing the modern English school—Ralph Vaughan Williams (1872–1958) and Benjamin Britten (1913–1976). Britten's works for the stage have established his reputation as one of the foremost opera composers of the era. Among his operas are *Peter Grimes* (1945, based on George Crabbe's poem *The Borough*), about an English fishing village, and *Billy Budd* (1951), after Herman Melville's story. Widely admired too are the lovely Serenade for tenor solo, horn, and string orchestra (1943) and the deeply moving *War Requiem* (1961). You will recall that Britten's *Variations and Fugue on a Theme of Purcell* (*The Young Person's Guide to the Orchestra*) was discussed earlier (see Chapter 9).

English school

Among the composers who came into prominence in Germany in the years after the First World War, Paul Hindemith (1895–1963) was the most significant. He left Germany when Hitler came to power—his music was banned from the Third Reich as "cultural Bolshevism"—and spent two decades in the United States, during which he taught at Yale University and at Tanglewood, Massachusetts, where many young Americans came under his influence.

German school

Carl Orff (1895–1982) took his point of departure from the clear-cut melodies and vigorous rhythms of Bavarian folk song. He is best-known in North America for his stirring cantata *Carmina burana* (1937), set to racy medieval lyrics. Kurt Weill (1900–1950) was one of the most arresting figures to emerge from Germany in the 1920s. For the international public, his name is indissolubly linked with *The Three-penny Opera* (1928), which he and the poet Bertolt Brecht adapted from *The Beggar's Opera* by John Gay. Frequent revivals have made this one of the century's most famous theater pieces.

Hungarian nationalism found two major representatives in Béla Bartók, whom we will study, and Zoltán Kodály (1882–1967). Both composers collected and studied traditional songs, and made the folk element prominent in their music. The Czech national school is well represented by Leoš Janáček (1854–1928), whose operas *Jenůfa* (1904) and *The Cunning Little Vixen* (1924) have found great favor with the American public. Spain contributed two important nationalists of the post-Romantic era—Isaac Albéniz (1860–1909) and Enrique Granados (1867–1916), both of whom paved the way for the major figure of the modern Spanish school, Manuel de Falla (1876–1946).

Other nationalists

Finland's Jean Sibelius (1865–1957) was an important figure during the 1920s and 1930s, especially in England and the United States. His Second

Symphony, Violin Concerto, and tone poem *Finlandia* remain popular. Carl Nielsen (1865–1931), a Danish composer, wrote six symphonies that have slowly established themselves in our concert life. Ernest Bloch (1880–1959), a native of Switzerland, was one of the few well-known Jewish composers who consciously identified himself musically with his cultural origins. In *Schelomo*—the biblical name of King Solomon—he produced a "Hebrew Rhapsody" for cello and orchestra that gave eloquent expression to his heritage, much as Arnold Schoenberg did a generation later in *A Survivor from Warsaw*.

SERGEI PROKOFIEV: HIS LIFE AND MUSIC

Sergei Prokofiev

"The cardinal virtue (or, if you like, vice) of my life has always been the search for originality. I hate imitation. I hate hackneyed methods. I do not want to wear anyone else's mask. I want always to be myself."

Sergei Prokofiev (1891–1953) was one of those fortunate composers who achieved popularity with both the general public and professional musicians. He appeared at a twilight moment in the history of Russian music, infusing it with a fresh but traditional air. Prokofiev was thirteen when he entered the St. Petersburg Conservatory, armed with the manuscripts of four operas, two sonatas, a symphony, and a number of piano pieces; Rimsky-Korsakov, who was one of the entrance examiners, exclaimed, "Here is a pupil after my own heart!"

At nineteen, Prokofiev made his first public appearance in St. Petersburg playing a group of his piano pieces. The dynamism of this music at once revealed a distinctive personal style. The works that followed—especially the Second Piano Concerto, the Second Piano Sonata, and the *Sarcasms* for piano—established the young composer as the "naughty boy" of Russian music, a role he thoroughly enjoyed.

Years outside Russia   The Revolution of 1917 caught Prokofiev unaware, since politics lay outside his sphere of interest. As living conditions grew more difficult, he decided to emigrate to the United States, where he would be able to work in peace. It became clear, however, that the conquest of the New World was not going to be as easy as he had imagined.

> I wandered through the enormous park in the center of New York and, looking up at the skyscrapers that bordered it, thought with cold fury of the marvelous American orchestras that cared nothing for my music, of the critics who

balked so violently at anything new, of the managers who arranged long tours for artists playing the same old hackneyed programs fifty times over.

There was nothing to do but admit defeat and look elsewhere.

In 1920, Prokofiev made Paris his home, with frequent journeys to the musical centers of Europe and the United States to perform his music. Yet the sense of being uprooted plagued him. "I've got to talk to people who are of my own flesh and blood, so that they can give me back something I lack here—their songs, my songs," he wrote a friend.

The years of wandering were followed by nineteen years back in Russia (except for professional trips abroad). During this period, he established his position as the leading composer of the Soviet school. As one who had voluntarily rejoined the Soviets when he might have made a career elsewhere, he was laden with honors by the regime and reaped considerable financial rewards. In 1943, he received the Stalin Prize for his Seventh Piano Sonata. The following year, he was awarded the Order of the Red Banner of Labor for outstanding service in the development of Soviet music.

Soviet years

Nevertheless, of all the Soviet composers, Prokofiev was the one who, because of his long residence abroad, was most closely associated with the Western influences that the regime considered opposed to socialist art. When the Central Committee of the Communist Party in 1948 accused the leading Soviet composers of "bourgeois formalism"—the conventional term for non-Soviet trends in art—Prokofiev was one of its main targets. The government showed its displeasure by ordering his works to be removed from the repertory, along with those of Shostakovich, Aram Khachaturian, and Nikolai Miaskovsky. However, as these composers happened to be the Big Four of Soviet music, the prohibition could not be maintained. After a few months, Prokofiev's works—first his ballets, then his symphonies—found their way back into the concert halls.

He died on March 5, 1953, at the age of sixty-two, one day after the death of the Communist Party leader, Joseph Stalin. The Soviet government withheld the news for forty-eight hours, presumably so that the one event would not overshadow the other.

Prokofiev himself has provided us with the best analysis of the elements of his style. "The first is Classical, originating in my early childhood when I heard my mother play Beethoven sonatas. It assumes a Neoclassical aspect in my sonatas or concertos, or imitates the Classical style of the eighteenth century." In the *Classical* Symphony, composed "as Haydn might have written it had he lived in our day," Prokofiev came as close as anyone in the twentieth century to recapturing the spirit of Haydn's effortless Allegros. The second element in his style he identified as the search for innovation. "At first this consisted in the quest for an individual harmonic language, but it was later transformed into a medium for the expression of strong emotions.

Classical elements

Search for innovation

"The third is the element of the toccata, or motor element, probably influenced by Schumann's Toccata, which impressed me greatly at one time." The toccata is associated with a strong rhythmic drive, generally of the "perpetual motion" type, which is favored in the music of our time. "The fourth element is lyrical. Since my lyricism has for a long time been denied appreciation, it has grown but slowly. But at later stages I paid more and more attention to lyrical expression.

"I should like to limit myself to these four elements, and to regard the fifth, that of the grotesque, which some critics try to foist on me, as merely a variation of the others. In application to my music, I should like to replace the word 'grotesque' with 'Scherzo-ness' or with the three words giving its gradations: 'jest,' 'laughter,' 'mockery.'" The composer stood in the forefront of those who attempted to broaden musical expression to include the comic and the mischievous. In his later years, his style mellowed into a compassionate humor.

Prokofiev became one of the most popular of twentieth-century composers, and a number of his works, among them the concert suites from the ballet *Romeo and Juliet*, have become "classics." In his later symphonies, he sought to recapture the heroic affirmation of the Beethovenian symphony. Of his operas, two in particular have found favor outside Russia: *The Love for Three Oranges* and *War and Peace*. The latter, based on Tolstoy's novel, is considered his masterpiece for the lyric theater.

Principal Works

Orchestral works, including 7 symphonies (No. 1, *Classical*, 1917); *Scythian Suite* (1915); *Peter and the Wolf* (with narrator, 1936); 5 piano concertos; 2 violin concertos; and 1 cello concerto

Operas, including *The Love for Three Oranges* (1921), *The Flaming Angel* (1923), and *War and Peace* (1943)

Ballets, including *The Prodigal Son* (1929), *Romeo and Juliet* (1938), and *Cinderella* (1945)

Choral music, including *Alexander Nevsky* (1939, cantata adapted from film score)

Chamber music, including string quartets and sonatas

Piano music, including 9 sonatas

Film music, including *Lieutenant Kije* (1933) and *Alexander Nevsky* (1938); incidental music; songs

Alexander's triumphant return to Pskov as depicted in **Sergei Eisenstein's** *great film*
Alexander Nevsky. (Museum of Modern Art Film Stills Archive, New York)

Alexander Nevsky

The decade preceding the outbreak of the Second World War saw mounting
tension throughout Europe as the Soviet Union was increasingly threatened
by Hitler's Germany. Thus a film based on the life of a folk hero who defeated
the Germans was bound to have a morale-raising effect on the Russian people. In 1938, the great director Sergei Eisenstein produced such a film about
Alexander Nevsky, the Grand Duke of Novgorod, who in 1240 defeated an
attacking Swedish army on the river Neva, and two years later repulsed German attackers in a battle on the frozen surface of Lake Chudskoye. Prokofiev
wrote the film score, which he later shaped into a cantata. (See CP 21 on
music for films, p. 626.) The project had the full support of the Soviet government—members of the Russian army even served as extras for the film.

The cantata, in seven movements, is scored for chorus, mezzo-soprano,
and orchestra. (See Listening Guide 64 for their titles.) We will hear the final
movement, *Alexander's Entry into Pskov.* The Grand Duke and his troops return triumphant from the decisive battle. A folk-song-like tune first heard in
the fourth movement reappears against brilliant orchestration. Throughout

this seventh movement, percussion punctuates the choral parts, which often separate into women's and men's voices.

Despite his subsequent difficulties with the Soviet government and its official doctrine of "socialist realism" (as opposed to the "bourgeois formalism" of the West), Prokofiev appears to have remained faithful to the aesthetic he adopted when he returned to Russia.

Listening Guide 64

CD: Chr/Std 7/58–61
Cassette: Chr/Std 7B/4

PROKOFIEV: *Alexander Nevsky*, Seventh Movement   (4:41)

Date of work: 1939

Genre: Cantata for chorus, mezzo-soprano, and orchestra, in 7 movements

Basis: Film score for *Alexander Nevsky* (1938), directed by Sergei Eisenstein

Movements:

I. *Russia Beneath the Yoke of the Mongols* (orchestral prelude)—portrays the desolation of the country under the foreign invaders
II. *Song About Alexander Nevsky*—celebrates Alexander's earlier victory over the Swedes
III. *The Crusaders in Pskov* (chorus)—depicts the brutal treatment of the people of Pskov by the Germans
IV. *Arise, People of Russia* (chorale)—rallies the people to rise up and defend the Motherland
V. *The Battle on the Ice*—spectacular orchestral movement, with choral chants; depicts the victory of the Russians as the Germans sink under the cracking ice
VI. *The Field of the Dead* (mezzo-soprano solo)—laments the fate of a fallen knight
VII. *Alexander's Entry into Pskov*—triumphal return of the conquering army

SEVENTH MOVEMENT: *Alexander's Entry into Pskov*

		Text	Translation	Description
		CHORUS OF RUSSIANS		
58	0:00	Na vyliki boi vykhodila Rus'.	Russia marched out to mighty battle.	Loud and stately chorus with orchestra, punctuated with percussion.
		Voroga pobyedila Rus'.	Russia overcame the enemy.	
		Na rodnoi zyemlye nye byvat' vragu.	On our native soil, let no foe exist.	
		Kto pridyot, budyet nasmyert' bit.	Whoever invades will be killed.	Quicker tempo, with bells and xylophone.
		WOMEN		
59	0:58	Vyesyelisya, poi, mat'rodnaya Rus'!	Be merry, sing, mother Russia!	Folklike melody sung by women's voices.

Na rodnoi Rusi nye byvat' vragu.	In our native Russia, let no foe exist.	
Nye vidat' vragu nashikh russikh syol.	Let no foe see our native villages.	
Kto pridyol na Rus', budyet nasmert' bit.	Whoever invades Russia will be killed.	

Opening of women's verse:

Nye vidat' vragu nashikh, russikh syol.	Let no foe see our native villages.	Men's voices answer the women; violins forecast the Motherland Russia theme, soon to be sung.	
Kto pridyot na Rus', budyet nasmert' bit.	Whoever invades Russia will be killed.		
Na Rusi rodnoi, na Rusi bol'shoi nye byvat' vragu.	In our native Russia, in great Russia, let no foe exist.	Motherland Russia theme, in 3 lower voices.	
60 1:47			Orchestral interlude; quick, imitative exchanges between instruments; woodwinds are featured.
61 2:37 Na Rusi rodnoi, na Rusi bol'shoi nye byvat' vragu.	In our native Russia, in great Russia, let no foe exist.	Motherland theme in unison, stately, with an animated orchestral accompaniment.	
Vyesyelisya, poi, mat' rodnaya Rus'!	Be merry, sing, mother Russia!		
Na vyelikii prazdnik sobralasya. Rus'.	At the mighty festival, all Russia has gathered together,	Chorale-like, very slow; stately brass, with much percussion; a grandiose ending.	
Vyesyelisya, Rus'! rodnaya mat'!	Be merry, Russia, mother of ours!		

Motherland theme, in altos and basses:

545

Béla Bartók

Study of folklore

BÉLA BARTÓK: HIS LIFE AND MUSIC

"What is the best way for a composer to reap the full benefits of his studies in peasant music? It is to assimilate the idiom of peasant music so completely that he is able to forget all about it and use it as his musical mother tongue."

It was the mission of Béla Bartók (1881–1945) to reconcile the traditional songs of his native Hungary with the main currents of European music. In the process, he created an entirely personal language and revealed himself as one of the major artists of the twentieth century.

Bartók was born in a small Hungarian town in which his father served as director of an agricultural school. He studied at the Royal Academy in Budapest, where he came in contact with the nationalist movement aimed at shaking off the domination of German musical culture. His interest in folklore led him to realize that what passed for Hungarian in the eyes of the world—the idiom romanticized by Liszt and Brahms and kept alive by café musicians—was really the music of Romany, or Gypsies. The true Hungarian idiom, he decided, was to be found only among the peasants. With his fellow composer Zoltán Kodály, he toured the remote villages of the country, determined to collect the native songs before they died out forever. "Those days I spent in the villages among the peasants," he wrote later, "were among the happiest of my life. In order to feel the vitality of this music one must . . . [come] to know it by direct contact with the peasants."

With the performance at the Budapest Opera of his ballet *The Wooden Prince* (1917), Bartók came into his own. Then in 1918, the fall of the Hapsburg monarchy released a surge of national sentiment that created a favorable climate for his music. In the following decade, Bartók became a leading figure in the musical life of his country.

The alliance between the Hungarian government and Nazi Germany on the eve of the Second World War confronted the composer with issues that he faced squarely. He protested the performances of his music on the Berlin radio and at every opportunity took an anti-Fascist stand. To go into exile meant surrendering the position he enjoyed in Hungary, but he would not compromise. "He who stays on when he could leave may be said to acquiesce tacitly in everything that is happening here," he said. Bartók came to the United States in 1940 and settled in New York City.

The American years were not happy ones. Sensitive and retiring, he felt uprooted, isolated in his new surroundings. He made some public appearances, playing his music for two pianos with his wife and onetime pupil, Ditta Pásztory-Bartók, but these barely provided for their needs.

Emigration to America

In his final years, Bartók suffered from leukemia and was no longer able to appear in public. Friends appealed for aid to the American Society of Composers, Authors, and Publishers (ASCAP), which granted funds that provided the composer with proper care in nursing homes and enabled him to continue writing to the end. A series of commissions from various sources spurred him to the composition of his last works, which rank among his finest. "The trouble is," he remarked to his doctor shortly before the end, "that I have to go with so much still to say." He died in New York City at the age of sixty-four.

Final years

The tale of the composer who spends his last days in poverty and embitterment only to be acclaimed after his death would seem to belong to the Romantic past, to the legend of Mozart and Schubert. Yet it was played out in twentieth-century America as well. Bartók's death brought about an almost immediate surge of interest in his music.

Like Stravinsky, Bartók carefully disclaimed the role of revolutionary. "In art there are only fast or slow developments. Essentially it is a matter of evolution, not revolution." Despite the newness of his musical language, his roots were in the Classical heritage, as witnessed by his adherence to the logic and beauty of Classical form.

Bartók found that Eastern European traditional music was based on ancient modes, unfamiliar scales, and nonsymmetrical rhythms. These features freed him in his composing from what he called "the tyrannical rule of the major and minor keys," and brought him to new concepts of melody,

Melody and harmony

Principal Works

Orchestral works, including *Music for Strings, Percussion, and Celesta* (1936), *Concerto for Orchestra* (1943), 2 violin concertos (1908, 1938), and 3 piano concertos (1926, 1931, 1945)

1 opera: *Bluebeard's Castle* (1918)

2 ballets: *The Wooden Prince* (1917) and *The Miraculous Mandarin* (1926)

Chamber music, including 6 string quartets (1908–39); *Contrasts* (for violin, clarinet, and piano, 1938); sonatas, duos

Piano music, including *Allegro barbaro* (1911) and *Mikrokosmos* (6 books, 1926–39)

Choral music, including *Cantata profana* (1930); folk song arrangements

Songs, including folk song arrangements

Cultural Perspective 15

BARTÓK—A ROVING COLLECTOR OF FOLK SONGS

What kinds of music did the Hungarian composer Béla Bartók hear in the Eastern European villages he visited? What are the essential ingredients of the traditional music of his native Hungary and neighboring regions? Bartók, along with fellow composer Zoltán Kodály (1882–1967), searched out and wrote down folk songs in an attempt to identify the national musics of various Eastern European cultures. The two took on this project not as composers but as folklorists who wanted to study traditional music scientifically. (Today, we would call them ethnomusicologists. The comparative study of musics of the world, focusing on the cultural context of performance, is known as ethnomusicology.) Their fieldwork, in the villages and countrysides of Eastern Europe, centered on the music of numerous distinct groups: Slovak, Romanian, Bulgarian, Serbian, Croatian, and Arab, as well as Hungarian. The many thousands of songs they collected reflect the very essence of these peoples—their social rituals (weddings, matchmaking, and dancing) and their religious ceremonies.

Bartók drew extensively in his compositions from the melodies, rhythms, and poetic structures of this rich body of traditional music. He was partial to modal scales, especially those typical of Slovak and Romanian melodies. But rhythm was the primary attraction of this body of folk music and dance. Bartók tried at times to imitate the vocal style of Hungarian music, which is based on free speech-rhythms and follows the natural inflection of the language. At other times, he used the irregular folk dance rhythms typical of Bulgarian music. These propelling rhythms were driven by additive meters built from unit groups of 2, 3, or 4. Thus instead of dividing a 9/8 meter into regular divisions of 3, he might build it from irregular groups of 2 and 3 (2 + 3 + 2 + 2, for example; see the discussion of additive meters on p. 10). From this folk legacy Bartók fashioned a unique musical style.

One type of music collected by Bartók was that of the Romanies, or Gypsies, a word that conjures up Hollywood-style images of traveling caravans full of roguish and colorful entertainers. In reality, this little-understood and itinerant group has a long and esteemed musical history. Believed to have originated in northern India, Romany peoples eventually settled throughout Europe and America. One of the most important and well-documented groups is the Hungarian Romanies, who were especially famous for their dance music, played by violinists and bagpipers. Bartók soon understood that theirs was not the traditional music he sought to collect but rather an urban, commercial style cultivated by professional performers. Beginning in the late eighteenth century, Romany bands were usually made up of two violins, a cimbalom (a zither-like instrument whose strings were struck), and a double bass. The Hungarian composer Franz Liszt, who also drew inspiration and themes from this music, publicly recognized the skill and musicianship of these performers in his book *The Gypsy in Music.* Gypsy ensembles remain popular in modern-day Hungary; they consist of professionally trained musicians playing all styles of music—art, traditional, and popular.

Terms to Note:

ethnomusicology
fieldwork
additive meter

Suggested Listening:

Bartók: *Music for Strings, Percussion, and Celesta,* Fourth Movement
Liszt: *Hungarian Rhapsody* No. 2
Folk songs collected by Bartók
Gypsy (Romany) music

Béla Bartók in 1907, recording Slovakian folk songs on an acoustic cylinder machine in the Hungarian village of Zobordarázs.

harmony, and rhythm. Bartók's harmony can be bitingly dissonant. Polytonality abounds in his work; but despite an occasional leaning toward atonality, he never wholly abandoned the principle of key.

Rhythmic innovations

Bartók's is one of the great rhythmic imaginations of modern times. His pounding, stabbing rhythms constitute the primitive aspect of his art. Like Stravinsky, Bartók sometimes changed the meter at almost every bar and frequently used syncopations and repeated patterns (ostinatos). He, along with Stravinsky, played a major role in the revitalization of European rhythm, infusing it with earthy vitality and tension.

Form

The composer was more traditional in his choices of form—his model was the Beethoven sonata, but more tightly structured. In his middle years, he came under the influence of Baroque music and turned increasingly from thinking harmonically to thinking linearly. The resulting complex texture is a masterly example of modern dissonant counterpoint.

Orchestration

Bartók departed from the orchestral sound of Strauss and Debussy to found a palette of colors all his own. His orchestration ranges from brilliant mixtures to threads of pure color that bring out the intertwining melody lines; from a hard, bright glitter to a luminous haze. A virtuoso pianist himself, he was one of the masters of modern piano writing; his works typify the twentieth-century use of the piano as an instrument of percussion and rhythm. And his six string quartets rank among the finest achievements of the century. He is best-known to the public by the three major works of his last period: the *Music for Strings, Percussion, and Celesta,* regarded by many as his masterpiece; the *Concerto for Orchestra,* a favorite with American audiences (and the work we will study); and his final effort, the Third Piano Concerto, an impassioned and broadly conceived work.

Bartók's music encompasses the diverse trends of his time: polytonality and atonality, Expressionism and Neoclassicism, folk dance and abstract music, the lyric and the dynamic. It ranges from the primitive to the intellectual, from program music to the abstract, from nationalism to the universal.

Concerto for Orchestra

In the summer of 1943, two years before his death from leukemia, Bartók received a visit from the conductor Serge Koussevitzky, who offered him a commission of $1,000 and a premiere by the Boston Symphony Orchestra for a new work. The terminally ill composer rallied his strength and set to work on the *Concerto for Orchestra,* which he completed in October of the same year. He wrote that "the mood of the work represents, apart from the jesting second movement, a gradual transition from the sternness of the first movement and the lugubrious death-song of the third to the life-assertion of the last." Of symphonic dimension, the work is called a concerto because of its tendency, as Bartók explained, "to treat the single orchestral instruments in a

---

In His Own Words

Many people think it is a comparatively easy task to write a composition on found folk tunes. . . . This way of thinking is completely erroneous. To handle folk tunes is one of the most difficult tasks; equally difficult, if not more so, than to write a major original composition. If we keep in mind that borrowing a tune means being bound by its individual peculiarity, we shall understand one part of the difficulty. Another is created by the special character of folk tune. We must penetrate it, feel it, and bring out its sharp contours by the appropriate setting. . . . It must be a work of inspiration just as much as any other composition.

concertante or soloistic manner." In other words, he used the term in its eighteenth-century meaning, although in this case, the virtuoso is the entire orchestra.

The concerto has five movements: the first, a spacious Introduction, is in sonata-allegro form and makes use of a folklike pentatonic scale; the second is a joking "game of pairs" with short sections, each of which features a different pair of wind instruments; the third, called *Elegia*, is a contemplative and rhapsodic nocturne, or "night music"; the fourth (which we will study) is a songful Intermezzo that separates the two serious movements surrounding it; and the fifth is a rhythmic and primitive-sounding folk dance set as a sonata allegro.

The fourth movement, titled *Interrupted Intermezzo*, opens with a plaintive tune in the oboe and flute whose pentatonic structure evokes a Hungarian folk song. The nonsymmetrical rhythm, alternating between 2/4 and 5/8 meter, gives the movement an unpredictable charm. A memorable broad theme is then heard in the strings, highly reminiscent of the song *You Are Lovely, You Are Beautiful, Hungary.* The mood is interrupted by a harsh clarinet melody borrowed from the Russian composer Dmitri Shostakovich's Symphony No. 7, a musical portrayal of the Nazi invasion of Russian in 1942. Bartók made an autobiographical statement in this movement: "The artist declares his love for his native land in a serenade, which is suddenly interrupted in a crude and violent manner; he is seized by rough, booted men who even break his instrument." The two opening themes eventually return in a sentimental declaration of the composer's love for his homeland.

Listening Guide 65

CD: Chr/Std 7/28–34, Sh 4/15–21
Cassette: Chr/Std 7A/9, Sh 4A/4

BARTÓK: *Interrupted Intermezzo*, from
Concerto for Orchestra   (4:20)

Date of work: 1943

Genre: Orchestral concerto

Movements:
1. Introduction, Allegro non troppo/Allegro vivace; sonata-allegro form
2. *Game of Pairs*, Allegretto scherzando; **A-B-A'** form
3. *Elegia*, Andante non troppo; in three episodes
4. *Interrupted Intermezzo*, Allegretto; rondo-like form
5. Pesante/Presto; sonata-allegro form

FOURTH MOVEMENT: *Interrupted Intermezzo*, Allegretto; rondo-like form, shifting meter (2/4, 5/8, 3/4, 5/8)

28 0:00 Dramatic 4-note introduction, unison in strings.

0:05 **A** section—plaintive, folklike tune, played by oboe in changing meter with asymmetrical rhythms:

Theme heard in flute and clarinets; dialogue continues in woodwinds and French horn.

29 1:00 **B** section—sweeping lyrical melody in violas, in shifting meter:

Violins take up lyrical theme an octave higher, with countermelody in violas; marked "calmo" (calm).

30 1:44 **A'** section—dissonant woodwinds lead to varied statement of opening theme; more chromatic.

31 2:04 **C** section—tempo picks up; clarinet introduces new theme (from Shostakovich symphony):

2:17 Dissonant punctuations in brass and woodwinds.

2:31 Theme parodied in violins.

32 2:44 Theme of **C** section introduced by tubas with theme in its original form, then heard in inversion in strings:

33 2:57 **B'** section—flowing **B** section theme returns in muted strings.

34 3:31 **A''** section—woodwinds with fragments of open theme; flute cadenza; leads into gentle closing.

552

75

The American Scene

"Armies of men . . . have turned to a better life by first hearing the sounds of a Salvation Army band. The next time you hear a Salvation Army band, no matter how humble, take off your hat."
—JOHN PHILIP SOUSA

Unlike the composers of the New England School (see p. 153), who derived much of their inspiration and techniques from European models, the two twentieth-century American masters we will study here based their works on popular and traditional music of their native land. The nationalism of Charles Ives, one of America's most original spirits, and Aaron Copland, one of its most prolific and gifted, takes us back to campground revival meetings, minstrel shows, old-time band concerts, and scenes from our Western frontiers. It is to these musical traditions that we now turn our attention.

POPULAR MUSIC IN LATE-NINETEENTH-CENTURY AMERICA

We have noted already the rise of devotional music—notably spirituals and gospel hymns—among African Americans and whites in the nineteenth century (see CP 12). Publishers reached out to the public by issuing books of folk hymns and so-called "white spirituals" with music printed in *shape-note* notation, a new, easy system designed for people lacking music literacy. The melodies of the shape-note hymns, which resemble those of the ballads and fiddle tunes of the era, are set in simple four-part harmonizations. Publications such as *The Easy Instructor* and *The Sacred Harp* disseminated this repertory from New England to rural as well as urban audiences in the South and Midwest, where the hymns were used in singing schools, churches, and social gatherings. As a result, a body of hymns and anthems has been preserved not only in devotional music books, but through a continued oral tradition; some of these works remain popular even today in gospel and contemporary Christian music arrangements.

Although the composers and lyricists of nineteenth-century gospel hymns

The title page to Stephen Foster's song Jeanie with the Light Brown Hair *(1854). (New York Public Library for the Performing Arts)*

Stephen Foster

are mostly forgotten today, one prophet of indigenous American song remains a household name: Stephen Foster (1826–1864), known for his lyrical ballads, minstrel show tunes, and poignant plantation songs. Born on the Fourth of July, on the fiftieth anniversary of the signing of the Declaration of Independence, Foster strove to write a simpler music that could be understood by all. In this effort, he was successful. Among his most popular songs are *Oh, Susanna* (1848) and *Camptown Races* (1850), both minstrel-show songs that remain in the common tradition; the well-known and highly nostalgic plantation songs *Old Folks at Home* (1851; the official state song of Florida) and *My Old Kentucky Home* (1853; the state song of Kentucky); and the timeless ballads *Jeanie with the Light Brown Hair* (1854) and *Beautiful Dreamer* (1864), the first a lament on the lost happiness in his marriage and the second, his last song, written in the style of an Italian air.

Although there is no evidence that Foster took a political stand on the abolition of slavery, his songs gradually moved from a depiction of African Americans as simple, good-hearted people, in stock minstrel-show tradition, to a more realistic image of a people experiencing pain, joy, and sorrow. *Angelina Baker* (1850), for example, is a slave's lament for a lover sent away, and *Oh! Boys, Carry Me 'Long* (1851) makes a request commonly heard in spirituals, for deliverance from pain through death. Stephen Foster, America's most beloved songwriter, died an alcoholic in 1864, alone and in poverty.

Concert bands

America's vernacular tradition included instrumental music as well, particularly performances by concert bands. An outgrowth of the British military band, wind groups thrived throughout the United States. These groups first served as regimental bands for colonial militia during the War of Independence; some continued after the war, and new ones were founded as well. One, the U.S. Marine Band (now called The President's Own), formed in 1798, comprised two oboes, two clarinets, two French horns, bassoon, and drums. The refinement of keyed brass instruments by the Belgian Adolphe Sax (inventor of the saxophone) revolutionized the makeup of bands; thus, by the Civil War era (1861–65), both Northern and Southern regiments marched to the sounds of brass groups. Many bands reorganized after the war as concert and dance ensembles; such was the case with the Union Army group under the direction of the virtuoso cornet player and bandmaster Patrick S. Gilmore. It was reportedly his Union band that first played the rousing *When Johnny Comes Marching Home*, to welcome back soldiers from North and South alike.

America's greatest bandmaster was undoubtedly John Philip Sousa (1854–1932), who conducted the U.S. Marine Band from 1880 to 1892 and later formed the incomparable Sousa's Band. Known as "the march king," Sousa wrote over 130 marches for band, as well as dance music and operettas. He toured North America and Europe extensively with his group, delighting audiences with his *Semper Fidelis* (1888), *The Washington Post* (1889), the ever-popular *Stars and Stripes Forever* (1897), and band arrangements of ragtime, the newest dance rage (see p. 568). Almost single-handedly, Sousa created a national music for America that continues to resonate in its concert halls, on its streets, in its sports stadiums, and in the hearts of its people.

John Philip Sousa

One New England musician born into this rich environment of inspirational hymns, patriotic songs, and especially brass bands—his father was a bandmaster—was Charles Ives, who never forgot his nineteenth-century vernacular heritage even while nurturing very modern tendencies.

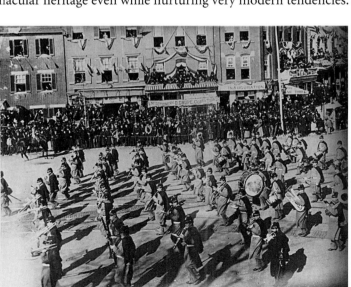

The United States Marine Band marches in parade, with its director, John Philip Sousa (1854–1932), playing cornet (in right front). (Harry Ransom Humanities Research Center, University of Texas, Austin)

Charles Ives

Career in business

Renown as composer

CHARLES IVES: HIS LIFE AND MUSIC

"The future of music may not lie in music itself, but rather in the way it encourages and extends, rather than limits, the aspirations and ideals of the people, in the way it makes itself a part with the finer things that humanity does and dreams of."

Charles Edward Ives (1874–1954) had to wait many years for recognition. Today he stands as the first great American composer of the twentieth century, and one of the most original spirits of his time.

Ives was born in Danbury, Connecticut. At thirteen, he held a job as church organist and arranged music for the various ensembles conducted by his father. At twenty, he entered Yale, where he studied composition with Horatio Parker. Ives's talent for music was evident throughout his four years at Yale; yet when he had to choose a career, he decided against a professional life in music, suspecting that society would not pay him for the kind of music he wanted to compose. He was right.

Ives entered the business world, and two decades later, he was head of the largest insurance agency in the country. The years it took him to achieve this success—roughly from the age of twenty-one to forty-two—were the years when he also wrote his music. He composed at night, on weekends, and during vacations, working in isolation, concerned only to set down the sounds he heard in his head.

The few conductors and performers he tried to interest in his compositions pronounced them unplayable. After a number of these rebuffs, Ives gave up showing his manuscripts. When he felt the need to hear how a piece sounded, he hired a few musicians to play it through. Except for these rare and inadequate performances, Ives heard his music only in his imagination, and continued to pile up one score after another in his Connecticut barn. When well-meaning friends suggested that he try to write music people would like, he could only respond, "I can't do it—I hear something else!"

Ives's double life as a business executive by day and composer by night finally took its toll. In 1918, when he was forty-four, he suffered a physical breakdown that left his heart damaged. Although he lived almost forty years longer, he produced nothing further of importance.

When Ives recovered, he faced the realization that the world of professional musicians was irrevocably closed to his ideas. Feeling that he owed it to his music to make it available to those who might be less conservative, he privately printed the *Concord* Sonata for piano and the *Essays Before a Sonata*, a kind of elaborate program note that formulated his views on life and art. These were followed by the *114 Songs*. The three volumes, which were distributed free to libraries, music critics, and whoever else asked for them, had no impact whatsoever on the concertgoing public. But they gained Ives the support of other experimental composers who were also struggling to make their way in an indifferent music world. The tide finally turned when the American pianist John Kirkpatrick, at a recital in New York's Town Hall in January 1939, played the *Concord* Sonata. Ives was then sixty-five. The piece was repeated several weeks later by Kirkpatrick and scored a triumph. The next morning, the critic Lawrence Gilman hailed the *Concord* Sonata as "the greatest music composed by an American."

Ives had already begun to exert an influence on the younger generation of composers, who found in his music a realization of their own ideals. Now he was "discovered" by the general public and proclaimed as the grand old man of American music. In 1947, his Third Symphony was performed and won a Pulitzer Prize. This story of delayed recognition was carried by newspapers throughout the country. Ives awoke at seventy-three to find himself famous. He died in New York City at the age of eighty.

Both personally and artistically, Ives was rooted in the New England tradition of plain living and high thinking that came to flower in the idealism of such writers as Nathaniel Hawthorne (*The Scarlet Letter*), Louisa May Alcott (*Little Women*), Ralph Waldo Emerson (*Essays*), and Henry David Thoreau (*Walden*). The sources of his tonal imagery are found in the music of his childhood: hymn tunes and traditional songs, the town band at holiday parades, the fiddlers at Saturday night dances, patriotic songs, sentimental parlor ballads, the melodies of Stephen Foster, and the medleys heard at country fairs and in small theaters.

New England tradition

Ives's keen ear caught the sound of untrained voices singing a hymn together—some, in their eagerness, straining and sharpening the pitch, others just missing it and flatting, so that in place of the single tone there was a cluster of tones that made a deliciously dissonant chord. Some voices were a trifle

Principal Works

Orchestral music, including 4 symphonies (1898, 1902, 1904, 1916), *Three Places in New England* (1914), *The Unanswered Question* (1908), and *The Fourth of July* (from *A Symphony: New England Holidays*, 1913)

Chamber music, including 2 string quartets and 4 violin sonatas

Piano music, including 2 sonatas (No. 2, *Concord*, 1915)

Choral music and many songs, including *General William Booth Enters into Heaven* (1914) and *The Things Our Fathers Loved* (1917)

Cultural Perspective 16

MUSIC AND THE PATRIOTIC SPIRIT

Have you ever been moved to tears by a patriotic song—perhaps your national anthem? Music has often fueled emotions, inciting acts of heroism and patriotism that are remembered for generations through song. We can hear several traditional songs of the Civil War echoing through the twentieth-century compositions of Charles Ives. Many tunes well-known to most of us had their origins in wartime as well. The colonial troops of the American Revolution marched to the fife-and-drum strains of *Yankee Doodle. Dixie* ("I wish I was in the land of cotton," written, ironically, by a Northerner) became a rallying cry of the Civil War's Confederacy sounded against the North's *Battle Hymn of the Republic* (a poem by author Julia Ward Howe, sung to the tune of *John Brown's Body*).

In the early twentieth century, songwriter George M. Cohan was so moved by the U.S. declaration of war against Germany in 1917 that he wrote *Over There* ("Send the word, over there, that the Yanks are coming"), a catchy song that caught on immediately with the American public and soldiers during the First World War. Likewise, songwriter Irving Berlin joined with singer Kate Smith in a 1938 radio broadcast on Armistice Day (now Veterans Day) to build patriotic support in the United States as the Second World War was looming. The song that captured the hearts of millions then was *God Bless America*, now considered by many the country's "second national anthem."

The national anthems of many countries, including the United States, were the direct result of wartime emotions. The lyrics of *The Star-Spangled Banner* were written in 1814 by a Baltimore attorney named Francis Scott Key during the English bombardment of Fort McHenry (a famous battle during the War of 1812). Key was aboard a small ship in the Chesapeake Bay, nervously watching the American flag over the fort and knowing that if it went down, so too would his beloved Baltimore. Thus the flag-inspired lyrics—"Oh, say, can you see, by the dawn's early light, what so proudly we hailed at the twilight's last gleaming? Whose broad stripes and bright stars through the perilous fight"—which he adapted to the disjunct tune of an English drinking song that now everyone finds difficult to sing. (The song was not adopted as the U.S. national anthem until 1931.) France's *La Marseillaise* is another example of a revolutionary anthem ("Allons, enfants de la patrie! Le jour de gloire est arrivé," or "Arise, children of the homeland! The day of glory has arrived"), as is Mexico's *Mexicanos, al grito de guerra* (*Mexicans, to the War Cry*), a spirited song of independence.

Happily, the patriotic spirit is alive in peacetime as well. It has produced such notable anthems as Britain's *God Save the*

Queen (or *King*)—the same tune to which we sing *America* ("My country, 'tis of thee") and the stately *Emperor's Hymn* by Haydn. The latter was originally adopted as the Austrian anthem but serves today as the national song of recently unified Germany, with the text "Einigkeit und Recht und Freiheit," or "Unity and right and liberty." Canada also recently adopted an anthem that draws together its multiethnic population—*O Canada*, written in 1880 by the French-Canadian Calixa Lavallée, was named the country's national hymn (in French and English) in 1980. The universality of music is illustrated in Israel's anthem, *Hatikvah* (*The Hope*), a moving poem of the Jewish people returning to their ancient homeland in the late nineteenth century, set to the melody of a haunting Bohemian folk song. In times of national crisis or pride, whether responding to a war or an Olympic victory, these memorable songs resound deep in the soul of a people.

Suggested Listening:

National anthems (of the United States, France, Mexico, Canada, Israel, Great Britain, Germany)

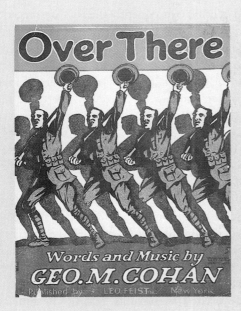

Sheet music for Over There, *by George M. Cohan, written to inspire American troops fighting in the First World War. The cover design is by the famous American illustrator* **Norman Rockwell.**

American Gothic, *by* **Grant Wood** *(1892–1942), is an example of regionalism, celebrating rural life in the United States. The painting is one of the most recognized in the world.* (Art Institute of Chicago)

ahead of the beat, others lagged behind; consequently the rhythm sagged and turned into a jumble of polyrhythms. Ives also heard the pungent clash of dissonance when two bands in a parade, each playing a different tune in a different key, came close enough together to overlap; he heard the effect of *quarter tones* (an interval half the size of a half step) when fiddlers at a country dance went a bit off pitch in their excitement. He remembered the sound of a wheezy harmonium (a reed organ) accompanying church hymns a trifle out of tune.

All these dissonances, Ives realized, were not exceptions; they were the norm of traditional American musical life. Thus he found his way to such

Polytonality and polyrhythm

concepts as polytonality, atonality, polyharmony, chord clusters based on the interval of a second, and polyrhythms. And this occurred in the last years of the nineteenth century, when Schoenberg was still writing in a post-Wagnerian idiom, and neither Stravinsky nor Bartók had yet embarked on a career in music. This lone musician, isolated from the public and his fellow composers, developed conceptions far ahead of his time and accurately forecast the paths that twentieth-century music would follow.

Orchestral and other works

The central position in Ives's orchestral music is held by the four symphonies. Among his other orchestral works are *Three Places in New England*, *The Unanswered Question*, and *A Symphony: New England Holidays*, a cycle of four symphonic poems. The Sonata No. 2 for piano—"Concord, Mass., 1840–1860"—which occupied him from 1909 to 1915, reflects various aspects of New England's culture. Its four movements are named after distinguished American authors: *Emerson, Hawthorne, The Alcotts*, and *Thoreau*. Ives also wrote a variety of songs, as well as chamber, choral, and piano compositions.

The Things Our Fathers Loved

One of Ives's most nostalgic songs, *The Things Our Fathers Loved* transports us back to another time in America's history. The text, written by the composer, reminisces on the music of bygone days in a medley of familiar tunes—some patriotic, some religious, some from the popular tradition—tinged with his own bittersweet harmonies. The song begins with a hint of *Dixie*, from Civil War times; this is quickly followed by a few notes of the Stephen Foster favorite *My Old Kentucky Home*. An American Protestant hymn called *Nettleton* is alluded to for a few bars, and then, as the tempo picks up, another Civil War rallying cry is sounded—*The Battle Cry of Freedom*, written in 1861 by George F. Root in response to President Lincoln's appeal for Northern army volunteers ("Yes, we'll rally 'round the flag"). For the climax, Ives quotes a lengthy section from the nineteenth-century gospel hymn *Sweet By-and-By*, sung at revival and prayer meetings (see Listening Guide 66 for these tunes). Throughout, the ear is jarred by "wrong" turns of lines and by a dissonant, and rather independent, piano part. The result is a song that illustrates well Ives's wholly original musical idiom.

The works of Charles Ives are now firmly established in contemporary concert life. Like the familiar melodies he cites in his music, he has become an American classic.

In His Own Words

Beauty in music is too often confused with something that lets the ear lie back in an easy chair. Many sounds that we are used to do not bother us, and for that reason we are inclined to call them beautiful. Frequently—possibly almost invariably—analytical and impersonal tests will show that when a new or unfamiliar work is accepted as beautiful on its first hearing, its fundamental quality is one that tends to put the mind to sleep.

Listening Guide 66

CD: Chr/Std 7/20–21
Cassette: Chr/Std 7A/7

IVES: *The Things Our Fathers Loved* (1:42)

Date: 1917 (published 1922)

Text: By Charles Ives

Medium: Voice and piano

Basis: Various American tunes (*Dixie, My Old Kentucky Home, Nettleton, The Battle Cry of Freedom, Sweet By-and-By*)

		Text	Description
20	0:00	I think there must be a place in the soul all made of tunes, of tunes of long ago;	Begins slowly, quoting opening of *Dixie*. One phrase of *My Old Kentucky Home* quoted.
	0:24	I hear the organ on the Main Street corner Aunt Sarah humming Gospels; summer evenings,	Rhythm from *My Old Kentucky Home* with new intervals. Reference to the hymn *Nettleton*.
21	0:53	the village cornet band, playing in the square. The town's Red, White, and Blue, all Red, White, and Blue. Now! Hear the songs! I know not what are the words, but they sing in my soul of the things our Fathers loved.	Cites opening of *The Battle Cry of Freedom*. Pace quickens. Repeats reference to *The Battle Cry of Freedom*. On the word "Blue," citation of complete chorus of *Sweet By-and-By*; continues until end.

Tunes cited compared with excerpts from song

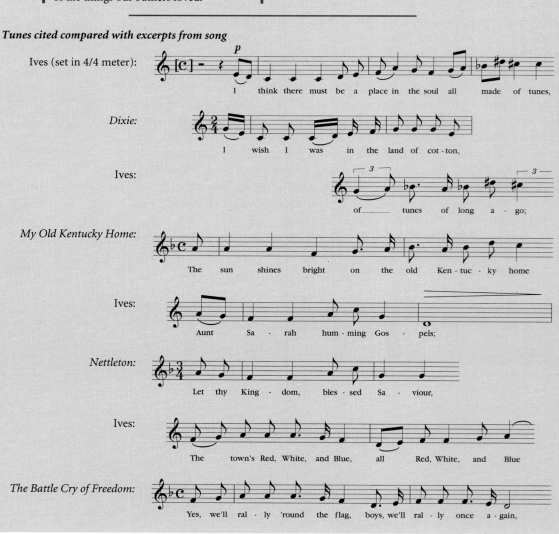

562

AARON COPLAND: HIS LIFE AND MUSIC

"I no longer feel the need of seeking out conscious Americanism. Because we live here and work here, we can be certain that when our music is mature it will also be American in quality."

Aaron Copland (1900–1990) has been generally recognized as the representative figure among contemporary American composers. In his music, he achieves the clarity and sense of balance that is regarded as the essence of the Classical temperament.

Copland was born "on a street in Brooklyn that can only be described as drab. . . . Music was the last thing anyone would have connected with it." During his early twenties, he studied in Paris with the famous teacher Nadia Boulanger; he was her first full-time American pupil. When Boulanger was invited to give concerts in New York, she asked Copland to write a work for her. He obliged with the *Symphony for Organ and Orchestra*. After the first performance, in 1925, conductor Walter Damrosch found it necessary to calm down his subscribers (contemporary American music was still a novelty to New York audiences). "If a young man at the age of twenty-five," he announced from the stage of Carnegie Hall, "can write a symphony like that, in five years he will be ready to commit murder." Luckily, Damrosch's prophecy was not fulfilled.

In his growth as a composer, Copland mirrored the dominant trends of his time. After his return from Paris, he turned to the jazz idiom, a phase that culminated in his brilliant Piano Concerto. Then followed a period during

Aaron Copland

Jazz idiom

Cultural Perspective 17

COPLAND LOOKS TO THE WILD WEST AND SOUTH OF THE BORDER

We will see that composer Aaron Copland was inspired by songs of the Western frontier, although he was born and raised in Brooklyn, New York. There is a wide repertory of traditional tunes of the West that have come down to us today. Some tell of famous outlaws such as Billy the Kid and Jesse James or of high-stakes gamblers like Wild Bill Hickok; others are work songs (*Git Along, Little Dogies*) or laments of death on the trail or in gunfights (*The Streets of Laredo*). In short, they narrate the way of life of the American cowboy. Traditional songs such as *Goodbye, Old Paint* suggest that a person's horse was not only a tool of the trade, but a trusted companion as well. ("Old paint" refers to a pinto horse, *pinto* being Spanish for "spotted"; see p. 25 for the tune and words.)

The Hollywood image of the American cowboy, with John Wayne always winning the fights against the bad guys, is somewhat distorted. Many of those roving the American frontier were Southerners— whites and African Americans—who lost their homes and families in the Civil War. It is through an ex-slave named Charley Willis that the song *Goodbye, Old Paint* is preserved today; Willis taught it to a ranch hand who, in old age, recorded it for folk song collector John Lomax. Other cowboys were Native Americans, and many were Chicanos (called *vaqueros*, the Spanish word for "cowboys"). Several commonly used words derive from the early days of Spanish colonization in the West: "lariat" (a rope) comes from *la reata*, and "chaps" (leather leg coverings) is short for *chaparreras*.

What of women in the West? Several were legendary: the expert markswoman Annie Oakley was originally from Cincinnati, at the edge of the frontier, and traveled as part of a Wild West show, while Calamity Jane came from the Dakota Territory (the Dakotas were not yet states) and reportedly could outshoot any man. (You may know that Annie Oakley inspired the well-known 1946 Broadway musical *Annie Get Your Gun*, by Irving Berlin.) Another heroine of frontier days was Emily West, an African-American woman who played a key role in the Battle of San Jacinto, in which the Texans defeated the Mexican army of General Antonio Lopez de Santa Ana. It is she, not a flower, who is the subject of *The Yellow Rose of Texas* ("the yellow rose of Texas beats the belles of Tennessee"—the allusion to "yellow" refers to the fact that she was of mixed Caucasian and African-American ancestry). Many more unnamed women braved the long and difficult trip west to establish a new life for their families. The familiar song *Sweet Betsy from Pike* praises one such courageous woman ("Oh, don't you remember Sweet Betsy from Pike, who crossed the big mountains with her lover Ike?").

Cowboy songs have been preserved for

us today through the efforts of folk song collectors and the media, especially the singing cowboys that were popular in 1930s and 1940s movies (Gene Autry, Roy Rogers, and Tex Ritter).

The lore of the West has intrigued artists as well, and several have left us vivid images of life of this earlier era. Most famous are the American painters Winslow Homer (1836–1910) and Frederic Remington (1861–1909), the latter well-known for his rough-and-tumble cowboys and cavalrymen and for his much-prized bronze sculptures like *Bronco Buster*.

Aaron Copland also looked to Latin America for traditional music. He toured Mexico and South America, visiting with such native composers as Carlos Chávez (1899–1978) and Alberto Ginastera (1916–1983), both of whom combined indigenous musics with European styles in their own compositions. Copland's orchestral work *El salón México* (1936) draws on the colorful sounds of Mexican dance music, as does his ballet suite *Billy the Kid*. This latter work incorporates the jarabe, a rural Mexican dance and musical form that has various sections in different tempos and meters. An exhibition dance, the jarabe is performed by a couple attired in gala dress—the man with wide-brimmed hat and chaps, the woman in a multi-colored, sequined skirt and shawl. Today, the jarabe is an urban form, accompanied by mariachi groups (with trumpets, violins, guitar, and guitarron, or bass guitar). Mariachi bands, originally from western Mexico, can be heard today throughout that country and in parts of the United States as well.

Terms to Note:

jarabe
mariachi

Suggested Listening:

Copland: *Street in a Frontier Town* from
   Billy the Kid, or *El salón México*
Traditional songs of the Old West
Mexican music (mariachi band, jarabe)
Works by Carlos Chávez or Alberto Ginastera

Copland's music for Billy the Kid *is as firmly rooted in uniquely American traditions as the cowboy bronzes of* **Frederic Remington** *(1861–1909), like* Bronco Buster. *(Amon Carter Museum, Fort Worth)*

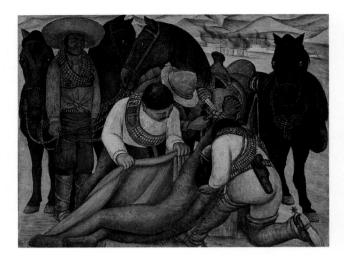

The murals of the Mexican painter **Diego Rivera** *(1886–1957) construct an eloquent narrative of his country's history that speaks to all peoples of Mexico.* The Liberation of Peon *(1931).* (Philadelphia Museum of Art; © Estate of Diego Rivera/licensed by VAGA, New York)

Neoclassical period

which Copland the Neoclassicist experimented with the abstract and produced the Piano Variations, *Short Symphony,* and *Statements for Orchestra.* "During these years I began to feel an increasing dissatisfaction with the relations [between] the music-loving public and the living composer," Copland wrote. "It seemed to me that we composers were in danger of working in a vacuum." He realized that a new public for contemporary music was being created by the radio, phonograph, and film scores. "It made no sense to ignore them and to continue writing as if they did not exist. I felt that it was worth the effort to see if I couldn't say what I had to say in the simplest possible terms." In this fashion, Copland was led to what became a most significant development after the 1930s: his attempt to simplify the new music so that it would communicate to a large public.

The 1930s and 1940s saw the creation of works that established Copland's

Principal Works

Orchestral music, including 3 symphonies, Piano Concerto (1926), *Short Symphony* (1933), *Statements for Orchestra* (1933–35), *El salón México* (1936), *A Lincoln Portrait* (1942), *Fanfare for the Common Man* (1942), and *Connotations for Orchestra* (1962)

3 ballets: *Billy the Kid* (1938), *Rodeo* (1942), *Appalachian Spring* (1944)

Film scores, including *The City* (1939), *Of Mice and Men* 1939), *Our Town* (1940), *The Red Pony* (1948), and *The Heiress* (1948)

Piano music, including Piano Variations (1930)

Chamber music; choral music and songs

popularity. *El salón México* (1936) is an orchestral piece based on Mexican melodies and rhythms. The three ballets, *Billy the Kid, Rodeo*, and *Appalachian Spring*, continue to delight an international audience. (The choreographer for *Rodeo*, Agnes de Mille, made innovations that opened a new era in American theater dance.) Among his film scores are *Quiet City, Of Mice and Men, Our Town, The Red Pony*, and *The Heiress*, the last of which brought him an Academy Award. He wrote two important works during wartime: *A Lincoln Portrait*, for speaker and chorus, with texts drawn from Lincoln's own speeches, and the Third Symphony. In *Connotations for Orchestra*, Copland clearly demonstrated that he could handle twelve-tone techniques.

Billy the Kid

For the ballet based on the saga of Billy the Kid, Copland produced one of his freshest scores. Several classic cowboy tunes are used in this work as a point of departure for his own creations; they flavor his music but are assimilated into his personal style rather than quoted literally.

Billy the Kid—the Brooklyn-born William Bonney—had a brief but intense career as a desperado and soon became one of the legends of the Wild West. The ballet touches on the chief episodes of his life. We see him first as a boy of twelve; when his mother is killed by a stray bullet in a street brawl, he stabs the man responsible for her death. Later, during a card game, he is accused of cheating and kills the accuser. Captured after a gun battle, he is put in jail, but he murders his jailer and gets away. A romantic interlude ensues when Billy joins his Mexican sweetheart in the desert. But he is tracked down and killed by his childhood friend Sheriff Pat Garrett. At the close, we hear a lament on the death of the notorious outlaw.

The concert suite Copland put together contains about two-thirds of the ballet. *The Open Prairie*, which serves as a prologue, evokes a remote and spacious landscape, a poetic symbol of all that is vast and unchanging. We will hear the first scene, *Street in a Frontier Town*, in which, as Copland explained, he used such tunes of the Wild West as *Goodbye, Old Paint; The Old Chisholm Trail; Git Along, Little Dogies; The Streets of Laredo*; and *Great Grand-Dad*. (See Listening Guide 67 for details.) But the composer decked them out with polyrhythms, polytonal harmonies, and dissonances made more striking because they fall on accented beats. The result is a music of powerful rhythmic thrust and vigorous physical activity, bursting with energy and excitement as it mounts to a *fortissimo* climax.

Music has a glorious way of leaping over barriers of race, religion, and nation. And so it was given to the son of Russian-Jewish immigrants growing up on the streets of Brooklyn to create a musical image of the American West, the prairie, and the cowboy that is heard and recognized worldwide.

In His Own Words

To explain the creative musician's basic objective in elementary terms, I would say that a composer writes music to express and communicate and put down in permanent form certain thoughts, emotions and states of being. These thoughts and emotions are gradually formed by the contact of the composer's personality with the world in which he lives. He expresses these thoughts (musical ones . . .) in the musical language of his own time. The resultant work of art should speak to men and women of the artist's own time with a directness and immediacy of communicative power that no previous art expression can give.

Listening Guide 67

CD: Chr/Std 8/9–13, Sh 4/22–26
Cassette: Chr/Std 8A/2, Sh 4A/5

COPLAND: *Billy the Kid*, Scene 1,
Street in a Frontier Town   (6:24)

Date of work: 1938 (ballet first performed); 1939 (orchestral suite)

Genre: Orchestral suite from ballet

Basis: Actual story of outlaw William Bonney (called Billy the Kid)

Sections of orchestral suite:

The Open Prairie	Gun Battle
Street in a Frontier Town	Celebration (after Billy's capture)
Prairie Night (Card Game at Night)	Billy's Death

Copland's notes on the ballet: *The ballet begins and ends on the open prairie. The first scene is a street in a frontier town. Cowboys saunter into town, some on horseback, others on foot with their lassos; some Mexican women do a jarabe, which is interrupted by a fight between two drunks. Attracted by the gathering crowd, Billy is seen for the first time, a boy of twelve, with his mother. The brawl turns ugly, guns are drawn, and in some unaccountable way, Billy's mother is killed. Without an instant's hesitation, in cold fury, Billy draws a knife from a cowhand's sheath and stabs his mother's slayers. His short but famous career has begun. In swift succession we see episodes in Billy's later life—at night, under the stars, in a quiet card game with his outlaw friends, hunted by a posse led by his former friend Pat Garrett, in a gun battle. A drunken celebration takes place when he is captured. Billy makes one of his legendary escapes from prison. Tired and worn out in the desert, Billy rests with his girl. Finally the posse catches up with him.*

Street in a Frontier Town; Moderato

9   0:00   Piccolo solo, with tune *Great Grand-Dad:*

      Other woodwinds join in dialogue.

0:21   New tune (paraphrased from *Git Along, Little Dogies*) in oboe and trumpet, almost in unison, with dissonance on strong beat (x):

0:45   *Great Grand-Dad* heard in piccolo, while strings enter with dissonant tune from above.

0:57   Alternation of two tunes—the first in woodwinds and strings, second in trombones.

10   1:10   Trumpet, with new, shifting-meter tune (4 + 3 + 4 + 3), and accompaniment in opposite meter (3 + 4 + 3 + 4):

1:15   Strings take up shifting-meter tune; brass and strings return to dissonant tune, which dies out.

1:48   Large chords played *fortissimo* in full orchestra, punctuated by bass drum; disjunct tune based on *The Old Chisolm Trail*.

11   1:58   Quick dance tune in strings in 4/4 (loosely based on *The Old Chisolm Trail*), accompanied by syncopated woodblock:

2:19   Trombones enter with tune from *The Streets of Laredo*:

2:28   Dance tune continues, with interjections of earlier dissonant tune in oboe and trumpet.

2:57   Opening tune heard in piccolo and clarinet, more animated, with grace notes and harmonics in strings and sleigh bells, followed by slower, legato melody in low strings and brass (based on *The Streets of Laredo*).

12   3:27   Mexican dance (jarabe) and finale; trumpet, with melody in 5/8 meter (*based on Git Along, Little Dogies*), accompanied by woodblock and gourd (accents shown with x's):

13   4:15   Violins enter with tune *Goodbye, Old Paint* in legato, 3/4 meter; alternate with oboe playing verse of same cowboy song:

5:24   *Goodbye, Old Paint* continues in fabric of complex polyphony; full orchestra plays tune, alternating chorus and verse; transformed as it builds to climax.

5:57   3 loud chords, followed by 2 low notes (gunshots), end section.

Popular Styles

76

Blues and Early Jazz

All riddles are blues,
And all blues are sad,
And I'm only mentioning
Some blues I've had.—MAYA ANGELOU

We have seen that a diversity of cultures met in the great melting pot that is America. Blues and jazz, rooted in the music of African Americans, were part and parcel of the American scene, and they captured the imagination of the world.

Jazz refers to a music created mainly by African Americans around the turn of the twentieth century as they blended elements drawn from African musics with the popular and art traditions of the West. One of the most influential early styles was ragtime, which gained popularity in instrumental ensemble arrangements by Scott Joplin.

SCOTT JOPLIN AND RAGTIME

Known as "the king of ragtime," Scott Joplin (1868–1917) was one of the first black Americans to gain importance as a composer. He was born in Texarkana, Texas, to a musical family. His father, a former slave, played violin, and his mother sang and played banjo, as did his brothers. Joplin began his musical instruction on the guitar and bugle, but soon showed such a gift for improvisation that he was given free piano lessons. He left home when he was only fourteen, after the death of his mother, and traveled throughout the Mississippi Valley playing honky-tonks and piano bars, and absorbing the current styles of folk and popular music. In 1885, he arrived in St. Louis, then the center of a growing ragtime tradition.

Ragtime (or "ragged rhythm") was originally a piano style marked by highly syncopated melodies. It first gained public notice as a form of instrumental ensemble music when Joplin and his small orchestra performed at the 1893 World Exposition in Chicago. Around this time, Joplin sought more formal musical training at the George R. Smith College in Sedalia, Missouri, where he studied music theory and composition. It was at a club in Sedalia that Joplin, surrounded by a circle of black entertainers, introduced his *Maple Leaf Rag*. Fame came to the composer in 1899, when the sheet music of the piece sold a million copies. Four years later, he wrote the first of his two operas, *A Guest of Honor*, but the work was never performed during his lifetime and is now lost. In 1906, Joplin moved from St. Louis to Chicago and ultimately to New York, where he was active as a teacher, composer, and performer. As an aid to amateur musicians, he published a series of piano exercises (1908) that offered drills for the tricky rhythmic patterns typical of the style.

Joplin strove to elevate ragtime from a purely improvised style to a more serious art form that could stand on a level with European art music and possibly become the basis for larger forms such as opera or the symphony. Realizing that he must lead the way in this merger of styles, he began work on his opera *Treemonisha*, which he finished in 1911. But the opera, produced in a scaled-down performance, was not well received, and Joplin fell into a severe depression from which he never fully recovered; he died in New York City on April 1, 1917. *Treemonisha* remained virtually unknown until its extremely successful revival in 1972 by the Houston Grand Opera. In 1976, nearly sixty years after his death, Joplin was awarded a Pulitzer Prize for his masterpiece.

Scott Joplin is best remembered today for his piano rags, some of which were recorded by the composer himself and preserved on punched paper rolls made in 1910 on a Steinway player piano. The rags reflect Joplin's preoccupation with classical forms. They exhibit balanced phrasing and key structures, combined with catchy, imaginative melodies. Like earlier dance forms, they are built in clear-cut sections, their patterns of repetition reminiscent of those heard in the marches of John Philip Sousa, whose own band frequently played arrangements of Joplin rags.

The *Maple Leaf Rag*, perhaps the best-known rag ever composed, is typical in its regular, sectional form. Quite simply, the dance presents a series of sixteen-measure phrases, called *strains*, in a moderate duple meter; each strain is

Scott Joplin

In His Own Words

What is scurrilously called ragtime is an invention that is here to stay. That is now conceded by all classes of musicians. . . . All publications masquerading under the name of ragtime are not the genuine article. . . . That real ragtime of the higher class is rather difficult to play is a painful truth which most pianists have discovered. Syncopations are no indication of light or trashy music. . . . Joplin ragtime is destroyed by careless or imperfect rendering, and very often players lose the effect entirely by playing too fast.

repeated before the next one begins. The *Maple Leaf Rag* established the form, with four strains; in this work, the opening idea returns once before a shift to the subdominant key area in the third strain (see Listening Guide 68). As in most rags, the listener's interest is focused throughout on the syncopated rhythms of the melodies, played by the right hand, which are supported by an easy, steady duple-rhythm accompaniment in the left hand.

Joplin's sophisticated piano rags brought him worldwide recognition. Their continued popularity nearly a century later confirms that they are the work of a master.

Listening Guide 68

CD: Chr/Std 7/11–15, Sh 4/27–31
Cassette: Chr/Std 7A/4, Sh 4A/6

JOPLIN: *Maple Leaf Rag*   (3:21)

Date of work: Published 1899

Genre: Piano rag

Performance: Piano roll of Joplin on 1910 Steinway player piano

Form: Sectional dance form; 4 sections, or strains (each of 16 measures), with repeats
(**A-A-B-B-A-C-C-D-D**)

Tempo: Tempo di marcia; 2/4 meter

| 11 | 0:00 | **A**—strain 1—syncopated middle-range ascending melody, accompanied by steady bass; begins with upbeat in bass; in A-flat major; performer adds ornamental flourishes in left hand: |

| | 0:22 | **A**—strain 1 repeated. |

| 12 | 0:44 | **B**—strain 2—similar syncopated pattern in melody; begins in higher range and descends; steady bass accompaniment; in A-flat major: |

| | 1:06 | **B**—strain 2 repeated. |

| 13 | 1:28 | **A**—return to strain 1. |

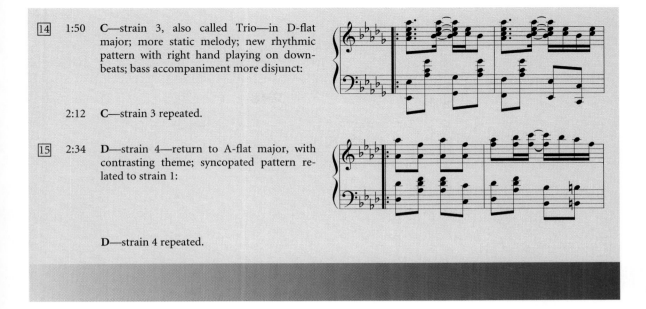

14　1:50　**C**—strain 3, also called Trio—in D-flat major; more static melody; new rhythmic pattern with right hand playing on down-beats; bass accompaniment more disjunct:

　　2:12　**C**—strain 3 repeated.

15　2:34　**D**—strain 4—return to A-flat major, with contrasting theme; syncopated pattern related to strain 1:

　　　　　D—strain 4 repeated.

BLUES AND NEW ORLEANS JAZZ

Blues is a truly American form of folk music based on a simple, repetitive po-etic-musical structure. The term refers to a mood as well as a harmonic pro-gression, which is usually twelve or sixteen bars in length. Characteristic is the *blue note*, a slight drop in pitch on the third, fifth, or seventh tone of the scale. A blues text typically consists of a three-line stanza of which the first two lines are identical. Its vocal style was derived from the work songs of Southern blacks.

Blues is a fundamental form in jazz. The music we call jazz was born in New Orleans through the fusion of such African-American elements as rag-time and blues with other traditional styles—spirituals, work songs, and shouts. (For more on the roots of jazz, see CP 18.) In all of these styles, the art of improvisation was crucially important. Performers made up their parts as they went along, often with several musicians improvising at the same time. This seemingly chaotic practice worked because all the players knew the basic rules—the tempo, the form, the harmonic progression, and the order in which instruments were to be featured. A twelve-bar blues progression fol-lowed a standard harmonic pattern (see p. 572).

New Orleans jazz actually depended on the players' multiple improvisa-tion to create a polyphonic texture. The trumpet or cornet played the melody or an embellished version; the clarinet was often featured in a countermelody above the main tune; the trombone improvised below the trumpet and sig-

Blues

New Orleans jazz

Twelve-Bar Blues Progression

Measure no.:	1	2	3	4
Harmony:	I (Tonic)			
Text:	I woke up this morn-ing	with an aw-ful ach-ing	head _____.	

	5	6	7	8
	IV (Subdominant)		I (Tonic)	
	I woke up this morn-ing	with an aw-ful ach-ing	head _____.	

	9	10	11	12
	V (Dominant)		I (Tonic)	
	My new man had left me just a	room and an emp-ty	bed _____.	

naled the chord changes; and the rhythm section—consisting of string bass or tuba, guitar or banjo, and drums—provided rhythmic and harmonic support. Among the greats of New Orleans jazz were Joseph "King" Oliver (cornet), Sidney Bechet (soprano saxophone), Ferdinand "Jelly Roll" Morton (piano), and Louis "Satchmo" Armstrong (trumpet).

LOUIS ARMSTRONG AND THE BLUES

"There's only two ways to sum up music: either it's good or it's bad. If it's good, you don't mess with it; you just enjoy it."

During the 1920s, New Orleans musicians traveled throughout the country—to New York, Chicago, Denver, and points west—spreading their new sound. One well-known musician, Louis Armstrong (1901–1971), settled in Chicago in 1922, joining the ten-piece New Orleans–style ensemble known as the King Oliver Creole Jazz Band. The young Armstrong, playing cornet, made his first recordings in 1923 with this group, and went on to revolutionize jazz.

Armstrong was unquestionably the most important single force in the development of early jazz styles. He was a great improviser who used a variety of mutes to expand the capacities of his cornet in range and tone color. To distinguish his unique melodic-rhythmic style of performance, his admirers coined the term "swing," which became a standard description of jazz. His **Scat singing** 1926 recording of *Heebie Jeebies* introduced *scat singing*, in which syllables without literal meaning (vocables) are set to an improvised vocal line. Ella Fitzgerald (1918–1996) later brought this technique to a truly virtuosic level.

The Hot Five in 1925: (left to right) Louis Armstrong, trumpet; Johnny St. Cyr, banjo; Johnny Dodds, clarinet; Kid Ory, trombone; and Lil Hardin Armstrong, piano.

In jazz, a *chorus* is a single statement of melodic-harmonic pattern, like a twelve-bar blues progression. Armstrong's style of jazz introduced a number of new features: stop-time choruses (solos accompanied by spaced staccato chords); double-time choruses, in which each beat of each measure was subdivided; a simple two- or four-beat meter based on evenly accented pulses; and solo rather than ensemble choruses. In his solos, only hints of the original tune are recognizable. Through these innovations, jazz was transformed into a solo art that presented improvised fantasias on chord changes rather than on a repeated melody.

Lillian Hardin's *Hotter Than That*

The pianist and composer Lillian Hardin (1898–1971) was one of the first women to rise to prominence in the jazz world. Born in Memphis, Tennessee, "Lil" Hardin studied piano and organ as a child, attended Fisk University, and later received a teacher's diploma from the Chicago College of Music. Although her family disapproved of popular music, Hardin claimed, "I was just born to swing, that's all." Her first job was as a "song plugger," selling sheet music at a music store in Chicago, where her family had moved. It was there that she met Jelly Roll Morton, possibly the greatest jazz pianist of her time. From him she learned the heavy-handed, rhythmic style of piano accompaniment that became her trademark.

For a few years, Hardin headed up her own band, then in 1921 joined the King Oliver Creole Jazz Band, one of the leading New Orleans–style groups. Shortly thereafter, Louis Armstrong was recruited to play in the band. Hardin and Armstrong hit it off right away and were married in 1924. She was highly influential in Armstrong's career during this period, teaching him how to read music and helping him start his own band. From 1925 to 1928, she played with two of his most famous groups, the Hot Five and the Hot Seven, for whom she wrote a number of her hit *charts* (a jazz term for an original score or an arrangement).

Louis Armstrong soon rose to stardom, but his marriage with Hardin failed. They separated in 1931 and divorced in 1938. Hardin continued a successful career, playing on Broadway, recording for Decca Records, and directing her own all-male band; she toured the United States, Canada, and Europe, and saw two of her songs—*Bad Boy* and *Just for a Thrill*—achieve huge success in the 1960s. She died in 1971 while performing in a memorial concert for her former husband.

Hardin's talents—she was a skillful and well-trained pianist—are not fully displayed on early recordings. She explained the practice of the time as follows: "It wasn't the style during the King Oliver days for the pianist to play many solos. . . . Sometimes I'd get the urge to run up and down the piano and make a few runs and things, and Joe [Oliver] would turn around, look at me, and say, 'We have a clarinet in the band.' "

Her compositions are innovative, with melodic and harmonic figurations atypical of the New Orleans style. She recorded two of her most famous works—*Struttin' with Some Barbeque* and *Hotter Than That*—in 1927 with Louis Armstrong and his Hot Five; both feature Armstrong's inventive improvisations set against Hardin's steady, driving accompaniment.

Hotter Than That is an upbeat tune set to a thirty-two-bar harmonic pattern with five choruses (see Listening Guide 69). After a lively eight-bar ensemble introduction, the first three choruses feature, in turn, Armstrong on cornet (a close, mellower-sounding relative of the trumpet), Johnny Dodds on clarinet, then Armstrong with a scat vocal. Each chorus is divided in half by a *break*, where the rhythmic accompaniment supporting the soloist stops momentarily. The fourth chorus, shortened to twenty measures, introduces a playful call-and-response between voice and guitar (featuring Lonnie Johnson), played out of time, after which Hardin firmly reestablishes the beat with a piano *vamp* (a repeated accompaniment pattern). The last chorus provides a brilliant climax that brings back the opening tune in the trombone, then in a full ensemble statement that is a fine example of *heterophony* (a texture in which two or more parts elaborate the same melody simultaneously, often the result of improvisation). A free guitar and cornet *tag* (the jazz term for a coda) close off this energetic work.

HARDIN: *Hotter Than That*, with Louis Armstrong and his Hot Five

(3:01)

Date: Recorded 1927

Form: 32-bar song form (Introduction and 5 choruses)

Tempo: Upbeat, in quick 4/4 time

Performers:

Louis "Satchmo" Armstrong, cornet and vocal   Lillian Hardin Armstrong, piano
Edward "Kid" Ory, trombone   Johnny St. Cyr, banjo
Johnny Dodds, clarinet   Lonnie Johnson, guitar

70	0:00	Introduction—8 bars long, features full ensemble with steady beat; in heterophonic texture.
71	0:09	Chorus 1—cornet solo by Armstrong, with rhythm accompaniment (piano and banjo); 32 bars long, in four 8-bar phrases:
	0:16	Solo cornet "break" in middle, leads into second half of chorus:
72	0:45	Chorus 2—clarinet solo with steady rhythm accompaniment; same structure as chorus 1, with clarinet "break" in middle.
	1:20	Voice (Armstrong) enters with "break" at end of chorus:
73	1:22	Chorus 3—scat singing solo (Armstrong) with banjo; piano drops out; 32 bars as above:
74	2:00	Chorus 4—voice and guitar in alternation, played out of time and with no accompaniment; shortened chorus of 20 bars; solo piano vamp pattern (Hardin) closes out chorus.

75 2:19 Chorus 5—trombone solo at beginning with rhythm accompaniment; cornet "break" brings in full ensemble in heterophonic statement.

2:52 Tag—guitar and cornet closing, played freely.

Duke Ellington

DUKE ELLINGTON AND THE BIG BAND ERA

"Somehow I suspect that if Shakespeare were alive today, he might be a jazz fan himself."

From the inspired, improvisational style of Louis Armstrong, we turn to the brilliantly composed jazz of Duke Ellington and the big band, or swing, era. Edward Kennedy "Duke" Ellington (1899–1974) was born in Washington, D.C., and was playing in New York jazz clubs by the 1920s. He became famous as a composer in the following decade. The advent of the big bands brought a greater need for arranged, or written-down, music, and Ellington played a major role in this development. A fine pianist himself, he was an even better orchestrator. As one of his collaborators remarked, "He plays piano, but his real instrument is the orchestra."

Ellington's orchestral palette was much richer than that of the New Orleans band. It included two trumpets, one cornet, three trombones, four saxophones (some of the players doubling on clarinet), two string basses, guitar, drums, vibraphone, and piano.

One of Ellington's best-known and most unpretentious works is *Ko-Ko*, originally written for his unfinished opera *Boola*. First recorded in 1940, *Ko-Ko* is a twelve-bar blues, expressively set in a minor key. In this work, the composer drew inspiration from the drum ceremonies based on African religious rites that used to take place in New Orleans's Congo Square.

Ko-Ko opens with a distinctive rhythmic pattern in the tom-tom and baritone saxophone that persists throughout the score (see Listening Guide 70). In both form and content, the piece is an accomplished jazz "composition." Its seven choruses continually build in dynamic, harmonic, and textural intensity. On the recording, solo choruses feature valve trombonist Juan Tizol, backed by the orchestra in a call-and-response exchange; trombonist Joe Nanton, with his characteristic plunger-mute style; Ellington on piano, with imaginative figurations that superimpose dissonant harmonies over the established E-flat-minor tonality; and bassist Jimmy Blanton, heard against the

In His Own Words

The word "improvisation" has great limitations, because when musicians are given solo responsibility they already have a suggestion of a melody written for them, and so before they begin they already know more or less what they are going to play. Anyone who plays anything worth hearing knows what he's going to play, no matter whether prepared a day ahead or a beat ahead. It has to be with intent.

full ensemble divided into choirs of varying tone colors. The final chorus, scored for full orchestra, sounds as though more instruments are playing than actually are. An **A-B-A** coda recapitulates the opening.

Ellington's multifaceted contribution influenced the world of jazz profoundly. As a composer, he brought his art to new heights and a newfound legitimacy; as an arranger, he left a rich legacy of works for a wide range of jazz groups; as a band leader, he served as teacher and model to a whole generation of jazz musicians. America's cultural heritage would have been far poorer without him.

Listening Guide 70

CD: Chr/Std 8/1–8, Sh 4/32–39
Cassette: Chr/Std 8A/1, Sh 4A/7

ELLINGTON: *Ko-Ko*   (2:39)

Date of work: 1940, first recorded by Duke Ellington and his Famous Orchestra

Form: 12-bar blues (Introduction, 7 choruses, and coda), E-flat minor

Soloists:
Juan Tizol, valve trombone
Joe "Tricky Sam" Nanton, trombone
Duke Ellington, piano
Jimmy Blanton, bass

1	0:00	**Introduction** (8 bars): Opening rhythm in tom-tom and baritone saxophone, set up against the trombone section.
2	0:12	**Chorus 1** (12 bars): Valved trombone, in syncopated call-and-response pattern with reeds.
3	0:31	**Chorus 2** (12 bars): Muted trombone, answered by brass section, moving bass line.
4	0:49	**Chorus 3** (12 bars): Muted trombone, growing in intensity and dynamics; mute placed tighter against bell for different timbre.
5	1:07	**Chorus 4** (12 bars): Piano solo interjects dissonant harmonies against increasing complexity in the reeds and brass, now set in a higher range.
6	1:25	**Chorus 5** (12 bars): Trumpets with main theme, at a higher pitch level; orchestra divided into 4 choirs (trombones, trumpets, reeds, rhythm).
7	1:43	**Chorus 6** (12 bars): Figure ascends through trombones and trumpets, then breaks for bass solo, heard against full orchestra with brilliant, thickly scored chords.
8	2:01	**Chorus 7** (12 bars): Full orchestra, richly scored to produce effect of larger ensemble. **Coda** (12 bars): Recapitulation of Introduction.

Cultural Perspective 18

The Roots of Jazz

Jazz has been viewed by many as a truly American art form, but in reality it draws together traditions from West Africa, Europe, and the Americas. The African origins of jazz evoke an earlier episode of American history: the slave trade from Africa. Many of the slaves brought to America came from the west coast of Africa, often called the Ivory or Gold Coast. It is not surprising, then, that studies comparing the musical traditions in sub-Saharan Africa with those in certain isolated regions of black America have confirmed many similarities. These include singing styles (call-and-response patterns and various vocal inflections) and storytelling techniques, traits that have remained alive for several centuries in both regions through oral tradition.

Black music in nineteenth-century America included dancing for ritual and ceremonial purposes and the singing of work songs (communal songs that synchronized the rhythm of group tasks) and spirituals (a kind of religious folk song, often with a refrain). West African religious traditions mingled freely with the Protestant Christianity adopted by some slaves. The art of storytelling through music, typical of many West African tribes, and praise singing (glorifying deities or royalty) were other traditions retained by slaves that would contribute to spirituals and blues. Although both men and women took part in praise singing—either could lead call-and-response ceremonial songs—the musical storyteller, called the griot, was always a male, whose mission it was to preserve and transmit the history, stories, and poetry of the people.

The city of New Orleans fueled the early sounds of jazz. There, in Congo Square, slaves met in the pre–Civil War era to dance to the accompaniment of all sorts of instruments, including drums, gourds, mouth harps, and banjos. Their music featured a strong underlying pulse over which syncopations and polyrhythmic elaborations took place. Melodies incorporated African-derived techniques such as rhythmic interjections, vocal glides, and percussive sounds made with the tongue and throat, and were often set in a musical scale with blue notes (lowered scale degrees on the third, fifth, or seventh of a major scale).

In the years after the Civil War and the Emancipation Proclamation (1863), a new style of music arose in Southern logging camps—country, or rural, blues, performed by a raspy-voiced male singer and, by the turn of the century, accompanied by a steel-string guitar. This music voiced the difficulties of everyday life in a continuation of the storyteller, or griot, tradition. The vocal lines featured melodic pitch bending, or blue notes, sung over repeated bass patterns. One of the greatest Mississippi blues singers was Charlie Patton.

Dance music also flourished among

Southern blacks, and one type in particular, ragtime, strongly influenced early jazz. Ragtime was the first African-American music to experience widespread popularity. This catchy style was soon heard across the country and in Europe, both as accompanied song and as solo piano music; we have already learned of Scott Joplin's important contribution to this genre. The rhythmic vitality of ragtime fascinated such art music composers as Debussy, who captured its spirit in *Golliwog's Cakewalk*, and Stravinsky, in *Ragtime for Eleven Instruments* (1918), *Piano-Rag-Music* (1919), and a dance in *The Soldier's Tale* (1918).

Terms to Note:

spiritual   blue note
call and response ragtime

Suggested Listening:

African-American spirituals or work songs
Rural blues (Charlie Patton)
Ragtime (Scott Joplin)
New Orleans jazz (Louis Armstrong's
    West End Blues)

The Bamboula, *danced in Congo Square, New Orleans, to the accompaniment of drums and singing, according to artist* **E. V. Kemble** *in 1885.*

LATER JAZZ STYLES AND PERFORMERS

"It's taken me all my life to learn what not to play."
—DIZZY GILLESPIE

Bebop

Cool jazz

West Coast jazz

Third stream jazz

By the end of the 1940s, musicians had become disenchanted with big band jazz. Their rebellion resulted in the new styles known as bebop and cool jazz. *Bebop* (also known as *bop*) was an invented word mimicking the two-note phrase that is the trademark of this style. Trumpeter Dizzy Gillespie, saxophonist Charlie Parker, and pianists Bud Powell and Thelonious Monk were among the leaders of the bebop movement in the 1940s. Over the next two decades, the term came to include a number of substyles such as *cool jazz* (the "cool" suggesting a restrained, unemotional manner), West Coast jazz, hard bop, and soul jazz. The principal exponent of cool jazz, a laid-back style characterized by lush harmonies, lowered levels of volume, moderate tempos, and a new lyricism, was trumpeter Miles Davis.

West Coast jazz is essentially a small-group, cool-jazz style featuring mixed timbres (one instrument for each color, without piano) and contrapuntal improvisations. Among the important West Coast ensembles that sprang up in the 1950s are the Dave Brubeck Quartet (with Paul Desmond on saxophone) and the Gerry Mulligan Quartet (with Chet Baker on trumpet). Mulligan (1927–1996) established a style noted for its use of walking bass lines (plucked on the string bass) and riffs backing up the solo instrument—in this case, either Baker on trumpet or Mulligan on baritone saxophone. (A *riff* is a short melodic ostinato frequently heard in jazz; it derives from West African call-and-response patterns.) A good example is the Mulligan Quartet's 1953 recording of *My Funny Valentine*, a well-known tune from a Broadway show of the 1930s. (See Listening Guide 71 in Chapter 77 for an analysis.)

In a 1957 lecture, composer and jazz historian Gunther Schuller put forth the idea that art music could learn from jazz, and vice versa. He coined the term *third stream*, holding that the first stream was classical music, the second jazz, and the third a combination of the other two. Although the designation referred mainly to the instruments used, it was soon extended to include other elements as well, such as the adoption by jazz performers of classical forms and tonal devices.

Schuller's idea was taken over by a number of jazz musicians, among them pianist John Lewis (b. 1920), who formed the Modern Jazz Quartet in answer to the growing demand for jazz on college campuses across the country. The ensemble played concerts that "swung" but also featured serious, composed works. Lewis's *Sketch*, recorded in 1959, combined the foursome of his jazz ensemble with the Beaux Arts Quartet, one of the finest string quartets in the country. More recently, trumpeter Wynton Marsalis demonstrated his mastery of both jazz and classical styles in his Pulitzer-Prize-winning jazz oratorio *Blood in the Fields* (1996) and his Stravinsky-inspired *A Fiddler's Tale* (1998).

By the 1960s, new experiments were in the making. A free-style avant-garde jazz emerged, with tenor saxophonist John Coltrane as its leading proponent. Also heard for the first time was a hybrid style known as *fusion*, which combined jazz improvisation with amplified instruments and the rhythmic pulse of rock. Trumpeter Miles Davis was an important catalyst in the advent of this style, and performers such as guitarist Jerry Garcia (1942–1995, of the Grateful Dead) and vibraphone player Gary Burton are modern-day exponents of the fusion sound. (Davis, Garcia, and Burton have all recorded separate arrangements of *My Funny Valentine*, demonstrating the show tune's adaptability and timelessness.)

Fusion

In the last several decades, jazz styles have taken conflicting turns. Modern bebop arose as a contemporary Neoclassical style of the 1980s, characterized by expanded tonalities, modal improvisation, and new forms merged with bebop's disjunct lines. Wynton Marsalis is one of the new voices of this Neo-classicism. Free jazz, founded by saxophonist Ornette Coleman in the 1960s, has developed alongside the more mellow, contemplative strains of new-age jazz, the latter best exemplified by saxophonist Paul Winter. New technologies, including MIDI (see CP 24) and interactive performance between musicians and computers, have opened a world of creative possibilities and sounds; meanwhile, other performers are looking back to the fundamentals of jazz, reinventing it for today's listeners.

Two Great Jazz Singers: Bessie Smith and Billie Holiday

Among the many outstanding performers in the world of jazz, two women—both African Americans—made an indelible mark. Bessie Smith (1894–1937) was arguably the greatest blues singer of all time. She began her professional career singing in cabarets and minstrel shows, and made her first blues recording in 1923, establishing herself as the most successful African-American recording artist of her era. She sang with the greats—Louis Armstrong, Benny Goodman, Fletcher Henderson, and many more. Her career was damaged by the Great Depression and her addiction to alcohol; the circumstances surrounding her premature death remain obscure. With her intense and emotionally charged style and wide, expressive range, she set the standard by which all other blues singers have been measured.

The legendary Billie Holiday (1915–1959) began to sing professionally in 1929 and made her first recording in 1933, with clarinetist Benny Goodman, with whom she would record many more times. Affected too by the Depression of the 1930s, Holiday suffered from a hopeless drug addiction. She was

The great blues singer Bessie Smith.

an original, noted for her melodic nuances and blues style, a languid, behind-the-beat rhythm. Among her most famous performances are renditions of *God Bless the Child*, *All of Me*, *These Foolish Things*, and the terrifying ballad *Strange Fruit*.

77

Musical Theater

"The hills are alive with the sound of music."
—OSCAR HAMMERSTEIN II

THE DEVELOPMENT OF AMERICAN MUSICAL THEATER

The American musical theater of today developed from the comic opera, or *operetta*, tradition of Johann Strauss Jr., Jacques Offenbach, and other Europeans. The genre was revamped to the American taste by composers such as

Victor Herbert (1850–1924), whose works include such charming items as *Babes in Toyland* (1903), *Mlle. Modiste* (1905), and *Naughty Marietta* (1910). The Broadway musical (or musical comedy) gradually evolved in the 1920s, with works like Sigmund Romberg's *Student Prince* (1924), set in a glamorized Old Heidelberg, and Jerome Kern's landmark *Show Boat* (1927), a tale of Mississippi River life that introduced the classic song *Ol' Man River*. In the ensuing decades, the musical established itself as America's unique contribution to world theater.

Early musicals

The musical depended on romantic plots in picturesque settings enlivened by comedy, appealing melodies, choruses, and dances. Within the framework of a thoroughly commercial theater, a group of talented composers and writers created a body of works that not only enchanted audiences of their time but lasted well beyond it. Among these were Burton Lane's *Finian's Rainbow* (1947), Cole Porter's *Kiss Me, Kate* (1948), Frank Loesser's *Guys and Dolls* (1950), Harold Rome's *Fanny* (1954), and Alan Jay Lerner and Frederick Loewe's *My Fair Lady* (1956).

Originally, the plots of musicals were contrived and silly, functioning mainly as scaffolding for the songs and dances. The emphasis gradually changed to present a more convincing treatment of character and situation, as composers began to turn to sophisticated literary sources for their plots. *Show Boat* was based on an Edna Ferber novel, *Kiss Me, Kate* on Shakespeare's *The Taming of the Shrew*, *Guys and Dolls* on the stories of Damon Runyon, *Fanny* on Marcel Pagnol's trilogy, and *My Fair Lady* on George Bernard Shaw's play *Pygmalion*. As the musicals' approach grew more serious, the genre outgrew its original limitations.

Sources of plots

George Gershwin's masterpiece *Porgy and Bess* (1935), an "American folk opera" based on the novel and play by DuBose and Dorothy Heyward, was so far ahead of its time that, despite its focus on African-American folk idioms, it did not become a success until a revival toured Europe in the 1950s. The work paved the way for such musicals as Leonard Bernstein's *West Side Story* (1957), one of the first to end tragically, and Jerry Bock's *Fiddler on the Roof* (1964), based on stories by the great Yiddish writer Sholem Aleichem. Both works won worldwide success, and both would have been unthinkable twenty years earlier because of the serious elements in their plots.

The composer Richard Rodgers collaborated with two talented lyricists during his long career to produce some of the best-loved musicals of the century. Along with Lorenz Hart, he created a string of successful Broadway shows, including *Babes in Arms* (1937), which we will study. After the death of Hart in 1943, Rodgers teamed up with Oscar Hammerstein II to write such unforgettable musicals as *Oklahoma!* (1943), *Carousel* (1945), *South Pacific* (1949), *The King and I* (1951), and *The Sound of Music* (1959). Here too the literary sources were of a high order. *Carousel* was based on Ferenc Molnár's *Liliom*, *Oklahoma!* on Lynn Riggs's *Green Grow the Lilacs*, *South Pacific* on the

Rodgers and Hammerstein

stories of James Michener, *The King and I* on *Anna and the King of Siam* by Margaret Landon, and *The Sound of Music* on the moving memoir of Baroness Maria von Trapp.

Stephen Sondheim

In the 1970s and 1980s, Stephen Sondheim brought the genre to new levels of sophistication in a series of works that included *A Little Night Music* (1973), *Sweeney Todd* (1979), *Sunday in the Park with George* (1983), and *Into the Woods* (1988). Sondheim continued to attract Broadway audiences of the following decade with *Assassins* (1990) and *Passion* (1994).

Andrew Lloyd Webber

A new era opened with the advent of rock musicals such as Galt MacDermot's *Hair* (1968), The Who's *Tommy* (1969; music and lyrics by Peter Townshend), and Andrew Lloyd Webber's *Jesus Christ Superstar* (1971). Suddenly the romantic show tunes to which millions of young Americans had learned to dance and flirt went completely out of fashion. After a while, however, melody returned. The British Lloyd Webber conquered the international stage with *Evita* (1978), *Cats* (1981), *Starlight Express* (1984), *The Phantom of the Opera* (1986), and *Sunset Boulevard* (1993)—works in which song and dance were combined with dazzling scenic effects, as in the court operas of the Baroque. Together with Frenchman Claude-Michel Schonberg's *Les Misérables* (1987), *Miss Saigon* (1988), and *Martin Guerre* (1996), the last two in collaboration with Alain Boublil, these musicals represented a new phenomenon. What had been almost exclusively an American product was now taken over by Europeans.

Recent musicals

Recently, many "classic" musicals have enjoyed successful revivals on Broadway: among these are *My Fair Lady, Guys and Dolls, Carousel, Show Boat, Chicago, Candide, The King and I,* and *Crazy for You,* an adaptation of Gershwin's *Girl Crazy* (1930). More recent American productions of note are *The Kiss of the Spider Woman* (1993) and *Steel Pier* (1996) by John Kander and lyricist Fred Ebb (whose earlier collaboration produced the 1966 musical *Cabaret*), and the Disney studio's *Beauty and the Beast* (1994), and *The Lion King* (1997), based on the animated films. With these works, Disney has not only reversed the standard order of a hit musical generating a film, but has opened up a new world of source material and writers.

Two newer musicals find their basis in older classics: Jonathan Larsen's hit show *Rent,* a modern rock opera inspired by Puccini's opera *La Bohème,* premiered on the hundredth anniversary of the Italian masterwork; and Stephen Flaherty's *Ragtime* (1996, with lyrics by Lynn Ahrens), a musical setting of the well-known novel *Ragtime* (1975), by E. L. Doctorow, derives from the syncopated rhythmic style of the turn-of-the-century dance craze. Dance has inspired a new type of musical in which choreography takes precedence over story line, as in *Bring in 'da Noise, Bring in 'da Funk* (1995), featuring tap star Savion Glover, and *Riverdance* (1994), with the sensational Irish step dancer Michael Flatley.

From the great American stage works mentioned above, we will consider two representative examples: Rodgers and Hart's *Babes in Arms* and Bernstein's *West Side Story*. Through them, we will see not only the musical growth of the Broadway tradition, but the significant interaction between jazz and the American musical theater.

RODGERS AND HART AND THE AMERICAN MUSICAL STAGE

"It is a pleasure to live at a time when songs can be both popular and intelligent."—LORENZ HART

One of the most gifted songwriting teams of the Broadway stage, Richard Rodgers and Lorenz Hart wrote nearly thirty shows between 1926 and 1943. In so doing, they single-handedly elevated the level of lyrics in musical comedy from clichés to more thoughtful poetry, leaving the world such favorite songs as *My Funny Valentine* and *Bewitched*, among many others.

Richard Rodgers (1902–1979) mostly taught himself the basics of composition. As a teenager, he was attracted to the musical stage works of Victor Herbert and Jerome Kern, and began writing music and lyrics for some off-Broadway productions. In 1918, he met Lorenz Hart (1895–1943) at Columbia University, where Hart was studying journalism. They achieved their first big hit in 1925 with the musical revue *Garrick Gaieties*. Soon they turned their attention to more serious musical plays that merged songs with drama and character development. Their most successful collaborations include *The*

Richard Rodgers at the piano, with Lorenz Hart.

Girl Friend (1926), *A Connecticut Yankee* (1927), *On Your Toes* (1936), *Babes in Arms* (1937), *I Married an Angel* (1938), *The Boys from Syracuse* (1938), and *Pal Joey* (1940). Rodgers and Hart also tried their hand at writing songs for film scores, and film versions were made of many of their stage works. Their career together was the subject of a 1948 film, *Words and Music*.

Rodgers and Hart songs typically feature sophisticated texts with multi-syllabic rhymes (where more than just the last syllable rhymes) and occasional internal rhymes; these are set to lyrical, small-ranged melodies accompanied by simple harmonies. *Babes in Arms*, one of their most appealing shows, is set in a fictional actors' colony called Seaport, and focuses on a group of adolescents who are left behind when their parents go on tour and who are thus forced to make it on their own. To demonstrate that they are capable of taking care of themselves, the young people set out to produce a show of their own. *My Funny Valentine*, a sentimental ballad, is sung by an itinerant traveler, Billie Smith, after she has her first lovers' quarrel with Val LaMar over whether two African-American youths should take part in the show. The rhythmic *Johnny One Note* spins a tale of a singer with a limited vocal range as a part of the show within the show, and later, when Billie decides to return to the road, she sings the catchy tune *The Lady Is a Tramp*.

Babes in Arms drew immediate praise from critics, who found the cast "as nice a group of youngsters as ever dove into an ice cream freezer at a birthday party." Its success was ensured shortly after its opening when all the competing shows closed, leaving it the only musical on Broadway in the summer of 1937. The sophisticated Rodgers and Hart score has inspired many pop and jazz arrangements of its songs, particularly its most famous ballad, *My Funny Valentine* (see Chapter 76 for a discussion of such jazz arrangements). We will hear both the memorable original version and a West Coast jazz rendition by the Gerry Mulligan Quartet (see Listening Guide 71).

Listening Guide 71   MW   CD: Chr/Std 7/62–69
Cassette: Chr/Std 7B/5–6

RODGERS: *My Funny Valentine*   (6:58)

Date of work: First performance on April 14, 1937

Text: Lorenz Hart

Genre: Musical theater song (solo voice and orchestra)

Form: Verse and refrain (**A-B-A′**)

VERSION 1: Vocal selection from *Babes in Arms* (4:04)

		Text	Description
			Brief orchestral introduction.
62	0:00	VERSE (Moderately) Behold the way our fine-feathered friend His virtue doth parade. . Thou knowest not, my dim-witted friend, The picture thou hast made. Thy vacant brow and thy tousled hair Conceal thy good intent. Thou noble, upright, truthful, sincere, And slightly dopey gent—you're . . .	Speechlike vocal line doubled by solo oboe; phrase endings punctuated by woodwinds and celesta.
63	1:04	REFRAIN (Slowing, with much expression) My funny Valentine, Sweet comic Valentine, You make me smile with my heart. Your looks are laughable, Unphotographable, Yet you're my favorite work of art.	**A**—lyrical, conjunct, with orchestra and celesta; C minor (8 measures). Variation of opening of refrain; C minor, transition to E-flat major (8 measures).
64	1:41	Is your figure less than Greek? Is your mouth a little weak? When you open it to speak, Are you smart?	**B**—more leaps in melody; in E-flat major (8 measures).
65	1:59	But don't change a hair for me. Not if you care for me. Stay, little Valentine, stay. Each day is Valentine's Day.	**A′**—variation of opening of refrain; return to C minor (12 measures).
66	2:28	REFRAIN repeated	Orchestral statement of **A** section; melody in low strings, accompanied by woodwinds and celesta.
67	3:01	Is your figure less than Greek . . .	Voice reenters with repeated text (**B** and **A′**); solo violin obbligato accompanies voice; climax on "Stay, little Valentine, stay"; orchestral closing with celesta leads to final chord.

Opening melody of refrain:

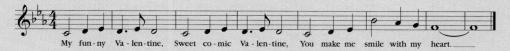

VERSION 2: Gerry Mulligan Quartet (2:54)

Date: Recorded January 1953
Style: West Coast jazz
Basis: Musical theater song (refrain only)

Performers:
Chet Baker, trumpet
Gerry Mulligan, baritone saxophone
Carson Smith, string bass
Chico Hamilton, drums

68	0:00	**Chorus 1**—trumpet solo throughout
		A section (8 measures)—trumpet solo, with plucked string bass accompaniment.
		(8 measures)—adds baritone saxophone.
		B section (8 measures)—bridge with all instruments.
		A′ section (12 measures)—variation of **A**.
69	2:01	**Chorus 2** (abridged)—baritone saxophone solo
		A′ section (8 measures)—baritone saxophone and string bass alone.
		(6 measures)—closing, all instruments.

LEONARD BERNSTEIN AND THE BROADWAY MUSICAL

Leonard Bernstein

"Any composer's writing is the sum of himself, of all his roots and influences."

In the same decade that West Coast jazz came to prominence, the composer-conductor Leonard Bernstein attempted another important union of jazz with musical theater. The result was *West Side Story*, a stage work that has achieved the status of a classic.

As a composer, conductor, educator, pianist, and television personality, Bernstein (1918–1990) enjoyed one of the most spectacular careers of our time. He was born in Lawrence, Massachusetts, the son of Russian-Jewish immigrants. At thirteen, he was playing piano with a jazz band. He entered Harvard at seventeen, where he studied composition with Walter Piston, attended the Curtis Institute in Philadelphia, and then became a disciple of the conductor Serge Koussevitzky. In 1943, when he was twenty-five, Bernstein was appointed assistant to Artur Rodzinski, conductor of the New York Philharmonic. A few weeks later, a guest conductor, Bruno Walter, was suddenly taken ill, and Rodzinski was out of town. With only a few hours' notice, **Conductor** Bernstein took over the Sunday afternoon concert, which was being broadcast coast to coast, and led a stunning performance. Overnight he became famous. Fifteen years later, he was himself named director of the New York Philharmonic, the first American-born conductor (and the youngest, at age forty) to occupy the post.

Composer As a composer, Bernstein straddled the worlds of serious and popular music. He was thus able to bring to the Broadway musical a compositional technique and knowledge of music that few of its earlier practitioners had possessed. In his concert works, he spoke the language of contemporary

590

music with enormous fluency—not as an experimenter but as one who, having inherited the great tradition, stamped it with his own personality. He possessed a genuine flair for orchestration—the balance and spacing of sonorities, the use of the brass in the high register, and the idiomatic writing that shows off each instrument to its best advantage all bespeak a master. His harmonic idiom is spicily dissonant, his jazzy rhythms have great vitality, and his melodies soar.

Bernstein's feeling for the urban scene—specifically that of New York City—is vividly projected in his theater music. In *On the Town* (a full-length version of his ballet *Fancy Free)*, *Wonderful Town,* and *West Side Story*, he created a sophisticated kind of musical theater that explodes with movement, energy, and sentiment. His death in October 1990 aroused universal mourning in the music world and beyond.

West Side Story

In *West Side Story*, Bernstein realized a dream: to create a musical based on the Romeo and Juliet story. This updated tale, with a book by playwright Arthur Laurents and lyrics by Stephen Sondheim (his first job as a lyricist), sets the saga amid turf wars of two rival street gangs in New York City. The hostility between the Jets (led by Riff) and their Puerto Rican rivals, the Sharks (led by Bernardo), is a modern-day counterpart of the feud between the Capulets and the Montagues in Shakespeare's play. In this tragic tale, Tony, one of the Jets, and Maria, Bernardo's sister, meet at a dance and immediately fall in love. Riff and Bernardo bring their two gangs together for a

Cultural Perspective 19

LATIN-AMERICAN DANCE MUSIC

The energetic rhythms of Leonard Bernstein's *West Side Story* do not sound particularly foreign to us, yet they are based on dances from a variety of Latin-American countries. Some dances, like the Brazilian samba and the Cuban rumba, began as rural music that was later popularized by urban bands. In the 1950s and 1960s, Americans and Europeans alike were dancing to the distinctive rhythms of the Cuban cha cha cha and mambo and the Brazilian bossa nova, all derived from earlier traditional styles. We noted previously that the Argentinian tango, a heated couple dance that had its origins in the poor neighborhoods of Buenos Aires, has remained popular through much of the twentieth century. The Afro-Cuban conga is a favorite Latin-American Carnival dance whose name is also applied to a long, single-headed drum used in much Latin-American popular music. The collective term "salsa" (Spanish for "sauce," as in "spicy") is sometimes used to label various contemporary styles loosely based on Afro-Cuban dance music.

More recent Latin-American types have also achieved international prominence. In the 1960s, a Jamaican style called ska became popular; it was characterized by quick, off-the-beat rhythms and was represented by such artists as the Skalites and Millie Small (whose hit song *My Boy Lollipop* had some success in the United States and Canada). Ska led the way for reggae, a Jamaican style of music that slows down the quick beat of ska and emphasizes the role of the bass, placing it in a complex rhythmic relationship with the other parts (see p. 609). Ska has recently undergone a revival; its feel-good mood and up-tempo rhythms have gained broad appeal. Among the most popular recording groups are The Mighty Mighty Bosstones, known for their hard-core punk ska.

Music of Latin America and the Caribbean has enjoyed continued popularity, in part because of its potential as

fight. When Tony tries to stop them, Riff is stabbed by one of the Sharks and Tony in turn kills Bernardo. Tony begs Maria for forgiveness, but the gang warfare mounts to a final rumble in which Tony is killed. This story of star-crossed lovers unfolds in scenes of great tenderness, with such memorable songs as *Maria, Tonight,* and *Somewhere* alternating with electrifying dance sequences choreographed by Jerome Robbins.

We will hear first the *Mambo,* a part of the dance scene where Tony meets

"dance-floor dynamite." A fad of the late 1990s, the macarena, is a Spanish dance that captured the attention first of Latin America and then of the world. The current rage for world beat music, which has opened the Western market to a myriad of new styles, has changed the sounds and rhythms of popular music forever and has brought Latin-American music into our everyday experience.

Terms to Note:

samba	bossa nova	ska
rumba	tango	reggae
cha cha cha	conga	macarena
mambo	salsa	world beat

Suggested Listening:

Bernstein: *West Side Story*
Latin-American dance music
Ska or reggae
Bob Marley and the Wailers

Jamaican reggae star Bunny Wailer (Livingston), who sang with the original Bob Marley and the Wailers, performing at Madison Square Garden in 1986.

Maria. When the lively Latin beat starts, the Jets and Sharks are on opposite sides of the hall. At the climax of the dance, Tony and Maria catch a glimpse of each other across the room. A *mambo* is an Afro-Cuban dance with a fast and highly syncopated beat; in Bernstein's dance, the bongos and cowbells keep the frenetic pulse under the shouts of the gang members and the jazzy riffs of the woodwinds and brass. The music dies away as Maria and Tony walk toward each other on the dance floor.

The *Tonight* Ensemble is set later the same evening, after a fire-escape version of Shakespeare's famous balcony scene, where Tony and Maria first sing their love duet. As darkness falls, the two gangs anxiously await the expected fight, each vowing to cut the other down to size. Underneath the gang music, an ominous three-note ostinato is heard throughout. Tony's thoughts are only of Maria as he sings the lyrical ballad *Tonight* (an **A-A′-B-A″** form) over an animated rhythmic accompaniment. The gang music returns briefly, after which Maria and later Tony repeat their love song, their voices soaring above the complex dialogue in an exciting climax to the first act.

West Side Story remains, more than forty years after its production, a timeless masterpiece of musical theater; its dramatic content, stirring melodies, colorful orchestration, and vivacious dance scenes continue to delight audiences of today.

Listening Guide 72

CD: Chr/Std 8/19–29, Sh 4/40–50
Cassette: Chr/Std, 8A/5–6, Sh 4A/8–9

BERNSTEIN: *West Side Story*, excerpts   (5:26)

Date: 1957
Genre: Musical theater

Characters:
Maria, a Puerto Rican girl, sister of Bernardo
Tony, member of the Jets
Anita, Puerto Rican girlfriend of Bernardo
Riff, leader of the Jets
Bernardo, leader of the Sharks

ACT I: *The Dance at the Gym, Mambo*   (1:48)

Tempo: Fast, with syncopated rhythms
Medium: Orchestra, with Latin rhythm section (including bongo drums and cowbells)

<table>
<tr><td>19</td><td>0:00</td><td>Percussion introduction, 8 bars, with bongos and cowbells; very fast and syncopated.</td></tr>
<tr><td></td><td>0:07</td><td>Brass, with accented chords; Sharks shout, "Mambo!"; followed by quieter string line, accompanied by snare drum rolls; accented brass chords return; Sharks shout, "Mambo!" again.</td></tr>
<tr><td></td><td>0:28</td><td>High dissonant woodwinds in dialogue with rhythmic brass.</td></tr>
<tr><td>20</td><td>0:33</td><td>Trumpets play riff over *fff* chords:</td></tr>
</table>

Woodwinds and brass alternate in highly polyphonic texture.

1:00   Rocking two-note woodwind line above syncopated low brass:

21   1:13   Solo trumpet enters in high range above complex rhythmic accompaniment:

Complex *fortissimo* polyphony until climax; rhythm slows as music dies away at close.

ACT I: *Tonight* Ensemble   (3:38)

Tempo: Fast and rhythmic
Setting: The neighborhood, 6:00–9:00 P.M. Riff and the Jets, Bernardo and the Sharks, Anita, Maria, and Tony all wait expectantly for the coming of night.

22   0:00   Short, rhythmic orchestral introduction featuring brass and percussion; based on 3-note ostinato:

Text	*Description*
RIFF AND THE JETS The Jets are gonna have their day Tonight.	Gangs sing in alternation, in marked recitative style:
BERNARDO AND THE SHARKS The Sharks are gonna have their way Tonight.	
RIFF AND THE JETS The Puerto Ricans grumble, "Fair fight." But if they start a rumble, We'll rumble 'em right.	
SHARKS We're gonna hand 'em a surprise Tonight.	
JETS We're gonna cut them down to size Tonight.	
SHARKS We said, "OK, no rumpus, No tricks." But just in case they jump us, We're ready to mix Tonight!	

23	0:42	

BOTH
We're gonna rock it tonight,
We're gonna jazz it up and have us
    a ball!
They're gonna get it tonight;
The more they turn it on, the harder
    they fall!
	Unison chorus, more emphatic and accented; with accented brass interjections.

JETS Well, they began it!	Antiphonal exchange between gangs; punctuated by sharp chords in orchestra.
SHARKS Well, they began it—	
BOTH And we're the ones to stop 'em once and for all, Tonight.	

24	1:08

ANITA Anita's gonna get her kicks Tonight. We'll have our private little mix Tonight. He'll walk in hot and tired, So what! Don't matter if he's tired, As long as he's hot, Tonight!	Opening melody now in uneven triplet rhythm; sung sexily: 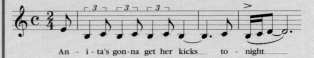

Reprise of song, in **A-A′-B-A″** form, lyrical vocal line over syncopated accompaniment:

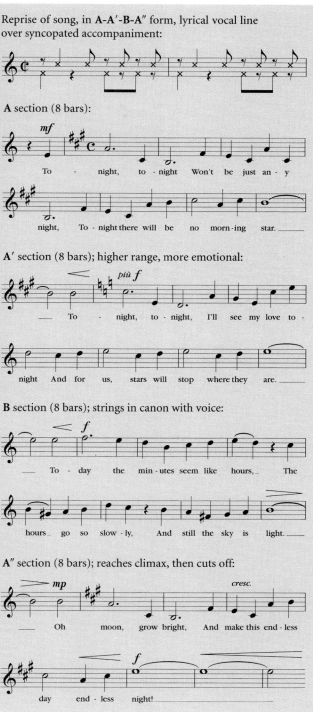

A section (8 bars):

A′ section (8 bars); higher range, more emotional:

B section (8 bars); strings in canon with voice:

A″ section (8 bars); reaches climax, then cuts off:

25	1:25	**TONY** Tonight, tonight, Won't be just any night, Tonight there will be no morning star.

Tonight, tonight,
I'll see my love tonight,
And for us, stars will stop where
they are.

26	1:51	Today the minutes seem like hours, The hours go so slowly, And still the sky is light . . .

Oh moon, grow bright,
And make this endless day endless
night!

27	2:14		Instrumental interlude.

RIFF *(to Tony)*
I'm counting on you to be there
Tonight!
When Diesel wins it fair and square
Tonight!
That Puerto Rican punk'll go down
And when he's hollered Uncle,
We'll tear up the town!

Return to opening idea, sung more vehemently.

Ensemble finale: Maria sings *Tonight* in high range, against simultaneous dialogue and interjections over the same syncopated dance rhythm that accompanied Tony's solo; dramatic climax on last ensemble statement of "Tonight!"

28	2:39	MARIA *(warmly)*
[A] Tonight, tonight	RIFF AND THE JETS
So I can count on you boy?

TONY *(abstractedly)*
All right.

Won't be just any night,

RIFF AND THE JETS
We're gonna have us a ball.

TONY
All right.

Tonight there will be no morning star.

RIFF
Womb to tomb!

TONY
Sperm to worm!

RIFF
I'll see you there about eight.

TONY
Tonight.

[A'] Tonight, tonight,

JETS
We're gonna rock it tonight!

I'll see my love tonight,

SHARKS
We're gonna jazz it tonight!

ANITA
Tonight, tonight,

And for us, stars will stop where they are.

Late tonight. We're gonna mix it tonight.

SHARKS
They're gonna get it tonight!

29	3:05	TONY AND MARIA
[B] Today the minutes seem like hours,	ANITA
Anita's gonna have her day,
Bernardo's gonna have his way tonight.

The hours go so slowly,

SHARKS
They began it. And we're the ones to
stop 'em once and for all!

And still the sky is light.

JETS
They began it. We'll stop 'em once and for all!

598

78

Rock and the Global Scene

"You know my temperature's risin',
The juke box's blowin' a fuse,
My heart's beatin' rhythm,
My soul keeps singin' the blues—
Roll over, Beethoven,
Tell Tchaikovsky the news."—CHUCK BERRY

The rise of rock and roll and its offspring rock is the most important music phenomenon of the past half century. Economically, rock music has grown into a multibillion-dollar industry; socially, it has had a far-reaching impact on the way people live, dress, talk, and even think; musically, it has dominated the popular scene for some forty years, and influenced virtually every other style of music—classical, jazz, country/western, and contemporary world beat. There is now a Rock and Roll Hall of Fame, which opened in 1995 in Cleveland, Ohio, to honor the superstars of the genre.

Rock and roll, which first came on the scene in the 1950s, was born of a union of African-American rhythm and blues with country/western and pop music. *Rhythm and blues,* popular from the late 1940s through the early 1960s, is a predominantly vocal genre, featuring a solo singer accompanied by a small group including piano, guitar (acoustic or electric), acoustic bass, drums, and tenor saxophone. Its harmonies and structure are clearly drawn from twelve-bar blues and thirty-two-bar pop song form (both of which we heard in Chapter 76). As the name implies, the style is characterized by a strong, driving beat, usually in a quadruple meter. Among the many great rhythm and blues performers were four African Americans: Bessie Smith (whom we encountered earlier as a blues singer), Big Bill Broonzy, B. B. King, and Joe Turner.

Rhythm and blues

The irrepressible Chuck Berry, seen in three typical positions.

Rock and roll   In the mid-1950s, rock and roll emerged as a form of rhythm and blues that crossed racial lines: white singers like Bill Haley (*Rock Around the Clock,* with the Comets, 1954), Elvis Presley (*Heartbreak Hotel, Hound Dog,* and *Don't Be Cruel,* all from 1956), and Jerry Lee Lewis (*Whole Lotta Shakin' Going On* and *Great Balls of Fire,* both from 1957) drew on elements of the black style. At the same time, African Americans like Chuck Berry (*Roll Over, Beethoven,* 1956), Fats Domino (*Blueberry Hill,* 1956), and Little Richard (*Long Tall Sally,* 1956) caught the attention of a white audience. The styles of Chuck Berry and Little Richard clearly derived from gospel music, and that of Jerry Lee Lewis was much influenced by country/western singers. The new sounds of rock and roll, belted out somewhat raspily and always in a lively manner, revolutionized the music industry's concept of markets, appealing to wide audiences across racial lines.

Soft rock   As hard-driving rock and roll declined in popularity around 1960, a gentler, more lyrical style, *soft rock,* found an audience. The medium of radio furthered the crooning styles of white singers Bobby Darin (*Splish, Splash,* 1958; *Dream Lover,* 1959), Neil Sedaka (*Calendar Girl,* 1960–61; *Breaking Up Is Hard to Do,* 1962), and Bobby Vinton (*Roses Are Red,* 1962; *Mr. Lonely,* 1964). Meanwhile, black America was listening to the sound of *soul* and *Motown* (from Motortown, or Detroit—a fusion of gospel, pop, and rhythm and blues). Top recording artists included Diana Ross and the Supremes (*Where Did Our Love Go,* 1964), James Brown (*Papa's Got a Brand New Bag,* 1965), Gladys Knight and the Pips (*I Heard It Through the Grapevine,* 1967), Aretha Franklin (*Respect,* 1967), and Stevie Wonder (*You Are the Sunshine of My Life,* 1973). Ray Charles (*I've Got a Woman,* 1965) is often considered to be the "father" of soul.

In the early 1960s, rock and roll was revitalized with the popularity of a new dance, the twist, and with the emergence of new groups, notably the Beach Boys in the United States and the Beatles, the Rolling Stones, and The Who in Britain. It was the Beatles who provided direction amid a variety of styles. In 1964, this group from Liverpool, England, took America by storm, performing at Carnegie Hall in New York, at the Washington Coliseum, and on television's highly popular *Ed Sullivan Show*. In 1964, the Beatles held the top five spots on the Billboard chart: *Can't Buy Me Love, Twist and Shout, She Loves You, I Want to Hold Your Hand,* and *Please Please Me.* This foursome— Paul McCartney on electric bass, George Harrison and John Lennon on amplified acoustic guitars, and Ringo Starr on drums—featured a strong rhythm section and a hard-driving beat, with John and Paul singing unison and two-part vocals in a high range, almost a falsetto.

The Beatles' success story continued through the decade because they had the creativity to experiment with other types of music. In Paul McCartney's lyrical ballad *Yesterday* (1965), the Beatles moved from rock and roll to a pop sound combined with string quartet; and in the albums *Rubber Soul* (1965) and *Revolver* (1966), the group adopted a new style, with more expressive lyrics, complex harmonies, and sophisticated recording techniques. George Harrison took up the Indian sitar (an instrument also used by a California folk-rock group, the Byrds) for the 1965 song *Norwegian Wood.* With these

The Beatles

The Beatles (Paul, Ringo, John, George) performing November 1963.

Rock new sounds, the old rock and roll was gone, and the more expressive style known as *rock* emerged.

In the late 1960s, the Beatles continued to express their individuality as well as their newfound interest in Eastern philosophy. *Hey Jude* (1968) was their biggest-selling single of all time; and the albums *Sgt. Pepper's Lonely Hearts Club Band* (1967) and *Abbey Road* (1969) were both stunning musical achievements that showcased their various songwriting abilities. Notable among the selections on these albums are John Lennon's *Lucy in the Sky with Diamonds*, Paul McCartney's *When I'm Sixty-Four*, and George Harrison's *Here Comes the Sun*. In 1970, the group broke up, its members going on to establish successful solo careers.

The Byrds Many of the expressive features of rock were molded by California bands, especially the Byrds. One of the most creative rock groups, the Byrds formed their band in Los Angeles in 1964 and soon became caught up in the politics of the San Francisco scene—the free speech movement and the protest of American involvement in the Vietnam War (1957–75). Their music combined the folk style of protest singers Bob Dylan and Joan Baez with the new

Folk rock sounds of rock, thereby creating *folk rock*. Their first release was their biggest hit: *Mr. Tambourine Man* (1965), set to words and music by Bob Dylan. This was followed in the same year by *Turn, Turn, Turn*, a Pete Seeger song with lyrics from the biblical book of Ecclesiastes. *Eight Miles High* (1966), one of the first recordings banned because of its drug references, displays highly adventuresome harmonic language.

Woodstock The culminating event for rock music in the 1960s was the Woodstock Festival, held in upstate New York in August 1969, where over 300,000 music fans gathered for four days of "peace, love, and brotherhood." Important performances were given there by The Who (*Summertime Blues*, with Peter Townshend's famous guitar-smashing routine), Joe Cocker (singing the Beatles' *With a Little Help from My Friends*), Country Joe and the Fish (with the antiwar song *What Are We Fighting For?*), Jimi Hendrix (known for his psychedelic blues-style rendition of *The Star-Spangled Banner*), Richie Havens (singing the spiritual *Sometimes I Feel Like a Motherless Child*), and a then unknown group named Santana (*Soul Sacrifice*), that went on to develop Latin rock. Other performers included the North Indian sitarist Ravi Shankar and folk singers Joan Baez and Arlo Guthrie. On the twenty-fifth anniversary of this festival, nostalgic re-creations took place in Bethel and Saugerties, New York, featuring some of the same performers.

The British invasion Meanwhile, the success of the Beatles in America had sparked a British invasion of rock groups—the Dave Clark Five (*Over and Over*, 1965), the Animals (*The House of the Rising Sun*, 1964), and especially the Rolling Stones (*I Can't Get No Satisfaction*, 1965). The Stones soon became the "bad boys" of rock: their lyrics, most by Mick Jagger, and their public behavior condoned sexual freedom, drugs, and violence. Openly sexual innuendo (*Let's Spend the*

Night Together) and tales of an LSD trip (*Something Happened to Me Yesterday*) are subjects typical of their songs. Their concert tours often sparked violence: at the Altamont Festival of 1969 (California's answer to Woodstock), a fan was murdered as Jagger sang *Sympathy for the Devil* to an out-of-control audience. But despite the negative image they acquired, the Rolling Stones opened the path more than any other group for new styles of the 1970s and 1980s: hard rock, punk rock, and heavy metal.

America's answer to this British invasion was *acid rock*—a style of music originating in San Francisco that focused on drugs, extremely high volume levels, instrumental improvisations, and new sound technologies. The Jefferson Airplane (*White Rabbit*, 1967), featuring female lead singer Grace Slick, made no pretense about their psychedelic lyrics, and the Grateful Dead, with Jerry Garcia on lead guitar, performed lengthy instrumental improvisations at deafening volume levels. Today, the Grateful Dead represent a counterculture, with a huge market for licensed memorabilia. In 1970–71, the music world was shaken by the alcohol- and drug-related deaths of three superstars: the phenomenal blues guitarist Jimi Hendrix, the raspy-voiced Janis Joplin, and the lead singer of the Doors, Jim Morrison. Each was only twenty-seven years old.

Acid rock

Psychedelic rock seemed destined to become a short-lived style, but Britain's Pink Floyd proved otherwise. Their 1973 album *Dark Side of the Moon*, with its ageless themes of madness and death, remained on the Top 40 charts for a record 751 weeks. A later gem, the two-album set *The Wall* (1980), ensured their place in the annals of rock.

THE ECLECTICISM OF THE 1970s

"I believe there can be no evolution without revolution. Why should we try to fit in?"—MICK JAGGER

Two eclectic styles of rock were developing in the early 1970s: *jazz rock* (later called *fusion*), featuring traditional jazz-style instruments (trumpet, trombone, saxophone, and flute) playing long, improvised melodic lines; and *art rock*, which used large forms, complex harmonies, and sometimes quotations from classical music. One of the most important jazz rock groups was Blood, Sweat, and Tears, whose 1969 album launched three hits—*You've Made Me So Very Happy*, *And When I Die*, and *Spinning Wheel*, the last of which epitomized the style with its improvised solos and walking bass line. The group Chicago (*Does Anybody Really Know What Time It Is?* 1971), which was more rock-oriented, was noted for its horn lines and vocal improvisations.

Jazz rock

Art rock

Art rock (sometimes called *progressive rock*) was largely a British style, pio-

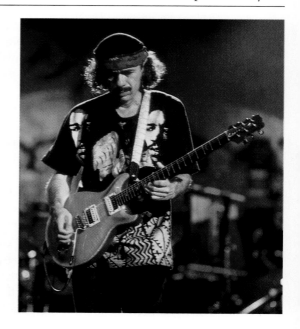

Guitarist Carlos Santana, who has remained a popular Latin rock and jazz musician for some twenty-five years, performing in Mexico City, 1993.

neered by the Moody Blues with their 1968 album *Days of Future Passed*, recorded with the London Symphony Orchestra. The Who experimented with opera, and the result was the first rock opera, *Tommy*, written by Peter Townshend and premiered in 1969. Three years later, keyboardist Keith Emerson together with Greg Lake and Carl Palmer produced a major art rock work based on a well-known suite by the Russian composer Musorgsky—*Pictures at an Exhibition*. One American who experimented with art rock's large forms was Frank Zappa (1940–1993), leader of the Mothers of Invention; Zappa invited listeners to dissect his music: "These things are so carefully constructed that it breaks my heart when people don't dig into them and see all the levels that I put into them."

Among the fusion bands that have remained popular is Santana, named after its leader-guitarist. The group started out as a California blues band to which Carlos Santana, the son of a Mexican mariachi musician, added Latin

Latin rock and African percussion instruments. The resulting style, called *Latin rock*, electrified the Woodstock audience. Santana's distinctive sound came from their instrumentation—conga drums (of African-Cuban origin, played with bare hands), maracas (Latin-American rattles), and timbales (small kettle-drums of Cuban origin)—their polyrhythmic drumming style, and their tight, Latin-style rhythms. A fine jazz guitarist, Carlos Santana has also recorded with many jazz artists. His band enjoyed international popularity in the early 1970s with such hit songs as *Evil Ways* (1969), *Black Magic Woman/Gypsy Queen* (1970), and *Guajira* (1971).

The 1970s and 1980s were characterized by a fragmentation of musical styles and a continual procession of new groups. Mainstream rock was represented by America (*A Horse with No Name*, 1972), The Eagles (*Hotel California*, 1972), and the Doobie Brothers (*Listen to the Music*, 1972), among others. The British once again invaded, this time with *heavy metal rock*, featuring simple, repetitive motives and loud, distorted instrumental solos. Led Zeppelin (*Whole Lotta' Love*, 1969) and Black Sabbath were the most important heavy metal bands of the 1970s. *Glitter rock*, a showy, theatrical style of performance, was best represented by Britain's outrageous David Bowie (*Diamond Dogs* album, 1974) and later by the talented keyboardist Elton John (*Bennie and the Jets*, from *Goodbye, Yellow Brick Road*, 1973). The ultimate rebellion came in the form of *punk rock*, a return to the basics of rock and roll—simple, repetitive, and loud—coupled with offensive lyrics and shocking behavior. Britain's Sex Pistols (*Anarchy in the U.K.* and *God Save the Queen*, both from 1977), featuring lead singer Johnny Rotten, was the first major punk group. They were followed by the Clash, who focused their music on the central issues of the punk rebellion: unemployment (*Career Opportunities*), violence (*Hate and War*), racism (*White Riot*), and police brutality (*Police and Thieves*). The last work is a *cover* (a recording that remakes an earlier recording by another singer or group) of a reggae hit.

Heavy metal rock

Glitter rock

Punk rock

Cover

Other reactions to the difficult times of the 1970s included the commercial dance music known as *disco*, and *reggae*, a Jamaican style with offbeat rhythms and chanted vocals that reflected the beliefs of a Christian religious movement known as Rastafarianism. Representative reggae groups included Bob Marley and the Wailers and Black Uhuru. The style was especially popular in Britain, where Eric Clapton's cover of Bob Marley's *I Shot the Sheriff* (1974) met with great success. A return to soft rock, yet another rejection of heavy metal and punk rock, was epitomized by such artists as the Carpenters (*We've Only Just Begun*, 1970) and Olivia Newton-John (*I Honestly Love You*, 1975), among others.

Disco and reggae

New wave, a direct outgrowth of punk rock, has been popular among British and American groups since the late 1970s, leading the way to a simpler, 1950s-based music. In Britain, the rock scene was set by Elvis Costello (backed up by the Attractions in *This Year's Model*, 1978) and Police, with lead singer Sting (*Roxanne*, 1978; *Every Breath You Take*, 1986). The New York City scene developed around a number of clubs in lower Manhattan, including CBGB's (Country, Blue Grass, and Blues), where Blondie debuted in 1975. Named for the attractive blond singer Deborah Harry, the group achieved commercial success with its album *Parallel Lines* (1978), and later turned to disco (*Heart of Glass*, 1980) and reggae styles (*The Tide Is High*, 1980). America's most influential new wave group was the Talking Heads, whose lyrics (by songwriter-singer David Byrne) focused on social commentary and whose style embraced third-world musics.

New wave

THE 1980S AND BEYOND

"Tonight I'm a rock and roll star."—NOEL GALLAGHER

Music videos The single most important development in the 1980s was the music video. Now, instead of the radio, the visual medium (and especially MTV, or Music Television, which premiered in August 1981 and launched its network of stars in January 1983) was the principal means of presenting music to the public. New and colorful performers like Duran Duran came on the scene, and an image- and fashion-conscious aesthetic soon dominated rock. One giant in the video arena was Michael Jackson, who had gained fame as a member of the Jackson Five (a group that carried on the Motown sound) and who then became a superstar in the 1980s. Jackson's album *Thriller* (1982–83) broke all previous sales figures; its hit songs included *The Girl Is Mine* (sung with Paul McCartney), *Billie Jean*, and *Beat It* (Jackson's version of the rumble scene from Bernstein's *West Side Story*). Jackson's fast dance style, together with his talent as a ballad singer, helps account for his continued popularity; his two-CD album *HIStory: Past, Present, and Future, Part 1*, topped the charts in 1995. Other Superstars of the 1980s include Bruce Springsteen (*Born in the USA*, 1984) and Madonna, who launched her first big hit with *Like a Virgin* (1984), which she followed with the eclectic album *True Blue* (1986). She has achieved great success, including a film career (*Evita*, 1996), based on her carefully developed image as a sex object.

Among the important groups in the late 1980s, two stand out. The Irish group U2 sounded a unified voice of political activism and personal spirituality in their collection *The Unforgettable Fire* (1984). Following a series of concerts for Live Aid and Amnesty International, the group achieved stardom with the 1987 Grammy-winning album *The Joshua Tree*, which included two major hits: *With or Without You* and *I Still Haven't Found What I'm Looking For*. The Los Angeles band Guns n' Roses, featuring outspoken lead singer Axl Rose and guitarist Slash, transcended their metal roots in *Appetite for Destruction* (1987) and *Use Your Illusion* (I and II, both from 1991), revealing an accessible style that is derivative of many of rock's greatest performers.

Rap The technological developments of the early 1980s, including the use of synthesizers and other electronic devices, paved the way for *rap*, a highly rhythmic style of musical patter that had been popular with New York audiences in the 1970s and later developed wider appeal. The group Run DMC (*Raising Hell*, 1986) was largely responsible for the commercialization of rap; their collaboration with Aerosmith on the cover recording of the 1977 hit song *Walk This Way* introduced the style to white audiences. Public Enemy, a

The Irish group U2, in concert at Zooropa in Rotterdam, the Netherlands, 1993.

group from Long Island, New York, produced several highly influential rap albums (*It Takes a Nation of Millions to Hold Us Back*, 1988; *Apocalypse 91: The Enemy Strikes Black*, 1991), and female rapper Queen Latifah made a strong case against the genre's frequent female bashing in *All Hail the Queen* (1989).

Rap in its diversified forms has continued as one of the most popular types of African-American music and has been imitated by white groups such as the Beastie Boys and Vanilla Ice. *Gangsta rap* of the 1990s has further dissem- inated the style through graphic descriptions of inner-city realities. Leaders in this style include N.W.A. (Niggas with Attitude), whose 1991 album *Efil4zag-gin* ("Niggaz 4 Life" backward) hit the top of the charts, and former N.W.A. rapper Ice Cube (*Death Certificate*, 1991). The violent shooting deaths of two well-known gangsta rappers, Tupac Shakur in 1996 and Notorious B.I.G. in 1997, has highlighted the violence associated with this musical style. B.I.G.'s last album, released after his murder, was appropriately titled *Life After Death* (1997).

Gangsta rap

Gansta rap is part of the much bigger hip-hop culture, the "urban alternative" rebellion of choice for many young people today. The riveting rhythms of hip hop have transcended racial boundaries; its sounds, slang, and fashions are now commonly featured on prime-time television, in movies, and in advertising.

The more mellow sounds of soul and rhythm and blues also have a strong following today, especially the music of Whitney Houston (*I Will Always Love You*, from the movie *The Bodyguard*, 1992), Mariah Carey (*Daydreams*, 1995), and the Motown-style quartet Boyz II Men (the album *II*, 1994). One of the most important forces behind the success of these performers is songwriter/producer/artist Kenneth "Babyface" Edmonds, who received record numbers of Grammy nominations in 1997 and 1998, including recognition for the best collaboration (with Stevie Wonder, in *Gone Too Soon*, a cover of a Michael Jackson tune), for the album of the year (*The Day*, 1998), and for the best song in a motion picture (*A Song for Mama*, sung by Boyz II Men in *Soul Food*, 1997).

Grunge rock

The late 1980s and early 1990s also saw the rise of a Seattle-based hybrid of punk and 1970s metal known as *grunge rock* (so-called after its harsh guitar sounds). Popular groups to come out of the grunge scene were Soundgarden, Nirvana, and Pearl Jam. Pearl Jam's *Ten* and Nirvana's *Nevermind* (1991) were huge hits, attracting widely diverse audiences. In 1994, when Nirvana was at the height of its popularity, guitarist-songwriter Kurt Cobain committed suicide; his untimely death at twenty-seven—the same age that signaled the end for Jimi Hendrix, Janis Joplin, and Jim Morrison—promoted sales of their last album, *Unplugged in New York* (1994). Pearl Jam has maintained a strong following with its more recent releases—*Vitalogy* (1994) and *Yield* (1998).

Among the newer alternative bands who have captured the spotlight are

Mariah Carey performing with Boyz II Men during the Grammy Awards, February 28, 1998.

The Smashing Pumpkins, whose 1995 album *Mellon Collie and the Infinite Sadness* exhibits a surprising breadth of styles. Popular groups representing the current English scene include Oasis (*Definitely Maybe*, 1994; *What's the Story / Morning Glory*, 1995), with well-crafted tunes by songwriter Noel Gallagher, and Bush (*Sixteen Stone*, 1995), which has been favorably compared with Nirvana.

Women musicians have come a long way in recent years, as evinced by the success of Courtney Love (a singer/actress and Kurt Cobain's widow) and Alanis Morissette (*Jagged Little Pill*, 1995), the first Canadian women to top the charts, and Celine Dion, who won a 1996 Grammy for *Falling into You* and who sang the award-winning song *My Heart Will Go On* in the blockbuster movie *Titanic* (1997). An all-female touring festival called Lilith Fair (which takes its name from a character in Jewish folklore who preceded Eve in the Garden of Eden), set up by the Canadian pop singer Sarah McLachlan and including Sheryl Crow, Jewel, Tracey Chapman, and Fiona Apple, is giving audiences the chance to see more of today's female music entertainers in live performances.

Women in rock

Recent years have seen a number of significant revivals as well. The Eagles regrouped for a tour (as well as a special performance at their induction into the Rock and Roll Hall of Fame) and for cutting the award-winning album *Hell Freezes Over* (1994); the Rolling Stones made several successful tours, the latest in 1997 (which Mick Jagger says is their last); and the Beatles, without John Lennon (who was shot and killed in 1980), reconstructed an old home demo to produce *Free as a Bird*, the opener to their chart-topping album of older songs *Anthology 1* (1995). England's Elton John has matured from his glitter rock days of the 1970s, writing memorable ballads for the soundtrack of Disney's delightful 1994 film *The Lion King* (*Can You Feel the Love Tonight?*) and for the Westminster Abbey funeral service of Diana, Princess of Wales (*Candle in the Wind*, 1997). American songwriter Bob Dylan has made a comeback as well, as a Kennedy Center honoree in the arts and compiler of a best-selling album, *Time out of Mind* (1997). The Dylan name promises to live on through his talented son, Jakob, guitarist with the group Wallflowers.

Revivals

At the forefront of older musical styles experiencing a new popularity is a punk-inspired ska, made popular by the Boston-based band The Mighty Mighty Bosstones (*Let's Face It*, 1997). The southern California group No Doubt has also helped to mainstream ska, with albums like *Tragic Kingdom* (1996).

This overview of rock has highlighted a mere handful of groups, those whose influence is difficult to challenge. Rock is unquestionably here to stay, but popularity in this genre is fleeting; only time will tell which current artists and styles will be remembered tomorrow.

WORLD BEAT

Today's most eclectic musical movement brings a new global perspective to the music listener. Not really a single style, this movement promotes popular music of the third world, ethnic and traditional music from all regions, and collaborations between Western and non-Western musicians. *World beat*, or *ethno-pop*, has been around for some time. In the 1950s, television fans heard Afro-Cuban music played by Desi Arnaz on the sitcom *I Love Lucy*, and enjoyed Harry Belafonte's vocal calypsos, a mixture of Jamaican and American styles. In the 1960s, the Brazilian bossa nova found favor (*The Girl from Ipanema*), and Ravi Shankar, along with the Beatles, brought Indian sitar music to the West.

The Chieftains and Irish Traditional Music

One style of world music that is enjoying immense popularity today is Irish traditional dance music. The best-known Irish band, The Chieftains, has been playing folk clubs and bars since the early 1960s, and more recently, touring all over the world as cultural ambassadors for their country. Their recordings not only demonstrate the authentic Irish style, but also show its adaptability to other traditional musics. In 1996, The Chieftains won a Grammy Award (their fifth) for their album *Pilgrimage to Santiago*, which merges Irish styles and instruments with music from Galicia, in northwest Spain. They have also been heard on a number of movie soundtracks, including *Barry Lyndon* (1975), *Far and Away* (1992), and *Rob Roy* (1995).

Irish instruments   The members are all virtuoso players of traditional Irish instruments. These include the *Irish*, or *Celtic, harp*, a small plucked harp with about thirty strings; *wooden flute*, a transverse instrument with one or more keys; *tin whistle*, a small, metal end-blown flute with finger holes; *uilleann*, or *union*, *pipes*, a type of bagpipe with an elbow-manipulated bellows rather than a blow pipe; *fiddle*, or violin; *bodhran*, a frame drum with a single goatskin head; and *concertina*, a small free-reed instrument similar to the accordion.

Irish dance types   Irish dance music generally falls into three categories: the *jig*, a lively dance that is often in compound meter; the *hornpipe*, a slower, more rhythmically articulated dance; and the *reel*, a moderately fast dance in duple meter. The reel is by far the most popular dance form—in an Irish club today, musicians might spend an entire evening playing only reels. Most dances have a two-part form (**A-B**) in which each part comprises eight measures broken into two similar four-measure phrases. Our example is a set of two reels that form a kind of miniature suite. The first tune, *The Wind That Shakes the Barley*, is well known to Irish enthusiasts; it unfolds in the standard two-part form, the

The Chieftains—Matt Molloy (wooden flute), Paddy Moloney (uilleann pipes), Kevin Conneff (bodhran), Sean Keane (fiddle), Derek Bell (in front, Irish harp), and Martin Fay (fiddle).

B section played in a range considerably higher than the first. The lively reel (of only sixteen measures) is repeated four times, with each new statement featuring a different solo instrument or combination. The wooden flute begins alone, but is joined in the **B** section by the fiddle and drum (bodhran). The pipes, with their unique nasal quality, provide a new timbre in the rousing third statement of the tune, and the full instrumental ensemble leads the fifth statement almost imperceptibly into the next tune. *The Reel with the Beryle* has a more disjunct melodic line that is introduced on the concertina. As in the first reel, the **B** section proceeds into a higher range, and its varied statements—five in all—feature different instrumental combinations.

The music of these two reels is essentially melodic, with little harmony or counterpoint. Like jazz, it relies on ornamentation, or melodic and rhythmic variations—such as filling in intervals and inserting *grace notes* (short decorative notes attached to the main pitches of the tune)—and on heterophonic performance (in which different players decorate the same line at the same time).

Together with the rise in popularity of Irish dance music has come an increased interest in traditional *step dancing*, in which dancers perform intricate footwork, similar to tap, while holding their arms straight down at their sides and keeping their backs perfectly straight. This dance style has been made world famous by Michael Flatley (known for his ability to tap twenty-eight times per second, according to *The Guinness Book of World Records*), who, after dancing for some years with The Chieftains, created the popular show *Riverdance* (1994). The wide acclaim accorded his recent theater piece, *Lord of the Dance* (1996), attests to the continued allure of this newest dance craze.

In His Own Words

The great leaders of the world should learn the tin whistle and have a party.
—*Paddy Moloney*

Step dancing

Listening Guide 73

CD: Chr/Std 8/66–75, Sh 4/51–60
Cassette: Chr/Std 8B/6, Sh 4A/10

The Wind That Shakes the Barley/The Reel with the Beryle, by The Chieftains   (2:54)

Genre: Irish traditional dance music; arranged by Mick Turbridy

Form: Two reels, each with 2 sections (**A** and **B**, 8 measures each)

Meter: Cut time (¢)

Texture: Heterophonic

Instruments: Wooden flute, fiddles (violins), tin whistle, bodhran (drum), uilleann pipes, Irish harp, concertina

---

The Wind That Shakes the Barley
Performance: Tune played five times
Phrase structure:
    A = a + a′ (two 4-measure phrases, second varied)
    B = b + b′ (two 4-measure phrases, second varied)

		Section	Instruments	Traditional tune *(recording features variations and ornamentation)*

66	0:00	1	**A:** a	Solo flute:	
			a′	Solo flute:	
			B: b	Fiddle, flute, bodhran:	
			b′	Fiddle, flute, bodhran:	
67	0:17	2	**A:** a	Fiddle, flute, bodhran	
			a′	Fiddle, flute, bodhran	
			B: b	Fiddle, flute, bodhran	
			b′	Ensemble	
68	0:34	3	**A:** a	Fiddle, flute, bodhran	
			a′	Ensemble	
			B: b	Pipes, harp, bodhran	
			b′	Pipes, harp, bodhran	

69	0:51	4	**A:**	a	Fiddle, flute, bodhran
				a′	Ensemble
			B:	b	Fiddle, flute, bodhran
				b′	Ensemble
70	1:08	5	**A:**	a	Pipes, harp, bodhran
				a′	Pipes, harp, bodhran
			B:	b	Ensemble
				b′	Ensemble

The Reel with the Beryle

Performance: Tune played five times
Phrase structure:

    A = a + a′ (two 4-measure phrases, second varied)
    B = b + c (two different 4-measure phrases)

			Section	Instruments	Traditional tune
71	1:25	1	**A:** a	Concertina, bodhran:	
			a′	Concertina, bodhran:	
			B: b	Fiddle, flute, bodhran, concertina:	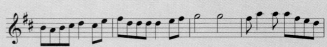
			c	Fiddle, flute, bodhran, concertina:	
72	1:42	2	**A:** a	Fiddle, flute, bodhran, concertina	
			a′	Fiddle, flute, bodhran, concertina	
			B: b	Ensemble	
			c	Ensemble	
73	1:59	3	**A:** a	Pipes, harp, bodhran	
			a′	Pipes, harp, bodhran	
			B: b	Ensemble	
			c	Ensemble	
74	2:16	4	**A:** a	Pipes, harp, bodhran	
			a′	Pipes, harp, bodhran	
			B: b	Ensemble	
			c	Ensemble	
75	2:33	5	**A:** a	Ensemble	
			a′	Ensemble	
			B: b	Ensemble	
			c	Ensemble	

Cultural Perspective 20

THE SOUNDS OF WORLD BEAT

If you visit your nearest CD store and browse through the international or world section, you are likely to find an overwhelming selection from all corners of the earth—chants by Tibetan monks, Bolivian panpipe ensembles, Javanese gamelan orchestras, folk songs from Bosnia and Herzegovina, Russian balalaika ensembles, ceremonial drumming from Ghana, and Navajo dance music, to name only a few possibilities. It seems that America is as hungry for world music as it is for pizza and sushi.

Where did a listening audience with such international tastes come from? This global awakening began with the wars of the mid–twentieth century, in which thousands of Americans were transported to far-off places (South Pacific islands, Vietnam, Iraq), and the public at home was made increasingly aware of these locales through the media. Global communications brought us vivid, next-day images from Vietnam and, some years later, live pictures from Kuwait. Another factor was the raised

sociopolitical consciousness of the 1960s and such historical events as Woodstock, where hundreds of thousands were moved by the performance of Indian sitarist Ravi Shankar playing a music to which they had had little prior exposure. Today, we can experience world musics first-hand through a transportation network that allows fast travel to all regions of the globe; meanwhile, at home, the media—radio, TV, video, movies, and the Internet—continually feed our appetite for new sounds. Recording companies are responding to increased consumer demand for world musics, producing all kinds of specialty collections as well as samplers for those who want a varied multicultural listening experience.

Does a recording of modern world music capture the essence of a culture's tradition? There are a number of historical field recordings by anthropologists and ethnomusicologists that carefully preserve traditional musics and ceremonies as they existed at the time of the recording. (We

Ladysmith Black Mambazo and Music of South Africa

Graceland

A famous and successful collaboration of differing musical cultures resulted in Paul Simon's album *Graceland* (1986), which featured various styles of South African music. Simon was especially attracted to a style known as "township jive," the street music of Soweto, and to the musicality of South

will study one such recording from the Republic of Uganda in a later chapter.) You can probably find some of these collections in your college or university library (the Nonesuch Explorer series and Folkways recordings are fairly standard). But music is a living art. Thus, despite efforts to preserve "authentic" musics of certain cultures, what we hear today is often a fusion of styles—traditional, art, and pop—from around the world. Some of these popular musics reflect the strong impact of Western rock—the recordings of Algerian musician Khaled Hadj Brahim exemplify this influence. Other styles, such as the South African music of Ladysmith Black Mambazo and the Irish dance music of The Chieftains (both of whom we will hear), cultivate more indigenous sounds, setting them in a contemporary idiom for today's avid listeners.

Suggested Listening:

South African music (Ladysmith Black Mambazo)
Irish music (The Chieftains)
Tibetan music (Gyütö monks)
Senegalese music (Youssou N'Dour)
Algerian music (Khaled Hadj Brahim)

The Gyütö monks from Tibet, famous for their extraordinary style of chanting Buddhist Tantras.

Africa's popular *a cappella* vocal group Ladysmith Black Mambazo. The album was politically controversial in the United States, since it violated commercial sanctions against South Africa's apartheid policy; in the end, however, it did much to further the cause of the black population there. Simon called on musicians from around the world, including the popular Senegalese singer Youssou N'Dour. The album also introduced to the Ameri-

Mbube

can public Ladysmith Black Mambazo, which went on to win the Grammy Award for the best traditional folk recording of 1988.

The South African choral singing heard on *Graceland* exemplifies a traditional style developed by Zulu migrant workers that came to be known as *mbube* (lion). This style was first introduced to the Western world in the early 1950s by the folk group the Weavers in *Wimoweh* (made better-known by the Tokens in 1961 as *The Lion Sleeps Tonight*), and is now familiar to many through the recordings of Ladysmith Black Mambazo. Originally sung in labor camps to alleviate loneliness, mbube singing became linked to protest against apartheid. The music features the call-and-response pattern typical of many African cultures, with the *a cappella* choral responses set in rich, close-knit harmonies sung in medium to slow tempos. Irregular phrasing and syncopated rhythms enliven the musical movement, and special effects such as trilled vocal glides and blues-style interjections are typical.

Ladysmith Black Mambazo has long been a voice for peace and freedom in South Africa; in the role of cultural ambassador, the group sang in Oslo, Norway, in December 1993, when Nelson Mandela and former South African president F. W. de Klerk were awarded the Nobel Peace Prize for their efforts to end apartheid. *Kangivumanga* (*I Disagreed*), by Joseph Shabalala, a professor at the University of Natal and the leader of Ladysmith Black Mambazo, presents a strong antiracist message, in Zulu and English, in the traditional *a*

Joseph Shabalala, founder and leader of the popular South African vocal group Ladysmith Black Mambazo.

South African songwriter and actress Tsidii Le Loka plays Rafiki, the baboon-shaman, in the spectacular Disney Broadway production of The Lion King *(1997). The score, with new music by Le Loka, evokes traditional African styles.*

cappella style. The voices move in parallel motion as they follow the natural rhythmic and melodic inflections of the words, exchanging ideas with the soloist. The group's polished style of singing, known as *iscathamiya* (stalking approach), exemplifies the urbanization of traditional choral music.

Listening Guide 74

CD: Chr/Std 8/76–78
Cassette: Chr/Std 8B/7

Kangivumanga (I Disagreed), by Ladysmith Black Mambazo

(5:09)

Date of work: Recorded 1996

Text and music: By Joseph Shabalala (in Zulu and English)

Genre: World beat, South African *mbube*

Singing style: Call and response; chorus in close harmony (*iscathamiya*, stalking approach)

Special effects: Vocal glides, trills, interjections, and nonlexical vocables

Medium: A *cappella* male vocal group (9 members), Joseph Shabalala, leader

76	0:00	Unkulunkulu wethu
		Ubaba wethu ungumdali wethu
		Nguye lo sithanda sonke
		Uma kukhon okonakele
		Masibuyele kwezomdabu
		Masilalele abadala
		Bathi akukho silima
		Sindlebende kwaso

77	0:33	Please note, when I say
		Our Creator, I do not
		Mean any particular race,
		Color, or creed. I love
		My brothers and sisters.
		Somebody was begging me
		To hate one of my brothers and sisters;
		I said no, no, no, never, never, never.

	1:16	Different colors [it] means nothing to me,
		Different languages [it] means nothing to me,
		Different names [it] means nothing to me.

78	1:31	Kukhona lomuntu okade engincenga
		Ethi phakathi kwabafowethu no dadewethu
		Angizonde omnye wo mina kangivumanga
		Chabobo ngike ngimbulale mina udadewethu
		Ngeke ngimbulale mina umzala wami
		Ngeke ngimbulale mina umfowethu
		Ngeke ngimbulale mina ugogo
		Ngeke ngimbulale mina umkhulu
		Ngeke ngimbulale mina ubaba
		Ngeke ngimbulale mina uma.

| | 2:36 | Different colors [it] means nothing to me, |
| | | Different names [it] means nothing to me. |

| | | Repeated Zulu text |

| | 4:40 | Different colors [it] means nothing to me, |
| | | Different names [it] means nothing to me. |

Unit XXV

The New Music

79

New Directions

"From Schoenberg I learned that tradition is a home we must love and forgo."—LUKAS FOSS

The term "new music" has been used throughout history. Nearly every generation of creative musicians produced sounds and styles that had never been heard before. All the same, the innovations of the past half century have outstripped the most far-reaching changes of earlier times, truly justifying the label "new music." In effect, we have witnessed nothing less than the birth of a new world of sound.

THE ARTS SINCE MID-CENTURY

The increasing social turmoil since the Second World War has inevitably been reflected in the arts, which are passing through a period of violent experimentation with new media, new materials, and new techniques. Artists are freeing themselves from every vestige of the past in order to explore new areas of thought and feeling.

A trend away from objective painting led to Abstract Expressionism in the

Abstract Expressionism

In Abstract Expressionism, space and mass become independent values, liberated from the need to express reality. Elegy to the Spanish Republic No. 18, *by* **Robert Motherwell** *(1915–1991).* (Museum of Modern Art, New York; © Dedalus Foundation/licensed by VAGA, New York)

United States during the 1950s and 1960s. In the canvases of such painters as Robert Motherwell and Jackson Pollock, space, mass, and color were freed from the need to imitate objects in the real world. The urge toward abstraction was felt equally in sculpture, as is evident in the work of such artists as Henry Moore and Isamu Noguchi. (See illustration on facing page.)

Pop Art

At the same time, a new kind of realism appeared in the art of Jasper Johns, Robert Rauschenberg, and their colleagues, who owed some of their inspiration to the Dadaists of four decades earlier. Rauschenberg's aim, as he put it, was to work "in the gap between life and art." This trend culminated in Pop Art, which drew its themes and techniques from modern urban life: machines, advertisements, comic strips, movies, commercial photography, and familiar objects connected with everyday living. A similar aim motivated Andy Warhol's *Four Campbell's Soup Cans*, Jim Dine's *A Nice Pair of Boots*, Rauschenberg's *First Landing Jump*, and Roy Lichtenstein's *Whaam!* (see p. 622).

Post-Modernism

Today, the term "Post-Modernism"—suggesting a movement away from formalism—is applied to a variety of styles, including conceptual art, minimalism, and environmental art. One of the most successful proponents of Post-Modernism is the architect Michael Graves, whose Humana Building in Louisville, Kentucky, features a monumental entrance and a lobby reminiscent of an ancient temple. A familiar Neoclassical structure of the Post-Modern era is I. M. Pei's *Grand Louvre Pyramid*, in Paris (see p. 625). Environmental art, sometimes called earthworks, is one manifestation of the minimalist movement, which advocates a bareness and simplicity (we will read about minimalism in music in Chapter 83). The artist Robert Smithson is well-known for *Spiral Jetty* (1970), an environmental sculpture in the Great Salt Lake, in Utah (see p. 628).

The feminist movement has affected mainstream developments in the art world since the late 1960s, by focusing attention on a lesser-known body of works and artists and on issues of gender. The collaborative projects led by Judy Chicago, carried out by teams of women artists, have contributed much to this movement: an example is the celebrated artwork *The Dinner Party* (1979), a triangular table with thirty-nine place settings, which pays homage to important women throughout history. Recently, serious attention has also been paid to the artistic achievements of America's diverse ethnic communities, especially the African-American, Latino, and Native American. The AIDS epidemic of recent decades has inspired a monumental example of public art—the AIDS Memorial Quilt, an ongoing community project intended to commemorate the many thousands who have died and to raise public awareness of this social crisis. (The 79,000 names on the quilt's 45,000 panels represent only a small fraction of the victims worldwide.)

A national art of *perestroika* (openness) has arisen in countries of the former Soviet Union. This new avant-garde style, essentially a deconstruction of the "official" Soviet art, can be seen in the works of the Russian artist Eric Bulatov. A nationalist style has developed in China as well; the canvases of Yu Youhan, for example, combine elements of pop art and the ancient Chinese art of block printing. In *Mao and Blonde Girl Analyzed* (1992; p. 623), the blond girl, symbolic of involuntary Westernization, is juxtaposed with a portrait of the Chinese leader.

In the field of literature, poetry has lent itself to the most widespread ex-

Feminist and ethnic art

Poetry

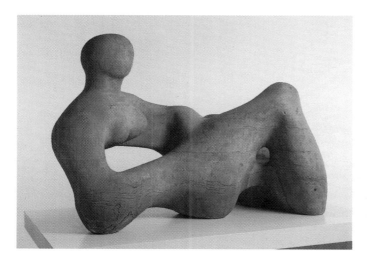

The urge toward abstraction has been felt by sculptors such as **Henry Moore** *(1898–1986). Recumbent Figure. (Tate Gallery, London)*

perimentation. Many poets face the contemporary world with a profound sense of alienation. Modern American verse ranges from complex intellectualism to the Whitmanesque exuberance of the "beat generation," with a great variety of forms. In recent years, the poetry and literature of various cultural groups has received widespread attention. Among these, African-American poet Maya Angelou, American Yiddish writer Isaac Bashevis Singer, and West Indian Derek Walcott have been awarded Nobel Prizes in literature.

Drama and the novel   Since drama and the novel are by their very nature based on an imitation of life, they have not remained indifferent to the new trends. The theater moved away from the social and psychological concerns that permeated the plays of Arthur Miller (such as *The Crucible*, 1953) and Tennessee Williams (*Cat on a Hot Tin Roof*, 1955) in the 1950s, turning instead to the "theater of the absurd," whose leading European proponents—Samuel Beckett (*Waiting for Godot*, 1956) and Eugene Ionesco (*Rhinoceros*, 1960)—viewed the world with a vast disillusionment. The spirit of the absurd also penetrated the novel; witness such works as *Catch 22* (1961), by Joseph Heller, and *Slaughterhouse Five* (1969), by Kurt Vonnegut, to name only two that caught the pulse of the 1960s.

Recent writers who have captured the attention of the literary world include British dramatist Tom Stoppard (*Rosencrantz and Guildenstern Are Dead*, 1967, based on two minor characters from Shakespeare's *Hamlet*), American playwright/screenwriter/actor Sam Shepard (*Buried Child*, 1978; *A Fool for Love*, 1983), and New York playwright Wendy Wasserstein (*The Heidi Chronicles*, 1989; *The Sisters Rosensweig*, 1993). Among the distinguished novelists of our time are Nobel laureates Saul Bellow (*Humboldt's*

Roy Lichtenstein *(1923–1997) fully embraced popular mass culture in his enlarged comic strips, such as* Whaam! *(1963). Acrylic on canvas.* (Tate Gallery, London)

In Mao and Blonde Girl Analyzed *(1992),* **Yu Youhan** *(b. 1943) combines elements of Chinese peasant paintings and pop art with Socialist Realism. Acrylic on canvas.*

Gift, 1976) and Toni Morrison (*Beloved,* 1987) as well as Pulitzer Prize winners John Updike (*The Centaur,* 1963; the *Rabbit* tetralogy, 1960–91) and Jane Smiley (*A Thousand Acres,* 1992), to name only a few. Latin-American writers who have risen to prominence include Gabríel Garcia Márquez, who has produced some of the great novels of our age (*One Hundred Years of Solitude,* 1967; *Love in the Time of Cholera,* 1985).

Linked to developments in modern theater is performance art, which combines visual stimuli with theater and music. The term "happening" was coined in the 1960s to describe this semi-improvised multimedia event, which was often highly dependent on audience participation. The experimental composer John Cage was intrigued by this art form, as is Laurie Anderson, who uses a combination of popular music, storytelling, comic routines, and high-tech equipment to address social issues (see p. 630).

Performance art

Several trends have changed the way we look at literature. For example, deconstruction, developed in the early 1970s, is based on the concept that any text can be understood to say something quite different from what it first appears to mean; a deconstructive interpretation focuses only on the text itself, without concern for external influences, such as its context. Feminine criti-

Literary criticism

cism, popular since the late 1960s, questions long-standing male interpretations of texts and attempts to describe experience as depicted in literature from the female point of view. (On feminism and music, see CP 3.)

New wave cinema

Finally, film—of all the arts the one most securely chained to popular storytelling—has also responded to the twin impulses of experimentation and abstraction. "New wave" directors include Jean-Luc Godard (*Breathless*, 1959), Federico Fellini (*La Strada*, 1959; *8½*, 1963), Michelangelo Antonioni (*Blowup*, 1966; *The Passenger*, 1975), and Louis Malle (*My Dinner with André*, 1981; *Au revoir, les enfants*, 1987). In films like Alain Resnais's *Last Year at Marienbad* (1962) and Ingmar Bergman's *Persona* (1966), the Abstract Expressionist urge was realized on the screen.

A number of national cinemas have come into their own in the past several decades. In the 1970s, German filmmakers, among them Rainer Werner Fassbinder (*The Marriage of Maria Braun*, 1978), were world leaders in the genre. Japanese and Chinese films have also received critical attention, especially those of China's Zhang Yimou (*Raise the Red Lantern*, 1991; *The Story of Qiu Ju*, 1992), which depict tragedies suffered under the Communists. Polish filmmaker Krzysztof Kieslowski has also presented poignant views of his native country throwing off Communist rule (*Three Colors* trilogy: *Blue*, 1993; *White*, 1994; *Red*, 1994). The genre of nonnarrative film is best exemplified by American Godfrey Reggio (*Koyaanisqatsi*, 1983; *Powaqqatsi*, 1988), whose visual collages soar against the minimalist music of Philip Glass. Such "art films" have given us profound insights into the lives of people all over the world. The long-term marriage of film and music in popular and art cultures is explored in CP 21.

The artworks mentioned above are only a few landmarks in the second half of the twentieth century, but they are enough to indicate that all the arts have become increasingly intellectual, experimental, and abstract.

TOWARD GREATER ORGANIZATION IN MUSIC

When Schoenberg based his twelve-tone method on the use of tone rows, he was obviously moving toward a much stricter organization of sound material. It remained for later generations to extend the tone-row principle to the elements of music other than pitch—such as durations (time values), dynamic values (degrees of loudness), or timbres. Registers and densities, types of attack, and sizes of intervals might also be organized serially. By thus extending the serial principle in all possible directions, a composer could

The Grand Louvre Pyramid, *at the entrance to the expansion of the Louvre, provides a Neoclassical skylight for viewing Paris's historic museum. It was designed by the Chinese-American architect* **I. M. Pei** *(b. 1917).*

achieve a totally organized fabric. This move toward *total serialism* resulted in an extremely complex, ultrarational music. The composers who embraced the idea, such as Pierre Boulez and Karlheinz Stockhausen, pushed the experience of listening to music to unprecedented limits.

Total serialism

TOWARD GREATER FREEDOM IN MUSIC

"My music liberates because I give people the chance to change their minds in the way I've changed mine."—JOHN CAGE

The urge toward a totally controlled music had its counterpart in the desire for greater, even total, freedom from all predetermined forms and procedures. Music of this type emphasizes the antirational element in artistic

MUSIC FOR FILMS

It is difficult to imagine a film or TV program today whose musical soundtrack—whether in the background or the foreground—does not affect and enhance our response to the on-screen visuals. We react accordingly, whether the music ominously forecasts the action—sounding the shark's rhythmic theme in *Jaws* just before an attack, for example—or ceremoniously announces the victor in battle, as in Luke Skywalker's triumph over Darth Vader in *Star Wars*. The music can even help viewers understand relationships between characters and complex details of plots, thus allowing us to enjoy foreign films as well as those in our own language.

Music has been linked with films from the very beginning: the silent movies of the early 1900s were accompanied by a pianist or organist playing from the theater pit, improvising music on the spot to enhance the action. The first full-length masterwork, *The Birth of a Nation* (1915), directed by D. W. Griffith, set technical and musical standards for silent films. This and similar movies were shown in some theaters to the accompaniment of live orchestras playing medleys of popular and classical works. The first "talkie," or film with spoken dialogue, was in fact a musical: *The Jazz Singer* (1927), starring the famous singer Al Jolson.

Most of the important early film composers were Europeans. Among those who wrote for silent films were Camille Saint-Saëns, Arthur Honegger, Darius Milhaud, Pietro Mascagni, and Jean Sibelius, all of whom are discussed elsewhere in this book. We have already noted a major contribution by the Russian composer Sergei Prokofiev. His first effort, commissioned by the director Feinzimmer, produced the score for *Lieutenant Kije* (1933), a satirical story of a soldier who never was. One of his most popular works, *Lieutenant Kije* illustrates Prokofiev's range of humorous expression in music. On a trip to the United States in 1936, the Russian master visited movie studios in Hollywood to study film music techniques. On his return to Russia, he was commissioned by Sergei Eisenstein to write the music for *Alexander Nevsky*. Prokofiev's masterful score heightens the intense drama of this film, especially in the magnificently visualized battle sequence where the attacking German army is swallowed by the cracking ice on Lake Chudskoye. Prokofiev and Eisenstein collaborated again to produce the epic two-part film *Ivan the Terrible* (1943, 1946).

While the American movie studios were leaders in the industry, music for films in the 1930s, 1940s, and 1950s was shaped largely byEuropean émigré composers, such as Erich Wolfgang Korngold (*The Adventures of Robin Hood, 1938*), Max Steiner (*King Kong,* 1933; *Gone with the Wind,* 1939; *Casablanca,* 1943; *The Big Sleep,* 1946), and Bernard Herrmann (*Citizen Kane,* 1941; *Vertigo,* 1958; *Psycho,* 1960; *Journey to the Center of the Earth,* 1959; *Fahrenheit 451,* 1966). Steiner's prolific output of film scores was astounding (over 200 in all!); furthermore, he introduced the concept of theme music—derived from Wagner's use of leitmotifs in opera—with "Tara's Theme" from *Gone with the Wind*. Many film composers have adopted this technique, including John Barry in the popular James Bond series and Henry Mancini in the hilarious Pink Panther movies.

Some films depend on well-known musical classics for their effect. Who can forget the association of Dukas's delightful *Sorcerer's Apprentice* with Mickey Mouse and his magic gone awry in the landmark animated movie *Fantasia* (1940)? Another of the film's musical episodes unites Stravinsky's revolutionary *Rite of Spring* with images of dinosaurs stalking the earth. The now-classic film *2001: A Space Odyssey* (1968) launched Richard Strauss's powerful tome poem *Thus Spake Zarathustra* onto the Top 40 charts and left an indelible connection for many between space flight and the elegant waltzes of Johann Strauss Jr.

Music for films is often original, newly created for each scene. One of the most successful and best-known film composers today is John Williams, who began his career writing for television. He moved from the popular 1960s TV series *Gilligan's Island* to the big screen, writing memorable scores for *Jaws* (1975), *Close Encounters of the Third Kind* (1977), and the ever-popular *Star Wars* trilogy (1977, 1980, 1983; all remastered in 1996–97). Like the great Leonard Bernstein (see p. 588), Williams's talents cross over into concert music—he recently wrote a concerto for the world-famous cellist Yo-Yo Ma—and conducting: he led the Boston Pops Orchestra from 1980 to 1995.

Today the masters of film music often rely on electronic and computer-generated sounds, both for special effects and to simulate an entire orchestra. Whatever the sound source, music is crucial to the full, multimedia experience of film, whether we are sitting in an IMAX wide-screen theater or watching a video in our own living room.

In this scene from Star Wars—*featuring Han Solo (Harrison Ford), Obi-Wan Kenobi (Alec Guinness), Luke Skywalker (Mark Hamill), and Chewbacca (Peter Mayhew)—John Williams's score heightens the drama as the starship* Millennium Falcon *is drawn into the tractor beam of the Death Star.*

The Spiral Jetty, *built in 1970 by* **Robert Smithson,** *is an environmental sculpture in the Great Salt Lake, Utah. It exemplifies the principles of bareness and simplicity that characterize the minimalist movement.*

experience: intuition, chance, the spur of the moment. Composers who wish to avoid the rational ordering of musical sound may rely on the element of chance and allow, for example, a throw of dice to determine rhythm and melody, or perhaps build their pieces around a series of random numbers generated by a computer. They may let the performer choose the order in which the sections are to be played, or indicate the general range of pitches, durations, and registers but leave it up to the performer to fill in the details. The performance thus becomes a musical "happening" in the course of which the piece is re-created afresh each time it is played.

Aleatoric music   Such indeterminate music is known as *aleatoric* (from *alea*, the Latin word for "dice"). In aleatoric music, the overall form may be clearly indicated, but the details are left to choice or chance. On the other hand, some composers, among them John Cage, will indicate the details of a composition clearly enough but leave its overall shape to choice or chance; this type of flexible

Open form   structure is known as *open form*. Related to these tendencies is the increased reliance on improvisation—a technique common in music of the Baroque and earlier eras and, of course, in jazz. Traditionally, improvisation consists of spontaneous invention within a known framework and a style, so that player and listener have fairly well defined ideas of what is "good" and what is "bad." In the more extreme types of aleatory music, no such criteria are set; anything that happens is acceptable to the composer.

A representative figure of this new freedom is Lukas Foss (b. 1922), whose *Time Cycle* (1960) and *Echoi* (1961–63) placed him in the forefront of those who were experimenting with indeterminacy, group improvisation, and fresh approaches to sound. Foss was also a leader in a trend adopted from the visual arts called *collage*, in which musical fragments from other composers' works are juxtaposed or overlapped within a new composition.

Contemporary attitudes have liberated not only forms but all the elements of music from the restrictions of the past. The idea that music must be based on the twelve pitches of the chromatic scale has been left far behind. Electronic instruments make possible the use of sounds that lie "in the cracks of the piano keys"—the *microtonal* intervals, such as quarter tones, that are smaller than semitones—and very skilled instrumentalists and vocalists have now mastered these novel scales.

Microtonality

THE INTERNATIONALISM OF THE NEW MUSIC

The Second World War and the events leading up to it disrupted musical life in Europe much more than in North America, with the result that the United States forged ahead in certain areas. The first composer to apply serial organization to dimensions other than pitch was the American Milton Babbitt, and the experiments of John Cage anticipated and influenced similar attempts abroad. Earle Brown (b. 1926) was the first to use open form; Morton Feldman (1926–1987) was the first to write works that gave the performer a choice. Once the war was over, the Europeans quickly made up for lost time. Intense experimentation went on in Italy, Germany, France, England, the Netherlands, and Scandinavia. Serial and electronic music have also taken root in Japan, while the music of the East has in turn influenced Western composers.

A number of Europeans have achieved international reputations. Luciano Berio (b. 1925) is a leading figure among the radicals of the post-Webern generation in Italy. He was one of the founders of the electronic studio in Milan, which became a center of avant-garde activity, and for several years taught composition at the Juilliard School in New York. Berio's music exemplifies three major trends in the contemporary scene—serialism, electronic technology, and indeterminacy. A characteristic work is his well-known

Luciano Berio

Mixed-media artist **Laurie Anderson,** *whose face is magnified in this scene from her film* Home of the Brave *(1986), is accompanied by two backup singers and a saxophonist.*

homage to Martin Luther King Jr., *Sinfonia* (1969), for orchestra, organ, harps, piano, chorus, and reciters.

Iannis Xenakis

The music of Greek composer Iannis Xenakis (b. 1922), who was trained as an engineer, expresses the close ties between music and science that characterize our time. Xenakis's music derives its very special sound from massed sonorities, prominent use of glissandos, and a texture woven out of individual parts for each instrument in the orchestra. In a search for new sonorities,

Krzysztof Penderecki

Krzysztof Penderecki (b. 1933), Poland's foremost composer, has written scores that include such noises as the sawing of wood and the clicking of typewriters. His choral music calls on singers to hiss, shout, whistle, articulate rapid consonants, and the like. In these techniques, he has been much influenced by Xenakis.

Karlheinz Stockhausen

The German composer Karlheinz Stockhausen (b. 1928) assumed leadership in the 1950s of an international group of composers who worked at an avant-garde radio station studio in Cologne, Germany. His works pursue the possibilities of serialism, aleatoric technique, improvisation, and electronic manipulation of prerecorded tape. Pierre Boulez, the most important com-

Pierre Boulez

poser of the French avant-garde, is widely known for his activities as a conductor and as head of IRCAM (the French government's institute for composition and acoustics). We will study a work by Boulez in the next chapter. The

Sofiya Gubaidulina

Russian composer Sofiya Gubaidulina (b. 1931) stands out as a leader among women on the international scene. She brings to modern techniques a strong spiritual element. In some vocal works, she gives the voice nontextual and highly emotional utterances. Her reputation was established by her Violin Concerto, entitled *Offertorium* (1980), which parodies J. S. Bach's *Musical Offering* in a Webernesque setting.

OTHER VOICES OF THE NEW MUSIC

Among the American composers who have made significant contributions to the development of new music is Elliott Carter (b. 1908), whose deeply profound and well-crafted works have been widely praised. Carter's dissonant chromaticism places him among the Abstract Expressionists. Some of his works employ a novel technique that he calls "metric modulation," in which fluctuating tempos help create the form of a piece.

Several composers have tried to reconcile serial procedures with tonality. None has played a more important role in this area than George Perle (b. 1915), who has retained the concept of tonal centers while using a language based on the twelve-tone scale. In 1986, Perle won the Pulitzer Prize for his Wind Quintet IV as well as a "genius" grant from the MacArthur Foundation. Before then, he was known chiefly for his books, including *Serial Composition and Atonality* (1962) and *Twelve-Tone Tonality* (1978).

Charles Wuorinen (b. 1938) started out from the sound world of Stravinsky, Schoenberg, and French composer Edgard Varèse (see p. 670) and found his way to the twelve-tone system in the 1960s. He freely adapts the procedures of serialism to the needs of a particular piece. A prolific composer, he has received his share of awards and honors, among them a Pulitzer Prize and a MacArthur grant. Ralph Shapey (b. 1921) directs the Contemporary Chamber Players at the University of Chicago. A disciple of Varèse, Shapey defines music as "an object in Time and Space: aggregate sounds structured into concrete sculptural forms." Although his output is mostly instrumental, he was one of the first American composers to treat the voice as an instrument, "using syllables in organized sound-structures."

Among women composers, Louise Talma (b. 1906), who studied with the French teacher Nadia Boulanger, is an important exponent of serialism. Much influenced by Stravinsky, Talma retains tonal qualities in her music while using advanced serial techniques as added unifying procedures. She is known for her choral works, including *La Corona* (1955) and an opera, *The Alcestiad* (1955–58), a collaboration with writer Thornton Wilder. Barbara Kolb (b. 1939), the first American woman to win the prestigious Prix de Rome, has developed a personal style of serialism. Her piano work *Appello* (1976), based on Pierre Boulez's *Structures* (1952), is written in a much more expressive style of serialism than the sparse pointillism of her model.

Elliott Carter

George Perle

Charles Wuorinen

Ralph Shapey

Louise Talma

Barbara Kolb

Cultural Perspective 22

CANADA'S VISION FOR A GLOBAL CULTURE

What significant contemporary musical trends are found in Canada? A huge, multi-ethnic country, Canada has established a national arts identity despite its linguistic and cultural divisions and its relative youth as a nation (it achieved independence in 1867). Thus while the traditional musics of Canada are widely varied—representing the French, British, Native American, and Inuit (Eskimo) cultures—its modern art music has presented a more unified and mainstream front.

Canadian composers are notable for their interest in avant-garde techniques. With the advent of electronic music in the 1950s, Canada was quick to respond with studios around the country—in Ottawa, Toronto, Montreal, and Vancouver. Composer John Weinzweig (b. 1913) first championed twelve-tone technique in Canada; he, along with Jean Papineau-Couture of the French-Canadian community, actively sought support for new music through an organization they headed, the Canadian League of Composers. The country also boasts one of the best music information centers in the world, devoted exclusively to the promotion and dissemination of music by Canadians. Another important music institution is the National Youth Orchestra of Canada, whose commitment to discovering and training young musicians has contributed significantly to the high quality of Canada's performance groups.

Most contemporary Canadian composers have felt the influence of one of the country's important thinkers, Marshall McLuhan (1911–1980), who early on saw the far-reaching consequences of electronic communication. McLuhan prophesied the coming of what he called a "global village," achieved through the mass media of radio, TV, films, and computers—in short, a new way of experiencing the world. He firmly believed, however, that the means of communication—the medium—had more influence than the actual message. (The commonly heard phrase "The medium is the message" is the title of a book by McLuhan.) His writings had a significant impact on composer John Cage, who included selected phrases in a verbal collage (published under the title *I-VI*, 1988–89).

One Canadian composer who has responded to the ideas of both McLuhan and Cage is R. Murray Schafer (b. 1933). His early interest in new techniques of sound, notation, and mixed media, especially theater, has led him to a world wide study of acoustic ecology. This project, known as World Soundscapes, explores the relationship between people and the sounds of the environment. Echoing McLuhan's concern for the impact of technology, Schafer has been actively recording and preserving the sounds of the world. Schafer also draws on the natural resources and native culture of his homeland, as in *The*

Princess of the Stars (1981), a drama based on a Native American legend that is performed outdoors, at dawn, on the shore of a lake. His works expand our established notions of performance ritual—that is, the place, time, and conventions of a concert.

Schafer has also influenced the arts in Canada as an educator. He has taught at universities on both coasts, in Newfoundland and British Columbia, and has worked extensively with children in order to develop their general awareness and receptiveness to sounds. Like McLuhan, Schafer has achieved a global view of sound through his inventory of worldwide soundscapes, which he hopes will change the relationship between humanity and the acoustic environment.

Suggested Listening:

Colin McPhee: *Nocturnes,* for chamber orchestra (1958)
Malcolm Forsyth: *Atayoskewin,* for orchestra (1984)
Jean Papineau-Couture: *Prouesse,* for solo viola (1986)
R. Murray Schafer: *Dream Rainbow Dream Thunder,* for orchestra (1986)
John Weinzweig: Divertimento No. 11, for English horn and orchestra (1989)
Harry Freedman: *Touchings,* percussion concerto (1989)
Alexina Louie: *Music for Heaven and Earth,* for orchestra (1990)

A Native American legend is the theme of R. Murray Schafer's Princess of the Stars, *performed at dawn at Two Jack Lake in the Canadian Rockies.*

It is impossible to name all the composers who have contributed to the myriad of contemporary styles and procedures. In the following chapters, we will explore a number of representative individuals who have helped shape and give expression to modern musical ideas.

80

The New Virtuosity of the Modern Age

Musical styles that differ so greatly from what is familiar call for a new breed of instrumentalists and vocalists to cope with their technical demands. We have only to attend a concert of avant-garde music to realize how far the art of piano playing or singing has moved from the world of Chopin or Schubert. The piano keyboard may be slammed with fingers, palm, or fist; or the player may reach inside to hit, scratch, or pluck the strings directly. A violinist may tap, stroke, or even slap the instrument. Vocal music runs the gamut from whispering to shouting, including all manner of groaning, moaning, or hissing along the way. Wind players have learned to produce a variety of double stops, subtle changes of color, and microtonal progressions; and the percussion section has been enriched by an astonishing variety of noisemakers creating special effects.

We will consider here four gifted singers, and then turn to the works of three creative minds whose music has demanded heightened levels of expression and virtuosity from such performers: the French composers Olivier Messiaen and Pierre Boulez, and the Polish musician Witold Lutosławski, each of whom has sounded an original voice in the diverse world of avantgarde music.

VIRTUOSO WOMEN SINGERS OF THE TWENTIETH CENTURY

Bethany Beardslee

Among the extraordinary virtuosos of the new music are four American women singers who have made a significant mark on the development of contemporary styles. Bethany Beardslee (b. 1927), a soprano who is widely admired for the silvery quality and wide range of her voice, presented the

American premieres of works by Schoenberg, Stravinsky, and Berg. In 1964, she was awarded a grant from the Ford Foundation to commission a work from Milton Babbitt. The resulting composition, *Philomel*, for soprano and prerecorded tape, is based on the Roman poet Ovid's tale of a princess who is raped by the king, has her tongue cut out, and is transformed into a nightingale so she can sing of her suffering. This violent story, really an antirape statement, is told through Beardslee's virtuosic distortions and fragmentation of her voice.

Equally noted for her vocal virtuosity was Cathy Berberian (1928–1983), a singer (and composer) who gained fame with her 1958 performance of *Aria*, by John Cage. In presenting the work, she had to create her own melody from the composer's purposely vague indications, singing a text in five languages and changing between numerous vocal styles, techniques, ranges, and imitations, including jazz, contralto, Sprechstimme, Marlene Dietrich (a pop singer known for her sensuous, husky voice), coloratura soprano, folk, Asian, baby, and nasal. Berberian was married for some years to the Italian composer Luciano Berio, who wrote many works for her, including *Circles* (1960).

Cathy Berberian

Phyllis Bryn-Julson (b. 1945) attracted the attention of her teacher Gunther Schuller with her phenomenal sight-reading ability and *perfect pitch* (the ability to sing any note without hearing it first). She can also sing *quarter tones* (an interval halfway between a half step), a technique called for in certain compositions inspired by non-Western musics. Her performance in 1966 with the Boston Symphony Orchestra of the suite from Alban Berg's opera *Lulu* showed off the ease with which she could sing the difficult intervals found in twelve-tone music.

Phyllis Bryn-Julson

The clear and versatile voice of mezzo-soprano Jan DeGaetani (1933–1989) can be heard on recordings of early music, Schubert Lieder, Stephen Foster songs, and many contemporary pieces (including the Ives song we studied). She premiered, among other works, the challenging song cycle *Ancient Voices of Children*, written in 1970 by George Crumb. (See Chapter 81 for a discussion of this work.) In 1973, DeGaetani was appointed to the faculty of the Eastman School of Music in Rochester, New York, and made her first appearance with the New York Philharmonic Orchestra. She sang regularly with the Contemporary Chamber Ensemble, with whom she made a famous recording of Schoenberg's *Pierrot lunaire*. She has greatly influenced the next generation of performers in her dual role as singer and teacher.

Jan DeGaetani

All of these women gained fame through their remarkable ability to sing avant-garde music, a talent that women musicians, especially sopranos, have developed far more than men. Contemporary music has thus created a great demand for certain female singers, and allowed them a venue for showing off their flexible voices and adventuresome spirits.

Olivier Messiaen and the Postwar Era

"My secret desire of enchanted gorgeousness in harmony has pushed me toward those swords of fire, those sudden stars, those flows of blue-orange lavas, those planets of turquoise, those violet shades, those garnets of long-haired arborescence, those wheelings of sounds and colors in a jumble of rainbows."

Olivier Messiaen

Olivier Messiaen (1908–1992), from the southern French city of Avignon, received his musical training at the Paris Conservatory, where he won most of the awards offered to students. At twenty-three, he became organist of the Church of the Trinity in Paris and five years later professor at two French schools. After serving in the army during World War II, he was appointed to the faculty of the prestigious Paris Conservatory. He later taught at summer schools at Tanglewood (in Massachusetts), at Darmstadt (in Germany), and at centers of contemporary music in North and South America.

Messiaen steadfastly maintained that art is the ideal expression of religious faith. A mystic and a visionary, he considered his religious feeling to be the most important aspect of his art, "the only one perhaps that I will not regret at the hour of my death." Works inspired by religious mysticism include his *Hymn to the Holy Sacrament* (1932, for orchestra), *Quartet for the End of Time* (1941), which we will study, and *Twenty Glances at the Infant Jesus* (1944, for piano).

Many streams of influence merge in Messiaen's art. A love of nature was reflected in his interest in bird songs, which he found an inexhaustible source of melody. He was also strongly drawn to the undulating and free melodic lines of Gregorian chant, the archaic sound of the medieval church modes, the subtle, nonsymmetrical rhythms of India, and the delicate bell sounds of the Javanese gamelan. All these strands are woven into the colorful tapestry of his *Turangalîla-Symphony*, a monumental orchestral work in ten movements. He also contributed highly important works to the twentieth-century literature for the organ and the piano.

Quartet for the End of Time

When the Second World War broke out, Messiaen, then thirty-one, was drafted into the army. In June 1940, he was captured by the Germans and transferred to a prisoner-of-war camp, Stalag VIIA, in Saxony. Among the prisoners were three other French musicians: a violinist, cellist, and a clarinetist. Messiaen began to write a chamber music piece for them, to which he

Principal Works

Orchestral music, including *Hymne au Saint Sacrement* (*Hymn to the Holy Sacrament*, 1932), *Turangalîla-Symphony* (1948), *Oiseaux exotiques* (*Exotic Birds*, 1956), *Chronochromie* (1960)

Chamber music, including *Quatuor pour la fin du temps* (*Quartet for the End of Time*, 1941)

Choral music, including *La transfiguration de Notre Seigneur Jésus-Christ* (*The Transfiguration of Our Lord Jesus Christ*, 1969)

Vocal music, including *Poèmes pour Mi* (1936), song cycle *Harawi* (1945); one opera, *St. François d'Assise* (1983)

Piano music, including *Vingt regards sur l'enfant Jésus* (*Twenty Glances at the Infant Jesus*, 1944)

Organ music, including *Le nativité du Seigneur* (*The Lord's Nativity*, 1935)

Theoretical works, including *La technique de mon langage musical* (*The Technique of My Musical Language*, 1944)

soon added a piano part. The composition of this monumental work's eight movements—the *Quartet for the End of Time*—helped sustain him through this terrible episode in his life. When the quartet was finished, Messiaen and his friends decided to organize a performance. The violinist and clarinetist had managed to hold on to their instruments; a cello was found in the camp, with one of its strings missing, and an old piano, "badly out of tune, with some keys sticking periodically." The concert took place on a bitterly cold night in January 1941, in front of five thousand prisoners from France, Belgium, and other countries.

This work, presented under such dramatic circumstances, was inspired by a passage in the Revelation of St. John, Chapter 10:

> I saw an angel full of strength descending from the sky, clad with a cloud and having a rainbow over his head. His face was like the sun, his feet like columns of fire. He set his right foot on the sea, his left foot on the earth, and, standing on the sea and the earth, he raised his hand to the sky and swore by Him who lives in the centuries of centuries, saying: *There shall be no more Time*, but on the day of the seventh Angel's trumpet the mystery of God shall be accomplished.

The following movement-by-movement description of the quartet includes the composer's own comments (in quotes):

Liturgy of Crystal. "Between three and four in the morning, the awakening of birds: a blackbird or a nightingale improvises, surrounded by a sonorous cloud of dust, by a halo of trills lost high up in the trees." The solo parts—

MESSIAEN: *Quartet for the End of Time*, Second Movement, *Vocalise for the Angel who announced the end of Time* (4:31)

Date of work: 1941

Medium: Chamber quartet—violin, clarinet, cello, and piano

Movements: 8
1. *Liturgy of Crystal*
2. *Vocalise for the Angel who announced the end of Time*
3. *Abyss of the birds*
4. *Interlude*
5. *Praise to the Eternity of Jesus*
6. *Dance of fury, for the seven trumpets*
7. *Glow of the rainbows for the Angel who announced the end of Time*
8. *Praise to the immortality of Jesus*

Vocalise for the Angel who announced the end of Time, 3/4 meter

| 16 | 0:00 | Powerful, dissonant chords in piano (Robuste, modéré; Vigorous, moderate) alternate with disjunct passages and trills in clarinet and fast string passages (Presque vif, joyeux; Fairly lively, joyous); loud dynamic level (*fff*); ascending run in piano like a lightning flash. |

| 17 | 0:56 | Angelic song, very lyrical, slow and distant (Presque lent, impalpable, lointain; Rather slow, imperceptible, distant), played by muted violin and cello (*sourdine*, muted) in double octaves; accompanied by soft chords in piano (like "drops of water in a rainbow"); very soft (*ppp*): |

clarinet and violin—are marked "like a bird." The movement fades from a *pianissimo* to a *ppp*.

Vocalise for the Angel who announced the end of Time. "The first and third sections, very short, evoke the power of this mighty angel. . . . On the piano, soft cascades of blue-orange chords envelop in their distant chimes the song of the violin and cello, which is almost like plainchant." We will hear this movement, in triple meter, which alternates between Robuste, modéré (Vigorous, moderate) and Presque vif, joyeux (Fairly lively, joyous). The violin and cello play an angelic song two octaves apart, accompanied by the piano's "drops of water in the rainbow." The might of the heavenly being is evoked through penetrating chords on the piano, played *fff*, at the opening and closing of the movement.

Abyss of the birds. "For clarinet solo. The abyss is Time, with its sorrows and lassitudes. The birds are the opposite of Time: our desire for light, for stars, for rainbows and jubilant vocalists!" The movement is marked Lent, expressif et triste (Slow, expressive and sad). A broad but desolate melody alternates with lighter passages that evoke the birds.

Interlude. "A Scherzo, more extrovert than the other movements, but attached to them by several melodic reminiscences." Messiaen wrote this section before he decided to add the piano to the ensemble.

Praise to the Eternity of Jesus. "Jesus is here considered as the Word. A long and infinitely slow phrase on the cello magnifies, with love and reverence, the eternity of this powerful and mild Word, 'whose years shall not be consumed.'" The movement, a lovely meditation, evokes the expressive quality of the cello.

Dance of fury, for the seven trumpets. "Rhythmically, this is the most characteristic movement. The four instruments in unison imitate the charm of bells and trumpets."

Glow of the rainbows for the Angel, who announced the end of Time. "Certain passages from the second movement return here. . . . In my dreams, I hear and see groups of chords and melodies, colors and familiar shapes. Then, after this transitory stage, I pass into the unreal and experience with ecstasy a whirling, a dancing interpenetration of superhuman sounds and colors. These swords of fire, these streams of blue-orange lava, these sudden stars—this is the glow, these are the rainbows!"

Praise to the immortality of Jesus. "This praise is love. Its slow rising toward the climax traces the ascent toward God, of the Child of God toward His Father, of the human-made God toward Paradise."

The quartet sums up Messiaen's many-faceted musical interests, but it also testifies to the courage of the human spirit in that the composer could rise above the dreadful conditions of Stalag VIIA to write so bold a work. Listeners can easily grasp the music's power and mysticism, whether or not they share the theology that inspired it.

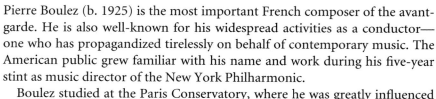

PIERRE BOULEZ AND THE FRENCH AVANT-GARDE

"I think that music should be magic and collective hysteria."

Pierre Boulez

Pierre Boulez (b. 1925) is the most important French composer of the avant-garde. He is also well-known for his widespread activities as a conductor—one who has propagandized tirelessly on behalf of contemporary music. The American public grew familiar with his name and work during his five-year stint as music director of the New York Philharmonic.

Boulez studied at the Paris Conservatory, where he was greatly influenced by the composer Messiaen. He subsequently fell under the spell of Debussy, then Stravinsky, and later, Webern, whose impact reached its height just after the Second World War. Taking Webern's later works as his point of departure, Boulez extended serial techniques to control not only pitch but rhythm, dynamics, texture—in short, he strove for total serialism of the elements. He was especially interested in rhythm, and wrote of one early work in which he tried "for the first time to articulate rhythmic structures, of which Messiaen had revealed to me the possibilities, upon classical serial structures."

The emotional content of Boulez's music extends from a gentle lyricism to a furious Expressionism. From Messiaen, he took over a fondness for bell and percussion sounds that evoke the *gamelan,* an orchestra made up largely of gongs and other metalophones (percussion instruments with tuned metal bars that are struck; see illustration on p. 491).

The Hammer Without a Master

Among Boulez's chief early works are three piano sonatas, *The Hammer Without a Master,* and *Fold upon Fold,* the latter two for voice and chamber ensemble. More recently, he has worked in combined media, such as orchestra with electronic equipment; one such piece, *Répons,* has undergone several recent revisions.

Boulez's best-known work, *The Hammer Without a Master,* a suite of nine movements based on three short poems by René Char, exhibits the chief traits of his style within a compact frame. We will study three movements—

the setting of the first poem, *Furious Artisans* (No. 3), and the Prelude (No. 1) and Postlude (No. 7), to the same poem (see Listening Guide 76).

The piece is scored for alto voice and six instruments, of which alto flute, guitar, and viola are most in evidence. These are supported by xylophone, vibraphone, and a group of unpitched percussion instruments. The full group never plays together; instead, each movement presents a different combination of instruments. The overall limpid and brilliant sound evokes the music of several non-Western cultures.

The vocal line displays the wide leaps we associate with twelve-tone music. Boulez does not attempt to make the words of the poem clear in his setting; "If you want to 'understand' the text," he says, "read it!" Char's poetry, though, is thoroughly surrealist in the violence of its images, and the reader may find the translation more than a little mystifying.

The Prelude, entitled *Before "Furious Artisans,"* is scored for alto flute, vibraphone, guitar, and viola. The tense, plucked-string sound of the guitar is reminiscent of the mandolin in certain works by Schoenberg and Webern. The dark hue of the viola contrasts with the lighter timbre of the flute. Boulez's serial technique, with its emphasis on dissonant intervals, makes for a highly uniform texture.

Like certain musics of East Asia, *Furious Artisans*, a duet between the voice and flute, proceeds in a free, improvisational manner that is both ornate and rhapsodic. The words seem to dissolve in music, an effect frequently heightened by the vowels' being extended over several notes. The voice, asked to sing in an enormously wide range with devilishly difficult intervals, is treated here as an instrument. The flute part, also very virtuosic, includes a technique known as *flutter tonguing* (in which the tongue is "fluttered" against the roof of the mouth).

The brief Postlude, *After "Furious Artisans,"* relates to the Prelude in both its interval structure and sound texture. The viola, however, is omitted in this movement. Since it does not follow *Furious Artisans* directly, it serves as a reminiscence.

In His Own Words

L'artisanat furieux is a purely linear piece. . . . Many listeners' first impression is primarily exotic; and in fact my use of xylophone, vibraphone, guitar, and percussion is very different from the practice of Western chamber music, closer in fact to the sound pictures of Far Eastern music, though the actual vocabulary used is entirely different. . . . I must acknowledge that I was influenced by non-European models in choosing this particular combination of instruments, the xylophone representing the African balafron, the vibraphone the Balinese gender, and the guitar recalling the Japanese koto. In fact, neither the style nor the actual use of these instruments has any connections with these different civilizations. My aim was rather to enrich the European sound vocabulary.

BOULEZ: *The Hammer Without a Master*
(*Le marteau sans maître*), Nos. 1, 3, 7   (5:12)

Date of work: 1953–54; revised 1957

Medium: Alto voice, alto flute, viola, guitar, vibraphone, xylophone, and unpitched percussion

Text: 3 poems by René Char, surrealist poet

Structure: 9 movements, with serial organization (indentations below line up related movements)
1. *Before "Furious Artisans" (Avant "L'artisanat furieux")*
   2. Commentary I on *Hangmen of Solitude (Bourreaux de solitude)*
  3. *Furious Artisans (L'artisanat furieux)*
    4. Commentary II on *Hangmen of Solitude*
     5. *Lovely Building and Forebodings (Bel edifice et les pressentiments), version première*
   6. *Hangmen of Solitude*
7. *After "Furious Artisans" (Après "L'artisanat furieux")*
   8. Commentary III on *Hangmen of Solitude*
    9. *Lovely Building and Forebodings, double*

|37|

1. *Before "Furious Artisans" (Avant "L'artisanat furieux")*   (1:46)

Medium: Alto flute, vibraphone, guitar, and viola
Tempo: Rapide (Quickly)
Description: Dialogue between 4 instruments, disjunct, with wide leaps; individual notes
    stand out; meter constantly shifts; viola alternates bowing and pizzicato.

Opening of first movement, showing exchanges between instruments:

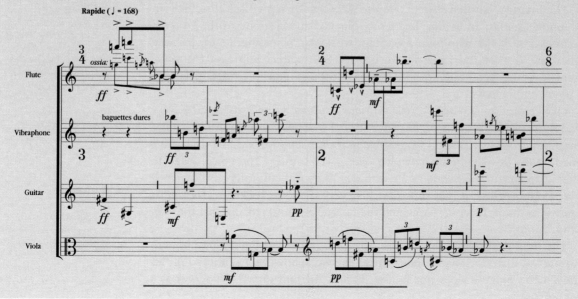

3. Furious Artisans (*L'artisanat furieux*)

(2:26)

Medium: Alto voice and flute
Tempo: Modéré sans rigueur (Moderate, without strictness)

Text
La roulotte rouge au bord du clou
Et cadavre dans le panier
Et chevaux de labours dans le fer à cheval
Je rêve la tête sur la pointe de mon couteau
   le Pérou

Translation
The red caravan at the prison's edge
and the corpse in the basket
and the work horses in the horseshoe
I dream of Peru with my head on the point of
   my knife

Description:
   Solo flute introduction, with wide-ranging leaps.

   Voice enters, unaccompanied, in chromatic, disjunct line, followed by flute with flutter tonguing on sustained note:

   Voice has grace notes on "du clou"; builds to climax with melody that reverses that of opening.

   Dialogue continues with imitation; voice enters on sustained pitch (C), flute enters on dissonant tone (C-sharp); duet transposes the 12-tone row.

   Closes with flutter tonguing on flute.

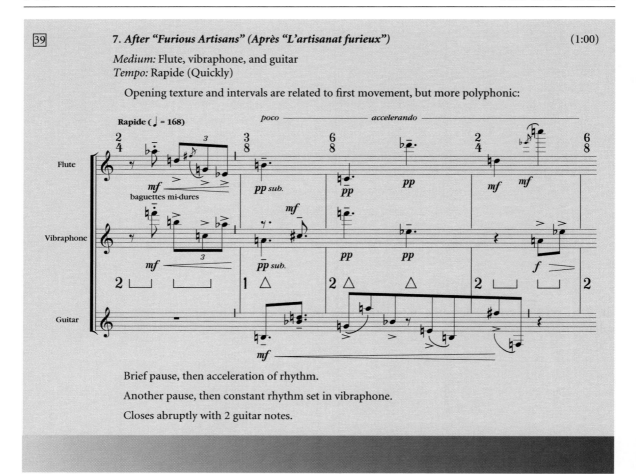

39 **7. *After "Furious Artisans" (Après "L'artisanat furieux")***   (1:00)

Medium: Flute, vibraphone, and guitar
Tempo: Rapide (Quickly)

Opening texture and intervals are related to first movement, but more polyphonic:

Brief pause, then acceleration of rhythm.

Another pause, then constant rhythm set in vibraphone.

Closes abruptly with 2 guitar notes.

Witold Lutosławski

WITOLD LUTOSŁAWSKI AND ALEATORIC MUSIC

"I . . . realized that I could compose music different from that of my past."

The Polish composer Witold Lutosławski (1913–1994), a prominent member of the European avant-garde, nevertheless found ways to combine contemporary procedures with elements drawn from more traditional styles.

Lutosławski's serial period began with *Funeral Music* (1958), a work written in a unique style that blends twelve-tone elements with chromatic harmony in elaborately contrapuntal textures abounding in canonic devices. He next fell under the influence of John Cage; it occurred to him while listening to Cage's Concerto for Piano and Orchestra (1960) that "I could progress toward the whole not from the small detail but the other way around—I could start out from chance and create order in it gradually." Lutosławski coined the term "aleatoric counterpoint" to indicate music in which the pitches for all the parts are written out, but the rhythms are improvised within given rules. (*Aleatoric,* you will recall, refers to indeterminate or random music in which certain elements are deliberately left to chance.)

An example of music written in this style is *Venetian Games*, a work that derives its title from the Festival of Contemporary Music in Venice, for which it was written. The first movement (which we will study) contains eight sections, labeled A–H. Here the orchestra is divided into two groups, winds and percussion pitted against the strings, one group alternating with the other. (See Listening Guide 77 for analysis.) The wind sections are written out; they often begin and end with a loud percussive chord. Their music is very active rhythmically, with a piano part added toward the end of the movement. The string sections throughout are aleatoric; in these sections, the composer strives for maximum freedom of choice. They feature dissonant chord clusters, with loud entries on notated pitches, some pizzicato. The woodwind-and-percussion sound at the beginning of the movement is balanced by string sound at the end; four percussion chords shape the final cadence, each softer than the one before.

The second movement ends with a passage for piano *ad libitum* (which means the pianist can play or omit that particular part). The third movement includes a free solo part for flute, with the entries of the other instruments decided by the conductor. Some passages have fixed time frames, while others are free. In the fourth movement, the opening and closing sections are notated, while the middle part is aleatoric.

Lutosławski's music shows how avant-garde elements can successfully combine with older styles, establishing him as one of the most interesting personalities on the contemporary scene.

Venetian Games

Listening Guide 77

CD: Chr/Std 8/14–15
Cassette: Chr/Std 8A/3

LUTOSŁAWSKI: *Venetian Games (Jeux vénitiens),* First Movement

(3:15)

Date of work: 1961
Movements: 4

FIRST MOVEMENT

Timed sections (A-H) alternate winds/percussion (A, C, E, G) and strings (B, D, F, H); string sections very free (aleatoric)

		Sections	Length	Description
14	0:00	A	(14″)	Woodwinds and percussion—closes with percussive chord.
	0:14	B	(32″)	Strings—individual entries on notated pitches; closes with high violin pitch.
	0:46	C	(21″)	Woodwinds and percussion, with timpani added—percussive chord begins and ends section.
15	1:07	D	(28″)	Strings—high, repeated notes, dissonant clusters.
	1:35	E	(7″)	Woodwinds, percussion, timpani, with brass added—begins with percussive chord.
	1:42	F	(2″)	Strings.
	1:44	G	(27″)	Woodwinds, brass, percussion, timpani, with piano added—begins with percussive chord.
	2:11	H	(64″)	Strings—closes with 4 percussion chords, growing progressively softer.

81

Contemporary Composers and Non-Western Styles

"I believe composers must forge forms out of the many influences that play upon them and never close their ears to any part of the world of sound."—HENRY COWELL

Throughout the course of history, the West has felt the influence of other cultures. Twentieth-century composers, as we have seen, found inspiration in the strong rhythmic features of songs and dances from the borderlands of

Western culture—southeastern Europe, Asiatic Russia, the Near East, and parts of Latin America (see world map at back of book). We have also noted how American musicians combined the powerful rhythmic impulse of African styles with the major-minor tonality of Western art music to produce the rich literature of spirituals, work songs, and shouts—and ultimately, ragtime, blues, jazz, swing, and rock.

A number of contemporary composers have responded in particular to the philosophy of the Far East, notably Zen Buddhism and Indian thought. Among them are three Californians whose work has attracted much notice: Henry Cowell, Harry Partch, and especially John Cage, whose name was associated with the avant-garde scene for over fifty years.

IMPORTANT EXPERIMENTERS

Henry Cowell (1897–1965) was drawn toward a variety of non-Western musics. His studies of the music of Japan, India, and Iran as well as rural Ireland and America led him to combine Asian instruments with traditional Western ensembles, as he did in his two koto concertos (1962 and 1965). (The koto, illustrated on p. 35, is a Japanese zither with thirteen strings stretched over bridges and tuned to one of a variety of pentatonic scales.) Cowell also experimented with foreign scales, which he harmonized with Western chords. The piano provided a medium for several of his innovations; two such innovations were *tone clusters*, groups of adjacent notes that are sounded with the fist, palm, or forearm, and plucking of the piano strings directly with the fingers.

Henry Cowell

Tone clusters

The piano also lent itself to experiments with new tuning systems. One of the first to attempt microtonal music for the piano was Charles Ives, who wrote for pianos tuned a quarter tone apart. But perhaps the most serious proponent of this technique was Harry Partch (1901–1974), who single-mindedly pursued the goal of a microtonal music. In the 1920s, he evolved a scale of forty-three microtones to the octave and adapted Hindu and African instruments to fit this tuning. Among his original idiophones are cloud-chamber bowls (made of glass), cone gongs (made of metal), diamond marimba (made of wood), and tree gourds. Such instruments make melody and timbre, rather than harmony, the focus of his music. Partch's performance group, called the Gate 5 Ensemble, played his works from memory; one example is *The Delusion of Fury* (1969), a large-scale ceremonial piece that employs elements of Japanese Noh drama in its first part, "On a Japanese Theme" (see illustration on p. 63), and demands that its instrumentalists make choral-voice sounds in the second part, which is titled "On an African Theme."

Harry Partch

Harry Partch with two of his remarkable musical instruments: a gourd tree and a cone gong.

THE MUSIC OF JOHN CAGE

"I thought I could never compose socially important music. Only if I could invent something new, then would I be useful to society."

John Cage

John Cage (1912–1992) represents the type of eternally questing artist who no sooner solves one problem than he presses forward to another. Born in Los Angeles, Cage attended Pomona College, then left school to travel in Europe. He exhibited an early interest in non-Western scales, which he learned from his mentor, Henry Cowell. Cage was also a student of Arnold Schoenberg and explored compositions with fixed tone rows, but eventually became persuaded that future advancement would occur through rhythm rather than pitch. This abiding interest in rhythm led him to explore the possibilities of percussion instruments. He soon realized that the traditional division between consonance and dissonance had given way to a new opposition between music and noise, as a result of which the boundaries of the one were extended to include more of the other. The composer prophesied in 1937 that "the use of noise to make music will continue and increase until we reach a music produced through the aid of electrical instruments, which will make available for musical purposes any and all sounds that can be heard."

In 1938, Cage invented what he called the "prepared piano," consisting of nails, bolts, nuts, screws, and bits of rubber, wood, or leather inserted at crucial points in the strings of an ordinary grand piano. From this instrument came a myriad of sounds whose overall effect resembled that of a Javanese *gamelan* (an ensemble made up of various kinds of gongs, xylophones, drums, bowed and plucked strings, cymbals, and sometimes singers). Cage wrote a number of works for the prepared piano, notably the set of *Sonatas and Interludes* (1946–48). The music reflects the composer's preoccupation with East Asian philosophy. "After reading the work of Ananda K. Coomaraswamy, I decided to attempt the expression in music of the 'permanent emotions' of Indian tradition: the heroic, the erotic, the wondrous, the mirthful, sorrow, fear, anger, the odious, and their common tendency toward tranquility." A quest for tranquillity pervaded Cage's life and work.

Prepared piano

Cage's interest in indeterminacy led him to compose works in which performers make choices by throwing dice. He also relied on the *I Ching* (Book of Changes), an ancient Chinese method of throwing coins or marked sticks for chance numbers, from which he derived a system of charts and graphs governing the series of events that could happen within a piece. He solved the problem of transferring indeterminacy to tape in *Fontana Mix* (1958), the first taped work to set conditions whose outcome could not be foreseen. These experiments established Cage as a decisive influence in the artistic life of the mid–twentieth century.

Indeterminacy

Cage maintained an intense interest in exploring the role of silence. "In this new music," he declared, "nothing takes place but sounds: those that are notated and those that are not. . . . There is no such thing as an empty space or an empty time. There is always something to see, something to hear. In fact, try as we may to make a silence, we cannot." Out of this intriguing observation came a piece, *4′33″*, without any musical content at all, consisting of four minutes and thirty-three seconds of "silence." Audience members are expected to become aware of the sounds in the hall or outside it, the beating of their hearts, or the sounds floating around in their imagination. The piece was first performed by the pianist David Tudor in 1952. He came out onstage, placed a score on the piano rack, sat quietly for the duration of the piece, then closed the piano lid and walked off the stage.

4′33″

Some critics considered the piece a hoax or a not-so-clever trick. Yet Cage viewed it as one of the most radical statements he had made (and he made many) against the traditions of Western music, one that raised profound questions. What is music, and what is noise? And what does silence contribute to music? In any case, *4′33″*, which can be performed by anyone on any instrument, always makes us more aware of our surroundings.

MULTICULTURAL INFLUENCES IN CONTEMPORARY SOCIETY

The impulse toward a world music sound has continued with such composers as Alan Hovhaness (b. 1911), Lou Harrison (b. 1917), Philip Glass, Terry Riley, and Steve Reich (on the last three composers, see pp. 681–82). Also in this category are several composers who drew on their Asian heritage as well as the traditions of the West; these include Chou Wen-chung (b. 1923), Toru Takemitsu (1930–1996), Yuji Takahashi (b. 1909), and Chinary Ung (b. 1942), whom we will study (see also CP 23 on modern Asian composers). The result of all this activity has been to open up to the West a new world of styles, techniques, and instruments.

We have in past chapters traced how artistic impulses from disparate cultures have steadily grown closer together. Having received powerful impetus during the Second World War, this trend has been further strengthened through air travel and the media of radio, television, the press, and the Internet, all of which have made the earth a smaller place. The result is that today, artists in general and musicians in particular are more exposed to multicultural influences than anyone in earlier times could have imagined.

We will study three modern representatives of this awakening: the American composer George Crumb, whose settings of the Spanish poet Federico García Lorca are enhanced by flamenco and East Asian music; the Hungarian György Ligeti, whose piano études assume the rhythmic complexity of certain African and Indonesian musics; and the Cambodian-American Chinary Ung, whose works express, in a Western pitch language, the gestures and timbres of Asian music.

GEORGE CRUMB'S ANCIENT VOICES OF CHILDREN

"Music [is] a system of proportions in the service of a spiritual impulse."

George Crumb

In recent years, George Crumb (b. 1929) has achieved a preeminence that is due partly to the emotional character of his music, which results from the composer's highly developed sense of the dramatic. His kind of romanticism is a rarity among composers of his generation. Crumb uses contemporary techniques for expressive ends that make an enormous impact in the concert hall. He has won numerous honors and awards and has been teaching composition at the University of Pennsylvania since 1965.

Crumb has shown a special affinity for the poetry of Federico García Lorca, the great poet who was killed by the Fascists during the Spanish Civil War. (The poet's mysterious death continues to capture the public's imagination in the recent movie *The Disappearance of García Lorca* [1997].) His Lorca cycles include *Ancient Voices of Children; Night Music I;* four books of madrigals; *Songs, Drones, and Refrains of Death;* and *Night of the Four Moons.*

Ancient Voices of Children is a cycle of songs for soprano, boy soprano, oboe, mandolin, harp, electric piano, and percussion (see Listening Guide 78). Like many contemporary composers, Crumb uses the voice here like an instrument, in a vocal style he describes as ranging "from the virtuosic to the intimately lyrical." He found his ideal interpreter in the mezzo-soprano Jan DeGaetani, discussed earlier as one of the great virtuoso singers of the century; her recording of the work remains as a model for all other interpreters.

The score abounds in unusual effects, many inspired by musics of distant cultures. The soprano opens with a fanciful *vocalise* (a wordless melody, in this case based on purely phonetic sounds) that is reminiscent of a rhapsodic East Asian melody. She sings into an electrically amplified piano, arousing a shimmering cloud of sympathetic vibrations. The pitch is "bent" to produce microtones, which typify some styles of Asian music. Included in the score are a toy piano, a harmonica, and a musical saw as well as a rich array of percussion instruments—many borrowed from other cultures—such as Tibetan prayer stones, Japanese temple bells, tuned tom-toms (high-pitched drums of

Federico García Lorca

Ancient Voices of Children

In His Own Words

In Ancient Voices of Children, *as in my earlier Lorca settings, I have sought musical images that enhance and reinforce the powerful yet strangely haunting imagery of Lorca's poetry. I feel that the essential meaning of this poetry is concerned with the most primary things: Life, death, love, the smell of the earth, the sounds of the wind and the sea. These ur-concepts are embodied in a language which is primitive and stark, but which is capable of infinitely subtle nuance.*

Principal Works

Orchestral music, including *Echoes of Time and the River* (1967) and *A Haunted Landscape* (1984)

Vocal music based on Lorca poetry, including *Night Music I* (1963); four books of madrigals (1965–69); *Songs, Drones, and Refrains of Death* (1968); *Night of the Four Moons* (1969); and *Ancient Voices of Children* (1970)

Chamber music, including *Black Angels* (1970), for electrified string quartet; *Lux aeterna* (*Eternal Light,* 1971), for voice and chamber ensemble (including sitar); *Vox balanae* (*The Voice of the Whales,* 1971), for amplified instruments; and *Quest* (1994), for guitar and chamber ensemble

Music for amplified piano, including 2 volumes of *Makrokosmos* (1972, 1973), *Music for a Summer Evening* (1974), and *Zeitgeist* (1988); piano music (*Processional,* 1984)

CRUMB: *Ancient Voices of Children*, First Movement   (4:30)

Date of work: 1970

Genre: Song cycle (5 songs and 2 instrumental interludes)

Text: Poems by Federico García Lorca

---

1. *The Little Boy Is Looking for His Voice (El niño busca su voz)*
Medium: Soprano, boy soprano, electric piano, harp, tam-tam (gong), other percussion

		Text	Translation	Description
40	0:00			Opens with an elaborate vocalise for soprano, including cries, trills, other vocal gymnastics; she sings into piano with pedal down for resonance.
41	2:47	El niño busca su voz. (La tenía el rey de los grillos.) En una gota de agua buscaba su voz el niño.	The little boy is looking for his voice. (The king of the crickets had it.) In a drop of water the little boy looked for his voice.	Strophe 1—sung by soprano alone with turns, trills, hisses; she continues with low-pitched recitation.
42	3:32	No la quiero para hablar; me haré con ella un anillo que llevará mi silencio en su dedo pequeñito.	I don't want it to speak with; I will make a ring of it so that he may wear my silence on his little finger.	Strophe 2—overlaps strophe 1; boy soprano sings offstage, through cardboard tube; folk-like character to melody.

Vocal line, at beginning of strophe 1:

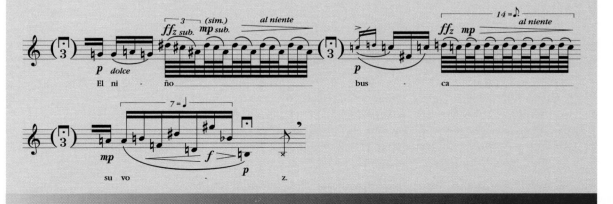

African origin), Latin-American claves (wooden clappers), and maracas (a kind of rattle). Also heard are marimba, vibraphone, sleigh bells, glockenspiel plates, tubular bells, and gong (tam-tam). The composer explained why he picked this unusual combination: "I was conscious of an urge to fuse unrelated stylistic elements . . . a suggestion of Flamenco with a Baroque quotation, or a reminiscence of Mahler with the Orient."

The first song from this cycle, *The Little Boy Is Looking for His Voice (El niño busca su voz*; Listening Guide 78), displays a free and fantastic character. The soprano part offers a virtuoso exhibition of what the voice can do in the way of cries, sighs, whispers, buzzings, trills, and percussive clicks. There are even passages marked "fluttertongue"—an effect we have hitherto associated only with instruments. Throughout, Crumb captures the improvisational spirit of flamenco song. The passion is here, the sense of mystery and wonder—but in a thoroughly twentieth-century setting.

In *Ancient Voices*, Crumb found the right music for the dark intimations of Lorca's poetry. The work has justly established itself as a prime example of contemporary imagination and feeling.

First song

GYÖRGY LIGETI'S *ETUDES FOR PIANO*

György Ligeti (b. 1923), left his native Hungary in 1956 to settle first in Vienna and later in Hamburg, Germany. He was also active at the electronic music studio in Cologne and taught summer courses at Darmstadt. In Darmstadt, he worked closely with other leaders of the European avant-garde such as Stockhausen and Boulez (to whom the piece we will study is dedicated). Ligeti belongs to the circle of composers who have tried to broaden the Schoenberg heritage by making it responsive to more recent currents. He has been especially interested in achieving with traditional instruments the finer gradations of sound made familiar by electronic music. Through tone clusters and amalgams of sound that create a flow of shifting densities and colors, Ligeti has gone beyond focusing on fixed, recognizable pitches to working with large clusters of tones.

György Ligeti

Ligeti developed a process of interweaving many separate strands into a complex polyphonic fabric, deriving the shape and momentum of the music from barely perceptible changes in timbre, dynamics, density, and texture. The result is a shimmering current of sound, to which he applied the term "micropolyphony." This style reached its fullest expression in his works of the early 1960s. He subsequently moved toward a style with more transparent textures and more clear-cut melodic, harmonic, and rhythmic contours.

Atmosphères, "for large orchestra without percussion," established Ligeti's

Atmosphères

Principal Works

Orchestral works, including *Apparitions* (1958–59), *Atmosphères* (1961), *Lontano* (1967), Piano Concerto (1985–88), and Violin Concerto (1990)

Chamber works, including Chamber Concerto (1970) and Trio for Violin, Horn, and Piano (1982)

Theater works, including *Aventures* (1962), *Nouvelles aventures* (1962–65), and *Le grand macabre* (1976)

Choral works, including *Lux aeterna* (*Eternal Light*, 1966) and *Magyar Etüdök* (*Hungarian Studies*, 1983)

Keyboard music, including *Etudes for Piano* (Book I, 1985; Book II, 1989–90)

position as a leader of the European avant-garde. Together with his choral work *Lux aeterna*, it was included in the soundtrack of the classic Stanley Kubrick film *2001: A Space Odyssey* (1968), making the composer's name familiar to an international public. In *Atmosphères*, Ligeti explored the region that lies between instrumental and electronic music. Although more than sixty individual lines can be identified in the score, what we hear is a murmurous continuum. As he put it, he was composing with blocks of sound—except that the blocks all merged into a continuous flow.

Ligeti's *Etudes for Piano* illustrate another of his interests—the manipulation of rhythm. In these pieces, Ligeti experimented with illusionary rhythm, where, for example, the listener perceives a work to be much slower than it is actually played because of the recurrence of certain accented notes. Inspiration for this rhythmic treatment came from a variety of sources, including a long-held fondness for paradoxes and mathematical puzzles and the musics he had studied of certain sub-Saharan African and Indonesian cultures. Around 1980, he became aware of the player-piano works written by Conlon Nancarrow (1912–1997), an American expatriate living in Mexico, who was able to attain levels of virtuosity in rhythm and polyphony that were impossible in live performance. By punching holes in piano rolls in a certain precise way, Nancarrow could superimpose elaborate rhythmic ratios that were then automatically played on the mechanical instrument. Ligeti sought to achieve a similar effect on a normal piano with a live person performing.

Disorder   The first étude from Book I, *Disorder* (*Désordre*), is the most rhythmically contorted of the set. Here, Ligeti combines two distinct musical processes: an additive metric pattern (5 + 3 or 3 + 5) and a simultaneous sounding of triple patterns in one of the pianist's hands and duple patterns in the other. (See Listening Guide 79 for analysis.) These techniques make for "disorder" in the piece—the hands do not always coincide in their accents, with one hand falling behind the other, then catching up again, then lagging once more. All this proceeds at a vigorous tempo, with strongly accented notes. Thus the music whizzes by at a speed at which the ear cannot possibly disentangle the complexities involved. What you will hear is a rhythmic drive and texture of extraordinary force and energy that builds to a furious climax in the upper register of the instrument, then vanishes. Ligeti's careful mathematical planning throughout the work, and his borrowing of African concepts of additive meter and polyrhythms, are obscured by the overall perception of chaos. At the same time, the work presses the pianist's virtuosic ability to new heights.

Listening Guide 79

CD: Chr/Std 8/30–32, Sh 4/64–66
Cassette: Chr/Std 8A/7, Sh 4B/2

LIGETI: *Disorder (Désordre), from Etudes for Piano*, Book I

(2:18)

Date of work: 1985

Medium: Solo piano

Form: Cycles of order and disorder, achieved through a mathematical system of accents

Tempo: Molto vivace, vigoroso, molto ritmico (Very fast, vigorous, and rhythmical)

---

30   0:00   Hands begin synchronized, with movement in eighth notes in groups of 8 (accents in patterns of 3 + 5 or 5 + 3), played legato, accents played *forte*; right hand gradually gets ahead of left by dropping one eighth note every 4 measures; dissonance increases.

Opening 7 measures, showing accents and divergence of parts:

0:30   Hands finally come together again with same accents; after 4 measures, same process be-
       gins with eighth notes in right hand.

0:37   Shift in rhythmic patterns: both hands begin shortening patterns at different rates; hands
       and accents synchronize in pattern of 4 eighths per measure (accented 1 + 3 or 3 + 1),
       then diverge again as groupings change.

31 0:49   Both hands converge, then begin patterns of 3, but these are not coordinated or accented
       the same; piece builds to *crescendo*; bass part (left hand) drops one octave lower.

       Hands continue to diverge, *fortissimo*; briefly synchronize, then diverge again.

1:18   Hands converge at *fff* marking with all notes heavily accented; piece reaches climax.

32 1:22   Intensity and volume let down; both hands in treble range synchronized for a long time,
       then diverge to more rhythmic complexity and increasingly dense texture.

       Piece ends with hands ascending to upper end of keyboard.

Music from Eastern Africa

We have noted that certain musical systems of Africa were highly influential
to the contemporary composer György Ligeti, in his *Etudes for Piano*. Let us
investigate some of these musical elements in an example from Uganda, one
of the regions that particularly interested Ligeti.

Uganda is a land-locked country in eastern Africa, bordering Kenya and
Lake Victoria (for location, see world map at back of book). The peoples of
Uganda—representing many different cultures—have felt significant outside
influences throughout their history; they have long had contact with the Arab
world and with Indonesia, and they were colonized by the British until they
gained independence in 1962. The modern Republic of Uganda was formerly
subdivided into a number of powerful kingdoms, each with its own court
and ruler. We will consider a piece that was originally court music, played by
a royal drum ensemble.

Among the types of musical instruments that can be associated with this
region of Africa are chordophones—musical bows, zithers, harps, lyres, and

fiddles; aerophones—flutes and both end-blown and side-blown trumpets; idiophones—log xylophones and plucked metal instruments called *lamellaphones*; and membranophones—pitched and unpitched drums. The court musicians of the former King (or *Kabaka*) of Buganda (a region of Uganda on Lake Victoria) included a private harpist, a flute ensemble (accompanied by drums), a xylophone group, a band of trumpeters, and an ensemble called the *entenga*. This last group, one of the most prestigious at court, consisted of six musicians playing fifteen drums: four played twelve melody drums that were graduated in size and were tuned to notes of a pentatonic scale, while the other two accompanied them on three unpitched bass drums (see Listening Guide 80 for this arrangement). These tuned conical drums, often called *drum chimes*, have cowhide skins laced tight over both open ends; they are played with long, curved beaters (see illustration below).

Like much of eastern Africa, this region developed pentatonic music. The tunes played by the drum ensembles come mostly from the vocal folk song literature. Our example, *Ensiriba ya munange Katego*, tells the story of a subchief named Kangawo, who wears a leopard-skin headband for good luck. One night, his precious headband disappears, and he feels so unprotected without his charm that he becomes ill and dies.

In the performance of *Ensiriba ya munange Katego*, the players of the melody drums enter one after the other, striking at the sides of their drums. The first melody player begins a pattern—let's call it A—which is then doubled an octave lower by the second player. The third drummer enters with two different patterns, B and C, one played in each hand. The fourth musician then joins in doubling pattern B. When the patterns are all established and the large bass drums have begun to punctuate the dense polyrhythmic

Members of the entenga drum chime ensemble of Uganda.

fabric that results, the players move their strokes to the middle of the drum heads, at which point the volume level grows and the pitches of the individual lines can be heard more easily (see Listening Guide 80). As in the Ligeti piano étude we studied, a carefully planned musical process produces what sounds somewhat chaotic to our ears. The selection ends with a release in intensity as the drummers drop out one by one.

This is music transmitted through an oral tradition, in which an apprentice learns the repertory and technique by sitting beside an accomplished drummer. Such tuned-drum ensembles are not unique to Uganda nor to this once-famous court. Similar instruments are found in south and southeast Asia as well, offering support to the theory that the musical cultures of eastern Africa and Asia are linked. Today, this drum ensemble is seldom played, except as a vestige of Uganda's rich cultural past.

Listening Guide 80

CD: Chr/Std 8/33–36, Sh 4/67–70
Cassette: Chr/Std 8A/8, Sh 4B/3

EASTERN AFRICAN MUSIC: *Ensiriba ya munange Katego*   (2:37)

Region: Kampala (former kingdom of Buganda), Uganda (Ganda tribe)

Function: Ceremonial court music

Characteristics: Pentatonic melodies with gapped scale (not equidistant intervals), polyrhythm

Melodic patterns: 3 basic patterns (A, B, C), played in 2 ½-octave range
    5 notes in lowest octave, with lines under numbers
    5 notes in middle octave, no lines
    2 notes (½ octave) in highest octave, with lines above notes

Medium: 12 tuned (melody) drums (4 players) and 3 bass drums (2 players)

Arrangement of drums and players:

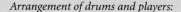

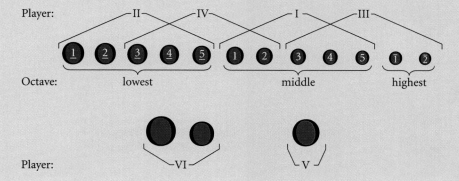

Who plays what:

Player	Drums	Pattern
I	① ② ③ ④ ⑤	A (24 notes long)
II	① ② ③ ④ ⑤	A′ (1 octave below A)
III	③ ④ ⑤ 1̄ 2̄	B and C
IV	3̲ 4̲ 5̲ 1 2	B′ (1 octave below B)
V	(large drum)	Punctuates patterns
VI	(two large drums)	Punctuates patterns

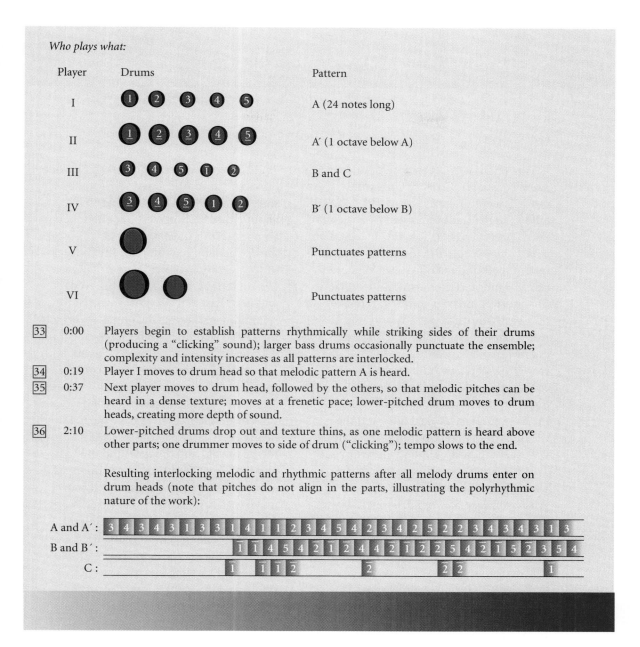

33 0:00 Players begin to establish patterns rhythmically while striking sides of their drums (producing a "clicking" sound); larger bass drums occasionally punctuate the ensemble; complexity and intensity increases as all patterns are interlocked.

34 0:19 Player I moves to drum head so that melodic pattern A is heard.

35 0:37 Next player moves to drum head, followed by the others, so that melodic pitches can be heard in a dense texture; moves at a frenetic pace; lower-pitched drum moves to drum heads, creating more depth of sound.

36 2:10 Lower-pitched drums drop out and texture thins, as one melodic pattern is heard above other parts; one drummer moves to side of drum ("clicking"); tempo slows to the end.

Resulting interlocking melodic and rhythmic patterns after all melody drums enter on drum heads (note that pitches do not align in the parts, illustrating the polyrhythmic nature of the work):

A and A′: 3 4 3 4 3 1 3 3 1 4 1 1 2 3 4 5 4 2 3 4 2 5 2 2 3 4 3 4 3 1 3

B and B′: 1̄ 1̄ 4 5 4 2 1̄ 2 4 4 2̄ 1̄ 2 2 5 4 2 1̄ 5 2 3 5 4

C: 1̄ 1̄ 1̄ 2 2 2̄ 2̄ 1̄

Chinary Ung's *Spiral*

A Cambodian-born composer, Chinary Ung (b. 1942) received a diploma from L'Ecole de Musique Phnom Penh before he emigrated to the United States in 1964. He then studied clarinet at the Manhattan School of Music

Cultural Perspective 23

EAST MEETS WEST: THE COMPOSER'S PERSPECTIVE

We are about to meet a contemporary Asian composer, Chinary Ung, whose music is a cultural mixture of styles. Ung follows in the tradition of the Japanese-born composer Toru Takemitsu, who won worldwide recognition for blending Eastern instruments and melodies into Western classical music. Takemitsu claimed that his first musical interests came from outside—the West—through post–World War II American military radio, and only later did he learn Japanese music. In 1967, the New York Philharmonic Orchestra commissioned Takemitsu's *November Steps,* in which two Japanese instruments—the biwa (a short-necked lute) and the shakuhachi (a bamboo flute)—play along with the standard symphony instruments.

Some Asian composers come to the United States in order to experience Western music first-hand. Chinese-born composer Chou Wen-chung, at Columbia University, has helped guide a generation of mainland Chinese composers who were cut off from the West by the Chinese Cultural Revolution. Among these are Bright Sheng, whose cello concerto *Spring Dreams* (1997) was written for cellist Yo-Yo Ma, accompanied by traditional Chinese orchestral instruments; and Tan Dun, whose opera *Marco Polo* (1996) explores another important intersection of Eastern and Western culture. Dun claims he is "most interested in the process of mingling the elements to find a new territory, a new sound that will work. . . . It's not really about either East or West but about being yourself." Dun's *Symphony 1997 (Heaven, Earth, Mankind)*, written for the transfer of sovereignty in Hong Kong from Great Britain to mainland China, mixes old and new, East and West. It is written for symphony orchestra (including a cello solo for Yo-Yo Ma meant to represent the universality of music), children's chorus, and imperial bells cast in the fourth century B.C.E. Dun views this work not as a political statement but as an expression of peace.

Traditional orchestras have sprung up in nearly every large city of China as a way to merge the old and the new, and the East and the West. Traditional instruments are grouped according to their sound source: metal (bells and gongs), skin (drums), silk (the pipa, a pear-shaped, plucked lute), gourd (the sheng, a mouth organ), and bamboo (the di, a bamboo flute). Instrumental training in China has been influenced by Western practices as well, with music conservatories replacing the older master-pupil tutorial system.

We have noted the attraction that the East has held for Western composers, including Mahler, Debussy, and Ravel at the turn of the twentieth century, and later the experimenters Henry Cowell, Harry Partch, and John Cage. Cowell attempted to wed Eastern and Western instruments in his two koto concertos, Partch was influenced by microtonal scales and Japanese Noh drama, and Cage turned to ancient Chinese writings for innovative methods of structuring his music. The 1960s era of exploration in concert music had its counterpart in popular music: the Byrds, a West Coast folk-rock group, were the first to use the Indian sitar, influencing the Beatles (*Norwegian Wood*, 1965), especially George Harrison, toward an Eastern sound and philosophy of life. These musical mergers, described by Chinary Ung in terms of the color green, which is achieved by mixing blue (Western) and yellow (Eastern) elements, bring us closer than ever to distant cultures and their art forms.

Terms to Note:

biwa	sheng
shakuhachi	di
pipa	Noh drama

Chinese-American composer Tan Dun and world-famous cellist Yo-Yo Ma discuss a music score.

Chinary Ung

and received a doctorate in composition in 1974 from Columbia University; he has studied composition with Chou Wen-chung, Mario Davidovsky, and George Crumb (whose *Ancient Voices of Children* we have heard). Ung has taught at the University of Pennsylvania, Northern Illinois University, Arizona State University, and (currently) the University of California at San Diego. The recipient of many awards, commissions for new works, and fellowships, including one to study traditional Cambodian music, Ung performs on the Cambodian xylophone (*roneat-ek*), lectures widely on Asian music, and has compiled several albums of Cambodian folk music.

Ung's works are strongly influenced by music of his native Cambodia (see world map). His chamber work *Mohori* (1974) draws its title from the Khmer word for the small orchestra of the royal palace, made up of voice with wind, string, and percussion instruments; the term also refers to a legendary bird, a figure in Khmer folk song. The work uses phonetics for emotional impact, just as Khmer singers interject speech sounds for emphasis. In *Khse Buon* (1980), for solo cello or viola, Ung evokes the sound of the *sarangi*, a bowed string instrument of India that allows for special improvisation techniques. The works in his *Spirals* series, of which we will study the first, are scored for diverse and often unusual combinations of instruments and explore one of Ung's characteristic compositional techniques, in which ideas return in various recombinations. Ung's music is lyrical and highly expressive. He uses Western instruments, harmonies based on Eastern pentatonic scales, and occasional pitch bending to create an exotic tapestry of sound that intertwines Asian and Western styles.

Spiral (1987), written for cello, piano, and percussion, provides an excellent introduction to Ung's music. Here, Ung combines Western pitch language, rhythmic structures, and notation to evoke the gestures (or melodic patterns) and timbres of Asian music. Described by one critic as "basically a lyric and pensive piece in an atonal style rife with exotic colors," *Spiral* has a haunting and elusive quality, flavored as it is with high-pitched pentatonicism, colorful special effects, freedom of rhythmic movement, and shifts of modes with no reference to a home key. The texture is largely heterophonic, with multiple lines blending and interweaving their strands against the occasional punctuation provided by the piano and percussion. The range of the cello is widened by the extensive use of *harmonics* (crystalline tones in a very high range, produced by lightly touching the string at certain points). Glissandos (rapid slides between pitches) and bent pitches (slight drops in pitch) on the cello invoke Eastern gestures as well, as does the brittle timbre of the various metallophones.

This emotion-filled work has been described as a possible eulogy for the millions killed in Ung's homeland at the hands of the Khmer Rouge regime (a genocidal horror that was dramatized in the 1984 movie *The Killing Fields*).

Listening Guide 81

CD: Chr/Std 8/49–54, Sh 4/71–76
Cassette: Chr/Std 8B/2, Sh 4B/4

UNG: *Spiral*, excerpt   (4:48)

Date of work: 1987

Medium: Chamber work for cello, piano, and percussion

Percussion instruments used:		*Special effects used on cello:*
glass wind chime	crotales	harmonics
metal wind chime	tubular bells	glissando
bell tree	vibraphone	tremolo
4 suspended cymbals	marimba	*sul ponticello* (played on the bridge)
sizzle cymbal	2 bongos	pizzicato
gong	4 tom-toms	*frappé* (struck)
2 tam-tams (gongs, high and low)	bass drum	*jeté* (bounced on the string)
		bent pitches
		rubato

Pentatonic scale on which opening section of *Spiral* is based (gaps are marked with brackets):

Note: C♯ can also be written as D♭ and D♯ as E♭.

49	0:00	Bright, brittle timbre, with instruments (cello, piano, crotales, vibraphone) mostly in unison on pentatonic line; opening cello line in high range with glissandos, slides, and harmonics (marked with small circle over notes); uses 4 of the 5 notes of pentatonic scale (A-D♯-E-G); changes meter in each measure:

	0:27	Piano and chimes punctuate main notes of tremolo on cello, then cello line descends to low range.
50	0:37	Slower, disjunct melody, in heterophonic texture, which in tempo and dynamics builds as piano and vibraphone combine in unison with cello.
	0:55	Cello solo broken off by marimba tremolo (*fff*), followed by plucked and struck chords on cello, and sharp strikes on tom-toms and bongos.
51	1:02	Short unmeasured section, in which cello holds an open fifth, punctuated by a low, thunking repeated note in piano; then cello bends pitches, followed by a long glissando up into the high range of harmonics:

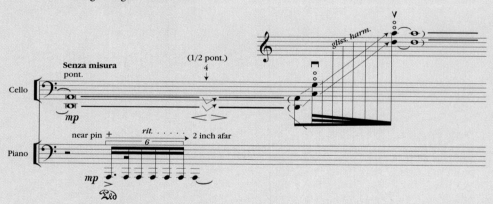

	1:15	Quicker tempo in more percussive style; dissonant chords on offbeats.
52	1:27	Cello enters with high-range lyrical melody reminiscent of opening:

	1:35	Returns to lower range, accompanied by tremolos.
	1:52	Bouncing effects with repeated notes on cello, imitated by piano and vibraphone; rhythmic chords introduce short marimba solo.
53	2:21	Singing cello melody, with slides between notes; sounds very Asian; with soft accompaniment outlining new pentatonic scale; played pizzicato inside piano:

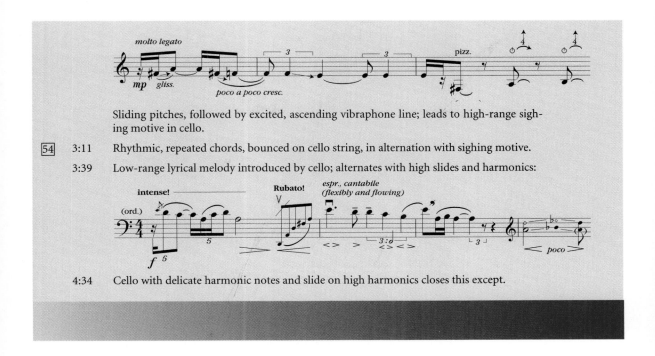

Sliding pitches, followed by excited, ascending vibraphone line; leads to high-range sighing motive in cello.

54 3:11 Rhythmic, repeated chords, bounced on cello string, in alternation with sighing motive.

3:39 Low-range lyrical melody introduced by cello; alternates with high slides and harmonics:

4:34 Cello with delicate harmonic notes and slide on high harmonics closes this except.

An Introduction to Chinese Traditional Music

Having been introduced to an example of Asian-inspired chamber music played on Western instruments (Chinary Ung's *Spiral*), with its unique melodic and timbral effects, we should now hear a traditional Asian work played on traditional instruments. For this purpose, we will listen to a well-known Chinese piece, *The Moon Reflected on the Second Springs.*

The musician who composed and first performed this work is known as Abing (1883–1950). According to the official biography written by a Chinese music historian, Abing's original name was Hua Yanjun, and he was born in Wuxi, in the eastern Chinese province of Jiangsu (see world map). Both his parents died when Abing was young; he was adopted by a Daoist monk, who taught him music. (*Daoism* is one of China's major philosophies and religions, based on the teachings of sixth-century-B.C.E. philosopher Lao-tse.) As an apprentice Daoist, Abing played in the wind and percussion ensemble of the local temple. He was eventually expelled from the Daoist group for playing this music in secular settings, and became a wandering street musician. In his mid-thirties, he went blind—some say as a result of contracting syphilis.

Abing was able to make a (meager) living by singing and playing the two-stringed fiddle (*erhu*) and the lute (*pipa*). In his music, much of it improvised on the spot, he sometimes narrated the day's news as he heard it at the opium houses. Shortly before his death in 1950, Abing taped six memorable solo works; *The Moon Reflected on the Second Springs* is the most famous.

Abing

665

Zhang Bao-li, playing the erhu.

Master yangqin player Yangqin Zhao in performance.

Oral transmission

Abing's pieces are viewed as traditional music because they were created through improvisation and thus took their shape gradually, and because they have been orally disseminated in differing versions, like folk music (in this case, they have also been written down for posterity). Today, Abing's music is highly revered; it forms part of the standard repertory at music conservatories for erhu and pipa players, further blurring the lines between art and traditional music.

This humble Chinese musician would have been surprised to read some accounts of his life, written under the Communist regime (which came to power in 1949), that have romanticized his life and made him out to be a revolutionary hero of the people. Questions have even arisen over the descriptive title of the work we will hear, which was probably given to the composition after a long period of performance and development. Although some have searched for political meaning behind the name, most scholars believe it refers to a scenic site outside the city of Wuxi, near the Second Springs pavilion.

Erhu

Yangqin

The Moon Reflected on the Second Springs was originally conceived for solo *erhu*, a bowed, two-string fiddle played resting upright on the upper leg, with a snakeskin-covered sound box and with its bow hairs fixed between the two strings. Our modern recorded version adds the *yangqin*, a hammered dulcimer with a trapezoidal sound box strung with metal strings that are struck (or hammered) with strips of bamboo. The work is based on a pentatonic scale (D-E-G-A-B) that uses only the intervals of major seconds and minor thirds (as shown in Listening Guide 82; this scale differs from the one used in Ung's *Spiral*, which includes a half step, or semitone).

The melody is made up of four musical phrases, which are repeated and ornamented with many types of embellishments (trills, slides, glissandos, grace notes, bent notes, and tremolos, among others) in a process beautifully described as "adding flowers" (*jia hua*). The haunting melody begins slowly, in a low range and rhythmically free, and then ascends very gradually and expressively. The yangqin adds depth to the linear movement, offering new melodic decoration and rhythmic pulses with its gently hammered tremolos.

The complete melodic outline of the work is heard four times, with newly invented ornamentation at each appearance. In this performance, a poignant climax is reached in the third statement of the melody, with the erhu "singing" out beautifully in the instrument's highest range. A final statement releases some of the tension and ends the work (in literary terms) with a *denouement* unlike some of the highly dramatic climaxes we have heard in Western music. The version we hear today of *The Moon Reflected on the Second Springs* has, like most traditional pieces, been shaped over several generations since its modest beginnings, when it was performed by a blind, gifted Chinese musician.

Listening Guide 82

CD: Chr/Std 8/55–58, Sh 4/77–80
Cassette: Chr/Std 8B/3, Sh 4B/5

ABING: *The Moon Reflected on the Second Springs* (*Er quan ying yue*)

(5:36)

Date: First recorded in 1950 by Abing

Medium: Erhu (2-string fiddle), with yangqin (hammered dulcimer)

Genre: Chinese traditional music, from Jiangsu region

Scale: Pentatonic (five-note), with pitches D-E-G-A-B

Form: 4 musical phrases, repeated and elaborated

Tempo: Slow, with very gradual acceleration

| 55 | 0:00 | Short, rhythmically free introduction by erhu is followed by lyrical melodic phrase 1, played in low range; accompanied by yangqin; ends on low G: |
| | 0:35 | Melodic phrase 2—begins up an octave, in middle range and louder, with brief counter-melody on yangqin; ends on sustained D: |

	0:48	Melodic phrase 3—higher range, begins with soft staccato note, ends on sustained pitch of G:	

	1:06	Melodic phrase 4—returns to middle range; serves as a short closing idea ending on D:	

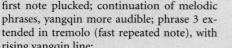

56	1:15	Returns to phrase 1 in low range, soft, with first note plucked; continuation of melodic phrases, yangqin more audible; phrase 3 extended in tremolo (fast repeated note), with rising yangqin line:	

57	2:30	Returns to phrase 1, in low range and with short opening notes; long elaboration of middle phrases, with statement of second idea in very high range; reaches climax and descends to cadence pitch of D.
58	4:08	Last statement of opening phrase, now with rising interval of sixth; more trills on erhu as melody climbs through phrases; ending is extended and tempo slows down; cadence pitch is on D.

82

Technology and Music

"I have been waiting a long time for electronics to free music from the tempered scale and the limitations of musical instruments. Electronic instruments are the portentous first step toward the liberation of music."—EDGARD VARÈSE

THE TECHNOLOGICAL REVOLUTION

The most demonstrably important development in art music of the 1950s and 1960s was the emergence of electronic music. The invention earlier in the century of such instruments as the electronic organ and the *ondes Martenot*—

which produced sounds by means of an electronic oscillator—predicted a future that was quickly realized by the booming revolution of technology.

The postwar emergence of electronic music falls into three stages. The first stage came with the use of magnetic tape recording, which was much more flexible as a medium for storing sounds than the lacquer-disc recording that had been used previously. Around 1947, a group of technicians at a Paris radio station, led by Pierre Schaeffer, were experimenting with what they called *musique concrète*, a music made up of natural sounds and disc recordings that were then altered by changing the playback speed. When the group began to use tape, they were able to cut and splice the sounds into new combinations.

Musique concrète

The possibility of using not only natural but also artificially generated sounds soon presented itself, and a wide variety of sound equipment came into use. Significant in this regard were the experiments begun around 1951 by Otto Luening and Vladimir Ussachevsky at Columbia University, and by Herbert Eimert and Karlheinz Stockhausen in Cologne. Within a few years, studios for the production of tape music sprang up in many of the chief musical centers of Europe and America. With the raw sound (either naturally or electronically produced) as a starting point, the composer could isolate its components, alter its pitch, volume, or other dimensions, play it backward, add reverberation (echo), filter out some of the overtones, or add other components by splicing and overdubbing. Even though all these operations were laborious and time-consuming—it might take many hours to process only a minute or two of finished music—composers hastened to try out and use the new medium.

The second stage in the technological revolution came with the development of *synthesizers*, which basically combine sound generators and sound modifiers in one package with a unified control system. The first was the RCA Electronic Music Synthesizer, unveiled in 1955; a more sophisticated model was installed four years later at the Columbia-Princeton Electronic Music Center in New York City. The synthesizer is capable of generating completely new sounds or combinations of sounds, with an infinite variety of pitches, durations, timbres, dynamics, and rhythmic patterns. This complex machine represented an enormous step forward in electronic music composition, since the composer was now able to control many of the characteristics beforehand and thus could bypass some of the time-consuming manual production techniques associated with tape-recorder music. The German composer Karlheinz Stockhausen (b. 1928), working in the Cologne studio, wrote two *Electronic Studies* (1953–54) built entirely from electronic sounds. He later produced his electronic masterpiece *Song of the Youths* (*Gesang der Jünglinge*, 1956) for vocal and recorded synthesized sounds, which marked the beginning of an enduring fascination with the electronic exploration of language.

Synthesizers

Cultural Perspective 24

MUSIC AND THE WORLD OF TECHNOLOGY

With the advent of such innovations as the electric guitar in the 1930s, making way for the digital sound synthesis of today, art and popular music have become highly dependent on electronic technology. Each new stage of development seems revolutionary before it becomes familiar and then obsolete, a sequence that occurs quickly in the modern world of electronics.

The ability to synthesize sounds has been crucial to both the popular performer and the electronic music composer. Commercial musicians continue to use keyboard synthesizers and samplers (devices that digitize, store, and play back sounds) in popular music and in film and TV scores. These electronic instruments can reproduce "real instrument" sounds and produce new sounds as well. A significant development in digital electronics, the adoption of MIDI (musical instrument digital interface) standards, allows a performer or composer to control a number of instruments either directly or through a computer, which becomes part of the musical process. The computer is capable of recording input,

reordering, transposing, superimposing, synchronizing, and playing back musical ideas in performance. Sources for MIDI input can be keyboards, guitars, winds, strings, or percussion instruments. This technology lets composers and performers interact with the computer and electronic musical instruments in live performance and in the studio.

We are all reaping the benefits of new music technologies. The quality and convenience of recordings has improved radically over the years. We have progressed from LPs and cassettes to various digital formats, including CDs (compact discs), DATs (digital audio tapes), MDs (mini-discs), and most recently, DVDs (digital video discs), each new format allowing storage of yet more data. We have "intelligent" interactive media at our fingertips, most notably with CD-ROM (CD–read only memory), CD-R (CD-writable), and now CD-RW (CD-re-writable); with the last of these, you can not only record your own CD, but rerecord it as many times as you wish. Today, multimedia

Because of its size and cost, the RCA machine at Columbia has remained unique; but advances in technology made possible smaller synthesizers that encompassed many of its features and added a few of their own. The cost of these synthesizers—in particular those manufactured by Moog, Buchla, and ARP—put them within reach of even small studios and individual composers.

on-demand services such as the Internet (a worldwide network of computer systems) and cable and satellite delivery systems provide easy access to interactive materials from all over the world.

Performers on tour can now record a new release via satellite link or the Internet without returning to the studio; and you can hear their latest hit on their website, download it to your system, listen to it, and even cut your own CD on your desktop. The world of technology promises more exciting media than we have yet imagined possible to enhance our listening pleasure and our ability to experience music actively.

Terms to Note:

synthesizer
sampler
MIDI
CD
DAT
MD
DVD
CD-ROM
CD-R
CD-RW
interactive media

A home studio with a MIDI-interfaced keyboard (Yamaha DX-7), sound mixer, and desktop computer.

Digital technology

The third stage of development involves the "digital revolution" that is still sweeping the electronic world. Digital circuits developed for computer systems have been adapted and refined for use in music. Digital technologies include MIDI communication standards, synthesis, sampling, and signal processing. Composers now have the ability to manipulate an unprecedented number of the parameters that make up a sound—pitch, timbre, duration, volume, and spacialization. A computer records, stores, retrieves, and manipulates sound in a fast and efficient manner. To hear the sound, the string of binary numbers is converted to an electrical signal that can be pushed through speakers, using a process known as digital-to-analog conversion.

A recent development, called virtual modeling, allows composers to use mathematical models that emulate and forecast the process by which real instruments produce sounds. Hybrid models can be made as well to create instruments that exist only in theory, such as a "bowed trombone." These technological advances have given composers even more control over their music and its performance, and have had an enormous impact on commercial music (see CP 24).

IMPORTANT FIGURES IN ELECTRONIC MUSIC

Edgard Varèse

One of the pioneers of electronic music was the French composer Edgard Varèse (1883–1965), who turned to this new medium relatively late in his life. His only completely electronic composition is *Poème electronique* (1958), a work commissioned for a sound and light show at a Brussels World Fair pavilion. The pavilion design, by the architect Le Corbusier, called for music to accompany projected images, so that visual and audio elements worked together to build a sensory environment. The music was composed on three audio channels, most of it directly onto tape. Varèse combined sounds of the human voice, treated electronically, with percussion and synthetic sounds created by an oscillator and several filters, and used a pulse generator to make drum sounds. Written when the composer was seventy-three, this landmark work heralded the musical sounds of the future.

Electronic music has two novel aspects. The most immediately obvious one, the possibility to create new sounds, has impelled many musicians to use the medium. Equally important, the composer of electronic music can work directly with the sounds and produce a finished work without the help of an intermediary performer.

However, combining electronic sounds with live music has also proved fertile, especially since many younger composers have been working in both media. Works for soloist and recorded tape have become common, even "concertos" for tape recorder (or live-performance synthesizer or computer) and orchestra. One important composer working in this mixed medium is

Mario Davidovsky

Mario Davidovsky (b. 1934); formerly professor of composition at Columbia University and director of the Columbia-Princeton Electronic Music Center in New York, he now teaches at Harvard University. Among his works for tape and live performer is a series known as *Synchronisms* (1963–88), dialogues for solo instrument and prerecorded tape. No. 1, for flute and tape, is particularly effective because of the flute's purity of tone, wide range of dynamics, and agility in pitch and articulation. "The attempt here," Davidovsky writes, "has been made to preserve the typical characteristics of the conventional instruments and the electronic medium respectively—yet to achieve integration of both into a coherent musical texture."

Another important voice in the field of electronic music is that of Milton Babbitt (b. 1916), who was one of the first to recognize its possibilities. Babbitt's early electronic works, composed at the Columbia-Princeton Electronic Music Center, reflect his interest in assuming total control of the final musical result. But it was never his intention that the synthesizer should replace the live musician. "I know of no serious electronic composer who ever asserts that we are supplanting any other form of music. . . . We're interested in increasing the resources of music." Like Davidovsky, he saw as the next step combining electronic music with live performers, an area in which he has contributed such pathbreaking works as *Philomel* (1964) and *Phonemena* (1974), both for soprano and tape. Babbitt has been a highly influential teacher at Princeton University to several generations of talented young composers.

Milton Babbitt

Pauline Oliveros (b. 1932), one of the more experimental contemporary composers, helped found the San Francisco Tape Center and became its director in 1966. She has explored mixed media and the possibilities of multichannel tape interacting with live performers and theatrical forms. Oliveros is also known for her experiments with live electronic music, in which sounds are generated and manipulated during the performance. Her developing interest in the 1970s in Asian culture and philosophy resulted in *Sonic Meditations* (1971–74), twenty-five pieces with verbal descriptions that suggest ways to make, hear, and think about sounds. Her later works look back to earlier techniques: *The Roots of the Moment* (1988), for example, combines an interactive electronic environment with a favorite instrument of hers, the accordion. A forerunner in the field of electronic music, Oliveros has strongly influenced the younger generation of composers.

Pauline Oliveros

Electronic music has permeated the commercial world of music making in a big way. Much of the music we hear today as movie and TV soundtracks is electronically generated, although some effects resemble the sounds of conventional instruments so closely that we are not always aware of the new technology. Popular music groups have been "electrified" for some years, but now most of them regularly feature synthesizers and samplers that both simulate conventional rock band instruments and produce altogether new sounds.

Paul Lansky

LANSKY: *NOTJUSTMOREIDLECHATTER*

"I like to project the idea that my electronic sounds don't have a supernatural origin, that they have a human origin."

Paul Lansky (b. 1944), a pioneer in digital sound synthesis, is one of the most prominent figures in the world of computer music. He studied composition with George Perle and Hugo Weisgall at Queens College in New York and with Milton Babbitt and Edward Cone at Princeton University, where he has taught since 1969. In addition to his composing, for which he has received many awards, fellowships, and commissions, Lansky has made notable contributions to music theory and music criticism.

Like most contemporary composers, Lansky has explored a number of different compositional methods. Some of his early works for chamber ensembles and solo instruments reflect his interest in a twelve-tone system. For the past twenty years, however, he has preferred the medium of computer-synthesized tape. In *Six Fantasies on a Poem by Thomas Campion* (1979), the composer captured and manipulated sounds of the human voice, using linear predictive coding (LPC)—analyzing a sound in order to reproduce it or to create new sounds by modifying some its properties.

Lansky fully embraced computer-assisted composition in *Idle Chatter* (1985) and its two sequels, *just_more_idle_chatter* (1987) and *Notjustmoreidlechatter* (1988). In these works, the computer participates in defining and creating the compositional procedures and the complex textures. *Notjustmoreidlechatter*, which we will consider, is unified by a simple recurring tonal bass progression, over which the listener hears thousands of unintelligible synthesized word fragments. The fragments first appear random, then the "chatter" seems to become almost understandable and "human"; but this perception is soon lost, and the listener abandons any hope of making sense out of the "text." Lansky uses LPC to produce a series of "frames," each of which contains information on the sound frequencies and timbral qualities that combine to make up speech at various moments. He then synthesizes a voice using these frames to control the filtering of an artificial sound produced by a buzz generator. White noise is mixed in to produce certain consonants, and the buzz generator controls the pitch and rhythm of the "words," giving a "humanness" to the computer-generated sounds. The resulting lively and engaging work draws the listener in to its varied speech sounds.

In one of his newest projects, the computer opera *Things She Carried* (1995–96, with collaborator Hannah MacKay), Lansky continued exploring the world of human sound. The opera is an eight-movement musical portrait that investigates what a particular woman notices, remembers, reads, knows, feels, likes, and carries in her purse.

Principal Works

Chamber/instrumental works, including 2 string quartets (1967, 1971/rev. 1977), *Crossworks* (1978, for piano, flute, clarinet, violin, cello), *As If* (1981–82, for string trio with computer-generated tape), *Hop* (1993, for marimba and violin)

Electronic/computer works, including *mild und leise* (1973), *Six Fantasies on a Poem by Thomas Campion* (1979), *As it grew dark* (1983), *Idle Chatter* (1985), *just_more_idle_chatter* (1987), *Notjustmoreidlechatter* (1988), *Smalltalk* (1988), *Not So Heavy Metal* (1989), *QuakerBridge* (1990), *The Sound of Two Hands* (1990), *Table's Clear* (1992), *Still Time* (1994), and *Things She Carried* (1995–96, computer opera)

Listening Guide 83

CD: Chr/Std 8/59–62
Cassette: Chr/Std 8B/4

LANSKY: *Notjustmoreidlechatter*, excerpt   (3:52)

Date of work: 1988

Medium: Computer-synthesized tape

Style: Human-like voice sounds, in polyphonic texture over slow, recurring harmonic progression

59	0:00	Fast chatter; irregular and syncopated accents over underlying harmonic progression with regular, "rock-like" feel (begins in G minor: i-VI-i-VII-i-IV-i-III-VII-i); sense of slow-moving "back-up voices" as harmony.
		Independent "voices" in different ranges emerge and are almost understandable.
60	0:57	Returns to opening G-minor progression and textures; continues with various harmonies and hints of individual voices.
61	2:03	Returns again to opening G-minor progression.
62	2:52	Begins to fade; low "rock-like" pulse is less strong and then stops; slow-moving "strings" are simulated in high range, alternating between two notes as texture thins; dynamics fade; voices more prominent and almost intelligible; recording fades.

83

Other Recent Trends

"The current state of music presents a variety of solutions in search of a problem, the problem being to find somebody left to listen."—NED ROREM

THE NEW ROMANTICISM

Serial, or twelve-tone, music, with its emphasis on intellectual and constructivist aspects (the highly structural use of all musical elements), has lost some favor in recent decades to a more eclectic synthesis of familiar styles known as the New Romanticism. A number of composers felt that the time had come to close the gap between themselves and the public by restoring music to its former position as "the language of the emotions," complete with appealing melodies, regular rhythms, lush harmonies, and rich orchestral colors.

The New Romanticism has taken a variety of forms. Some composers have combined the general harmonic language of the Romantic era with other current trends, such as the New Virtuosity (see p. 632). Others have used the Romantic style or the works of a particular composer more literally. As usual, there are no clear dividing lines. Many works that are labeled as examples of the New Romanticism share techniques with serial and aleatoric music and employ the new instrumental possibilities that have opened up since the middle of the century.

Samuel Barber

The New Romanticism had an important precursor in Samuel Barber (1910–1981), whose music, suffused with feeling, leans toward the grand gestures of nineteenth-century tradition. Several of his works achieved enormous popularity, among them the light-hearted Overture to *The School for Scandal* (1932) and the elegiac *Adagio for Strings* (1936). Although his works from the 1940s on feature more "modern" harmony and scoring, his successful opera *Vanessa* (1958), on a libretto by Gian Carlo Menotti, was praised as "highly charged with emotional meaning."

Ned Rorem

Ned Rorem (b. 1923), one of the most distinguished composers of his generation, has written widely in all genres, from chamber and orchestral music to opera. His songs are in the line of descent from the great French art song of the post-Romantic period. A talented writer, Rorem has published several books of criticism and memoirs in the form of diaries.

One of the leading exponents of the New Romanticism is the Scottish-born composer Thea Musgrave (b. 1928). She is best-known for her stage works—operas and ballets. *Mary, Queen of Scots* (1977) is a highly accessible tonal opera that draws on the history of the composer's native land. A figure from American history serves as the heroine in her opera *Harriet, the Woman Called Moses* (1985)—Harriet Tubman, who escaped from slavery and helped establish the Underground Railroad. Musgrave's most recent opera, *Simón Bolívar* (1995), brings to the stage the bloody story of South America's fight for independence from Spain. In addition to composing, Musgrave has conducted numerous orchestras and opera companies in the performances of her own works.

Thea Musgrave

Of a more recent generation of composers interested in the New Romanticism, David Del Tredici (b. 1937) stands out for the broad lyric appeal of his music. He spent some years writing large works for soprano and orchestra inspired by Lewis Carroll's *Alice's Adventures in Wonderland* and *Through the Looking Glass.* Two such compositions, *Final Alice* (1976) and *In Memory of a Summer Day* (1980), have found special favor with the public.

David Del Tredici

Joan Tower (b. 1938) has written some outstanding works that pay homage to influential composers through the techniques of parody and quotation. Her Piano Concerto (1985) honors Beethoven by making prominent use of ideas from three of his piano sonatas, and her chamber work *Petroushskates* (1980) draws inspiration from Stravinsky's ballet *Petrushka* (as well as the imagery of figure skating). The first American to win the Grawemeyer Award, Tower has written numerous orchestral works, concertos, and chamber pieces, and a ballet, *Stepping Stones* (1993).

Joan Tower

Among the most accessible works of the New Romantic idiom are those of John Corigliano (b. 1938), whose music displays an imaginative use of contemporary techniques. His major works include *The Naked Carmen* (1970), an "eclectic rock opera" fashioned after Bizet, and *The Ghosts of Versailles* (1991), commissioned by the Metropolitan Opera in New York. The latter work, with a highly original libretto by William Hoffman, was a resounding success at its premiere. Two recent works by Corigliano are dedicated to AIDS victims: the Symphony No. 1 (subtitled the *AIDS* Symphony), premiered at the Kennedy Center in Washington, D.C., in 1995; and the cantata *Of Rage and Remembrance* (1996), based on the third movement of the *AIDS* Symphony, with a text that combines an emotionally intense poem by William Hoffman with a litany of victims' names. In the finale of the cantata, the chanted names change with each performance, as chorus members remember their own friends lost to this modern-day plague.

John Corigliano

Amid the late-twentieth-century composers whose experiments have produced such a wide variety of styles, Ellen Taaffe Zwilich (b. 1939) has chosen

Ellen Taaffe Zwilich

to continue the great tradition of the symphony. In 1975, Zwilich became the first woman to earn a doctorate in composition from the Juilliard School in New York. She was also the first woman to win a Pulitzer Prize in composition, granted in 1983 for her Symphony No. 1 (1982). Zwilich's loyalty to traditional forms and her reaffirmation of tonality has endeared her to concert audiences and musicians alike.

Tobias Picker

Tobias Picker (b. 1954) belongs to that fortunate breed of artists to whom recognition comes early enough to be enjoyed. His First Symphony was commissioned by the San Francisco Symphony in 1982, when he was twenty-eight. *Keys to the City* (1982), really his second piano concerto, was written for the one-hundredth anniversary of the Brooklyn Bridge; a performance of this work, with the composer as soloist, was broadcast on national television. His opera *Emmeline* (1996), commissioned by the Santa Fe Opera and with a libretto by J. D. McClatchy, effectively brings to the stage Judith Rossner's novel of the same name. Picker's style is marked by grand gesture, sweeping melodies, expressive harmonies, and virtuoso instrumental writing, all of which rank him with the New Romantics.

LIBBY LARSEN AND QUOTATION MUSIC

"I try to study the culture I live in and to use the rhythms and the phrasing of the culture in my music."

Libby Larsen

Libby Larsen (b. 1950) is one among only a handful of composers who make a living from their creative work rather than from holding an academic position. Raised in Minneapolis, Larsen studied composition at the University of Minnesota with Dominick Argento and Paul Fetler. She co-founded the Minnesota Composers Forum at the age of twenty-two, and from 1983 to 1987 she served as composer-in-residence for the Minnesota Orchestra. Larsen has received numerous commissions and awards, and her output of compositions spans most genres. She strives to "find ways of creating simple concepts" to make her music accessible to the general audience and to further explore the sonic environment of the concert hall. Her works are characterized by melodic artistry and a careful harmonic architecture. In her chamber music, Larsen shows a special affinity for the flute, which she uses to evoke popular and traditional styles of music.

Some of Larsen's compositions express her interest in illuminating strong-minded women—among them *Songs from Letters* (1989), a song cycle set to letters that sharpshooter Calamity Jane wrote to her daughter; *Ghosts of Old Ceremonies* (1991), an orchestral work with dancers based on experiences of women pioneers in the Old West; the oratorio *Coming Forth into Day* (1986), set to a text partly written by Jihan Sadat, widow of the slain leader of Egypt;

Principal Works

Orchestral music, including *Symphony: Water Music* (1985), *What the Monster Saw* (1987), *Ghosts of Old Ceremonies* (1991, with dancers), and *Song-Dances to the Light* (1995)

Chamber music, including *Ulloa's Ring* (1980, flute and piano) and *Aubade* (1982, solo flute)

10 operas, including *Beauty and the Beast* (1989) and *Frankenstein, the Modern Prometheus* (1990), and *Eric Hermannson's Soul* (1996)

Choral music, including the oratorio *Coming Forth into Day* (1986), *Missa Gaia: Mass for the Earth* (1991–92), *Seven Ghosts* (1995, with brass choir), and *Billy the Kid* (1997, with large chorus and The King's Singers)

Vocal music, including *Three Rilke Songs* (1977, for soprano, harp, flute, guitar); song cycles, including *Sonnets from the Portuguese* (1989, soprano and chamber orchestra on poems by Elizabeth Barrett Browning), and *Songs from Letters* (1989, after Calamity Jane)

and the one-act opera *Eric Hermannson's Soul* (1996), adapted from a short story by Willa Cather. The murder trial of O. J. Simpson seemed to Larsen to elevate the image of the antihero, and she responded with *Seven Ghosts*, a work for chorus and brass choir that celebrates seven heroes of the past: revolutionary poet Phillis Wheatley, President George Washington, author Harriet Beecher Stowe, Swedish singer Jenny Lind, astronomer Clyde Tombaugh, aviator Charles Lindbergh, and jazz artist Louis Armstrong.

One of Larsen's most significant works, the opera *Frankenstein, the Modern Prometheus* (1990), takes a new perspective on novelist Mary Shelley's classic. She began work on the opera with an orchestral study, *What the Monster Saw*, that told the story from the monster's point of view. The completed, rock-inspired stage work features multidimensional video effects, reflecting her interest in capturing a contemporary audience. Larsen is a strong advocate for musical institutions—notably symphony orchestras and opera companies—and for the wide acceptance of contemporary American art music.

Symphony: Water Music

As someone who grew up in the "land of a thousand lakes," Larsen found it natural to seek inspiration for her music in the environment. The four movements of her pictorial *Symphony: Water Music* resemble four unframed portraits of "the motions and rhythms of nature."

In Her Own Words

I want to give the listener not the sound of a bird as much as the feeling of flying; not the footsteps on a mountain so much as the sense of climbing, not the boat on water so much as the water itself. . . . I came to this view—that the response to nature matters more in music than the thing in nature—innocently enough. As a Minnesotan and a Norwegian by heritage, nature is dear—for half the year there is little sound or movement, and the overwhelming white background heightens one's awareness of each small irregularity or contrast or surprise.

Commissioned by the Minnesota Orchestra to celebrate the tercentenary of George Frideric Handel's birth (in 1685), this work pays homage to one of Larsen's favorite composers by incorporating fragments from his *Water Music* in the first movement, *Fresh Breeze* (the movement we will study; see Listening Guide 84). The soft opening chord that emerges in the strings "attempts to capture that fresh, oscillating, crystalline vibrancy of water moved by constant wind." The gestures move around the orchestra with constantly changing colors—the horns and harp, then the high woodwind trills amid the mellow, dark violas. Her orchestral palette makes prominent use of percussive metallic sounds, produced by vibraphone, marimba, orchestral bells, crotales, bell tree, triangle, and wind chimes.

Throughout the movement, the brass instruments intone fragments from Handel's *Water Music*, especially the hornpipe we heard earlier (p. 450). Near the end, we hear a clear statement of Handel's majestic theme, rendered in turn by various instruments. The parodying of Handel's suite is a technique known as *quotation music*. Here, Larsen pays musical homage to the earlier masterpiece while retaining her own unique sound and personality.

The second movement, *Hot, Still*, opens with a solo flute phrase that conjures up a summer breeze. The flickering in the woodwinds brings to mind the gently rippling surface of the water, and the low, heavy brass and strings suggest the lethargy of the lake on a hot and humid August day. *Wafting*, according to Larsen, suggests "tiny scatter squalls and cats' paws creating puffs on the water just before a front moves in"; the trumpets and horns set the pace for a rhythmically complex scherzo. *Gale*, the closing movement, features sharp dynamic contrasts that muster the fury of a violent summer storm, rather than delineating a sequence of events. This impressionistic evocation of water-filled landscapes is clearly the work of one who knows and respects the forces of nature.

Listening Guide 84

CD: Chr/Std 8/63–65, Sh 4/81–83
Cassette: Chr/Std 8B/5, Sh 4B/6

LARSEN: *Symphony: Water Music*, First Movement   (5:01)

Date of work: 1985
Occasion: 300th anniversary of the birth of Handel, commissioned by the Minnesota Orchestra
Genre: Program symphony
Structure: 4 movements (fast-slow-presto-fast)

1. *Fresh Breeze*   3. *Wafting*
2. *Hot, Still*   4. *Gale*

Theme from hornpipe, in Handel's *Water Music*:

Fresh Breeze, from *Symphony: Water Music*, 6/8 meter

63 0:00 Introductory section, features syncopated string line punctuated with trills in the woodwinds and harp glissandos, over pedal note (G).

0:17 French horns and cellos introduce motive related to hornpipe theme:

French horns

0:33 String flourish leads to syncopated trumpet idea (muted), from last notes of French-horn theme:

Trumpets

Trumpets answered by fast, repeated-note figure in French horns, accompanied by woodwind trills and jangling bell tree.

0:42 Swirling string lines with sixteenth notes and trills, followed by restatement of trumpet motive (without mutes); swirling strings ascend to *fff* climax.

1:05 Trumpets play more extended version of main theme (now clearly based on Handel's hornpipe), leading to full orchestral climax:

Trumpets

64 1:14 Change of tempo (slower, *poco meno mosso*) and shift to 4/4 meter; plucked strings and woodwinds exchange short motive idea (2 notes, ascending stepwise); marimba, harp, and vibraphone featured.

1:25 Lyrical oboe solo, begins with extended note, answered by other woodwinds:

Oboe

1:41 Rhythmic pulses in low instruments alternate with 2-note motive and trills.

2:02 Return of oboe solo; builds to dissonant climax with wavering strings (similar to opening).

65	3:07	Return of trumpet theme, now more triumphant, with swirling strings and woodwind trills.
	3:13	Whole orchestra trades off trumpet theme; first trombones, then strings and woodwinds; overlapping statements of theme, accompanied by gong, build in momentum and volume.
	4:16	Coda extends trills and offbeat pulses in double basses until end; final chime strike closes movement.

MINIMALISM AND POST-MINIMALISM

"Now that things are so simple, there's so much to do."
—MORTON FELDMAN

Independently of the New Romantics, another group of composers found their own way to simplify the musical language. They stripped their compositions down to the barest essentials in order to concentrate the listener's attention on a few basic details. This urge toward a minimal art, which first found expression in painting and sculpture, became a significant force in contemporary music during the 1970s.

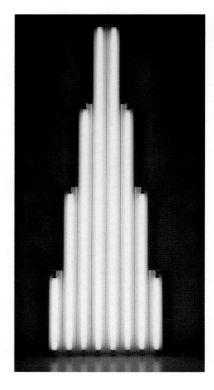

Untitled (Monument for V. Tatlin, 1964), *by* **Dan Flavin,** *an eight-foot structure of cool, white fluorescent light, is a distinctive example of imaginative minimalism.*

The salient feature of *minimalist music*, as it has come to be known, is the repetition of melodic, rhythmic, and harmonic patterns with very little variation. The music changes so slowly that it can have a hypnotic effect, and indeed the term "trance music" has attached itself to some works of the minimalists. But it is a label they reject because, as they point out, their material is selected most carefully and worked out in highly disciplined procedures. One can say, however, that in minimalist music, time moves at a different pace from what most of us are accustomed to.

In simplifying melody, rhythm, and harmony within an unwavering tonality, the minimalists have turned away from the complex, highly intellectual style of the serialists. They reject the heritage of Schoenberg and Webern just as they do the cerebral preoccupations of Boulez and Babbitt. Instead, they open themselves to modes of thought emanating from Third World countries—especially the contemplative art of India and the quasi-obsessive rhythms of some African cultures—and to jazz, pop, and rock. Although influenced by the early ideas of John Cage, minimalists for the most part reject his interest in indeterminacy and chance. They prefer to control their sounds.

There are several kinds of minimalist music. In some works, the pulse is repeated with numbing regularity. Others are very busy on the surface, though the harmonies and timbres change very slowly. Terry Riley (b. 1935) **Terry Riley** introduced the element of pulse and the concept of tiny motivic cells that repeat in his ninety-minute masterwork *In C* (1964). Influenced by the music of the Far East, by ragtime and jazz, and by the theories of John Cage, Riley has employed elements of performer choice in electronic music, along with improvisation.

The most widely known minimalists are Steve Reich, whom we will study, and Philip Glass (b. 1937). Glass's career began conventionally enough, at the **Philip Glass** University of Chicago and the Juilliard School, after which he went off to Paris on a Fulbright Scholarship to study with Nadia Boulanger. It was she who imparted to him, as he put it, "the skills that make music go." Even more decisive was his contact with the Indian sitar player Ravi Shankar (see illustration on p. 54), reflecting the composer's fascination with non-Western music. "And, of course, I was also hearing the music of Miles Davis, of John Coltrane, and the Beatles." When he returned to New York, he became convinced that "modern music had become truly decadent, stagnant, uncommunicative. Composers were writing for each other and the public didn't seem to care." It was out of this conviction that Glass evolved his own style, drawing on the musical traditions of India and Africa as well as the techniques of rock and progressive jazz. His most important works include *Glassworks* (1983) and his operas *Einstein on the Beach* (1976), *Satyagraha* (1980), and *Akhnaten* (1984).

A composer was bound to appear who, in seeking to expand the expressive range of minimalist music, would respond to the emotional impulses of the

John Adams

New Romantics. Such a new voice belonged to John Adams (b. 1947), the best-known of the post-minimalists. Adams's music is more personal than that of his predecessors. He attracted much attention with his opera *Nixon in China* (1987), a fruitful collaboration with the imaginative director Peter Sellars and the poet Alice Goodman, which is set in Beijing during the three-day visit of President Nixon in November 1972. This work was followed by *The Death of Klinghoffer* (1991), an opera on a more explosive issue—the killing of a wheelchair-bound Jewish tourist by Arab terrorists. His *Short Ride in a Fast Machine* (1986) is an exuberant work for large orchestra and two synthesizers that stems from the extroverted side of Adams's personality.

Yet another style of minimalism that has developed, mostly at the hands of European composers, is a nonpulsed music inspired by religious beliefs and expressed in deceptively simple—and seemingly endless—chains of lush modal or tonal progressions. The major representatives of this deeply medi-

Spiritual minimalism

tative music, often referred to as *spiritual minimalism,* are Arvo Pärt (b. 1935), an Estonian composer who combines the mysticism of Russian Orthodox rituals with elements of Eastern European folk music in his sacred choral works *Passio* (1982) and *Miserere* (1989); the Polish composer Henryk Górecki (b. 1933), whose Symphony No. 3 (for soprano and orchestra, 1976) features modern sound masses couched in a slow-moving triadic, tonal musical language; and John Taverner (b. 1944), an English composer whose style combines elements of New Romanticism with a devout spiritualism. Taverner's powerful choral work *Song for Athene* was heard by millions at the close of the funeral service for Princess Diana on September 6, 1997; its text, "Alleluia. May flights of angels sing thee to thy rest," is drawn from Shakespeare's *Hamlet* and from the Orthodox Vigil Service.

STEVE REICH'S *CITY LIFE*

Steve Reich

Steve Reich (b. 1936) is widely regarded as one of the principal figures of minimalism in music. A native of New York City, Reich studied percussion and piano as a youth. He attended Cornell University as a philosophy major, then returned to New York and the Juilliard School to study composition with William Bergsma and Vincent Persichetti. In 1961, he entered Mills College in Oakland, California, where he took classes with Darius Milhaud and Luciano Berio. While in California, Reich developed an interest in electronic composition, jazz, Balinese gamelan music, and African drumming.

His earliest works, music featuring taped sounds for several underground films, led to one of his most famous tape works, *Come Out*, in which he manipulated speech fragments looped for infinite repetition and overlapping, a process known as *phasing*. Reich recalls the effect he experienced while listen-

<hr>

Principal Works

Orchestral music, including *Music for a Large Ensemble* (1979), *Eight Lines* (1983, orchestral revision of Octet), and *The Four Sections* (1987)

Choral/vocal music, including *Tehillim* (voices and amplified chamber ensemble, 1981) and *The Desert Music* (for amplified choir and orchestra, 1982–84)

Chamber works, including *Piano Phase* (2 pianos or marimbas, 1967), *Violin Phase* (violin and tape, 1967), *Drumming* (percussion and chamber ensemble, 1971), *Music for Mallet Instruments, Voices, and Electric Organ* (1973), Octet (1979), *Variations for Winds, Strings, and Keyboards* (1980), *Different Trains* (string quartet and tape, 1988), and *City Life* (1995)

Multimedia works, including *The Cave* (video/music theater, in collaboration with Beryl Korot; 1993)

Other: *Come Out* (tape, voice of Harlem Six member Daniel Hamm; 1966), *Clapping Music* (4 hands, no piano; 1972), and a book, *Writings about Music* (1974)

<hr>

ing to his early phase pieces on headphones: "The sensation I had in my head was that the sound moved over to my left ear, moved down to my left shoulder, down my left arm, down my leg, out across the floor to the left and finally began to reverberate, [eventually coming] back together in the center of my head." Reich's phase music developed in complexity and diversity from *Clapping Music* (1972), for two performers, to *The Desert Music* (1983), setting poetry of William Carlos Williams for amplified chorus and orchestra. In the 1970s, with landmark minimalist works such as *Music for Mallet Instruments, Voices, and Electric Organ*, he introduced harmonic modulation into his essentially repetitive structures.

Reich's music was strongly influenced by some nontraditional music training, including studies in drumming at the Institute for African Studies at the University of Ghana (1970), in Balinese gamelan performance in Seattle and Berkeley (1973–74), and in Hebrew cantillation, or biblical chanting (in New York and Jerusalem, 1976–77). "I studied Balinese and African music because I love them," he said, "and also because I believe that non-Western music is presently the single most important source of new ideas for Western composers and musicians."

In 1970, Reich achieved a long-standing goal: to study music in Ghana. "I

Study in Ghana

was overwhelmed by their music, [it was] like being in front of a tidal wave." Reich learned that in Ghanaian drumming (and especially that of the Ewe tribe), the ensemble is held together by a basic rhythm called a "timeline," over which each musician plays a repeated rhythmic pattern, with the most complex performed by the group leader, or master drummer. The essential organization of the music is thus multilinear—each line contributes a simple pattern resulting in a complex fabric of parts. On his return to the United States, Reich wrote *Drumming* (1971), a work for percussion ensemble—including drums, bells, and maracas (rattles made from gourds)—that draws heavily on the cyclic structures and polyrhythms he heard in Ghana.

In recent years, Reich has moved toward composing larger works. *City Life* (1995), which we will study, is one of his longest ensemble pieces, and his multimedia work *The Cave* (1993) is his most ambitious project yet. The latter, completed in collaboration with his wife, video artist Beryl Korot, calls for live singers, a small ensemble of musicians, and five oversized video screens showing snippets of taped interviews with Israelis, Palestinians, and Americans. The music is constructed from "speech melodies," and the mosaic-like libretto is based on the Koran, the Bible, and the videotaped interviews. The "cave" in question is the burial site of Abraham, in the town of Hebron in the Holy Land. One critic has called this work "a tantalizing glimpse of what opera might be like in the twenty-first century."

Reich's *City Life*, for woodwinds, string quartet, contrabass, two pianos, two samplers (programmable keyboards in which a key can reproduce and modify a prerecorded sound), and percussion, resulted from a joint commission by the Ensemble Modern (in Frankfurt), the London Sinfonietta, and the Ensemble Intercontemporain (in Paris). Its five-movement structure forms an arch, with the center and two outer movements based on speech samples. For the first movement, Reich taped the sales pitch of a street vendor in Lower Manhattan: "Check it out." The third movement, with its manipulated text, "It's been a honeymoon—can't take no mo'," was recorded at an African-American political rally in New York City. In the final movement, Reich used speech samples drawn from live field communications of the New York City Fire Department on the day of the World Trade Center bombing, February 25, 1993. The second and fourth movements incorporate sampled urban noises rather than speech.

City Life opens with an introductory section featuring sustained chords that seems to pay homage to the American composer Aaron Copland, whom we studied earlier. Soon, however, the momentum quickens with a three-note ascending motive that permeates the entire fabric of the movement. This motive derives from the linear and rhythmic contour of the words "check it out," as shouted by the street vendor. The essence of minimalism is a short, insistent idea; here, the idea is the three-note motive and its inver-

In His Own Words

The idea that any sound may be used as part of a piece has been in the air during much of the twentieth century. From the use of taxi horns in Gershwin's An American in Paris *through Varèse's sirens . . . Cage's radio, and rock and roll's use of all of the above and more starting at least in the 1970s, and more recently in rap music, the desire to include everyday sounds in music has been growing. The sampling keyboard now makes this a practical reality. In* City Life, *not only samples of speech but also car horns, door slams, air brakes, subway chimes, pile drivers, car alarms, heartbeats, boat horns, and fire and police sirens are part of the fabric of the piece. . . . The prerecorded sounds here are played live in performance on two sampling keyboards. . . . "loaded" with sounds, many recorded by myself in New York City.*

sion, which form the basis for a disjunct line. Soon the samplers enter with the text, punctuated by special "street" effects. Instruments then enter with overlapping statements, in and out of phase with the main motive, producing a dense polyphonic texture. Throughout, the persistent motive is heard in the instruments and sampled voice, taking on new melodic shapes with each change of key. Finally, the drive lets up, and the nostalgic chords of the opening return, guiding the movement to a familiar close.

Listening Guide 85

CD: Chr/Std 8/43–48, Sh 4/84–89
Cassette: Chr/Std 8B/1, Sh 4B/7

REICH: *City Life*, First Movement

(5:57)

Date: 1995

Instrumentation: 2 flutes, 2 oboes, 2 clarinets, 2 vibraphones, 2 pianos, 2 samplers, percussion (cymbals, snare drum, bass drum), string quartet, and contrabass

Movements:
1. "Check it out"
2. Pile driver/alarms
3. "It's been a honeymoon—can't take no mo'"
4. Heartbeats/boats & buoys
5. "Heavy smoke"

FIRST MOVEMENT: "Check it out"

Special effects sampled: Text phrase "check it out," door slam, bus air, subway air, car motor, car horn, car over manhole, subway chime, tire skid

43	0:00	Introductory section with homophonic (chordal) texture, all parts moving together slowly, with very short phrases, in shifting meters; violin line represents melodic idea; no sampled effects:
44	0:39	Disjunct, quick-paced rhythmic idea introduced (and heard throughout movement); 3-note ascending motive at beginning previews "music" for text; inversion of 3-note figure follows:

0:46 First statement of "check it out," based on 3-note motive, followed immediately by door slam; piano has motivic idea:

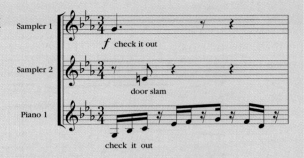

Texture becomes more polyphonic as motive moves throughout instruments, overlapping in statements, producing phasing effect; special effects heard (door slam, bus and subway air):

1:18 Overlapping statements of "check it out"; strings mimic voice, but change interval from rising third to fourth; instruments now "out of phase" as rhythmic idea is displaced in the measure:

Texture continues to become denser as more instruments take up rhythmic idea in overlapping statements; car horn and car motor added to effects; piece builds to sudden change of key center.

45 1:57 "Check it out" motive now heard with new intervals, in smaller and more chromatic range, punctuated by door slam:

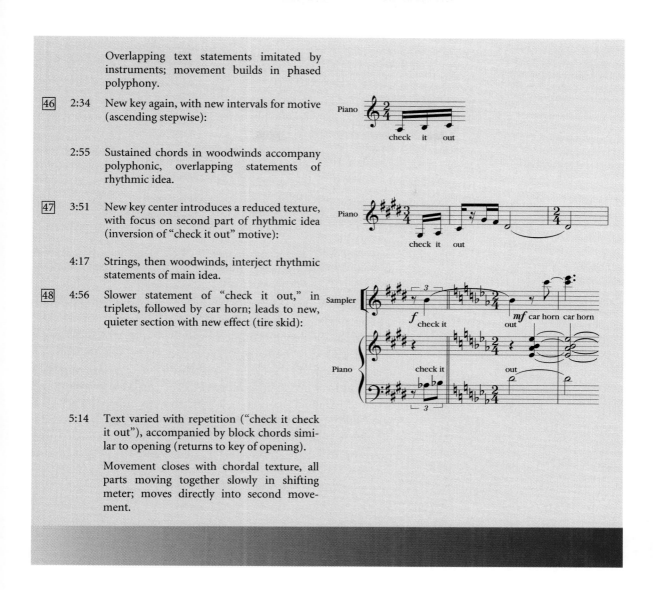

46	2:34	New key again, with new intervals for motive (ascending stepwise):
	2:55	Sustained chords in woodwinds accompany polyphonic, overlapping statements of rhythmic idea.
47	3:51	New key center introduces a reduced texture, with focus on second part of rhythmic idea (inversion of "check it out" motive):
	4:17	Strings, then woodwinds, interject rhythmic statements of main idea.
48	4:56	Slower statement of "check it out," in triplets, followed by car horn; leads to new, quieter section with new effect (tire skid):
	5:14	Text varied with repetition ("check it check it out"), accompanied by block chords similar to opening (returns to key of opening).
		Movement closes with chordal texture, all parts moving together slowly in shifting meter; moves directly into second movement.

Overlapping text statements imitated by instruments; movement builds in phased polyphony.

Minimalist music has had wide appeal with popular-music audiences, in part because it is easily accessible and its non-Western sense of time lends a certain mysterious aura. With fewer minute details on which to concentrate, listeners can easily grasp the composition as a whole. Minimalism can be directly linked to rock and, to a lesser extent, jazz, as both styles are based on the repetition of a limited harmonic idea. Rock groups of the 1970s, such as Pink Floyd and the Talking Heads (with minimalist composer Brian Eno), led the way for the new-age music of today, which offers a soothing audio environment. Reich's minimalism, like new-age music, achieves a trancelike quality that is generated by the repetitive structures and constantly shifting variation techniques we associate with certain world musics.

Coda

"Just listen with the vastness of the world in mind. You can't fail to get the message."—PIERRE BOULEZ

These pages have included a variety of facts—historical, biographical, and technical—that have entered into the making of music and that we must consider if we seek to listen intelligently to music. Like all books, this one belongs to the domain of words, and words have no power over the domain of sound. They are helpful only insofar as they lead us to enjoy the music.

The enjoyment of music depends on perceptive listening, which (like perceptive anything) is achieved gradually, with practice and effort. By studying the circumstances out of which a musical work issued, we prepare ourselves for its multiple meanings; we open ourselves to that exercise of mind and heart, sensibility and imagination, that makes listening to music a unique experience. But in building up our musical perceptions—that is, our listening enjoyment—let us always remember that the ultimate wisdom rests neither in dates nor in facts. It is to be found in one place only: the sounds themselves.

Appendix I

Musical Notation

THE NOTATION OF PITCH

Musical notation presents a kind of graph of each sound's duration and pitch. These are indicated by symbols called *notes*, which are written on the *staff*, a series of five parallel lines separated by four spaces:

Staff

The positions of the notes on the staff indicate the pitches, each line and space representing a different degree of pitch.

A symbol known as a *clef* is placed at the left end of the staff to determine the relative pitch names. The *treble clef* (&) is used for pitches within the range of the female singing voices, and the *bass clef* (℈) for a lower group of pitches, within the range of the male singing voices.

Clefs

Pitches are named after the first seven letters of the alphabet, from A to G. (From one note named A to the next is the interval of an octave.) The pitches on the treble staff are named as follows:

Pitch names

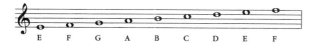

E   F   G   A   B   C   D   E   F

And those on the bass staff:

G   A   B   C   D   E   F   G   A

For pitches above and below these staffs, short extra lines called *ledger lines* can be added:

Middle C—the C that, on the piano, is situated approximately in the center of the keyboard—comes between the treble and bass staffs. It is represented by either the first ledger line above the bass staff or the first ledger line below the treble staff, as the following example makes clear. This combination of the two staffs is called the *great staff* or *grand staff*:

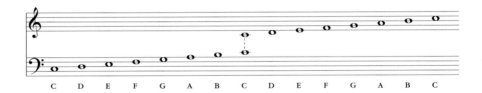

Accidentals   Signs known as *accidentals* are used to alter the pitch of a written note. A *sharp* (♯) before the note indicates the pitch a half step above; a *flat* (♭) indicates the pitch a half step below. A *natural* (♮) cancels a sharp or flat. Also used are the *double sharp* (×) and *double flat* (♭♭), which respectively raise and lower the pitch by two halftones—that is, a whole tone.

Key signature   In many pieces of music, where certain sharped or flatted notes are used consistently throughout, these sharps or flats are written at the beginning of each line of music, in the *key signature*, as seen in the following example of piano music. Notice that piano music is written on the great staff, with the right hand usually playing the notes written on the upper staff and the left hand usually playing the notes written on the lower:

THE NOTATION OF RHYTHM

The duration of each musical tone is indicated by the type of note placed on the staff. In the following table, each note represents a duration, or *value*, half as long as the preceding one:

Note values

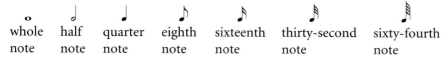

| whole note | half note | quarter note | eighth note | sixteenth note | thirty-second note | sixty-fourth note |

In any particular piece of music, these note values are related to the beat of the music. If the quarter note represents one beat, then a half note lasts for two beats, a whole note for four; two eighth notes last one beat, as do four sixteenths. The following chart makes this clear:

Notes   *Beats*
(in quadruple time)

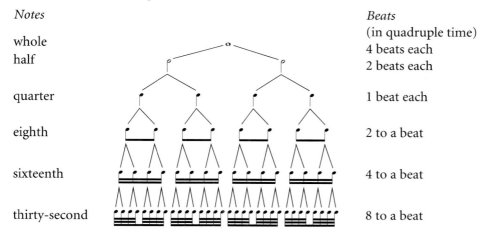

whole — 4 beats each
half — 2 beats each
quarter — 1 beat each
eighth — 2 to a beat
sixteenth — 4 to a beat
thirty-second — 8 to a beat

When a group of three notes is to be played in the time normally taken up by only two of the same kind, we have a *triplet*:

Triplet

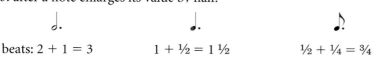

If we combine successive notes of the same pitch, using a curved line known as a *tie*, the second note is not played, and the note values are combined:

Tie

beats: 4 + 4 = 8   2 + 4 = 6   1 + ½ = 1 ½

A *dot* after a note enlarges its value by half:

Dot

beats: 2 + 1 = 3   1 + ½ = 1 ½   ½ + ¼ = ¾

Rests Time never stops in music, even when there is no sound. Silence is indicated by symbols known as *rests*, which correspond in time value to the notes:

whole	half	quarter	eighth	sixteenth	thirty-second	sixty-fourth
rest	rest	rest	rest	rest	rest	rest

Time signature The metrical organization of a piece of music is indicated by the *time signature*, which specifies the meter: this appears as two numbers written as in a fraction. The upper numeral indicates the number of beats within the measure; the lower one shows which note value equals one beat. Thus, the time signature 3/4 means that there are three beats to a measure, with the quarter note equal to one beat. In 6/8 time, there are six beats in the measure, each eighth note receiving one beat. Following are the most frequently encountered time signatures:

duple meter	2/2	2/4	
triple meter	3/2	3/4	3/8
quadruple meter		4/4	
sextuple meter		6/4	6/8

Measures and bar lines The examples below show how the system works. Notice that the *measures* are separated by a vertical line known as a *bar line*; a measure is sometimes referred to as a *bar*. As a rule, the bar line is followed by the most strongly accented beat, the ONE.

Sur le pont d'Avignon, French children's song

Clef: Treble
Key signature: None = key of C major
Meter: Duple (2/4)
Other features: Begins with pick-up note (upbeat)

Home on the Range, American song of the West

deer   and the   an - te - lope   play,   where

sel - dom   is   heard   a dis - cour - ag - ing   word   and   the

skies   are   not   clou - dy   all   day.

Clef: Bass
Key signature: 1 flat (B♭) = key of F major
Meter: Triple (3/4)
Other features: Pick-up note, dotted rhythms, and ties

Auld Lang Syne, Scottish traditional song

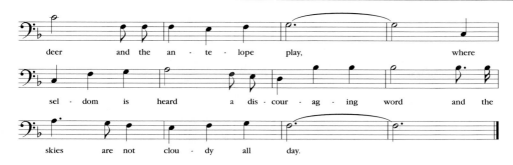

Should   auld   ac - quain - tance   be   for - got,   and__ nev - er brought to   mind,   Should

auld   ac - quain - tance   be   for - got   and__ days   of auld   lang   syne?

Clef: Treble
Key signature: 1 sharp (♯) = key of G major
Meter: Quadruple (4/4)
Other features: Pick-up note, dotted rhythms

Greensleeves, English traditional song

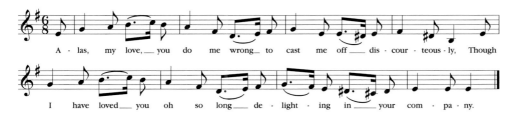

A - las,   my love,__ you   do   me wrong__ to   cast   me off __ dis - cour - teous - ly, Though

I   have loved__ you   oh   so   long__ de - light - ing in __ your   com - pa - ny.

Clef: Treble
Key signature: 1 sharp (♯) = key of E minor
Meter: Sextuple (6/8)
Other features: Pick-up note, dotted rhythms, and accidentals (D♯ and C♯)

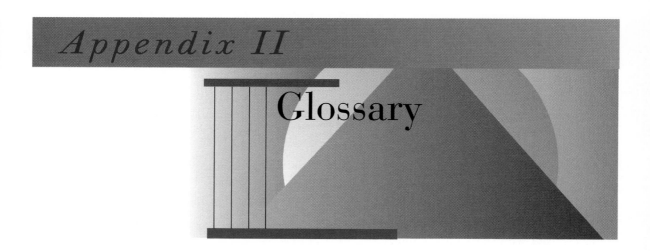

Appendix II

Glossary

absolute music   Music that has no literary, dramatic, or pictorial program. Also *pure music*.

a cappella   Choral music performed without instrumental accompaniment.

accelerando   Getting faster.

accent   The emphasis on a beat resulting in that beat's being louder or longer than another in a measure.

accompagnato   Accompanied; also a *recitative* that is accompanied by orchestra.

accordion   A musical instrument with a small keyboard and free-vibrating metal reeds that sound when air is generated by pleated bellows.

acid rock   Genre of American rock that emerged in the late 1960s, often associated with psychedelic drugs. Its style featured heavy amplification, instrumental improvisation, new sound technologies, and light shows.

adagio   Quite slow.

additive meter   Patterns of beats that subdivide into smaller, irregular groups (e.g., 2 + 3 + 2 + 3 = 10); common in certain Eastern European musics.

ad libitum   Indication that gives the performer the liberty to omit a section or to improvise.

aerophone   Instrument that produces sound by using air as the primary vibrating means, such as a flute, whistle, or horn.

agitato   Agitated or restless.

Agnus Dei   A section of the Mass; the last musical movement of the *Ordinary*.

aleatory   Indeterminate music in which certain elements of performance (such as pitch, rhythm, or form) are left to choice or chance.

alla breve   See *cut time*.

allegro   Fast, cheerful.

allemande   German dance in moderate duple time, popular during the Renaissance and Baroque periods; often the first movement of a Baroque *suite*.

alto   Lowest of the female voices. Also *contralto*.

andante   Moderately slow or walking pace.

answer   Second entry of the subject in a *fugue*, usually pitched a fourth below or a fifth above the subject.

anthem   A religious choral composition in English; performed liturgically, the Protestant equivalent of the *motet*.

antiphonal   Performance style in which an ensemble is divided into two or more groups, performing in alternation and then together.

antique cymbals   Small disks of brass, held by the player one in each hand, that are struck together gently and allowed to vibrate.

arabesque   Decorative musical material or a composition based on florid *embellishment*.

aria   Lyric song for solo voice with orchestral accompaniment, generally expressing intense emotion; found in *opera, cantata*, and *oratorio*.

arioso   Short, aria-like passage.

arpeggio   Broken chord in which the individual tones are sounded one after another instead of simultaneously.

Ars Antiqua   French sacred polyphonic musical style from the period c. 1160–1320.

Ars Nova   Fourteenth-century French polyphonic musical style whose themes moved increasingly from religious to secular.

art rock   Genre of rock that uses larger forms and more complex harmonies than other popular styles; occasionally quotes examples from classical music. Also *progressive rock*.

a tempo   Return to the previous tempo.

atonality   Total abandonment of *tonality* (centering in a key). Atonal music moves from one level of dissonance to another, without areas of relaxation.

attaca   "Attack," proceed without a pause between movements.

augmentation   Statement of a melody in longer note values, often twice as slow as the original.

aulos   Double-reed pipe; played for public and religious functions in ancient Greece.

bagpipe   Wind instrument popular in Eastern and Western Europe that has several tubes, one of which plays the melody while the others sound the *drones*, or sustained notes; a windbag is filled by either a mouth pipe or a set of bellows (*uilleann pipes*).

balalaika   Guitar-like instrument of Russia with a triangular body, fretted neck, and three strings; often used in traditional music and dance.

ballade   French poetic form and chanson type of the Middle Ages and Renaissance with courtly love texts. Also a Romantic genre, especially a lyric piano piece.

ballad opera   English comic opera, usually featuring spoken dialogue alternating with songs set to popular tunes; also called dialogue opera.

ballet   A dance form featuring a staged presentation of group or solo dancing with music, costumes, and scenery.

banjo   Plucked-string instrument with round body in the form of a single-headed drum and a long, fretted neck; brought to the Americas from Africa by early slaves.

baritone   Male voice of moderately low range.

baritone horn   See *euphonium*.

bas   Medieval category of soft instruments, used principally for indoor occasions, as distinct from *baut*, or loud, instruments.

bass   Male voice of low range.

bass clarinet   Woodwind instrument of the clarinet family with the lowest range.

bass drum   Percussion instrument played with a large, soft-headed stick; the largest orchestral drum.

basse danse   Graceful court dance of the early Renaissance; an older version of the *pavane*.

basso continuo   Italian for "continuous bass." See *figured bass*. Also refers to performance group with a bass, chordal instrument (harpsichord, organ), and one bass melody instrument (cello, bassoon).

bassoon   Double-reed woodwind instrument with a low range.

bass viol   See *double bass*.

beat   Regular pulsation; a basic unit of length in musical time.

bebop   Complex jazz style developed in the 1940s. Also *bop*.

bel canto   "Beautiful singing"; elegant Italian vocal style characterized by florid melodic lines delivered by voices of great agility, smoothness, and purity of tone.

bell tree   Long stick with bells suspended from it, adopted from *Janissary music*.

bellows   An apparatus for producing air currents in certain wind instruments (accordion, bagpipe).

bent pitch   See *blue note*.

big band   Large jazz ensemble popular in 1930s and 1940s, featuring sections of trumpets, trombones, saxophones (and other woodwinds), and rhythm instruments (piano, double bass, drums, and guitar).

binary form   Two-part (A-B) form with each section normally repeated. Also *two-part form*.

biwa   A Japanese lute, similar to the Chinese *pipa*.

blue note   A slight drop of pitch on the third, fifth, or seventh tone of the scale, common in blues and jazz. Also *bent pitch*.

blues   African-American form of secular folk music, related to jazz, that is based on a simple, repetitive poetic-musical structure.

bodhran   Hand-held frame drum with a single goatskin head; used in Irish traditional music.

bongo   A pair of small drums of differing pitches; held between the legs and struck with both hands; of Afro-Cuban origin.

bop   See *bebop*.

bossa nova   Brazilian dance related to the *samba*, popular in the 1950s and 1960s.

bourrée   Lively French Baroque dance type in duple meter.

branle   Quick French group dance of the Renaissance, related to the *ronde*.

brass instrument   Wind instrument with a cup-shaped mouthpiece, a tube that flares into a bell, and slides or valves to vary the pitch. Most often made of brass or silver.

brass quintet   Standard chamber ensemble made up of two trumpets, French horn, trombone, and tuba.

break   Jazz term for a short improvised solo without accompaniment that "breaks" an ensemble passage or introduces an extended solo.

bridge   Transitional passage connecting two sections of a composition; also *transition*. Also the part of a string instrument that holds the strings in place.

bugle   Brass instrument that evolved from the earlier military, or field, trumpet.

Burgundian chanson   Fifteenth-century French composition, usually for three voices, some or all of which may be played by instruments. Also *chanson*.

cadence   Resting place in a musical phrase; music punctuation.

cadenza   Virtuosic solo passage in the manner of an improvisation, performed near the end of an aria or a movement of a concerto.

cakewalk   Syncopated, strutting dance of nineteenth-century origin; developed among Southern slaves in a parody of white plantation owners.

call and response   Performance style with a singing leader who is imitated by a chorus of followers. Also *responsorial singing*.

canon Type of polyphonic composition in which one musical line strictly imitates another at a fixed distance throughout.

cantabile Songful, in a singing style.

cantata Vocal genre for solo singers, chorus, and instrumentalists based on a lyric or dramatic poetic narrative. It generally consists of several movements including recitatives, arias, and ensemble numbers.

cantor Solo singer or singing leader in Jewish and Christian liturgical music.

cantus firmus "Fixed melody," usually of very long notes, often based on a fragment of Gregorian chant that served as the structural basis for a polyphonic composition, particularly in the Renaissance.

capriccio Short lyric piece of a free nature, often for piano.

carol English medieval strophic song with a *refrain* repeated after each stanza; now associated with Christmas.

cassation Classical instrumental genre related to the *serenade* or *divertimento* and often performed outdoors.

castanets Percussion instruments consisting of small wooden clappers that are struck together. They are widely used to accompany Spanish dancing.

castrato Male singer who was castrated during boyhood to preserve the soprano or alto vocal register, prominent in seventeenth-and early eighteenth-century opera.

celesta Percussion instrument resembling a miniature upright piano, with tuned metal plates struck by hammers that are operated by a keyboard.

cello See *violoncello*.

celtic harp See *Irish harp*.

chaconne Baroque from similar to the *passacaglia*, in which the variations are based on a repeated chord progression.

chamber choir Small group of up to about twenty-four singers, who usually perform *a cappella* or with piano accompaniment.

chamber music Ensemble music for up to about ten players, with one player to a part.

chamber sonata See *sonata da camera*.

chanson French polyphonic song, especially of the Middle Ages and Renaissance, set to either courtly or popular poetry. See also *Burgundian chanson*.

chart Colloquial or jazz term for a score or arrangement.

chimes Percussion instrument of definite pitch that consists of a set of tuned metal tubes of various lengths suspended from a frame and struck with a hammer. Also *tubular bells*.

Chinese block Percussion instrument made from a hollowed rectangular block of wood that is struck with a beater.

choir A group of singers who perform together, usually in parts, with several on each part; often associated with a church.

choral Baroque congregational hymn of the German Lutheran church.

chorale prelude Short Baroque organ piece in which a traditional chorale melody is embellished.

chorale variations Baroque organ piece in which a chorale is the basis for a set of variations.

chord Simultaneous combination of three or more tones that constitute a single block of harmony.

chordal Texture comprised of chords in which the pitches sound simultaneously; also homorhythmic.

chordophone Instrument that produces sound from a vibrating string stretched between two points; the string may be set in motion by bowing, striking, or plucking.

chorus Fairly large group of singers who perform together, usually with several on each part. Also a choral movement of a large-scale work. In jazz, a single statement of the melodic-harmonic pattern.

chromatic Melody or harmony built from many if not all twelve semitones of the octave. A *chromatic scale* consists of an ascending or descending sequence of semitones.

church sonata See *sonata da chiesa*.

clarinet Single-reed woodwind instrument with a wide range of sizes.

clavecin French word for "harpsichord." See *harpsichord*.

claves A Cuban clapper consisting of two solid hardwood sticks; widely used in Latin-American music.

clavichord Stringed keyboard instrument popular in the Renaissance and Baroque that is capable of unique expressive devices not possible on the harpsichord.

clavier Generic word for keyboard instruments, including harpsichord, clavichord, piano, and organ.

closed ending Second of two endings in a secular medieval work, usually cadencing on the final.

coda The last part of a piece, usually added to a standard form to bring it to a close.

codetta In sonata form, the concluding section of the *exposition*. Also a brief coda concluding an inner section of a work.

collage A technique drawn from the visual arts whereby musical fragments from other compositions are juxtaposed or overlapped within a new work.

collegium musicum An association of amateur musicians, popular in the Baroque era. Also a modern university ensemble dedicated to the performance of early music.

comic opera See *opéra comique*.

commedia dell'arte Type of improvised drama popular in sixteenth- and seventeenth-century Italy; makes use of stereotyped characters.

common time See *quadruple meter*.

compound meter Meter in which each beat is subdivided into three rather than two.

computer music A type of electro-acoustic music in which computers assist in creating works through sound synthesis and manipulation.

con amore with love, tenderly.

concertante Style based on the principle of opposition between two dissimilar masses of sound; concerto-like.

concert band Instrumental ensemble ranging from forty to eighty members or more, consisting of wind and percussion instruments. Also *wind ensemble*.

concertina Small, free-reed, bellows-operated instrument similar to an accordion; hexagonal in shape, with button keys.

concertino Solo group of instruments in the Baroque *concerto grosso.*

concerto Instrumental genre in several movements for solo instrument (or instrumental group) and orchestra.

concerto form Structure commonly used in first movements of concertos that combines elements of Baroque *ritornello* procedure with *sonata-allegro form.* Also *first-movement concerto form.*

concerto grosso Baroque concerto type based on the opposition between a small group of solo instruments (the *concertino*) and orchestra (the *ripieno*).

concert overture Single-movement concert piece for orchestra, typically from the Romantic period and often based on a literary program.

conductor Person who, by means of gestures, leads performances of musical ensembles, especially orchestra, bands, or choruses.

con fuoco With fire.

conga Afro-Cuban dance performed at Latin-American Carnival celebrations. Also a single-headed drum of Afro-Cuban origin, played with bare hands.

conjunct Smooth, connected melody that moves principally by small intervals.

con passione With passion.

consonance Concordant or harmonious combination of tones that provides a sense of relaxation and stability in music.

continuous bass See *basso continuo.*

continuous imitation Renaissance polyphonic style in which the motives move from line to line within the texture, often overlapping one another.

contrabass See *double bass.*

contrabassoon Double-reed woodwind instrument with the lowest range in the woodwind family. Also *double bassoon.*

contralto See *alto.*

contrapuntal Texture employing counterpoint, or two or more melodic lines.

cool jazz A substyle of *bebop*, characterized by a restrained, unemotional performance with lush harmonies, moderate volume levels and tempos, and a new lyricism; often associated with Miles Davis.

cornet Valved brass instrument similar to the trumpet but more mellow in sound.

cornetto Early instrument of the brass family with woodwind-like finger holes. It developed from the cow horn, but was made of wood.

Council of Trent A council of the Roman Catholic Church that convened in Trent, Italy, from 1543 to 1565 and dealt with Counter-Reformation issues, including the reform of liturgical music.

counterpoint The art of combining in a single texture two or more melodic lines.

countermelody An accompanying melody sounded against the principal melody.

countersubject In a figure, a secondary theme heard against the subject; a countertheme.

country-western Genre of American popular music derived from traditional music of the rural South, usually vocal with an accompaniment of banjos, fiddles, and guitar.

courante French Baroque dance, a standard movement of the *suite*, in triple meter at a moderate tempo.

cover Recording that remakes an earlier, often successful, recording with a goal of reaching a wider audience.

cowbell Rectangular metal bell that is struck with a drumstick; used widely in Latin-American music.

Credo A section of the Mass; the third musical movement of the *Ordinary.*

crescendo Growing louder.

crossover Recording or artist that appeals primarily to one audience but becomes popular with another as well (e.g., a rock performer who makes jazz recordings).

crotales A pair of small pitched cymbals mounted on a frame; also made in chromatic sets.

crumhorn Early woodwind instrument, whose sound is produced by blowing into a capped double reed and whose lower body is curved.

cut time A type of duple meter interpreted as 2/2 and indicated as ¢; also called *alla breve.*

cyclical form Structure in which musical material, such as a theme, presented in one movement returns in a later movement.

cymbals Percussion instruments consisting of two large circular brass plates of equal size that are struck sidewise against each other.

da capo An indication to return to the beginning of a piece.

da capo aria Lyric song in ternary, or **A-B-A**, form, commonly found in operas, cantatas, and oratorios.

decrescende Growing softer.

development Structural reshaping of thematic material. Second section of *sonata-allegro form*; it moves through a series of foreign keys while themes from the exposition are manipulated.

dialogue opera See *ballad opera.*

diatonic Melody or harmony built from the seven tones of a major or minor scale. A *diatonic scale* encompasses patterns of seven whole tones and semitones.

Dies irae Chant from the *Requiem Mass* whose text concerns Judgment Day.

diminuendo Growing softer.

diminution Statement of a melody in shorter note values, often twice as fast as the original.

disco Commercial dance music popular in the 1970s, characterized by strong percussion in a quadruple meter.

disjunct Disjointed or disconnected melody with many leaps.

dissonance Combination of tones that sounds discordant and unstable, in need of resolution.

divertimento Classical instrumental genre for chamber ensemble or soloist, often performed as light entertainment. Related to *serenade* and *cassation.*

Divine Offices Cycle of daily services of the Roman Catholic Church, distinct from the *Mass*.

doctrine of the affections Baroque doctrine of the union of text and music.

dodecaphonic Greek for "twelve-tone"; see *twelve-tone music*.

dolce Sweetly.

dolente Sad, weeping.

dominant The fifth scale step, *sol*.

dominant chord Chord built on the fifth scale step, the V chord.

double bass Largest and lowest-pitched member of the bowed string family. Also called *contrabass* or *bass viol*.

double bassoon See *contrabassoon*.

double exposition In the concerto, twofold statement of the themes, once by the orchestra and once by the soloist.

double-stop Playing two notes simultaneously on a string instrument.

doubles Variations of a dance in a French keyboard suite.

down beat First beat of the measure, the strongest in any meter.

drone Sustained sounding of one or several tones for harmonic support, a common feature of some folk musics.

dulcimer Early folk instrument that resembles the *psaltery*; its strings are struck with hammers instead of being plucked.

duple meter Basic metrical pattern of two beats to a measure.

duplum Second voice of a polyphonic work, especially the medieval *motet*.

duration Length of time something lasts; e.g., the vibration of a musical sound.

dynamics Element of musical expression relating to the degree of loudness or softness, or volume, of a sound.

embellishment Melodic decoration, either improvised or indicated through *ornamentation* signs in the music.

embouchure The placement of the lips, lower facial muscles, and jaws in playing a wind instrument.

Empfindsamkeit German "sensitive" style of the mid-eighteenth century, characterized by melodic directness and homophonic texture.

encore "again"; an audience request that the performer(s) repeat a piece or perform another.

English horn Double-reed woodwind instrument, larger and lower in range than the oboe.

entenga Tuned drum from Uganda; the royal drum ensemble of the former ruler of Buganda.

episode Interlude or intermediate section in the Baroque *fugue*, which serves as an area of relaxation between statements of the subject.

equal temperament Tuning system based on the division of the octave into twelve equal half steps; the normal system used today.

erhu Bowed, two-string fiddle from China, with its bow hairs fixed between the strings; rests on the leg while playing.

espressivo Expressively.

ethnomusicology Comparative study of musics of the world, with a focus on the cultural context of music.

ethno-pop See *world beat*.

étude Study piece that focuses on a particular technical problem.

euphonium Tenor-range brass instrument resembling the tuba. Also *baritone horn*.

exoticism Musical style in which rhythms, melodies, or instruments evoke the color and atmosphere of far-off lands.

exposition Opening section. In the *fugue*, the first section in which the voices enter in turn with the subject. In *sonata-allegro form*, the first section in which the major thematic material is stated. Also *statement*.

falsetto Vocal technique whereby men can sing above their normal range, producing a lighter sound.

fantasia Free instrumental piece of fairly large dimensions, in an improvisational style; in the Baroque, it often served as an introductory piece to a fugue.

fiddle Colloquial term for *violin*; often used in traditional music.

figured bass Baroque practice consisting of an independent bass line that often includes numerals indicating the harmony to be supplied by the performer. Also *thorough-bass*.

film music Music that serves either as background or foreground for a film.

first-movement concerto form See *concerto form*.

first-movement form See *sonata-allegro form*.

fixed forms Group of forms, especially in medieval France, in which the poetic structure determines musical repetitions. See also *ballade, rondeau, virelai*.

flat sign Musical symbol (b) that indicates lowering a pitch by a semitone.

fluegelhorn Valved brass instrument resembling a bugle with a wide bell, used in jazz and commercial music.

flute Soprano-range woodwind instrument, usually made of metal and held horizontally.

flutter tonguing Wind instrument technique in which the tongue is fluttered or trilled against the roof of the mouth.

folk music. See *traditional music*.

folk rock Popular music style that combines folk music with amplified instruments of rock.

form Structure and design in music, based on repetition, contrast, and variation; the organizing principle of music.

formalism Tendency to elevate formal above expressive value in music, as in Neoclassical music.

forte (f) Loud.

fortissimo (ff) Very loud.

four-hand piano music Chamber music genre for two performers playing at one or occasionally two pianos, allowing home or salon performances of orchestral arrangements.

free-verse rhythm A free-flowing, nonmetric line in which movement is linked to the text inflections, as in Gregorian chant.

French horn Medium-range valved brass instrument that can be played "stopped" with the hand as well as open. Also *horn*.

French overture Baroque instrumental introduction to an opera, ballet, or suite, in two sections: a slow opening followed by an Allegro, often with a brief return to the opening.

frequency Rate of vibration of a string or column of air, which determines pitch.

fugato A fugal passage in a nonfugal piece, such as in the development section of a *sonata-allegro form.*

fuging tune Polyphonic, imitative setting of a *hymn* or *psalm*, popular in Great Britain and the United States from the eighteenth century.

fugue Polyphonic form popular in the Baroque era in which one or more themes are developed by imitative counterpoint.

fusion Style that combines jazz improvisation with amplified instruments of rock.

gagaku Traditional court music of Japan.

galliard Lively, triple-meter French court dance.

gamelan Musical ensemble of Java or Bali, made up of gongs, chimes, metallophones, and drums, among other instruments.

gavotte Duple-meter Baroque dance type of a pastoral character.

genre General term describing the standard category and overall character of a work.

Gesamtkunstwerk German for "total artwork"; a term coined by Richard Wagner to describe the synthesis of all the arts (music, poetry, drama, visual spectacle) in his late operas.

gigue Popular English Baroque dance type, a standard movement of the Baroque *suite*, in a lively compound meter.

gioioso Joyous.

glee club Specialized vocal ensemble that performs popular music, college songs, and more serious works.

glissando Rapid slide through pitches of a scale.

glitter rock Theatrical, flamboyant rock style popular in the 1970s.

glockenspiel Percussion instrument with horizontal, tuned steel bars of various sizes that are struck with mallets and produce a bright metallic sound.

Gloria A section of the Mass; the second musical movement of the *Ordinary.*

Goliard song Medieval Latin-texted secular song, often with corrupt or lewd lyrics; associated with wandering scholars.

gong Percussion instrument consisting of a broad circular disk of metal, suspended in a frame and struck with a heavy drumstick. Also *tam-tam.*

gospel music Twentieth-century sacred music style associated with Protestant African Americans.

grace note Ornamental note, often printed in small type and not performed rhythmically.

Gradual Fourth item of the *Proper* of the Mass, sung in a *melismatic* style, and performed in a *responsorial* manner in which soloists alternate with a choir.

grand opera Style of Romantic opera developed in Paris, focusing on serious, historical plots with huge choruses, crowd scenes, elaborate dance episodes, ornate costumes, and spectacular scenery.

grave Solemn; very, very slow.

Gregorian chant Monophonic melody with a freely flowing, unmeasured vocal line; liturgical chant of the Roman Catholic Church. Also *plainchant* or *plainsong.*

ground bass A repeating melody, usually in the bass, throughout a vocal or instrumental composition.

grunge rock Contemporary Seattle-based rock style characterized by harsh guitar chords; hybrid of *punk rock* and *heavy metal.*

guitar Plucked-string instrument originally made of wood with a hollow resonating body and a fretted fingerboard; types include acoustic and electric.

habanera Moderate duple-meter dance of Cuban origin, popular in the nineteenth century; based on characteristic rhythmic figure.

half step Smallest interval used in the Western system; octave divides into twelve such intervals; on the piano, the distance between any two adjacent keys, whether black or white. Also *semitone.*

harmonica Mouth organ; a small metal box on which free reeds are mounted, played by moving back and forth across the mouth while breathing into it.

harmonics Individual pure sounds that are part of any musical tone; in string instruments, crystalline tones in the very high register, produced by lightly touching a vibrating string at a certain point.

harmonium Organ-like instrument with free metal reeds set in vibration by a bellows; popular in late-nineteenth-century America.

harmony The simultaneous combination of notes and the ensuing relationships of intervals and chords.

harp Plucked-string instrument, triangular in shape with strings perpendicular to the soundboard.

harpsichord Early Baroque keyboard instrument in which the strings are plucked by quills instead of being struck with hammers like the piano. Also *clavecin.*

haut Medieval category of loud instruments, used mainly for outdoor occasions, as distinct from *bas*, or soft, instruments.

heavy metal Rock style that gained popularity in the 1970s, characterized by simple, repetitive ideas and loud, distorted instrumental solos.

heptatonic scale Seven-note scale; in non-Western musics, often fashioned from a different combination of intervals than major and minor scales.

heterophonic Texture in which two or more voices (or parts) elaborate the same melody simultaneously, often the result of improvisation.

homophonic Texture with principal melody and accompanying harmony, as distinct from *polyphony*.

horn See *French horn.*

hornpipe Country dance of British Isles, often in a lively triple meter; optional dance movement of solo and orchestral Baroque suite; a type of duple-meter hornpipe remains popular in Irish traditional dance music.

hymn Song in praise of God; often involves congregational participation.

idée fixe "Fixed idea"; term coined by Berlioz for a recurring musical idea that links different movements of a work.

idiophone Instrument that produces sound from the substance of the instrument itself by being struck, blown, shaken, scraped, or rubbed. Examples include bells, rattles, xylophones, and cymbals.

imitation Melodic idea presented in one voice and then restated in another, each part continuing as others enter.

improvisation Creation of a musical composition while it is being performed, seen in Baroque ornamentation, cadenzas of concertos, jazz, and some non-Western musics. See also *embellishment.*

incidental music Music written to accompany dramatic works.

inflection Small alteration of the pitch by a microtonal interval. See also *blue note.*

instrument Mechanism that generates musical vibrations and transmits them into the air.

interlude Music played between sections of a musical or dramatic work.

intermezzo Short, lyric piece or movement, often for piano. Also a comic interlude performed between acts of an eighteenth-century *opera seria.*

interval Distance and relationship between two pitches.

inversion Mirror or upside-down image of a melody or pattern, found in fugues and twelve-tone compositions.

Irish harp Plucked-string instrument with about thirty strings; used to accompany Irish songs and dance music (also *celtic harp*).

isorhythmic motet Medieval and early Renaissance motet based on a repeating rhythmic pattern throughout one or more voices.

Italian overture Baroque overture consisting of three sections: fast-slow-fast.

Janissary music Music of the military corps of the Turkish sultan, characterized by percussion instruments such as triangle, cymbals, bell tree, and bass drum as well as trumpets and double-reed instruments.

jarabe Traditional Mexican dance form with multiple sections in contrasting meters and tempos, often performed by *mariachi* ensembles.

jazz A musical style created mainly by African Americans in the early twentieth century that blended elements drawn from African musics with the popular and art traditions of the West.

jazz band Instrumental ensemble made up of reed (saxophones and clarinets), brass (trumpets and trombones), and rhythm sections (percussion, piano, double bass, and sometimes guitar).

jia hua Literally, "adding flowers"; an embellishment style in Chinese music using various ornamental figures.

jig A vigorous dance developed in the British Isles, usually in compound meter; became fashionable on the Continent as the *gigue*; still popular as an Irish traditional dance genre.

jongleurs Medieval wandering entertainers who played instruments, sang and danced, juggled, and performed plays.

jongleuresses Female *jongleurs*, or wandering entertainer/minstrels.

jota A type of Spanish dance song characterized by a quick triple meter and guitar and castanet accompaniment.

karaoke "Empty orchestra"; popular nightclub style from Japan where customers sing the melody to accompanying prerecorded tracks.

kettledrums See *timpani.*

key Defines the relationship of tones with a common center or tonic. Also a lever on a keyboard or woodwind instrument.

keyboard instrument Instrument sounded by means of a keyboard (a series of keys played with the fingers).

keynote See *tonic.*

key signature Sharps or flats placed at the beginning of a piece to show the key of a work.

Klangfarbenmelodie Twentieth-century technique in which the notes of a melody are distributed among different instruments, giving a pointillistic texture.

koto Japanese plucked-string instrument with a long rectangular body, thirteen strings, and movable bridges or frets.

lamellophone Plucked idiophone with thin metal strips; common throughout sub-Saharan Africa.

lamentoso Like a lament.

largo Broad; very slow.

Latin rock Subgenre of rock featuring Latin and African percussion instruments (*maracas, conga drums, timbales*).

legato Smooth and connected; opposite of *staccato.*

Leitmotif "Leading motive," or basic recurring theme, representing a person, object, or idea, commonly used in Wagner's operas.

libretto   Text, or script, of an opera, prepared by a librettist.

Lied   German for "song"; most commonly associated with the solo art song of the nineteenth century, usually accompanied by piano.

Lieder   Plural of *Lied*.

lining out   A call-and-response singing practice prevalent in early America and England; characterized by the alternation between a singer leader and a chorus singing heterophonically.

lute   Plucked-string instrument of Middle Eastern origin, popular in western Europe from the late Middle Ages to the eighteenth century.

lyre   Ancient plucked-string instrument of the harp family, used to accompany singing and poetry.

lyric opera   Hybrid form combining elements of *grand opera* and *opéra comique* and featuring appealing melodies and romantic drama.

madrigal   Renaissance secular work originating in Italy for voices, with or without instruments, set to a short, lyric love poem; also popular in England.

madrigal choir   Small vocal ensemble that specializes in *a cappella* secular works.

maestoso   Majestic.

Magnificat   Biblical text on the words of the Virgin Mary, sung polyphonically in church from the Renaissance on.

major scale   Scale consisting of seven different tones that comprise a specific pattern of whole and half steps. It differs from a minor scale primarily in that its third degree is raised half a step.

mambo   Dance of Afro-Cuban origin with a characteristic quadruple-meter rhythmic pattern.

mandolin   Plucked-string instrument with a rounded body and fingerboard; used in some folk musics and in *country-western* music.

maracas   Latin-American rattles (*idiophones*) made from gourds or other materials.

march   A style incorporating characteristics of military music, including strongly accented duple meter in simple, repetitive rhythmic patterns.

marching band   Instrumental ensemble for entertainment at sports events and parades, consisting of wind and percussion instruments, drum majors/majorettes, and baton twirlers.

mariachi   Traditional Mexican ensemble popular throughout the country, consisting of trumpets, violins, guitar, and bass guitar.

marimba   Percussion instrument that is a mellower version of the *xylophone*; of African origin.

masque   English genre of aristocratic entertainment that combined vocal and instrumental music with poetry and dance, developed during the sixteenth and seventeenth centuries.

Mass   Central service of the Roman Catholic Church.

mazurka   Type of Polish folk dance in triple meter.

mbube   "Lion"; *a cappella* choral singing style of South African Zulus, featuring call-and-response patterns, close-knit harmonies, and syncopation.

measure   Rhythmic group or metrical unit that contains a fixed number of beats, divided on the musical staff by bar lines.

medium   Performing forces employed in a certain musical work.

melismatic   Melodic style characterized by many notes sung to a single text syllable.

melody   Succession of single tones or pitches perceived by the mind as a unity.

membranophone   Any instrument that produces sound from tightly stretched membranes that can be struck, plucked, rubbed, or sung into (setting the skin in vibration).

meno   Less.

mesto   Sad.

metallophone   Percussion instrument consisting of tuned metal bars, usually struck with a mallet.

meter   Organization of rhythm in time; the grouping of beats into larger, regular patterns, notated as *measures*.

metronome   Device used to indicate the tempo by sounding regular beats at adjustable speeds.

mezzo forte (*mf*)   Moderately loud.

mezzo piano (*mp*)   Moderately soft.

mezzo-soprano   Female voice of middle range.

micropolyphony   Twentieth-century technique encompassing the complex interweaving of all musical elements.

microtone   Musical interval smaller than a semitone, prevalent in some non-Western musics and in some twentieth-century art music.

MIDI   Acronym for musical instrument digital interface; technology standard that allows networking of computers with electronic musical instruments.

minimalist music   Contemporary musical style featuring the repetition of short melodic, rhythmic, and harmonic patterns with little variation. See also *spiritual minimalism*.

Minnesingers   Late medieval German poet-musicians.

minor scale   Scale consisting of seven different tones that comprise a specific pattern of whole and half steps. It differs from the major scale primarily in that its third degree is lowered half a step.

minuet and trio   An A-B-A form (**A** = minuet; **B** = trio) in a moderate triple meter; often the third movement of the Classical *sonata cycle*.

misterioso   Mysteriously.

modal   Characterizes music that is based on modes other than major and minor, especially the early church *modes*.

mode   Scale or sequence of notes used as the basis for a composition; major and minor are modes.

moderato   Moderate.

modified strophic form   Song structure that combines elements of strophic and through-composed forms; a variation of strophic form in which a section might have a new key, rhythm, or varied melodic pattern.

modulation The process of changing from one key to another.

molto Very.

monody Vocal style established in the Baroque, with a solo singer and instrumental accompaniment.

monophonic Single-line texture, or melody without accompaniment.

monothematic Work or movement based on a single theme.

morality play Medieval drama, often with music, intended to teach proper values.

motet Polyphonic vocal genre, secular in the Middle Ages but sacred or devotional thereafter.

motive Short melodic or rhythmic idea; the smallest fragment of a theme that forms a melodic-harmonic-rhythmic unit.

movement Complete, self-contained part within a larger musical work.

MTV Acronym for music television, a cable channel that presents non-stop *music videos*.

muses Nine daughters of Zeus in ancient mythology; each presided over one of the arts.

musical Genre of twentieth-century musical theater, especially popular in the United States and Great Britain; characterized by spoken dialogue, dramatic plot interspersed with songs, ensemble numbers, and dancing.

musical saw A handsaw that is bowed on its smooth edge; pitch is varied by bending the saw.

music drama Wagner's term for his operas.

music video Video tape or film that accompanies a recording, usually of a popular or rock song.

musique concrète Music made up of natural sounds and sound effects that are recorded and then manipulated electronically.

mute Mechanical device used to muffle the sound of an instrument.

nakers Medieval percussion instruments resembling small kettledrums, played in pairs; of Middle Eastern origin.

neumatic Melodic style with two to four notes set to each syllable.

neumes Early musical notation signs; square notes on a four-line staff.

new age Style of popular music of the 1980s and 1990s, characterized by soothing timbres and repetitive forms that are subjected to shifting variation techniques.

New Orleans jazz Early jazz style characterized by multiple improvisations in an ensemble of cornet (or trumpet), clarinet (or saxophone), trombone, piano, string bass (or tuba), banjo (or guitar), and drums; repertory included *blues*, *ragtime*, and popular songs.

new wave Subgenre of rock popular since the late 1970s, highly influenced by simple 1950s-style *rock and roll*; devel-

oped as a rejection of the complexities of *art rock* and *beauty metal*.

ninth chord Five-tone chord spanning a ninth between its lowest and highest tones.

nocturne "Night piece"; common in the nineteenth century, often for piano.

Noh drama A major form of Japanese theater since the late fourteenth century; based on philosophical concepts from Zen Buddhism.

nonmetric Music lacking a strong sense of beat or meter, common in certain non-Western cultures.

non troppo Not too much.

oboe Soprano-range, double-reed woodwind instrument.

octave Interval between two tones seven diatonic pitches apart; the lower note vibrates half as fast as the upper and sounds an octave lower.

ode Secular composition written for a royal occasion, especially popular in England.

offbeat A weak beat or any pulse between the beats in a measured rhythmic pattern.

ondes Martenot Electronic instrument that produces sounds by means of an oscillator.

open ending The first ending in a medieval secular piece, usually cadencing on a pitch other than the final.

open form Indeterminate contemporary music in which some details of a composition are clearly indicated, but the overall structure is left to choice or chance.

opera Music drama that is generally sung throughout, combining the resources of vocal and instrumental music with poetry and drama, acting and pantomime, scenery and costumes.

opera buffa Italian comic opera, sung throughout.

opéra comique French comic opera, with some spoken dialogue.

opera seria Tragic Italian opera.

oral tradition Music that is transmitted by example or imitation and performed from memory.

oral transmission Preservation of music without the aid of written notation.

oratorio Large-scale dramatic genre originating in the Baroque, based on a text of religious or serious character, performed by solo voices, chorus, and orchestra; similar to opera but without scenery, costumes, or action.

orchestra Performing group of diverse instruments in various cultures; in Western art music, an ensemble of multiple strings with various woodwind, brass, and percussion instruments.

orchestral bells See *chimes*.

orchestration The technique of setting instruments in various combinations.

Ordinary Sections of the Roman Catholic Mass that remain the same from day to day throughout the church year, as distinct from the *Proper*, which changes daily according to the liturgical occasion.

ordre See *suite.*

organ Wind instrument in which air is fed to the pipes by mechanical means; the pipes are controlled by two or more keyboards and a set of pedals.

organal style *Organum* in which the Tenor sings the melody (original chant) in very long notes while the upper voices move freely and rapidly above it.

organum Earliest kind of polyphonic music, which developed from the custom of adding voices above a plainchant; they first ran parallel to it at the interval of a fifth or fourth and later moved more freely.

ornamentation See *embellishment.*

ostinato A short melodic, rhythmic, or harmonic pattern that is repeated throughout a work or a section of one.

overture An introductory movement, as in an opera or oratorio, often presenting melodies from arias to come. Also an orchestral work for concert performance.

panpipe Wind instrument consisting of a series of small vertical tubes or pipes of differing length; sound is produced by blowing across the top.

pantomime Theatrical genre in which an actor silently plays all the parts in a show while accompanied by singing; originated in ancient Rome.

part song Secular vocal composition, unaccompanied, in three, four, or more parts.

partia See *suite.*

pas de deux A dance for two that is an established feature of classical ballet.

passacaglia Baroque form (similar to the *chaconne*) in moderately slow triple meter, based on a short, repeated base-line melody that serves as the basis for continuous variation in the other voices.

passepied French Baroque court dance type; a faster version of the *minuet.*

passion Musical setting of the Crucifixion story as told by one of the four Evangelists in the Gospels.

pastorale Pastoral, country-like.

pavane Stately Renaissance court dance in duple meter.

pedal point Sustained tone over which the harmonies change.

penny whistle See *tin whistle.*

pentatonic scale Five-note pattern used in some African, Far Eastern, and Native American musics; can also be found in Western music as an example of exoticism.

percussion instrument Instrument made of metal, wood, stretched skin, or other material that is made to sound by striking, shaking, scraping, or plucking.

performance art Multimedia art form involving visual as well as dramatic and musical elements.

perpetuum mobile Type of piece characterized by continuous repetitions of a rhythmic pattern at a quick tempo; perpetual motion.

phasing A technique in which a musical pattern is repeated and manipulated so that it separates and overlaps itself, and then rejoins the original pattern; getting "out of phase" and back "in sync."

phrase Musical unit; often a component of a melody.

pianissimo (*pp*) Very soft.

piano (*p*) Soft.

piano Keyboard instrument whose strings are struck with hammers controlled by a keyboard mechanism; pedals control dampers in the strings that stop the sound when the finger releases the key.

pianoforte Original name for the *piano.*

piano quartet Standard chamber ensemble of piano with violin, viola, and cello.

piano quintet Standard chamber ensemble of piano with two violins, viola, and cello.

piano trio Standard chamber ensemble of piano with violin and cello.

piccolo Smallest woodwind instrument, similar to the flute but sounding an octave higher.

pipa A Chinese lute with four silk strings; played as solo and ensemble instrument.

pitch Highness or lowness of a tone, depending on the frequency (rate of vibration).

pizzicato Performance direction to pluck a string of a bowed instrument with the finger.

plainchant See *Gregorian chant.*

plainsong See *Gregorian chant.*

poco A little.

polka Lively Bohemian dance; also a short, lyric piano piece.

polonaise Stately Polish processional dance in triple meter.

polychoral Performance style developed in the late sixteenth century involving the use of two or more choirs that alternate with each other or sing together.

polyharmony Two or more streams of harmony played against each other, common in twentieth-century music.

polyphonic Two or more melodic lines combined into a multivoiced texture, as distinct from *monophonic.*

polyrhythm The simultaneous use of several rhythmic patterns or meters, common in twentieth-century music and in certain African musics.

polytextual Two or more texts set simultaneously in a composition.

polytonality The simultaneous use of two or more keys, common in twentieth-century music.

portative organ Medieval organ small enough to be carried or set on a table, usually with only one set of pipes.

positive organ Small single-manual organ, popular in the Renaissance and Baroque eras.

prelude Instrumental work intended to precede a larger work.

prepared piano Piano whose sound is altered by the insertion of various materials (metal, rubber, leather, and paper) between the strings; invented by John Cage.

presto Very fast.

program music Instrumental music endowed with literary or pictorial associations, especially popular in the nineteenth century.

program symphony Multimovement programmatic orchestral work, typically from the nineteenth century.

progressive rock See *art rock.*

Proper Sections of the Roman Catholic Mass that vary from day to day throughout the church year according to the particular liturgical occasion, as distinct from the *Ordinary,* in which they remain the same.

Psalms Book from the Old Testament of the Bible; the 150 psalm texts, used in Jewish and Christian worship, are often set to music.

psaltery Medieval plucked-string instrument similar to the modern zither, consisting of a sound box over which strings were stretched.

punk rock Subgenre of rock popular since the mid-1970s, characterized by loud volume levels, driving rhythms, and simple forms typical of earlier rock and roll; often contains shocking lyrics and offensive behavior.

pure music See *absolute music.*

quadrivium Subdivision of the seven liberal arts; includes the mathematical subjects of music, arithmetic, geometry, and astronomy.

quadruple meter Basic metrical pattern of four beats to a measure. Also *common time.*

quadruple stop Playing four notes simultaneously on a string instrument.

quadruplum Fourth voice of a polyphonic work.

quartal harmony Harmony based on the interval of the fourth as opposed to a third; used in twentieth-century music.

quotation music Music that parodies another work or works, presenting them in a new style or guise.

raga Melodic pattern used in music of India; prescribes pitches, patterns, ornamentation, and extramusical associations such as time of performance and emotional character.

regime Late-nineteenth-century piano style created by African Americans, characterized by highly syncopated melodies; also played in ensemble arrangements. Contributed to early jazz styles.

range Distance between the lowest and highest tones of a melody, an instrument, or a voice.

rap Subgenre of rock in which rhymed lyrics are spoken over rhythm tracks; developed by African Americans in the 1970s and widely disseminated in the 1980s and 1990s.

rebec Medieval bowed-string instrument, often with a pear-shaped body.

recapitulation Third section of *sonata-allegro form,* in which the thematic material of the *exposition* is restated, generally in the tonic. Also *restatement.*

recitative Solo vocal declamation that follows the inflections of the text, often resulting in a disjunct vocal style; found in opera, cantata, and oratorio.

recorder End-blown woodwind instrument with a whistle mouthpiece, generally associated with early music.

reed Flexible strip of cane or metal set into a mouthpiece or the body of an instrument; set in vibration by a stream of air.

reel Moderately quick dance in duple meter danced throughout the British Isles; the most popular Irish traditional dance type.

refrain Text or music that is repeated within a larger form.

regal Small medieval reed organ.

reggae Jamaican popular music style characterized by off-beat rhythms and chanted vocals over a strong bass part; often associated with the Christian religious movement Rastafarianism.

register Specific area in the range of an instrument or voice.

registration Selection or combination of stops in a work for organ or harpsichord.

relative key The major and minor key that share the same key signature; for example, D minor is the relative minor of F major, both having one flat.

repeat sign Musical symbol (‖: :‖) that indicates repetition of a passage in a composition.

Requiem Mass Roman Catholic Mass for the Dead.

resolution Conclusion of a musical idea, as in the progression from an active chord to a rest chord.

response Short choral answer to a solo *verse;* an element of liturgical dialogue.

responsorial singing Singing, especially in Gregorian chant, in which a soloist or a group of soloists alternates with the choir. See also *call and response.*

restatement See *recapitulation.*

retrograde Backward statement of melody.

retrograde inversion Mirror image and backward statement of a melody.

rhythm The controlled movement of music in time.

rhythm and blues Popular African-American music style of the 1940s through 1960s featuring a solo singer accompanied by a small instrumental ensemble (piano, guitar, acoustic bass, drums, tenor saxophone), driving rhythms, and blues and pop song forms.

ring shout Religious dance performed by African-American slaves, performed with hand clapping and a shuffle step to spirituals.

ripieno The larger of the two ensembles in the Baroque *concerto grosso.* Also *tutti.*

ritardando Holding back, getting slower.

ritornello Short, recurring instrumental passage found in both the aria and the Baroque concerto.

rock and roll American popular music style first heard in the 1950s; derived from the union of African-American *rhythm and blues, country-western,* and pop music.

rock band Popular music ensemble that depends on amplified strings, percussion, and electronically generated sounds.

romance Originally a ballad; in the Romantic era, a lyric instrumental work.

ronde Lively Renaissance "round dance," associated with the outdoors, in which the participants danced in a circle or a line.

rondeau Medieval and Renaissance fixed poetic form and chanson type with courtly love texts.

rondo Muscial form in which the first section recurs, usually in the tonic. In the Classical *sonata cycle*, it appears as the last movement in various forms, including **A-B-A-B-A, A-B-A-C-A,** and **A-B-A-C-A-B-A.**

roneat-ek Cambodian xylophone with 21 tuned wooden keys.

rosin Substance made from hardened tree sap, rubbed on the hair of a bow to help it grip the strings.

round Perpetual canon at the unison in which each voice enters in succession with the same melody (for example, *Row, Row, Row Your Boat*).

rounded binary Compositional form with two sections, in which the second ends with a return to material from the first; each section is usually repeated.

rubato "Borrowed time," common in Romantic music, in which the performer hesitates here or hurries forward there, imparting flexibility to the written note values. Also *tempo rubato*.

rumba Latin-American dance of Afro-Cuban origin, in duple meter with syncopated rhythms.

rural blues American popular singing style with raspy-voiced male singer accompanied by acoustic steel-string guitar; features melodic *blue notes* over repeated bass patterns.

sackbut Early brass instrument, ancestor of the trombone.

sacred music Religious or spiritual music, for church or devotional use.

salsa "Spicy"; collective term for Latin-American dance music, especially forms of Afro-Cuban origin.

saltarello Italian "jumping dance," often characterized by triplets in a rapid 4/4 time.

samba Afro-Brazilian dance, characterized by duple meter, responsorial singing, and polyrhythmic accompaniments.

sampler Electronic device that digitizes, stores, and plays back sounds.

Sanctus A section of the Mass; the fourth musical movement of the *Ordinary*.

sarabande Stately Spanish Baroque dance type in triple meter, a standard movement of the Baroque *suite*.

sarangi Bowed chordophone from north India with three main strings and a large number of metal strings that vibrate sympathetically.

saxophone Family of single-reed woodwind instruments commonly used in the concert and jazz band.

scale Series of tones in ascending or descending order; may present the notes of a key.

scat singing A jazz style that sets syllables without meaning (*vocables*) to an improvised vocal line.

scherzo Composition in **A-B-A** form, usually in triple meter; replaced the *minuet and trio* in the nineteenth century.

secco Operatic *recitative* that features a sparse accompaniment and moves with great freedom.

Second Viennese School Name given to composer Arnold Schoenberg and his pupils Alban Berg and Anton Webern; represents the first efforts in twelve-tone composition.

secular music Nonreligious music; when texted, usually in the vernacular.

semitone Also known as a *half step*, the smallest interval commonly used in the Western musical system.

sequence Restatement of an idea or motive at a different pitch level.

serenade Classical instrumental genre that combines elements of chamber music and symphony, often performed in the evening or at social functions. Related to *divertimento* and *cassation*.

serialism Method of composition in which various musical elements (pitch, rhythm, dynamics, tone color) may be ordered in a fixed series. See also *total serialism*.

seventh chord Four-note combination consisting of a triad with another third added on top; spans a seventh between its lowest and highest tones.

sextuple meter Compound metrical pattern of six beats to a measure.

sforzando (*sf*) Sudden stress or accent on a single note or chord.

shakuhachi A Japanese end-blown flute.

shamisen Long-necked Japanese *chordophone* with three strings.

shape note Music notation system originating in nineteenth-century American church music in which the shape of the note heads determines the pitch; created to aid music reading.

sharp sign Musical symbol (♯) that indicates raising a pitch by a semitone.

shawm Medieval wind instrument, the ancestor of the oboe.

sheng A reed mouth organ from China.

side drum See *snare drum*.

simple meter Grouping of rhythms in which the beat is subdivided into two, as in duple, triple, and quadruple meters.

sinfonia Short instrumental work, found in Baroque opera, to facilitate scene changes.

Singspiel Comic German drama with spoken dialogue; the immediate predecessor of Romantic German opera.

sitar Long-necked plucked *chordophone* of northern India, with movable frets and a rounded gourd body; used as solo instrument and with *tabla*.

ska Jamaican urban dance form popular in the 1960s, influential in *reggae*.

slide trumpet Medieval brass instrument of the trumpet family.

snare drum   Small cylindrical drum with two heads stretched over a metal shell, the lower head having strings across it; played with two drumsticks. Also *side drum*.

soft rock   Lyrical, gentle rock style that evolved around 1960 in response to hard-driving *rock and roll*.

sonata   Instrumental genre in several movements for soloist or small ensemble.

sonata-allegro form   The opening movement of the sonata cycle, consisting of themes that are stated in the first section (*exposition*), developed in the second section (*development*), and restated in the third section (*recapitulation*). Also *sonata form or first-movement form*.

sonata cycle   General term describing the multimovement structure found in sonatas, string quartets, symphonies, concertos, and largescale works of the eighteenth and nineteenth centuries.

sonata da camera   Baroque chamber sonata, usually a suite of stylized dances. Also *chamber sonata*.

sonata da chiesa   Baroque instrumental work intended for performance in church; in four movements, frequently arranged slow-fast-slow-fast. Also *church sonata*.

sonata form   See *sonata-allegro form*.

song cycle   Group of songs, usually *Lieder*, that are unified musically or through their texts.

soprano   Highest-ranged voice, normally possessed by women or boys.

sousaphone   Brass instrument adapted from the tuba with a forward bell that is coiled to rest over the player's shoulder for ease of carrying while marching.

spiritual   Folklike devotional genre of the United States, sung by African Americans and whites.

spiritual minimalism   Contemporary musical style related to *minimalism*, characterized by a weak pulse and long chains of lush progressions—either tonal or modal.

Sprechstimme   A vocal style in which the melody is spoken at approximate pitches rather than sung on exact pitches; developed by Arnold Schoenberg.

staccato   Short, detached notes, marked with a dot above them.

statement   See *exposition*.

stile concitato   Baroque style developed by Monteverdi, which introduced novel effects such as rapid repeated notes as symbols of passion.

stile rappresentativo   A dramatic *recitative style* of the Baroque period in which melodies moved freely over a foundation of simple chords.

stopping   On a string instrument, altering the string length by pressing it on the fingerboard. On a horn, playing with the bell closed by the hand or a mute.

strain   A series of contrasting sections found in rags and marches; in duple meter with sixteen-measure themes or sections.

string instruments   Bowed and plucked instruments whose sound is produced by the vibration of one or more strings. Also *chordophone*.

string quartet   Chamber music ensemble consisting of two violins, viola, and cello. Also a multimovement composition for this ensemble.

string quintet   Standard chamber ensemble made up of either two violins, two violas, and cello or two violins, viola, and two cellos.

string trio   Standard chamber ensemble of two violins and cello or violin, viola, and cello.

strophic form   Song structure in which the same music is repeated with every stanza (strophe) of the poem.

Sturm und Drang   "Storm and stress"; late-eighteenth-century movement in Germany toward more emotional expression in the arts.

style   Characteristic manner of presentation of musical elements (melody, rhythm, harmony, dynamics, form, etc.).

subdominant   Fourth scale step, *fa*.

subdominant chord   Chord built on the fourth scale step, the IV chord.

subject   Main idea or theme of a work, as in a fugue.

suite   Multimovement work made up of a series of contrasting dance movements, generally all in the same key. Also *partita* and *ordre*.

swing   Jazz term coined to described Louis Armstrong's style; more commonly refers to big-band jazz.

syllabic   Melodic style with one note to each syllable of text.

symphonic poem   One-movement orchestral form that develops a poetic idea, suggests a scene, or creates a mood, generally associated with the Romantic era. Also *tone poem*.

symphony   Large work for orchestra, generally in three or four movements.

syncopation   Deliberate upsetting of the meter or pulse through a temporary shifting of the accent to a weak beat or an offbeat.

synthesizer   Electronic instrument that produces a wide variety of sounds by combining sound generators and sound modifiers in one package with a unified control system.

tabla   Pair of single-headed, tuned drums used in north Indian classical music.

tabor   Cylindrical medieval drum.

tag   Jazz term for a coda, or a short concluding section.

tala   Fixed time cycle or meter in Indian music, built from uneven groupings of beats.

tambourine   Percussion instrument consisting of a small round drum with metal plates inserted in its rim; played by striking or shaking.

tam-tam   See *gong*.

Te Deum   Song of praise to God; a text from the Roman Catholic rite, often set polyphonically.

tempo   Rate of speed or pace of music.

tempo rubato   See *rubato*.

tenor   Male voice of high range. Also a part, often structural, in polyphony.

tenor drum Percussion instrument, larger than the snare drum, with a wooden shell.

ternary form Three-part (A-B-A) form based on a statement (A), contrast or departure (B), and repetition (A), Also *three-part form.*

terraced dynamics Expressive style typical of Baroque music in which volume levels shift based on the playing forces used.

tertian harmony Harmony based on the interval of the third, particularly predominant from the Baroque through the nineteenth century.

texture The interweaving of melodic (horizontal) and harmonic (vertical) elements in the musical fabric.

thematic development Musical expansion of a theme by varying its melodic outline, harmony, or rhythm. Also *thematic transformation.*

thematic transformation See *thematic development.*

theme Melodic idea used as a basic building block in the construction of a composition. Also *subject.*

theme and variations Compositional procedure in which a theme is stated and then altered in successive statements; occurs as an independent piece or as a movement of a *sonata cycle.*

theme group Several themes in the same key that function as a unit within a section of a form, particularly in *sonata-allegro form.*

third Interval between two notes that are two diatonic scale steps apart.

third stream Jazz style that synthesizes characteristics and techniques of classical music and jazz; term coined by Gunther Schuller.

thorough-bass See *figured bass.*

three-part form See *ternary form.*

through-composed Song structure that is composed from beginning to end, without repetitions of large sections.

timbales Shallow, single-headed drums of Cuban origin, played in pairs; used in much Latin-American popular music.

timbre The quality of a sound that distinguishes one voice or instrument from another. Also *tone color.*

timbrel Ancient percussion instrument related to the tambourine.

timpani Percussion instrument consisting of a hemispheric copper shell with a head of plastic or calfskin, held in place by a metal ring and played with soft or hard padded sticks. A pedal mechanism changes the tension of the head, and with it the pitch. Also *kettle-drums.*

tin whistle Small metal end-blown flute commonly used in Irish traditional music.

toccata Virtuoso composition, generally for organ or harpsichord, in a free and rhapsodic style; in the Baroque, it often served as the introduction to a *fugue.*

tom-tom Cylindrical drum without snares.

tone A sound of definite pitch.

tonal Based on principles of major-minor tonality, as distinct from *modal.*

tonality Principle of organization around a tonic, or home, pitch, based on a major or minor scale.

tone cluster Highly dissonant combination of pitches sounded simultaneously.

tone color See *timbre.*

tone poem See *symphonic poem.*

tone row An arrangement of the twelve chromatic tones that serves as the basis of a *twelve-tone* composition.

tonic The first note of the scale or key, *do.* Also *keynote.*

tonic chord Triad built on the first scale tone, the I chord.

total serialism Extremely complex, totally controlled music in which the twelve-tone principle is extended to elements of music other than pitch.

traditional music Music that is learned by *oral transmission* and is easily sung or played by most people; may exist in variant forms. Also *folk music.*

tragédie lyrique French serious opera of the seventeenth and eighteenth centuries, with spectacular dance scenes and brilliant choruses on tales of courtly love or heroic adventures; associated with J.-B. Lully.

transition See *bridge.*

transposition Shifting a piece of music to a different pitch level.

tremolo Rapid repetition of a tone; can be achieved instrumentally or vocally.

triad Common chord type, consisting of three pitches built on alternate tones of the scale (e.g., steps 1-3-5, or *do-mi-sol*).

triangle Percussion instrument consisting of a slender rod of steel bent in the shape of a triangle, struck with a steel beater.

trill Ornament consisting of the rapid alternation between one tone and the next above it.

trio sonata Baroque chamber sonata type written in three parts: two melody lines and the *basso continuo;* requires a total of four players to perform.

triple meter Basic metrical pattern of three beats to a measure.

triple-stop Playing three notes simultaneously on a string instrument.

triplet Group of three equal-valued notes played in the time of two; indicated by a bracket and the number 3.

triplum Third voice in early polyphony.

tritonic Three-note scale pattern, used in the music of some sub-Saharan African cultures.

trobairitz Female *troubadours,* composer-poets of southern France.

trombone Tenor-range brass instrument that changes pitch by means of a movable double slide; there is also a bass version.

troubadours Medieval poet-musicians in southern France.

trouvères Medieval poet-musicians in northern France.

trumpet Highest-pitched brass instrument that changes pitch through valves.

tuba Bass-range brass instrument that changes pitch by means of valves.

tubular bells   See *chimes.*

tutti   "All"; the opposite of solo. See also *ripieno.*

twelve-bar blues   Musical structure based on a repeated harmonic-rhythmic pattern that is twelve measures in length (I-I-I-I-IV-IV-I-I-V-V-I-I).

twelve-tone music   Compositional procedure of the twentieth century based on the use of all twelve chromatic tones (in a *tone row*) without a central tone, or *tonic,* according to prescribed rules.

two-part form   See *binary form.*

uilleann pipes   Type of bellows-blown bagpipe used in Irish traditional music; bellows are elbow-manipulated.

union pipes   See *uilleann pipes.*

unison   Interval between two notes of the same pitch; the simultaneous playing of the same note.

upbeat   Last beat of a measure, a weak beat, which anticipates the downbeat.

vamp   Short passage with simple rhythm and harmony that introduces a soloist in a jazz performance.

verismo   Operatic "realism," a style popular in Italy in the 1890s, which tried to bring naturalism into the lyric theater.

verse   In poetry, a group of lines constituting a unit. In liturgical music for the Catholic Church, a phrase from the Scriptures that alternates with the *response.*

Vespers   One of the *Divine Offices* of the Roman Catholic Church, held at twilight.

vibraphone   A percussion instrument with metal bars and electrically driven rotating propellers under each bar that produces a *vibrato* sound, much used in jazz.

vibrato   Small fluctuation of pitch used as an expressive device to intensify a sound.

vielle   Medieval bowed-string instrument; the ancestor of the violin.

Viennese School   Title given to the three prominent composers of the classical era: Haydn, Mozart, and Beethoven.

viola   Bowed-string instrument of middle range; the second-highest member of the violin family.

viola da gamba   Family of Renaissance bowed-string instruments that had six or more strings, was fretted like a guitar, and was held between the legs like a modern cello.

violin   Soprano, or highest-ranged, member of the bowed-string instrument family.

violoncello   Bowed-string instrument with a middle-to-low range and dark, rich sonority; lower than a viola. Also *cello.*

virelai   Medieval and Renaissance fixed poetic form and chanson type with French courtly texts.

virtuoso   Performer of extraordinary technical ability.

vivace   Lively.

vocable   Nonlexical syllables, lacking literal meaning.

vocalise   A textless vocal melody, as in an exercise or concert piece.

volume   Degree of loudness or softness of a sound. See also *dynamics.*

waltz   Ballroom dance type in triple meter; in the Romantic era, a short, stylized piano piece.

West Coast jazz   Jazz style developed in the 1950s, featuring small groups of mixed timbres playing contrapuntal improvisations; similar to *cool jazz.*

whole step   Interval consisting of two half steps, or *semitones.*

whole-tone scale   Scale pattern built entirely of whole-step intervals, common in the music of the French Impressionists.

wind ensemble   See *concert band.*

woodwind   Instrumental family made of wood or metal whose tone is produced by a column of air vibrating within a pipe that has holes along its length.

woodwind quintet   Standard chamber ensemble consisting of one each of the following: flute, oboe, clarinet, bassoon, and French horn (not a woodwind instrument).

word painting   Musical pictorialization of words from the text as an expressive device; a prominent feature of the Renaissance madrigal.

work song   Communal song that synchronized group tasks.

world beat   Collective term for popular third-world musics, ethnic and traditional musics, and eclectic combinations of Western and non-Western musics. Also *ethno-pop.*

xylophone   Percussion instrument consisting of tuned blocks of wood suspended on a frame, laid out in the shape of a keyboard and struck with hard mallets.

yangqin   A Chinese hammered dulcimer with a trapezoidal sound box and metal strings that are struck with bamboo sticks.

zither   Family of string instruments with sound box over which strings are stretched; they may be plucked or bowed. Zithers appear in many shapes and are common in traditional music throughout Europe, Asia, and Africa.

Appendix III

Attending Concerts

Even with all the many ways now available to hear fine-quality recorded music, nothing can equal the excitement of a live concert. The crowded hall, the visual as well as aural stimulation of a performance, even the element of unpredictability—of what might happen on a particular night—all contribute to the unique communicative powers of people making music. There are, however, certain traditions surrounding concerts and concertgoing: the location of the most desirable seats, the way performers dress, the appropriate moments to applaud, are but a few. These conditions differ somewhat between concerts of art music and of popular styles. Understanding the various traditions can contribute to your increased enjoyment of the musical event.

CHOOSING CONCERTS, TICKETS, AND SEATS

Widely diversified musical events, performed by groups ranging from professional orchestras and college ensembles to church choirs, can be found in most parts of the country. It may take some research to discover the full gamut of concerts available in your area. Both city and college newspapers usually publish a calendar of upcoming events; these are often announced as well on the local radio stations. Bulletin boards on campus and in public buildings and stores are good places to find concert announcements. Often a music or fine arts department of a college will post a printed list of future events featuring both professional and student performers.

Ticket prices will vary considerably, depending on the nature of the event and the location of the theater. Many fine performances can be heard for a small admission price, especially at college and civic auditoriums. For an orchestra concert or an opera in a major metropolitan area, you can expect to pay anywhere from $20 to $75 or more for a reserved seat. The first rows of the orchestra section, located at stage level, and of the front balcony or loge are usually the most expensive. Although many consider it desirable to sit as close as possible to the performers, you are actually better off sitting in the middle of the hall to hear a proper balance, especially of a large ensemble. Today, most new concert halls are constructed so that virtually all seats are satisfactory. For the opera, many people bring opera glasses or binoculars if they are sitting some distance from the stage.

Concert tickets may be reserved in advance as well as purchased at the door. Often, reduced prices are available for students and senior citizens. Tickets reserved by telephone, or charged to a credit card, are generally not refundable; they are held at the box office in your name.

PREPARING FOR THE CONCERT

You may want to find out what works will be performed at an upcoming concert so that you can read about them and their composers in advance. If this book does not provide enough background, visit your campus or local public library or ask your instructor for assistance. If you plan to attend an opera, it is especially helpful to read an overview of the plot, since productions are often sung in the original language of the work. Fortunately, many American and Canadian opera houses today run simultaneous English translations above the stage or on seat backs, a practice that can increase our comprehension and enjoyment enormously.

Suitable attire for a concert depends somewhat on the degree of formality and the location of the event. Although strict traditions of concert dress have long since broken down, you will not feel out of place if you are neatly dressed. If you are attending an opening night of an opera, musical, or orchestra season, or if you have seats in a box or founder's circle, you will find most people wearing formal evening dress. But more usually, dress will be less formal.

ARRIVING AT THE CONCERT

Plan to arrive at a concert at least twenty minutes before it is scheduled to begin. This is particularly important if the seating is open—that is, nonreserved by seat number—so that you can choose your location. The time before a performance is often when people meet with friends, or enjoy a beverage at the lobby bar.

Concert programs are generally passed out (and sometimes sold) in the lobby or handed to you by the usher showing you to your seat. The program provides important information about the pieces being performed and about the performers. Often you will find English translations of vocal texts as well.

Should you arrive after the performance has begun, you may not be able to enter the hall until the first break in the music. This may occur after the first piece, or following the first movement of a large-scale work. Being late can mean missing as much as twenty minutes or more of a concert. When you finally do enter the hall, it is considerate to take a seat as quickly and quietly as possible.

THE CONCERT PROGRAM

The following is a sample program for an orchestra concert such as you might find at your college or in your community. When laid out in the traditional manner, the program provides the audience with a good deal of information about the concert and, for the informed listener, sets certain expectations for the upcoming sequence of musical events.

PROGRAM

Overture to *A Midsummer Night's Dream*   Felix Mendelssohn
                    (1809–1847)

Symphony No. 41 in C major, K. 551 (*Jupiter*) W. A. Mozart
  Allegro vivace   (1756–1791)
  Andante cantabile
  Menuetto (Allegretto) & Trio
  Finale (Molto allegro)

INTERMISSION

Concerto No. 1 for Piano and Orchestra   P. I. Tchaikovsky
 in B-flat minor, Op. 23   (1840–1893)
  Allegro non troppo e molto maestoso;
   Allegro con spirito
  Andante simplice; Prestissimo; Tempo I
  Allegro con fuoco
     Barbara Allen, piano

The University Symphony Orchestra
Eugene Castillo, conductor

A glance at the program confirms that three works will be performed. The concert will open, as is often the case, with an overture. The title of this work implies that it has a literary basis: Shakespeare's well-known play *A Midsummer Night's Dream*. In other words, this is a programmatic piece. Since no subdivisions or internal tempo markings are noted, you can expect it to be a one-movement work. The program also provides dates for the composer, Felix Mendelssohn, which establish him as an early Romantic master. (Since we study Mendelssohn, you could read about him in advance in this book.)

The concert will continue with a symphony by the eighteenth-century composer Mozart. The work's title suggests that Mozart wrote many symphonies; what we would not know without reading about him is that this is his last. You can further note that the symphony is in the key of C major and has a catalog number of 551 (assigned by a bibliographer named Köchel).

The program reveals that the symphony is in four sections, or movements, with contrasting tempo indications for each movement. The tempo pattern of fast (Allegro vivace)-slow (Andante cantabile)-moderate dance (Menuetto & Trio)-fast (Molto allegro) matches the plan for the sonata cycle; thus, the work is typical in its overall structure. (You can read more about the sonata cycle and the forms of individual movements in Chapter 28.)

The second half of the concert will be devoted to a single multimovement work—a piano concerto by the late-nineteenth-century composer Tchaikovsky. (You may notice different spellings for Tchaikovsky and other Russian composers on some programs, owing to varied ways of transcribing their names.)

This concerto appears to be a three-movement work, falling again into a standard format (fast-slow-fast). The tempo markings for each movement are, however, much more descriptive than those for the Mozart symphony, using words like "maestoso" (majestic), "con spirito" (with spirit), and "con fuoco" (with fire). This is typical of the Romantic era, as is the work's somber minor key. In the concerto, your interest will be drawn sometimes to the soloist, performing virtuoso passages and cadenzas, and at other times to the orchestra.

In addition to the works to be performed, the printed program may include short notes about each composition and biographical sketches of the soloist and the conductor. Traditionally, the names of all the ensemble members are also listed, along with upcoming concert dates.

DURING THE PERFORMANCE

Certain concert conventions come into play when the performance begins. The house lights will generally go down for the entrance of the performers or the opening of the curtain. Large ensembles, such as an orchestra or chorus, will usually be onstage at this time. The orchestra takes this opportunity to tune their instruments, cued by the *concertmaster* or *concertmistress* (the first chair, first violinist) asking for a pitch from the oboe player. It is customary to applaud the entrance of the conductor or any soloists. There will then be a moment's pause for complete quiet before the concert begins.

Knowing when to applaud during a concert is important. Generally, one applauds after complete works such as a symphony, a concerto, a sonata, or a song cycle; it is inappropriate to clap between movements of a multimovement work. Sometimes, short works are grouped together on the program, suggesting that they are a set. In this case, applause is suitable at the close of the group. If you are unsure, follow the lead of others in the audience. This is also sound advice for performances in a church, where people often feel reluctant to applaud until the close of a performance, if at all. One notable exception to the rule of avoiding applause during a work is at the opera, where it is traditional to interrupt with applause after a particularly fine delivery of an aria or an ensemble number.

Most concerts have an intermission, which is indicated on the program. (At the opera, there may be two or more, one after each act.) This is the only time that it is appropriate to leave one's seat or the theater. After about fifteen minutes, the theater manager will signal the audience to return to their seats, by either flashing the lights or ringing a bell.

The Performers

Newcomers to the concert hall are often surprised at the way the performers are dressed. For many years, it has been traditional for ensemble players to wear black—long dresses or pantsuits for the women, tuxedos or tails for the men. While this may seem overly formal, it is still customary, since dark, uniform clothing will minimize visual distraction. Soloists may dress more colorfully.

The behavior of the performers on the stage is often as formal as their dress. The entire orchestra often stands at the entrance of the conductor, who shakes the hand of the first violinist before beginning. A small group, such as a string quartet, will often bow to the audience in unison. Normally a performer will directly address the audience only if, at the close of the program, an additional piece or two is demanded by the extended applause. In this case, the *encore* (French for "again") is generally announced.

It may surprise you to see that some musicians, particularly pianists, singers, and other soloists, perform from memory. To perform without music requires intense concentration and necessitates many arduous hours of study and practice.

This brief explanation is intended to remove some of the mystery surrounding concertgoing. The best advice that can be given is to take full advantage of the opportunities available—try something completely unfamiliar, perhaps the opera or the symphony, and continue enjoying concerts of whatever music you already like!

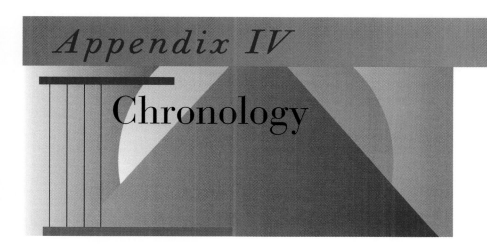

Appendix IV
Chronology

WORLD EVENTS	COMPOSERS	PRINCIPAL FIGURES
		Virgil (70–19 B.C.E.) Roman poet
44 C.E. *Augustus, first Emperor of Rome.*		
476 C.E. *Fall of Roman Empire.*		Li Po (c. 700–762) Chinese poet
800 *Charlemagne crowned first Holy Roman Emperor.*	HILDEGARD OF BINGEN (1098–1179)	
	PEROTIN (fl. c. 1200) COUNTESS OF DIA (fl. c. 1210) MONIOT D'ARRAS (fl. 1213–1239)	Eleanor of Aquitaine (c. 1122–1204 Queen of France and England Kublai Khan (1214–1294) Emperor of China
1260 *Kublai Khan founds Yuan dynasty in China.*		Dante Aligheri (1265–1321) Italian poet
1270 *Last Crusade to the Holy Land.*		
1271 *Marco Polo embarks for China.*	GUILLAUME DE MACHAUT (c. 1300–1377)	Ambrogio Lorenzetti (d. 1348?) Italian painter Francesco Petrarch (1304–1374) Italian poet and scholar Giovanni Boccaccio (1313–1375) Italian writer
	FRANCESCO LANDINI (c. 1325–1397)	
1337 *Beginning of the Hundred Years' War between England and France.*		Geoffrey Chaucer (c. 1345–1400) English poet
1347 *Black Death begins.*	JOHN DUNSTABLE (c. 1390–1453) GUILLAUME DU FAY (c. 1397–1474) GILLES BINCHOIS (c. 1400–1460)	Donatello (c. 1386–1466) Florentine sculptor

WORLD EVENTS	COMPOSERS	PRINCIPAL FIGURES
1415 *John Huss burned for heresy. Henry V defeats French at Agincourt.*	ANTOINE BUSNOIS (d. 1492) JOHANNES OCKEGHEM (c. 1420–c. 1495) ROBERT MORTON (c. 1430–78[+?])	
1431 *Joan of Arc executed.*		François Villon (1431–c. 1465) French poet
	JOSQUIN DESPREZ (c. 1440–1521)	
1453 *Fall of Constantinople to Turks.*		Leonardo da Vinci (1452–1519) Italian painter and scientist
1456 *Gutenberg Bible printed.*	JACOB OBRECHT (c. 1457–1505) MARCHETTO CARA (c. 1465–1525)	Desiderius Erasmus (c. 1466–1536) Dutch humanist and scholar Niccolò Machiavelli (1469–1527) Italian statesman
	BARTOLOMEO TROMBONCINO (c. 1470–1535)	Albrecht Dürer (1471–1528) German painter Nicolas Copernicus (1473–1543) Polish astronomer Isabella d'Este (1474–1539) Italian patroness of the arts Michelangelo (1475–1564) Italian sculptor, painter, architect, and poet Martin Luther (1483–1546) German religious reformer Raphael (1483–1520) Italian painter
1492 *Columbus discovers the New World. Death of Lorenzo di Medici. Expulsion of Jews from Spain.*	CLEMENT SERMISY (1490–1562)	
1501 *First book of printed music published by Petrucci in Florence.*		
1506 *St. Peter's church begun by Pope Julius II.*	THOMAS TALLIS (c. 1505–1585) JACOB ARCADELT (c. 1505–c. 1560)	
1509 *Henry VIII becomes King of England.*		
1513 *Ponce de León discovers Florida. Balboa reaches Pacific.*		
1517 *95 Theses of Martin Luther.*	TIELMAN SUSATO (c. 1515–1568)	
1519 *Cortéz begins conquest of Mexico.*	GIOVANNI DA PALESTRINA (c. 1525–1594)	Pierre de Ronsard (1524–1585) French poet
1534 *Henry VIII becomes head of Church of England.*	ROLAND DE LASSUS (c. 1532–1594)	Pieter Brueghel (1525–1569) Flemish painter
1541 *De Soto discovers the Mississippi.*	WILLIAM BYRD (1543–1623) GIULIO CACCINI (1545–1618)	El Greco (c. 1541–1614) Italian painter
1545 *Council of Trent begins.*	TOMÁS LUIS DE VICTORIA (c. 1549–1611) LUCA MARENZIO (1553–1599)	Miguel de Cervantes (1547–1616) Spanish novelist Edmund Spenser (1552–1599) English poet
1556 *Worst earthquake death toll (830,000 in northeastern China).*	GIOVANNI GABRIELI (c. 1557–1612) THOMAS MORLEY (1557–1603)	

WORLD EVENTS	COMPOSERS	PRINCIPAL FIGURES
1558 *Elizabeth I becomes Queen of England.*		
	CARLO GESUALDO (1560–1613) JACOPO PERI (1561–1633)	
		Galileo Galilei (1564–1642) Italian astronomer William Shakespeare (1564–1616) English dramatist
	CLAUDIO MONTEVERDI (1567–1643)	
1572 *St. Bartholomew's Eve Massacre.*		
	JOHN WILBYE (1574–1638)	John Donne (1573–1631) English metaphysical poet Ben Jonson (1573–1637) English dramatist
	THOMAS WEELKES (c. 1575–1623)	Peter Paul Rubens (1577–1640) Flemish painter
	ORLANDO GIBBONS (1583–1625) HEINRICH SCHÜTZ (1585–1672)	
1587 *Mary, Queen of Scots executed.*	FRANCESCA CACCINI (1587–1630)	
1588 *Drake defeats Spanish Armada.*		Hendrik Terbruggen (1588–1629) Dutch painter
1590 *First three books of Spenser's* Faerie Queene *published.*		
		René Descartes (1596–1650) French mathematician and philosopher
1601 *Shakespeare,* Hamlet.		Anthony van Dyck (1599–1641) Flemish painter
1606 *William Jansz discovers Australia.*	GIACOMO CARISSIMI (1605–1674)	Rembrandt van Rijn (1606–1669) Dutch painter
1607 *First European settlement in America founded at Jamestown, Virginia.*		Pierre Corneille (1606–1684) French dramatist
1609 *Henry Hudson explores the Hudson River.*		John Milton (1608–1674) English poet
1611 *King James Version of Bible.*		
1620 *Mayflower Compact. Plymouth settled.*	BARBARA STROZZI (1619–c. 1663) ISABELLA LEONARDA (1620–1704) JEAN-BAPTISTE LULLY (1632–1687)	Jan Vermeer (1632–1675)
1636 *Harvard established as first college in America.*	DIETRICH BUXTEHUDE (1637–1707)	Dutch painter
1640 *The Bay Psalm Book, first book printed in American colonies.*		Jean Racine (1639–1699) French playwright
1642 *Puritan Revolution begins in England. French found Montreal.*		
1643 *Reign of Louis XIV begins.*		
1648 *Peace of Westphalia ends Thirty Years' War.*		
1649 *Period of the Commonwealth begins in England.*	ARCANGELO CORELLI (1653–1713)	
	HENRY PURCELL (1659–1695)	
1664 *New Amsterdam becomes New York.*		
	ELISABETH-CLAUDE JACQUET DE LA GUERRE (c. 1666–1729)	
1665 *Milton's* Paradise Lost.		

WORLD EVENTS	COMPOSERS	PRINCIPAL FIGURES
	FRANÇOIS COUPERIN (1668–1733)	Joseph Addison (1672–1719)
	ANTONIO VIVALDI (1678–1741)	English essayist
1682 *Reign of Peter the Great (Russia) begins.*	GEORG PHILLIP TELEMANN (1681–1767)	Richard Steele (1672–1719)
	JEAN-PHILIPPE RAMEAU (1683–1764)	Irish-born playwright
1684 *Newton's theory of gravitation.*	JOHN GAY (1685–1732)	Jean Antoine Watteau (1684–1721)
	JOHANN SEBASTIAN BACH (1685–1750)	French painter
	DOMENICO SCARLATTI (1685–1757)	
	GEORGE FRIDERIC HANDEL (1685–1759)	
		Alexander Pope (1688–1744)
		English poet and satirist
		Voltaire (1694–1778)
		French poet and satirist
1702 *Start of War of the Spanish Succession.*	GIOVANNI BATTISTA PERGOLESI	Giovanni Antonio Canal (1697–1768)
	(1710–1736)	Italian painter
	WILHELM FRIEDEMANN BACH (1710–1784)	Jean Jacques Rousseau (1712–1778)
		Swiss-born French philosopher and composer
1714 *Queen Anne succeeded by George I, Handel's patron.*	CHRISTOPH WILLIBALD GLUCK (1714–1787)	Francesco Guardi (1712–1793)
	CARL PHILLIP EMANUEL BACH (1714–1788)	Italian painter
1715 *First Opéra Comique founded. Reign of Louis XV begins.*		Thomas Gray (1716–1771)
	JOHANN STAMITZ (1717–1757)	English poet
1719 *Herculaneum and Pompeii rediscovered. Classical revival.*		Joshua Reynolds (1723–1792)
		English portrait painter
1732 *Linnaeus's System of Nature. George Washington born.*	JOSEPH HAYDN (1732–1809)	Pierre-Augustin Caron de Beaumarchais (1732–1799)
	JOHANN CHRISTIAN BACH (1735–1782)	French playwright
1737 *San Carlo Opera House, Naples, opened.*		
1743 *Thomas Jefferson born.*	MARIANNE VON MARTINEZ (1744–1812)	
	MADDELENA LOMBARDINI SIRMEN	Francisco Goya (1746–1828)
	(1745–1818)	Spanish painter
	WILLIAM BILLINGS (1746–1800)	Jacques-Louis David (1748–1825)
		French painter
		Johann Wolfgang von Goethe (1749–1832)
		German poet
		Evariste-Désiré de Parny (1753–1814)
1752 *Franklin's discoveries in electricity.*	MUZIO CLEMENTI (1752–1832)	French poet
		William Blake (1757–1827)
1756 *Opening of Seven Years' War (in America, the French and Indian War).*	WOLFGANG AMADEUS MOZART (1756–1791)	English poet and painter
1759 *Wolfe captures Quebec.*	MARIA THERESIA VON PARADIS (1759–1824)	Robert Burns (1759–1796)
		Scottish poet
		Friedrich von Schiller (1759–1805)
		German dramatist
1762 *Catherine the Great crowned Empress of Russia.*	LUIGI CHERUBINI (1760–1842)	Katsushioka Hokusai (1760–1849)
		Japanese artist
1769 *Watt's steam engine.*		
1770 *Boston Massacre.*	LUDWIG VAN BEETHOVEN (1770–1827)	William Wordsworth (1770–1850)
		English poet
1771 *First edition, Encyclopaedia Britannica.*		Sir Walter Scott (1771–1832)
		Scottish writer

WORLD EVENTS	COMPOSERS	PRINCIPAL FIGURES
		Samuel Taylor Coleridge (1772–1834)
		English poet
1775 *American Revolution begins.*	GASPARO SPONTINI (1774–1851)	Caspar David Friedrich (1774–1840)
		German painter
		J. M. W. Turner (1775–1851)
1776 *Adam Smith's* The Wealth of Nations.		English painter
Declaration of Independence signed.		E. T. A. Hoffmann (1776–1822)
		German writer
		John Constable (1776–1837)
		English landscape painter
1778 *La Scala Opera opened in Milan.*	NICCOLÒ PAGANINI (1782–1840)	Jean Ingres (1780–1867)
	CARL MARIA VON WEBER (1786–1826)	French painter
1787 *Constitutional Convention.*		Lord Byron (1788–1824)
		English poet
1789 *French Revolution begins.*		Alphonse Lamartine (1790–1869)
		French poet
1791 *Bill of Rights.*	GIACOMO MEYERBEER (1791–1864)	
	GIOACCHINO ROSSINI (1792–1868)	Percy Bysshe Shelley (1792–1822)
	LOWELL MASON (1792–1872)	English poet
1793 *Eli Whitney's cotton gin.*		
		John Keats (1795–1821)
1796 *Jenner introduces vaccination.*		English poet
		Jean Baptiste Corot (1796–1875)
		French landscape painter
	GAETANO DONIZETTI (1797–1848)	Heinrich Heine (1797–1856)
	FRANZ SCHUBERT (1797–1828)	German poet
		Ferdinand Victor Eugene Delacroix
		(1798–1863)
		French painter
		Alexander Pushkin (1799–1837)
		Russian poet and novelist
		Honoré de Balzac (1799–1850)
		French novelist
1800 *Laplace's mechanistic view of the*		Alexander Dumas the elder (1800–1870)
universe.	VINCENZO BELLINI (1801–1835)	French novelist
		Victor Hugo (1802–1885)
		French writer
1803 *Louisiana Purchase.*	HECTOR BERLIOZ (1803–1869)	Prosper Mérimée (1803–1870)
	JOHANN STRAUSS (father) (1804–1849)	French writer
	MIKHAIL GLINKA (1804–1857)	Ralph Waldo Emerson (1803–1882)
	FANNY MENDELSSOHN HENSEL	American poet and philosopher
	(1805–1847)	Aurore Dudevant, alias George Sand
		(1804–1876)
		French novelist
		Henry Wadsworth Longfellow (1807–1882)
		American poet
		Honoré Daumier (1808–1879)
		French painter
	FELIX MENDELSSOHN (1809–1847)	Edgar Allen Poe (1809–1849)
		American poet and writer
	FRÉDÉRIC CHOPIN (1810–1849)	
	ROBERT SCHUMANN (1810–1856)	
	FRANZ LISZT (1811–1886)	
1812 *Napoleon invades Russia. War of 1812.*		Georg Büchner (1813–1837)
	RICHARD WAGNER (1813–1883)	German playwright
	GIUSEPPE VERDI (1813–1901)	
1815 *Battle of Waterloo, Congress of*		Charlotte Brontë (1816–1855)
Vienna.		English novelist

WORLD EVENTS	COMPOSERS	PRINCIPAL FIGURES
		Henry David Thoreau (1817–1862)
		American naturalist and poet
	CHARLES GOUNOD (1818–1893)	Emily Brontë (1818–1848)
		English novelist
		Marius Petipa (1818–1910)
		French choreographer
1819 *First steamship to cross Atlantic.*	JACQUES OFFENBACH (1819–1880)	Walt Whitman (1819–1892)
	CLARA SCHUMANN (1819–1896)	American poet
1821 *First women's college in America* *established.*	PAULINE VIARDOT-GARCIA (1821–1910)	Charles Baudelaire (1821–1867)
		French poet
		Feodor Dostoevsky (1821–1881)
	CÉSAR FRANCK (1822–1890)	Russian novelist
1823 *Monroe Doctrine.*	ÉDOUARD LALO (1823–1892)	
1824 *Bolívar liberates South America.*	BEDŘICH SMETANA (1824–1884)	Alexander Dumas the younger (1824–1895)
	JOHANN STRAUSS (son) (1825–1899)	French writer
	STEPHEN COLLINS FOSTER (1826–1864)	Henrik Ibsen (1828–1906)
		Norwegian poet and playwright
		Leo Tolstoi (1828–1910)
1829 *Independence of Greece.*	WILLIAM MASON (1829–1908)	Russian novelist
	LOUIS MOREAU GOTTSCHALK (1829–1869)	
1830 *First railroad, Liverpool-Manchester.* *July Revolution in France.*		Emily Dickinson (1830–1886)
		American poet
		Camille Pissarro (1830–1903)
		French painter
1832 *Morse invents telegraph.*		Edouard Manet (1832–1883)
		French painter
1833 *Slavery outlawed in British Empire.*	JOHANNES BRAHMS (1833–1897)	
1834 *McCormick patients mechanical* *reaper.*	ALEXANDER BORODIN (1834–1887)	James Whistler (1834–1903)
		American painter
		Edgar Degas (1834–1917)
		French painter
	CAMILLE SAINT-SAËNS (1835–1921)	Mark Twain (1835–1910)
		American author
	LÉO DELIBES (1836–1891)	
1837 *Queen Victoria ascends the throne.*	MILY BALAKIREV (1837–1910)	
	GEORGES BIZET (1838–1875)	H. H. Richardson (1838–1886)
		American architect
1839 *Daguerreotype invented. New York* *Philharmonic Society and Vienna* *Philharmonic founded.*	MODEST MUSORGSKY (1839–1881)	Paul Cézanne (1839–1906)
		French painter
	PETER IL YICH TCHAIKOVSKY (1840–1893)	Auguste Rodin (1840–1917)
		French sculptor
		Claude Monet (1840–1926)
		French painter
		Thomas Hardy (1840–1928)
		English novelist and poet
	ANTONÍN DVOŘÁK (1841–1904)	Berthe Morisot (1841–1895)
		French painter
		Pierre Auguste Renoir (1841–1919)
		French painter
	ARTHUR SULLIVAN (1842–1900)	Stéphane Mallarmé (1842–1898)
	JULES MASSENET (1842–1912)	French Symbolist poet
	EDVARD GRIEG (1843–1907)	Henry James (1843–1916)
		American novelist
	NIKOLAI RIMSKY-KORSAKOV (1844–1908)	Paul Verlaine (1844–1896)
		French poet

WORLD EVENTS	COMPOSERS	PRINCIPAL FIGURES
		Friedrich Nietzsche (1844–1900)
		German philosopher
		Henri Rousseau (1844–1910)
		French primitive painter
	GABRIEL FAURÉ (1845–1924)	Mary Cassatt (1845–1926)
1846 *Repeal of Corn Laws. Famine in Ireland.*		American painter
1848 *Revolution throughout Europe. Gold Rush in California. Marx's Communist Manifesto.*		Paul Gauguin (1848–1903) French painter
	VINCENT D'INDY (1851–1931)	
1852 *Second Empire under Napoleon III. Stowe's Uncle Tom's Cabin.*	ARTHUR FOOTE (1853–1937)	Vincent van Gogh (1853–1890) Dutch painter
1854 *Commodore Perry opens Japan to the West. Crimean War.*	LEOŠ JANÁCEK (1854–1928) GEORGE CHADWICK (1854–1931) JOHN PHILIP SOUSA (1854–1932)	
1855 *Charge of the Light Brigade.*	ERNEST CHAUSSON (1855–1899)	
		Louis H. Sullivan (1856–1924) American architect George Bernard Shaw (1856–1950) Irish dramatist and critic
1857 *Dred Scott decision.*	EDWARD ELGAR (1857–1934) CECILE CHAMINADE (1857–1944) RUGGERO LEONCAVALLO (1857–1919)	
1858 *Covent Garden opened as opera house.*	GIACOMO PUCCINI (1858–1924) ETHEL SMYTH (1858–1944)	
1859 *Darwin's* Origin of Species. *John Brown raids Harper's Ferry.*		Georges Seurat (1859–1991) French painter
	HUGO WOLF (1860–1903) ISAAC ALBÉNIZ (1860–1909) GUSTAV MAHLER (1860–1911)	Anton Chekhov (1860–1904) Russian writer
1861 *Serfs emancipated in Russia. American Civil War begins.*	EDWARD MACDOWELL (1861–1908)	Frederic Remington (1861–1909) American painter and bronze artist
	CLAUDE DEBUSSY (1862–1918) FREDERICK DELIUS (1862–1934)	Gustav Klint (1862–1918) Austrian artist Maurice Maeterlinck (1862–1949) Belgian poet and dramatist Gabriele D'Annunzio (1862–1938) Italian poet and dramatist
1863 *Emancipation Proclamation.*	PIETRO MASCAGNI (1863–1945)	Edvard Munch (1863–1944) Norwegian Expressionist painter
	RICHARD STRAUSS (1864–1949)	Henri de Toulouse-Lautrec (1864–1901) French painter
1865 *Civil War ends. Lincoln assassinated.*	PAUL DUKAS (1865–1935) JEAN SIBELIUS (1865–1957)	Rudyard Kipling (1865–1936) English novelist and poet
1866 *Transatlantic cable completed.*	ERIK SATIE (1866–1925)	H. G. Wells (1866–1946) English novelist
1867 *Marx's* Das Kapital *(vol. I). Alaska purchased.*	AMY CHENEY BEACH (1867–1944)	Luigi Pirandello (1867–1936) Italian dramatist Frank Lloyd Wright (1867–1959) American architect
	SCOTT JOPLIN (1868–1917)	Maxim Gorky (1868–1936) Russian writer
1869 *Suez Canal completed.*	ALBERT ROUSSEL (1869–1937) WILL MARIAN COOK (1869–1944)	Henri Matisse (1869–1954) French painter
1870 *Franco-Prussian War. Vatican Council proclaims papal infallibility.*		

WORLD EVENTS	COMPOSERS	PRINCIPAL FIGURES
1871 *William I of Hohenzollern becomes German emperor. Paris Commune. Unification of Italy. Stanley and Livingston in Africa.*	RALPH VAUGHAN WILLIAMS (1872–1958)	Marcel Proust (1871–1922) French novelist Theodore Dreiser (1871–1945) American novelist Sergei Diaghilev (1872–1929) Russian impresario Piet Mondrian (1872–1946) Dutch painter
1873 *Dynamo developed.*	MAX REGER (1873–1916) SERGEI RACHMANINOFF (1873–1943) DANIEL GREGORY MASON (1873–1953) ARNOLD SCHOENBERG (1874–1951) CHARLES IVES (1874–1954)	Willa Cather (1873–1947) American novelist Gertrude Stein (1874–1946) American poet W. Somerset Maugham (1874–1965) English novelist and playwright
1875 *New Paris Opera opened.*	MAURICE RAVEL (1875–1937)	Rainer Maria Rilke (1875–1926) German poet
1876 *Telephone invented. Bayreuth theater opened. Battle of Little Bighorn.*	MANUEL DE FALLA (1876–1946) CARL RUGGLES (1876–1971)	
1877 *Phonograph invented.*		Isadora Duncan (1878–1927) American dancer
	OTTORINO RESPIGHI (1879–1936)	Paul Klee (1879–1940) Swiss painter
1880 *Irish insurrection.*	ERNEST BLOCH (1880–1959)	Michel Fokine (1880–1942) Russian-born American dancer and choreographer
1881 *Czar Alexander II assassinated. President Garfield shot. Panama Canal begun. Boston Symphony founded.*	BÉLA BARTÓK (1881–1945) GEORGES ENESCO (1881–1955)	Pablo Picasso (1881–1973) Spanish artist
1882 *Berlin Philharmonic founded. Koch discovers tuberculosis germ.*	NATHANIEL DETT (1882–1943) IGOR STRAVINSKY (1882–1971) ZOLTÁN KODÁLY (1882–1967)	Virginia Woolf (1882–1941) English novelist Georges Bracque (1882–1963) French painter Edward Hopper (1882–1967) American painter
1883 *Brooklyn Bridge opened. Metropolitan Opera opened. Amsterdam Concertgebouw founded.*	EDGARD VARÈSE (1883–1965) ANTON WEBERN (1883–1945) ABING (HUA YANJUN, 1883–1950)	Franz Kafka (1883–1924) Bohemian writer
1884 *Pasteur discovers inoculation against rabies.*	CHARLES T. GRIFFES (1884–1920) ALBAN BERG (1885–1935) JELLY ROLL MORTON (1885–1941) WALLINGFORD RIEGGER (1885–1961)	Amadeo Modigliani (1884–1920) Italian painter and sculptor Sinclair Lewis (1885–1951) American novelist Sonia Delaunay (1885–1979) Russian-born French painter
1886 *Statue of Liberty unveiled in New York Harbor.*		Wassily Kandinsky (1886–1944) Russian-born French painter Diego Rivera (1886–1951) Mexican painter Oskar Kokoschka (1886–1980) German Expressionist painter
1887 *Daimler patents high-speed internal combustion machine. Artistic Secession movement in Vienna.*	HEITOR VILLA-LOBOS (1887–1959)	Juan Gris (1887–1927) Spanish painter Marcel Duchamp (1887–1968) French-born American painter

WORLD EVENTS	COMPOSERS	PRINCIPAL FIGURES
		Georgia O'Keeffe (1887–1986)
		American painter
1888 *Eiffel Tower. Brazil becomes a republic.*	FLORENCE PRICE (1888–1953)	Hans Arp (1888–1966)
	MAX STEINER (1888–1971)	French sculptor
1889 *Paris World Exhibition.*		Jean Cocteau (1889–1963)
		French writer and film director
		Marc Chagall (1889–1985)
		Russian-born French artist
1890 *Journey around world completed in 72 days.*	BOHUSLAV MARTINU (1890–1959)	Vaslav Nijinsky (1890–1950)
	SERGE PROKOFIEV (1891–1952)	Russian dancer
		Grant Wood (1891–1942)
1892 *Duryea makes first American gas buggy.*	ARTHUR HONEGGER (1892–1955)	American painter
	DARIUS MILHAUD (1892–1974)	
	GERMAINE TAILLEFERRE (1892–1983)	
	LILI BOULANGER (1893–1918)	Joan Miró (1893–1983)
	DOUGLAS MOORE (1893–1969)	Spanish painter
1894 *Nicholas II, last czar, ascends throne.*	BESSIE SMITH (1894–1937)	Martha Graham (1894–1991)
	WALTER PISTON (1894–1976)	American choreographer
		Aldous Huxley (1894–1963)
		English novelist
1895 *Roentgen discovers X-rays. Marconi's wireless telegraphy. First African American awarded Harvard Ph.D.*	PAUL HINDEMITH (1895–1963)	Lorenz Hart (1895–1943)
	WILLIAM GRANT STILL (1895–1978)	American lyricist
	CARL ORFF (1895–1982)	Oscar Hammerstein II (1895–1960)
		American lyricist
		Robert Graves (1895–1985)
		English poet
	HOWARD HANSON (1896–1981)	F. Scott Fitzgerald (1896–1940)
	ROGER SESSIONS (1898–1985)	American novelist
	VIRGIL THOMSON (1896–1989)	
1897 *Queen Victoria's Diamond Jubilee.*	ERICH WOLFGANG KORNGOLD (1897–1957)	
	HENRY COWELL (1897–1965)	
1898 *The Curies discover radium. Spanish-American War.*	GEORGE GERSHWIN (1898–1937)	Sergei Eisenstein (1898–1948)
	ROY HARRIS (1898–1979)	Russian film director
	LILLIAN HARDIN (1898–1971)	Bertolt Brecht (1898–1956)
		German playwright and poet
		Ernest Hemingway (1898–1961)
		American novelist
		Alexander Calder (1898–1976)
		American artist, pioneer of Kineficart
		Henry Moore (1898–1986)
		English sculptor
1899 *Boer War. First International Peace Conference at The Hague.*	E. K. ("DUKE") ELLINGTON (1899–1974)	Federico García Lorca (1899–1936),
	CARLOS CHÁVEZ (1899–1978)	Spanish poet and playwright
	RANDALL THOMPSON (1899–1984)	
	FRANCIS POULENC (1899–1963)	
1900 *Boxer Insurrection in China.*	COLIN McPHEE (1900–1964)	Thomas Wolfe (1900–1938)
	AARON COPLAND (1900–1990)	American novelist
	ERNST KRENEK (1900–1991)	
	KURT WEILL (1900–1950)	
1901 *Queen Victoria dies, Edward VII succeeds.*	RUTH CRAWFORD (1901–1953)	
	LOUIS ARMSTRONG (1901–1971)	
	HARRY PARTCH (1901–1974)	
	RICHARD RODGERS (1902–1979)	John Steinbeck (1902–1968)
	WILLIAM WALTON (1902–1983)	American novelist
		Langston Hughes (1902–1967)
		American poet and playwright

WORLD EVENTS	COMPOSERS	PRINCIPAL FIGURES
1903 *Wrights' first successful airplane flight.*		Barbara Hepworth (1903–1975) English sculptor Mark Rothko (1903–1970) American Abstract Expressionist painter
1904 *Russo-Japanese War.*	LUIGI DALLAPICCOLA (1904–1975)	Isamu Nuguchi (1904–1988) American sculptor Salvador Dali (1904–1989) Spanish painter George Balanchine (1904–1983) Russian choreographer Willem de Kooning (1904–1997) Dutch-born American Abstract Expressionist painter Isaac Bashevis Singer (1904–1991) American Yiddish writer
1905 *Sigmund Freud founds psychoanalysis. First Russian Revolution.*	MARC BLITZSTEIN (1905–1964)	Jean-Paul Sartre (1905–1980) French philosopher and novelist
1906 *San Francisco earthquake and fire.*	LOUISE TALMA (1906–) DMITRI SHOSTAKOVICH (1906–1975) MIRIAM GIDEON (1906–)	
		W. H. Auden (1907–1973) English poet and dramatist Lillian Hellman (1907–1984) American playwright
1908 *Model-T Ford produced.*	ELLIOT CARTER (1908–) OLIVIER MESSIAEN (1908–1992)	Richard Wright (1908–1960) American novelist
1909 *Peary reaches North Pole. National Association for the Advancement of Colored People (NAACP) founded.*	YUJI TAKAHASHI (1909–) SAMUEL BARBER (1910–1982)	Agnes de Mille (1909–1993) American choreographer Jean Genet (1910–1986) French writer
1911 *Amundsen reaches South Pole.*	ALAN HOVHANESS (1911–) BERNARD HERRMANN (1911–1975) VLADIMIR USSACHEVSKY (1911–1990)	Marshall McLuhan (1911–1980) Canadian writer Tennessee Williams (1911–1983) American playwright Romare Bearden (1911–1988) African-American artist
1912 *China becomes republic. Titanic sinks. James Thorpe stripped of Olympic medals.*	JOHN CAGE (1912–1992) CONLON NANCARROW (1912–1996)	Jackson Pollock (1912–1956) American artist Eugene Ionesco (1912–1994) Romanian-born French dramatist
	WITOLD LUTOSLAWSKI (1913–1994) BENJAMIN BRITTEN (1913–1976)	
1914 *Panama Canal begins. World War I begins.*		Dylan Thomas (1914–1953) Welsh poet and playwright
1915 *Lusitania is sunk.*	BILLIE HOLIDAY (1915–1959) DAVID DIAMOND (1915–) GEORGE PERLE (1915–)	Arthur Miller (1915–) American playwright Robert Motherwell (1915–) American Abstract Expressionist painter
	MILTON BABBITT (1916–) ALBERTO GINASTERA (1916–1983)	
1917 *U.S. enters World War I. Russian Revolution. Prohibition Amendment.*	LOU HARRISON (1917–)	Andrew Wyeth (1917–) American painter I. M. Pei (1917–) Chinese-born American architect
1918 *Kaiser abdicates. World War I ends in armistice.*	LEONARD BERNSTEIN (1918–1990)	Ingmar Bergman (1918–) Swedish filmmaker

WORLD EVENTS	COMPOSERS	PRINCIPAL FIGURES
1919 *Treaty of Versailles. Mussolini founds Italian Fascist Party.*		J. D. Salinger (1919–) American novelist Merce Cunningham (1919–) American dancer and choreographer
1920 *Women's suffrage: Nineteenth Amendment passed.*	CHARLIE PARKER (1920–1955) RALPH SHAPEY (1921–)	Federico Fellini (1920–1993) Italian filmmaker Richard Wilbur (1921–) American poet
1922 *Discovery of insulin. First woman U.S. senator.*	LUKAS FOSS (1922–) IANNIS XENAKIS (1922–)	Kurt Vonnegut (1922–) American novelist
1923 *USSR established.*	MEL POWELL (1923–1998) GYÖRGY LIGETI (1923–) CHOU WEN-CHUNG (1923–) NED ROREM (1923–) LUIGI NONO (1924–1990) JULIA PERRY (1924–1979) LUCIANO BERIO (1925–) PIERRE BOULEZ (1925–) GUNTHER SCHULLER (1925–) EARLE BROWN (1926–) MORTON FELDMAN (1926–1987) BETSY JOLAS (1926–)	Denise Levertov (1923–) American poet Norman Mailer (1923–) American novelist Roy Lichtenstein (1923–) American painter Robert Rauschenberg (1925–) American artist Andy Warhol (1926–1987) American pop artist and film director Allen Ginsberg (1926–1997) American "Beat-generation" poet
1927 *Lindbergh's solo flight across Atlantic. Babe Ruth sets home-run record.*		John Ashbery (1927–) American poet Günter Grass (1927–) German novelist Neil Simon (1927–) American dramatist
	THEA MUSGRAVE (1928–) KARLHEINZ STOCKHAUSEN (1928–)	Maya Angelou (1928–) American writer Edward Albee (1928–) American dramatist Gabriel García Márquez (1928–) Colombian novelist
	GEORGE CRUMB (1929–)	Adrienne Rich (1929–) American poet Claes Oldenburg (1929–) American artist
1930 *The planet Pluto discovered.*	TORU TAKEMITSU (1930–1996)	Derek Walcott (1930–) West Indian poet and playwright Jean-Luc Godard (1930–) French filmmaker Jasper Johns (1930–) American painter Harold Pinter (1930–) English dramatist
1931 *Japan invades Manchuria. Empire State Building is completed.*	DAVID BAKER (1931–) LUCIA DLUGOSZEWSKI (1931–) SOFIA GUBAIDULINA (1931–) PAULINE OLIVERAS (1932–) JOHN WILLIAMS (1932–)	Alvin Ailey (1931–1989) American choreographer Toni Morrison (1931–) African-American novelist John Updike (1932–) American novelist
1933 *Franklin D. Roosevelt inaugurated. Hitler becomes dictator of Germany.*	KRZYSZTOF PENDERECKI (1933–) MARIO DAVIDOVSKY (1934–) R. MURRAY SCHAFER (1933–) MORTON SUBOTNIK (1933–) PETER MAXWELL DAVIES (1934–)	Yevgeny Yevtushenko (1933–) Soviet poet Inamu Amiri Baraka (Le Roi Jones) (1934–), American poet Michael Graves (1934–) American postmodern architect

WORLD EVENTS	COMPOSERS	PRINCIPAL FIGURES
	TERRY RILEY (1935–)	Jim Dine (1935–) American artist
1936 *Spanish Civil War. Sulfa drugs introduced in the U.S.*	STEVE REICH (1936–)	Frank Stella (1936–) American artist
1937 *Japan invades China. Amelia Earhart disappears over Pacific.*	DAVID DEL TREDICI (1937–) PHILIP GLASS (1937–)	Tom Stoppard (1937–) Czech-born English playwright Lanford Wilson (1937–) American playwright David Hockney (1937–) British painter
	JOAN TOWER (1938–) CHARLES WUORINEN (1938–) JOHN CORIGLIANO (1938–)	Robert Smithson (1938–1973) American "land artist"
1939 *World War II starts. Germany invades Poland, Britain and France declare war on Germany, Russia invades Finland.*	ELLEN TAAFFE ZWILICH (1939–) BARBARA KOLB (1939–)	Alan Ayckbourn (1939–) British dramatist Judy Chicago (1939–) American artist
1940 *Roosevelt elected to third term. Churchill becomes British prime minister.*		Pina Bausch (1940–) German choreographer and dancer
1941 *U.S. attacked by Japan, declares war on Japan, Germany, Italy.*		
1943 *Germans defeated at Stalingrad and in North Africa. Italy surrenders.*	CHINARY UNG (1942–) MEREDITH MONK (1943–)	
1944 *D-Day. Invasion of France.*	PAUL LANSKY (1944–)	Sam Shepard (1943–) American playwright and actor
1945 *Germany surrenders. Atom bomb dropped on Hiroshima. Japan surrenders. Roosevelt dies.*		Anselm Kiefer (1945–) German Neoexpressionist painter Rainer Werner Fassbinder (1946–1982) German film and stage director
	LAURIE ANDERSON (1947–) JOHN ADAMS (1947–)	Steven Spielberg (1947–) American filmmaker
1948 *Gandhi assassinated. Nation of Israel established.*	ANDREW LLOYD WEBER (1948–)	Mikhail Baryshnikov (1948–) Russian-born American dancer
1949 *Communists defeat Chiang Kai-shek in China. USSR explodes atom bomb. NATO begins.*	ALEXINA LOUIE (1949–)	
1950 *North Korea invades South Korea.*	STEPHEN SONDHEIM (1930–) LIBBY LARSEN (1950–)	Wendy Wasserstein (1950–) American playwright
1952 *Eisenhower elected president. Elizabeth II crowned Queen of England.*	OLIVER KNUSSEN (1952–) TOD MACHOVER (1952–) TOBIAS PICKER (1954–)	
1955 *Warsaw Pact signed. Salk serum for infantile paralysis.*	STEVEN MACKEY (1956–)	
1957 *First underground atomic explosion. Russians launch the first satellite, Sputnik I.*		
		Peter Sellars (1958–) American stage director

WORLD EVENTS

1959   *Alaska becomes 49th state. Castro victorious in Cuba. Hawaii becomes 50th state.*

1960   *Kennedy elected president.*

1963   *Cuban missile crisis. Algeria declared independent of France. Vatican II begins.*

1963   *Kennedy assassinated. Lyndon Johnson becomes president.*

1964   *Passage of Civil Rights Act. Beatles take U.S. by storm.*

1965   *First walk in space. Alabama civil rights march.*

1966   *Indira Gandhi elected Prime Minister of India.*

1967   *Israeli-Arab Six-Day War. First successful heart transplant.*

1968   *Richard M. Nixon elected president. Martin Luther King Jr. and Robert F. Kennedy assassinated. My Lai massacre.*

1969   *American astronauts walk on moon. Woodstock Festival.*

1970   *U.S. intervention in Cambodia. Nobel Prize in literature to Solzhenitsyn.*

1971   *26th Amendment gives 18-year-olds the right to vote.*

1972   *Richard Nixon reelected.*

1973   *"Watergate Affair" begins. Vice President Agnew resigns. Roe vs. Wade decision on abortion rights.*

1974   *President Nixon resigns. First home computers sold.*

WORLD EVENTS

1975   *Francisco Franco dies. Vietnam War ends. Regime of Khmer Rouge begins in Cambodia.*

1976   *Viking spacecraft lands on Mars. Mao Zedong dies. Jimmy Carter elected president.*

1977   *New Panama Canal Treaty signed. Menachem Begin named Israeli prime minister.*

1978   *John Paul II first Polish pope.*

1979   *Shah of Iran deposed. Major nuclear accident at Three-Mile Island.*

1980   *Ronald Reagan elected president. Margaret Thatcher elected Prime Minister of Britain.*

1981   *First woman appointed to Supreme Court. Egyptian President Sadat assassinated. First AIDS cases reported.*

1983   *First woman astronaut into space. U.S. invades Grenada.*

1984   *Reagan reelected president. AIDS virus identified. Bishop Tutu wins Nobel Peace Prize.*

1985   *Reagan-Gorbachev summit meeting.*

1986   *Space shuttle Challenger crew dies in launching disaster. Iran-Contra scandal revealed.*

1988   *George Bush elected president. Mikhail Gorbachev named Soviet president.*

1989   *Polish Solidarity trade union legalized. Berlin Wall dismantled. Chinese military massacre in Tiananmen Square. Exxon Valdez oil spill in Alaska.*

WORLD EVENTS

1990   *Reunification of Germany.*

1991   *Soviet Union dissolved; Commonwealth of Independent States formed. Persian Gulf War. Pan Am flight 103 explodes over Lockerbie, Scotland.*

1922   *Bill Clinton elected president. Rodney King beating sets off Los Angeles riots. Hurricane Andrew devastates coasts of Florida and Louisiana.*

1993   *North American Free Trade Agreement (NAFTA) ratified. Bombing of New York World Trade Tower. Middle East peace accord of Palestinian self-rule. Nelson Mandela and F. W. deKlerk awarded Nobel Peace Prize.*

1994   *First free elections in South Africa. Civil war in Rwanda leaves 500,000 dead. Major earthquake rocks Los Angeles. Three planets discovered outside solar system.*

1995   *Israeli Prime Minister Yitzak Rabin assassinated. Oklahoma City Federal Building bombed. Million Man March in Washington, D.C.*

1996   *Bill Clinton reelected president. Microscopic life investigated on Mars. Bosnian collective presidency established.*

1997   *China's Deng Xiaoping dies. Transfer of sovereignty in Hong Kong. Diana, Princess of Wales, and Mother Theresa die. Tony Blair elected Prime Minister of Britain (Labor Party in rule).*

1998   *Frank Sinatra dies. Peace accord in Ireland. Indonesian President Suharto resigns.*

Acknowledgments

PHOTOGRAPHS

Page xxx: Kevin Fleming/Corbis; p. xxxi: AP/Wide World Photos; p. xxxiii: photo by Dana Ross; facing page 1: Sonia Delaunay. *Electric Prisms.* 1914. Musée National d'Art Moderne, Centre Georges Pompidou, Paris. photo: Scala/Art Resource, NY; © L & M Services, BV. Amsterdam 98705; p. 2: Jeremy Horner/Corbis; p. 7: Danny Lehman/Corbis; p. 10: National Monuments Record, S. Smith Collection, RCHME © Crown; p. 13: Courtesy of the Trustees, National Gallery, London; p. 18: Paul Klee. *Neighborhood of the Florentine Villas.* 1926. Musée National d'Art Moderne, Centre Georges Pompidou, Paris. © 1998 Artists Rights Society (ARS), New York/VG Bild-Kunst, Bonn; p. 26 (left): Corbis-Bettmann; p. 26 (right): Indian Tourist Board; p. 30: Giraudon/Art Resource, NY; p. 39 (top): M. Jorge Reinhardt; p. 40 (left): © Martha Swope; p. 40 (right): Arthur Elgort; p. 41 (left): Warner Brothers; p. 41 (right): Mariedi Anders; p. 43 (top, left): Brian Davis; p. 43 (top, right): Lisa Kohler; p. 43 (bottom, right): Philadelphia Orchestra; p. 45 (top, left): Nubar Alexanian; p. 45 (bottom, left): Fritz Curzon; courtesy Gallo & Giordano; p. 47: Ludwig Drum Company; p. 49; Christian Steiner; p. 51: Dave Bartruff/Corbis; p. 52: Christian Steiner; p. 54: Alan Koslowski; p. 55: Orchestre Symphonique de Montréal; p. 57: Courtesy Indiana University School of Music; p. 58: Reuters/Corbis-Bettmann; p. 63: Morton Beebe—S.F/Corbis.

Facing p. 67: Caspar David Friedrich. *Journey Above the Clouds.* 1818. Kunsthalle, Hamburg; photo: Elke Walford; p. 68: The Louvre, Paris; © R.M.N.; p. 69: Honoré Daumier. *The Third-Class Carriage.* Oil on canvas, 25¾ × 35½". The Metropolitan Museum of Art, New York, Bequest of Mrs. H.O. Havemeyer, 1929; The H.O. Havemeyer Collection; p. 74: Lebrecht Collection, London; p. 75: Freies Deutsches Hochstift-Goethemuseum, Frankfort; photo: Ursula Edelmann; p. 78: Germänische Nationalmuseum, Nuremberg; p. 80: Schubert Museum, Vienna; p. 82: Bayer. Staatsgemäldesammlungen, Schack-Galerie, Munich; photo: ARTOTHEK; p. 85: Corbis-Bettmann; p. 89: Corbis-Bettmann; p. 91: John Constable. *Hampstead Heath with Harrow in the Distance.* c. 1821. Oil on paper on canvas, 26 × 31.3 cm. © The Cleveland Museum of Art, 1998, Gift of Mr. and Mrs. J.H. Wade, 1916.1027; p. 92: from *Klavierwerke* by Fanny Hensel, edited by Fanny Kistner-Hensel, Munich: © G. Henle Verlag, Munich; reproduced with permission of G. Henle Verlag; p. 95: The Metropolitan Museum of Art, New York. Gift of Mrs. Henry McSweeny, 1959; photo: Sheldon Collins; p. 97 (bottom): Corbis-Bettmann; p. 105: Corbis-Bettmann; p. 114: Henry Fuseli: *Tatiana and Bottom.* c. 1790. Oil on canvas, 217.2 × 275.6 cm. Tate Gallery, London; photo: Tate Gallery, London/Art Resource, NY; p. 116 (bottom): Corbis-Bettmann; p. 118: Francisco Goya. *Witches' Sabbath.* c. 1819–23. Museo del Prado, Madrid; p. 123: Corbis-Bettmann; p. 125: Wolfgang Kaehler/Corbis; p. 126: © Martha Swope; p. 137: Lebrecht Collection, London; p. 152: Royal College of Music, London; p. 158: The Museum of London Picture Library; p. 163: Corbis-Bettmann; p. 169: Deutsches Theatermuseum, Munich; p. 171: Corbis-Bettmann; p. 173: Museo Teatrale alla Scala, Milan; p. 176: Corbis-Bettmann; p. 183: Richard Wagner-Museum, Luzern, Switzerland; p. 185: Courtesy of the Archives of the Richard Wagner Museum, Bayreuth; p. 193: © Isabella Stewart Gardner Museum, Boston; p. 202: Courtesy Christian Steiner; p. 208: © Martha Swope; facing p. 211: Romare Bearden. *Mary Lou Williams: The Piano Lesson.* c. 1984. Lithograph. Hampton University Museum, Hampton, Virginia. © Romare Bearden Foundation/Licensed by VAGA, New York, NY.

Facing p. 233: David. *Mars Disarmed by Venus and the Graces.* 1824. Musées Royaux des Beaux-Arts de Belgique, Bruxelles; p. 235: courtesy of the University of Virginia; p. 236: Huntington Library and Art Gallery, San Marino, California/SuperStock, Inc.; p. 241: The New York Public Library,

Aster, Lenox and Tilden Foundations; p. 244: Corbis-Bettmann; p. 248: Mozarteum, Salzburg; p. 255: Zentralbibliothek, Zurich; p. 260: © I Busz Hungarian Travel Company; p. 269: Lebrecht Collection, London; p. 271: Beethoven-Haus, Bonn; p. 279: Mozarteum, Salzburg; photo: O. Anrather; p. 289: Topkapi Sarayi Museum, Istanbul; p. 290: Bibliothèque Nationale, Paris; p. 298: Historisches Museum der Stadt Wien; p. 303: Deutsches Theatermuseum, Munich; p. 316: Joseph Wright of Derby. *Outlet of Wyburn Lake.* 1796. Oil on canvas, 22¼ × 30½″. The Nelson-Atkins Museum of Art, Kansas City, Missouri. Bequest of Milton McGreevy.

Facing p. 323: Raphael. *Galatea.* Villa Farnesina, Rome. Scala/Art Resource, NY; p. 325: Mimmo Jodice/Corbis; p. 327: Scala, Art Resource, NY; p. 331: Hugh Rooney, Eye Ubiquitious/Corbis; p. 337: courtesy of the Library of the Hungarian Academy of Sciences, Budapest; p. 343: Heidelberg University Library; p. 350: The British Library (Harley MS 4425, f.12v); p. 354: British Library, MS ADD. 24098. fol.19vi; p. 353: Erich Lessing/Art Resource, NY; p. 359: © The British Museum, London; p. 360: Giraudon/Art Resource, NY; p. 361: Scala/Art Resource, NY; p. 362: Musea Wuyts-Van Campen en Baron Caroly, Lier; p. 366: Bibliothèque Nationale, Paris; p. 375: © Photo thèque des Musées de la Ville de Paris; photo: Ladet; p. 379: Musée Du Berry, Bourges; p. 380: courtesy RCMI; p. 386 (top): Scala/Art Resource, NY; p. 386 (bottom): Hamburg Kunsthalle, photo: Elke Walford.

Facing p. 389: Hendrik Terbruggen. *Duet.* The Louvre, Paris. Scala/Art Resource, NY; p. 390: Michelangelo. *Studies for the Lybian Sibyl.* The Metropolitan Museum of Art, Purchase, 1924, Joseph Pulitzer Bequest; p 391: Peter Paul Rubens. *The Garden of Love.* c. 1638. Museo del Prado, Madrid. Scala/Art Resource, NY; p. 394: El Greco. *View of Toledo.* Oil on canvas, 47¾ × 42¾″. The Metropolitan Museum of Art, New York. H.O. Havemeyer Collection, Bequest of Mrs. H.O. Havemeyer, 1929; p. 399: Collection of Janos Scholz, New York; p. 401: Scala/Art Resource, NY; p. 404: Beth Bergman; p. 416: Staatliche Museen zu Berlin—Preußischer Kulturbesitz, Nationalgalerie, Berlin. © Bildarchiv Preußischer Kulturbesitz, Berlin, 1998, photo: Jorg P. Anders; p. 432: AP/Wide World Photos; p. 433 (bottom): The Metropolitan Museum of Art, Crosby Brown Collection of Musical Instruments, 1889; photo by Sheldon Collins; p. 434: The Metropolitan Museum of Art, New York; p. 436: Alte Pinakothek, Munich; p. 446: Louis Carmontelle. *The Three Daughters of the Composer Royer.* Musée Carnavalet, Paris. Giraudon/Art Resource, NY; p. 448: Corbis-Bettmann; p. 452: Scala/Art Resource, NY; p. 457: Josef Albers. *Fugue.* 1925. Opaque glass, red paint, oil, 24.5 × 66 cm. Öffentliche Kunstsammlung, Basel, Kunstmuseum, photo: Öffentliche Kunstsammlung, Basel, Martin Bühler. © 1998 The Josef and Anni Albers Foundation/Artists Rights Society (ARS), New York; p. 461: National Gallery, London; p. 464: Tate Gallery, London/Art Resource, NY.

Facing p. 469: Pablo Picasso. *Harlequin.* Paris, late 1915. Oil on canvas, 6′¼″ × 41⅜″. The Museum of Modern Art, New York. Acquired through the Lillie P. Bliss Bequest. Photograph © 1998 The Museum of Modern Art, New York. © 1998 Estate of Pablo Picasso/Artists Rights Society (ARS), New York; p. 472: Austrian Museum of Applied Arts, Vienna; p. 478: courtesy Boosey & Hawkes; p. 482: Claude Monet. *Impression, Sunrise.* 1873. Oil on canvas, 17¾ × 21¾″. Musée Marmottan. Paris; p. 483: Edgar Degas. *The Dance Class.* The Metropolitan Museum of Art, New York, Bequest of Mrs. Harry Payne Bingham, 1986; p. 485: Mary Cassatt. *The Boating Party.* 1893/94. Oil on canvas, 35 7/16 × 46⅛″. National Gallery of Art, Washington, D.C., Chester Dale Collection. photo: © 1998 Board of Trustees, National Gallery of Art, Washington, D.C.; p. 489: Hokusai. *The Hollow of the Wave off Kanagawa.* The Metropolitan Museum of Art, New York; Bequest of Mrs. H.O. Havemeyer, 1929, The H.O. Havemeyer Collection; p. 491: photo by Jack Vartoogian; p. 497: Henri Rousseau. *The Sleeping Gypsy.* 1897. Oil on canvas, 51″ × 6′7″. The Museum of Modern Art, New York; Gift of Mrs. Simon Guggenheim. Photograph © 1998 The Museum of Modern Art, New York; p. 498: Natalia Goncharova. *Spanish Dancer with Shawl.* Musée National d'Art Moderne, Paris. Photo: SEF/Art Resource, NY. © 1998 Artists Rights Society (ARS), New York/ADAGP, Paris; p. 501: photo by Lee Boltin; p. 502: Paul Gauguin. *Orana Maria.* 1891. Oil on canvas, 44¾ × 34½″. The Metropolitan Museum of Art, New York. Bequest of Sam A. Lewisohn, 1951; p. 503: Joan Miró. *Dutch Interior I.* 1928. Oil on canvas, 36⅛ × 28¾″. The Museum of Modern Art, New York. Mrs. Simon Guggenheim Fund. Photograph © 1998 The Museum of Modern Art, New York. © 1998 Artists Rights Society (ARS), New York/ADAGP, Paris; p. 504: Oskar Kokoschka. *Knight Errant (Der irrende Ritter).* 1915. Oil on canvas, 35¼ × 70⅛″. The Solomon R. Guggenheim Museum, New York, photograph by David Heald, © The Solomon R. Guggenheim Foundation, New York. © 1998 Artists Rights Society (ARS), New York/Pro Litteris, Zurich; p. 506: Pieter Cornelis Mondrian. *Composition No. 10—Pier and Ocean.* 1915. Collection Kröller-Müller Museum, Otterlo, The Netherlands. © 1998 Mondrian/Holtzman Trust—Artists Rights Society (ARS), New York; p. 513: Alexander Benois. *Set design for the Butter Week Fair, Scenes 1 and 4 from Petrushka.* Accession #1933.402, The Ella Gallup Sumner and Mary Catlin Sumner Collection, Wadsworth Athenaeum, Hartford, Conn.; photo © Wadsworth Athenaeum, Hartford, Conn.; p. 520: Arnold Schönberg Center, Vienna; p. 527: Vasily Kandinsky. *Panel for Edwin R. Campbell (Painting No. 199).* 1914. Oil on canvas, 64⅛ × 48⅜″. The Museum of Modern Art, New York, Nelson A. Rockefeller Fund (by exchange). Photograph © 1998 The Museum of Modern Art, New York. © 1998 Artists Rights Society (ARS), New York/ADAGP, Paris; p. 535: Georges Seurat. *Study for "Sunday Afternoon on the Island of La Grande Jatte."* Oil on canvas, 27¾ × 41″. The Metropolitan Museum of Art, New York. Bequest of Sam A. Lewisohn, 1951; p. 538: Pablo Picasso. *Guernica.* 1937. Oil on canvas, 11′6″ × 25′8″. Museo Nacional Centro de Arte Reina Sofia, Madrid. Photo: Art Re-

Funny Valentine": Words by Lorenz Hart. Music by Richard Rodgers. Copyright © 1937 by Williamson Music and The Estate of Lorenz Hart in the United States. Copyright renewed. All rights on behalf of The Estate of Lorenz Hart, administered by WB Music Corp. International copyright secured. All rights reserved. © 1937 (renewed) Chappell & Co. Rights for extended renewal term in U.S. controlled by The Estate of Lorenz Hart (administered by WB Music Corp.) and Family Trust U/W Richard Rodgers and the Estate of Dorothy F. Rodgers (administered by Williamson Music). All rights reserved. Used by permission. Warner Bros. Publications U.S. Inc., Miami, FL 33014; pp. 594–99: Leonard Bernstein, *West Side Story*. © Copyright 1956, 1957 by The Estate of Leonard Bernstein and Stephen Sondheim. Copyright renewed. Reprinted by permission of Leonard Bernstein Music Publishing Company LLC, publisher, and Boosey & Hawkes, Inc., sole agent.

Pp. 638–39: Olivier Messiaen, *Quartet for the End of Time (Quatuor pour la fin du temps)*. © 1942 Durand S.A. Used by permission. Sole agent USA Theodore Presser Company; pp. 642–44: Pierre Boulez, *Le marteau sans maître (The Hammer Without a Master)*. © Copyright 1954 by Universal Edition (London) Ltd., London. Final version: © Copyright 1957 by Universal Edition (London) Ltd., London. © Copyrights renewed. *Poems de René Char*: © Copyright 1964 by Jose Corti Editeur, Paris. © Copyright renewed. All rights reserved. Used by permission of European American Music Distributors Corporation, sole U.S. and Canadian agent for Universal Edition (London) Ltd., London; p. 652: George Crumb, *Ancient Voices of Children*. Copyright © 1970 by C. F. Peters Corporation, 373 Park Avenue South, New York, NY 10016. Reprinted with permission of the publishers who published the score of the complete work under Peters Edition No. 66303; pp. 655–56: György Ligeti, *Etudes Pour Piano*, Premiere Livre. © B. Schott's Söhne, Mainz, 1986. All rights reserved. Used by permission of European American Music Distributors Corporation, sole U.S. and Canadian agent for B. Schott's Söhne, Mainz; pp. 663–65: Chinary Ung, *Spiral*. Copyright © 1989 by C.F. Peters Corporation, 373 Park Avenue South, New York, NY 10016. International copyright secured. All rights reserved; pp. 680–82: Libby Larsen, *Symphony: Water Music*. Copyright 1984 by E.C. Schirmer Music Co. Inc., for all countries. A division of ECS Publishing; pp. 687–89: Steve Reich, *City Life*. © Copyright 1994, 1998 by Hendon Music Inc., a Boosey & Hawkes Company. Reprinted by permission.

TRANSLATIONS

Pages 347–48: Moniot d'Arras, "Ce fut en mai," translation by W. D. Snodgrass. Reprinted by permission of W. D. Snodgrass; pp. 307–14: Wolfgang Amadeus Mozart, *Le Nozze di Figaro*. Translation © by Lionel Salter; pp. 517–18: Igor Stravinsky, *Petrushka*. Translation reprinted from *Notes: Quarterly Journal of the Music Library Association*, by permission of the Music Library Association; pp. 529–32: Alban Berg, *Wozzeck*. Translation by Sarah E. Soulsby. See acknowledgment above; pp. 544–45: Sergei Prokofiev, *Alexander Nevsky*. Translation by Steven Ledbetter; reprinted by permission of the Boston Symphony Orchestra, Inc; p. 652: Federico García Lorca, "El niño busca su voz," from *Obras Completas* (Galaxia Gutenberg, 1996 edition). © Herederos de Federico García Lorca. Translation by W. S. Merwin, © W. S. Merwin and Herederos de Federico García Lorca. All rights reserved. For information regarding rights and permissions for works by Federico García Lorca, please contact William Peter Kosmas, Esq., 8 Franklin Square, London W14 9UU, England. Reprinted by permission.

Index

Definitions of terms appear on pages indicated in **bold type;** *italic* page numbers refer to illustrations. The abbreviation *fc.* refers to unpaginated illustrations facing the indicated page.

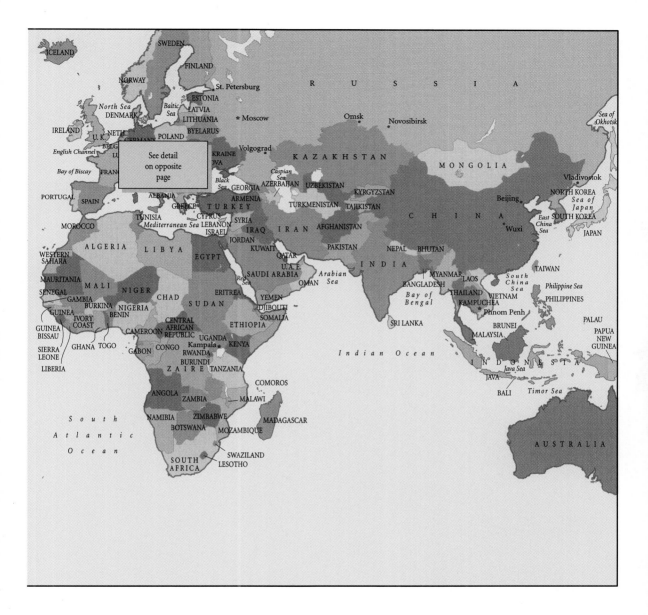

ICELAND

SWEDEN

FINLAND

NORWAY

St. Petersburg

R   U   S   S   I   A

ESTONIA
North Sea   Baltic
DENMARK   Sea
LATVIA

Moscow

Omsk

Novosibirsk

Sea of
Okhotsk

IRELAND
U.K.   NETH.
GERMANY   POLAND

LITHUANIA
BYELARUS

KRAINE
OVA

KAZAKHSTAN

MONGOLIA

Vladivostok

English Channel
BELG
LU

See detail
on opposite
page

Bay of Biscay   FRAN

Volgograd

Caspian
Sea
AZERBAIJAN   UZBEKISTAN
Black
Sea   GEORGIA

KYRGYZSTAN

TAJIKISTAN

Beijing

NORTH KOREA
Sea of
Japan
SOUTH KOREA

PORTUGAL
SPAIN

ALBANIA
GREECE
TUNISIA

ARMENIA
TURKMENISTAN

C   H   I   N   A

Wuxi

East
China
Sea
JAPAN

TURKEY
CYPRUS
Mediterranean Sea   LEBANON
ISRAEL

SYRIA
IRAQ
JORDAN

IRAN

AFGHANISTAN

MOROCCO

WESTERN
SAHARA

ALGERIA

LIBYA

EGYPT

KUWAIT
QATAR
U.A.E.
SAUDI ARABIA
Red
Sea   OMAN

PAKISTAN

NEPAL   BHUTAN

I   N   D   I   A

TAIWAN

MAURITANIA

MALI

NIGER

CHAD

Arabian
Sea

BANGLADESH

MYANMAR   LAOS

South
China
Sea

Philippine Sea

SENEGAL
GAMBIA
GUINEA
BISSAU
GUINEA

BURKINA
IVORY
COAST

NIGERIA
BENIN

SUDAN

ERITREA
YEMEN
DJIBOUTI
SOMALIA

Bay of
Bengal

THAILAND
KAMPUCHEA

VIETNAM

Phnom Penh

PHILIPPINES

SIERRA
LEONE

GHANA   TOGO

CENTRAL
AFRICAN
REPUBLIC
CAMEROON
GABON   CONGO

ETHIOPIA

UGANDA
Kampala
RWANDA
BURUNDI

KENYA

SRI LANKA

Indian   Ocean

BRUNEI
MALAYSIA

PALAU

PAPUA
NEW
GUINEA

LIBERIA

Z   A   I   R   E   TANZANIA

COMOROS

I   N   D   O   N   E   S   I   A

Java Sea

South
Atlantic
Ocean

ANGOLA

NAMIBIA

ZAMBIA

BOTSWANA

ZIMBABWE

MALAWI

MOZAMBIQUE

MADAGASCAR

JAVA

BALI

Timor Sea

AUSTRALIA

SOUTH
AFRICA

SWAZILAND
LESOTHO